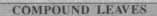

COMPOUND LEAVES

palmately lobed

pinnate

bipinnate

palmate

reniform

sagittate

hastate

peltate

deltoid

spatulate

rhombic

sinuate

undulate

lobed

cleft

parted

umbel

cyme

head

spathe & spadix

ligulate

bilabiate

papilionaceous

PERENNIALS FOR AMERICAN GARDENS

PERENNIALS
FOR AMERICAN
GARDENS

Ruth Rogers Clausen and Nicolas H. Ekstrom

RANDOM HOUSE NEW YORK

Library of Congress Cataloging-in-Publication Data
Clausen, Ruth Rogers.
Perennials for American gardens.
Bibliography;
Includes index.
1. Perennials—United States.   2. Perennials—
United States—Pictorial works.   1. Ekstrom, Nicholas H.
II. Title.
SB434.C58   1989   635.9′32′0973   88-43209
ISBN 0-394-55740-9

Manufactured in the United States of America
Typography and binding design by J.K. Lambert
2 4 6 8 9 7 5 3
First Edition

For all who create gardens

CONTENTS

PREFACE   ix

INTRODUCTION   xi

    Nomenclature   xi
    Hardiness   xii
    Arrangement of Alphabetical Entries   xvi
    Rapid Reference Lines   xvi

ALPHABETICAL ENTRIES   3

APPENDICES   579

    Gardening with Perennials   579
        Soil   579
        Planting   580
        Selection   581
        Maintenance   582

    Sources of Plant Material   587
        Nurseries and Seedsmen   587
        Specialist Societies   591

    Display Gardens   592

GLOSSARY   598

BIBLIOGRAPHY   604

INDEX OF SYNONYMS   608

INDEX OF COMMON NAMES   620

PREFACE

With the blossoming of American interest in gardens, and in perennials in particular, we felt that the time had come for a comprehensive work on ornamental perennials, addressing the special needs of Americans gardening in our varied climates.

This concept has resulted in the most extensive and up-to-date treatment of perennials and subshrubs suitable for all areas of the United States.

Perennials for American Gardens is intended as a practical working tool for professionals, nurserymen, landscape architects, and designers, as well as serious amateurs, indeed all students of ornamental horticulture.

We describe over 400 genera, and several thousand species, cultivars, and hybrids. Our principal concern is with the plants themselves, not with basic techniques of gardening.

This book is the product of long personal experience gardening in different parts of this country and in Europe, and of many years of careful research.

Some readers may find flaws and omissions, for which we accept full responsibility. This vast country encompasses so many singular local conditions that some of our recommendations may, at times, have to be interpreted broadly.

We are grateful to innumerable friends and colleagues who provided assistance and encouragement throughout the project, as well as those who allowed us to take photographs in their gardens: Rupert Barnaby, Sidney Baumgartner, Pierre Bennerup, Alan Bloom, John Bond, Ruth Borun, Jane Brennan, J. Kenneth Burras, Francis H. Cabot, Philip Chandler, Beth Chatto, Tom Christopher, Donald Clausen, James Compton, the late Jean Delacour, the late T. H. Everett, Air Commodore and Mrs. Noel Fresson, Bob Grimes, Brett Hall, Miss Elizabeth C. Hall, David Harrington, the late Lester Hawkins, Peter Healing, Penelope Hobhouse, the staff of the Horticultural Society of New York, Simon Irwin, Christopher Lloyd, the late Robert Long, Pamela Lord, Lothian Lynas, Fred and Mary Ann McGourty, Lynden Miller, Kathy Musial, the late John H. Nally, the staff of the library of the New York Botanical Garden, Andrew and Dodo Norton, Arthur H. Ode, Jr., Marshall Olbrich, Charles O'Neill, the Lady Anne Palmer, Larry G. Pardue, Nancy Goslee Power, John F. Reed, Mrs. J. H. Robinson, Christine Rosmini, Elizabeth Scholtz, Ronald Sidwell, Dr. J. A. Smart, David Smith, Marco P. Stufano, Bill and Linda Teague, Carl Totemeier, Rosemary Verey, Philip and Pat Vlasto, Dick Weaver, Simon and Philippa Wills, and Linda Yang.

Special thanks are due Earl and Eloise Dibble, and Vicki Ferreniea for the use of their photographs of *Alpinia, Doronicum, Galax, Lathyrus, Perovskia, Smilacina,* and *Vernonia.*

We wish to express our appreciation to Helen F. Pratt and Susan P. Urstadt, our literary agents, and to Jason Epstein, our editor, to Kassie Evashevski, associate editor, and to J. K. Lambert, designer, as well as to the staff of Random House.

Our families have been unfailing in their patience and support throughout this lengthy project and have earned our perennial gratitude.

INTRODUCTION

Flowering plants are divided into categories according to the duration of their normal life cycle. Annuals arise from seed, produce their flowers and fruit, and then die, all within a single season. Biennials take two years to complete the cycle. Perennials continue to flower and seed, year after year, sometimes for many years.

This work includes herbaceous perennials and subshrubs. Herbaceous perennials usually do not form woody tissue. Normally, they die down at some period of the year, in response to temperature, moisture, or light, and renew activity in the following growing season. Some may develop woody tissue under certain environmental conditions. Subshrubs display some woodiness at all times.

A complete listing of perennials is beyond the scope of this or any other work. This is a personal selection. We have chosen to include only plants which, in our opinion, have significant ornamental merit. Specialized groups such as bulbs, grasses, and aquatics warrant separate treatment; alpines and other plants of diminutive stature, as well as some traditionally considered ground covers, have been omitted.

Most of the plants listed are available from commercial nurseries or seed companies, although some are elusive. Others may only be found through specialized plant societies, which have seed and/or plant exchange lists. A few of the rarest are traded only between collectors.

Perennials have an important place in every garden, formal or informal. They are appropriate not only for borders and beds, herbaceous or mixed, but also for rock and herb gardens, woodland, and wild and native plant gardens. The bolder sorts can serve effectively as accents in the landscape. Perennials also furnish the majority of flowers for cutting.

NOMENCLATURE

The Latin binomial system of naming plants is used throughout this work. This is the internationally accepted method, both botanically and horticulturally. Each name consists of the generic name, which is always capitalized; the specific epithet or species name follows and, according to current practice, is in lower case: e.g., *Paeonia lactiflora*. Occasionally the specific epithet is followed by a Latin subspecies or variety (var.) name. In the text, note is made of widely used but obsolete synonyms, which were at one time valid botanical names. Where a botanical name has been traditionally but erroneously applied, it is noted by the qualifier "Hort." The phrase "of gardens," often seen in the literature, has the same meaning.

A cultivar name, capitalized and enclosed in single quotation marks, refers to a horticultural, cultivated, or garden variety. Usually it is given by the original propagator, and is often registered. It applies to the progeny of a hybrid, garden form, sport, or clone, normally propagated vegetatively; it may or may not reproduce true from seed.

Some plants result from crossing two genera, species, or cultivars. These hybrids are identified by the use of an "x" in the Latin binomial. In intergeneric hybrids, the "X" precedes the generic name, which is a composite of the generic names of the parent plants. E.g., X *Heucherella* is a hybrid between *Heuchera* and *Tiarella*. In interspecific hybrids, the "x" is inserted between the genus and the specific epithet, e.g., *Epimedium* x *rubrum (E. alpinum* x *E. grandiflorum)*. Where the parentage is known, it is noted.

Common names are included if they are well known or of interest. However, they are not reliable for identification purposes. Frequently the same common name is used for different plants. E.g., Bluebell refers to *Endymion* in England and to *Mertensia* in the United States; Dusty Miller is widely used for species of *Artemisia, Centaurea,* and *Senecio.*

Each genus belongs to a botanical family, which is noted on the genus line in the alphabetical entries. This name bears the suffix "-aceae" in all but eight cases, where the old family name has been conserved, e.g., Cruciferae. However these have also been given new names to conform to the rule: Brassicaceae may be used interchangeably with Cruciferae. Here, the conserved family names have been retained. Family affiliation is based primarily on floral characteristics. It is good practice for gardeners to be comfortable with families. Often it is found that genera belonging to the same family have similar cultural requirements.

The rules pertaining to the naming of plants are established by the International Code of Botanical Nomenclature and the International Code of Nomenclature for Cultivated Plants.

HARDINESS

It is of paramount importance for a gardener considering the purchase of plants or seeds to know whether particular species will survive under the climatic and environmental conditions of his garden. The measure of the plants' resistance to these is called hardiness.

Hardiness is popularly understood to mean only the cold tolerance of a plant. Every plant has a genetically determined resistance to a specific degree of cold. Undoubtedly this is the most important factor; however, several others, either alone or in combination, significantly affect the survival of perennials.

Soil Type

Possibly the next in importance is soil type, as it affects drainage or water retention.

Both heavy soils with a high clay content, which do not drain freely, and excessively light soils, where water retention is poor, will adversely influence cold weather survival. Dry fall conditions, due to low rainfall or insufficient watering, put added stress on plants. They enter the winter in a weakened condition and with a reduced ability to tolerate low temperatures. This is compounded by wind, which causes further drying out, as well as possible erosion of soil from around the crowns.

Poor drainage, regardless of its cause, is lethal to many perennials during their period of dormancy. This condition is known as "wet feet."

Snow

This insulating blanket, sometimes called "poor man's mulch," protects the roots from heaving and drying out, caused by thawing and refreezing during sunny winter days and frigid nights. Furthermore it discourages precocious growth. These problems can be alleviated by winter mulching after the ground is thoroughly frozen. Wind may remove the natural mulch of snow cover.

Microclimates

Within each climatic area, microclimates occur which deviate from the surrounding macroclimate. They vary in size, from a corner of a particular garden to an extensive area, such as that surrounding a lake. Local temperatures are affected by altitude, aspect, exposure or shelter, and the proximity of bodies of water.

Winter Dormancy

As we have seen, plants can be adversely affected by low temperature. However, for some plants, a degree of cold is necessary for their well-being. These plants must undergo a period of dormancy, naturally induced by low temperatures. In areas with mild winters, such plants will not bloom satisfactorily without special attention. Some can be forced into dormancy by gradually withholding water.

Summer Hardiness

While little work has been done on this aspect of hardiness, it is well known that many plants will not tolerate excessive heat. High temperatures, especially if unrelieved by nighttime cooling or in combination with high humidity, prevent success with certain perennials. (See Hardiness, under Rapid Reference Lines.) Experience, under your own conditions, may show that a particular plant is more or less tolerant than suggested. Southwestern gardeners, in the hottest of the low-lying interior areas, are cautioned that very few perennials are adapted to survive their torrid climate.

Zones of Hardiness

Although many factors influence the hardiness of perennials, cold remains the overriding determinant of survival. In order to provide guidelines to the geographical limits of particular species, zone maps have been devised using average annual minimum temperatures as their sole criterion.

There are at present two main hardiness zone maps in use in the United States. The

USDA (United States Department of Agriculture) map and the Arnold Arboretum (Harvard University) map are ten-zone systems. In both, Zone 1 covers areas with an average annual minimum temperature below −50° F. They increase in increments of 5° to 15° to Zone 10, which has an average annual minimum temperature of 30° F to 40° F. The USDA zones may be further subdivided by 5° increments into a and b subzones. E.g., Zone 5a covers −20° F to −15° F. Zones 1 and 2 are predominantly Canadian. The two systems are compared in the following chart:

USDA		ARNOLD ARBORETUM
Below −50° F	Z1	Below −50° F
−50° F to −40° F	Z2	−50° F to −35° F
−40° F to −30° F	Z3	−35° F to −20° F
−30° F to −20° F	Z4	−20° F to −10° F
−20° F to −10° F	Z5	−10° F to −5° F
−10° F to 0° F	Z6	−5° F to 5° F
0° F to 0° F	Z7	5° F to 10° F
10° F to 20° F	Z8	10° F to 20° F
20° F to 30° F	Z9	20° F to 30° F
30° F to 40° F	Z10	30° F to 40° F

Always determine which system is being used when consulting a book or garden catalog. The USDA and Arnold Arboretum maps are a rough guide at best, since they cover huge areas and are based on average, rather than actual, minimum temperatures. They do not take into account small-scale variations in altitude or other factors that affect local climate.

As a result of the inadequacy of these systems, attempts have been made to devise one more accurate.

The Sunset *New Western Garden Book* details a zone system used in *Sunset* magazine and Sunset books, and in some other western publications. It is a twenty-four-zone system, and applies only to the western states. It is not compatible with the USDA and Arnold Arboretum systems, as it relies on other criteria in addition to average annual minimum temperature.

Ortho Books has recently published the Ortho Growing Zone System, based on observed plant use rather than on climate. It is too early to judge whether it will prove useful.

The USDA is currently collecting information from gardeners nationwide for a new system. It will include data based on plant observations.

It is apparent that all these systems have major flaws. However, since it is the most flexible and widely used, particularly by nurserymen, we have opted for the USDA system. Gardeners are advised, however, to take into account their own local microclimatic conditions.

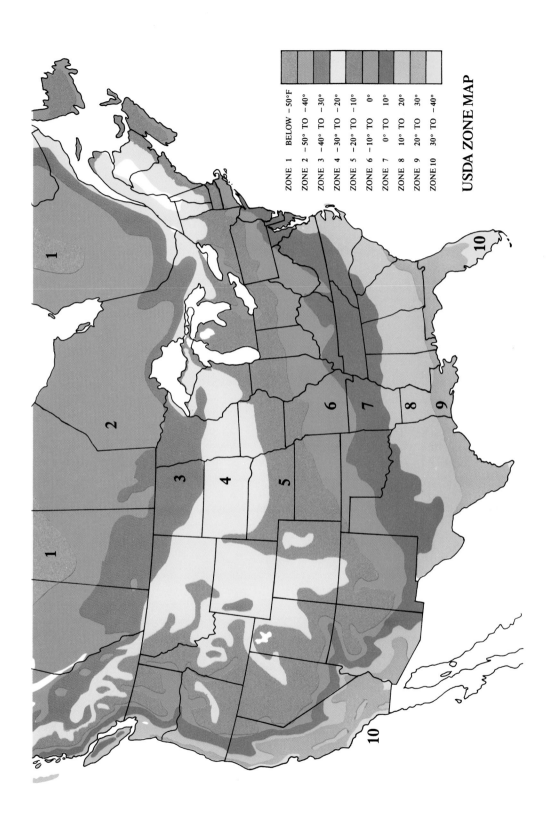

USDA ZONE MAP

ZONE 1 BELOW – 50°F
ZONE 2 – 50° TO – 40°
ZONE 3 – 40° TO – 30°
ZONE 4 – 30° TO – 20°
ZONE 5 – 20° TO – 10°
ZONE 6 – 10° TO 0°
ZONE 7   0° TO 10°
ZONE 8   10° TO 20°
ZONE 9   20° TO 30°
ZONE 10 30° TO – 40°

ARRANGEMENT OF ALPHABETICAL ENTRIES

This volume lists over 400 genera in alphabetical order.

The genus name is printed in boldface italic capitals and is followed by the family name. The total number of species in the genus is listed in brackets; usually only a few have ornamental value. If a common name is popularly applied to the entire genus, it is noted on this same line. General comments pertinent to the genus are found in this section when appropriate; they are not repeated under the individual species entries.

The species name, in boldface italics, or occasionally a cultivar name, in single quotes, is followed by two lines of symbols and abbreviated information designed for rapid reference. The text begins, in each case, with any widely accepted common names, followed by Latin synonyms enclosed in square brackets (see Nomenclature section). Descriptions under each entry may include general appearance and habit; arrangement, shape, size, and texture of the leaves; type of inflorescence; shape and size of the individual flower. Notes and comments on cultural preferences and problems as well as suggested plant combinations may be added. Note is made of the country of origin. The species entry concludes by listing important cultivars and strains, subspecies and varieties.

RAPID REFERENCE LINES

FLOWER COLOR   **FLOWERING TIME**   **HEIGHT/SPACING**
SUN/SHADE NEEDS   **HARDINESS**   **PROPAGATION/AVAILABILITY**

Flower Color

Generally confined to a single word; more detailed information is given in the description.

Flowering Time

Flowering seasons occur in different months in various parts of the country. It is therefore impossible to give precise blooming times by month. We have opted to indicate flowering time by substituting the terms "spring, late spring," etc., using them as growing seasons rather than as periods designated by the calendar. Reference to local nurseries and their catalogs should supply additional regional information. In practice, actual flowering times fluctuate somewhat from year to year, depending on local weather conditions.

SP = spring **SU** = summer **F** = fall **W** = winter
E = early **L** = late
LSP/ESU = late spring or early summer
SP–SU = spring through summer

Height/Spacing

The first figures indicate the average range in height of a mature plant in flower, under garden conditions. This is meant to serve only as a guide, since environmental factors or seasonal conditions may cause a plant to grow much larger than usual or fail to reach its potential.

The second figures indicate the suggested planting distance. Perennials seldom reach their potential girth until they are well established, at least in their second or third season. Gardeners who require "instant displays," or need a ground cover, may plant more closely than recommended.

Sun/Shade Needs

Indicated thus:

Full sun = ○
Partial shade = ◑
Full shade = ●

While large numbers of plants seem to prefer an open position in full sun, many will tolerate partial shade or even thrive there. This condition of partial shade is not the same as half shade, where areas are blocked by shadows for some part of the day, e.g., morning shade with full afternoon sun. A full shade condition exists where the sun is blocked throughout the day. As long as there is plenty of light from the sky, many plants will thrive. Although a full sun position may be recommended for a particular plant, good gardeners will not be deterred by less than ideal conditions. Most plants are flexible in their requirements.

Hardiness

The hardiness zone numbers refer to the USDA map on page xv and the detailed discussion of hardiness on pages xii-xiv. The precise hardiness of many perennials has not been determined. Despite the fact that we have included zone ranges for each species listed, it is expected that many will survive in somewhat colder or warmer areas, with good culture. These hardiness zone numbers should serve only as a guide. Many plants, listed as hardy in z3, will indeed survive in Canadian z2 gardens.

Many perennials will not tolerate a combination of high heat and humidity; others are impervious. In an attempt to alert gardeners to this aspect of hardiness, we have devised the following code: H denotes those most sensitive to these difficult conditions, T those most tolerant. H indicates that a plant will not tolerate hot, humid conditions in any of our warmer zones, e.g., z10-5/H. A plant with such a zone rating will tolerate the dry heat of a Southern California summer, but will thrive neither in the humidity of z10 in Florida nor in z9 in Georgia. T indicates that a plant is tolerant of the hot and humid summers of southern Florida and the Gulf Coast, e.g., z10-5/T. Plants lacking both the H and T symbols are intermediate in their tolerance of hot, humid summers. A plant with a rating of z10-5 will tolerate a hot, dry climate, and may survive in z9 in Georgia, but will not adapt to southern Florida and the Gulf Coast.

Propagation

The letter symbols refer to the most usual methods of propagation:

C = Stem Cuttings
D = Division
R = Root Cuttings
S = Seed

Availability in the United States

**** = Common
*** = Available
** = Hard to find
* = Rare

PERENNIALS
FOR AMERICAN
GARDENS

Acanthus spinosissimus

Unsurpassed for strong, sculptural effects, these plants form mounds of arching, long-stalked foliage. The large oblong leaves are variously cut, lobed, or even deeply pinnately divided. Irregular flowers, in dense, erect, stiff spikes to 1.5′ long, are borne well above the foliage. The corolla is tubular, with a large 3-lobed lower lip. It is subtended by spine-tipped bracts and a large calyx lobe; another much enlarged calyx lobe forms a hood. In warm regions, the Bear's-Breeches flower in late spring to early summer, elsewhere in midsummer. In the colder zones, mulch well. They are probably hardier than commonly thought, their hardiness depending to a great extent on culture. All species must have well-drained soils, and are especially averse to wet winter conditions. Provide some shade in the hottest areas. Invasive. Slugs and snails can be a problem. *A. dioscoridis, A. hirsutus,* and *A. syriacus* are small ornamental species well worth looking for, but rare in cultivation and rather temperamental.

---

balcanicus	**PINK**	**LSP/SU**	**4′–5′/2′–3′**
	○ ◑	**Z10-6/H**	**DRS ∗∗**

[*A. longifolius*]. Leaves 2′–3′ long, narrower than in the other species; pinnately divided, with the individual lobes always narrowed at the base. Corolla purplish pink, with darker calyx lobes. Very free flowering. Southeastern Europe.

---

mollis	**WHITE**	**LSP/SU**	**4′–5′/3′**
	○ ◑	**Z10-8/H**	**DRS ∗∗∗∗**

Bear's-Breech. This most commonly cultivated species has shiny, dark green leaves up to 2′ long by 1′ wide, varying from shallow lobed to deeply cut. The corolla is usually white, sometimes pink. The prominent calyx lobes are purplish. Not only are this and *A. spinosissimus* extremely variable, but there are also numerous intermediate natural and garden hybrids. Mediterranean region.
———— 'Latifolius' [*A. latifolius, A. lusitanicus* Hort.]. Large leaves, usually not deeply lobed. Hardier than the species, to Z6.

---

spinosissimus	**WHITE**	**LSP/SU**	**3′–4′/2′–3′**
	○ ◑	**Z10-7/H**	**DRS ∗∗∗**

[*A. spinosus*]. A most variable plant. Leaves pinnately dissected, with the lobes further divided, almost Thistle-like; more or less spiny. Flower spikes often more slender than in the other species; corolla white, calyx lobes purple tinged. Eastern Mediterranean.

The attractive foliage and durable flowers of the stalwart Yarrows are an indispensable feature of summer gardens. They are also excellent for cutting and drying. Their erect stems are sufficiently sturdy to need staking only rarely. Most have feathery or ferny foliage, pinnately dissected into slender segments. Small flower heads, composed of a few short, blunt rays surrounding a little tuft of disk florets, crowd into dense, flat or convex corymbs. These sun lovers are undemanding, resistant to drought once established, and intolerant only of heavy, wet soils. Most are vigorous and need to be divided every 2–3 years. Easily propagated from seed or by division. In addition to _A. tomentosa,_ the Yarrows boast any number of low-growing species suitable for rock gardens, including _A. ageratifolia, A. clavennae,_ and _A._ x _lewisii_ 'King Edward.' The horticultural taxonomy of the genus is badly in need of revision.

clypeolata **Hort.**	YELLOW	SU	**1.5′–2′/1′–1.5′**
	○	Z10-3/T	DS ✳✳

Silvery gray, finely dissected leaves, to 13″ long, smaller above. The bright yellow flower heads are in 2″ corymbs. A parent of several superior hybrids. The southeastern European species _A. clypeolata_ is not in cultivation.

'Coronation Gold'	YELLOW	SU	**3′/1.5′**
	○	Z10-3/T	D ✳✳✳✳

A. clypeolata Hort. x _A. filipendulina._ This superb hybrid much resembles the latter parent, but has finer, grayer foliage. Its smaller, bright yellow corymbs are only 3″ wide.

filipendulina	YELLOW	SU	**3.5′–4′/1.5′–2′**
	○	Z10-3/T	DS ✳✳✳✳

Fern-Leaf Yarrow. [_A. eupatorium_]. Erect, and the tallest of the Yarrows, with elegant ferny foliage. Linear leaves, to 10″ long, pinnately divided into narrow, toothed segments. Slightly convex 4″–5″ corymbs of golden yellow flower heads. May need staking. Striking against a background of _Miscanthus sinensis_ 'Variegatus.' Asia Minor. 'Gold Plate,' with 6″ corymbs, and 'Parker's Variety,' both 4′–5′ tall, are popular cultivars.

grandifolia	WHITE	SU-LSU	**3′–4′/2′–3′**
	○	Z10-3	DS ✳

This lush, bushy plant, with handsome gray green ferny foliage, is unaccountably neglected by American gardeners. The large leaves, ovate in outline, are boldly pinnately dissected, lobed and toothed. Modest corymbs of white flower heads. Undoubtedly as tough as the other Yarrows. Southeastern Europe, Asia Minor.

millefolium	WHITE	SU-EF	**2′–2.5′/2′**
	○	Z10-3/T	DS ✳✳✳✳

Weedy and invasive, the Common Yarrow is not a fit subject for gardens, but several of its cultivars and hybrids have undeniable merit. The narrow leaves, to 8″ long, are

2 to 3 times pinnately divided into thread-fine segments. Convex 2″ corymbs of white, rarely pink or red, ¼″ flower heads. Europe, Western Asia.

———— var. *californica* 'Island Pink' [*A. borealis* 'Island Pink']. A pink-flowered variant, from Santa Cruz Island, selected by the Santa Barbara Botanic Garden. 2′ tall. Very long blooming.

———— 'Cerise Queen' has bright rose pink flower heads.

———— 'Fire King.' Crimson flowers.

———— 'Lilac Queen' has lilac flowers.

———— 'Red Beauty' is similar to 'Fire King'.

———— 'Rosea' has soft pink flower heads.

———— 'Rubra' is red flowered.

A. 'Schwefelblüte' ['Flowers of Sulfur'] is probably a hybrid with *A.* x *taygetea.* New German hybrids with *A.* x *taygetea* include pink 'Apfelblüte' ['Appleblossom'], brilliant red 'Fanal' ['The Beacon'], sulfur yellow 'Hoffnung' ['Great Expectations,' 'Hope'], and salmon pink 'Lachsschoenheit' ['Salmon Beauty'].

Achillea filipendulina 'Gold Plate'

| 'Moonshine' | YELLOW | SU | 2'/1.5' |
| | ○ | ZI0-3/T | D **** |

This Alan Bloom hybrid, involving *A. clypeolata* Hort., *A.* x *taygetea,* and
A. 'Schwefelblüte,' has finely dissected gray green foliage, and lemon yellow flower
heads in 2½" corymbs. It contrasts better with *Salvia* x *superba* than the brighter
yellow *A.* 'Coronation Gold,' an often recommended but rather crude combination.

| *ptarmica* | WHITE | SU | 1.5'–2'/2' |
| | ○ | ZI0-3/T | DS **** |

Sneezeweed, Sneezewort. Only the double-flowered forms of this invasive and untidy
species deserve garden space. Narrow, sessile, small-toothed 1"–4" leaves. Loose co-
rymbs of ½"–¾" flower heads, with white rays and greenish disks. Asia, Europe.
————— 'The Pearl' ['Boule de Neige']. Pristine white double flower heads.
————— 'Perry's White' is slightly taller. It may be a double-flowered cultivar of
A. sibirica, a species with sharply lobed leaves.

| x *taygetea* | YELLOW | SU | 1.5'/1.5' |
| | ○ | ZI0-3/T | DS *** |

Probably a hybrid of *A. clypeolata* Hort. and *A. millefolium,* and not to be confused
with the Greek species *A. taygetea.* Finely dissected, gray green foliage. Flat 1½"–2"
corymbs of sulfur yellow flower heads.

| *tomentosa* | YELLOW | SU | 1'/1.5' |
| | ○ | ZI0-3 | DS *** |

Woolly Yarrow is a spreading plant, with woolly, narrow, bipinnately dissected leaves.
Dense corymbs of tiny bright yellow flower heads. Useful for edging and rock gardens.
Europe, Western Asia.

ACONITUM, Ranunculaceae. (100)   Monkshood

The common names Monkshood or Helmet Flower refer to the characteristic 1" high
hooded or helmet-shaped flowers. These are borne in usually erect racemes or panicles.
The attractive alternate foliage is lobed or sometimes deeply cleft. All are easy to grow
in fertile, cool, and moisture-retentive soil. Mulch in the spring. The tuberous roots
resent disturbance, but need division every 3–4 years. In the north, Aconites may be
planted in sunny or shaded positions, but in warmer zones they do not tolerate full sun.
All their parts are dangerously poisonous, the roots in particular. Never plant them
where children play, near vegetable gardens, or other places where they might be eaten
inadvertently.

| *anthora* | YELLOW | SU | 2'/1.5' |
| | ○ | Z9-2/H | DS *** |

Pyrenees Monkshood. Several erect stems, heavy with very finely divided 2"–5" leaves;

each division deeply cleft twice, into linear lobes. The rounded, pale yellow ½"–¾" flowers are arranged in spikelike racemes. Southern Europe.

x *bicolor*	BLUE	SU/F	3'/2'
	○ ◑	Z9-2/H	D ***

[*A. stoerkianum, A. cammarum, A. napellus bicolor*]. Assumed to be hybrids of *A. napellus* and *A. variegatum.* Plants may be erect and somewhat stiff, or more loosely branching. The glossy, dark green 2"–3" leaves are deeply fingered, with 5–7 toothed lobes.

——————— 'Bicolor.' Loosely branched, to 4' in height. White flowers edged with blue, in midsummer. May need staking.

——————— 'Bressingham Spire' has violet blue flowers; very long-blooming. Compact, with erect 3' stems which seldom need staking. Introduced by Alan Bloom, it is one of the best of the genus.

——————— 'Newry Blue,' a little taller than the last, but with the same strong upright habit. Early, dark blue flowers. Superior for cutting.

carmichaelii	BLUE	LSU/EF	4'/2'
	○ ◑	Z9-2/H	DS ***

Azure Monkshood. [*A. fischeri*]. A handsome, erect but somewhat rigid, clump-former, with dark green glossy foliage. The leaves are cleft, nearly to the base, into three primary segments, each further lobed and toothed. The purplish blue flowers, taller than broad, like Roman helmets, are arranged in stiff, sparsely branched panicles. A good cut flower. Combines well with *Anemone* x *hybrida* 'September Charm.' China.

——————— *wilsonii* [*A. carmichaelii* var. *wilsonii*]. Amethyst blue flowers on stems to 6' tall. May need staking.

henryi 'Spark's Variety'	BLUE	SU	3'–5'/2'
	○ ◑	Z9-2/H	D ***

Autumn Monkshood. [*A. autumnale, A. californicum, A. napellus* 'Sparks' Variety']. Similar to *A. carmichaelii,* but with slender, tapering stems and thinner leaves; blooms earlier in the season. Intense dark violet blue flowers in large, loose, widely branched panicles. China.

napellus	BLUE	SU/LSU	3'/2'
	○ ◑	Z9-2/H	DS ***

Common or English Monkshood, Helmet Flower. The leafy stems of this elegant plant are erect, and seldom need staking. Slightly pubescent, the 2"–4" leaves are completely divided into 3 parts, each cleft again into toothed, lanceolate ¼" segments. The helmets of the violet blue flowers are broader than tall, arranged in crowded racemes, on much-branched stems; terminal raceme much longer than the laterals. Cut back after flowering for later flushes of bloom. Probably the most poisonous of the genus, and a source of the drug aconite. Northern Europe.

——————— 'Albus' has white flowers on 3'–4' stems.

——————— 'Carneum' is pink flowered. 3'–4'. Best in cool zones.

Aconitum x *bicolor*

| *vulparia* | YELLOW | SU/EF | 3′–5′/1.5′ |
| | ○ ◑ | Z9-2/H | DS ** |

[*A. lycoctonum*]. Upright, or sometimes sprawling, with many branched stems. Its glabrous dark green leaves are deeply slashed, lobed and toothed. The cream flowers, about ¾″ tall, rounded at the top and constricted in the middle, crowd into terminal racemes. Europe. *A.* 'Ivorine' may belong here, or may be a hybrid. It is compact, with erect spikes of off-white flowers, on 2′–3′ stems in late spring into summer.

ACTAEA, Ranunculaceae. (8)   Baneberry

Baneberries naturalize well, particularly in woodland gardens where the soil is cool and moist. Their handsome leaves are large and finely dissected. Short spires of minute white flowers create a foamy effect, followed by decorative but poisonous berries.

| *pachypoda* | WHITE | LSP/ESU | 2′/1.5′ |
| | ● | Z9-2 | DS *** |

Doll's Eyes, White Baneberry, Cohosh. [*A. alba*]. This erect plant has bright green, glabrous, ternately compound leaves; each lobe deeply toothed, even incised or cleft. Loose clusters of striking, dead white fruits, pea sized and spherical, with a persistent purple stigma; their thick pedicels are red. Wonderful with late-blooming white lilies. Eastern North America.

Actaea pachypoda

rubra	WHITE	LSP/ESU	1.5′/1′
	●	Z9-2	DS ✱✱✱

Red Baneberry, Snakeberry. [*A. spicata* var. *rubra*]. Bushy, with ferny foliage, hairy beneath along the veins. Glistening and red, the elliptical ½″ berries are borne on slender green pedicels, in short spikes, high above the foliage. Northern North America.

ACTINOTUS, Umbelliferae. (10)

helianthi	WHITE	LSP/SU	1.5′–2′/2′
	○	Z10-9/H	CDS ✱✱

Flannelflower. A most unusual plant. Erect, with sparse gray green woolly herbage. The leaves are ternately divided into narrow-lobed segments. The minute greenish flowers are crowded into a domed inflorescence surrounded by a 4″ involucre of large white green-tipped flannely bracts which give the plant a deceptively Daisy-like appearance. Cut back hard after flowering. Well-drained soil. Thrives both on the coast and in hot, dry inland areas. Often grown as an annual. Australia.

ADENOPHORA, Campanulaceae. (40)   Ladybells

confusa	BLUE	SU	1′–1.5′/1′
	○ ◑	Z9-3	CS ✱✱✱✱

Ladybells. [*A. farreri*]. This charming plant has upright, usually branched stems, and kidney-shaped basal leaves. Numerous alternate 1½″–3″ stem leaves, narrowly ovate to elliptic, and finely toothed. The nodding, broadly bell-shaped flowers are deep blue, to ¾″ long, arranged in loose racemes. The fleshy roots resent disturbance. Prefers a deep, well-drained soil. Easy to grow from seed. These slight plants need to be grouped for effect. China. Several other Asiatic species should find their way into our gardens before too long.

liliifolia	BLUE	SU	2′–3′/1′
	○ ◑	Z9-3	CS ✱✱✱

[*A. communis, A. stylosa*]. This similar European species is often difficult to distinguish from *A. confusa*. Its stem leaves are 3″ long, wedge shaped and deeply toothed. The nodding light blue bells are gently lobed and fragrant. Free flowering. Central Europe.

ADONIS, Ranunculaceae. (40)   Pheasant's Eye

As one of the earliest of the herbaceous perennials to bloom, Pheasant's Eyes make fine companions for spring bulbs, or they can be massed in informal areas; particularly

Adenophora confusa

effective in the shade of deciduous trees. Plant in fall, in fertile, humusy soil. In Z5 or colder, a winter mulch of pine needles is beneficial. Fertilize after flowering, before the foliage dies down. Propagate by careful division of the thonglike roots in spring; seed in spring or fall. Poisonous.

amurensis	YELLOW	ESP	1′–1.5′/6″
	○ ◑	Z8-4	DS ✳✳

Pheasant's Eye. [*A. dahurica*]. Erect, usually with many branched stems. The alternate, ternately compound 3″–6″ leaves are triangular overall; each segment further divided. They appear mostly after the flowers, and die down in warm weather. Solitary, brilliant golden flowers, to 2″ across, with many rounded petals; blackish in bud. They are the first of the genus to bloom, sometimes even through the snow. There are several Japanese cultivars, but these are presently scarce in the trade. Northeastern Asia.
——————— 'Pleniflora' is a double-flowered form.

vernalis	YELLOW	ESP	9″–1′/6″
	○ ◑	Z8-3	DS ✳✳

Spring Adonis. Similar to *A. amurensis,* but with mostly unbranched stems. Its very finely dissected fernlike foliage is sessile, reduced to scales at the base. The butter yellow 2″–3″ flowers have many pointed petals. A dressing of lime is recommended. Europe.

AEONIUM, Crassulaceae. (40)

Although closely related to the Sempervivums, these shrubby plants resemble them little. Aeoniums display a wide range of habits. One group of species develops strong, sometimes branched stems, topped with large rosettes of alternately arranged, fleshy leaves. Another type consists of low bushy plants, their many branches ending in smaller rosettes of succulent foliage. The starry 6- to 12-parted flowers congregate in panicles, at times quite large, arising from the center of the rosettes. All species are tender and withstand only a few degrees of frost. A sharply draining soil is essential. Propagate from seed or most easily from cuttings. Aeoniums assort well with other succulents, but in general appeal more to collectors than to gardeners. They hybridize readily, and both species and hybrids are much confused in the trade. The short-stemmed velvety rosettes of *A. canariense,* the giant of the genus, eventually reach 2.5′–3′ across. Its pyramidal panicles of sulfur yellow flowers rise high on slender stalks.

| *arboreum* | YELLOW | W-ESP | 2′–3′/2′ |
| | ○ ◑ | ZI0/H | CS ✶✶✶✶ |

Stout, branched stems, each topped with a flat 6″–8″ rosette of shiny wedge-shaped 2″–3″ leaves, edged with fine hairs. Bright yellow ¾″ flowers, in long-stalked, pointed 4″ panicles. Morocco. The cultivars are more widely grown than the species. The purple-leaved forms are particularly effective against a contrasting background of glaucous Agaves, or interplanted with *Limonium perezii.*
———— 'Atropurpureum' has dark purple foliage.
———— 'Foliis Purpureis' includes a group of purple-leaved forms.
———— 'Foliis Variegatis' covers several variegated cultivars: the leaves of one have a whitish edge, those of another a yellow center.
———— 'Zwartkop' has glossy purplish black foliage.

Aeonium arboreum 'Atropurpureum'

x *floribundum*	YELLOW	SP-LSP	1'/1.5'
	○ ◑	Z10/H	C ****

A. simsii x *A. spathulatum.* This popular, free-blooming hybrid branches into a bushy mound of small rosettes; oblong 1"–1½" leaves, striped with dark glands. Dense clusters of golden yellow ½" flowers. Modest *A. simsii,* which recalls a Houseleek rather than an Aeonium, seems an unlikely parent.

haworthii	VARIOUS	SP	1'–2'/1'–2'
	○ ◑	Z10/H	CS ****

Pinwheel forms a spreading mound of much-branched stems, covered in small, loose rosettes of foliage. The pointed, obovate 1"–2" leaves are glaucous, blue green, and edged in red. Foot-long, branching flower stalks, with bractlike leaves, end in small clusters of pale yellow or rose pink flowers. Canary Islands. Two similar, slightly smaller species, both with pinkish white flowers, are commonly grown: *A. decorum* has noticeably scaly stems; *A. castello-paivae* has grayer foliage and blooms later.

sedifolium	YELLOW	SP	6"–1'/1'–1.5'
	○ ◑	Z10/H	CS ****

This densely bushy subshrub branches and rebranches into numerous twiglets, each tipped with a small loose rosette of glossy foliage. The club-shaped ½" leaves, striped with red, are glandular and sticky to the touch. Bright yellow flowers in small clusters, barely above the foliage. Canary Islands.

tabuliforme	YELLOW	SU	6"/1'
	○ ◑	Z10/H	CS ***

The perfect, single rosette of crowded pale green leaves lies flat on the ground, or in older plants is raised on a short stem. The wedge-shaped 3"–6" leaves are edged with pale hairs. Light yellow ⅔" flowers, in a foot-long panicle. This curious species, remarkable enough to merit inclusion here, is limited in its use to rock gardens and wall plantings. Canary Islands.

undulatum	YELLOW	SP	3'–4'/2'–3'
	○ ◑	Z10/H	CS ***

Saucer Plant. [*A. pseudotabuliforme* Hort.]. Resembles *A. arboreum,* at a first glance, except that its stems are unbranched; new stems arise directly from the rootstock below ground. It may, in time, reach the considerable height of 10'. Large rosettes of red-edged, sometimes undulate, 4"–8" leaves. Long conical panicles of bright yellow ¾" flowers. Canary Islands.

AETHIONEMA, Cruciferae. (70)   Stonecress

The Stonecresses are compact evergreen subshrubs, particularly useful in rock gardens or walls, and the taller species at the front of the border. They are quite variable from

Aethionema iberideum

seed, and good selections should be sought. Must have free-draining soil and lime. All benefit from a light shearing after the blooms fade. Rare *A. iberideum* is prostrate.

| *coridifolium* | PINK | ESU | 8″–10″/1′–1.5′ |
| | ○ | Z9-5/H | CDS ✳✳ |

Lebanon Stonecress. [*A. jacunda, Iberis jacunda*]. Erect rounded tufts with mostly unbranched flowering stems. Its narrow, fleshy, blue green ⅓″–⅔″ leaves grow mostly on the nonflowering stems. The clusters of small mauve or dusty pink cruciform flowers crowd into 1″ terminal racemes. Lebanon, Turkey, Asia Minor.

| *grandiflorum* | PINK | ESU | 1.5′/1.5′ |
| | ○ | Z9-5/H | CDS ✳✳ |

Persian Stonecress. [*A. pulchellum*]. Erect, but sometimes spreading, with simple or branched stems. The glaucous gray green leaves are linear-oblong, to 1½″ in length. Pink cruciform ¼″ flowers are arranged in loose racemes, which elongate to 3″ as the lower flowers fade. Similar to *A. coridifolium,* but distinguished by its flat, rather than convex-concave silicles (fruits). Middle East.

| x *warleyense* | PINK | ESU | 8″/1′–1.5′ |
| | ○ | Z9-5 | C ✳✳✳✳ |

[*A. warleyense, A.* ‘Warley Rose’]. Probably *A. armenum* x *A. grandiflorum.* A beautiful mounded compact plant. The foliage is steel blue and broader than that of *A. grandiflorum.* The deep pink ¼″ flowers, with lighter veining, crowd into dense clusters which do not lengthen with age. Variable; select a good form. More tolerant of warm climates than the species.

AGAPANTHUS, Liliaceae. (9)	Blue African Lily

Elegant and stately, the Blue African Lilies are striking subjects from southern Africa for our warmer gardens. In less favored areas, they make fine container plants for conservatories and terraces. Attractive to butterflies. Good for cutting. Some species are evergreen, others deciduous. Some of the evergreen kinds are root hardy but not leaf hardy in slightly colder regions; the deciduous are usually more cold tolerant. The genus is confused taxonomically due to both variation and free hybridizing among the species. It is probable that most material offered for sale is of hybrid origin. Generally the leaves are strap shaped, often arching and glossy, arising from thick fleshy rootstocks; in time, they make large handsome clumps. Well above them, large umbels of blue, purplish, or white flowers rise on sturdy, erect, or leaning scapes, which in some species may bear a hundred or more short-pedicelled flowers. These are usually funnelform with 6 tepals joined into a perianth tube below. Blue African Lilies are easy, tolerant of most soils, and of drought once established, although most will not bloom well if kept too dry prior to flowering time. Ideally, the soil should be deep, well drained, and fertile, with enough humus to keep it moist throughout the growing season; container-grown plants must have a coarser free-draining soil. An annual feeding at the start of the growing season is recommended. Division of the heavy roots is only necessary after several years or to increase stock. Plants may also be started from seed, but will take three or more years to reach flowering size. Unless the seed has been collected from isolated plants, the seedlings will be quite variable and not reliably true to species. Beware of planting too deeply. Deadhead regularly. Agapanthus seldom need to be staked, and are free of pests and diseases. Shelter from intense sun. Where winters are cold, potted plants should be kept, slightly moist, in a frost-free place.

---

africanus	BLUE	SU	1.5'–2'/2'
	○	Z10-9	DS ***

Blue African Lily, Lily of the Nile, Dwarf Agapanthus. [*A. umbellatus* Hort.]. This variable evergreen has 2-ranked, channeled erect leaves, 1' or more in length by ½"–1" wide. Small rounded umbels of as many as thirty 1"–2" flowers. The spreading perianth segments, thick and of a waxy texture, are deep blue with a darker stripe down the center. The species itself is probably seldom grown, but many plants are listed under this name in the trade. Cape Peninsula.

---

campanulatus	BLUE	SU	1.5'–3'/1.5'
	○	Z10-8	DS **

Bell Agapanthus. Deciduous. Another variable species, divided into subspecies botanically. Ssp. *campanulatus* [*A. campanulatus*] has leaves to 1.5' long by ½"–1" wide. The bell-shaped 1"–2" perianths are pale to medium blue, in flattened umbels atop 3.5' scapes. Natal. Blooming slightly earlier, ssp. *patens* [*A. umbellatus globosus*] is a more refined plant with narrower, slightly glaucous leaves. Neat, rounded umbels. The pale to deep blue perianth segments, darkly striped down the middle, flare widely at the mouth. There are white-flowered forms of both subspecies. Orange Free State, Lesotho.

| x 'Headbourne Hybrids' | BLUE | SU-EF | 3'–4'/2' |
| | ○ | Z10-8 | D ** |

This fine strain of hybrids was raised in England by the Hon. Lewis Palmer, and is becoming increasingly popular in American gardens. The parentage includes *A. campanulatus, A. inapertus,* and *A. praecox,* and possibly some other species. In some, the

Agapanthus 'Headbourne Hybrid'

leaves are fully deciduous; others are more or less evergreen. The evergreen types are probably root hardy at least to Z8; deciduous sorts are reputed to survive in Z6, with winter protection. The colors range from white and pale grayish blue to strong deep blues; many selections have been named. Seed offerings are of mixed colors and habits. All have spherical 5″–8″ umbels of flowers on strong but leaning scapes. The perianths flare broadly, but are not reflexed.

'Alice Gloucester' has creamy white flowers in large umbels. Early flowering. 3′ tall.

'Blue Giant.' Rich blue flowers on 4′ scapes.

'Bressingham Blue' may be the deepest blue-flowered cultivar. 2.5′–3.5′ in height.

'Cherry Holley' has very dark blue flowers; repeat blooms. 2.5′.

'Loch Hope.' A dark blue late bloomer with large umbels. 3′.

'Luly.' Light blue flowers on 3′ stems.

'Rosemary' has pale bluish gray flowers. 3′ in height.

'Snowy Owl' is a good white-flowered selection.

praecox	BLUE	LSU-EF	3′–5′/2′
	○	Z10-9	DS ∗∗∗

Common Agapanthus, Blue African Lily. [*A. umbellatus*]. This evergreen species has also been split into subspecies due to its variability. Ssp. *orientalis* [*A. orientalis*] is probably the most widely grown. It produces dense clumps of arching strap-shaped leaves, 2′ or more in length by 2″–3″ wide. The compact, rounded umbels, to 8″ across, are composed of a hundred or more medium blue flowers. They are borne on strong smooth scapes which lean toward the sun. The perianth segments flare widely, and are about 3″ long. There are several forms, including one with white flowers. Eastern Cape. Ssp. *praecox* is a larger version of the species, and several of the older garden forms probably belong here. 'Aureovittatus' has striped variegated leaves; 'Monstrosus' has very large umbels, and bluish green leaves; and 'Giganteus' has massive flower heads, of over 200 flowers! Ssp. *minimus* [*A. umbellatus minimus*] is much smaller, with narrower leaves, and pale blue umbels of flowers atop 2′ scapes. 'Peter Pan' is a widely grown cultivar. 'Storms River' and 'Adelaide' are South African selections. Eastern Cape.

AGAVE, Agavaceae. (300)	Century Plant

Regardless of their size, which ranges from monumental to pygmy, the sculptural rigor of the Century Plants fits them best for use as accent plants: the smaller species in rock gardens and borders, the larger in association with architectural features or as landscape specimens. Most flower so rarely that they are best regarded as foliage plants. Their tough, succulent evergreen leaves, in dense to loose rosettes, are usually armed with a terminal spine as well as marginal prickles. The foliage of most is basal; few have stems of any length. Spikes, racemes, or panicles, on stout stalks, arise from the center of the rosettes or more rarely from the leaf axils. The flowers are mostly funnelform, with 6 tepals, usually united below into a tube. The stamens are prominently exserted.

Some Agaves bloom only once, when mature, and then die; in others, the rosette that has bloomed dies but is survived by offsets. The species which produce axillary flowering stems may bloom annually, or at longer intervals. Flowering time is extremely variable, and is probably affected by environmental factors. Although most Agaves are native to warm, arid regions, a few will endure considerable cold; some will also thrive in the hot, humid climate of southern Florida and the Gulf Coast. A well-drained soil is their only common requirement. They are drought resistant, but maintain their looks best if watered periodically during dry weather. Readily propagated from offsets, also by bulbils formed in the flower axils of some species, or from seed. Agave weevils can be a fatal pest. Nearly all have ornamental merit; the following species are commonly available.

americana	FOLIAGE	LSP-ESU	4'–6'/6'
	○ ◑	ZI0-8/T	DS ✶✶✶✶

Century Plant, Maguey, American Aloe. [*A. americana* var. *americana*]. Arching gray green leaves, to 6' long by 10" wide, armed with a terminal spine and marginal teeth. The massive, paniculate inflorescence of pale yellow 2½"–3½" flowers rises 15'–25' high. Dies after flowering, but offsets freely. Mexico.

———————— var. *expansa* has erect foliage.
———————— var. *picta.* The leaves are edged in pale yellow.
———————— 'Marginata' has yellow leaf margins.
———————— 'Medio-Picta' has a broad yellow stripe down the center of the leaf.
———————— 'Striata.' The leaves are striped with yellow and white.
———————— 'Variegata' has twisted leaves, with a wide yellow margin.

Agave americana var. *picta*

attenuata

FOLIAGE	LSU-F	3′–5′/3′–4′
○ ◑	ZI0	DS ****

Foxtail Agave. Loose rosettes of glaucous pale green foliage, developing a stout stem with age. The pointed ovate 1.5′–2.5′ leaves, with slightly wavy margins, lack a terminal spine. The slender, dense 6′–10′ raceme of greenish yellow 1½″–2″ flowers arches gracefully. May produce bulbils. Shade from intense sun in hot areas. Mexico.

deserti

FOLIAGE	SP-LSP	1.5′–2′/2′
○ ◑	ZI0-8	DS ***

Glaucous gray or blue green, lanceolate 1′–1.5′ leaves, with a terminal spine and marginal teeth. The narrow, paniculate inflorescence of yellow flowers is borne on a slender stalk 8′–12′ tall. Offsets prolifically. Southwestern United States, Mexico.

filifera

FOLIAGE	SU	1′/1′–1.5′
○ ◑	ZI0-9/T	DS ***

Dense rosettes of medium to dark green, lanceolate 1′ leaves, with a sharp terminal spine, and loose marginal threads. The tapering 6′–8′ spike is crowded with reddish 1½″ flowers. Offsets readily. Mexico.

parryi

FOLIAGE	LSP-SU	1.5′–2′/2′–2.5′
○ ◑	ZI0-8	DS ***

Compact rosettes of glaucous gray green ovate leaves, with a dark brown spine and teeth. Yellow 2½″–3″ flowers in a broad, stout panicle, 12′–18′ tall. Suckers freely. Southwestern United States.
———— var. *huachucencis* [*A. huachucencis*] is somewhat more robust in all its parts.

shawii

FOLIAGE	LSU-ESP	1.5′–2′/2′
○ ◑	ZI0	DS ***

Compact rosettes on stems variable in length. Light green to green ovate 8″–20″ leaves, spined and toothed. Awkward panicles of yellow or reddish 3″–4″ flowers, 6′–12′ tall. Suckers readily. Southern California, Baja California.

stricta

FOLIAGE	SU-F	1.5′–2′/1.5′–2′
○ ◑	ZI0-9/T	DS ***

Hedgehog. Crowded globose rosettes, on thick stems, decumbent and branching with age. Straight linear 1′–1.5′ leaves, with a sharp terminal spine. The slender 5′–8′ spike bears small red to purplish flowers. Offsets freely. Mexico. *A. striata* is closely related.

victoriae-reginae

FOLIAGE	SU	6″–9″/1′
○ ◑	ZI0-9/T	DS ****

Compact rosettes of broadly ovate 6″–9″ leaves, dark green with white markings, and armed with a short black spine. The slender 9′–15′ raceme is crowded with greenish 1½″ flowers, tinged with red or purple. Multiplies by offsets. This extremely variable species now includes *A. fernandi-regis*. Mexico.

| *vilmoriniana* | FOLIAGE | SP | 3′–4′/4′–6′ |
| | ○ ◑ | Z10-9 | DS ∗∗∗ |

Octopus Agave. Light green to yellow green, arching twisted foliage, in a single loose rosette. The linear-lanceolate 3′–6′ leaves are spine tipped, and edged with a narrow brown border. Yellow 1½″ flowers in a slender 9′–15′ spike. Some plants bear numerous bulbils in the axils of the flowers. Mexico.

AJUGA, Labiatae. (40)   **Bugleweed**

The Bugleweeds are low, creeping or clump-forming plants, excellent as ground covers. The opposite leaves are frequently evergreen where winters are not too severe. The 2-lipped, irregular flowers, borne in the axils of the bracts, are arranged in verticillasters, in terminal spikes. Numerous cultivars are available in different flower colors, or with striking foliage variations. The nomenclature of these is rather confused and may overlap. Aphids, mildew, and crown rot can be problems, the last largely controlled by removal of fallen leaves in autumn.

| *genevensis* | BLUE | LSP/ESU | 8″–1′/1′ |
| | ○ | Z10-2/H | DS ∗∗∗∗ |

Geneva Bugleweed. [*A. alpina, A. rugosa*]. Clump-forming, with erect flower spikes. The leaves are oblong-elliptic, with coarsely toothed margins. Verticillasters, of 6 or more flowers, form loose spikes, denser toward the top. Prefers dryish soil conditions. Europe.
———— 'Brockbankii' is shorter, with dark blue flowers.
———— 'Pink Beauty' has pink flowers on 6″–8″ stems.

| *pyramidalis* | BLUE | LSP/ESU | 6″–1′/8″ |
| | ○ ◑ | Z9-2 | DS ∗∗∗∗ |

A neat clump-former. Its glossy ovate to obovate leaves are slightly toothed, and sessile or on short petioles. The verticillasters of royal blue flowers crowd into dense, erect spikes. Prefers a damp, moisture-retentive soil. Does not spread. Europe.
———— 'Metallica-Crispa.' The leaves are reddish brown with a metallic glint, turning purplish in the fall; crisped margins. 6″ tall.

| *reptans* | BLUE | LSP/ESU | 4″–8″/8″ |
| | ○ ● | Z10-3/H | DS ∗∗∗∗ |

Common Bugleweed, Carpet Bugleweed. [*A. repens*]. A prostrate spreading plant, with fast-growing stolons. Leaves obovate to oblong-elliptic, wavy margined, and on winged petioles below; elliptic or ovate, and sessile above. The verticillasters, of usually 6 blue purple flowers, are crowded into rigid vertical spikes. This species will tolerate dry shade, but soils with plenty of moisture-retentive organic matter are ideal; in either sun

Ajuga reptans

Ajuga reptans 'Multicoloris'

or shade. Often becomes invasive, but the cultivars are more compact. Europe.

———— 'Alba.' Dark green foliage and white flowers. 8″ tall.

———— 'Bronze Beauty.' ['Atropurpurea,' 'Purpurea']. Purple flowers with bronzy purple leaves. 6″ tall.

———— 'Burgundy Glow.' Tricolored foliage: pink edged with cream, new growth burgundy. Blue flowers. Intolerant of dry conditions. 4″ mats.

———— 'Multicoloris.' ['Rainbow,' 'Multicolor']. Very shiny foliage; tricolored, bronze and/or dark bronzy green, mixed with red, cream, or yellow. Deep blue flowers. Particularly showy in fall. 4″ high.

———— 'Rosea.' Green foliage, with spikes of pink flowers on 8″ stems.

———— 'Variegata.' ['Albovariegata,' 'Silver Beauty']. Gray green leaves, edged and splashed with cream. Flowers blue. Tolerates deep shade. 4″ tall.

These cultivars are quite variable, and good forms should be selected.

ALCEA, Malvaceae. (60)	Hollyhock

Often listed under *Althaea,* Hollyhocks have larger sessile or very short-stalked flowers, arranged in spikelike racemes. The central, staminal columns of their open, cup-shaped flowers are 5-sided rather than cylindrical. Hollyhocks are tall, strict plants with large, long-petioled basal leaves and unbranched stems; the alternate stem leaves are reduced. They require moist, well-drained soil. Susceptible to rust and leaf spot; slugs and Japanese beetles may also be troublesome. Though short-lived perennials, they are best treated as biennials. A few of the numerous strains will flower the first year from very early seeding. A popular old-fashioned plant for cottage gardens, but also stately at the back of the border.

rosea	VARIOUS	SU/F	5′–10′/3′
	○	Z10-2/H	DS ****

Hollyhock. [*Althaea rosea*]. Basal clumps of coarse, hairy 6″–8″ leaves, more or less heart shaped, with 5–7 shallow lobes. The tall, stout, leafy stems end in 2′ racemes of 3″–5″ flowers, which open from the bottom up; long blooming. Single and double forms in mixed or individual shades of red, pink, yellow, and maroon are available, as well as the modern strains. Probably of hybrid origin. China.

STRAINS:

'Chaters Double' is mostly double flowered, on 6′ stems. Available in mixed or separate colors.

'Majorette' has double, laced blooms in pastel colors. 2′–3′ in height.

'Powder Puffs' has fully double flowers in mixed colors. 6′–8′ tall.

Alcea rosea

The Lady's-Mantles are frustratingly difficult to classify. They reproduce by apomixis: they can produce fertile seed without pollination. All offspring are genetically identical to the parent plant. Every slight local variation results in a distinct population, many of which have been given specific names. Are these species or just populations? Is *A. mollis* just a variant of the ubiquitous *A. vulgaris?* The Alchemillas form sprawling clumps of long-stalked, rounded leaves, palmately lobed or divided, and often somewhat toothed. The leaves, variably hairy and somewhat scalloped and cupped, are admired for their ability to hold a glistening pearl of rainwater after a shower. The tiny apetalous green or yellow green flowers are borne above the foliage in frothy compound cymes. These hardy plants need a well-drained but moist soil, and some shading in hot areas. Watch out for self-sown seedlings. Plants of the *A. alpina* group, 6″–12″ tall, have leaves palmately divided to the base into 5–7 leaflets. Lovely 6″ tall *A. erythropoda* has scalloped blue green leaves and lime green flowers. Diminutive *A. pectinata* of Mexico is a charming ground cover for our Z10-9 western gardens.

mollis	YELLOW	LSP/ESU	1′–2′/1.5′
	○ ◑	Z9-3/H	DS ****

Lady's-Mantle. This is the plant commonly found in English gardens, and the most ornamental. The gray green small-toothed leaves, to 6″ wide, are lobed ⅓ way to the base, and densely felted with soft hairs. Produces many stems of lime green flowers. Asia Minor. *A. vulgaris,* widely distributed in the northern Temperate Zone, is perhaps slightly smaller, with less woolly foliage, and yellow green flowers. Both are good for cutting and drying.

Alchemilla mollis

This diverse genus of succulents exhibits an astonishing range of forms: from large trees with massive trunks, to branching shrubs and vines, to short-stemmed or stemless plants. These last are suitable for flower beds and rock gardens. Usually, the fleshy, brittle, sharp-pointed leaves are armed with marginal teeth or spines, and are arranged in rosettes. The showy flowers are borne in terminal or axillary racemes or panicles, on long scapes. The perianth is cylindrical, of 6 tepals, free or united toward the base. Unlike Agaves, which they sometimes resemble superficially, Aloes flower every year. All require a sharply draining soil, but otherwise are undemanding. They are quite tender, and withstand only a few degrees of frost. Aloes combine appropriately with other succulents and xerophytes.

| *aristata* | RED | W/SP | 1′–1.5′/1′ |
| | ○ ◑ | Z10-9/T | DS **** |

Lace Aloe, Torch Plant. Its crowded stemless rosette offsets prolifically. The lanceolate 4″ leaves are decorated with white spots or tubercles, an apical tuft of hairs, and white marginal teeth. Racemes of orange red 1¼″ flowers in a branched inflorescence. *A. brevifolia* has glaucous gray green toothed leaves in a looser rosette, and simple racemes of red flowers, intermittently throughout the year. Variously called Crocodile-Jaws, Hedgehog, or Spider Aloe, *A. humilis* forms clumps of rosettes. Its lanceolate-ovate 4″ leaves are covered with tubercles and armed with white marginal teeth. Green-tipped red 1½″ flowers in long racemes. The glaucous gray green 6″ leaves of *A. pratensis* are lanceolate to lanceolate-ovate, edged with brown-spined white teeth. Its compact raceme of green-tipped, orange red 1½″ flowers blooms in early spring, on a 2′ scape. *A. virens* spreads by offsets to form broad clumps of small rosettes. Its narrowly lanceolate 8″ leaves are edged with white teeth. Short racemes of red 1½″ flowers, on 2′ scapes. All are South African.

| *barbadensis* | YELLOW | SP/SU | 2′–3′/1.5′–2′ |
| | ○ ◑ | Z10-9/T | DS **** |

Barbados Aloe, Medicinal Aloe. [*A. perfoliata* var. *vera, A. vera*]. Commonly grown, both as an ornamental and for its curative properties. The glaucous gray green, lanceolate 1′–2′ leaves, with white to reddish teeth, form stemless rosettes. Slender 2′–3′ racemes of yellow 1″ flowers. Multiplies readily by offsets. Probably native to the Canary Islands, Madeira, and the Cape Verde Islands.

| *striata* | RED | LW/ESP | 3′/2′ |
| | ○ ◑ | Z10-9/T | S **** |

Coral Aloe. [*A. hanburiana*]. Coarse rosettes of broadly ovate, toothless 1.5′ leaves, striated, and edged in red. The short decumbent stem elongates to 3′ with age. Short racemes of coral red 1¼″ flowers, in a widely branching panicle. South Africa. *A. berhana* is a more graceful plant, with orange red flowers in a similar inflorescence, and small-toothed, narrowly lanceolate leaves. In time, *A. nobilis* forms long decumbent stems, ending in rosettes of dark green foliage. Its lanceolate-ovate 8″ leaves are

Aloe pratensis

spine tipped, and edged with horny yellow teeth. Dense racemes of red 1½″ flowers, in a 2′ panicle. Long blooming in late spring. South African, possibly of hybrid origin.

| *variegata* | PINK | LW/ESP | 1′/1′ |
| | ○ ◑ | Z10-9/T | DS **** |

Partridge-Breast, Tiger Aloe. Stemless rosettes of 3-ranked, triangular-lanceolate 4″–6″ leaves. The blade is rimmed and spotted in white, its margin horny and round toothed. Loose racemes of pink or dull red 1½″ flowers, on 1′ scapes. Exceptionally drought resistant. South Africa.

ALONSOA, Scrophulariaceae. (10)

| *warscewiczii* | RED | SU | 2′–3′/1′–1.5′ |
| | ○ | Z10-9 | CS *** |

Mask Flower. [*A. grandiflora* Hort.]. This most commonly grown species is bushy, with erect, branching, angled stems. The small, opposite leaves are ovate and toothed. Resupinate, scarlet or bright red ¾″ flowers in loose racemes. Corolla slightly asymmetrical, flattened with a very short tube. Well-drained but rich soil. Most often grown as an annual. There is a dwarf form about 1′ tall. Peru.

ALPINIA, Zingiberaceae. (250)   Ginger Lily

These tall, erect plants with leafy stems are useful near watersides and for creating a tropical effect. Large, shiny, lanceolate leaves sheathe the stems. The showy inflorescence is a nodding terminal raceme. Evergreen in frost-free areas; the roots will survive lows of about 15°F. Need rich soil and frequent watering. Remove canes which have flowered. Malayan *A. mutica* is less commonly grown.

| *purpurata* | RED | SU/LSU | 8′–15′/2′–3′ |
| | ○ ◑ | Z10-9/T | DS *** |

Red Ginger has leaves to 2.5′ long. The showy inflorescences are composed of small inconspicuous white flowers subtended by large overlapping red bracts. Pacific Islands.

| *zerumbet* | PINK | SU/LSU | 8′–12′/2′–3′ |
| | ○ ◑ | Z10-9/T | DS *** |

Shellflower, Shell Ginger. [*A. speciosa, A. nutans* Hort.]. Leaves 2′ long by 5″ wide, ribbed with parallel veins. The flower buds, white, well flushed with pink, open to reveal a small corolla and an irregularly campanulate, petaloid 2″ staminode. This shell-like staminodal lip is yellow, and beautifully patterned in red and brown. Flowers fragrant. There is a cultivar with white-variegated foliage. Eastern Asia.

Alonsoa warscewiczii

Alpinia purpurata

ALSTROEMERIA, Alstroemeriaceae. (60)   **Peruvian Lily**

All of the Peruvian Lilies are native to South America. They thrive out of doors mostly in our warmer regions, but some are hardy to Z7, or in colder zones if mulched heavily. Otherwise, they may be grown as container plants, to furnish cool conservatories or garden rooms. They add an exotic touch to flower borders and make excellent cut flowers. Leafy, bushy clumps develop from thick fibrous roots. The narrow leaves taper to a curiously twisted petiole, which holds the leaves in an inverted position. Most of the slender, erect stems are topped with bracted corymbs of showy, Lily-like flowers, but some are nonflowering. Each trumpet-shaped flower is composed of 6 separate, usually unequal, perianth parts, clawed at the base. Propagation by division is often recommended, but must be done with great care as the roots are very deep and brittle. Seed sown as soon as it is ripe usually germinates readily, but stored seed is very erratic. Plant roots at least 6″–8″ deep in early fall, in very well-drained, sandy but fertile soil. Alstroemerias resent disturbance. Provide some shade from intense sun.

---

aurantiaca   **ORANGE**   **SU**   **3′/1′**
                                 ○ ◑   **Z10-7**   **DS ***

The hardiest and most vigorous of the species has spreading, running roots, which may be invasive. The strong stems are well clothed in short-petioled lanceolate leaves, to 4″ long below, and grayish green underneath. Loose, multibranched umbels of 1½″–2″ flowers; perianth segments brilliant orange, the upper two splashed and spotted with red. Conspicuous drooping stamens. A parent of the 'Parigo' hybrids, bred for the cut flower trade by Jan Goemans in Holland. There are several named cultivars, as yet unavailable to gardeners. This breeding program was inspired by the fine hybrid 'Walter Fleming' ['Orchid'], which is the mainstay of the Alstroemeria cut flower industry. Chile.

——————— 'Aurea' is more golden than orange.

——————— 'Dover Orange' has rich orange flowers.

——————— 'Lutea' is a choice yellow form.

Ligtu **Hybrids**	VARIOUS	ESU	2′–4′/1.5′
○ ◑		ZI0-7	DS ✳✳✳

A. ligtu x *A. haemantha.* Similar to *A. aurantiaca,* but with flowers in a wide range of pinks, flame reds, apricots, yellows, and creams, with beautiful dark markings. The loose clusters of fifteen or more 1½″ flowers are supported on wiry stems. After blooming, the plants go dormant, leaving a gap in the border. However, since they are planted so deeply, it is easy to fill in with annuals or other perennials that will provide interest later. Self-seeds freely.

psittacina	RED	SU-F	2′–3′/1′
○ ◑		ZI0-8	DS ✳✳

Parrot Flower. [*A. pulchella*]. This easy, compact species is evergreen in mild areas. Its lanceolate 3″ leaves are stalked on the sterile stems, sessile on the flower stems. The exotic-looking 1¾″ flowers are brownish red, tipped with green, in clusters of 4 or more. Brazil.

Alstroemeria hybrid

ALTHAEA, Malvaceae. (12)

Distinguished from *Alcea* by having racemes or panicles of stalked flowers, rather than a spikelike inflorescence. Its cup-shaped flowers have a cylindrical, staminal column. The leaves are alternate. This easy plant is appropriate for informal parts of the garden. *Malva sylvestris* 'Zebrina' is frequently listed incorrectly as *A. zebrina*.

cannabina	PINK	SU	5′–6′/4′
	○	Z9-3	DS ***

[*A. narbonensis*]. Erect and wiry. The pubescent leaves are deeply palmately lobed into fingers, and irregularly toothed. Each rose pink ½″ flower has a maroon eye and staminal column, and is carried on a long, sometimes branched, peduncle, in axillary clusters or terminal panicles. Southern Europe.

officinalis	PINK	SU	3′–4′/2′
	○	Z9-3	DS ***

Marsh Mallow. [*A. kragujevacensis, A. taurinensis*]. A gray, soft-velvety plant of upright habit. Its triangular-ovate 1″–3″ leaves are coarsely toothed or shallowly 3 to 5 lobed. The short-stalked rose or sometimes mauve 1″–2″ flowers are solitary or in clusters, in the upper leaf axils. Particularly tolerant of seaside conditions and drought. The roots were used in making marshmallow confections. Europe.

ALYSSUM, Cruciferae. (160)   Madwort

Madworts are mostly suitable for rock gardens, though the larger ones may also be sited at the front of the border. They form loose rosettes of silvery, pubescent foliage, and bloom with tiny yellow, pink, or white cruciform flowers, in elongating terminal racemes. Best in sunny or open places. Soils should be lean and extremely well drained; somewhat tolerant of drought. Shear after flowering. *A. alpestre, A. borzaeanum, A. condensatum,* and *A. wulfenianum,* too small for inclusion here, will appeal to rock garden enthusiasts. Erect *A. murale* [A. *agenteum*] appears to be unavailable here.

montanum	YELLOW	SP/SU	10″–1′/1′
	○	Z9-3	S ***

[*A. pedemontanum*]. Sprawling, with semiprostrate shoots forming a grayish white mat. The alternate, oblong-linear leaves are ¾″–1″ long. Fragrant, bright mustard yellow flowers. Several other species are similar. Excellent in rock walls. Europe.

spinosum	WHITE	LSP/SU	1′–2′/1.5′
	○	Z10-7	CS **

[*Ptilotrichum spinosum*]. This spiny, mounding subshrub has silvery white stems and spines, and lanceolate to spatulate 2″ leaves. The fragrant white or pinkish flowers are in short racemes. *A. s.* 'Roseum' is superior to the species. It makes a compact 8″–12″

Althaea officinalis

plant, with lavender or purplish pink flowers. Provides interest throughout the winter. Mediterranean.

AMSONIA, Apocynaceae. (20)

tabernaemontana	BLUE	ESU	2′–3′/2′–3′
	○ ◑	Z9-3	CDS ****

Blue Star, Blue Dogbane. Erect, rather stiff clumps. The glossy, entire, oblong-elliptic 3″–6″ leaves, are usually arranged alternately along the stem. Light blue, starlike ½″ flowers, steely blue in bud, are borne terminally in pyramidal clusters, similar to related *Rhazya orientalis.* An excellent low-maintenance perennial for moist, fertile soils. Good for cutting; sear the base of the stems to prevent "bleeding." Northeastern and central United States. *A. t. salicifolia* [*A. salicifolia*] has somewhat narrower leaves. Other species suitable for the wild garden include *A. ciliata, A. hubrectii,* and *A. ludoviciana.*

ANACYCLUS, Compositae. (25)

depressus	WHITE	ESU	10″–12″/2′
	○	Z10-6/H	S ***

Mt. Atlas Daisy. [*A. pyrethrum* var. *depressus*]. Slender, prostrate or ascending stems radiate from a matlike rosette of gray green ferny foliage. The alternate 1″–1½″ leaves are pinnately dissected 2–3 times, with pointed lanceolate segments. Terminal and usually solitary, the Daisy-like 1″–2″ flower heads have yellow disks and white ray flowers, purple or reddish beneath. The contrasting reverse of the rays is most conspicuous when the flower heads close on cloudy days and in the evening, or in the bud stage. Demands neutral to alkaline soils, with sharp drainage; intolerant of wet winter conditions. Morocco.

ANAGALLIS, Primulaceae. (30)

monelli	BLUE	SU	1′–1.5′/1′–1.5′
	○	Z10-7	CDS ***

This tender relative of the common annual Scarlet Pimpernel has erect to decumbent stems, and ovate to oblong 1″ leaves which are opposite or whorled. The slender-stalked, axillary ¾″ flowers are gentian blue, reddish beneath. Corolla rotate and 5 parted. There are less attractive pink, reddish, and purplish forms. Of very easy culture. Often, and perhaps better, grown as an annual. The flowers fail to open on cloudy days.

Alyssum murale

Amsonia tabernaemontana

Anagallis monelli

A. m. linifolia [*A. grandiflora, A. linifolia*] has linear to linear-lanceolate leaves. Mediterranean region.

——————— 'Phillipsii.' To 1′ tall. Deep gentian blue flowers.

ANAPHALIS, Compositae. (35)	Pearly Everlasting

Pearly Everlastings are grown not only for their showy clusters of white buttonlike flowers, but for their woolly-white or silvery foliage. The alternate, entire leaves heavily clothe the stems. Each diskoid flower head is surrounded by showy, strawlike white bracts. Easy to grow in average well-drained soil, they are also tolerant of drought and strong sun. An excellent fresh or dried cut flower.

margaritacea	WHITE	LSU/F	1′–3′/1′
	○	Z9-3	DS ✶✶✶✶

Common Pearly Everlasting. The erect, sometimes branched, white-woolly stems become rust-colored with age. The numerous, linear to narrowly lanceolate 3″–5″ leaves are green, or sparsely covered with white hairs on top, thickly felted beneath. Numerous gray white ¼″–½″ flower heads arranged in flattish, terminal corymbs. The most drought-tolerant species. May become invasive. Northern United States, Europe, eastern Asia.

margaritacea yedoensis	WHITE	SU/F	2.5'/1'
	○	Z9-3	D ****

Japanese Pearly Everlasting. [*A. yedoensis, A. cinnamomea*]. Similar to *A. margaritacea,* but with silver-edged, dark gray foliage, and larger clusters of chalk white flower heads. Combines well with *Veronica* 'Icicle' in the white garden. Himalayas.

triplinervis	WHITE	LSU/EF	1.5'–2'/1'
	○	Z9-3	DS ****

Of similar robust, upright habit. The numerous pubescent obovate to elliptic stem leaves may reach 8″ long by ¾″ wide; heavily gray-felted underneath. Grayish white flower heads, to ¾″ in diameter, cluster into 2″ corymbs. Tolerant of rather damp soils and lightly dappled shade; will not endure drought. Himalayas.

———— 'Summer Snow.' Pearly white flowers in late summer. At 10″ tall, it makes a good ground cover.

ANCHUSA, Boraginaceae. (50)

In spite of their rather ungainly habit, Anchusas are invaluable in the summer garden for their rich, intensely blue flowers. These are salverform or funnel shaped, and arranged in scorpioid cymes. They require deep, fertile soil which is moisture retentive,

Anaphalis margaritacea

but they will die out if waterlogged. Fertilize in spring and again during the growing season; water deeply in dry weather. Useful as filler plants as well as for cut flowers.

azurea	BLUE	ESU	3′–5′/1.5′
	○	Z10-3	DRS ****

Italian Bugloss, Italian Alkanet. [*A. italica*]. Somewhat coarse with erect or floppy stems. The hispid leaves, sessile or with winged petioles, are alternate, oblong to lanceolate; the lower ones may reach 1.5′ long. Cymes of bright blue to purplish Forget-Me-Not flowers, to ¾″ across, in large panicles. The numerous cultivars must be propagated vegetatively. Not for the Deep South. Mediterranean.

———— 'Dropmore.' This old cultivar has been largely replaced by improved selections. Deep blue flowers, in mid to late summer. Needs staking. 4′–5′ in height.

———— 'Little John,' Dwarf Alkanet, has deep blue flowers, from late spring through early fall. Evergreen to Z6. 1′–1.5′ tall.

———— 'Loddon Royalist.' A rich purplish blue refinement on 'Dropmore.' Bushy and well branched, to 3′ tall.

———— 'Royal Blue.' ['Dropmore Royal Blue']. Intensely blue flowers, on 3′ stems. Introduced by Sutton's Seed Company.

A. barrelieri, Early Bugloss, has blue ¼″ flowers with a white eye, in late spring. 2′ tall. Seldom grown in the United States. Europe, Asia Minor.

Anchusa azurea 'Sutton's Royal Blue'

Japanese Anemones are deservedly popular for their splendid late summer and early fall display, and for their durable and attractive foliage. The other species are mostly smaller, early season bloomers. Anemones have mostly basal foliage, either palmately divided or lobed and toothed, or sometimes palmately compound, with separate leaflets. The smaller stem leaves form an involucral whorl below the flowers, and often quite remote from them. Solitary or in loose clusters, on long, erect stalks, the flowers are apetalous. At times numerous, the showy, usually spreading petaloid sepals encircle a crowded ring of small stamens and a central cone or knob of pistils.

| *blanda* | BLUE | LW/ESP | 6″–8″/4″ |
| | ○ ◑ | Z10-6 | DS **** |

Greek Windflower carpets the ground with dainty foliage; its softly hairy leaves, 3″ wide, are dissected into 3 deeply cut segments. The sky blue 1½″–2″ flowers consist of 9–14 narrow sepals; white, pink, and dark blue forms are available. Southeastern Europe, Asia Minor. *A. apennina* differs in minor details. Plant in fall; soak the tuberous roots overnight beforehand.

| *coronaria* | VARIOUS | ESP | 6″–1.5′/8″–1′ |
| | ○ | Z10-7/H | DS **** |

The Poppy Anemone, rarely grown as a species, has been replaced in gardens by cultivars, and by hybrids with *A. pavonina* and *A. hortensis.* The species has deeply lobed biternate leaves, and deeply divided involucral leaves. Each stem ends with a solitary 1½″–2½″ flower; the red, pink, white, or violet elliptic sepals, numbering 5–8, surround a dark eye. Southern Europe, Asia Minor. Florists' Anemones resemble their principal parent, but may have even larger flowers, in a wide range of vibrant colors. The 'de Caen' strain has large single flowers; the 'St. Brigid' strain has semidouble or double flowers. Named individual selections from these popular strains are sometimes available. The Peacock Anemone, *A. pavonina,* usually represented in gardens by its 'St. Bavo' strain, has coarser foliage. Its leaves are parted into 3–5 toothed segments; the stem leaves are entire, or barely lobed. Scarlet, pink, or purple 1″–2″ flowers, with a variable number of white-clawed sepals, around a dark eye. Southern Europe, Asia Minor. *A. hortensis* [*A. stellata*] resembles this last in foliage. Its lilac or rose flowers have 12–19 narrow sepals. Southern Europe. Scarlet-flowered *A.* x *fulgens* is probably a hybrid of *A. hortensis* and *A. pavonina.* All of them like well-drained, organically rich soils in a sunny position, perhaps sheltered from the hottest midday sun. Plant the tubers 2″ deep in the fall, in warm to moderate climates, in early spring, in cold winter areas; overnight soaking is strongly recommended.

| *hupehensis* | PINK | LSU | 1.5′–2′/1.5′ |
| | ○ ◑ | Z10-6 | DRS * |

Japanese Anemone. Similar in habit and foliage to *A.* x *hybrida.* The rounded, rose pink sepals number 5–6 and are flushed with red on the outside. Central China.

———— 'Superba' is more vigorous than the species. 2.5′ tall.

——— var. *japonica* [*A. japonica, A. nipponica*] usually has 20 or more narrow, carmine rose sepals; it blooms a little later. Not as rare as the species. Southern China.

| **x** *hybrida* | VARIOUS | LSU-F | 3′–5′/2′ |
| | ○ ◑ | Z10-6 | DR **** |

Japanese Anemone. [*A. elegans, A. japonica* Hort.]. *A. hupehensis* var. *japonica* x *A. vitifolia.* Nearly all of the Japanese Anemones presently found in gardens and in the trade, often under the name *A. japonica,* are hybrids and belong here. The only exceptions are *A. hupehensis, A. tomentosa,* and *A. vitifolia,* less frequently cultivated species. All like deep, moisture-retentive soils. Apply a heavy winter mulch in cold zones. Afford some shading from midday sun, especially in hot areas. These low-maintenance plants are essentially free from pests and diseases, seldom need staking, and require division only every 3–4 years. Excellent for cutting. These hybrids spread to form substantial mounds of foliage, borne low to the ground. The large leaves are palmately compound, with three ovate, lobed and toothed leaflets, only slightly hairy beneath. Above, the branching stems end in lovely, open 2″–3″ flowers. Their broad petaloid sepals may number anywhere from 6–20, most commonly from 7–9. The numerous cultivars come in white and many shades of pink, in single, semidouble, and double.

——— 'Alba' has white flowers.

——— 'Bressingham Glow' has rose red semidouble flowers, on 2′ stems. An Alan Bloom selection.

——— 'Honorine Jobert.' The oldest white cultivar. 3′ tall.

——— 'Krimhilde' has salmon flowers. 2′ tall.

——— 'Margarete.' A deep pink semidouble. 3′–3.5′ tall.

——— 'Mont Rose.' Rose, double flowers. 2.5′ tall.

——— 'Prinz Heinrich' ['Prince Henry']. Deep rose, double flowers.

——— 'Queen Charlotte' is a pink semidouble. 3.5′ tall.

——— 'September Charm,' sometimes listed under *A. hupehensis,* has silvery pink flowers. 2.5′ tall.

——— 'Whirlwind' is a white semidouble. 3′–4′ tall.

| **x** *lesseri* | VARIOUS | LSP/ESU | 1′–1.5′/1′ |
| | ○ ◑ | Z9-5 | D ** |

A. multifida x *A. sylvestris.* Rounded in outline, the ferny basal leaves, to 5″ across, are deeply lobed into irregular segments. The glossy foliage is somewhat hairy along the margins and veins. Erect stalks bear solitary 1½″–2″ flowers, with 5–8 sepals; they vary in color from white to yellow, pink, red, and purple, although deep rose pink and red are most common. This free-flowering plant often reblooms in the fall.

| *magellanica* **Hort.** | WHITE | ESU | 1′–1.5′/1′ |
| | ○ ◑ | Z9-5 | DRS *** |

May be only a variety of *A. multifida,* which it much resembles. The ternate leaves are further divided into linear lobes. Cream white to pale yellow ½″–1″ flowers, followed by woolly seed heads. Southern South America.

| *narcissiflora* | WHITE | LSP/ESU | 1′–1.5′/1.5′ |
| | ○ ◑ | Z9-5 | DRS * |

This compact plant has long-stalked leaves of rounded outline, divided into 3–5 segments, each further lobed or toothed. The umbel-like clusters of flowers are subtended by a bold involucral ruff. Its white or cream 1″–1½″ flowers are sometimes flushed with purple outside. Eurasia.

| *polyanthes* | WHITE | ESU | 1′–1.5′/1.5′ |
| | ○ ◑ | Z9-6 | DRS * |

Long-stalked, hairy leaves, 2″–4″ wide, lobed into 5–7 toothed segments. White 1″–1½″ flowers, with 4–7 sepals, on wiry, branching stems. Not in the first rank of Anemones, but useful for its graceful effect. Himalayas.

| *pulsatilla* | PURPLE | ESP/SP | 1′/1′ |
| | ○ ◑ | Z9-6/H | DRS **** |

Pasque-Flower. [*Pulsatilla amoena, P. vulgaris*]. Erect stems, interrupted by a delicate involucre, produce solitary flowers early, at half their mature height, and before the basal foliage has fully developed. The ferny 4″–6″ leaves are tripinnately divided into linear segments. The campanulate 2½″ flowers, with 6 sepals, vary from light to dark purple. In sunlight the entire plant glistens with long silky hairs. All species of the Pasque-Flower group have feathery fruits, a trait which, in the eyes of some authorities, relegates them to a separate genus. Well-drained, dryish soils. Best propagated from seed. Europe. Some cultivars may in fact be hybrids with other European species.

———— 'Alba' is white flowered.

———— 'Rubra' has reddish purple flowers.

A. nuttalliana [*Pulsatilla nuttalliana*], of northwest North America, is similar. Its foliage develops before blooming time.

| *sylvestris* | WHITE | SP | 1′–1.5′/1′ |
| | ◑ | Z9-3 | DRS **** |

Snowdrop Anemone has running roots, and rapidly colonizes open woodlands in well-drained, humusy soils. It has only a few basal leaves, divided into 3–5 toothed segments, hairy beneath; the stem leaves are similar. Fragrant, nodding, white 1½″ flowers, with 5 sepals. May rebloom periodically throughout the summer and again in the fall. Europe, Asia.

———— 'Flore Pleno' has double flowers.

———— 'Grandiflora' ['Macrantha']. Its larger flowers may reach 3″ across.

A. canadensis, 1′–2′ tall, favors moist soils. Its flowers face upward rather than nod, but otherwise it is very much an American version of *A. sylvestris.* Extremely variable *A. nemorosa,* the European Wood Anemone, is a charming, little plant, of similar use. Reaching 10″ in height, it has 3 to 5 parted leaves, with deeply lobed segments. The nodding 1″ flowers, usually with 6 sepals, may be white, pink, or blue, sometimes double. European *A. ranunculoides,* only 8″ tall at most, has toothed 3 to 5 parted leaves. It has yellow 1″ flowers; 'Flore Pleno' [var. *pleniflora*] is double flowered. 'Superba' has bronze foliage.

Anemone tomentosa

| *tenuifolia* | PINK | W/ESP | 1′–1.5′/1′–1.5′ |
| | ◑ | Z10-9/H | S * |

Cape Anemone. [*A. capensis*]. This subshrub has evergreen leaves, with 2–3 deeply lobed segments. Silky pale pink or mauve 3″ flowers, paler inside, with as many as 20 narrow sepals. Well-drained but moist soil. South Africa.

| *tomentosa* | PINK | SU/LSU | 3′–4′/2′ |
| | ○ ◑ | Z10-4 | DRS *** |

[*A. vitifolia* Hort.]. Earlier to flower than the other Japanese Anemones. Similar in habit and foliage to *A.* x *hybrida,* but the stems and undersides of the leaves are thickly covered with whitish hairs. Each 2″–3″ flower has 5–6 pale rose sepals. Northern China.

——————— 'Robustissima' is usually listed under *A. vitifolia,* but undoubtedly belongs here.

| *vitifolia* | WHITE | EF | 3′–4′/1.5′ |
| | ○ ◑ | Z10-7 | DRS ** |

Similar in habit to *A.* x *hybrida.* Its leaves are not palmately compound like those of the other Japanese Anemones, but are deeply lobed and resemble grape leaves. The white 2″–3″ flowers usually have 5 sepals. Unaccountably confused with *A. tomentosa.* Northern India, Burma, Western China.

ANEMONOPSIS, Ranunculaceae. (1)

| *macrophylla* | BLUE | SU/LSU | 2′–3′/1.5′ |
| | ◑ | Z9-6/H | DS ** |

False Anemone. This graceful woodland plant much resembles the Japanese Anemones. The mass of the foliage is borne low to the ground; above rise slender stems of nodding flowers. The long-stalked 10″ leaves are triangular in outline, and bipinnately or ternately compound; jaggedly toothed 2″–4″ leaflets. Loose racemes of pale lavender blue, waxy 1½″ flowers. The unusual flowers are composed of 7–10 large, spreading, petaloid sepals surrounding a cup-shaped corolla of about 10 smaller, darker blue petals. Likes cool, moist conditions, and a porous, humusy soil. Japan.

ANGELICA, Umbelliferae. (50)

| *archangelica* | WHITE | SU | 5′–7′/3′ |
| | ○ ◑ | Z9-4 | S *** |

Wild Parsnip, Archangel. [*A. officinalis, Archangelica officinalis*]. An imposing, erect plant with heavy stems and elegant, thrice-compound leaves. Terminal and compound 3″–6″ umbels of small greenish white flowers. Cut back before seed formation to extend

Angelica archangelica

the life of the plant; short-lived at best. Useful for its architectural effect in the border. A bold cut flower. All parts of the plant are aromatic and have culinary uses. Europe, Asia.

ANGELONIA, Scrophulariaceae. (30)

salicariifolia	BLUE	SU/LSU	1.5′–2.5′/1′
	○ ◑	Z10-9/T	CS **

[*A. grandiflora* Hort.]. This tender perennial, sticky-pubescent throughout, sends up a sheaf of slender, erect stems clothed in narrow 1″–3″ leaves edged with fine teeth. The lower leaves are opposite, the upper sometimes alternate. Graceful racemes of asymmetrical violet blue ¾″ flowers. The short-tubed corolla is 2 lipped; upper lip 2 lobed, lower 3 lobed and oblong. Often grown as an annual. Long flowering. West Indies and northern South America.

ANIGOZANTHOS, Haemodoraceae. (10)   Kangaroo Paw

The Kangaroo Paws of southwestern Australia form clusters of narrow, leathery, dark green leaves. Erect flower stems rise well above the foliage, and in some species are branched; upper stems often quite woolly. The inflorescence is a one-sided spike or raceme of densely woolly flowers; corolla tubular, split nearly to the base on one side, and 6-lobed. These handsome plants will tolerate at most only a few degrees of frost. They prefer full sun and well-drained soils. All are susceptible to a serious fungus disease which causes black spots on the leaves and stems; treat with a fungicide. Also subject to attack by snails and slugs. They make excellent and long-lasting cut flowers. Several other species are quite ornamental but rarely found in cultivation here: *A. rufus* and the smaller *A. gabrielae, A. humilis* and *A. preissii,* as well as numerous new hybrids.

flavidus	YELLOW	LSP-F	4′–6′/2′
	○ ◑	Z10-9/H	DS ****

[*A. coccineus*]. Long, very narrow 2′–3′ leaves. This, the commonest species, has branching flower stems with woolly branchlets. The 1½″ flowers are extremely variable, most often yellow green, but also yellow, buff, orange, to dark rust red. (The red-flowered form is at times listed incorrectly as *A. coccineus.*) Hybridizes easily. Cut back spent flower stems to encourage continued flowering. Southwestern Australia. Smaller *A. pulcherrimus* is quite similar. *A.* 'Pink Joey' resembles *A. flavidus,* but has beautiful soft pink flowers.

Anigozanthos flavidus

| *manglesii* | GREEN | LSP-F | 2′–3′/1.5′ |
| | ○ ◑ | Z10/H | DS *** |

Narrow, gray green 1′–1.5′ leaves. Unbranched or forked woolly red flower stems. The inflorescence is a terminal raceme of woolly, tubular 2½″ flowers, green with red bases; flower lobes strongly reflexed. Divide every 2–3 years to maintain vigor. *A. bicolor* is similar but smaller. Southwestern Australia.

ANTHEMIS, Compositae. (100)   Chamomile

One of the best of the Daisies, Anthemis vary greatly in habit. Some make good border plants, while others are excellent as ground covers. The stems and alternate, pinnately divided leaves, sometimes with a silvery sheen, are strongly aromatic. Yellow disk florets surrounded by yellow or white ray florets, in radiate flower heads. They bloom so abundantly, and for so long, that the plants are short-lived. Prefer a slightly alkaline, dry soil; easy in sunny positions. Mildew may be a problem where air circulation is poor. Excellent for cutting.

| *cupaniana* | WHITE | ESU | 1′–1.5′/3′ |
| | ○ | Z10-5/H | DS *** |

This low, spreading plant forms loose mats over several square feet. Its ferny gray green leaves are evergreen in mild areas. The white 2″ Daisies are carried on wiry stems, well above the foliage. Particularly useful for hot, dry situations. Italy.

| *marschalliana* | YELLOW | SU | 1′/1′ |
| | ○ | Z10-4/H | DS *** |

[*A. biebersteiniana, A. rudolphiana*]. Multibranched stems, with beautiful, finely cut, silvery foliage in low mounds. Their erect flower stems bear solitary, clear yellow 1″ Daisies. Caucasus.

| *sancti-johannis* | ORANGE | SU | 2′/2′ |
| | ○ | Z10-5/H | CDS **** |

St. John's Chamomile. This upright and bushy plant is covered with soft hairs. Its grayish, pinnately divided leaves may reach 5″ long; upper leaves smaller. The flower heads, to 2″ wide, are composed of orange rays around a dark yellow disk. A prolific and continuous bloomer, and an excellent cut flower. Deadhead regularly. Balkans.

| *tinctoria* | YELLOW | LSP-EF | 1.5′–3′/2.5′ |
| | ○ | Z10-3/H | CDS **** |

Golden Marguerite, Ox-eye Chamomile. Bushy, with strong, erect stems, and finely dissected, pinnate leaves, woolly-pubescent beneath. The long-lasting 1½″ flower heads, with bright yellow ray florets, make this a fine cut flower. The extended flowering time may exhaust the plant; cut back the spent blooms to promote healthy basal growth.

Anthemis sancti-johannis

Since the species is short-lived, the new basal shoots may be rooted to bloom the following season. Numerous cultivars. Central and southern Europe, Asia.

———— 'Beauty of Grallagh.' ['Grallagh (or Grallach) Gold']. This British selection has large, deep golden yellow flower heads on 2′–3′ stems.

———— 'Kelwayi' has bright lemon yellow 2″ daisies. 2.5′–3′ in height.

———— 'Moonlight.' Soft pale yellow heads on 1.5′ stems.

———— 'Mrs. E. C. Buxton.' Lemon yellow flowers. Excellent for cutting. 2′–2.5′ tall.

———— 'Pale Moon.' Paler than 'Moonlight' fading to ivory. 2′–2.5′ in height.

ANTHERICUM, Liliaceae. (50)			Spider Plant

These graceful and elegant plants deserve to be more widely grown. Tufts of narrow basal leaves rise from fleshy or tuberous roots. Their slender scapes bear starry white flowers in loose terminal racemes. Culture is easy in rich, moist but light soils. Sow seed as soon as it is ripe.

liliago	WHITE	ESU	3′/1′
	○ ◑	Z9-3	DS **

St. Bernard's Lily. The gray green linear leaves, to 1′ long by 1″ wide, give this clump-former an attractive, vase-shaped habit. The pure white 1″ flowers are fragrant, and held on unbranched scapes well above the foliage. Useful as a cut flower. Europe.

Anthericum liliago major

——————— *major* [*A. algeriense*] has larger snow white flowers on 2.5′ stems, in midsummer.

ramosum	WHITE	SU	2′/1′
	○ ◑	Z9-4	DS **

Similar to *A. liliago* but shorter. Wiry, branched scapes bear numerous small, dainty white flowers, over a long but slightly later season. Europe.

AQUILEGIA, Ranunculaceae. (100)	Columbine

The graceful Columbines are old-fashioned favorites; some have been in cultivation in cottage and physic gardens for hundreds of years. They form erect clumps of basal foliage and slender, branching, leafy stems. Their ferny, compound leaves are 1 to 3 times ternately divided; the delicate leaflets are usually 3-lobed at their apical end. Erect or nodding, the flowers are complex in structure. Five usually spreading petaloid sepals alternate with 5 true petals, around a tuft of numerous stamens. Each petal is composed of a blade or limb, and a backward projecting spur, both of which vary in size and shape from species to species. In mild climates, Columbines can be grown in full sun; elsewhere most prefer partial shade. They thrive in quite ordinary soil, provided it is sufficiently well drained. Self-seed abundantly. Leaf miners are their only serious problem and must be controlled early, as they disfigure the foliage. These free-flowering plants tend to exhaust themselves, and are best replaced every 4–5 years. In gardens, Columbines hybridize with abandon if different species are grown close together, and will not come true from seed. On the other hand, this tendency has facilitated the development of many superb hybrid forms.

alpina	BLUE	ESU-SU	1′–2′/1′
	○ ◑	Z10-3	DS **

This mountain species has biternate leaves, with leaflets deeply divided into narrow lobes. Nodding bright blue or blue and white 2″–3″ flowers, with spreading sepals, and short, straight to recurved spurs. Switzerland.

———— var. *superba* is larger than the species.

———— 'Hensol Harebell,' a hybrid of *A. alpina* and *A. vulgaris,* may reach 3′ in height. Most often deep blue, it is as variable as *A. vulgaris,* and is also seen in blue and white, purplish red, lilac, and pink and white.

caerulea	BLUE	SP-ESU	1.5′–2.5′/1′–1.5′
	○ ◑	Z10-3	DS ****

Rocky Mountain Columbine, downy in its upper parts, has thin biternate leaves. Its erect 2″–3″ flowers have blue sepals; the petals have white blades, and long, straight or flaring, blue spurs. When its flowers are a true blue, it is one of the loveliest of Columbines; unfortunately they are often of a muddy, lavender shade. There are also white and pale yellow forms. Rocky Mountains.

Aquilegia chrysantha

canadensis	BICOLOR	LSP-ESU	1′–2′/1′
	○ ◑	Z10-3	DS ✴✴✴✴

Wild Columbine has biternate leaves, with deeply lobed leaflets. The nodding 1½″ flowers, several to a stem, have straight red sepals; the petals have a yellow limb, and long vertical red spurs. Var. *flavescens* has all-yellow flowers; var. *nana* only reaches 1′ in height. Another form has salmon red flowers. Eastern and central North America. *A. formosa* and *A. formosa* var. *truncata* [*A. californica*], 2′–3′ tall, are western versions of *A. canadensis,* but differ in having widely spreading sepals.

chrysantha	YELLOW	SP-ESU	2.5′–3.5′/1.5′–2′
	○ ◑	Z10-3	DS ✴✴✴✴

Golden Columbine branches freely. Its thin leaves are 2 to 3 times ternate, the leaflets downy on their undersides. Numerous erect 2″–3″ flowers with pale yellow sepals; darker yellow petal blades, and spurs which are long and spreading. Arizona, New Mexico, and Mexico. Its cultivars include white-flowered 'Alba,' double 'Alba Plena,' and 'Flore Pleno' with double yellow flowers. Closely related *A. longissima,* from Texas and Mexico, has slender 3½″–6″ spurs. Plants sold under this name are usually *A. chrysantha.*

flabellata	BLUE	SP-LSP	1′–1.5′/1′
	○ ◑	Z10-3	DS ✴✴✴✴

[*A. akitensis, A. fauriei, A. japonica*]. Glaucous, blue green, ternate to biternate leaves with broad, blunt-lobed leaflets. Nodding 1½″ flowers, with purplish blue to lilac sepals, yellow-tipped, lilac petals, and short recurved lilac spurs. Japan.

————— 'Alba' has white flowers.

————— 'Nana' is similar to the species, but barely reaches 1′ in height.

————— var. *pumila* is a white-flowered dwarf. Possibly the same plant as 'Nana Alba.' May be sold as *A. akitensis* Hort., *A. akitensis* var. *kurilensis* Hort., or *A. f.* var. *kurilensis.*

glandulosa	BLUE	SP-LSP	1′/1′
	○ ◑	Z10-3	DS ✴✴

Biternate leaves, with narrow leaflets. Nodding to semierect bright blue 1¾″ flowers, with spreading sepals, and very short reflexed spurs. Siberia.

————— var. *jacunda* is somewhat smaller. Its blue flowers have white petals.

x *hybrida*	VARIOUS	SP-ESU	2′–3′/1.5′
	○ ◑	Z10-5	DS ✴✴✴✴

Numerous hybrids of mixed and uncertain parentage, separated into long-spurred and short-spurred hybrids. The long-spurred are derived from several American species including *A. caerulea, A. canadensis, A. chrysantha, A. formosa,* and *A. longissima;* the short-spurred, from crossing these with *A. vulgaris.* A bewildering range is offered in the trade as plants or seed, in single or mixed colors and strains. Most come true from reliable commercial seed, but not from seed harvested in gardens. The 'Biedermeier' strain has flowers in many colors with white-tipped petals; its compact 1.5′ plants bloom profusely. 'Crimson Star' or 'Red Star' have red sepals, white petals with a red basal spot, and long red spurs. 2.5′ tall. 'Mrs. Scott Elliot' is an old strain in pastel shades. 2.5′–3′ tall. Flowers of the 'McKana Giants' strain are long spurred, bicolored in lilac and white, red and yellow, shades of pink, and other combinations, on 2.5′ stems. 'Nora Barlow' has fully double, spurless flowers, with soft red petals tipped with white. It undoubtedly has *A. vulgaris* in its ancestry. 2′–2.5′ tall. 'Snow Queen' has pure white flowers with long spurs. 2.5′ in height.

| *skinneri* | BICOLOR | SP-ESU | 2′–3′/1′–1.5′ |
| | ○ ◑ | Z10-3 | DS ** |

Branching stems; thin triternate leaves. Nodding 1½″ flowers, with yellow green erect to spreading sepals, short petal blades, and long straight red spurs. New Mexico. 'Flore Pleno' has double flowers.

| *viridiflora* | BICOLOR | SP-LSP | 1′–1.5′/1′ |
| | ○ ◑ | Z10-3 | DS ** |

[*A. atropurpurea, A. lutea*]. Substantial biternate leaves. The small nodding to semierect fragrant flowers have green sepals, yellow green to brownish purple limbs, and short straight spurs. A most curious, if unspectacular, plant. Siberia, China.

| *vulgaris* | VARIOUS | SP-ESU | 1′–2′/1′ |
| | ○ ◑ | Z10-3 | DS *** |

European Crowfoot, Garden Columbine, Granny's Bonnet. This variable species has biternate leaves, hairy on their undersides. The numerous nodding 1½″–2″ flowers have spreading sepals, and very short recurved spurs, ending in a knob. Colors range through purple, violet, purplish red, crimson, pink, and white. Europe. Cultivars and hybrids abound, some with semidouble, double, and spurless flowers. It is a parent of the short-spurred hybrids, as well as of 'Hensol Harebell.' *A. v.* var. *nivea* ['Munstead White'] has pure white flowers on 3′ stems.

ARABIS, Cruciferae. (100)   Rockcress

Many of the Rockcresses are only suitable for rock gardens, but those listed below are substantial enough to use at the front of the border. They form tufts or mats of often hairy evergreen leaves, above which rise loose racemes of fragrant cruciform flowers. Best in sunny locations with lean well-drained limy soil. Shear after flowering to control straggliness.

| x *arendsii* | PINK | SP | 6″–9″/1′ |
| | ○ | Z9-4 | CD **** |

A. caucasica x *A. aubrietioides*. This hybrid is similar in habit and appearance to *A. caucasica*, but has pink flowers.

Arabis caucasica

————— 'Rosabella' makes compact, light green hummocks of foliage; rose pink flowers.

————— 'Spring Charm' is bushy, with large carmine flowers.

blepharophylla	PINK	SP	6″–1′/1′
	○	Z9-6/H	CDS ✳✳✳

California Rockcress, Rose Cress. Flat rosettes of dark green oblong 2″–3″ basal leaves. Unbranched stems topped with short heavy clusters of purplish pink flowers. California.

caucasica	WHITE	SP	6″–9″/1′
	○	Z10-4/H	CDS ✳✳✳✳

Wall Rockcress, Caucasian Rockcress. [*A. albida, A. billardieri, A. alpina* Hort.]. Procumbent cushions of rapidly spreading rosettes. The pubescent, gray green 1″–3″ leaves are ovate to oblong, coarsely toothed at the tips. Chalk white ½″–1″ flowers are arranged in elongating racemes. Eastern Mediterranean, Iran.

————— 'Flore Pleno.' A double-flowered form; in bloom slightly later and much longer than the species.

————— 'Variegata' has leaves variegated with cream. Striking during the winter. Single white flowers.

————— 'Snow Cap' blooms freely, with single white flowers.

————— 'Snow Peak.' Single white flowers; very compact. 4″ tall.

procurrens	WHITE	SP	6″–I′/I′
	○ ◐	Z9-3	CDS ****

[*A. mollis* Hort.]. A stoloniferous plant forming low mats of glossy, bright green, persistent foliage. Its pointed basal leaves are smooth above, hairy underneath along the veins and margins. The erect flower stems bear few narrowly ovate leaves, and end in elongating racemes of pure white ¾″ flowers. Spreads vigorously, even in very dry, poor soils. Southern Europe.

ARCTOTHECA, Compositae. (6)

calendula	YELLOW	ALL YEAR	I′/I.5′
	○	ZI0-9/H	D ****

Cape Weed. [*Cryptostemma calendulaceum, Arctotis calendulacea*]. This sprawling ground cover forms mats of rather coarse basal foliage. The irregularly and deeply lobed gray green lyrate leaves are rough and hairy above, hoary below. Bright yellow 2″ flower heads are borne singly on slender hairy stems. It flowers profusely, especially through spring and early summer. A tough evergreen, it is useful for covering slopes and other open areas. Once established it needs little watering or maintenance. Spreads readily, so avoid growing where it will compete with less aggressive plants. Tolerates only a few degrees of frost. The clone grown in southern California is self-sterile and will not produce seed; it is propagated by division. The seed-grown annual form has become a major pest in its native environment. South Africa.

Arctotheca calendula

Although these African Daisies are perennial, they are best grown as annuals, as they bloom most profusely in their first year. The bulk of their vegetative growth is produced in winter and early spring, when they need to be well watered; at other times they are quite drought resistant. Flowering takes place in spring to early summer. In cold climates, set out young plants in early spring for later bloom. Propagate by seed or, where it is desired to preserve a particular color form, by cuttings. Grow in full sun, in soil amended with organic matter and sand to be free draining. Plants which are being retained should be cut back hard after flowering. (See *Venidium* and X *Venidio-arctotis.*)

acaulis	YELLOW	SP-ESU	1'/1'
	○	ZI0-9/H	CS ****

African Daisy. [*A. scapigera*]. Spreading rosettes of all-basal foliage. The variable 6"–8" leaves are pinnatifid to lyrate, with undulate margins; green or gray green and hairy above, gray-woolly beneath. The Daisy-like 3" flower heads, subtended by an involucre of several rows of bracts, are solitary on long stalks; the ray florets are golden yellow, black at the base, and flushed with red beneath; the disk is purplish black. South Africa. *A. breviscapa* is similar, but only some 6" tall. Its smaller flower heads have orange yellow rays and brownish disk florets. Hybrids of uncertain parentage are available as seed or plants, in a range of appealing colors: white, cream, yellows and orange, pinks and red, purple. These hybrids self-sow readily, but do not come true, and usually revert to yellow.

Arctotis acaulis hybrid

| *stoechadifolia* | CREAM | SP-ESU | 1.5'–2.5'/1.5' |
| | ○ | Z10-9/H | CS **** |

Blue-Eyed Arctotis, Trailing Arctotis. Decumbent to ascending branched stems, with gray green woolly foliage. The alternate oblong to obovate leaves, to 4" long, are pinnatifid or lyrate, and often toothed. Many 3" flower heads, with cream or white rays, yellow at the base and reddish underneath, surrounding violet blue disks. South Africa. As with *A. acaulis,* there are numerous hybrids of undetermined origin, in a wide range of colors.

———— var. *grandis* [*A. grandis*] is an altogether larger version of the species.

ARISAEMA, Araceae. (190)

While similar to related *Arum,* Arisaema differs in having divided leaves, which appear with or following the flowers. The spathe and spadix, which constitute the inflorescence, are typical of the Aroids. Spikes of decorative berries appear later. They need fertile, moisture-retentive soil with plenty of humus in light shade. Bait for slugs. Fall planting is recommended. Several other handsome Asian species such as *A. sikokianum, A. ringens,* and *A. consanguineum* are unfortunately scarce in the trade.

| *candidissimum* | WHITE | SU | 1'/1' |
| | ◑ | Z9-7 | DS ** |

Late to emerge but worth waiting for, the beautiful white 6" spathes are delicately striped with green outside, pink within. The large, handsome 3-lobed leaves appear after the flowers, and provide color in the fall. Not difficult to grow in spite of its exotic appearance. Plant in a position sheltered from drying winds. In time, spreads to make fine stands. Western China.

| *dracontium* | GREEN | ESU | 2'–3'/1.5' |
| | ◑● | Z9-4 | DS ** |

Dragon Arum, Green Dragon, Dragonroot. Each of the clustered corms produces a single, long-petioled leaf. The blade is divided into many pointed segments, each to 9" long. Resembling a long yellow whip, the spadix protrudes several inches from the narrow pointed green spathe, which envelops its base. Orange berries. Northeastern and central United States.

| *triphyllum* | PURPLE | SP | 1'/1' |
| | ◑● | Z9-4 | DS **** |

Jack-in-the-Pulpit, Indian Turnip. [*A. atrorubens*]. Its rounded tuberous root usually produces two 3-lobed leaves, on 1' petioles, which elongate after flowering time. The drooping spathe, varying in color from purple striped with light green to solid pale green, forms a canopy over the spadix. The spadix is purple or sometimes green. Often these variations are classified as subspecies. The large vermilion red berries provide food for wildlife. Best in woodland or native plant gardens. Northeastern United States.

Arisaema triphyllum

Aristea ecklonii

Aristolochia clematitis

ARISTEA, Iridaceae. (50)

This African genus includes some elegant plants for southern gardens and for conservatories in colder areas. The erect linear leaves are mostly basal and 2-ranked. Flowers generally blue; the 6-parted perianths, very short tubed and regular. Best propagated from seed grown in pots, since the roots resent disturbance; superior selections must be divided. Aristeas are undemanding and deserve to be more widely grown.

ecklonii	BLUE	ESU	1.5′–3′/2′
	○	Z10-9	DS **

Thick rhizomes give rise to fans of basal leaves, 1′–2′ long by about ½″ wide. Smaller stem leaves are borne on the upright branched stalks. These are topped with dainty open panicles of bright blue ½″–¾″ flowers with purple stamens. The individual flowers are short-lived but abundant, so blooming time is extended. As the perianths fade, they twist spirally, as in *Sisyrinchium,* a close relative. A variable but valuable species for the sunny flower border or rock garden, in average soil. Water during dry periods. Possibly hardy to Z8. Southern Africa. *A. thyrsiflora* [*A. major*] has thick, robust 3′–6′ stems, topped with narrow panicles, which may reach 9″ in length. The fragrant flowers are a little larger, with bluish purple stamens.

ARISTOLOCHIA, Aristolochiaceae. (200)

clematitis	YELLOW	SU	1.5′–4′/2′
	○	Z9-5/H	D **

One of the few nonclimbing species of this genus. Its numerous smooth stems are erect, well clothed in opposite triangular to heart-shaped leaves, on short petioles. Clusters of small dull yellow flowers arise from the axils. The petaloid calyx is tubular with a slightly bulbous base, spoon shaped at the tip; petals absent. Interesting and unusual. Possibly invasive. Europe.

ARMERIA, Plumbaginaceae. (80)   Thrift

Thrift or Sea Pinks make neat tufts of grassy evergreen foliage. Tough, wiry, leafless stems hold dense globular heads, composed of small spikes of pink or white flowers, well above the leaves. The heads are surrounded underneath, by an involucre of papery or chaffy bracts, sometimes sheathing the top of the scape. Individually, the flowers are small, with 5 spreading petals joined below into a tube. Excellent for edging, at the front of the border or in the rock garden. Thrifts demand only free drainage and a sunny position. Tolerant of seaside conditions and poor soil. Divide in the fall when necessary. *A. juniperifolia* [*A. caespitosa, Statice caespitosa*] is outstanding for the rock garden.

| *maritima* | PINK | LSP-ESU | 6″–1.5′/1′ |
| | ○ | ZI0-3 | DS **** |

Sea Pink, Thrift. This extremely variable species is split, by some authorities, into numerous forms, varieties, and subspecies; these hybridize freely, often making definitive identification impossible. Rounded clumps of bluish green linear leaves, to 4″ long. The hairy or smooth scapes support flower heads about 1″ across. Color varies from deep pink to the palest pink or even white. Look for a good selection or cultivar. Northwestern Europe, Iceland.

————— 'Alba' has white flowers and dark green leaves. 5″ tall.
————— 'Corsica' is a deep salmon pink. Late blooming. 6″ high.

Armeria maritima 'Vindictive'

——————— 'Düsseldorf Pride.' Masses of carmine red flowers on compact plants. Z9-5. 8″ in height.

——————— 'Laucheana.' [*A. m.* forma *laucheana, A. laucheana* Hort.]. Deep rose red flowers. Reblooms intermittently. 4″–6″ tall.

——————— 'Vindictive' has strong, vivid pink flowers.

plantaginea	PINK	SU	2′/1′
	○	Z10-6	DS ***

Plantain Thrift. [*A. montana, A. rigida, A. stenophylla*]. Similar to the next species, but with narrower leaves. Western Europe.

——————— 'Bees' Ruby' has shocking pink flowers; reblooms. 1.5′.

——————— 'Royal Rose.' Rich, medium pink flowers. Reaches to 15″.

pseudoarmeria	PINK	ESU	2′/1′
	○	Z10-6	DS ***

Pinkball Thrift. [*A. cephalotes, A. formosa* Hort., *A. latifolia*]. Robust clumps of oblanceolate leaves, to 10″ long. The flowers are on longer stems; useful for cutting. The 'Formosa' hybrid strain ranges in color from carmine to white; 2′ stems. Portugal.

——————— 'Rubra' has rose pink flowers above green mats of foliage. 10″–12″ tall.

ARMORACIA, Cruciferae. (3)

rusticana variegata	FOLIAGE	SP	2′–3′/1′–2′
	○	Z10-3/H	DR **

Variegated Horse-Radish makes crowded stands of erect, stalked, mostly basal leaves. Grown for its foliage, this ornamental form of the common Horse-Radish has large oblong variously lobed toothed leaves, to 15″ long, variegated in beautiful cream and green marbled patterns. Tiny white 4-petaled flowers in unappealing panicled racemes. Likes deep, rich, moist soil. May become invasive. Will not thrive in hot, damp climates. Very attractive to slugs and snails. Southeastern Europe.

ARNICA, Compositae. (30)

montana	YELLOW	LSP/SU	1′–2′/1′
	○	Z9-6/H	DS **

Grouped into a low, basal rosette, the oblong to oblanceolate, opposite leaves are hairy, at times weakly toothed, to 5″ long; stem leaves smaller, usually limited to one pair. The stout, straight stems bear one or more Daisy-like, yellow to orange yellow 2″–3″ flower heads. Free-draining but moist, lean soils; becomes rangy if grown in rich soil. Mountains of Europe. There are also several North American species not totally devoid of ornamental qualities.

Armoracia rusticana variegata

ARTEMISIA, Compositae. (400)   **Mugwort**

The Wormwoods furnish gardeners with some of the most beautiful of all foliage plants. Not only are they attractive in their own right, but they are invaluable as foils to plants of stronger coloration. Their gray or silver leaves relieve the monotony of the green herbage of most garden plants, and form useful backgrounds for delicate specimens. Many are excellent for cutting and drying. In habit, they vary from tall erect border subjects, to low mounding plants, suitable for edging and as ground covers. The alternate leaves, more often than not, are lobed or dissected. The insignificant yellow to white diskoid flower heads nod in sparse panicles; they add little to, or even detract from, the ornamental effect. As their reflective foliage suggests, these are sun-loving plants, but most will also tolerate very light shade. They thrive in ordinary soil, which must drain well, as none will countenance wet winter conditions. Few adapt to hot, humid summers. Easily propagated by division or cuttings, some by seed.

---

abrotanum	FOLIAGE	SU	3′–5′/1.5′–2′
	○	ZI0-6/H	CD ✶✶

Old-Man, Southernwood. [*A. procera*]. This aromatic subshrub has erect branching stems and feathery, gray green 1½″–2½″ leaves, 1 to 3 times pinnately dissected into linear lobes. Tiny nodding yellowish flowers in loose panicles. Prune back in spring. Southern Europe.

Artemisia lactiflora

absinthum	FOLIAGE	SU	2′–4′/2′–3′
	○	Z10-4/H	CD ***

Absinthe, Common Wormwood. Silvery-white throughout, this upright, well-branched subshrub has both stems and foliage coated with silky hairs. The delicate 1½″–4″ leaves are 2 to 3 times pinnately dissected below, less divided above. Grayish flower heads in leafy panicles. Europe.
———— 'Lambrook Silver,' one of Margery Fish's superior selections, is readily available. Taller 'Lambrook Giant' does not appear to be in the trade here.
A. 'Powis Castle' is considered a hybrid between *A. absinthum* and *A. arborescens*. A bushy 2′–3′ plant, with feathery foliage. Probably hardy to Z7. It rarely flowers.

arborescens	FOLIAGE	SU/LSU	2′–3′/2′
	○	Z10-9/H	CD **

A tender evergreen with spidery silver foliage, clothed in silky hairs. Leaves to 4″ long, 1 to 3 times pinnately dissected into linear lobes. Leafy panicles of tiny yellow flower heads. Mediterranean.

lactiflora	WHITE	SU	4′–6′/2′
	○ ◑	Z10-4/H	D ***

White Mugwort differs from the other species in having dark green foliage, paler beneath, and ornamental flowers, on sturdy, erect stems. The lower leaves, to 9″ long, are coarsely pinnately divided; the upper leaves are smaller. Graceful tapering 1′–2′

Artemisia schmidtiana 'Silver Mound'

panicles of minute cream white flower heads. An excellent plant for the back of the border. Requires a moister, richer soil than the other Wormwoods. China.

ludoviciana	FOLIAGE	SU	2′–3.5′/2′–3′
	O	Z10-5/H	D ****

[*A. l.* var. *gnaphalodes*, *A. gnaphalodes*, *A. palmeri* Hort., *A. purshiana*]. Stands of simple erect stems, with mostly lanceolate, silvery gray 1½″–4″ leaves, sometimes toothed or lobed. Large panicles of whitish flower heads. Central and Western North America. A variable species, with many subspecies or varieties, as well as cultivars, all much confused in the trade. 'Purshiana' and 'Valerie Finnis' are listed, but are of uncertain status.

———— *albula*. [*A. albula*]. This southwestern subspecies has blunter, somewhat revolute leaves, only ⅜″–¾″ long. Two popular cultivars, 'Silver King,' and slightly shorter 'Silver Queen,' both with silvery white foliage, undoubtedly belong here, although they have considerably longer leaves than the wild form.

pontica	FOLIAGE	SU	1.5′–3′/1.5′
	O	Z10-5/H	D **

Ferny, 2 to 3 times pinnately divided, hoary 1½″–2″ leaves, broadly ovate to triangular in outline. Long, loose panicles of nodding whitish yellow flower heads. Invasive. Southeastern and central Europe.

pycnocephala	FOLIAGE	LSP/SU	1′–2′/2′
	O	Z10-8/H	D ***

A coastal native, with attractive foliage, but an unruly habit. Its erect to ascending stems are crowded with small, hairy, gray leaves, 1 to 3 times pinnately dissected into linear lobes. Slender panicles of yellow flower heads. Cut back annually for neatness. Central California to Oregon.

schmidtiana	FOLIAGE	LSU/EF	1′–2′/1.5′
	O	Z10-4/H	D ****

This formal plant makes a rounded mound of silvery silky-haired foliage. The leaves, to 1¾″ long, are dissected into linear segments and are so crowded that they appear to be in rosettes. Yellowish heads in pyramidal panicles. Satisfactory only in full sun and lean soil. Trim to keep shapely. Japan.

———— 'Nana' is a dwarf form, only a few inches high.

———— 'Silver Mound.' Most commonly grown; it has largely replaced the species. 1′ tall.

A. frigida is similar in effect.

splendens Hort.	FOLIAGE	SU	1′–1.5′/1′–1.5′
	O	Z10-5/H	CD ***

The bushy little plants sold under the names *A. canescens*, *A. splendens*, and *A. versicolor* are seldom reliably identified. All have attractive, finely dissected silvery foliage, and can be used in similar ways.

stellerana	FOLIAGE	SU	1.5'–2.5'/2'–3'
	○	Z10-4/H	CD ***

Beach Wormwood, Dusty Miller, Old-Woman. Unlike similar *Senecio cineraria,* also called Dusty Miller, this species is extremely hardy. Densely felted throughout, with white hairs. The coarsely lobed, pinnatifid 2"–4" leaves are ovate to oblong in outline. Yellow ¼" flower heads in slender, dense panicles. Northeastern Asia, eastern North America.

ARTHROPODIUM, Liliaceae. (10)

cirrhatum	WHITE	LSP	3'/2'
	○ ◑	Z10-8	DS **

Renga Lily has arching evergreen leaves, to 2' long by 2½" wide, in a dense basal clump. Branching, open panicles of white 1" flowers, with 6 spreading tepals, are borne on long slender scapes, well above the bold mass of foliage. Likes a well-drained but fertile soil. Slugs and snails can be a problem. New Zealand.

ARUM, Araceae. (12)

These unusual plants are valued for their Calla-like flowers, and for the striking red berries which follow. The handsome, arrow-shaped, basal foliage emerges in late summer, persists through the winter, and then disappears after flowering time. The variously colored inflorescence consists of spathe and spadix, typical of the family. Male and female flowers, both fertile and sterile, are borne on the spadix, usually below a slight constriction in the spathe. Similar to *Arisaema.* Arums are suitable for open woodland gardens or for planting in light shade, where the soil is deep and somewhat damp. Best combined with a summer ground cover. Beware of slugs.

creticum	YELLOW	SP	1.5'/1'
	○ ◑	Z9-7/H	DS **

Of upright habit, its shiny, dark green, hastate leaves, to 5" long, appear in late summer on long petioles. The goblet-shaped 3"–6" spathes are greenish white, somewhat drooping and fragrant; the bright yellow spadix is erect, about half as long as the spathe. Under favorable conditions, deep red berries develop later. Shade in hot areas. Crete.

italicum	WHITE	LSP	1.5'/1'
	○ ◑	Z10-6/H	DS ***

Italian Arum. The long-petioled leaves, with pale green midribs and undulate margins, flare widely at the base. Large, pale, greenish white spathes, upright in bud, droop with

Arum creticum

age. Each encircles a stumpy, cream yellow spadix, barely half as long as the spathe. Spikes of orange red berries show in the early fall. Southeastern Europe.

————— 'Marmoratum' [*A. p. marmoratum* Hort.] has larger and broader leaves, with the main veins finely traced in cream or gray. Scarce.

————— 'Pictum' [*A. i. italicum*], not to be confused with fall-blooming *A. pictum*, has very shiny spear-shaped leaves, with bold cream veining and marbling, rimmed by a narrow green border. Showy red fruits form in late summer. Prized by flower arrangers. A miniature form is sometimes found.

ARUNCUS, Rosaceae. (3)

dioicus	WHITE	SU	4′–7′/3′
	○ ◑	Z9-3	DS ****

Goatsbeard. [*A. sylvester, Spirea aruncus*]. Erect, shrublike, with many branching stems. The compound leaves are bi- or tripinnate; ovate to lanceolate leaflets, doubly toothed, prominently veined and rough to the touch. Above the copious foliage rise large, feathery, Astilbe-like, branched panicles. The tiny white flowers are 5-petaled; male and female flowers on separate plants. The showier males make better garden subjects. Rich, moist soil. Trouble-free. Northern Hemisphere.

————— *astilboides,* a dwarf variety. 2′ tall. Japan.

————— 'Kneiffii,' with dainty narrow leaflets. 3′ tall.

Aruncus dioicus

ASARUM, Aristolochiaceae. (75)   Wild Ginger

The Wild Gingers, native to woodland areas of the North Temperate Zone, are grown chiefly as foliage ground covers. Creeping rhizomatous roots send up groups of 1–3 long-petioled, usually heart-shaped leaves; evergreen or nearly so in some species, fully deciduous in others. Curious purplish brown flowers, borne almost at ground level, are hidden by the foliage. The corolla is absent or vestigial; the calyx, bell shaped and deeply 3 lobed, with flaring or reflexed lobes. Slugs and snails must be controlled.

canadense	BROWN	SP	6″/8″–1′
	◑●	Z9-2	DS ∗∗∗

Canada Wild Ginger, Canada Snakeroot. The deciduous, heart-shaped leaves, about 6″ across, on hairy 1′ petioles are paired. Between them arise purplish brown 1″ flowers, with pointed reflexed lobes. New Brunswick south to North Carolina and Missouri.

caudatum	BROWN	SP	7″–9″/8″–1′
	◑●	Z9-6	DS ∗∗

British Columbia Wild Ginger. This western native is semievergreen except in cold winters. Its long, creeping rhizomes spread widely. The paired, kidney-shaped 6″ leaves, hairy along the veins and underneath, are carried on 7″ petioles. The calyx lobes extend into long tails. British Columbia to California.

Asarum europaeum

europeum	BROWN	SP	5″–6″/8″–1′
	◑●	Z8-4	DS ✳✳✳✳

European Wild Ginger. A choice evergreen, with uniform, dark green, polished foliage. Leaves in pairs, heart shaped with wavy margins, to 3″ across, on 5″–6″ petioles. The small greenish brown drooping flowers are inconspicuous. Spreads rapidly to create a handsome ground cover in humusy soils, but not where soil is dry. Plant no more than 1″ deep. Europe.

hartwegii	BROWN	SP	4″–6″/1′
	◑●	Z9-5	DS ✳✳✳

Cyclamen-Leaved Ginger. One of our most beautiful native plants. Its evergreen kidney-shaped leaves, about 5″ across on 8″ petioles, are dark green, strikingly marbled with silver along the veins, hairy beneath. Flowers similar to those of *A. caudatum.* California, Oregon.

shuttleworthii	BROWN	ESU	8″/1′
	◑●	Z9-7	DS ✳✳✳

Mottled Wild Ginger. [*Hexastylis shuttleworthii*]. A variable species, with fragrant, usually evergreen, cordate leaves, to 3″ across, either gray spotted or solid green. The vase-shaped, 2″ flowers have flaring lobes, and are violet spotted inside. Well adapted to southern gardens. Virginia to Georgia, Alabama. Little Brown Jugs, *A. arifolium*

[*Hexastylis arifolia*], native from Virginia to Florida and Alabama, blooms a little earlier, with an abundance of jug-shaped 1″ flowers. Its evergreen triangular leaves are usually blotched. *A. virginicum* [*Hexastylis virginica*], Virginia Wild Ginger, is also similar. Its thick evergreen leaves are paler along the veins. Somewhat hardier. Virginia to South Carolina, Tennessee.

ASCLEPIAS, Asclepiadaceae. (200)	Milkweed

"Familiarity breeds contempt"—thus we neglect these handsome native plants in favor of the more exotic; nevertheless many are worthy of a place in the garden, both for their flowers and their foliage. Milkweeds are stiffly erect, sturdy plants with substantial leaves mostly opposite or whorled. Many small colorful flowers are borne in compact terminal or axillary umbels. The complex and unusual flowers consist of a corolla with 5 sharply reflexed lobes, and a slender column topped by a corona, which together enclose the fused sexual parts. The corona itself is composed of 5 erect hoods each usually armed with a pointed horn. Their familiar pods or follicles contain numerous seeds tufted with silky hairs. Milkweeds resent transplanting; they are best container grown. Plant several together for effect.

curassavica	RED	SU	3′–3.5′/1.5′
	○	Z10-8/T	RS ✳✳✳

Bloodflower. This tropical plant has gone wild in our most southern states. Its glossy, opposite leaves, to 5″ long, are elliptic-lanceolate. Loose umbels of brilliant flowers; corolla red, corona orange. South America.

hallii	PINK	SU	1′–1.5′/1′
	○	Z9-4	RS ✳✳

Sometimes branching at the base and with large gray green lanceolate to narrowly ovate leaves. Corolla rose pink, corona greenish white. Much admired by English gardeners. Rocky Mountains.

incarnata	PINK	SU	4′–5′/1.5′
	○	Z10-3/T	RS ✳✳✳

Swamp Milkweed has opposite, linear to elliptic 3″–6″ leaves, and small tight umbels of bright pink, or rarely white, flowers. A useful plant for wet areas. Eastern and central North America.

speciosa	PINK	LSP/SU	2′–3′/1.5′–2′
	○	Z9-3	RS ✳✳✳

Large gray green woolly ovate leaves. Rose pink flowers in tight umbels. A superior ornamental. Northwestern and north central United States. *A. purpurascens* has less woolly foliage, and flowers of a deeper rose. Somewhat taller, *A. syriaca,* the Common Milkweed, is similar, but has disappointingly dull, purplish pink flowers.

Asclepias purpurascens

tuberosa	ORANGE	SU	1'–2.5'/1.5'
	○	ZI0-3/T	RS ****

Butterfly Weed. Clumps of stout stems crowded with narrow 2″–4″ leaves. Brilliant orange flowers in tight 2″ umbels. Free-flowering. Likes well-drained sandy or gravelly soil. Drought tolerant. There are also red and yellow flowered forms. Eastern and central North America.

ASPERULA, Rubiaceae. (90) Woodruff

The Woodruffs are seldom grown in this country outside of herb and rock gardens, but several are quite suitable for the flower garden. They have mostly square stems, interrupted by tiers or whorls of leaves. The numerous small flowers are funnel form, with 4 flaring lobes, as distinct from *Galium,* which has rotate flowers.

gussonii	PINK	SU	6″–9″/1'
	○	Z9-5	DS **

[*A. suberosa*]. This perfectly charming low tufted plant has softly woolly gray leaves, in closely set whorls of 4–5. Delicate pink flowers, about ¼″–½″ long, cluster at the tips of the stems. Resents winter wetness and probably is suitable only for scree gardens or alpine houses. Sicily.

Asperula tinctoria

| *tinctoria* | WHITE | SU | 1′–2′/1′ |
| | ○ | Z9-7 | DS ∗∗ |

Dyer's Woodruff. [*Galium triandrum*]. Rounded clumps of weak, tangled stems bearing whorls of 4–6 short linear bright green leaves. The branching clusters of small pure white flowers, produce an airy effect, useful in borders. Tolerant of dry soils. Europe.

| *taurina* | WHITE | SU | 1′/1′ |
| | ○ | Z9-6 | DS ∗∗ |

Erect and more robust than the other species. The leaves, in whorls of 4, are ovate and slightly glossy. Dense heads of white flowers are borne in the leaf axils. Southern Europe.

ASPHODELINE, Liliaceae. (15) Jacob's Rod

Jacob's Rods increase slowly and in time, make good-sized clumps. Soil must be well drained. Planting and division are best in the fall.

| *liburnica* | YELLOW | SU | 2′–2.5′/1′ |
| | ○ ◑ | Z8-6 | DS ∗∗ |

[*Asphodelus liburnicus*]. Similar to *A. lutea*. The linear 4″–5″ leaves are borne only on

Asphodeline liburnica

the lower part of the delicate stems. Branched racemes of pale yellow flowers, subtended by small bracts. Southeastern Europe.

lutea	YELLOW	LSP-ESU	3′–4′/1′
	○ ◐	Z8-6	DS ***

Jacob's Rod, King's Spear, Yellow Asphodel. [*Asphodelus luteus*]. Stiff, unbranched stems, heavily clothed in gray green linear 8″–10″ leaves, rise from the rhizomatous rootstock. The shiny, fragrant, starlike 1″ flowers, subtended by buff-colored ¾″ bracts, congregate into tubular 1′–1.5′ racemes. Striking in a monochromatic grouping with *Euphorbia polychroma* and *Potentilla fruticosa.* Mediterranean region.

ASPHODELUS, Liliaceae. (15)

albus	WHITE	ESU	3′–5′/1′
	○	Z9-5	DS ***

Asphodel. Heavy clumps of triangular, linear leaves, to 2′ long, rise from thick, tuberous roots. The terminal racemes of flowers, supported by stiff, unbranched scapes, rise well above the foliage. The white to pale buff pink funnelform flowers, to ¾″ across, are subtended by brown bracts. Most suitable for informal plantings. Southern Europe.

ASTER, Compositae. (500)

Hardy Asters are a large and important genus, which includes some of the most valuable plants for summer and fall gardens. They range in height from 6″–12″ dwarfs, well suited for the front of the border or rock garden, to 6′–7′ giants. The Michaelmas Daisies rise, stately and bold, behind more modest perennials or among shrubs. Many of our native species serve well in wild or native plant gardens. All have usually alternate, undivided leaves, narrow and sometimes toothed. Most of the species have numerous radiate (seldom diskoid) flower heads, arranged in panicles, corymbs, or racemes; a few have solitary heads. Backing each flower head are several rows of variously shaped, leafy, involucral bracts. The central yellow, or sometimes purplish, disk is surrounded by one or more rows of white, pink, red, purple, or blue ligulate ray florets; only clear yellow and orange are absent. The one exception is Goldilocks, *A. linosyris* [*Crinitaria linosyris, Linosyris vulgaris*], which has puffy yellow diskoid heads on 2′ stems. Other yellow-flowered species, previously grouped under *Aster,* now belong with *Chrysopsis;* intergeneric hybrids with *Solidago* are known as X *Solidaster.* The species, easily propagated from seed, often self-sow readily. Most of the ornamentals are hybrids, and must be propagated vegetatively, usually by division. All the Michaelmas Daisies (mainly *A. novae-angliae* and *A. novi-belgi* hybrids) require frequent division at least every two years, in spring or fall, to maintain vigor and to curb their wandering rhizomes. Most Hardy Asters thrive in well-enriched fertile but rather

Asphodelus albus

dry soils, but too little moisture, as well as stagnant air, favor attacks from powdery mildew. The hybrids seem particularly susceptible to this serious problem, to the point that some gardeners avoid the genus altogether; an unfortunate reaction, since most of the species are resistant. Combat powdery mildew with regular applications of fungicide and by thinning out young growth for better air circulation. Water deeply during dry spells, but avoid wetting the foliage, as with Garden Phlox. The tall kinds, particularly those with large, heavy clusters of flowers, need strong support. Protect from intense sun in the hottest climates.

x *alpellus* **Hort.**	BLUE	ESU	1′–1.5′/1′
	○	Z9-4	D ✳✳✳

A. alpinus x *A. amellus.* This hybrid is best known for its cultivar 'Triumph,' sometimes listed as a cultivar of *A. amellus.* It makes neat, low clumps of hoary, green, lanceolate foliage, above which rise strong stems, supporting fragrant violet blue flower heads with orange disks. Long-blooming, particularly where summers are cool.

alpinus	BLUE	LSP-ESU	6″–1′/1′
	○	Z9-4	CDS ✳✳✳✳

Basal clumps of light gray green, spatulate, decurrent leaves, to 2″ long. Several sturdy stems, each bearing a few smaller sessile leaves, end in solitary, yellow-eyed, violet blue 1″–3″ daisies. Prefer well-drained, limy soil. Best where winters are cold. Rocky Mountains, Europe. There are several reliable cultivars, but mixed blues, lavenders, pinks, and purples are usually offered in the trade.
———— 'Dark Beauty' has deep blue flowers, on 6″–12″ stems.
———— 'Goliath' has soft blue daisies. 15″ tall.
———— 'Happy End.' Semidouble, lavender flowers. 1′ high.

amellus	PURPLE	LSU-EF	1.5′–2′/1.5′
	○ ◑	Z10-4	CDS ✳✳

Italian Aster forms bushy clumps of strong, branched stems, clothed in rough, hoary green, oblong-lanceolate leaves, the lower to 6″ long. Terminal clusters of fragrant, violet purple 1½″–2″ flowers, with yellow centers. Divide in spring. Slow to establish and sometimes temperamental. Drought resistant. A very long-blooming plant for the front of the border. Italy.
———— 'Framfieldii.' Lilac heads, on 2′ stems.
———— 'Rudolph Goethe' has striking deep lavender flowers.
Native *A. spectabilis,* the Seaside Aster, also has large, deep violet to purple flowers, in late summer and fall. Its leafy flower clusters bloom above dark green tufts of long-petioled, lanceolate 3″–4½″ leaves. Its creeping rhizomes help to control erosion. Tolerant of sandy, acid soils, as well as poor, heavy ones. Coastal Massachusetts to North Carolina.

divaricatus	WHITE	LSU-EF	1′–2.5′/1.5′
	◑●	Z9-3	DS ✳✳

White Wood Aster. [*A. corymbosus*]. This woodlander, much appreciated as an ornamental in Europe, is useful for brightening shady corners, notably in city gardens. Loose clumps of almost black, rather sprawling, twiggy stems. The long-petioled, smooth 5″–7″ leaves are heart shaped and toothed; the sessile upper leaves, reduced. Mostly terminal, flat-topped clusters of white ½″–1″ flower heads; few rayed, with red or yellow centers. In bloom for several weeks. Tolerant of dry shade. Best planted in groups of three or more, and allowed to flop over stronger plants, such as Bergenias, a favorite combination of Gertrude Jekyll. Southern Canada, eastern United States.

ericoides	WHITE	SU-F	1′–3′/1.5′
	○	ZI0-3	DS **

Heath Aster. [*A. multiflorus*]. Several upright or sprawling, much-branched stems grow from a rhizomatous rootstock. The basal leaves are hairy and spatulate, to 3″ long; on the crowded stems, they are stiff and Heath-like, only ¼″ wide, and usually early deciduous below. Countless delicate white ½″ daisies, in multiple spreading, often one-sided sprays. May need staking, but otherwise carefree. Maine to Minnesota, south to Florida.
———— 'Cinderella' is superior to the species. 2.5′ tall.
Similar *A. lateriflorus* 'Horizontalis' is also trouble-free. Its stiff, very twiggy, almost shrublike 2′–3′ stems have tiny toothed variable leaves, dark green, turning to copper in fall. A profusion of mauve starry ¼″ flowers, with rosy pink disks, blooms well into the fall.

x *frickartii*	LAVENDER	ESU-F	2′–3′/1.5′
	○ ◑	ZI0-5/H	CD ****

A. thompsonii x *A. amellus*. Considered one of the best of all herbaceous perennials. It forms loose bushy mounds of numerous, much-branched stems, with dark green, rough-hairy, oblong to ovate 1″–2½″ leaves. Solitary at the ends of the branches, the lavender blue 2½″ daisies have bright yellow centers. The fragrant blooms cover the plants throughout summer and fall, almost year round in mild climates. Excellent for cutting. Somewhat resistant to mildew. In cold climates, mulch in winter with evergreen boughs. Divide every 3–4 years, preferably in spring.
———— 'Mönch' starts into bloom later and is considered a superior selection. Well-branched, sturdy and upright stems. Very floriferous, with large lavender blue daisies.
———— 'Wonder of Staffa' has clear lavender blue 2½″ heads on erect, branched 3′ stems, throughout summer and fall. Not necessarily superior to the ordinary hybrid.
x 'Flora's Delight' (*A. thompsonii* 'Nanus' x *A. amellus*) has gray green foliage on bushy 1.5′ stems. Masses of pale lilac flowers, with large yellow disks, bloom for several months. Cut back after flowering to maintain vigor. A fine Alan Bloom selection.

liniarifolius	MAUVE	SU-EF	1′–2′/1′
	○	ZI0-3	D **

Stiff Aster, Savoryleaf Aster, Bristle Aster. Neat clumps of strict, well-branched stems, covered with rough, stiff, linear 1″–1½″ leaves. The yellow-eyed lavender pink to violet ¾″–1″ flower heads usually cluster in terminal corymbs. Plants with white, purple, or pink flowers are available. Divide in spring. Eastern and central United States.

novae-angliae	VIOLET	LSU-F	3′–6.5′/2′
	○	Z9-4	D ✶✶✶✶

New England Aster, Michaelmas Daisy. The robust clumps of vertical, thick, rather woody stems, branching and rough-hairy above, are crowded with gray green foliage. The upper leaves are sessile, stem clasping, and broadly lanceolate, 4″–5″ long by ½″–1″ wide; rough-hairy above, softly hairy beneath. The lowermost leaves drop early. Long-blooming, loose leafy corymbs of 1″–2″ daisies, each with numerous narrow rays and yellow disks, surrounded below by sticky leaflike involucral bracts. Very tolerant of wet soils. Somewhat resistant to mildew. Eastern and central United States.

————— 'Alma Potschke' has beautiful warm pink flowers, on 3′ stems, for 6 weeks or more.

————— 'Harrington's Pink' open its clear pink blooms later than the other cultivars. Requires division less frequently than most. 3′–4′ tall.

————— 'September Ruby.' Cerise flowers on 4′ stems.

————— 'Treasurer' has masses of deep lilac flowers. 3.5′–4′.

novi-belgi	VIOLET	LSU-F	1′–4′/1.5′
	○	Z9-4	D ✶✶✶✶

New York Aster, Michaelmas Daisy. Variable in habit, but with mostly stout hairless stems. The narrowly lanceolate 2″–5″ leaves are also smooth, usually toothed, and only slightly clasping. Deep violet 2″ flowers, with reflexed involucral bracts. Eastern United States. This species and *A. novae-angliae* have been hybridized extensively, particularly with *A. dumosus, A. ericoides,* and *A. laevis. A. subspicatus* [*A. douglasii*] was used in developing the compact 'Oregon-Pacific' strain. These breeding programs have resulted in a broad range of cultivars. Divide often, replanting the healthy outer portions, which rapidly make robust plants. Moist, fertile soil is best for these Asters; fertilize sparingly to avoid soft, rank, disease-prone growth. Spray regularly for mildew. Except where the growing season is short, pinch the young shoots at about 6″ and again later to force bushy, compact growth; blooming will be delayed slightly. Brush stake the taller cultivars.

'Alert' has deep crimson flowers on 10″–15″ stems.

'Boningdale White.' Semidouble to double clean white flowers. 3.5′–4′ in height.

'Jenny' makes tight 12″–15″ mounds, covered with cerise flowers.

'Marie Ballard' is an old cultivar, but one of the loveliest. Large double powder blue flowers on 4′ stems.

'Patricia Ballard.' Almost fully double pink flowers. 3′ tall.

'Sailor Boy' has large navy blue flowers. 3′ tall.

'Winston Churchill' blooms early with nearly red flowers. 1.5′.

thompsonii	MAUVE	SU-F	1′–3′/1.5′
	○	Z9-5	D ✶✶✶

A parent of *A.* x *frickartii.* This most satisfactory plant is usually offered in its dwarf form, 'Nanus.' It has a neat, bushy habit, with hairy, gray green foliage, early deciduous below. The vertical stems bear clasping, broadly ovate 3″–4″ leaves, with triangular

Aster thomsonii

bases, and 8–12 usually shallow teeth. Sky blue or pale lilac flower heads reach 1″–2″ or more across and bloom in succession until cut down by frost. Himalayas.

| *tongolensis* | VIOLET | SU | 1′–1.5′/1′ |
| | ○ | Z9-3 | D *** |

[*A. subcaeruleus*]. Dark green mats or tufts of sessile, rather hairy, oblong-spatulate to oblong-lanceolate 3½″–5″ leaves, which are mostly toothless. The solitary 2″ flower heads have blue to violet rays and orange or yellow disks. Fine as edging plants, in the rock garden or as cut flowers. Well-drained, fertile soil. Divide after flowering or in late summer. Western China to India.
————— 'Berggarten.' This German cultivar has lavender blue 2″ daisies, with an orange center. 1.5′.
————— 'Napsbury.' Often sold as *A. yunnanensis* 'Napsbury.' A superior selection, with deep lavender blue, orange-eyed 2″ daisies on 15″–18″ stems.
————— 'Wartburg Star.' Large violet blue flowers with gold disks. 1.5′–2′.
Similar Asian species include *A. yunnanensis, A. diplostephioides,* and *A. farreri.*

| *umbellatus* | WHITE | LSU-LF | 3′–4′/2′ |
| | ○ | Z9-3 | D ** |

Flat-Topped Aster. Close, bushy plants, with smooth or minutely hairy wiry stems. The rough-margined, tapered, lanceolate to ovate 2″–6″ leaves are smaller and early deciduous below. Dense, flat-topped corymbs of sparsely rayed, white ¾″ flower heads with yellow eyes. Thrives in damp soil. Blooms with the Cardinal Flower, *Lobelia cardinalis,* and continues well into late fall. Eastern Canada to Georgia, west to Illinois, Minnesota.

ASTILBE, Saxifragaceae. (25)

Gardening in shaded areas would not be the same without these rewarding plants. Their excellent foliage, in low, leafy clumps, is mostly basal. The leaves are divided several times into toothed leaflets or, more rarely, are just lobed or toothed. On slender stems, the tapering plumy panicles are composed of a multitude of tiny flowers, usually with 4–5 petals and twice as many stamens. Astilbes like deep, organically rich, moist soils, well drained, especially in winter. All thrive in semishade, in sheltered positions, but will grow in full sun in moderate climates. They do not tolerate the high summer temperatures of our warmest zones, either arid or humid. They can be grown in coastal areas of California, tempered by a marine influence, but will have a shortened life span. These vigorous plants normally need division every third year; fertilize in the spring. Eastern *A. biternata* and Nepalese *A. rivularis,* both 5′–6′ tall, are more valued for their handsome foliage than for their rather understated flowers.

| **x** *arendsii* | VARIOUS | ESU/LSU | I.5′–4′/I.5′–2.5′ |
| | ○ ◑ | Z8-4 | D **** |

This group of hybrids, the results of numerous crosses involving *A. chinensis* var. *davidii, A. japonica, A. thunbergii,* and *A. astilboides* Hort. (probably a variant of *A. japonica*), covers a great range. They vary in all respects: in size, in the appearance and color of their foliage, and in the shape and color of their inflorescences, as well as in flowering time. The ferny compound leaves may be matte or glossy; some, in plants with deep pink to red flowers, are dark green, or tinged with brown or purple. Occasionally grown as a species, white-flowered *A. japonica* blooms early. Its cultivars with purple or variegated foliage are of particular interest.

————— 'Avalanche.' White. 2.5′–3′. Midseason.
————— 'Bremen.' Bright red. 3′. Early.
————— 'Bressingham Beauty.' Rich pink. 3′. Late.
————— 'Bridal Veil' ['Brautschleir']. White. 2′. Midseason.
————— 'Cattleya.' Rose pink. 3′. Early.
————— 'Deutschland.' White. 2′. Early.
————— 'Erica.' Pink. 2.5′. Midseason.
————— 'Etna.' Dark red. 2′. Early.
————— 'Europa.' Light pink. 2′. Early.
————— 'Fanal.' Red. 2′. Early.
————— 'Federsee.' Bright pink. 3′. Early.
————— 'Irrlicht.' White. 2′. Early.
————— 'Koblenz.' Red. 2′. Early to late.
————— 'Montgomery.' Red. 2′–2.5′. Early.
————— 'Ostrich Plume' ['Straussenfeder']. Pink. 3′. Midseason.

Astilbe x *arendsii* 'Montgomery'

———— 'Peach Blossom.' Light pink. 2'. Midseason. *A. chinensis* x *A. japonica;* correctly *A.* x *rosea* 'Peach Blossom.'

———— 'Professor van der Wielen.' White. 4'. Midseason.

———— 'Red Sentinel.' Carmine red. 2.5'–3'. Midseason.

———— 'Rheinland.' Deep rose. 2'. Early.

———— 'Snow Drift.' Pristine white. 2'. Early.

———— 'White Gloria.' Cream white. 2'. Midseason.

chinensis 'Pumila'	PINK	SU-LSU	1'/1'
	○ ◑	Z8-4	D ****

This tough little plant may be a hybrid. It spreads readily, forming a dense mat of sharply incised compound leaves. Over a long season, it bears many stiff, erect panicles of deep magenta pink flowers. Unfortunately, the lower flowers turn brown while the upper are still in bud. Late-blooming 'Finale' reaches 1.5' in height and has graceful panicles of pale mauve pink flowers. Other selections are less readily available.

simplicifolia hybrids	VARIOUS	ESU/SU	1'–1.5'/1'
	○ ◑	Z8-4	D ****

Diminutive *A. simplicifolia* of Japan differs from most other Astilbes in not having compound foliage. Its arching panicles of white flowers are pretty enough, but it is best known as a parent of several excellent hybrids, to which it has contributed its small stature. In most cases, the other parents are *A.* x *arendsii* or *A.* x *rosea (A. chinensis* x *A. japonica).* Lacking a name of their own, these hybrids are usually listed as if they were merely cultivars of *A. simplicifolia.*

———— 'Atrorosea' bears its bright pink flowers in early summer. 1.5' tall.

———— 'Praecox Alba' is white. 1' tall.

———— 'Sprite' *(A. simplicifolia* x *A. glaberrima saxosa)* has loose panicles of shell pink flowers, in midseason, over dark green foliage. 10" tall. An Alan Bloom selection. The *A.* x *crispa* hybrids are thought to result from crossing *A. simplicifolia* and *A.* x *arendsii.* 'Perkeo,' only 10" tall, has jagged dark green foliage. Its panicles of bright pink flowers bloom in early to mid summer.

taquetii 'Superba'	PINK	LSU	3'–4'/2'–3'
	○ ◑	Z8-4	D ****

[*A. chinensis taquetii* 'Superba']. This selection has large, broad, compound leaves, with double-toothed leaflets. Its narrow panicles of vivid magenta pink flowers are borne, high above the mass of foliage, on strong, erect stems. One of the latest of the Astilbes to bloom. It is more tolerant of heat and drought than most of the *A.* x *arendsii* hybrids.

ASTRANTIA, Umbelliferae. (9)   Masterwort

The Masterworts are charming cottage garden flowers, with mostly basal foliage, palmately lobed or divided. Slender, erect and branching flowering stems each bear several flower heads. The inflorescences are compact, domed umbels of tiny flowers, surrounded by a collar of stiff, petallike bracts. Need evenly moist, rich soil. Excellent for cutting.

| *carniolica* | WHITE | SU | 1′–1.5′/1′ |
| | ○ ◑ | Z9-4/H | DS ** |

This small species has deeply 3- to 5-lobed leaves, with ovate and toothed lobes. Bracts shorter than the flowers. Europe.
———— *rubra.* Flowers crimson. Delicate, slow to establish.

| *major* | WHITE | SU | 2′–3′/1′–1.5′ |
| | ○ ◑ | Z9-4/H | DS *** |

This most commonly cultivated species has deeply lobed 3″–6″ leaves of rounded outline. The lobes, numbering 3–7, are obovate to lanceolate and coarsely toothed. Flower heads to 1½″ across of greenish white or pinkish florets. The greenish white lanceolate bracts, sometimes flushed with pink or green tipped, are as long as or longer than the flowers. Europe.
———— *alba* has all-white flowers and bracts.
———— *carinthiaca* [*A. m. involucrata* Hort.] has larger bracts.
———— 'Margery Fish.' Quite close to the species. Said to be longer-flowering. Name sometimes misapplied to 'Shaggy.'
———— *rubra* has rose pink bracts.
———— 'Rosensinfonie.' An excellent form with rose pink bracts.
———— 'Shaggy' is a cultivar of *A. m. carinthiaca* with very long irregular bracts.
———— 'Sunningdale Variegated' ['Variegata']. Leaves irregularly edged and splashed with yellow. Shade from strong sun.

| *maxima* | PINK | SU | 1.5′–2.5′/1′–1.5′ |
| | ○ ◑ | Z9-4/H | DS ** |

[*A. helleborifolia*]. Leaves trifoliate. Flower heads rose pink. The bracts are longer than the flowers, and edged with sharp teeth. Southern Europe, Caucasus.

AUBRIETA, Cruciferae. (12)

Ideal at the front of the border, in the rock garden, or as an underplanting for spring bedding. Aubrietas form low evergreen mats of hairy gray green foliage, abundantly covered with pink to purple cruciform flowers. The numerous cultivars and seed strains are probably hybrids with *A. deltoidea.* These are variable, but particular selections are easily propagated from cuttings. In warm zones treat as biennials.

| *deltoidea* | VARIOUS | SP | 6″/1′ |
| | ○ ◑ | Z9-4/H | CS **** |

False Rockcress. Sprawling or trailing leafy plants. The short-stalked leaves are spatu-

Astrantia major 'Rosensinfonie'

Aubrieta deltoidea 'Gloriosa'

late to rhomboid, with 2–3 large teeth. Loose racemes of pink to purple ¾ " flowers are held above the foliage. Shear after flowering. They require well-drained light soil; excellent in stone walls. Best where summers are moderate. Mediterranean, Asia Minor.

——————— 'Borsch's White.' Possibly the only white-flowered cultivar.
——————— 'Gloriosa' has large, soft rose flowers.
——————— 'Greencourt Purple.' Double bluish purple flowers.
——————— 'Mrs. Rodewald.' Large carmine flowers.
——————— 'Purple Gem' is purple flowered.
——————— 'Variegata' has blue flowers, with silvery white-margined foliage.

STRAINS:

'Royal Cascade' has flowers in soft pinks and purples on trailing stems. Sometimes separate color selections, such as 'Red Cascade,' are offered. 4″ tall.

AURINIA, Cruciferae. (7)

Indispensable in the spring garden, Basket-of-Gold adds bold sweeps of color to the rock garden or the front of the border. It is particularly effective tumbling over low walls and next to steps or pathways. A position in full sun, in lean, very well-drained soil, produces neat, compact plants; rich soil results in untidy, sprawling plants with

Aurinia saxatilis

soft growth. This low-maintenance plant provides a wonderful contrast to early spring-flowering bulbs. May be treated as a biennial for spring bedding. Other species sometimes grown, include *A. corymbosa* [*Alyssum corymbosum*] and *A. petraea* [*Alyssum edentulum*].

saxatilis	YELLOW	ESP	1′–2′/1′
	○	ZI0-4	S ****

Basket-of-Gold, Goldentuft, Gold Dust. [*Alyssum saxatile*]. Dense hummocks of mealy gray persistent foliage grow from a rather woody base. The spatulate 2″–5″ leaves are softly hairy and sinuate; stem leaves smaller. Fragrant masses of brilliant yellow ¼″ cruciform flowers arranged in dense panicles cover the whole plant. Shear back hard after flowering to shape and prevent self-seeding. Europe. Alpine *Alyssoides utriculata* [*Vesicaria utriculata*], of similar appearance, is noteworthy for the inflated bladderlike ½″ pods which follow the flowers.

———— 'Citrinum.' ['Sulphureum,' 'Luteum']. Pale citrus yellow flowers on 8″–10″ stems.

———— 'Compactum' has a neater, more compact habit.

———— 'Compactum Flore-Pleno.' Bright yellow double flowers. Compact. Propagate from cuttings.

———— 'Dudley Neville Variegated.' The beautifully variegated foliage makes this a lovely, all-season plant. Cuttings only.

———— 'Silver Queen' is compact, with buttery yellow flowers on 8″ stems.

———— 'Sunnyborder Apricot' has apricot-tinted flowers on 8″–10″ stems.

———— 'Variegatum.' Leaves variegated with yellow. Propagate from cuttings.

Baileya multiradiata

BAILEYA, Compositae. (4)

multiradiata	YELLOW	SP-F	1.5′/1′–1.5′
	○	Z10-6/H	S ∗∗∗

Desert Marigold is erect to decumbent, and has beautiful silver gray woolly foliage. The alternate leaves are pinnate; the upper few, entire. Daisy-like, bright yellow 1½″–2″ flower heads are carried singly on long, bare stalks. This long-flowering plant of deserts and dry areas needs a well-drained sandy soil, and will not succeed in areas with hot, humid summers. In the wild, where it grows to an altitude of 5,000′, it is quite hardy. In gardens, its hardiness depends on cultural and climatic conditions. Often grown as an annual. Southwestern United States, Mexico.

BALLOTA, Labiatae. (35)

pseudodictamnus	FOLIAGE	LSP-SU	1′–2′/1.5′–2′
	○	Z10-8	CD ∗∗

This compact plant, with white-woolly stems and foliage, provides a gentle contrast to stronger colors in the garden. The opposite 1″–1½″ leaves are ovate to rounded, finely wrinkled and round-toothed. Axillary whorls of insignificant white flowers with purple spots; corolla 2 lipped, the lower lip 3 lobed. Needs very sharp drainage. Protect from winter wetness. Crete. *B. acetabulosa* from Greece is quite similar.

BALSAMORHIZA, Compositae. (12)			Balsamroot

hookeri	YELLOW	SP	1′/1′–1.5′
	○	Z10-4	S ***

Balsamroot has ferny, pinnately divided lanceolate leaves, to 1′ long, in a broad basal rosette; quite variably hairy. Many solitary clear yellow 1½″–3″ flower heads on leafless stems. Both this and the following species need well-drained soil and abhor wet winter conditions. The long taproots make transplanting difficult; plants should be container grown. Slow-growing. Northwestern and north central United States.

sagittata	YELLOW	SP/ESU	2′–2.5′/1.5′
	○	Z10-4	S ***

Oregon Sunflower. Broad basal rosettes of handsome hastate leaves, to 1′ long, with a silvery pubescence, mostly on the undersides, which diminishes with age. Each of the numerous bare flower stalks bears a large dark yellow 2½″–4″ sunflower. North central and Western United States.

BAPTISIA, Leguminosae. (35)	False Indigo

These handsome natives have erect, branching stems, alternate trifoliate leaves, and long racemes of Pea-like flowers. Of easy culture, but dislike lime; resent root disturbance. *B. perfoliata* is useful for cutting. Several other species and hybrids are occasionally grown, but are of modest horticultural interest.

Baptisia australis

| *australis* | BLUE | ESU | 3′–6′/3′ |
| | ○ ◑ | ZI0-3/T | DS **** |

Blue False Indigo, Blue Wild Indigo. [*B. exaltata, B. caerulea, B. versicolor*]. This most ornamental species has blue green foliage with obovate leaflets to 3″ long. Terminal racemes of indigo blue 1″ flowers, followed by attractive seedpods; both good for cutting. Drought resistant. May need staking. The few listed cultivars are not notably superior. Eastern United States. Of similar habit, white-flowered *B. pendula* from North Carolina grows 2′–3′ tall.

| *leucantha* | WHITE | ESU | 3′–6′/2′ |
| | ○ ◑ | ZI0-3/T | DS ** |

White False Indigo has glaucous leaves, with obovate to oblanceolate wavy leaflets, to 2½″ long. White 1″ flowers sometimes tinged with purple. *B. alba* and *B. leucophaea* are also white flowered. United States.

| *tinctoria* | YELLOW | ESU | 2′–4′/2′ |
| | ○ ◑ | ZI0-3/T | DS *** |

This bushy plant has blue green foliage; blunt, obovate leaflets, to 1″ long. Many sparsely flowered racemes of small bright yellow flowers. Less ornamental than *Thermopsis*. Eastern to central United States.

BELAMCANDA, Iridaceae. (2)

| *chinensis* | ORANGE | SU | 2′–3′/1′ |
| | ○ ◑ | ZI0-5/T | DS **** |

Blackberry Lily, Leopard Flower. [*Pardanthus chinensis*]. Erect, rising somewhat stiffly from heavy rhizomes. The sword-shaped, equitant leaves are similar to those of related *Iris*. The blooms, to 2″ across, are on wiry, forked stems; their showy perianth segments brightly splashed and spotted with yellow and crimson. Later, the fruit capsules split to expose shiny black fleshy seeds, valued for dried winter arrangements. China. The Candy Lilies, X *Pardancanda norrisii (Pardanthopsis dichotomus [Iris dichotoma]* x *Belamcanda chinensis),* are quite similar in habit and foliage. Their spotted and striped flowers display a wide range of colors from white and cream to orange, reds, and purples. They bloom freely through the summer and fall on 3′ stems. Bred by Dr. Jim Alston.

BELLIS, Compositae. (15)

| *perennis* | VARIOUS | LSP/ESU | 6″/6″–8″ |
| | ○ ◑ | ZI0-3/H | DS **** |

English Daisy, Bachelor's Buttons. Makes a basal rosette of spatulate, often hairy,

Belamcanda chinensis

Bellis perennis

leaves. Garden forms have solitary Daisy-like flowers, to 2″ across, often double or semidouble, in white, pinks, reds, and crimson. Numerous strains are available. Excellent for edging or as an underplanting for spring-blooming bulbs. Usually treated as a biennial. Europe, Western Asia.

STRAINS:

'Carpet.' Red, rose, or white 1″ double blooms on 4″ stems.
'Monstrosa' has 3″ double flowers in the usual color range. 8″ tall.
'Pomponette' is semidouble, with 1½″ blooms with quilled rays. 6″ in height.

BERGENIA, Saxifragaceae. (12)

[*Megasea, Saxifraga*]. The Bergenias have both handsome foliage and flowers. Although suited to the front of the flower border, they are perhaps at their best when used as a ground cover along pathways, or under shrubs or trees in shady places. Their thick, creeping rhizomes spread slowly to produce solid clumps, but are not invasive. The foliage of most species is more or less evergreen, and often becomes deeply colored when temperatures drop. The bold, sometimes leathery leaves, shaped like oars or paddles, are prized by flower arrangers. Strong stems bear clusters of waxy flowers in spring, often repeated with a second flush later in the season. The individual ¼″–½″ flowers are Saxifrage-like, and range from white to deep purplish red. Tolerant of a wide range of soils, but too rich a diet results in soft, leafy growth at the expense of good flowering. They prefer some shade, but will also thrive in full sun if the soil is sufficiently deep and moist. The best winter color occurs in exposed positions. Slugs need control, especially in damp places. Cut back if the stems become leggy, and divide as clumps become crowded. Since they cross-fertilize readily, there are numerous hybrids, some of uncertain origin. These must be propagated vegetatively. Some of the best are listed following the species. Not for southern Florida and the Gulf Coast.

ciliata	PINK	ESP	1′/1.5′
	◗	Z10-6	DS ****

Winter Begonia. [*B. ligulata*]. The spreading, densely hairy 9″–12″ leaves are almost circular, with toothed margins. The foliage is damaged by frost, although the roots are hardy. Large elegant clusters of fragrant pale pink flowers, which darken with age; calyces red. Pakistan.
——————— *ligulata* has nearly white flowers, with rosy calyces. The leaves are hairy only along the margins.
B. stracheyi is similar but smaller, and flowers in late spring.

cordifolia	PINK	SP	1.5′–2′/2′
	◗	Z10-3	DS ****

Heart-Leaved Bergenia. A strong grower with shiny, thick, Cabbage-like 1′ leaves, cordate at the base; bright green, but turning bronzy in cold weather. Deep pink flowers, with rosy calyces, cluster on thick, branched stems among the foliage. Siberia.

——————— *purpurea* ['Purpurea']. The leaves are larger and reddish, becoming purplish in winter. Red flower stalks, to 2′ tall, hold vivid purplish red flowers well above the foliage.

——————— 'Perfecta' is somewhat taller than the species. Rosy red flowers and purplish leaves. A Dutch introduction.

| *crassifolia* | MAGENTA | SP | 1′/1.5′ |
| | ◑ | Z10-4 | DS **** |

Winter-Blooming Bergenia, Pigsqueak. [*B. bifolia*]. Similar to *B. cordifolia*, but with smaller, spoon-shaped leaves, wedge shaped at the base, turning deep pink in winter. Its compact clusters of nodding rose purple flowers are on short branches. Siberia.

——————— *pacifica* has broader leaves.

| *purpurascens* | PINK | SP | 1′/1′ |
| | ◑ | Z9-4 | DS *** |

[*B. delavayi, B. beesiana*]. Especially valued for its glossy, dark green, upright foliage. The leaves are ovate-elliptic, with hairy margins. In cold weather, they turn almost crimson, mahogany beneath. Deep pink, nodding flowers on purple red stems rise well above the foliage. Himalayas to China.

Cultivars/Hybrids:

'Abendglocken.' ['Evening Bells']. Rose pink flowers; red winter foliage. 15″ tall.

'Abendglut' ['Evening Glow'] has deep purple flowers; its smaller leaves are maroon brown in winter. 10″ in height.

'Ballawley.' ['Delbees']. Crimson flowers. Tall, bright green leaves turning coppery in winter. Protect from cold winds. An Irish hybrid. Stems to 2′.

Bergenia 'Morgenröte'

'Bressingham Salmon' has salmon pink flowers. Foliage flushed pink in winter. Late flowering. One of several Bloom introductions. 1′ tall.

'Bressingham White.' Robust, pure white flowers. Early. 1.5′–2′.

'Morgenröte' ['Morning Red'] has purplish red flowers. One of the best. 15″ in height.

'Silberlicht.' ['Silver Light']. White flowers, pink tinged with age. Dark calyces. 1′ tall.

'Sunningdale.' Carmine red flowers on red stalks. Deep red winter foliage. Late blooming. 1.5′ stems. A Graham Thomas introduction.

BESCHORNERIA, Agavaceae. (10)

yuccoides	GREEN	SP/SU	**4′–6′/3′**
	○	Z10-8	DS ***

An imposing accent plant, which forms a rosette of narrow gray green 2′ leaves, less rigid than those of Yuccas. Erect or arching, the coral red stalked panicles have large red bracts and many drooping branchlets. The pendent, yellow green, funnelform 2″ flowers are followed by attractive bronze capsules. Needs good drainage, but enjoys a fertile soil. Several other similar species are rarely cultivated. This is the hardiest. Mexico.

BISCUTELLA, Cruciferae. (40)

frutescens	YELLOW	SP	**1.5′/1′**
	○	Z9-6	S **

Grouped low rosettes of grayish green felted foliage. The leaves are ovate to fiddle shaped, to 8″ long, with interesting wavy margins. Masses of cruciform ¼″ flowers are arranged in loose corymbs. The dried pods are useful for winter arrangements. For the front of the border or rock garden. Prefer limy, well-drained soils. Spain.

BLANDFORDIA, Liliaceae. (4)   Christmas Bells

Christmas Bells flower for the holidays only in the Antipodes; in American gardens, they bloom in late spring or early summer. Their slender, 2-ranked, evergreen leaves, triangular in cross section, are mostly basal. The racemes of pendent flowers rise on erect scapes, longer than the foliage. Brilliantly colorful, tubular or funnelform corollas, with 6 short lobes. Best in well-drained, but moist, acid soils; can also be grown under damper conditions and in bog gardens. Light shading from direct sun is advisable. Commonly raised from seed; they take 3–4 years to reach flowering size. With the exception of *B. punicea,* they do not deserve their difficult reputation.

Beschorneria yuccoides

Bletilla striata

grandiflora	RED	SP-ESU	1.5'–2.5'/1'–1.5'
	○ ◑	ZI0-9/H	DS **

[*B. flammea*]. Basal tufts of grassy, linear leaves, with crenulate margins. Loose racemes of funnel-shaped 1½″–2½″ flowers; corolla red, with short yellow lobes. There is also an all-yellow form. Australia.

nobilis	RED	SP-ESU	1.5'–2.5'/1'–1.5'
	○ ◑	ZI0-9/H	DS **

Herbage similar to that of *B. grandiflora*. Cylindrical red ¾″–1¼″ flowers tapering toward the base; corolla lobes yellow or yellow and green. Australia. *B. cunninghamii* is slightly larger in all its parts, but otherwise quite similar. Its leaf margins are entire. Tasmanian *B. punicea* [*B. marginata*] has strap-shaped leaves and numerous tubular red 1½″ flowers, yellow on the inside. Rather temperamental.

BLETILLA, Orchidaceae. (9)

striata	PURPLE	ESU	1.5'/9″
	◑	ZI0-8	D ***

Chinese Ground Orchid. [*B. hyacinthina, Bletia hyacinthina, B. striata*]. Each fleshy subterranean pseudobulb produces 3–5 pleated, broadly linear leaves, to 8″ long, papery

Boltonia asteroides 'Snowbank'

in texture. Wiry stems bear loose racemes of several 1½″ nodding flowers. The petals and sepals are deep purplish pink; the lip is paler with dark markings. Plant the pseudobulbs in masses, not more than 1″–2″ deep, in friable, highly organic soil. Best under light shade. They must never dry out. Top dress in the fall with leaf mold, and give winter protection where frost may occur. China, Japan, Korea.

———————— 'Alba' has white flowers. May be difficult to find.

———————— 'Albo-striata.' Foliage edged with white. Purple flowers. Scarce.

BOLTONIA, Compositae. (10)

| asteroides | VARIOUS | LSU/F | 4′–7′/2′–4′ |
| | ○ ◑ | Z10-3/T | DS **** |

[*B. glastifolia*]. These bold, Aster-like natives have strong, erect stems, much-branched above. The linear to oblanceolate, small-toothed, gray green leaves are up to 5″ long. Numerous ¾″ flower heads in loose panicles; disk florets yellow, ray florets white, pink, lilac, or purplish. Of easy culture in ordinary soil. Divide regularly every 2–3 years. May need staking, particularly in light shade. Plant several in a group at the back of the border, or naturalize in the landscape. Eastern and central United States.

———————— var. *latisquama*. [*B. latisquama*]. Larger flower heads, to 1″ or wider, in a denser inflorescence. Violet blue. Central United States. Its cultivar 'Nana' is 2′–3′ tall, with pink ray florets.

———————— 'Snowbank' reaches 4′ in height. White ray florets. Does not need staking.

BORAGO, Boraginaceae. (3)

| laxiflora | BLUE | ESU-F | 1.5′/2′ |
| | ○ | Z10-8 | S ** |

Rather unruly, but eminently worth growing for the superb azure blue of its dainty flowers. The basal foliage is coarse; leaves small, ovate to oblong, and hairy. The trailing hispid stems bear loose nodding cymes of small, 5-lobed campanulate flowers. Grow only in sharply drained poor soil. Water sparingly. Provide some shade in the hottest areas. Self-seeds readily. Corsica.

BROWALLIA, Solanaceae. (8)

| speciosa | BLUE | SP-F | 2′–2.5′/1′ |
| | ○ ◑ | Z10-9 | CS **** |

Bush Violet. Arching or pendulous; often woody at the base. Its pointed, ovate leaves are bright green and smooth, to 2½″ long. The showy purplish blue 1″–1½″ flowers

Borago laxiflora

are salverform and 5 lobed; solitary in the upper leaf axils. Provide deep fertile soil; avoid overfertilizing, which causes excessive foliage at the expense of flowers. Colombia. Browallias are frequently treated as annuals and are particularly useful for containers, bedding displays, and indoor pot plants. Many cultivars and strains are available, some taking advantage of the drooping habit for special use in hanging baskets.

———— 'Alba' has pure white flowers.

———— 'Major' has larger flowers then the species.

STRAINS:

'Troll.' A neat, compact strain with blue or white flowers. Slower growing than most; excellent for bedding displays. 6″–10″ tall.

'Bell' is particularly good for hanging baskets. Available in individual colors. 12″–15″ tall.

BRUNNERA, Boraginaceae. (3)

| *macrophylla* | BLUE | LSP-ESU | 1.5′/2′ |
| | ○ ◑ | Z10-3/H | DRS **** |

Siberian Bugloss. [*Anchusa myosotidiflora*]. Large, neat clumps of dark green, roughly hairy, basal foliage. The long-petioled, broadly heart-shaped leaves are 6″–8″ wide, more at maturity, and conspicuously net veined. They emerge along with the flowers, and expand to their full size only after the blooms have faded. The alternate, stem leaves are ovate and much smaller. Slim, hairy stems bear loose sprays of intensely blue ¼″ Forget-Me-Not flowers well above the foliage. They bloom as well in sun as in shade. The soil should be fertile and moist, particularly in sunny positions. Slugs may need control. Propagate in early spring; only by division of the fleshy roots, in the case of cultivars. Splendid as a specimen plant, in groups in the border, or massed as a ground cover under deciduous trees, especially beside water. A superior low-maintenance plant. Self-seeds freely. Eastern Mediterranean, western Siberia.

———— 'Hadspen Cream' is similar to 'Variegata,' with cream-bordered leaves. This and the next are British introductions.

———— 'Langtrees.' Leaves speckled with silvery gray, particularly toward the margins.

———— 'Variegata' has beautiful creamy white bands along the leaf margins. The variegated areas are prone to burning by wind and sun. In a cool, sheltered place, it makes an elegant specimen plant.

BULBINE, Liliaceae. (55)

These succulent plants have long, fleshy, linear to lanceolate leaves arising from their base, from short or creeping stems. Each tall, slender scape bears a long, tapering raceme of small, starry, 6-tepaled flowers, which open from the bottom up. Most easily distinguished from *Bulbinella* by its stamen filaments, which are densely bearded. Tolerant of heat and drought. Easy to grow and satisfied with even poor soils, which nevertheless must be well drained. Deadhead to prevent prolific self-seeding and for appearance. Good as cut flowers.

alooides		YELLOW	LW-ESP	1.5′–2′/1′–2′
	○ ◐		Z10-9/H	DS **

Its tuberous roots produce evergreen, Aloe-like rosettes of lanceolate, basal leaves. One or more slender scapes rise from the center of each rosette, each bearing a narrow raceme of ¼″ flowers. Amenable to most soils and situations. Spreading. South Africa.

bulbosa		YELLOW	LW	1.5′–2′/1′
	○ ◐		Z10-9/H	DS **

The bulblike tuber underlies a tuft of narrow basal leaves, to 16″ long. The slender scape reaches 2′ high and supports a loose raceme of starry 1″ flowers. Well-drained soils. Similar but smaller, *B. semibarbata* has 3 bearded and 3 naked staminal filaments. Both are Australian.

caulescens		YELLOW	LW-ESP	1.5′–2′/1.5′–2′
	○ ◐		Z10-9/H	DS ***

[*B. frutescens*]. The running, horizontal stems send up sprays of foot-long, linear, light

Bulbine bulbosa

green leaves, fleshy and rather lax. Slender racemes of starry yellow 1″ flowers on long scapes. It eventually spreads to cover large areas. South Africa.

BULBINELLA, Liliaceae. (13)

Differs from *Bulbine* mainly in having naked, not bearded, staminal filaments. The racemes are indeterminate, as are those of *Bulbine,* but broader in proportion to their length and more closely flowered.

| *floribunda* | YELLOW | W/ESP | 1.5′–2.5′/1′–1.5′ |
| | ○ ◑ | Z10-9/H | DS *** |

[*B. robusta, B. robusta* var. *latifolia, B. setosa*]. Has narrow, strap-shaped, deeply grooved, sheathing, basal leaves, to 2′ long. The base of the plant is cluttered with the fibrous remains of old leaves. The long, robust scapes end in substantial racemes, some 6″ long. The starry, 6-tepaled ¼″ flowers are usually yellow, but may be orange or white. Likes a sandy soil, enriched with a goodly amount of organic matter. The foliage dies down following flowering, and the plant goes dormant for some months during spring and summer. Remove dead foliage. Water well when new leaves appear, and during the growing and flowering seasons; withhold water during dormancy. Divide when clumps become crowded. Superb, long-lasting cut flowers. South Africa. *B. cauda-felis* [*B. caudata*] makes slender racemes of pure white flowers. This beautiful plant does not appear to be in cultivation in this country.

| *hookeri* | YELLOW | ESU/SU | 1.5′–2.5′/1′–1.5′ |
| | ○ ◑ | Z9-8/H | DS *** |

[*Chrysobactron hookeri*]. Arching linear leaves, to 1′ or longer. Broad racemes of starry, 6-tepaled flowers, to ¼″ or slightly wider, on stout scapes. Prefers a porous but moist soil; will also grow in drier sites. New Zealand.

BUPLEURUM, Umbelliferae. (100)   Thoroughwax

The Umbellifers are not generally known for spectacular floral effects, but the discreet charm of these plants will appeal to collectors of the unusual. Both are useful to flower arrangers.

| *angulosum* | YELLOW | SU | 1.5′/1′ |
| | ○ ◑ | Z9-4/H | DS * |

The lanceolate leaves, to some 6″ long, are crowded into a dense basal tuft. Several slender branching stems, with a few small clasping leaves, carry the flowers well above the mass of the foliage. The loose compound umbels are subtended by leaflike bracts. The small secondary umbels are composed of a tight cluster of minute yellow flowers

Bulbinella hookeri

Bupleurum angulosum

Calamintha grandiflora

subtended by a collar of larger rounded pale jade green bracts about ¾ ″ wide. Slow growing. Evergreen in mild-winter areas. This mountain plant is unlikely to be tolerant of hot, or hot and humid summers. Pyrenees, northeastern Spain.

| *falcatum* | YELLOW | SU-LSU | 2′–3′/1.5′–2′ |
| | ○ ◑ | Z9-4 | DS ∗ |

This extremely variable plant has narrowly ovate, stalked basal leaves and slender clasping stem leaves. The branching stems bear compound bracted umbels of tiny yellow flowers. Long flowering. Short-lived, but self-sows freely. Central and southern Europe, Asia.

| **CALAMINTHA, Labiatae. (7)** | | | **Calamint** |

| *grandiflora* | PINK | SU | 1′–2′/1.5′ |
| | ○ | Z10-5 | CDS ∗∗ |

Calamint. [*Satureja grandiflora*]. This erect, bushy little plant excels at the front of the border. Its opposite 2″–3″ leaves are ovate and strongly toothed. Sparsely flowered axillary cymes. The bright pink 1″–1½ ″ flowers are 2 lipped, the lower lip much longer and 3 lobed. Easy, but likes good drainage and a warm site. Southern Europe.

———————— 'Variegata' makes a lively show with leaves irregularly spattered with cream.

nepeta nepeta	WHITE	SU-EF	I′–1.5′/I′–1.5′
	○	ZI0-5	CDS **

[*C. nepetoides*]. A compact plant with erect stems and opposite, ovate, round-toothed, hairy ¾″ leaves. The long cymes bear a multitude of tiny white or pale lilac 2-lipped flowers. Well-drained soil. Plant alongside paths, where a passing touch will release the delightful scent of the foliage. Southern Europe.

CALLISIA, Commelinaceae. (8)

[*Spironema, Rectanthera*]. Inch Plants, native to tropical areas of the Americas, are suitable for growing out of doors, only in frost-free climates. In colder zones, they make good conservatory plants, and the trailing species adapt well to hanging baskets. They are related and somewhat similar to Wandering Jew. Conspicuously jointed and sheathed by the leaf bases at the nodes, the fleshy stems are sprawling or prostrate. The alternate leaves are oblong-lanceolate, decreasing in size along the stem. White, pink, or blue flowers, in paired, bracted, scorpioid cymes, are borne at the tips of the stems and in the upper leaf axils. As is typical of the family, the flowers have parts in threes; their sepals are papery, their petals of equal size. Easy to grow in average soil. Shade from very hot sun. Propagate from cuttings.

Caltha palustris 'Monstruosa'

elegans	WHITE	F-W	1'–2'/1.5'
○ ●		ZI0-9/T	C **

Striped Inch Plant. Sometimes listed incorrectly as *Setcreasea striata*. This velvety-haired plant has branched, ascending stems. Its 2-ranked leaves may reach 3" long and over 1" wide; they are dark green, elegantly silver striped above and purplish beneath, the margins fringed with hairs. The white ¾" flowers have petals longer than the sepals. Southern Mexico.

fragrans	WHITE	SU	2'–3'/3'
○ ●		ZI0-9/T	C **

[*Spironema fragrans, Tradescantia dracaenoides*]. The succulent, branched stems root along their length and quickly make wide-spreading plants. They are well clothed in thick, slightly boat-shaped leaves, smooth green above and purplish beneath. The lower leaves are about 1½" wide and may reach 10" long, and form dense rosettes of foliage. Long reddish purple stems, topped with large branched clusters of fragrant white flowers, develop only if the plants are sufficiently watered. Unusual as a ground cover or at the front of the border. Mexico.

———— 'Melnickoff' [*Spironema melnickoffii*] has foliage striped longitudinally with buff or brown.

CALTHA, Ranunculaceae. (20)   Marsh Marigold

Marsh Marigolds are handsome plants with bold, bright green foliage and showy, Buttercup-like flowers. They are at home in damp or boggy places near ponds or streams, although they will also thrive in drier areas if shaded from full sun. Soil must be rich in organic matter and never be allowed to dry out.

palustris	YELLOW	ESP	1'–2'/1.5'
◑ ●		ZI0-3	DS ****

Marsh Marigold, Kingcup, Cowslip. [*C. parnassifolia*]. Mounded clumps of glossy rounded leaves, heart shaped at the base, on long succulent stems. Many bright yellow 1" flowers are supported on hollow, branched stems above the foliage, in terminal and axillary clusters. Well adapted to positions under deciduous trees, where they are shaded when the trees leaf out. Europe, northern United States, Canada.

———— 'Alba' is white flowered.

———— 'Monstruosa' ['Multiplex,' 'Monstrosa-Plena,' 'Flore-Pleno'] has fully double 1½" pompomlike flowers. Longer in bloom than the species.

polypetala	YELLOW	ESP	2'–3'/3'
◑ ●		ZI0-3	DS **

A vigorously spreading, often sprawling plant, with lustrous dark green leaves, to 1' across. Not as floriferous as *C. palustris,* but the larger 3" blooms appear earlier. Tolerates somewhat drier soil conditions. Caucasus.

The Bellflowers present an astonishing array of valuable ornamentals, ranging in habit from stately border plants to rock garden specimens. *Campanula* is unusual among genera, in having such a high proportion of plants of merit. Their basal leaves often differ in shape from the alternate leaves along the stems, and are mostly larger and longer-petioled. The flowers are commonly borne in racemes; sometimes they are solitary or in spikes, panicles, or clusters. The corollas vary from campanulate to rotate; their 5 lobes, from shallow to deep. With the exception of a few alpine species, Campanulas are easy to please. They thrive in sun, or light shade in hot climates, in well-drained, fertile, preferably neutral to alkaline soils. Slugs and snails are their only serious enemies. The species are easily propagated by seed, cuttings, or division; cultivars and hybrids, vegetatively. Canterbury-Bells, biennial *C. medium* and its many forms, are essential features of cottage gardens. Monocarpic *C. thyrsoides,* rough-hairy throughout, bears a short stiff spike of crowded 1″ flowers, exceptional among those of Campanulas for their yellow color. Its foliage, mostly basal, is narrowly lanceolate. Var. *carniolica* ['Carniolica'] has longer spikes. European Alps. Extensive selection and breeding of the popular favorites has resulted in an abundance of cultivars and hybrids. Only the best are detailed below. Enthusiasts are referred to the magnum opus *Campanulas* by H. Clifford Crook.

alliariifolia	WHITE	LSP-ESU	1.5′–3′/1.5′
	○ ◑	Z10-3	CDS ***

Woolly throughout. Its petiolate basal leaves, to 10″ long, are ovate-cordate to kidney shaped, with rounded teeth; the sessile stem leaves, much smaller and ovate. Sometimes branched above, the stems bear one-sided racemes of nodding white 1″–2″ bells with short lobes. Not in the first rank of Bellflowers, but useful for the wild garden. Asia Minor, Caucasus.

carpatica	BLUE	LSP-SU	8″–1.5′/1′–1.5′
	○ ◑	Z10-3	CDS ****

Carpathian Bellflower, Tussock Bellflower. Spreading clumps of leafy, branching stems. Coarsely toothed, ovate 1″–1½″ leaves on long stalks below, short ones above. The solitary, erect, broadly campanulate 1″–2″ flowers are borne freely on slender axillary stalks. Carpathian Mountains.
———— var. *alba* ['Alba'] has white flowers.
———— var. *turbinata* [*C. turbinata*], smaller than the type, has gray green foliage and more bell-shaped deep purplish blue flowers. Its form *pallida* has light blue flowers.
———— 'Blue Carpet.' A blue-flowered dwarf.
———— 'Blue Clips' has medium blue flowers.
———— 'China Doll' is compact, with lavender blue flowers.
———— 'Wedgwood Blue' is a dwarf, with bright violet blue flowers.
———— 'White Carpet.' A white-flowered dwarf.
———— 'White Clips' is white flowered.

| *cochleariifolia* | BLUE | LSP-SU | 6"/1' |
| | ○ ◑ | Z10-6 | CDS **** |

[*C. bellardii, C. pusilla*]. This mountain plant forms spreading mats, with small, few-toothed ovate leaves, narrowly lanceolate above. One or more per stem, the nodding, bell-shaped ¾" flowers vary from purplish blue to pale blue. Free blooming. Best for rock gardens and walls. Europe.

——————— var. *alba* has white flowers.

| *collina* | BLUE | LSP | 1'/1' |
| | ○ ◑ | Z10-3 | CDS *** |

Forms a low clump of long-petioled, ovate-oblong 2"–3" leaves, downy and sharp toothed. One-sided racemes of deep purplish blue, bell-shaped 1½" flowers. Caucasus.

| *glomerata* | PURPLE | SP-SU | 1'–3'/1.5'–2' |
| | ○ ◑ | Z10-3 | CDS **** |

Clustered Bellflower forms clumps of erect stems and long-stalked, hairy, toothed, ovate 4"–5" basal leaves. The stem leaves are sessile or even clasping, and smaller. Funnel-shaped ¾"–1" flowers, in dense but somewhat clumsy terminal and axillary clusters, subtended by leafy bracts. Free blooming. Europe, Asia.

——————— var. *acaulis* has short stems, barely taller than the basal foliage.

——————— var. *alba* is white flowered.

——————— var. *dahurica*. Deep violet purple flowers on 1' stems.

Campanula lactiflora 'Loddon Anna'

———— 'Crown of Snow' ['Schneekrone'], with white flowers, just exceeds 1.5′ in height. More graceful in habit.

———— 'Joan Elliott' has violet purple flowers. 1.5′ tall.

———— 'Superba' has violet blue flowers on 3′ stems.

lactiflora	BLUE	LSP-LSU	3.5′–5′/2′
	○ ◑	Z10-6	CDS ✱✱✱

Its erect, branching stems are clothed in sessile, sharp-toothed, narrowly lanceolate 2″–3″ leaves. Large, heavy, broadly conical panicles of light to dark blue or white flowers. The open, bell-shaped corolla is deeply lobed, about 1″ across. Usually needs staking. Caucasus.

———— 'Loddon Anna' has pale pink flowers.

The following excellent English cultivars are not yet available here: 'Pouffe,' with pale blue flowers, on 1′ stems, is an Alan Bloom selection; 'Pritchard's Variety' has violet blue flowers on 3′ stems.

latifolia	BLUE	SU	3′–4′/2′
	○ ◑	Z10-3	CDS ✱✱✱✱

This bold plant forms clumps of sturdy, erect, unbranched stems, clothed in rather coarse, toothed, ovate leaves, to 6″ long. The upper leaves are smaller and narrower. Short, leafy, terminal racemes of purplish blue 1¼″ flowers. The corolla is campanulate, with pointed, reflexed lobes. Europe, Asia.

———— 'Alba' is white flowered.

———— 'Macrantha' has darker, purplish blue flowers.

persicifolia	BLUE	SU	2′–3′/1′–1.5′
	○ ◑	Z10-3	CDS ✱✱✱✱

Peach-Leaved Bellflower, Willow Bellflower. [*C. grandis, C. latiloba*]. Vertical stems, clothed in small-toothed, linear to lanceolate leaves, arise from basal rosettes of larger, round-toothed, narrowly oblanceolate 4″–8″ leaves. Loose racemes of bell-shaped 1½″ flowers, erect to nodding, on weak pedicels. Europe, North Africa, Asia. Innumerable cultivars in white and various shades of blue, as well as semidoubles and doubles.

———— 'Alba' has white flowers.

———— 'Blue Gardenia' has double blue flowers.

———— 'Telham Beauty' has large light blue flowers.

———— 'White Pearl' is a double.

The plant once known as *C. latiloba* [*C. grandis*] is now included under *C. persicifolia*, although it is coarser and more robust, and has sessile, more broadly campanulate flowers. Its cultivars 'Highcliffe,' 'Percy Piper,' and lilac pink 'Hidcote Amethyst' are still often sold under the old name.

portenschlagiana	BLUE	LSP-SU	6″–9″/1′
	○ ◑	Z10-5	CDS ✱✱✱✱

[*C. muralis*]. Forms a low mound of long-stalked basal leaves, rounded in outline, but very coarsely and irregularly toothed. The stem leaves are similarly rounded or ovate.

The procumbent stems end in clusters of upfacing, broadly campanulate, light purplish blue 1″ flowers, with blunt, reflexed lobes. Free blooming. Yugoslavia.

——————— var. *alba* has white flowers.

poscharskyana	BLUE	LSP-ESU	6″/1.5′
	○ ◑	Z10-3	CDS ****

Spreading, prostrate to decumbent stems, with long-stalked, coarsely toothed ovate 1″ leaves, narrower and smaller above. Loose panicles of starry, broadly campanulate lavender blue 1¼″ flowers, with long, pointed, reflexed lobes. Blooms profusely. Best suited to walls and rock gardens. Yugoslavia. *C. elatines* var. *garganica* [*C. garganica*] is similar, but has gray-hairy foliage and purplish blue flowers. *C. elatines* is more compact than its variety. All are closely related botanically. Southeastern Europe.

punctata	VARIOUS	SU	1′–2′/1.5′
	○ ◑	Z10-3	CDS **

Erect to arching stems. The sharp-toothed, ovate to heart-shaped 3″–5″ leaves are concentrated below; the stem leaves are smaller, narrower, and tend toward sessile. Its nodding, tubular, bell-shaped 2″ flowers, with short, blunt lobes, vary from white to lilac or pink and are usually well spotted inside with red or purple. Japan, Siberia. 'Alba' is white flowered; 'Rubriflora' has rosy purple blooms. Somewhat taller *C.* x *burghaltii* is thought to be a hybrid of *C. punctata* with *C. latifolia.* It has pale lavender to grayish blue bells, 3″ or more in length, with small spurs projecting from the sinuses between the corolla lobes. Propagated by division. Its scarcity is inexplicable, as it has long been in cultivation. Rare *C. takesimana,* from Korea, much resembles *C. punctata.* Its flowers are white, finely mottled with lilac outside and spotted with maroon inside.

pyramidalis	BLUE	SU	4′–6′/2′
	○	Z10-8	S ***

Chimney Bellflower is short-lived and often grown as a biennial. Its erect, branched stem is well clothed below in sharp-toothed, ovate 2″ leaves, decreasing above in size and length of petiole. The racemes of open, bell-shaped 1″ flowers, pale blue, with deep, flaring lobes, are grouped into pyramidal panicles. One of the most beautiful of Campanulas. Usually requires staking. Southern Europe.

——————— var. *alba* ['Alba'] has white flowers.
Closely related *C. versicolor,* from Greece, is more reliably perennial. It forms a clump of several stems, reaching 4′ in height. Its flowers, deep blue in the throat, shade to pale blue or white at the edge.

rapunculoides	VIOLET	SU	2′–4′/2′–3′
	○ ◑	Z10-3	CDS ****

Creeping Bellflower, Rover Bellflower. This ineradicable but beautiful weed spreads aggressively by rhizomes. It must never be introduced into gardens, except into the wildest areas. Its erect stems are clothed below in round-toothed, ovate to cordate 1″–3″ leaves, above in sessile, sharp-toothed, lanceolate-ovate leaves larger than the lower. Long, graceful racemes of sharply lobed, funnelform 1″ flowers. Europe, Asia.

| *rotundifolia* | BLUE | LSP-SU | 6″–1.5′/1′–1.5′ |
| | ○ ◑ | Z10-3 | CDS **** |

Bluebell, Bluebells-of-Scotland, Harebell. Only its long-petioled, toothed, basal leaves are round, but usually these are early-deciduous. Linear to lanceolate 1½″–3″ leaves clothe its many wiry, erect stems. Solitary or in racemes, the bell-shaped, blue 1″ flowers are upright to nodding. A variable group of plants with numerous local forms throughout the Northern Hemisphere.

———— 'Alba' is white flowered.

———— 'Olympica' has large flowers.

| *tommasiniana* | BLUE | SU | 6″–1′/1′ |
| | ○ ◑ | Z10-5 | CDS ** |

Erect to sprawling, branched stems, thick with Willow-like, linear-lanceolate 1″–2″ leaves, only very lightly toothed. The nodding, tubular, pale lavender blue ¾″ flowers, with short, spreading lobes, crowd toward the ends of the branches. Somewhat stiff in habit, but pleasantly so. Italy.

| *vidalii* | WHITE | SU | 2′–3′/1.5′–2′ |
| | ○ ◑ | Z10-9/H | CS ** |

This branching subshrub with grooved stems has fleshy, toothed, oblong to spatulate 3″–4″ leaves, nearly linear and smaller above. Waxy white or very pale pink 1½″–2″ bells, constricted at the center, nod in rather stiff panicles. Azores.

CANNA, Cannaceae. (60)

Cannas are currently enjoying a renewal of their popularity, due to the breeding of dwarf strains and new cultivars in subtler hues. They are native to tropical parts of South America and Asia, and are at their best planted in mixed borders or in containers around pools and patios, where they provide a tropical accent. However, they should be used with restraint, as their lush flamboyance can be overpowering. Commonly considered hardy only in warm areas, the recent strains are said to survive temperatures of 0° F. with heavy winter protection. The unbranched, fleshy stems are stout and erect, sheathed by the bases of the huge leaves. Their Banana-like foliage is alternate, paddle shaped, and usually smooth, with conspicuous veins; evergreen in frost-free areas. The flashy, irregular flowers are arranged in terminal spikes. Flower parts are in threes; the sepals usually small and green, the petals long and narrow, green or colored. In most, the showy parts of the flower are petaloid staminodes; the fertile stamen is less conspicuous. The lip, sometimes reflexed, is formed by the innermost staminode. One or two of the species have large, attractive seed capsules. Cannas are greedy feeders and must be supplied with well-manured, deep, fertile soil that neither dries out nor remains wet for any length of time. In colder regions cut back to about 6″ when the tops become frosted; lift and store in a cool, dry place. Start into growth like Dahlias, and plant out only when the soil has warmed up. Propagation is by division at planting time or from seed, soaked overnight or scarified prior to sowing. Maintenance is minimal apart from regular feeding and deadheading of spent blooms. Slugs need control.

x *generalis*	VARIOUS	SU-F	1.5′–9′/1.5′–3′
	○	Z10-8/T	DS ✳✳✳

[*C.* x *hortensis*]. Contains the numerous modern hybrids and hybrid strains, as well as the 'Crozy' strain. Their parentage includes *C. flaccida, C. coccinea, C. indica,* and others, but it is not accurately documented. These crosses vary greatly in height and have green, bronzy, or purplish foliage. The flowers are about 4″ across, with 4 erect staminodes. Among the giant 6′–9′ hybrids, 'Le Roi Humbert' ['Red King Humbert'] is a gaudy scarlet with reddish leaves; 'City of Portland' has rose pink flowers and 'The President' is bright red, both with green leaves. The semidwarf types grow about 3′–5′ tall and are represented by 'The Ambassador,' carmine with bronze leaves, and 'Stadt Fellbach,' apricot, and 'Richard Wallace,' lemon yellow, both with green foliage. The Orchid Cannas *(C.* x *orchioides*) also belong here. Their flowers are tubular at the base with reflexed petals, and may reach 6″ across. Popular cultivars, 3′ or less in height, include 'Lucifer' with red and yellow flowers, 'Eureka,' almost white, and 'Cupid,' a soft creamy pink, all with green foliage; 'Rosever' has rounded, deep rose flowers, and reddish stems and leaves. The 'Pfitzer Dwarf' strain, developed in Germany, grows about 2′–2.5′ tall. 'Crimson Beauty,' 'Salmon Pink,' and 'Primrose Yellow' are available cultivars. The 'Grand Opera Series,' 2′ tall, and the 'Seven Dwarfs' strain, about 1.5′ in height, are both offered in mixed colors.

glauca	YELLOW	SU	4′–6′/3′
	○	Z10-9/T	DS ✳

Its elegant, glaucous, bluish green leaves are rimmed with white and pointed at the tips. The slender, pale yellow flowers have a quiet charm lacking in the gaudy hybrids. The 3 staminodes are obovate, about 3″ long, the lip narrow and notched. West Indies, South America.

indica	RED	LSU	3′–6′/2′–3′
	○	Z10-9/T	DS ✳✳

Indian Shot. A substantial plant with glabrous, bronze, or green 1.5′ leaves. Stiffly erect racemes of small flowers; each has 3 bright red 2″–3″ staminodes and an orange lip and throat sometimes speckled with red. Naturalized in parts of the South. Central and South America, West Indies.
——————— 'Purpurea' has strongly purple-flushed leaves.

iridiflora	PINK	LSU-F	5′–10′/3′
	○	Z10-9/T	DS ✳✳

Most graceful of all the species. The huge oblong bluish green leaves may reach 2′ in length, sometimes woolly underneath when young. Soft rosy pink tubular flowers, about 1½″ long, hang in showy, scarcely branched racemes, subtended by grayish bracts. The petals, joined into a corolla tube, flare widely at the mouth; the 3 rounded

Canna indica

staminodes may reach 5″ in length, and the end of the lip is cleft. The cultivar *C. i.* 'Ehemannii' is usually grown. Peru.

warscewiczii	RED	LSU	5′–6′/3′
	○	Z10-9/T	DS *

A handsome species with glabrous, purplish green stems and purple-rimmed green foliage. The leaves are oblong, heart shaped at the base, to 1.5′ long. Its bright purplish red 3″ flowers, in simple racemes, have oblanceolate staminodes; the arching and reflexed ligulate lip is notched at the tip. Following the flowers, handsome light crimson prickly seed capsules, about ½″–1″ across, extend the season. Costa Rica, Brazil.

Cardamine pratensis 'Flore-Pleno'

CARDAMINE, Cruciferae. (100)			**Bittercress**

Commonly known as Bittercress, Cuckoo Flower, or Lady's Smock, this genus is lumped by some authorities with *Dentaria*. Charming in wet places beside streams or ponds. Seldom offered in catalogs.

latifolia	PURPLE	LSP	1.5'/2'
	◑	Z9-3/H	D ∗∗

Evergreen mats of Cress-like foliage. The showy panicles of deep pink or purple flowers are more robust than those of the following species. Pyrenees.

pratensis	LAVENDER	SP-LSP	1'/1'
	◑	Z9-3/H	DS ∗∗

Cuckoo Flower, Lady's Smock. Slender and erect, with fresh green, odd-pinnate leaves; those at the base are long stalked, with several pairs of rounded leaflets, the terminal

Carlina acaulis acaulis

leaflet larger and toothed. The short-petioled stem leaves have linear leaflets. Elongating terminal racemes of clear lavender, pink, or white Mustard-like ½″–¾″ flowers on slender stems. Europe, Asia, northern United States, Canada.

———— 'Flore-Pleno' has double lilac flowers like tiny rosettes.

C. kitaibelii, from the European Alps, has loose panicles of pale yellow flowers on 1′ stems.

CARLINA, Compositae. (20)

acaulis simplex	WHITE	LSP/SU	1′/1′
	○	Z9-5/H	S ✴

[*C. acaulis caulescens* Hort., *C. acaulis* 'Caulescens,' *Cirsium acaule*]. A low-growing Thistle-like plant, with pinnately lobed, spiny 6″ leaves forming stiff rosettes. One or more stems bear 5″ flower heads, singly or in corymbs. The large circle of white or reddish disk flowers is surrounded by stiff, papery, involucral bracts. Well-drained, preferably limy soil. Dislikes root disturbance. A mountain plant most unlikely to thrive in hot, damp areas. Europe. *C. a. acaulis* is stemless or nearly so.

CARPOBROTUS, Aizoaceae. (29)

One of many genera of mostly South African plants, among them *Drosanthemum, Lampranthus, Malephora,* and *Oscularia,* once grouped under *Mesembryanthemum*

Carpobrotus edulis

and still popularly known as Mesembs, or Ice Plants. Although *Mesembryanthemum* itself is only grown as an oddity, the others all include species that are highly decorative and useful in warm, dry regions. All of these plants have succulent, opposite leaves, in pairs that are usually somewhat joined at the base. The flowers are Daisy-like in appearance, but differ in being individual flowers, rather than flower heads composed of many ray and disk flowers. With age, they build up a thick thatch of dead stems which is both unsightly and a fire hazard. For these reasons, it is worthwhile replacing plantings every fourth year from cuttings, which root with astonishing ease, or from flats of inexpensively purchased plants. Bare patches are easily repaired in the same way. *Carpobrotus* is coarser than most, but useful as a ground cover and on slopes. It is tolerant of both drought and salt, but will perform better if given some water during hot, dry spells. Well-drained soils.

| *chilensis* | PINK | SU | 6″–9″/1′–1.5′ |
| | ○ | Z10-9/H | CS ✳✳✳✳ |

Sea Fig. The trailing stems of this native plant form extensive mats. Short, straight, 3-angled succulent leaves, to 2″ long. Magenta pink 3″ flowers. Often mislabeled as *C. aequilaterus,* which is a red-flowered species from Australia. Oregon to Baja California, Chile.

| *edulis* | YELLOW | LW-LSP | 6″–9″/1.5′–2′ |
| | ○ | Z10-9/H | CS ✳✳✳✳ |

Hottentot Fig. [*Mesembryanthemum edule*]. A mat-forming plant, with long, stout, trailing stems. Succulent, 3-angled, curving leaves, to 4″ long. The terminal, solitary 3″ flowers are pale straw yellow aging to pink; there are also pink to purplish forms. Scattered flowers over a long blooming season. Fruit edible. South Africa. Less often

Cassia hebecarpa

found in cultivation are *C. acinaciformis* with purple 5″ flowers and *C. muirii* with magenta pink 4″ flowers.

CASSIA, Leguminosae. (500)   Senna

| *hebecarpa* | YELLOW | SU | 3′–6′/2′ |
| | ○ ◑ | ZI0-3 | S ** |

Wild Senna is sturdy, erect, and shrublike in appearance. The alternate leaves are pinnate, with 8–10 pairs of delicate, light green, oblong to elliptic ¾″–2″ leaflets. Many-flowered axillary racemes form a large terminal panicle. The individual 1″ flowers are nearly regular and 5 petaled. This species is more heavily flowered than *C. marilandica*. Prefers well-drained soil. Useful as an accent plant or at the back of the border. Eastern to central United States.

| *marilandica* | YELLOW | SU | 3′–6′/2′ |
| | ○ ◑ | ZI0-3/T | S ** |

Wild Senna. Similar to *C. hebecarpa*, but has wider seedpods and 4–8 pairs of leaflets per compound leaf. Central and southern United States.

CATANANCHE, Compositae. (5)

| *caerulea* | BLUE | SU-EF | 2′/1′ |
| | ○ | ZI0-4/H | DRS **** |

Cupid's Dart makes neat clumps of slender, gray green, lanceolate leaves, to 1′ long. The solitary 2″ flower heads are held on very long stalks above the foliage. Lavender blue with a darker eye, the blooms are composed of strap-shaped florets, pinked at the apex, and surrounded by an involucre of strawlike, scaly bracts. An excellent cut flower, either fresh or dried. Drought resistant, but intolerant of "wet feet." The plants are short-lived, and benefit from frequent division. Plant in groups of at least 3. Self-seeds freely. Southern Europe.
———— 'Alba' has silvery white flowers.
———— 'Blue Giant.' Cornflower blue with navy centers.

CATHARANTHUS, Apocynaceae. (5)

| *roseus* | PINK | SU-F | 1′–2′/2′ |
| | ○ ◑ | ZI0/T | CS **** |

Madagascar Periwinkle, Rose Periwinkle. [*Ammocalis rosea, Lochnera rosea, Vinca rosea*]. An erect, bushy plant with pairs of glossy and fleshy oblong 1″–3″ leaves. The

Catananche caerulea

Catharanthus roseus 'Carpet Pink'

salverform, Phlox-like 1″–1½″ flowers are usually mauve pink or white, often with a darker eye. Invaluable for its long and colorful display in frost-free areas. Very tolerant of high temperatures and humidity. In colder zones, treat as an annual. Must not dry out. Madagascar, India.

——————— 'Bright Eye.' White flowers with a carmine eye. Dwarf.

——————— 'Pink Panther' has clear rose red flowers, with a darker eye. 10″–12″ tall.

STRAINS:

'Magic Carpet' has flowers in white and shades of pink and rose. Very heat tolerant. 6″–9″ in height.

CAUTLEYA, Zingiberaceae. (5)

These plants of tropical aspect form stiff stands of erect stems, bracted at the base and clothed in large, prominently veined, 2-ranked leaves. The complex, asymmetrical flowers are borne in the axils of bracts, in long terminal spikes. Each flower has a short-tubed corolla, with 3 nearly equal-sized petals, the upper one slightly hooded. Three petal-like staminodes, the lower much enlarged into a 2-lobed lip. A porous soil, well-enriched with moisture-retaining organic matter, is a must. Only for areas with mild winters and gentle summers. In colder climates, the rhizomes can be lifted and kept in cool but frost-free storage.

| *gracilis* | YELLOW | SU/LSU | 1.5′/1′ |
| | ○ ◑ | Z10-8/H | DS ** |

[*C. lutea*]. The sessile, ovate to lanceolate leaves, to 8″ long, are purple or streaked with reddish brown beneath. The calyx is purplish red; the corolla, yellow, 1½″ long. Himalayas.

| *spicata* | YELLOW | LSU | 2′/1.5′ |
| | ○ ◑ | Z10-8/H | DS *** |

Its foot-long, lanceolate to oblong-lanceolate leaves are not colored on their undersides. Red or green floral bracts. Dark yellow flowers in a dense spike. Himalayas.

——————— 'Robusta.' [*C. robusta* Hort., *C. s.* 'Autumn Beauty']. Sturdier than the species. Maroon bracts.

CELMISIA, Compositae. (60)

These evergreen New Zealand natives, with stiff, often silvery foliage and bold Daisy-like flower heads are temperamental plants, only suited to the mild climates of northern California and the northwest coast. Mostly they are grown by rock gardeners and other

Cautleya spicata 'Robusta'

collectors of rare plants, but a few are amenable to more general cultivation. They like a well-drained, gritty soil, but one that is neither poor nor devoid of moisture. Fresh seed is essential for success, or propagate from cuttings. Several smaller species are well worth trying, among them *C. hieracifolia* and *C. hookeri*. Perhaps hardier than indicated, especially under ideal conditions and in the hands of very skillful gardeners.

| *coriacea* | WHITE | ESU/SU | 1′–3′/2′ |
| | ○ | Z9-8/H | CS ✷✷ |

The most impressive as well as the easiest species. The short-stemmed clumps form rosettes of leathery, silver-skinned, furrowed 8″–2′ lanceolate leaves, densely clothed in silvery hairs beneath. The solitary Daisy-like flower heads, 1½″–4″ or more across, rise on woolly 1′–3′ scapes. The disk flowers are yellow; the pure white rays slender and numerous. Spreads by runners. *C. c.* var. *stricta* has narrower, more silvery leaves. New Zealand.

| *spectabilis* | WHITE | ESU/SU | 1′/1′ |
| | ○ | Z9-8/H | CS ✷✷ |

Crowded, narrow, silvery, basal leaves, to 6″ or longer, furrowed above and densely felted beneath, with white or buff hairs. Solitary 1½″–2″ flower heads, on scapes taller than the foliage. Mat forming, it will eventually cover a large area. *C. s.* var. *magnifica* is altogether larger than the species. New Zealand.

Celmisia coriacea

CENTAUREA, Compositae. (600)   **Knapweed**

The Knapweeds or Hardheads are generally easy, hardy plants for the border or wild garden. Many are excellent for cutting; some dry well. The alternate leaves of varied shapes are often silvery or even felted, with hairs on one or both sides. The Thistle-like flower heads lack true ray florets, but frequently the outermost florets are large and petaloid, sometimes frilled or fringed. The flower heads are surrounded by an involucre of papery or sometimes prickly bracts, which may also be fringed. They do best in full sun and prefer well-drained, sweet soils. Most are quite tolerant of dry soils, but not of "wet feet" in winter. Feed annually in the spring. Maintenance is minimal, and except for *C. montana,* division is necessary only every 3 or 4 years. The early bloomers are best divided in the fall.

| *dealbata* | PINK | SU | 1.5′–2.5′/2′ |
| | ○ | Z9-3 | DRS **** |

Persian Cornflower. The branched, erect or sometimes flopping stems are leafy. Their foliage is pinnately cleft into coarsely toothed oblong lobes; tomentose beneath. The petioled lower leaves may reach 1.5′; the upper leaves, usually sessile and smaller. Solitary and terminal, the Cornflower-like 2″–3″ flower heads are lavender to rosy pink; their enlarged outer florets and involucral bracts are deeply fringed. Iran, Asia Minor.

C. pulcherrima, from the Caucasus mountains, is similar, with purple flowers on unbranched stems.

———— *steenbergii* [*C. steenbergii* Hort.] has rosy crimson flowers above grayish leaves. A vigorous grower, which may become invasive.

gymnocarpa	PINK	SU	1.5′–3′/1′
	○	Z10-9	CS ****

Velvet Centaurea, Dusty Miller. [*C. argentea*]. This lovely subshrub is valued for its neat clumps of deeply cut, silvery white, felted foliage. Its bipinnately divided leaves may reach 8″ in length. The pale purplish pink flower heads, about 1½″ wide, have large marginal florets. The flowers, of secondary value, are sometimes sheared off to groom the plants. Capri. *C. cineraria* [*C. rutifolia, C. candidissima*] and *C. ragusina* closely resemble *C. gymnocarpa;* all are often lumped under the common name of Dusty Miller. None is hardy in the north, where they are usually propagated from cuttings taken in spring. They thrive in dry, rather poor soils.

hypoleuca	PINK	ESU	1.5′–2.5′/1.5′
	○	Z9-3	DRS ****

Erect, with smooth, dull green foliage, white-woolly beneath. Lower leaves lyrate, to 1′ long; stem leaves oblong and smaller. The lavender or rosy pink flower heads may reach 2″ across, and have large frilled outer florets. Asia Minor.

———— 'John Coutts' [*C. dealbata* 'John Coutts']. Leaves bluish white underneath. Deep rose pink flowers. Repeats bloom. Sometimes invasive. A Graham Thomas selection.

macrocephala	YELLOW	SU	2′–4′/2′
	○	Z9-3	DS ****

Yellow Hardhead. This bold if rather coarse plant makes splendid clumps of strong stems. The large, rough, saw-toothed leaves are broadly lanceolate. Spherical rusty buds open to bright lemon yellow 3″–4″ thistles, good for cutting. Caucasus. *C. glastifolia* [*Chartolepis glastifolia*] from central Europe is more refined, with silvery buds and pale yellow flowers on branched stems. Late summer blooming.

montana	BLUE	ESU-EF	1′–2′/2′
	○ ◑	Z10-3/H	D ****

Mountain Bluets, Perennial Cornflower. From stolons rise clumps of more or less erect stems. Numerous broadly lanceolate 5″–7″ leaves are lightly covered with silvery hairs above, more thickly beneath. The bright purplish blue, Cornflower-like 1½″–3″ flower heads are solitary and terminal, with spidery, deeply fringed marginal florets. The bracts on the egg-shaped involucre are conspicuously fringed in black. Very long blooming, but more useful as a filler than as a specimen plant. May become invasive, particularly in good soil. Divide every 2–3 years. Europe.

———— 'Alba' has white flowers.

———— 'Rubra.' Dark rose flowers.

nigra	VIOLET	SU	2.5'/1.5'
	○	Z10-5/H	D **

Black Knapweed, Spanish Buttons. Rather coarse, with elliptic to lanceolate basal leaves and smaller oblong stem leaves. The purplish Thistle-like 1½" flower heads are encircled by ovoid dark brown involucres. Probably only for the wild garden. Europe.

pulchra major Hort.	PINK	SU	2.5'/1.5'
	○	Z10-8/H	DRS **

This comely plant has attractive lobed leaves, rounded at the tips; dark silver above, white-felted beneath. Its unbranched stems are topped with large, fuzzy, purplish pink flower heads, each surrounded by rounded, brown and papery, glistening involucral scales. *C. cynaroides* [*Cnicus centauroides, Leuzea centauroides, Rhaponticum cynaroides*], native to the Pyrenees, is quite similar, though a little coarser, and 2'–3' tall. Its pinnately divided foliage, green above and grayish beneath, is deeply cleft into coarsely toothed, pointed lobes. Narrow, shiny bracts, with tan margins, encircle globose, purple 2" thistles. European *C. rhaponticum* [*Rhaponticum cynaroides scariosum*] is larger, but similar to the last. Its leaves are only sometimes lobed. Plant in bold clumps for the most striking effect from the purplish flower heads.

ruthenica	YELLOW	LSU	3'–4'/2'
	○	Z9-5/H	DRS **

More refined than some, this plant produces slender branched clumps of rich green ferny foliage, grayish beneath. Narrow corymbs of soft yellow 2½" flower heads, each bounded by a buff-colored, papery involucre. Eastern Europe.

Centaurea pulchra major Hort.

CENTRANTHUS, Valerianaceae. (12)

[*Kentranthus*]. Though native to warm Mediterranean regions, Red Valerian is a reliable border or cutting garden plant under a wide range of climatic conditions. Red, pink, or white flowers crowd into large, rounded, terminal heads, showy for much of the summer. In mild regions, where blooming begins early in the season, cutting back the spent stems will encourage a second flush. Well-drained, average soil is best; poor soil produces more compact plants, even suitable for the rock garden. Though tolerant of drought conditions, watering during dry periods promotes less woody growth. This short-lived perennial is best propagated from basal cuttings in spring. The flower color of seed-grown plants is variable.

ruber	RED	LSP-EF	1.5′–3′/1′–1.5′
○ ◑		Z10-4/H	CS ✱✱✱

Red Valerian, Jupiter's-Beard, Fox's-Brush, Keys-of-Heaven. [*Valeriana rubra, V. coccinea*]. Glabrous bushes of lax or erect stems, often woody at the base, are clothed with pairs of sessile, gray green leaves; fleshy and ovate, to 4″ long. The tiny ½″ flowers, clustered into large heads, have narrow, 5-lobed corolla tubes, spurred at the base. They are fragrant and vary from carmine to rosy pink. It self-seeds freely and has become naturalized locally in parts of California. Southern Europe, North Africa to Asia Minor. *C. angustifolius* and *C. longiflorus* are quite similar.

———— 'Albus' is white flowered.

———— 'Atrococcineus' is a deep brick red.

———— 'Coccineus' has deep pink flowers.

———— 'Roseus' [*Valeriana rosea* Hort.] has rose pink flowers.

Centranthus ruber

Centratherum sp.

CENTRATHERUM, Compositae. (20)

One South American species, not authoritatively identified, has aroused the interest of southern California gardeners in recent years. This agreeable, bushy little plant has ascending to erect, branched stems, reaching about 1′ in height and spreading to 1′ or more. The ovate 1″–1½″ leaves are alternate, coarsely toothed and deeply veined. Purplish pink Thistle-like 1″ flower heads. Thrives in full sun. It is not tolerant of drought, and must be watered in dry weather. Pinch to encourage fullness. Easily propagated from seed or cuttings.

CEPHALARIA, Dipsacaceae. (65)

gigantea	YELLOW	SU	6′/3′
	○	Z10-3	DRS ✱✱✱

[*C. tatarica* Hort.]. This erect, bushy plant has opposite and pinnately compound leaves, with ovate-lanceolate, toothed leaflets. Slender, upright, branching flower stems rise far above the mass of foliage, and bear Scabiosa-like, pale yellow 2″ flower heads. The tiny florets are 4-parted, the marginal ones larger. A graceful addition to the back of the border, where it will benefit from the shelter and support of neighboring plants. May need some staking; otherwise easy and undemanding. Caucasus.

Cephalaria gigantea

CERASTIUM, Caryophyllaceae. (60)

The silvery white carpets of foliage and starry white flowers of Snow-in-Summer are a familiar sight on many a sunny bank or in rock gardens. It is especially effective tumbling over walls, and its tendency to spread makes it a useful ground cover. Good drainage is its only requirement; tolerant even of pure sand. Shear after flowering for neatness.

biebersteinii	WHITE	ESU	4″–1′/2′
	○	ZIO-3	DS ***

Taurus Cerastium. Superior to the following favorite. Compact, with its stems and

Cerastium tomentosum

lanceolate 2″ leaves, densely covered with white hairs. Its somewhat larger flowers are arranged in cymes of 3–5. Mountains of Asia Minor.

tomentosum	WHITE	LSP-ESU	6″–12″/2′
	○	ZI0-3	DS ****

Snow-in-Summer. [*C. columnae*]. Rampant with prostrate, free-branching, grayish stems. The hairy, gray, opposite ½″–1″ leaves are linear to lanceolate, and form dense mats. Above these rise wiry 8″–12″ stems, topped by clusters of as many as 15 flowers. The star-shaped ¾″ blooms are pure white, with rounded and deeply notched petals. Very aggressive; the less invasive cultivars are preferable for the rock garden. Southern Europe.

———— *columnae* is more refined. It forms 4″ mounds of foliage.

———— 'Silver Carpet' has frosty white herbage. 8″ tall.

———— 'Yo-Yo' is free flowering. It has very fine silver foliage. 10″ in height.

CERATOSTIGMA, Plumbaginaceae. (8)

plumbaginoides	BLUE	LSU/F	1′/1.5′
	○ ◑	ZI0-5	CD ****

Leadwort, Plumbago. [*Plumbago larpentae*]. A low, spreading plant, somewhat woody at the base. The alternate ¾″–2″ leaves, obovate and fringed with hairs, become tinged

Ceratostigma plumbaginoides

with red in the fall. Terminal clusters of deep blue ½″ flowers; corolla salverform and 5-parted, bracts and calyx rusty red. Needs well-drained soil, especially in winter, and plenty of organic matter. Mulch in colder areas. In warm climates, where it does not die back naturally, cut back hard at the end of the season. A useful late- and long-flowering plant for the front of the border. China. The small shrub *C. willmottianum* (Z10-7) is an excellent subject for the mixed border. *C. griffithii* is more compact.

CHEIRANTHUS, Cruciferae. (10)   Wallflower

Wallflowers are closely related to *Erysimum,* and several species have now been moved to that genus. *Cheiranthus* is distinct in having nectaries only at the base of the outer stamens and by having only 1–2 rows of seeds in each cell. The freely branching stems bear narrow evergreen 2″–3″ leaves. Mostly fragrant, the cruciform flowers are arranged in dense, terminal panicles.

'Bowles Mauve'	LILAC	SU/F	2′–2.5′/1.5′
	○	Z10-6/H	C ***

[*C.* 'Bowles Purple', *Erysimum linifolium* 'E. A. Bowles']. Bushy mounds, often woody at the base. Its erect stems are well clothed in dark gray green linear leaves. The lovely, rich, clear mauve ½″ flowers, purple in bud, are arranged in elongating racemes. Very long blooming; shearing in midsummer forces a good flush of fall bloom. Protect from strong winds. Possibly a hybrid.

cheiri	YELLOW	SP	1′–2.5′/1′
	○ ◑	Z10-8/H	CS ****

English Wallflower. [*C. senoneri*]. An upright, bushy plant, becoming somewhat woody at the base. The alternate, gray green 3″ leaves are narrowly lanceolate, pointed at the tip. Spikes of fragrant yellow and brown 1″ flowers rise on leafy stems. In Europe, the popularity of English Wallflowers for bedding with spring bulbs has led to extensive breeding work, resulting in many cultivars and strains. They are readily overwintered, with protection in colder climates, where they are usually grown as biennials. Soil should be sweet and very well drained. Southern Europe.

—————— 'Blood Red' blooms early, with rich red flowers on 15″ stems.
—————— 'Cloth of Gold' has deep golden yellow flowers. 1.5′.
—————— 'Primrose Bedder.' Pale yellow flowers. 1′ in height.
—————— 'Rose Queen.' Rose pink flowers with apricot overtones. 1.5′.
—————— 'Vulcan' is a very popular, deep crimson cultivar. 12″–15″ stems.

'Harper Crewe'	YELLOW	SP-ESU	10″–12″/12″
	○	Z10-6/H	C **

This short-lived, bushy subshrub becomes leggy with age. Similar in foliage to *C. cheiri*. Its stems are leafy, topped by spires of small, deep yellow double flowers. Excellent in dry, rocky places, with alkaline soil. Replace with rooted cuttings as older plants get straggly. Greece.

Cheiranthus 'Bowles Mauve'

| x *kewensis* | BICOLOR | LW/ESP | 2'/1' |
| | ○ | Z9-8/H | C ** |

Winter Wallflower. [*C. cheiri* x *C. semperflorens*]. This hybrid has fragrant, bicolored 1" flowers; in bud, they are mostly rust brown, opening to orange brown and aging to lilac purple. Bred at the Royal Botanic Gardens, Kew.
——————— 'Variegatus' is similar, but with brightly variegated yellow and dark green leaves.

| *semperflorens* | BICOLOR | SP | 2'-3'/1.5' |
| | ○ | Z10-8/H | CS ** |

[*C. mutabilis*]. Herbaceous to subshrubby, with very dark green, somewhat hairy leaves. The striking bicolored flowers open very pale yellow, shortly becoming purple and sometimes rust colored. The buds are dark crimson. Morocco.
——————— 'Wenlock Beauty' has larger bronzy purple flowers.

CHELONE, Scrophulariaceae. (6)   Turtlehead

The Turtleheads form robust, rather stiff clumps of many stems bearing pairs of dark green, lustrous leaves. Crowded into compact terminal spikes, the unusual 1" flowers have curved, tubular, 2-lipped corollas, subtended by several sepal-like bracts (as distinct from *Penstemon*). The species are all quite similar and, although not as showy as some genera, are useful additions to the garden. Chelones will serve in the border, if the soil is sufficiently moist, but are perhaps at their best near streams or ponds. Mildew can be troublesome, if soil is dry and air circulation poor; otherwise they are easy, low-maintenance plants.

| *glabra* | WHITE | SU-F | 2'-3'/2' |
| | ○ ◑ | Z9-3/H | CDS *** |

Turtlehead, Snakehead, Balmony. The vigorous clumps of upright stems are well clothed in more or less sessile, lanceolate 6"-8" leaves. White flowers often flushed with pink. Divide when clumps become too large. Eastern United States.

| *lyonii* | PINK | LSU-F | 2'-4'/2' |
| | ◑ | Z10-4/H | CDS *** |

Distinguished from *C. glabra* by its ovate, coarsely toothed 4"-6" leaves. The clear pink flowers are excellent for cutting. Will not tolerate full sun, particularly in warm zones. Southern United States.

| *obliqua* | PURPLE | LSU-F | 2'-3'/2' |
| | ○ ◑ | Z9-3 | CDS *** |

This is the most ornamental species. Foliage similar to *C. glabra*, but short petioled. The corolla is rosy purple. Highly weather resistant and very long blooming. Central to southeastern United States.

Chelone lyonii

CHRYSANTHEMUM, Compositae. (200)

This large and diverse genus boasts many of the most popular ornamentals for perennial and mixed borders, edgings, rock gardens, and containers, as well as for cut flowers. Most are easy to grow in sunny positions, in well-drained but not overly rich soils. The taller types require staking. Chrysanthemums usually have upright, free-branching stems, often woody below. Their foliage, arranged in a basal rosette and/or alternately on the stem, is strongly aromatic in some species, less so in others; entire, lobed or pinnatifid, each division further lobed or toothed. Terminal, solitary, or in corymbs, the radiate flower heads, in all colors except blue, vary in size from ¾" to 5" or even 6" across. The heads are backed by overlapping rows of almost translucent buff-colored involucral bracts. Some authorities recognize only 5 species in the genus, putting the rest under other genera, such as *Leucanthemum, Dendranthema,* and *Pyrethrum.*

arcticum	WHITE	F	6"–1'/1'
	○	Z9-2/H	CDS ✳✳✳

Arctic Daisy forms wide, low clumps of ascending stems. Dark green and leathery, the spatulate 1"–3" leaves are pinnately divided into 3–5 shallow lobes, each deeply toothed; the lower leaves, as broad as long. Their stiff, erect flower stems, bearing a few smaller, linear leaves, end with solitary 1"–2" daisies; pink-tinged white rays and yellow disks. Extremely late blooming; in short-season climates, it may not bloom before being cut

Chrysanthemum corymbosum

down by hard frost. Alaska, Kamchatka. Taller *C. yezoense* from Japan is commonly offered as *C. arcticum*. It is a more robust plant, with smaller, long-petioled leaves. Each peduncle ends in 3 flower heads.

coccineum	VARIOUS	LSP-ESU	1'–2.5'/1.5'
	○	Z10-4	DS ****

Painted Daisy, Pyrethrum, Persian Insect Flower. [*Pyrethrum roseum*]. This slight, seldom-branched plant has dainty, finely cut, fernlike leaves, to 3" or longer below, reduced above. Wiry, unbranched flower stalks support solitary, yellow-eyed 2"–3" daisies. Single, Anemone-centered, and double forms are available in pinks, reds, and white. Superb for cutting. The plants do not ship well, and are best bought locally, preferably in bloom; they are offered usually in mixed colors. Soil must be very well drained and fairly rich; water during dry periods. Protect from severe cold and winter wetness. Cut the flower stems to the ground, as the blooms fade, to force another flush. Brush stake the taller cultivars. Divide every fourth year, preferably in spring, except in mild climates. Susceptible to attack by red spider mites and aphids. Propagate named cultivars vegetatively; seedlings tend to be inferior and may have deformed flowers. A source of the insecticide Pyrethrin. Iran, Caucasus.

————— 'Crimson Giant.' Single cerise flower heads. 3' or more tall.
————— 'Eileen M. Robinson.' Salmon pink heads on 2' stems.
————— 'James Kelway' has scarlet to crimson flowers with bright yellow disks. 1.5'.
————— 'Princess Mary' has double shell pink heads. 2' tall.
————— 'Robinson's Crimson.' Single crimson flower heads on 2' stems.
————— 'Robinson's Pink' has single medium pink heads. 2' tall.
————— 'Snowball' is a double-flowered white cultivar. 2.5'.

corymbosum	WHITE	SU	1'–3'/1'
	○	Z10-6	DS **

Thick clumps of sturdy stems, well branched above, with bipinnately dissected 6" leaves. Flat, loose terminal clusters of white-rayed 1" daisies with yellow disks. Caucasus.

frutescens	VARIOUS	LW-SU	2'–3'/3'
	○	Z10-9/T	CD ***

Marguerite, Paris Daisy. [*Anthemis frutescens* Hort.] Subshrubby at the base, it rapidly forms neat, rounded clumps of well-branched stems. The bipinnatifid 2"–4" leaves, essentially ovate in outline, emit a strong odor when bruised, which some find unpleasant. Its numerous 1½"–2½" daisies, supported by strong, straight stems, may be single, double, or Anemone-centered, in white, yellows, or pinks. Flowering time varies according to climate and treatment of the plants; in cold regions, they are popular for containers in cool conservatories and sunrooms or are treated as annuals. Maintain bushiness and extend the long flowering period by regularly but lightly cutting back the new growth; do not prune into old wood. Deadhead frequently. Prefers a free-draining but well-enriched soil; water deeply during periods of drought and fertilize lightly throughout the flowering season. Best propagated from cuttings. Canary Islands.

——————— 'Champagne Daisy' has pink, Anemone-centered 2″ flowers.
——————— 'First Love' has Anemone-centered lilac flowers.
——————— 'Honeymoon.' Large single yellow daisies with a yellow eye.
——————— 'Jamaica Primrose' has single pale yellow flower heads.
——————— 'Snow White.' Anemone-centered white flowers.

| *leucanthemum* | WHITE | ESU | 1′–2′/1′ |
| | ○ | Z10-3/T | CDS *** |

Oxeye Daisy, Field Daisy, White Daisy. [*Leucanthemum vulgare*]. Low mats of deep green, spoon-shaped leaves, to 6″ long, round-toothed or gently lobed. Sessile and much smaller, the oblong upper leaves are blunt toothed or even pinnatifid. Terminal and solitary, its yellow-eyed, white 1″–2″ daisies top long, mostly unbranched stems. Oxeye Daisies have become widely naturalized, due to their spreading, rhizomatous rootstocks and their prolific seeding. Europe, Asia.

| **x** *morifolium* | VARIOUS | LSU-F | 1′–6′/1.5′ |
| | ○ | Z10-4 | CDS **** |

Garden Chrysanthemums, Florists' Chrysanthemums. [*C.* x *hortorum*]. This vast, extremely variable hybrid complex is the result of breeding and selection over hundreds of years in the Orient, Europe, and North America. Its ancestry is variously considered to include *C. indicum* [*Dendranthema indicum*], *C. lavandulifolium* [*D. lavandulifolium*], *C. chanetti* [*D. chanetti*], *C. japonense, C. makinoi,* and *C. ornatum.* Most "Garden Mums" are vigorous clump-formers, with sturdy, upright or sprawling, branched, often woody stems. Their thick aromatic leaves, to 3″ long, frequently gray with hairs beneath, are lanceolate to ovate in outline, divided into entire or toothed lobes. The flower heads, in a full range of colors and many forms, vary from 1″ buttons to 6″ "footballs." The flower types have been divided into 13 classes by the National Chrysanthemum Society, whose members grow and train plants for exhibition through its local chapters. Vast numbers of plants are raised annually for the florist trade, mostly under glass. Each year in late summer, home owners buy pots of "Garden Mums" in bud by the million to brighten their fall gardens. Most have been raised from rooted cuttings taken early in the year and sold by specialist companies to be grown on. Rooted cuttings or small plants are also available during the summer by mail order or at local garden centers. Plant out before the hot weather; in cold zones, delay planting these soft cuttings until all danger of frost has passed. To encourage compact, bushy growth, regularly pinch the stems to 6 or 7 leaves, until about July fourth where the season is short, but until the end of July in long-season climates; the cushion types are self-pinching. Brush stake the taller sorts. It is probably best to buy new plants each year, although Chrysanthemums are easy to overwinter, with light protection in cold climates. Divide every 1–2 years to maintain vigor, and replant into rich, well-drained soil. The range of cultivars appears unending, with new ones available each season. Most nurseries and garden centers carry a full line of "mums" in assorted colors, flower types, heights, and flowering times; it is usually best to buy locally.

Chrysanthemum x *morifolium* cvs.

| *nipponicum* | WHITE | F | 1.5′–2.5′/2′ |
| | ○ | Z10-5/T | C **** |

Nippon Daisy, Nippon Oxeye Daisy. This almost glabrous subshrub forms substantial bushes of well-branched stems, often bare of foliage along their lower third. The thick, glossy, dark green 2″–3½″ leaves are sessile, spatulate, and coarsely blunt toothed toward their apex. Masses of terminal, long-stalked, solitary, Shasta-like 2½″ daisies, with green-tinged disks, cover the plants for many weeks. Best propagated from cuttings taken in the spring or from naturally layered stems. In mild climates, the stems do not die down and should be cut to the ground before new growth commences. Extremely tolerant of seaside conditions. In long-season regions only, pinch several times to promote compact growth; where the season is short, this operation may delay blooming until the buds are frosted. Plant as a specimen or accent plant, behind shorter plants, which will hide its unattractive "legs." Pest- and disease-free. Coastal Japan.

| *parthenium* | WHITE | SU-EF | 1′–3′/1′ |
| | ○ ◑ | Z10-4 | CDS *** |

Feverfew. [*Matricaria capensis* Hort., *M. eximia* Hort., *M. parthenoides* Hort., *Parthenium matricaria, Pyrethrum parthenium*]. Short-lived. Pungently aromatic, ferny foliage covers these neat, well-branched plants. Almost glabrous above, hairy beneath, the bright green pinnatifid leaves, to 3″ long, are broadly ovate to oblong in outline, further lobed or divided and toothed. Its buttonlike ½″–¾″ heads, with yellow disks surrounded by short, blunt, white rays, crowd into numerous corymbs. Best in light, sandy soil. Mulch for winter protection in cold climates where not reliably hardy. Self-seeds very freely; has become naturalized over much of North America. Divide annually in spring or fall. Propagate by division from summer cuttings or seed. Southeastern Europe, Caucasus.

———— 'Aureum,' Golden Feather, has chartreuse yellow foliage. Popularly grown as an annual for bedding.

———— 'Golden Ball' has small, double, golden yellow flowers on compact 1′ bushes.

———— 'Tom Thumb White Stars' is a fine edging plant, covered with white buttons for several weeks.

———— 'Ultra Double White.' Fully double flower heads. 15″–18″ tall.

| x *rubellum* Hort. | PINK | SU-LSU | 1′–2.5′/2′ |
| | ○ | Z10-4 | D *** |

[*C. erubescens* Hort., *C. zawadskii latilobum*]. These tough plants, which spread readily by rhizomes, form neat clumps of bushy, branched stems. Often pubescent, the long-petioled, wedge-shaped 1½″ leaves are bipinnate, with narrow, toothed segments; the upper leaves, reduced and lobed. Few to many-flowered, loose sprays of single 2½″–3½″ daisies, with narrow pink rays. An easy-to-grow border plant and valuable cut flower. Japan, Korea, northern China, Manchuria. Considered a parent, along with *C.* x *morifolium,* of the very hardy, variously colored Korean hybrids.

———— 'Clara Curtis' has rose pink daisies on 2′–3′ stems.

———— 'Mary Stoker.' Buff-colored flowers.

| x *superbum* | WHITE | ESU-F | 1′–3′/1.5′–2′ |
| | ○ ◑ | Z10-5 | CDS ✱✱✱✱ |

Shasta Daisy, Pyrenees Chrysanthemum. [*C. maximum* Hort.]. *C. lacustre* x *C. maximum.* Indispensable for its long display of showy blooms; also valuable for arrangements. Vigorous, bushy clumps of sturdy stems, with smooth, often lustrous dark green foliage. The coarsely toothed leaves are oblanceolate, petioled, to 1′ long below; lanceolate, sessile, and reduced above. Terminal and solitary, the long-stalked flower heads may reach 5″–6″ across, with numerous white rays surrounding a central yellow disk. Thrives in full sun or light shade; doubles must be shaded from intense sun. Short-lived, particularly in hot climates; divide in spring or fall every 2–3 years to retain vigor and compactness. Rich, very well-drained soil; water regularly and feed throughout the growing season for quality flowers. Deadhead for appearance and to extend blooming time. Tall cultivars may be pinched once or twice to keep plants compact, which results in more numerous but smaller flowers. Disbud for larger blooms. Susceptible to verticillium wilt and to attack by aphids.

———— 'Aglaya' has frilly, double 3″ flower heads on 1.5′–2′ stems.

———— 'Alaska.' Single 2″ daisies on 2′ stems. Reblooms if cut back after the first flush. Hardy to Z4.

———— 'Canary Bird.' Rather shaggy, semidouble heads, yellowing at the center. 1′–1.5′ in height.

———— 'Cobham Gold' has cream-colored flowers, with a pale yellow raised central crest. 15″–2′ tall.

———— 'Esther Read.' Double flower heads on 1.5′–2′ stems. This old standby was the first double-flowered cultivar.

———— 'Little Miss Muffet' has semidouble flowers on 12″–14″ stems.

———— 'Majestic' may have the largest single daisies of all, 4″–6″ across on 2′ stems.

———— 'Thomas Killen' has large single flowers, with a cream crest in the center, giving it the appearance of a double flower. 1.5′ tall.

———— 'Wirral Supreme' has largely replaced similar 'Esther Read.' 2.5′ in height. Tolerant of less than ideal conditions.

| *uliginosum* | WHITE | F | 5′–8′/2′ |
| | ○ | Z9-5 | CD ✱✱ |

High Daisy, Hungarian Daisy. [*C. serotinum, Tanacetum serotinum*]. Bushy, upright clumps of strong stems, well branched above. The slender, lanceolate 4″ leaves are coarsely dentate; the stem leaves are smaller. Numerous yellow-eyed daisies, to 3″ across. A striking companion for late-blooming Aconitums. Seldom needs staking. Central Europe.

| *weyrichii* | WHITE | F | 1′–1.5′/1′ |
| | ○ | Z8-3 | CDS ✱✱✱ |

Miyabe. Creeping clumps of branched or simple purple-tinged stems, with thick, deep green foliage. Their long-stalked lower leaves have rounded blades, which are palmately 5 cleft; the short-petioled or sessile smaller upper leaves are pinnately lobed or entire.

The yellow-eyed white daisies, almost 2″ in diameter, mature to pink. A fine ground cover, especially attractive with late-blooming dwarf Asters; also good for cutting. Japan.

———— 'Pink Bomb' has large pink flowers. 8″–10″ tall.

———— 'White Bomb.' One of the last of the Daisies to bloom. Pure white heads, pink tinged with age. Very free blooming until hard frost. 1′ tall.

CHRYSOGONUM, Compositae. (1)

virginianum	YELLOW	SP-F	4″–1′/1′
	○ ◑	Z10-5/T	DS ****

Goldenstar is a variable little plant, useful for edging or as a ground cover. Its branching stems as well as its leaves are hairy. The opposite 1″–3½″ leaves are ovate, with crenate margins. The starry 1½″ flower heads are usually solitary, terminal, or axillary. The tuft of disk flowers is surrounded by 5 ray florets, toothed on the ends. Evergreen in the south. At its best in average soils, with adequate moisture. Very long-flowering, especially in cooler areas. Pennsylvania to Florida and Louisiana.

Chrysogonum virginianum

Chrysopsis mariana

CHRYSOPSIS, **Compositae**. (30)			**Golden Aster**

These bright yellow Aster-like natives are valuable for their extremely long period of bloom at the end of the season. They are suitable for the border or wild garden, and require little attention. Very tolerant of dry, sandy soil and exposed positions. Benefit from a spring mulch. Divide in spring.

mariana	YELLOW	LSU-F	$1'$–$2'$/$1.5'$
	○	Z9-4	DS ****

Maryland Aster. [*Heterotheca mariana*]. Usually erect, the silky stems are well clothed in toothed, lanceolate 6″ leaves and topped with crowded clusters of bright yellow 1½″ flower heads. Eastern United States, Texas.

villosa	YELLOW	LSU-F	$1'$–$5'$/$2'$
	○	Z10-4	DS ***

Golden Aster, Hairy Goldaster. [*Heterotheca villosa*]. A most variable species. It is bold and bushy, with strong, usually branched stems. The pointed, lanceolate 2″–3½″ leaves may be toothed. Wide corymbs of solitary, brilliant yellow 1½″ flower heads. Pinch as for Asters during the growing season. May need staking. Western and central United States.

———— 'Golden Sunshine' has clear yellow flower heads on 5.5′ stems. A fine cut flower.

Cichorium intybus

CICHORIUM, Compositae. (9)

intybus	BLUE	SU	3′–5′/1.5′–2′
	○	ZI0-3	DRS ✳✳✳

Chicory is a widely naturalized weed. The basal clump of oblong to oblanceolate, lobed or toothed leaves gives rise to unattractive, rangy, branched stems. Its upper leaves are much reduced. Dandelion-like 1½″ heads consisting of only ray flowers. The unprepossessing habit of this plant is redeemed by the loveliest true sky blue flowers unfortunately closing by noon. Prefers a rather poor, well-drained, alkaline soil. Perhaps one day hybrids with other species will yield plants of more pleasing habit. The roots are used as a coffee substitute, the leaves as salad greens. Europe, North Africa, western Asia.

———————— 'Albus.' White flowers.

———————— 'Roseus.' Pink flowered.

CIMICIFUGA, Ranunculaceae. (15) Bugbane

The stately Bugbanes form large clumps of Astilbe-like foliage, above which rise tall spires of white flowers. The small, individual flowers are apetalous; the petaloid sepals drop quickly. Only the numerous stamens remain to create the fluffy effect so attractive in these plants. The species are all quite similar. Dramatic among shrubs, grouped at the back of the border or in open woodlands. Soils should be deep, well-drained, and humusy. In spite of their height, staking is seldom necessary; maintenance is minimal.

dahurica	WHITE	LSU	3'–5'/3'
	○ ◑	Z9-3	DS **

Seldom grown, this species spreads into wide clumps. Its foliage is similar to *C. racemosa,* but the leaflets are heart shaped at the base. The elegant flower stems branch widely; their cream white florets are evenly spaced on the arching inflorescence. Flowers a little later than *C. racemosa.* Siberia.

racemosa	WHITE	SU	3'–8'/2'
	○ ◑	Z10-3/H	DS ****

Bugbane, Black Cohosh, Black Snakeroot. The dark green 1.5' leaves are divided and subdivided into threes; the leaflets are broadly oval, coarsely toothed along the margins. Wandlike 2.5' racemes of fragrant flowers top wiry, branched stems; the side branches bloom later. Attractive fruits follow. Northeastern United States. Similar *C. americana* is native to mountain regions of the eastern United States.

———————— *cordifolia* [*C. cordifolia*] resembles the species, but has pale green flowers and smaller leaves. Virginia, Tennessee, North Carolina.

simplex	WHITE	F	2'–4'/2'
	○ ◑	Z9-3/H	DS ****

Kamchatka Bugbane. [*C. foetida* var. *intermedia*]. A beautiful plant with compound ferny foliage. The compact arching racemes, crowded with pure white flowers, are effective for several weeks. Lovely with *Helenium* 'Butterpat.' China.

———————— 'Elstead.' This outstanding British selection blooms very late in the season. 4'–6' tall. Worth tracking down!

———————— 'White Pearl' ['The Pearl'] has very large, white bottlebrushes, followed by lime green fruits. 3'–4' high.

simplex ramosa	WHITE	F	5'–8'/3'
	○ ◑	Z9-3/H	D **

[*C. ramosa*]. Flowering later, but similar to the species. A taller plant, with large,

Cimicifuga racemosa

tripinnate foliage. The well-branched, canelike, reddish stems bear narrow, erect, cream white 1′ inflorescences. Superb.

———— 'Atropurpurea' has dark purple foliage and stems, in striking contrast to the cream white flower spikes.

CIRSIUM, Compositae. (150)			Thistle

Most American gardeners associate Thistles with cow pastures rather than with flower gardens; nevertheless, some are quite ornamental and are valued by Europeans for the sculptural quality of their spiny, dissected foliage. The leaves are mostly basal, the stem leaves alternate. Each of the decorative flower heads has a crowded tuft of long, tubular, disk florets surrounded at the base by an involucre of several rows of often spiny bracts. They thrive in full sun, in ordinary porous but moisture-retentive soils. One of the most attractive species, East Asian *C. rhinoceros,* deserves to be introduced into American gardens. From a basal rosette, it forms a pyramid of leaves gradually decreasing in size up the stem. The leaves, lanceolate in outline, are pinnately divided. The angular, spine-tipped lobes are folded upward along their lower edge to form a spine-tipped crest on each side of the main leaf axis. The purplish pink flower heads are in terminal and axillary clusters. Lanceolate spine-tipped involucral bracts, longer than the florets, age to reddish brown.

japonicum	PINK	SU	3′-4′/2′
	O	ZIO-5	DS ***

Erect, with mostly basal, spiny foliage; obovate to oblong in outline, the pinnately divided leaves reach 1′ in length. The clasping, oblong stem leaves, also deeply cut, are smaller. Pink or purplish pink 1½″–2″ flower heads, solitary or in clusters of 2–3. Japan.

rivulare	PURPLE	SU-EF	2′-3′/2′
	O	ZIO-4	DS **

Forms clumps of erect stems, with mostly basal foliage. The bristly, pinnately divided leaves are densely hairy underneath. Stems essentially leafless. Purple or pink 1½″ flower heads, grouped in clusters of up to 8. Central Europe.

———— *atropurpureum* [*C. r.* 'Atropurpureum,' *Cnicus atropurpureus*], with deep wine red flowers, is the best form. It does not seem to be available in this country.

CLEMATIS, Ranunculaceae. (200)	

Known chiefly for its vining species, this genus also includes several erect perennials. They have opposite, usually compound leaves, and solitary or panicled, apetalous flowers. Four or five large petaloid sepals surround a central mass of white or yellow

Cirsium rhinoceros

Clematis x *eriostemon* 'Hendersonii'

stamens. The fruits of some species are decorative; each seed is adorned with feathery plumes. In spite of their reputation for favoring alkaline soils, Clematis will flourish under neutral or even slightly acid conditions. A cool root run and moist fertile soil, well enriched with leaf mold, are essential. Monthly feedings throughout the growing season are beneficial. Effective in sunny or lightly shaded borders and among shrubs. Light staking is usually necessary; pea sticks are best. American species include *C. freemontii,* with small, nodding, urn-shaped purple flowers and leathery, undivided leaves, and similar *C. ochroleuca. C. scottii* [*C. douglasii scottii, Viorna scottii*] is superior to both. All three are charming in the wild or native plant garden.

heracleifolia	BLUE	LSU	2'–4'/4'
	○ ◑	Z9-3/H	CDS ***

This bushy plant forms substantial, leafy mounds, subshrubby at the base. Erect stems carry pairs of palmately divided leaves, each with 3 broadly ovate, coarsely toothed leaflets; the largest, central one, to 5″ long. Small groups of fragrant, tubular 1″ flowers with strongly reflexed, light blue sepals cluster in tiers in the upper leaf axils and at the tips of the stems. In gardens, it is largely replaced by its cultivars and *C. h. davidiana.* China.

———— 'Crepuscule' has heavy clusters of Hyacinth-like, lavender blue flowers with curled sepals. May reach 4'–5' in height.

———— *davidiana* [*H. davidiana*] blooms earlier with dense clusters of more open, deep blue, fragrant flowers. Showier than the species. Up to 4' tall.

———— 'Robert Brydon.' ['Mrs Robert Brydon']. Pale blue flowers on 2' stems.

——— 'Wyevale' has clusters of larger deep blue flowers. This plant reaches 2'–3' in height and breadth. Both this and 'Robert Brydon' are considered to be cultivars of *C. h. davidiana* or seedlings of *C. x jouiniana* (*C. heracleifolia davidiana* x *C. vitalba*) or *C. x bonstedtii* (*C. heracleifolia davidiana* x *C. stans*). Under favorable conditions both may reach 6' or more.

integrifolia	BLUE	SU	2'–5'/4'
	○ ◐	Z9-3/H	DS **

Woody below, this softly hairy plant usually sprawls, and its appearance is improved if it is lightly supported with pea sticks. The wiry stems are clothed in pairs of thin, dark green, undivided 2"–4" leaves; sessile, ovate to oblong, and conspicuously veined. Solitary and terminal, the nodding ½"–1" flowers are urn shaped, with flaring, slightly twisted, lavender to violet blue sepals. An attractive companion for *Allium christophii*. Southern Europe, Asia. The hybrid *C. x eriostemon* 'Hendersonii' (*C. integrifolia* x *C. viticella*) is sometimes listed as a cultivar of *C. integrifolia*. It is similar, but often preferred due to its larger, indigo blue flowers and extended blooming period through late summer.

recta	WHITE	LSP-SU	2'–5'/2'
	○ ◐	Z9-3/H	CDS ***

Ground Clematis. Upright or scrambling, with pinnately divided leaves. Its 5–9 ovate leaflets are 1"–2" long, pointed and short stalked. Innumerable fragrant white starry 1" flowers are borne in large clusters, followed by silvery seed heads. The effect is frothy and light, particularly effective behind low shrubs, over which the plant can ramble. Requires support. Often used as a filler plant in borders. A double form *C. r.* 'Plena' appears to have been lost to the trade. Southern Europe.

——— *mandshurica* [*C. mandshurica*] is decumbent, with 2.5' long stems.

——— 'Purpurea' has pure white flowers and deep purple leaves. The foliage color varies, so select a good form. Blooms in summer on 3'–4' stems.

CLIVIA, Amaryllidaceae. (4)   Kaffir Lily

These impressive but rather graceless evergreen plants are great favorites of gardeners in our warmest areas, for their spectacular floral displays in shade or semishade. The flowers are followed by very ornamental persistent red berries. The thick, glossy, strap-shaped basal leaves form stiff, dense clumps. Crowded umbels of large, colorful, 6-tepaled flowers are borne on stout scapes, usually about as tall as the foliage. They do best in light, organically rich soils; fertilize before and during flowering. Water well when actively growing and in dry summer weather, then give plants a rest. These easy plants need dividing only when they become so overcrowded that flowering is reduced. They are easily propagated by division of their fleshy, shallow roots; from fresh seed, young plants will take several years to reach flowering size. Tolerant of a few degrees of frost, if under the protection of overhanging trees. Slugs and snails are a serious problem.

| *gardenii* | ORANGE | LW | 1'–2'/1.5'–2' |
| | ◐● | Z10-9 | DS ∗∗ |

A less showy species, with loose umbels of 10–14 pendulous, tubular 2″–3″ flowers, yellow or orange with green tips. South Africa.

| *miniata* | ORANGE | LW/ESP | 1.5'–2.5'/1.5'–2' |
| | ◐● | Z10-9 | DS ∗∗∗∗ |

Kaffir Lily. [*Imantophyllum miniatum*]. Its leaves are 1.5'–2.5' long by 2″ wide. Rounded umbels of 12–20 erect, funnel-shaped 3″ flowers, orange or red, often with yellow throats. The popularity of this spectacular species has led to the development of many superior cultivars; these are selections, not hybrids. *C.* x *cyrtanthiflora* (*C. miniata* x *C. nobilis*) is intermediate between its parents in size and number of flowers. It bears umbels of drooping, tubular, salmon to flame-colored flowers. South Africa.

———— var. *citrina* [*C. miniata* var. *flava, C. miniata* 'Citrina'] has clear yellow flowers and yellow berries.

———— 'Striata' has variegated leaves.

| *nobilis* | ORANGE | SP/ESU | 1'–1.5'/1.5' |
| | ◐● | Z10-9 | DS ∗∗∗ |

Its leaf margins are rough to the touch. Dense umbels of 20–40 or more drooping tubular yellow or orange 1″–1½″ flowers with green tips. South Africa.

Clivia miniata

Codonopsis clematidea

CODONOPSIS, Campanulaceae. (32) Bonnet Bellflower

Bonnet Bellflowers are choice, seldom-grown plants, prized by specialists. The genus includes several twining species, as well as erect perennials. These too may eventually twine, particularly in moist shade, but drier soil conditions appear to discourage this weak growth. They thrive where soil is sandy and acid and in the peat garden.

| *clematidea* | BLUE | LSU | 2'–4'/2' |
| | ○ ◑ | Z9-5/H | S ** |

Erect clumps, which tend to sprawl as the stems become top-heavy. The pubescent, gray green 1″ leaves are lanceolate to ovate, and essentially opposite. Nodding ice blue 1″ flowers are carried on softly hairy stems well above the foliage. Their calyx lobes are reflexed. The corolla is broadly campanulate, delicately traced inside with darker veins and maroon bandings, with orange nectaries at the base. Only when planted on a bank or wall and viewed from below can one appreciate their full beauty. Faded flowers are rather unsightly. The foliage emits a foxy odor when bruised. Asia.

| *ovata* | BLUE | MSU | 1'–2'/1' |
| | ○ ◑ | Z9-5/H | S * |

Often confused with similar *C. clematidea,* this is an erect, very pubescent plant, with small ovate leaves and nodding pale blue, bell-shaped 1″ flowers on almost leafless stems. The inside of the corolla is veined in dark blue or purple. Himalayas.

COLEUS, Labiatae. (150)

Native to the Old World tropics, these Nettle-like plants make striking displays in frost-free areas. Elsewhere they are grown as annuals. Best known are those with exotically colored and patterned foliage, although some with attractive flowers deserve more attention. All have square, somewhat fleshy stems and opposite, toothed leaves, characteristic of the Mints. Blue or purplish flowers, grouped in verticillasters, are borne in terminal racemes or panicles. The corollas are tubular and 2 lipped; the upper lip sometimes 2 lobed, the lower 3 to 4 lobed. Coleus thrive in well-drained but moisture-retentive soil, in light shade. Pinch to force bushy growth. When grown for their foliage, it is best to remove the flowers to maintain a compact habit. *C. amboinicus* [*C. aromaticus*], Spanish Thyme, probably native to Indonesia, is grown as a culinary herb.

autranii	PURPLE	SU	2′–3′/2′
	◑	Z10	CDS **

Upright clumps, with leafy stems, hairy at the nodes. The long-petioled, broadly ovate leaves may reach 5″ in length; dark green and pubescent above, paler and hirsute beneath. Violet or light purple ½″–¾″ flowers cluster in 6- to 10-flowered verticillasters, in large showy panicles. Ethiopia.

x *hybridus*	FOLIAGE	SU	1′–5′/1.5′
	◑	Z10	CS ****

Common Coleus. This highly variable group is grown for its dramatic foliage. Its exact parentage is open to question, but undoubtedly includes *C. blumei* (now probably out of cultivation) and *C. pumilus*. Free branching and erect or trailing, the plants are lush with 2″–4″ leaves, generally ovate in outline. The leaf margins are typically round toothed, but strains with elaborately frilled and/or cut edges are available. The range of colors and patterns seems endless, and new selections abound. Remove the spikes of small flowers to encourage compact, vegetative growth. Excellent for bedding, as specimen plants, for containers or hanging baskets. A selection of the some of the best cultivars include:
————— 'Concord' with rich purple, velvety leaves on green 2′ stems. Introduced by Color Farm.
————— 'Highland Fling.' The red stems bear yellow leaves splashed with light green. A Japanese selection.
————— 'Molten Lava' has very dark red and carmine red leaves with a narrow, deep red margin. 8″–10″ tall.
————— 'Pagoda' has yellow leaves blotched with red. A strong grower from Japan. 1.5′–2′ tall.
————— 'Red Monarch.' Beautiful, unpatterned, deep vermilion foliage on 2′ stems.
————— 'Salmon Lace' has reflexed leaves, salmon pink at the centers, edged with lacy markings and veined in green and cream. From Japan.
————— 'Scarlet Poncho' is a trailer, with bright red leaves rimmed with gold. 12″.

Coleus x *hybridus*

'Carefree' is a dwarf strain, with Oak-like leaves, marked with red, green, cream, and brown. 8″ tall.

'Fashion Parade.' A good mix, with multi-colored leaves in various shapes, some frilled and lace-edged.

'Rainbow' has medium-sized leaves, in bright color combinations. 15″–18″ tall.

'Saber Leaf Mixed' has long, narrow leaves, in bright colors. Bushy and late flowering. 8″ in height.

'Wizard Mixed,' dwarf and well branched, with a variety of leaf markings, in monochromes and bicolors; lime green to deep bronze.

| *lanuginosus* | LILAC | SU | 1′–2′/1.5′ |
| | ◗ | ZIO | CS ✳✳ |

Its upright to decumbent stems rise from tuberous roots. The green, softly hairy, ovate leaves may reach 3″ in length. Long panicles of whorled, pale lilac flowers. Central Africa.

| *pumilus* | BLUE | SU | 6″–3′/1.5′ |
| | ◗ | ZIO | CS ✳✳ |

Dwarf Coleus. [*C. rehneltianus*]. The decumbent stems root along their length. The small and rounded ¾″–1½″ leaves, crenate or dentate, are variously patterned in dark purple, rimmed in green. Fragrant, but insignificant, blue flowers. Philippines, Indonesia.

———— 'Lord Falmouth' has ruby leaves, rosy pink at the center.

──────── 'Red Trailing Queen'. Foliage with purple centers aging to mahogany, and rimmed with green.

thyrsoideus	BLUE	W	4'–7'/2'–3'
	◖	Z10	CS **

Flowering Bush Coleus. Its erect, sticky stems are subshrubby at the base. The dull green foliage is grayish beneath and covered with sticky hairs; leaves coarsely crenate and heart shaped, 2"–5" long. The many-flowered verticillasters, of royal blue ½" flowers, are arranged in showy narrow panicles. Central Africa.
C. shirensis, from the same region, has paler blue flowers, in 8"–15" panicles. Both are useful for northern greenhouse displays.

COMMELINA, Commelinaceae. (100)

coelestis	BLUE	SU	1.5'/1'–1.5'
	○	Z10-8/T	CDS **

Blue Spiderwort, Mexican Dayflower. Related to and reminiscent of *Tradescantia,* from which it differs in having flowers with 2 large petals and 1 much smaller one, instead of 3 equal-sized petals. It forms a clump of erect, jointed stems clothed in clasping, alternate leaves. The shiny, oblong-lanceolate leaves may reach 7" in length. The tightly clustered, bright blue 1" flowers emerge, one at a time, from an enclosing, spathelike bract. Each flower lasts only one day, but the plant is long blooming. In colder areas, dig and store the roots as with *Dahlia.* Mexico.
──────── 'Alba' has white flowers.
──────── 'Variegata' has blue and white variegated flowers.

CONVALLARIA, Liliaceae. (1)

majalis	WHITE	LSP	8"/1'
	◖●	Z9-3/H	D ****

Lily-of-the-Valley. Two or three stiffly erect, parallel-veined leaves, on short, sheathing petioles. The dark green, often glossy 6"–9" leaves are elliptic. Angular stems bear slightly arching one-sided racemes of flowers, each subtended by a small, pale green, lanceolate bract. The deliciously fragrant, nodding, bell-shaped ¼" blooms flare into 6 reflexed lobes at the mouth. Globular pale orange to red berries follow. Plant the fleshy rhizomes or "pips" horizontally about 1" deep in very early spring or fall. Divide to increase stock or when the beds flower poorly due to overcrowding. An excellent ground cover, particularly in humusy soil, until late summer when the foliage becomes shabby. Invasive under favorable conditions, but it can be temperamental. Mulch heavily with well-rotted manure or compost in the fall. The rootstocks and berries are poisonous. Europe, Asia.

———— 'Aureo-variegata' ['Striata,' 'Variegata,' 'Lineata'] has bold foliage longitudinally striped in cream. White flowers.

———— 'Fortunei Giant Bells' has larger flowers and leaves. May be synonymous with *C. m.* 'Fortin's Giant.' A little later to flower.

———— 'Prolificans' [*C. m. flore-plena*] is a double-flowered form.

———— 'Rosea' has soft lavender pink flowers, but is a rather muddy color.

CONVOLVULUS, Convolvulaceae. (225)

althaeoides	PINK	SU	6″/1.5′–2′
	○	ZI0-7	CDS **

Trailing stems and gray green foliage. The lower leaves are deeply round lobed; the upper leaves, finely divided, either palmately or pinnately. Its pink, funnelform 1″–2″ flowers are beautifully set off by the silvery foliage. Light, well-drained soils. Southern Europe.

cneorum	WHITE	LSP-SU	2′–4′/2′–3′
	○	ZI0-7	CDS ****

Silverbush is an erect, evergreen subshrub. Its small, alternate, lanceolate to oblong leaves are covered with silky, silver-gray hairs. Clusters of 1½″–2″ funnel-shaped white

Convolvulus mauritanicus

or pink-tinged flowers with yellow throats. This long-flowering plant is prized for its superb shimmering foliage. Needs well-drained, light soil. Prune heavily after flowering to keep plant compact. Southern Europe.

| *mauritanicus* | BLUE | LSP-SU | 1′/2′–3′ |
| | O | Z10-8 | CDS **** |

Ground Morning-Glory has trailing stems. Its alternate, hairy, gray green, ovate leaves are evergreen, ½″–1½″ long. Small clusters of lavender blue funnelform 1″ flowers. Well-drained, light soil. Do not overwater. Prune hard before new spring growth begins. An excellent, long-flowering plant for edging, ground cover, or walls. North Africa.

COREOPSIS, Compositae. (120) — Tickseed

The Tickseeds are useful, long-flowering North American natives, with yellow, Daisy-like flower heads. All are of extremely easy culture. *C. grandiflora* and *C. lanceolata* are quite similar, and there is considerable confusion over the ancestry of garden forms and hybrids of these two species. The superior named cultivars should be propagated vegetatively, as they are very variable from seed. Deadhead for the sake of appearance and continued flowering.

| *auriculata* | YELLOW | LSP-F | 1.5′/1′–1.5′ |
| | O | Z10-4/T | DS *** |

A bushy little plant with long, erect stalks bearing solitary flower heads. Ovate leaves to 5″ long, usually with one or a pair of earlike leaflets at the base. The orange yellow 2″ flower heads have 8 ray florets, toothed at the tip. Spreading. Southeastern United States.

———— 'Nana.' Excellent 6″ dwarf.

| *gigantea* | YELLOW | ESP/SP | 3′–4′/2′–3′ |
| | O | Z10-9/H | S ** |

[*Leptosyne gigantea*]. Occasionally reaching 10′ in height, this ungainly plant develops a succulent trunk to 4″ thick, branching at the top. The branches bear tufts of foot-long, ferny, bipinnate leaves with linear segments and corymbose clusters of 2″–3″ yellow flower heads on long stalks. Dormant most of the year, it leafs out with the winter rains and flowers in early spring. For naturalizing in coastal areas. Southern California, Baja California.

| *grandiflora* | YELLOW | ESU/SU | 1′–2′/2′–3′ |
| | O | Z10-5/T | DS **** |

A somewhat hairy plant with branching stems, leafy to the top. Its leaves are opposite; the basal and lower leaves, lanceolate to spatulate, the upper leaves, 3 to 5 parted, with lanceolate to linear lobes. Bright yellow 1½″–2½″ flower heads on very long stalks.

Coreopsis maritima

The toothed ray flowers usually number 8. Long-blooming. Tends to sprawl unless grown in full sun and poor soil. Divide often. There are many cultivars; whether they should be listed here or under *C. lanceolata* is problematical. Southern United States, north to Missouri.

———— 'Goldfink.' A compact dwarf, 8″–10″ tall.
———— 'Sunburst' has large, semidouble flowers.
———— 'Sunray,' 1.5′–2′ tall with double flowers.

lanceolata		YELLOW	ESU/SU	1′–2′/2′–3′
		○	Z10-5/T	DS ****

Very similar to *C. grandiflora,* this somewhat hairy plant has mostly basal foliage. Opposite 2″–6″ leaves, oblong-spatulate to lanceolate, rarely with small lateral lobes. The yellow 1½″–2½″ flower heads are borne on long peduncles; ray flowers usually 8 toothed. Long flowering. Culture as for *C. grandiflora.* Southern United States, north to Michigan.

———— 'Grandiflora' has larger flower heads.

maritima		YELLOW	ESP-SU	1′–3′/1′–2′
		○	Z10-9/H	S ***

Sea Dahlia. [*Leptosyne maritima*]. Many branching stems. Yellow green, slightly succulent bipinnate leaves, to 6″ long, with linear segments. Large clear yellow 2½″–4″

daisies, on long stems. Often grown as an annual. Excellent for cutting. Southern California, Baja California.

rosea	PINK	LSU/F	1′–2′/1′
	○	Z8-3/T	DS ***

The only moisture-loving Coreopsis is this small, erect, branching plant. Opposite leaves, 1″–2″ long; the upper linear, the lower bipinnate or tripinnate, with linear segments. Short-stalked 1″ flower heads with yellow disks and pink ray florets. There is a white-flowered form, *C. r.* 'Alba,' and an earlier flowering dwarf, *C. r.* 'Nana.' North America.

verticillata	YELLOW	SU-F	1′–3′/2′
	○	Z10-3/T	DS ****

Thread-Leaf Coreopsis. This most superior perennial is an erect, densely bushy plant with branching stems. The opposite, sessile 2″–3″ leaves are palmately divided into 3 parts and further dissected into narrowly linear segments. Bright yellow 1″–2″ daisies, in loose corymbs. Flowers long and profusely. Spreading, sometimes invasive. Drought resistant. Slow to appear in the spring. Protect young plants from rabbits. Southeastern United States.
——————— 'Golden Shower' ['Golden Showers']. Flowers brighter than the species.
——————— 'Grandiflora.' Larger flowered than the species.
——————— 'Moonbeam.' 2′ tall with pale yellow flowers.
——————— 'Zagreb.' 1′–1.5′ tall. Not always reliably dwarf.

CORONILLA, Leguminosae. (20) Crown Vetch

cappadocica	YELLOW	ESU/SU	1′/1.5′
	○	Z10-7	CDS **

Prostrate, or nearly so, it forms a dense mat of glaucous, odd-pinnate, compound leaves, each composed of 9–11 small obovate leaflets. Bright yellow Pea-like ½″ flowers in small, umbellate clusters on long axillary stalks. A well-behaved plant for the edge of the border or the rock garden. Asia Minor.

varia	PINK	LSP/SU	1′–2′/2′
	○ ◑	Z10-3	CDS ****

Crown Vetch is a coarse, unruly and invasive plant which would be scorned by gardeners were it not so useful as a ground cover. Excellent for poor dry soils and to control erosion on slopes and roadsides. It has odd-pinnate, compound leaves with 11–25 small, oblong to obovate leaflets. Crowded clusters of pink or white Pea-like ½″ flowers. Europe.
——————— 'Aurea' has golden foliage.
——————— 'Penngift.' Pink and white flowers from early summer through fall. Developed by Pennsylvania State University.

Coronilla varia

Corydalis lutea

CORYDALIS, Fumariaceae. (300)

These relatives of *Dicentra* form low, leafy mounds of attractive, ferny, pinnately compound foliage. The small asymmetrical flowers, in compact racemes, are 4 petaled, the outer 2 larger, one of them spurred. Most do best in semishade, in a light, well-drained soil that does not dry out. Seed, even when fresh, is difficult to germinate. Plant in rock gardens, cottage gardens, or at the front of the border. Few of the species are cultivated in this country, and only one, *C. lutea,* is common. The tuberous kinds, such as *C. bulbosa* and *C. cava,* both with purplish pink flowers, die down by midsummer. Himalayan *C. cashmeriana* has beautiful bright blue flowers, but is a temperamental plant suited only to mild climates, such as that of the Pacific Northwest.

lutea	YELLOW	SP-F	12″–15″/1′
	○ ●	Z10-5/H	DS ****

The neat mound of durable foliage is covered in bloom for many months. Stems numerous. Fresh green leaves, glaucous beneath, 2 to 3 times pinnate; leaflets roughly elliptic, entire or lobed. Long-stalked, axillary racemes of golden yellow ¾″ flowers. Often grown in walls and between paving stones. Europe. *C. ochroleuca* is similar, but its leaves are glaucous on both sides. Yellowish white flowers. Southeastern Europe. Yellow-flowered *C. cheilanthifolia* and *C. saxicola* are gardenworthy Chinese species.

nobilis	YELLOW	ESP-LSP	1.5′–2.5′/1′–1.5
	○ ◑	Z10-3/H	DS *

Erect stems, sparsely clothed in glaucous pinnate to bipinnate leaves, with lobed leaflets. Bright yellow 1″ flowers, tipped with brown, in dense, crowded, long-stalked racemes. The best of the genus, but unfortunately rare. Central Asia.

COSMOS, Compositae. (25)

atrosanguineus	MAROON	SU-F	2.5′/1′
	○	Z10-7/H	CDS **

Black Cosmos. [*Bidens atrosanguinea*]. This unusual, long-blooming plant, with flowers smelling strongly of chocolate, resembles *Dahlia* more than the annual *Cosmos*. From tuberous roots, it forms bushy clumps with smooth, pinnate leaves, each segment broadly lanceolate and sometimes lobed. Slender, wiry stems support the 1″–1½″ flower heads well above the foliage. The velvet-textured ray florets are an intense dark maroon, the disks darker still. Deep, moisture-retentive, but not wet soils. Heavy winter mulching is necessary in colder zones, or the tubers can be lifted and stored. Light brush staking is recommended. Excellent as a cut flower. Mexico. Commonly grown as an annual, *C. diversifolius* has 2″ flowers, with yellow disks and lilac pink ray flowers, on 2.5′ stems. Mexico.

Cosmos atrosanguineus

COTULA, Compositae. (60)

coronopifolia	YELLOW	ESP-F	6″–1′/1′–1.5′
	○	Z10-9	RS ✳✳✳

Brass-Buttons is semisucculent, with foot-long, branching, decumbent to ascending stems. The alternate leaves, to about 3″ long, are linear-oblong to oblanceolate, sometimes entire, but more often coarsely lobed. Rounded, bright yellow ½″ diskoid flower heads with enlarged marginal florets, on terminal or axillary stalks. Long blooming. Thrives in moist or wet ground, an unusual habitat for a Composite, but can be grown elsewhere if well watered. The other species in cultivation, mostly from New Zealand, are prostrate plants, suitable only for rock garden conditions. South Africa.

CRAMBE, Cruciferae. (20)

cordifolia	WHITE	LSP/ESU	4′–7′/3′
	○	Z9-6	RS ✳✳✳

Colewort. The large, up-to-2′-long, heart-shaped basal leaves, on long stalks, form a loose, low mound of handsome foliage. The leaves are variously lobed, coarsely toothed, somewhat hairy and wrinkled. A stout, many-branched, pale green stem rises high, bearing a huge, Gypsophila-like cloud of minute, 4-petaled, white flowers. Likes deep, well-drained, moderately alkaline soil. May need staking. The conspicuous foliage is often disfigured by insects, which are easily controlled by spraying. This superb but neglected plant may be hardier than generally thought. *C. orientalis* is decorative but rarely seen. Caucasus.

maritima	WHITE	LSP/ESU	2′–3′/2′
	○	Z9-6	RS ✳✳✳

Sea Kale. This ornamental vegetable makes a floppy mound of fleshy, glaucous, blue green basal foliage. The large, stalked, oblong leaves are variably lobed and crisped. Small, white, 4-petaled ½″ flowers crowd into slightly domed, corymbose racemes borne on thick stems. Culture as for *C. cordifolia*. The blanched young shoots are eaten as a vegetable. Europe.

CRASPEDIA, Compositae. (70)

glauca	YELLOW	ESP/LSU	1′–1.5′/1.5′–2′
	○ ◑	Z10-9/H	CDS ✳✳

[*C. uniflora*]. This variable species forms basal clumps of hairy, lanceolate to oblong leaves, reaching 10″ in length; the stem leaves are smaller and alternate. Each of the numerous scapes ends in a crowded, ovoid ¾″–1½″ inflorescence, composed of several clustered flower heads. The small tubular disk florets vary from white to pale yellow

Crambe cordifolia

to orange. Needs a well-drained soil. A taller form from Tasmania reaches 3′ in height. Australia, New Zealand.

| *globosa* | YELLOW | SP/SU | 1.5′–3′/1′–1.5′ |
| | ○ ◐ | Z10-9/H | DS ✳✳✳ |

Crowded into a basal clump, the narrow leaves, to 1′ long, are densely clothed in silvery hairs. Each tall, wiry scape bears a dense, spherical 1″ inflorescence, compounded of several flower heads. Bright yellow tubular disk florets. Excellent for cutting or drying. Plant in a sheltered spot; taller plants tend to blow over in the wind, and staking is both impractical and unattractive. Australia.

CRASSULA, Crassulaceae. (300)

This variable, predominantly southern African genus, ranges from large, shrubby species to small succulents. Excellent information on the latter, highly regarded by specialists and collectors, may be obtained from the Cactus and Succulent Society of America or the International Cactus and Succulent Society. A few subshrubby species are well suited to warm zone gardens, where they are especially effective planted in groups. Evergreen and fleshy, Crassulas have opposite, sessile leaves, which often taper toward the base but then join together, surrounding the stem. The stems and foliage of many species are compressed into attractive basal rosettes, which elongate at flowering time. The tiny flowers are 5 parted, mostly white, pink, or red, and arranged in loose clusters, or crowded into large, showy corymbs. Of easy culture, Crassulas require only a light, well-drained soil enriched with humus. They should be moderately supplied with water during the growing season, but are quite tolerant of drought when resting. The listed plants are increased by stem or leaf cuttings.

| *multicava* | PINK | LW-ESP | 1′/1′ |
| | ○ ◐ | Z10-9 | CS ✳✳✳ |

Fairy Crassula. [*C. quadrifida*]. Subshrubby at the base, with upright or trailing stems. Its glabrous, obovate 1″–3″ leaves are dark green, rimmed and dotted with red; the short petioles of each pair join together at the stem. Delicate, airy sprays of 4-petaled flowers, white tinged with red, top the gracefully branching, slender pink stems. Spreads freely by dropping minute plantlets from the flower panicles; the decumbent stems also root along their length. An excellent ground cover; the flowers are good for cutting. Eastern Cape Province, southern Natal.

| *perfoliata* var. *falcata* | RED | SU-F | 1.5′–4′/2′ |
| | ○ | Z10-9 | CS ✳✳✳ |

Airplane Plant, Sickle Plant, Scarlet Paintbrush. [*C. falcata, Rochea falcata*]. This splendid species has thick, stiff, mostly unbranched stems, shrubby at the base and largely obscured by the foliage. The very succulent, gray green 3″–4″ leaves, much reduced above, are oblong, sickle shaped, and triangular in cross section, and clasp the stem. Masses of scarlet flowers crowd into large, showy, flattened clusters, each 6″ or more across. These bloom over several weeks, and are useful for cutting. Choose a position where the roots can be shaded and kept cool, while the vegetative parts of the plant are in full sun. Best propagated from leaf cuttings, rooted in sand. Eastern Cape Province. *C. perfoliata* var. *miniata,* the Pointed-Leaf Red Crassula, has similar flowers, but its 4″–6″ leaves are green, lanceolate, and pointed. These are in pairs, channeled on their upper surface, and arranged at right angles up the stem. *C. p.* var. *perfoliata* has white flowers. There are hybrids between the several varieties.

CREPIS, Compositae. (200)

incana	PINK	ESU/SU	I′/I′
	○	ZI0-7/H	DRS ***

Hawk's Beard. Long, oblanceolate, basal leaves, to 5″, pinnately parted or divided and toothed; also somewhat pubescent. Many simple or branched stems bear lovely, clear pink, Dandelion-like 1½″ flower heads. Needs well-drained soil and dislikes hot, humid conditions. Greece.

Crepis incana

Cynara cardunculus

CYNARA, Compositae. (11)

Although the Artichoke and the Cardoon find their usual place in the vegetable garden, both are also highly ornamental and deserve space in the flower garden as bold accent plants. They need a well-drained, rich soil and an occasional deep watering. Both benefit from fertilizing and mulching. Provide some shade in the hottest areas. In colder climates, cut back in fall and mulch well, or overwinter roots indoors in a cool place. Spray or hose down for aphids, bait for slugs and snails; susceptible to leaf spot diseases. *C. hystrix* is a rangy plant, but has floral bracts beautifully flushed with pink. Good for cutting.

| *cardunculus* | PURPLE | SU | 6'–8'/3'–4' |
| | ○ | Z10-6 | DRS **** |

Cardoon makes a fountain of arching, stalked leaves, silvery gray green above, white-woolly below. The variable leaves are armed with strong spines, and are deeply to pinnately lobed, each further lobed or coarsely toothed; lower leaves, to 3' long, stem leaves, much smaller. Very stout, branching flower stems bear Artichoke-like 2"–3" buds which open into purplish blue, Thistle-like flower heads, with overlapping, spine-tipped involucral bracts. Southern Europe.

scolymus	PURPLE	SU	3′–5′/3′–4′
	○	Z10-6	DRS ✳✳✳✳

Artichoke forms a domed mound of arching gray green foliage. Its leaves are variable, much like those of *C. cardunculus,* but generally spineless. The flower buds, to 6″ wide, open into huge, Thistle-like, purplish blue heads. The immature flower heads are the artichokes of gastronomy. Not known to grow in the wild; probably of garden origin.

CYNOGLOSSUM, Boraginaceae. (60)

nervosum	BLUE	SU	2′–2.5′/2′
	○ ◑	Z9-4/H	DRS ✳✳✳

Hound's Tongue. A much-branched, erect plant with hairy stems and oblong 6″–10″ leaves. Terminal, scorpioid cymes of rich, gentian blue Forget-Me-Not flowers bloom over a long period. In warm climates, they will not tolerate full sun. Moisture-retentive soil is a must, but floppy stems will result if it is too rich. Grown lean, *Cynoglossum* should not need staking. Lovely with *Achillea* x *taygeta.* Himalayas. Blooming in the spring on dry slopes, *C. grande* is native to California and Washington. It has hairy basal leaves and true blue ½″ flowers on smooth 2.5′ stems. European *Solenanthus apenninus* is quite similar, though seldom grown in this country.

CYPRIPEDIUM, Orchidaceae. (50)   Lady's Slipper

Among our best-loved American natives, Lady's Slipper Orchids are also found in parts of Europe and Asia. They have softly pubescent leaves, which are strongly ribbed and pleated along their length. Solitary, or grouped in sparse, terminal racemes, each flower has 3 spreading sepals, the 2 lowest often joined, and 2 petals. The inflated lip is pouchlike, and forms a trap for pollinating insects, bees in particular. Lady's Slippers are highly prized by gardeners, not only for their unusual beauty, but also because of their challenging culture. They are extremely difficult to establish, and demand precisely the right soil and environment. Propagation from seed is almost impossible, so that stock must be obtained by dividing established plants or by digging from the wild. Unfortunately, in their desire for these special plants, many have overlooked the problems of their culture, digging indiscriminately, only to have them succumb when planted in the garden. As a result, the species have become increasingly rare. Responsible gardeners must discourage buying plants from nurseries which collect their material from the wild, unless rescued from an endangered site. It is heartening that this genus responds well to tissue culture; in the future, there should be an ample supply. Plant in the fall; divide in spring. In addition to the native species, there are several from China and Japan worth seeking, though rarely available here. *C. japonicum* is perhaps the best of the genus. Its large flowers have drooping, pale green petals and sepals, red spotted at the base, and a bladderlike pink and white marbled and ribbed pouch.

C. macranthum resembles a more robust *C. calceolus,* with flowers ranging from white to brownish purple.

| *acaule* | PINK | LSP-SU | 1′–1.5′/9″ |
| | ● | z8-3/H | D ✳✳✳ |

Pink Lady's Slipper, Moccasin Flower. [*Fissipes acaulis*]. The tuberous root gives rise to a pair of pleated, oval, basal leaves, to 8″ long by 3″ wide. The showy, solitary flower may reach 5″ across, borne on a scape 1′ or more long. The narrow 2″ sepals and petals are brownish to maroon, sometimes twisted; the deep rose, rarely white, bladderlike pouch is prominently veined and deeply creased down the front. Temperamental and very demanding. Soil must be humusy and acid; well drained but never drying out or becoming flooded. Plant the crown no more than 1″ deep; mulch well with pine needles. Northeastern United States, Canada.

| *calceolus* | YELLOW | SP-SU | 9″–2.5′/1′ |
| | ◑ | z8-3/H | D ✳✳✳ |

Yellow Lady's Slipper, Yellow Moccasin Flower. This highly variable species is split into several varieties by taxonomists. The typical form, *C. c.* var. *calceolus,* from Europe and Asia, is rarely grown in American gardens; the bigger, native Large Yellow Lady's Slipper, *C. c.* var. *pubescens* [*C. parviflorum* var. *pubescens, C. pubescens*], being grown instead. This sturdy plant has hairy, elliptic 8″ leaves, often undulate along their margins. Each stem ends in 1 or 2 slightly fragrant, large yellow flowers. The yellowish green or brownish sepals and petals are streaked with brown, the latter spirally twisted; the 1½″–2″ pouch is a soft lemon yellow, veined in purple. Woodlands of eastern North America. *C. c.* var. *parviflorum* [*C. parviflorum*], the Small Yellow Lady's Slipper, is smaller throughout, with more fragrant flowers. Its petals and sepals are maroon, its narrower, bright yellow 1″ lip veined in maroon. Swamps of eastern and central North America. These two varieties are often lumped under the name *C. pubescens.* Both are rather variable, and intermediate forms are not unusual. They are probably the easiest of the Slipper Orchids, tolerating both neutral and barely acid soils; good garden loam, enriched with leaf mold or humus, is satisfactory, provided that it never dries out or becomes flooded. Mulch annually.

| *californicum* | YELLOW | LSP-SU | 1′–3′/1′ |
| | ◑● | z9-5 | D ✳✳ |

Each stem, furnished with several hairy, oval 6″–8″ leaves, sports up to 10 or more flowers, about 1″ across, in the axils of leafy bracts. Both sepals and petals are yellowish brown, the pouch white or pink, speckled with brown. Plant in wet or even boggy soil. Resents disturbance. California, Oregon.

| *reginae* | PINK | ESU | 2′–2.5′/1′ |
| | ◑ | z8-4 | D ✳✳ |

Showy Lady's Slipper. [*C. hirsutum, C. spectabile*]. The most elegant of the North American species. Stout clumps of hairy, leafy stems, each topped with 1–3 flowers. The stem-clasping, elliptic to ovate leaves may exceed 8″ long by 4″ wide. The large,

Cypripedium calceolus var. *pubescens*

handsome 2″–3″ wide flowers have white petals and sepals; the deep rose-flushed lip is inflated like a rubber raft. Must have very moist, even boggy conditions, but the crowns must never be submerged. An open position, with neutral to alkaline soil, appears to be most suitable. Tricky under the best of circumstances. Eastern and central North America.

DACTYLORHIZA, Orchidaceae (30)   **Marsh Orchid**

[*Dactylorchis*]. Marsh Orchids or Spotted Orchids are suitable for the border or woodland garden, where they provide an exotic display of rich color in early summer. Their fingerlike tubers produce stiff, stout stems, topped by robust spikes of as many as 80 birdlike flowers; in varying shades of violet or purple, often with dark markings on the lower lip. The leaves are strap shaped, large and clasping below, often chocolate or purple spotted. Soil must be deep, rich, damp, and peaty. Generous dressings of well-rotted compost will encourage the plants to spread. *Dactylorhiza* is seldom grown in the United States, but well worth tracking down. Fall planting is recommended. Possibly hardier than expected.

elata	PURPLE	SU	2.5′–3′/1′
	◑	Z9-7	D **

Algerian Marsh Orchid. Stately and robust, with dark green unspotted leaves. The stems end in massive, cylindrical 8″–9″ spikes of close-set ¾″ flowers; purplish violet, with darker spots on the lower lip. Lovely in open woods. North Africa, southern France, Spain, Portugal. *D. praetermissa* [*Orchis praetermissa*], the Southern Marsh

Dactylorhiza praetermissa

Orchid, is similar and blooms in early summer. This northern European native favors damp soils.

foliosa	PURPLE	SU	I′–2′/I′
	◑	Z9-7	D **

Madeiran Marsh Orchid. [*D. maderensis, Orchis foliosa*]. Perhaps the easiest of the genus to cultivate, it is often confused with *D. elata*. Its leaves are also unspotted, but are glossy and broader, with less acute tips. The crowded pyramidal spikes are usually 3″–6″ long; each deep purple flower, darkly speckled and spotted, is somewhat smaller and broader. Madeira. Also similar, *D. majalis,* the Broad-Leaved Marsh Orchid, is native to western and central Europe, and is distinguished by the heavy chocolate markings on its leaves.

x *grandis*	PURPLE	SU	2′–2.5′/I′
	◑	Z9-7	D *

D. maculata x *D. praetermissa*. A strong-growing hybrid, usually with spotted leaves. The spikes of deep purplish pink flowers may reach 8″ long.

DAHLIA, Compositae. (27)

Dahlias, together with Chrysanthemums and Asters, form the backbone of the fall garden, providing brilliant displays of color until cut down by frost. Although hardy out of doors only in warm zones, they are grown extensively elsewhere, the fleshy tubers either protected by a heavy winter mulch or overwintered dry in a frost-free place. The hollow stems, both well branched and woody at the base, are swollen at the nodes. The odd-pinnate leaves, with mostly ovate, toothed or cut leaflets, are opposite. On long stalks, the radiate flower heads have a central tuft of yellow disk florets surrounded by a row of spreading ray flowers. In semidouble and double horticultural forms, some or all of the disk florets are replaced by rays. Dahlias range in color from white, through pinks and lavenders, yellows and oranges, to reds and maroon, in monochromes and bicolors; only true blue is missing. The flower heads are encircled by 2 rows of involucral bracts; the outer row, leafy and fleshy, the inner scalelike, enlarging as the flowers fade. Dahlias are gross feeders and need deep, porous, very well-enriched soil and plenty of moisture. Avoid high-nitrogen fertilizers, which cause excessive leafy growth at the expense of bloom. The tall kinds require stout stakes, best inserted at planting time, to avoid impaling the growing tubers. Protect from slugs. Where the plants are lifted for the winter, start them into growth in a box of damp peat moss, sand, or ashes. Once the young shoots appear, they must have adequate light and nutrients to avoid weak, etiolated growth; harden them off gradually prior to planting out of doors, after the last frost date. Propagation is by seed, division of the tubers, or by soft cuttings taken from young shoots. Most are very floriferous, blooming for weeks on end, particularly if deadheaded regularly. One of the best cut flowers. Only a few of the species are grown today, having been replaced by the vast range of horticultural forms,

Dahlia 'Dr. John Grainger'

cultivars, and hybrids. This is not the place for a detailed discussion of these. Further information may be obtained from the American Dahlia Society, the Canadian Chrysanthemum and Dahlia Society, and from specialist nurseries listed in the Appendix. Dahlias range in height from 1'–2' dwarfs, mostly used for bedding or at the front of the border, to 6' giants, used for background displays, as well as for hedges and screens. The societies have developed a precise classification system for the varied flower forms. Categories include small pompoms and Anemone-centered types, ball, single, collarette, semicactus and cactus, and large and small, formal and informal decoratives. In exhibition, and flower show work, these classes are followed stringently.

| *coccinea* | RED | LSU-F | 2'–10'/2' |
| | ○ | Z10-9 | CD ** |

A slender, glaucous or red-stemmed plant, branching above. The petioled, glabrous or hairy leaves, to 10" long, vary from entire to bipinnate or tripinnate, with toothed, narrowly ovate leaflets. Yellow, orange, or scarlet 2½"–3" flower heads, with 8 ray florets, on long, stiff peduncles. Probably one of the parents of the modern garden hybrids. Mexico, Central America, northern South America.

| *imperialis* | VARIOUS | LF | 6'–10'/3' |
| | ○ | Z10-9 | CD ** |

Bell Tree Dahlia, Candelabra Tree, Tree Dahlia. [*D. maxonii*]. The massive, 4- to 6-angled brown stems are Bamboo-like, branched above; its younger stems, glaucous green. Including the petiole, the 2 or 3 times pinnate leaves may reach 3' in length, and are almost as wide, with 9–15 toothed, ovate primary leaflets. The panicled inflorescence has abundant gently nodding, somewhat bell-shaped 4"–7" flower heads with white, lavender, or purplish rays. There are double-flowered forms in white and pink. Breaks reliably from the roots, if the tops are frosted. In frost-free zones, cut down to 6" after flowering. May reach 20' or more under ideal conditions. Protect from strong winds. Mexico, Guatemala, Central America.

| *merckii* | LAVENDER | F | 2'–3'/2' |
| | ○ | Z10-9 | CD ** |

Bedding Dahlia. This compact, glabrous plant has well-branched red stems. The bipinnate leaves, on hollow petioles, have narrow, pinnately dissected leaflets. Above the foliage, numerous long, slim, branched flower stalks end in 8-rayed lavender or lavender-flushed white 1"–3" flower heads. May reach 5'–6' when grown under the best conditions. Probably an ancestor of the modern dwarf bedding Dahlias. Mexico.

DATISCA, Datiscaceae. (2)

| *cannabina* | YELLOW | SU | 5'–7'/3'–4' |
| | ○ | Z10-8 | DS ** |

This handsome foliage plant has many strict stems, bushy with alternate, odd-pinnate

Datisca cannabina

leaves. Sharp pointed and toothed, the 7–13 lanceolate leaflets may reach 4″ in length. Its tiny, apetalous, male and female flowers are borne on separate plants; the male, in inconspicuous clusters, the more ornamental female, in slight racemes, in the axils of the upper leaves. Likes well-enriched, porous soils. Possibly hardier than indicated. In spite of its name, it bears little resemblance to *Cannabis*—you won't risk arrest by growing it! An excellent but little-known plant for the back of the border, similar in use to *Artemisia lactiflora*. Asia Minor to India.

DEINANTHE, Saxifragaceae. (2)

Rarely grown in this country, these quietly distinguished plants thrive in cool, moist, sheltered locations in semishade. They need a temperate climate. From creeping rhizomes, single, erect stems rise to form loose clumps; grouped toward the top of each stem are several handsome opposite leaves and a loose terminal corymb of nodding open flowers. The inflorescence bears both decorative bisexual flowers, and smaller sterile ones on the periphery. The fertile flowers have 5 waxy petals surrounding a wide ring of small crowded stamens and a prominent central style. The sterile flowers have 2–3 petaloid sepals.

| *bifida* | WHITE | SU/LSU | 1.5′–2′/1.5′ |
| | ☽ | Z9-6/H | DS * |

As the specific epithet implies, the leaves are bifid, deeply cleft at the apex into 2 symmetrical halves. They are rough textured, coarsely lobed and toothed, to 8″ long. The white flowers are smaller than those of *D. caerulea;* their stamens are yellow. Japan.

| *caerulea* | BLUE | SU/LSU | 1.5′/1.5′ |
| | ☽ | Z9-6/H | DS * |

Broadly ovate, coarsely toothed leaves to 10″ long. The pale violet blue 1¼″ flowers are borne on reddish stalks; blue stamens. *D. c.* 'Alba' is an even rarer white-flowered form. China.

DELPHINIUM, Ranunculaceae. (250)   Larkspur

Delphiniums are the first plants to come to mind when we think of traditional perennial gardens. The tall *D. elatum* hybrids form the keystone of many a summer border. They, as well as the shorter hybrid types and species, are prized for the exceptional beauty and rare colors of their flowers. Few serious gardeners forgo the pleasure of growing them, despite the wide range of problems attendant on their culture. Larkspurs form clumps of more or less erect, sometimes branching stems. The foliage is either basal or alternate; the leaves, palmately lobed or divided. The flowers are borne in loose to crowded spikes or racemes, at times grouped into panicles. Their complex, asymmetrical flowers are composed of 5 petaloid sepals, one of them spurred. Of the 2–4 true petals, only the small blades, sometimes called the "bee," are visible, crowded into the throat of the flower. The spurs of the upper 2 petals are hidden within the spurred sepal. Numerous stamens are spirally arranged around 1–5 pistils. In some horticultural forms, the petaloid sepals and petals may be numerous. The Delphinium Society publishes an extensive yearbook, and makes seed available to members.

| *x belladonna* | VARIOUS | SP/SU | 3'–4'/2' |
| | ○ | Z10-3/H | DS *** |

This group of hybrids is derived from crosses between *D. elatum* and *D. grandiflorum,* and perhaps *D. cheilanthum* [*D. formosum* Hort.] as well. They resemble the tall *D. elatum* hybrids, but with finer foliage, and lack a dominant central raceme. Over a long season, they produce numerous looser racemes of single to semidouble 1½"–2" flowers, in white and a full range of pale to very dark blues. These shorter plants seldom need staking, but otherwise are similar to the *D. elatum* hybrids in their cultural requirements.
———————— 'Belladonna' is light blue.
———————— 'Bellamosa' ['Bellamosum'] is dark blue.
———————— 'Casa Blanca' has pure white flowers.
———————— 'Cliveden Beauty' is light blue.
The 'Connecticut Yankee' strain, bred by Edward Steichen, is said to be the result of crossing *D.* x *belladonna* with *D. tatsienense.* These bushy, freely branching plants are only 2'–2.5' in height. Their charming single flowers may be white or shades of blue, lavender, or purple.

| *cardinale* | RED | SP/SU | 3'–6'/2' |
| | ○ | Z10-8/H | S ** |

Erect stems, simple or branching above. The basal leaves, 2"–8" wide, are palmately divided into 5 segments, each 3 lobed. The stem leaves are parted into 5–7 deeply cleft segments. Loose racemes or panicles of 1" flowers, with red sepals and yellow, red-tipped petals. Blooms the first year from seed, but is not an easy plant. California, Baja California.

| *elatum* **hybrids** | VARIOUS | SP/SU | 3'–8'/2'–3' |
| | ○ | Z10-3/H | CS **** |

The species *D. elatum* from Siberia, now rare in cultivation, is considered to be the principal ancestor of our magnificent modern hybrids. It is probable that their other forebears were *D. exaltatum* and *D. cheilanthum* [*D. formosum* Hort.]. Their precise parentage is obscure; breeding work has proceeded for some 150 years, early records are lacking, and some of the species involved appear to have been confused at the time. *D. grandiflorum* and others also may be implicated. The old-fashioned English Delphiniums flowered only in white and shades of blue. Many named cultivars were bred, and traditionally were propagated by cuttings. Later, the 'Pacific' hybrids were developed in California by Frank Reinelt. He concentrated on expanding the range of

Delphinium elatum hybrid 'Thundercloud'

separate colors of his seed strains. His introduction of native species weakened the perenniality of his lines, which were treated as annuals. Today true 'Pacific' hybrids are no longer available; those now offered are merely progeny of the original crosses and are much more variable. In an effort to increase the range and intensity of colors, 'Pacific' blood was introduced into some English and European lines. The constitution of some has suffered as a result. The English firm of Blackmore and Langdon, which introduced many of the most magnificent named cultivars over several generations, now supplies some of the strains available in this country. These and other seed strains are the principal means of Delphinium production today. Breeding continues; Dr. R. A. H. Legro is perfecting cultivars in the red color range, but these are not yet commercially available. *D. elatum* hybrids form clumps of several erect stems, abundantly clothed in dark green, deeply divided foliage. Above rise stately, cylindrical racemes, densely crowded with single or semidouble 2"–3" florets. Their color range is extensive: whites, near pinks, lavenders, mauves, purples and every shade of blue, often with contrasting bees. Delphiniums are greedy plants, and demand well-drained, rich soil, heavily amended with organic matter. Regular fertilizing is essential for superior bloom. Each plant produces several shoots, but is only able to support a few. Thin young plants to 2–3 shoots, when these are 6" tall; older plants can sustain 4–5 or more. For best effect, each stem must be staked individually, tied at 1' intervals. Remove spent racemes at their base, not only for neatness, but to prevent seed formation and to encourage the development of lateral spikes. Regrettably, Delphiniums are subject to a number of pests and diseases. Of these, slugs and snails are the most widespread, and are extremely destructive. A conscientious, regular spray program, including a miticide, insecticide, and fungicide, will serve to control the most common problems. Propagation is by seed, which must be of good quality and obtained from a reliable source. Seed-grown plants are readily available from nurseries. Favorite selections can be increased vegetatively by cuttings of new, young shoots. Delphiniums do best where summers are moderate and winters cold. Elsewhere they are most successful when treated as annuals.

STRAINS:

'Blackmore and Langdon.' Mixed colors. Exceptionally large flower spikes.
'Blue Fountains' is a mixed dwarf strain from Blackmore and Langdon. 2.5'–3' tall.

'PACIFIC' HYBRIDS:

'Astolat.' Lavenders to near pinks with a contrasting bee.
'Black Knight.' Deep violet with a black eye.
'Blue Bird.' Medium blue with a white bee.
'Galahad' is all-white.
'Summer Skies' has sky blue flowers with a white eye.

| *grandiflorum* | BLUE | SP/SU | 1'–2'/1'–1.5' |
| | O | Z10-3/H | S *** |

[*D. chinense, D. sinense*]. A diffuse, freely branching plant. The leaves are palmately divided into linear segments; the lower leaves are petioled, the upper, sessile. Loose

Delphinium tatsienense

racemes of blue, violet, or white 1″–1½″ flowers. Short-lived; often treated as an annual or biennial. Flowers the first year from an early seeding. Deadhead for continued bloom. China, Siberia.

————— 'Blue Elf' has blue flowers. Only about 1′ tall.

————— 'Blue Mirror' is gentian blue. 2′ tall.

nudicaule	RED	SP/SU	1′–2′/1′
	○ ◑	Z10-6/H	S **

Erect to ascending stems. The mostly basal 1″–4″ leaves are cleft into 3–5 rounded segments, broader than those of *D. cardinale.* Orange red to red 1″ flowers with yellow petals in a sparse inflorescence. Difficult. Most suitable for native plant gardens. California, Oregon.

semibarbatum	YELLOW	SP/SU	1′–2′/1′
	○	Z10-8/H	S *

[*D. zalil, D. sulphureum* Hort.]. Simple to lightly branched stems, with leaves palmately divided into narrow segments. Long racemes of clear yellow 1″–1¼″ flowers. Rare and temperamental. Needs a very well-drained soil. Iran.

tatsienense	BLUE	SP/SU	1.5′–2′/1′–1.5′
	○	Z10-6/H	S **

Similar to *D. grandiflorum,* but hairy throughout. Its rough leaves are deeply divided into 3 segments. Branched racemes of long-spurred, intense blue flowers, about 1¼″ long. Short-lived. Western China.

Best where winters are mild and summers cool, Toothworts or Pepperroots are charming in the wild garden, in front of shrubs, or in the flower garden. They thrive with little attention in fertile, damp soil. Distinguished from closely related *Cardamine* by their scaly, tuberous roots, which are white and toothlike. Elongating racemes of cruciform flowers rise above the handsome compound foliage. The American Toothworts are barely worthy of garden space, except in native plant areas.

digitata	PINK	SP	1.5′/1′
	◑●	Z9-7/H	D ✻✻

[*Cardamine pentaphyllos*]. Dense clumps of rather fleshy stems. Large, digitate leaves, with 3–5 ovate to obovate deeply serrate leaflets, about 2″ long. The slightly nodding racemes of 12 or more, rose or purplish pink ½″–¾″ blooms, open from the bottom. Particularly attractive planted under *Viburnum* x *burkwoodii*. Southern Europe.

pinnata	WHITE	SP	1.5′–2′/1′
	◑●	Z9-7/H	DS ✻✻

[*Cardamine heptaphylla*]. A slightly larger species, which makes bold clumps of stems, leafy at the top. Their dark green, odd-pinnate leaves have 7 ovate to elliptic toothed leaflets. Terminal racemes of pure white ¼″–½″ flowers, which contrast gracefully with its own foliage and with spring bulbs. European Alps to the Pyrenees.

Dentaria digitata

Dianella caerulea

Flax Lilies are useful border plants for our warmer gardens and good conservatory plants in colder climates. Grasslike foliage, sheathing at the base, rises from their spreading rhizomes. The loose panicles of many small, nodding Lily-like flowers, are followed by striking bright blue berries. The soil should be rich and fertile. Mature plants will tolerate drought, but ample moisture ensures a good crop of berries. Protect from searing sun.

caerulea	BLUE	SU	2′/1.5′
	O	Z10-8	DS **

Paroo Lily. Tufts of 1.5′ leaves, rough with small teeth along the midrib and edges. The bright blue or whitish flowers are only ¼″ wide, but the panicles may reach 1′ in length. Lustrous royal blue berries. Australia. *D. ensifolia* [*D. nemerosa, Dracaena ensifolia*], Umbrella Dracaena, has panicles of similar flowers atop stems to 6′ high. Its lower stems are leafy. Australia, Hawaii, China, eastern Africa.

revoluta	BLUE	SU	2′–4′/1′
	O	Z10-8	DS **

Black Anther Flax Lily. Tussocks of basal 2′–3′ leaves, with revolute and saw-toothed margins. Large panicles of deep purplish blue 1″ flowers, with dark brown or black anthers. The blue berries are rather small. Tolerant of dry soils. Southeastern Australia, Tasmania. *D. tasmanica* has purplish or grayish foliage in tussocks, and large graceful panicles of ¾″ flowers on 4′–5′ stems. Its bright blue ¾″ berries last throughout the summer. Tasmania.

Carnations, Cloves, and Pinks, and other members of this genus, have been grown over centuries for their attractive, deliciously fragrant flowers which are prized for cutting. Today, Carnations, *D. caryophyllus* and its hybrids, are grown almost exclusively under glass for the cut flower trade. In mild winter regions, they are sometimes used in gardens, but are untidy and seldom satisfactory. Other, less commercial species, predominantly those from alpine regions, adapt well to rock gardens and walls, and make attractive edging plants. They are quite variable and interbreed freely, resulting in much confusion in nomenclature. In the trade, named selections are often attributed to one species or another, when in fact they are hybrids, albeit of unknown or confused parentage. Mat forming, mounding, or with upright but lax flowering and vegetative stems, Dianthus have pairs of grassy, usually glabrous leaves, often joining at the base and sheathing a swollen node. The terminal flowers are grouped into few- to many-flowered panicles, cymes, or heads, or may be solitary; mostly white or shades of pink and red, often with a contrasting eye, seldom lavender or yellow. The tubular calyx is 5 lobed, subtended by one or more pairs of bracts; typically, the corolla is composed of 5 free, clawed petals, frilled, fringed, or toothed at the apex; the horticultural forms often have many more. In some species, the throat is bearded. All require a sunny position in fast-draining, neutral to alkaline, sandy loam. Poor drainage and wet crowns during the winter will surely kill many of the lowest-growing kinds. Pests and diseases are few. Propagation is easy; seed is best sown in spring, but as is usual, named selections and cultivars must be propagated vegetatively. Cuttings, preferably taken with a heel, as well as pipings and layers all root with ease throughout the growing season. Heel cuttings are taken from short side shoots, which are stripped downward from the stem, retaining a small part as a "heel." Pipings are tip cuttings, which break off within the node when pulled from the top, resulting in a very soft, easily rooted base; extra care must be taken that they do not dry out during the rooting period. The longer, lax stems root quite readily when layered. On the underside, cut through ⅓ to ½ the diameter of the stem at a 45° angle, open the wound, and peg it down into a friable medium; sever once rooted.

x *allwoodii* Hort.	VARIOUS	SU	1′–1.5′/1.5′
	○	Z10-4/H	C ****

Cottage Pink, Border Carnation, Allwood Pink. D. caryophyllus x D. plumarius. Usually this very large and variable group of hybrids forms vigorous tufts of glaucous, bluish gray foliage. The fragrant, solitary 1½″–2″ flowers may be single, semidouble, or fully double, often patterned or zoned, many with fringed petals. Very long blooming, particularly if deadheaded regularly. Provide a humus-rich soil and add lime if it tends toward acid. Increase by layers.

——————— 'Aqua' has pure white double flowers on 10″–12″ stems.

——————— 'Doris' has very fragrant, semidouble salmon pink flowers with a darker eye. Z9-5/H. An Allwood Brothers selection.

——————— 'Essex Witch.' Semidouble, medium pink flowers, with petals darker at the center and finely fringed at the edge. Sweet-smelling. Less tolerant of high temperatures. Z9-3/H.

——————— 'Her Majesty' has double white flowers with cut petals.

——————— 'Ian.' Double red flowers rimmed in crimson. Z9-5/H.

——————— 'Robin' has double flowers in salmon to scarlet.

STRAINS:

'Alpinus.' This fine strain makes neat, compact mounds of blue green, linear foliage, above which single, very fragrant flowers bloom throughout the summer until frost. Offered in mixed pinks and reds, many frilled, fringed, or with a darker eye. Select in bloom if possible. 6″–12″ tall.

barbatus	VARIOUS	LSP-ESU	1′–2′/2′
	○	Z10-4/H	CDS ****

Sweet William. Popular in cottage gardens for hundreds of years, these are short-lived perennials or biennials, often treated as annuals. They have strong, often stout stems, with pairs of glossy, dark green, lanceolate 4″ leaves. Their many-flowered, flat-topped or domed, terminal 3″–6″ cymes are dense and leafy. Lightly scented, bearded inside,

Dianthus deltoides

and sometimes fringed, the individual flowers are ½″–1″ or more across and range in color from white through pinks and reds to purplish crimson; they are frequently varicolored. The numerous strains, including dwarf and double-flowered ones, are mostly offered in mixed colors. Dramatic when massed in a mosaic or oriental carpet effect. Long lasting as cut flowers. Remove spent stems to ground level to maintain vigor and reduce self-seeding. Propagate the selections vegetatively. Divide frequently or replace after 2–3 years. Rich, moist, but well-drained soil. Best where summers are cool and winters mild. Naturalized in parts of North America. Central and southern Europe, Russia, China.

——————— 'Scarlet Beauty' has red 1″ flowers. 1′–1.5′ tall.

——————— 'Newport Pink' is similar with coral flowers.

STRAINS

'Double Midget' has double flowers on 4″–6″ stems.
'Excelsior.' A good mixture of rich colors. More fragrant than most. 1.5′ stems.
'Indian Carpet' is a dwarf strain, only 8″ tall.

| *deltoides* | VARIOUS | LSP-SU | 6″–1.5′/1′ |
| | ○ ◑ | Z10-3/H | CS ✳✳✳ |

Maiden Pink is variable, usually forming wide mats of loose, bright green herbage. The small, linear to lanceolate leaves are often hairy along their margins. Their slender, sparsely leaved flower stems usually fork toward the top and end in solitary, slightly fragrant ¾″ flowers. They range in color from purple through reds and pinks to white, with a dark, pale-spotted band at the base of the sharply toothed petals. Gritty, alkaline soil. Crown rot may be a problem. Protect with evergreen boughs in cold winter climates. Reliable and long blooming. Cut back spent blooms hard for neatness, vigor, and to curtail self-seeding. Blooms by midsummer from an early seeding; earlier if sown the previous fall. Tolerant of very light shade. Europe. Earlier blooming *D. arenarius* has slightly larger, fragrant, deeply fringed white flowers; it requires a slightly shaded position. Northern Europe.

———— 'Albus' has single white flowers. 6″ tall.

———— 'Brilliant.' Double, bright crimson flowers. 6″–8″.

———— 'Samos' has deep green leaves and rich crimson flowers on 9″ stems.

gratianopolitanus	PINK	SP	6″–12″/12″
	○	Z10-5/H	CS ***

Cheddar Pink. [*D. caesius, D. suavis*]. Neat, dense mounds of evergreen, glaucous blue gray, linear foliage, which in time forms large mats. The vegetative stems are lax, usually unbranched or nearly so; the wiry flower stems bear solitary, fragrant, single ½″–¾″ flowers, bearded at the throat, mostly with toothed petals. Blooms intermittently until frost. Top dress with lime chips to sweeten the soil and facilitate surface runoff. Southern England, east to Poland, Ukraine.

———— 'Petite' is a dwarf, covered with tiny, bright pink flowers. 3″ tall.

———— 'Splendens' has red flowers over tight buns of foliage.

———— 'Tiny Rubies' makes low mats of gray green foliage; fully double, rich pink flowers on 4″ stems.

knappii	YELLOW	SP	1.5′/1.5′
	○	Z9-3/H	CS ***

The only available yellow-flowered species has an unfortunately awkward habit. It is slightly pubescent, with pale green or somewhat glaucous, grayish herbage. The wiry stems, branchless or forked above, are sparsely clothed in linear 2½″ leaves. Their clusters of 4–10 soft yellow ¾″ flowers are unscented. Floriferous for some time, but never puts on a full display. Best in an informal grouping rather than as a specimen. Often grown as an annual. Yugoslavia.

plumarius	PINK	SU-F	6″–1′/8″
	○	Z10-4/H	C ****

Cottage Pink, Grass Pink, Scotch Pink. This species, long cultivated, is involved in the development of many of the modern dwarf hybrids, particularly the so-called Cottage Pinks, Border Pinks, and Old Laced Pinks. It makes wide, loose hummocks of glabrous and glaucous, gray herbage. The narrowly lanceolate leaves are conspicuously veined and keeled beneath, the lower to 4″ long. Above, supported on wiry 10″–12″ stalks, bloom clusters of 2–5 spicily fragrant, single, semidouble or double 1″–1½″ flowers. Their petals are usually deeply fringed to ⅓ of their length; the throat is bearded with long hairs. Very long-blooming, particularly if deadheaded regularly; cut back the spent stems almost to ground level. Mulch with evergreen boughs in cold winter areas. Needs moist, humusy soil, sweetened with lime. Eurasia.

————— 'Agatha' has semidouble, purplish pink flowers with a crimson eye. 8″ tall.

————— 'Mrs. Sinkins' is a much-loved old cultivar. Her fully double white flowers are intensely fragrant. The calyx tends to split, causing the flowers to "blow." Largely replaced by more modern selections.

————— 'White Ladies' has fragrant double white flowers.

STRAINS:

'Sonata' is reputed to be a superior form of 'Spring Beauty.' Earlier blooming, with a larger percentage of fully double flowers.

'Spring Beauty.' A good mixture of clove-scented semidouble and double flowers, in white, pinks, and reds, many zoned, often with frilled petals. Z9-3/H.

superbus	VARIOUS	SU	I′–2′/I.5′
	○	Z9-4/H	CS **

Lilac Pink. Another variable species, which makes tufts of mostly green, linear-lanceolate 2″ leaves. Decumbent and woody below, branching above, the stems end in loose clusters of 2–12 fragrant, shaggy, pale lilac to rose purple I½″–2″ flowers; deeply fringed petals and hairy throats. Floriferous to the point of exhaustion, this plant is short-lived and often treated as a biennial. Rich, moist soil. Europe, eastern Asia to Japan. The 'Loveliness' strain (crossed with *D.* x *allwoodii*) makes neater plants, with spidery pink, red, or purple flowers. Best treated as biennials.

DIASCIA, Scrophulariaceae. (5I)   Twinspur

Several of these long-blooming South African plants have become fashionable in recent years and well deserve their popularity. They form low clumps of erect to decumbent, usually branching, slender stems, arising from a crown. The small opposite and decussate leaves are well spaced. Flat or slightly cupped flowers, in various shades of pink, rose, or salmon, are borne in terminal and axillary racemes. The corolla is 2 lipped, the upper lip 2 lobed, the lower 3 lobed, with 2 small spurs. Diascias thrive in sun or partial shade, in well-drained, fertile soil, and must not be allowed to dry out. Cut back at the end of the season. They are intolerant of extreme heat as well as combined heat and humidity. Unreliably winter hardy; their hardiness is much affected by factors other than cold. Losses are unpredictable and frequent. Twinspurs are best propagated by cuttings, as they are often lost when divided. They seldom set seed outside of their native environment, but are easily raised from seed when it is available. Often grown as bedding plants from overwintered cuttings, when they must be planted more closely. The species are much confused in gardens and in the trade. Many are not easily distinguished by laymen, differing only in minor details of flower structure and leaf shape. *D. barberae,* the first species to be grown outside of South Africa but not one

Diascia stachyoides

of the finest, is often sold under the name *D. cordata;* most references describe it as an annual, although it is in fact perennial. The true *D. cordata* does not appear to be in cultivation. *D. vigilis,* described below, is usually sold under the invalid name *D. elegans. D. flanaganii,* a fine plant indeed, is no longer considered distinct from *D. stachyoides.* Hybrid *D.* 'Ruby Fields,' according to its breeder John Kelly, resulted from crossing *D. cordifolia (D. cordata?)* with *D. barberae.* Its deep rosy salmon flowers, compact habit, and hardiness make it one of the best. Readily available.

---

fetcaniensis		PINK	SP-EF	**1.5′/1.5′**
		○ ◑	ZI0-8/H	C ∗∗

This compact plant, with branching stems, is glandular-hairy throughout. Its broadly ovate ¾″–1″ leaves, cordate at the base, are gently toothed. The short, terminal racemes of concave rose pink ¾″–1″ flowers are followed by axillary racemes. South Africa.

---

integerrima		PINK	SP-EF	**1.5′/1.5′–2′**
		○ ◑	ZI0-8/H	C ∗∗

Upright to decumbent, branching stems, with linear to narrowly lanceolate ½″–1½″ leaves, only slightly toothed toward the base. Slender, erect racemes of rose pink ¾″ flowers. Tolerates drier conditions than most. Considered the best garden subject in its native land. South Africa.

---

rigescens		PINK	SP-EF	**1.5′/1.5′**
		○ ◑	ZI0-8/H	C ∗∗∗

This robust and vigorous species has sturdy stems, well clothed in sessile ¾″–2½″

leaves. Their ovate blades are fleshy, edged with small teeth. Its dense, crowded 6″ racemes of sharp rose pink ½″–¾″ flowers raise it above all other Diascias. South Africa.

| *vigilis* | PINK | SP-EF | 1′–1.5′/1.5′ |
| | ○ ◐ | Z10-8/H | C ✳✳ |

[*D. elegans* Hort.]. Substantial, ovate ½″–2″ leaves, edged with sharp teeth. Terminal and axillary, slender racemes of pale pink ¾″–1″ flowers. Graceful and well behaved. South Africa.

DICENTRA, Fumariaceae. (20)   Bleeding-Heart

The beloved Bleeding-Hearts are appropriate for the foreground of borders or for less formal use in cottage or wildflower gardens. These easy plants will thrive where their simple requirements are met. They need a very well-drained, humusy soil and will not survive in ground that remains wet. They prefer some shade, especially in hot areas. Short-lived in mild winter climates. Some species spread readily by means of tubers; those with rhizotomous roots do so less. Propagation is by division or seed; plants grown from seed are slow to mature. The ferny, ternately dissected or compound foliage is mostly basal; when present, stem leaves are alternate. Heart- or pantaloon-shaped flowers are borne in racemes or panicles above the foliage. The flattened, irregular corolla consists of 2 outer and 2 inner petals; the outer petals are pouched or spurred at the base, with spreading or recurved tips; the inner petals protrude slightly. Western *D. chrysantha* reaches 5′ in height and bears panicles of bright yellow flowers. It is temperamental outside of its native environment. Rare in cultivation.

| *cucullaria* | WHITE | ESP | 8″–12″/1′ |
| | ◐ ● | Z9-3/H | DS ✳✳✳ |

Dutchman's-Breeches. The basal foliage arises from small tubers. Racemes of small white nodding flowers; corolla pantaloon shaped, with long, spreading spurs; outer petals tipped with yellow. Dies down by midsummer. Suitable only for wildflower gardens. Eastern and central North America. Squirrel Corn, *D. canadensis,* has purple-tinged, greenish white, narrowly heart-shaped flowers.

| *eximia* | PINK | SP-SU | 1′–1.5′/1′–1.5′ |
| | ◐ ● | Z10-3/H | DS ✳✳✳✳ |

Fringed Bleeding-Heart, Wild Bleeding-Heart. Neat mounds of all basal foliage, finely dissected into toothed segments. Leaves broadly ovate in outline, variably gray green and glaucous. The narrowly heart-shaped ¾″–1″ flowers, pink to light reddish purple, nod in loose panicles on slender, watery scapes. The tips of the outer petals flare and are longer than those of *D. formosa.* May rebloom in late summer or early fall. Eastern United States. Many of the cultivars listed in the trade under *D. eximia* or *D. formosa* are of uncertain origin, and cannot be assigned to either of these species with any degree of confidence; in addition, there are hybrids between the two. Both cultivars and hybrids are more readily available than the true species. Most of the hybrids are more tolerant of direct sun.

————— 'Alba' has white flowers.

————— 'Bountiful' has blue green foliage and carmine red flowers.

————— 'Zestful.' Rose pink flowers.

D. 'Luxuriant,' reputedly a hybrid between *D. eximia* and *D. peregrina,* has blue green foliage and carmine flowers. Free blooming.

formosa	PINK	SP-ESU	1′–1.5′/1′–1.5′
	◑ ●	ZI0-3/H	DS ****

Western Bleeding-Heart. Quite as variable as *D. eximia* and indistinguishable from it, except by an expert. Some authorities say it is smaller, others larger; its foliage may be slightly less finely dissected, the flowers a little smaller. The spreading tips of its outer petals are usually a little shorter. Flowers pink to deep rose. Western United States.

————— 'Sweetheart' has white flowers.

————— *oregana* is a smaller plant. Its flowers have cream or pale yellow outer petals and rose-tipped inner petals. This subspecies is said to be involved in some of the hybrids. Northern California, Southern Oregon.

spectabilis	PINK	SP-LSP	2′–3′/1.5′
	◑ ●	ZI0-3/H	DS ****

Bleeding-Heart. This garden favorite has a looser habit and less finely dissected foliage

Dicentra spectabilis 'Alba'

than the other species. Upper stems reddish and leafy. One-sided racemes of pendent, broadly heart-shaped 1″ flowers; outer petals rose pink, with strongly reflexed tips, inner petals white and exserted. Tolerates sun in gentle climates. Dies back by midsummer, leaving an awkward gap which needs to be concealed by plants which develop later, such as Hostas, Astilbes, and ferns. Eastern Asia.

————— 'Alba' has pure white flowers.

DICHORISANDRA, Commelinaceae. (30)

These tropical perennials have stout, erect, rarely branching stems, sheathed with large, glossy, alternate leaves. The terminal inflorescences are thyrses, some 6″ long. The blue to purplish blue ½″ flowers are nearly regular. Each has 3 slightly unequal, persistent, fleshy sepals; the 2 upper petals overlap, the lower is reflexed. These tender plants withstand only a few degrees of frost and may go dormant in cool weather. They need a rich, humusy soil, fertilizing and plenty of water in summer, and even an occasional misting. Allow to rest in winter.

reginae	BLUE	LSU/F	2′–3′/1.5′–2′
	◑●	Z10/T	CDS ***

Queen's Spiderwort. [*Tradescantia reginae*]. The 2-ranked, lanceolate leaves, to 6″ long, are streaked with silver when young. Its conical thyrses are more compact than those of *D. thyrsiflora*. Sepals streaked with purple; deep purple blue petals, white at the base. Peru.

thyrsiflora	BLUE	LSU/F	3′–4′/1.5′–2′
	◑●	Z10/T	CDS ***

Blue Ginger has glossy green leaves, to 6″ or more, spirally arranged around its thick stems. Long inflorescences, more open than those of *D. reginae*. Ribbed sepals; purple blue petals. Brazil.

DICLIPTERA, Acanthaceae. (150)

suberecta	RED	SP-F	1′/1.5′
	○◑	Z10-9	CS **

[*Jacobinia suberecta*]. A compact, leafy little plant. Both the arching stems and the opposite, ovate 1½″–2½″ leaves are densely gray-woolly. The orange red 1¾″ flowers are borne profusely in loose cymes. Corolla tubular and 2 lipped, with exserted stamens. Long flowering. Well-drained soil, enriched with organic matter. Water regularly during the blooming season. Uruguay.

Dichorisandra reginae

Dictamnus albus 'Purpureus'

DICTAMNUS, Rutaceae. (I)

This extremely long-lived plant is one of the best perennials for low-maintenance gardens. It can safely be left to itself for many years, only resenting disturbance. While slow to become established, the Gas Plant spreads gradually and makes a handsome specimen for the flower border in sun or light shade; it is even tolerant of occasionally dry conditions if the soil is fertile. The foliage remains attractive throughout the season. Lovely with Bearded Iris and Campanulas.

albus	WHITE	LSP/SU	2′–3′/2.5′
	○	Z9-2/H	RS ***

Gas Plant, Burning Bush, Dittany, Fraxinella. [*D. fraxinella, D. f. albus*]. A robust plant with vertical stems and aromatic foliage. The dark green, slightly glossy, alternate leaves are odd-pinnate, with as many as eleven 2″–3″ leaflets. The showy, pure white, asymmetrical flowers are arranged in terminal racemes. Each flower has 5 petals, the lowermost one drooping, and conspicuous upward curving stamens. In bloom only for about 2 weeks, but attractive, star-shaped seedpods follow. The seeds are strongly fragrant of citrus. Poisonous. Southern Europe, Asia.

———— *caucasicus* is a larger plant with longer racemes. 3′–4′ tall.

———— 'Purpureus' [*D. a. ruber, D. f. ruber*] has mauve purple flowers with darker veins on 3′ stems.

———— 'Rubra' has rosy pink flowers veined with purple. 3′.

These handsome Iris-like plants have been segregated from *Moraea* because they grow from rhizomatous roots rather than from corms. They spread to form large clumps of stiff, erect, linear to sword-shaped evergreen leaves, usually in 2-ranked fans. The branching scapes, about as tall as the foliage, bear lovely flowers, reminiscent of Japanese Iris. Each is composed of 6 spreading tepals, the 3 outer segments larger, and often colored at the base. They surround an erect, petaloid, 3-parted style or crest. The individual flowers last only for one day, but new ones open daily. Long blooming, predominantly in spring and summer, with some flowers produced all year in mild areas. As the common name Fortnight Lily suggests, the heaviest flowering occurs in flushes, at more or less biweekly intervals. These are rewarding and easy plants, quite tolerant of neglect. Provide a well-drained soil, preferably enriched with organic matter. Water during dry spells. Division is needed infrequently, only when clumps become overcrowded.

bicolor	YELLOW	ESP-SU	2′–2.5′/2′
	○ ◑	ZI0-9/H	DS ****

[*Moraea bicolor*]. Stiff, linear, light green leaves. Branching scapes, topped with several pale yellow 2″ flowers. The tepals are rounded, the outer segments marked at the base with a dark brown blotch and small orange spots. South Africa. There are several hybrids between *D. bicolor* and *D. vegeta,* mostly more vigorous and free flowering than either species. 'Lemon Drop' has cream-colored flowers; the outer perianth segments marked with lemon yellow. 'Orange Drop' has cream flowers marked basally with orange.

Dietes vegeta

| *grandiflora* | WHITE | SP-SU | 3'–4'/2' |
| | ○ ◑ | ZIO-9/H | DS ** |

Dark green, sword-shaped leaves which, in this species alone, are not 2 ranked. Branched stems of large white 3"–4½" flowers with orange yellow and brown basal spots and crests striped with violet. The scapes produce flowers over several years; do not cut back after blooming, but remove only the individual spent flowers. South Africa.

| *robinsoniana* | WHITE | ESP-SU | 3'–6'/3'–4' |
| | ○ | ZIO/H | DS ** |

Wedding Lily. [*Iris robinsoniana, Moraea robinsoniana*]. Large clumps of tall, erect, linear to sword-shaped leaves, resembling those of *Phormium tenax.* The stout scapes support much-branched panicles, bearing as many as a hundred blooms. Beautiful 3" flowers, pure white or very faintly flushed with pale yellow at the base of the outer tepals. Well-drained, organically rich soil; water well during dry spells. It is unaccountable that this spectacular plant is not grown more widely in southern California gardens. Australia.

| *vegeta* | WHITE | ESP-SU | 2'–2.5'/2' |
| | ○ ◑ | ZIO-9/H | DS **** |

African Iris, Fortnight Lily. [*D. catenulata, D. iridoides, Moraea catenulata, M. iridoides, M. vegeta*]. The most commonly grown species. Crowded fans of stiff, narrow leaves. Branched scapes, usually taller than the foliage, bear 3–4 white or very pale lavender 2½" flowers. The outer tepals are marked with a long yellow blotch; the crest is lavender blue. Do not remove flowering stems after blooming, as they continue to produce flowers for several years; deadhead by breaking off spent flowers. South Africa.
————— 'Johnsonii' is a larger plant with 4" flowers.

DIGITALIS, Scrophulariaceae. (19)   Foxglove

These garden favorites have alternate leaves, the lower ones usually grouped into large basal rosettes, especially in younger plants; the upper smaller and mostly sessile. The thimble-shaped flowers are borne in crowded, usually one-sided racemes. The corolla is 4 lobed and 2 lipped, the lower lip, somewhat to much longer than the upper. Evergreen in mild areas. Several species are sources of the drug digitalis, and are highly poisonous. All are of easy culture, and thrive in porous but moist soils, well enriched with organic matter. In hot areas, shade lightly. Mulch after the ground freezes, to discourage crown rot in wet winters. Often grown as biennials. Will often reflower if cut back. Bait for snails and slugs where necessary. Best known is the biennial *D. purpurea,* the Common Foxglove, which occasionally survives as a short-lived perennial. Its flowers are purplish pink. There is also a white form, as well as many named cultivars and strains.

Digitalis ferruginea

ferruginea	YELLOW	LSP/SU	3'–4'/1'–1.5'
	○ ◑	Z10-4/H	DS ***

Rusty Foxglove has lanceolate leaves, to 7" long. Its yellow to yellow red ⅔" flowers are much veined in rust, especially within; the lower corolla lip is very long and hairy. Southeastern Europe, central Asia.

grandiflora	YELLOW	LSP/SU	2'–2.5'/1'–1.5'
	○ ◑	Z10-3/H	DS ****

Yellow Foxglove. [*D. ambigua*]. The shiny, conspicuously veined, ovate-lanceolate 8"–10" leaves have small, sharp teeth, and are sparsely hairy on their undersides. Hairy, pale yellow 2" flowers with brown veining inside. Europe, Western Asia.

lanata	WHITE	LSP/SU	2'–3'/1'
	○ ◑	Z10-4/H	DS ***

Grecian Foxglove is an erect, woolly plant, with sessile, gray green, lanceolate leaves. The white or yellowish 1" flowers, in a long, crowded raceme, are veined with brown or purple inside and out; the long, recurved lower lip is pale gray. Southeastern Europe.

lutea	YELLOW	LSP/SU	2'–3'/1'
	○ ◑	Z10-3/H	DS ***

Small Yellow Foxglove. The ovate-lanceolate leaves are sometimes toothed. Its long, slender, nodding racemes bear many pale yellow 1" flowers, with somewhat recurved corolla lobes. Seeds itself very freely. A more graceful plant than *D. grandiflora*. Southern Europe, northern Africa.

x *mertonensis*	PINK	LSP/SU	2'–3'/1'–1.5'
	○ ◑	Z10-5/H	DS ***

[*D. grandiflora* x *D. purpurea*]. This sturdy plant is a tetraploid hybrid, but comes true from seed. It has large, broadly ovate, toothed leaves, coarse with netted veining. Its racemes are crowded with large coppery pink flowers, each 2" or more in length. Prefers partial shade. Divide after flowering.

parviflora	BROWN	LSP/SU	2'–3'/1'
	○ ◑	Z10-4/H	DS **

Gray green, lanceolate to oblanceolate leaves. Each raceme is densely crowded with small, tubular ½" flowers, with bronze or brown corollas. Northern Spain.

DIPHYLLEIA, Berberidaceae. (3)

cymosa	WHITE	LSP	2'–3'/1'–2'
	○ ◑	Z8-6	DS **

Umbrella Leaf is an unusual and seldom grown native of cool woodlands in our southeastern states. Each stout rhizome gives rise to a single, long-petioled, basal leaf;

its peltate blade, which may reach 2' across, is deeply cleft into 2 segments, each gently lobed and toothed. The flower stalks bear 2 smaller but more deeply lobed alternate leaves, the lower slightly larger than the upper. The clusters of white, 6-parted ½"–¾" flowers are not especially decorative, but are followed by striking sapphire blue ⅓"–½" berries on red pedicels. Best where soil is damp and abundantly enriched with organic matter. Its bold foliage serves as a distinctive ground cover. Appalachian Mountains. *D. grayi* and *D. sinensis* are similar species from Asia.

DIPLARRENA, Iridaceae. (2)

moroea	WHITE	SP/ESU	2'/1.5'
	○	Z10-9	DS **

Butterfly Flag. [*D. moraea* Hort.]. Tussocks of evergreen, somewhat stiff, Iris-like leaves, 1'–2' long by ½" wide. The spikes of fragrant 1"–2" flowers, subtended by 2" bracts, are borne on wiry scapes, just above the foliage. The flowers consist of 3 broad, white petaloid perianth lobes, one larger, surrounding 3 much smaller, narrow lobes, sometimes tinged with bluish purple or yellow. The individual flowers are short-lived, but bloom in succession over a long season. An unusual and charming low-maintenance plant for gardens with light sandy soil, enriched with humus. Protect from more than slight frost. In late winter, the clumps of short, creeping rhizomes may be divided, or lifted for indoor bloom. The bronze-leaved form is quite scarce. Southeastern Australia, Tasmania. Taller *D. latifolia,* considered by some to be a variety of *D. moroea,* has wider leaves. Its flowers are on longer scapes. Tasmania. The genus was previously spelled *Diplarrhena.*

DODECATHEON, Primulaceae. (15)   **Shooting Star**

Sometimes known as American Cowslips, Shooting Stars are native plants, with a basal rosette of foliage and umbels of nodding, dart-shaped flowers. Many are true alpines. Summer dormant. Suitable for informal areas of the garden and for the rock garden. Most prefer rich, woodland soil which does not dry out. Very slow to come from seed. May be difficult.

jeffreyi	PINK	LSP	6"–2'/1'
	◑●	Z9-5/H	DS **

Sierra Shooting Star. [*D. tetrandrum*]. Variable, but distinguished from the next species by its longer basal leaves. These are not tinged with red, but may be hairy. The flowers are similar, magenta to very pale pink, with conspicuously thick stigmas. Western United States.

Dodecatheon meadia

| *meadia* | PINK | LSP | 1′–2′/1′ |
| | ◑● | Z9-4 | DS *** |

Common Shooting Star. Smooth, lanceolate to spatulate leaves, to 1′ long, frequently red at the base. Its umbels of many nodding ½″–1″ flowers rise on slender, arching pedicels atop sturdy, reddish scapes. Flower color ranges from almost white to deep rose. The corolla is strongly reflexed, and reveals a pointed beak of purple stamens, ringed with yellow. Variable. Keep moist and well mulched, until the foliage dies down in hot weather. Pennsylvania to Georgia, Texas.

DORONICUM, Compositae. (35)   Leopard's Bane

The earliest of the daisies to bloom, Leopard's Bane provides a welcome contrast to late spring bulbs, both in the garden and as a cut flower. Its bright yellow flower heads are held well above the low mounds of fresh green foliage, which usually dies down in hot weather. Divide every 3–4 years. Best in light shade with woodland-type soil. Easy.

| *cordatum* | YELLOW | SP | 1′–2′/1′ |
| | ◑ | Z9-4 | DS **** |

Caucasian Leopard's Bane. [*D. caucasicum, D. columnae, D. cordifolium*]. Low clumps of kidney-shaped, toothed, basal 2″–3″ leaves from underground stolons. The alternate stem leaves are ovate and petioled below, lanceolate and clasping above. Its sturdy stems bear solitary, bright yellow daisies, often 2″ wide. Southeastern Europe, Asia Minor.

———— 'Finesse' has flowers about 3″ in diameter on 1.5′–2′ stems. A little later to bloom.

———— 'Magnificum' has larger flower heads. 2′–2.5′ tall.

———— 'Miss Mason' ['Mme. Mason'] has somewhat more persistent foliage, with wavy margins. Very early and free flowering. Cut back for second flush of bloom. Tolerates full sun in the north. Probably a hybrid. 1.5′–2.5′ in height.

———— 'Spring Beauty' ['Frühlingspracht'] is double flowered; even earlier than the last. 1.5′ tall.

| *pardalianches* | YELLOW | LSP | 3′–4′/2′ |
| | ◑ | Z9-4 | DS ** |

Goldbunch Leopard's Bane, Great Leopard's Bane. A hairy plant, with heart-shaped, dentate, basal leaves on long petioles. Branched stems bear several canary yellow flower heads, somewhat smaller than those of *D. plantagineum.* May become invasive, but excellent to naturalize in lightly shaded areas. Europe.

| *plantagineum* | YELLOW | SP | 2′–4′/2′ |
| | ◑ | Z9-4 | DS *** |

Plantain Leopard's Bane, Showy Leopard's Bane. This rather coarse, tuberous-rooted

Doronicum cordatum 'Magnificum'

plant has long-petioled, hairy, ovate to elliptic leaves with wavy, dentate margins; upper stem leaves sessile. The large Daisy-like flower heads, to 3″ across, are mostly solitary. Europe.

———————— 'Harpur Crewe' [*D. excelsum, D. p.* 'Excelsum']. Flowers may reach 4″ wide, several per stem. An elegant, vigorous plant. Blooms later then *D. cordatum*. 5′ tall.

DORYCNIUM, Leguminosae. (15)

hirsutum	WHITE	SU	1′–2′/2′
	○	Z10-5	DS **

The numerous slender leafy shoots of this graceful subshrub arise from a woody base. Small, softly hairy, pale gray green leaves, with 5 obovate leaflets, the basal pair much reduced. Several white or pale pink Pea-like flowers are crowded into 1½″ clusters. A beautiful, soft, frothy plant to drape over stones in the rock garden or over the edge of a border. Likes well-drained, rather poor soil. Southern Europe.

DRACUNCULUS, Araceae. (2)

vulgaris	BROWN	ESU	3′/1′
	◑	Z10-8	D ***

Dragon Plant. [*Arum dracunculus*]. Its tuberous roots give rise to a strong, straight stem, sheathed by the long, spotted petioles of the leaves. The leaf blades are large and

Dorycnium hirsutum

Dracunculus vulgaris

fan shaped, cleft to the base, with lanceolate 6″ lobes and mottled with white. The enormous, velvety, mahogany brown spathe, 1.5′ or more long, is crisped along the margins. Erect and club shaped, the almost black spadix sometimes reaches 1′ in length. This sinister-looking inflorescence is vile smelling. Spikes of red berries follow, after which the whole plant dies down for a period of dormancy. May be hardy in sheltered places in z7. Culture as for *Arum.* A very rare white form is known. Mediterranean.

DROSANTHEMUM, Aizoaceae. (95)

Densely covered in dazzling flowers, these branching, succulent subshrubs make a spectacular display in our Mediterranean climate gardens, during their unfortunately short flowering season. The succulent leaves and new stems of *Drosanthemum* are covered with papillae, or glassy beads, from which they derive their popular name of Ice Plants. Beautiful, Daisy-shaped flowers, with slender, glossy petals. Drought resistant. Well-drained soils. Older plants eventually become scruffy and less floriferous, and should be replaced with cuttings or new plants. (See *Carpobrotus.*)

| *floribundum* | PINK | LSP/ESU | 6″/1′–1.5′ |
| | ○ | Z10-9/H | CS ✳✳✳✳ |

An excellent ground cover, with trailing stems, short leaves, only ½″ long, and profusely borne, pale pink ¾″ flowers. South Africa.

Drosanthemum speciosum

| *hispidum* | PURPLE | LSP/ESU | 1.5'–2'/3'–4' |
| | O | ZI0-9/H | CS ✶✶✶✶ |

Sprawling stems and stubby, cylindrical 1″ leaves, at times tinged with red. Dazzling, light purple 1″ flowers densely cover the plant with a sheet of bloom. South Africa.

| *speciosum* | RED | SP | 1.5'–2'/3'–4' |
| | O | ZI0-9/H | CS ✶✶✶✶ |

Dewflower. Slender stems becoming quite woody at the base. Blunt, semicylindrical ¾″ leaves. Brilliant orange red or scarlet 2″ flowers with white centers. More difficult to propagate from cuttings than the other species. South Africa.

DUDLEYA, Crassulaceae. (40)

These relatives of *Echeveria* are grown mostly by collectors of succulents. A few of the larger species are adaptable to ornamental use in our warm, dry, southwestern gardens. They look best in rocky or gravelly surroundings, or near architectural features such as pathways, steps, or stone walls. They can be used effectively to break up monotonous carpets of drought-resistant ground covers. For both horticultural and aesthetic reasons, plant in association with other xerophytic plants; succulents can look positively ridiculous combined with more verdant perennials. Thick, fleshy leaves, often coated with a waxy, powdery bloom, form one or more substantial rosettes. In time, some species develop a short, simple or branched stem. The flower stalks, adorned along their length with fleshy, bractlike leaves, arise from the lower leaf axils; they end in paniculate or cymose clusters, each branch of which is a cincinnus. The campanulate corolla has 5 erect or spreading petals joined near the base. Porous, but not poor soils. Water sparingly. Easy to propagate by cuttings and offsets, also by seed, but be aware that these plants hybridize freely.

| *brittonii* | YELLOW | SP | 2'–3'/1.5' |
| | O | ZI0-9 | CS ✶✶✶ |

[*D. grandis* Hort., *D. ingens* Hort.]. The usually solitary rosette of leaves reaches 1.5' in diameter. Essentially stemless at first, it develops a substantial 1'–2' stem in older plants. Pointed oblong leaves, to 8″ or even 10″ long, densely coated with a white bloom. The 1'–3' flower stalks, often several to a plant, are well clothed in bractlike leaves. Tight clusters of pale yellow ½″ flowers. Baja California. *D. pulverulenta* [*Echeveria pulverulenta*] is similar, with looser, branching clusters of nodding red ½″–¾″ flowers. It blooms a little later. Southern California, Baja California. Variable *D. caespitosa* [*Cotyledon caespitosa, C. californica, Echeveria cotyledon, E. laxa*] has branching stems, pointed oblong leaves to 8″ long, and tight clusters of white to yellow or red ½″ flowers on 1'–2' stems. Late spring or early summer. Central California. *D. virens* [*Cotyledon viscida* var. *insularis, Echeveria albida, Stylophyllum virens*] is an unruly, clump-forming plant with narrow leaves to 10″ long; the small flowers, white to yellow and

Dudleya brittonii

red with flaring petals, are in modest clusters on stems reaching 2′ in length. Southern California.

ECHEVERIA, Crassulaceae. (100)　　　　　　　　　**Hens-and-Chickens**

Known as Hens-and-Chickens, although the name is applied even more frequently to *Sempervivum,* these succulents are stemless or may have short, sometimes branched, stems. The fleshy oblong to obovate leaves are grouped into neat rosettes or, less often, alternately arranged along the stems. They are densely hairy in one of the 3 subgenera into which the genus is divided. The flower stalks, with fleshy, bractlike leaves, arise from the lower leaf axils. Varied inflorescences, including clusters of cincinni as in related *Dudleya,* spikes, racemes, or thyrses. The flowers have 5 fleshy, erect petals joined at the base and spreading only slightly at the tip. The enthusiasm of collectors notwithstanding, most of these succulents are suitable only for rock gardens and container gardens. Most are small plants with compact rosettes of leaves, often multiplying prolifically by offsets to form spreading colonies, suitable on a very small scale as ground covers or edging plants. Mexican *E. agavoides prolifera* forms small rosettes of red-tipped leaves. Wiry, reddish 1′ stems bear a few red flowers with yellow-tipped petals in springtime. Hybrid *E.* 'Set-Oliver' *(E. harmsii* x *E. setosa)* has densely hairy, obovate leaves. Its branched flower stalks bear yellow-tipped, red 1″ flowers in late fall or early winter.

Echeveria agavoides prolifera

| *gibbiflora* | RED | F-EW | 2′–3′/1.5′–2.5′ |
| | O | ZI0-9 | CS *** |

This astonishing plant may exceed 3′ in height, not including the flowering stems. The rosette, perched on a thick stem, reaches 2.5′ across. The foot-long, obovate to spatulate leaves are somewhat wavy edged, gray green or tinged with purple. Wandlike 5′ flower stalks branch into several cincinni of ¾″ red flowers. Mexico. Many cultivars are grown: 'Metallica' with purple foliage, changing to bronze; 'Pallida' with pale green leaves; and 'Carunculata,' which could only appeal to someone with a flawed sense of beauty, has ugly warts on its leaves.

ECHINACEA, Compositae. (3)

| *purpurea* | PURPLE | SU | 2′–5′/1.5′–2′ |
| | O | ZI0-3/T | DS **** |

Purple Coneflower, Hedgehog Coneflower. [*Rudbeckia purpurea, Brauneria purpurea*]. A sturdy, rather coarse, hairy plant with leafy, branching stems. The dark green long-petioled leaves, to 8″ in length, are broadly lanceolate, roughly toothed; stem leaves narrower, almost entire, and often sessile. Its solitary, Daisy-like flowers may reach 6″ across. Their showy, slightly reflexed to drooping rays vary from purplish pink to almost white. Stiff, orange bracts protrude from the raised mahogany-colored disk, which becomes conical as it matures. An easy low-maintenance plant for perennial or mixed beds, and often included in sunny, meadow-garden seed mixtures. Excellent for cutting. Attractive to butterflies. Both mildew and Japanese beetles may need control. Central and eastern United States.
——————— 'Bright Star' has bright rosy pink rays with maroon disks. 2.5′–3.5′ tall.
——————— 'Robert Bloom.' Crimson purple rays with an orange disk. Free-branching. Flowers over a long period. A selection from Alan Bloom.
——————— 'The King' is deep coral crimson with a brown center on 3′ stems. Inferior to 'Robert Bloom.'
——————— 'White Lustre' ['White King'] has large cream white flowers with bronze disks. 2.5′ tall.
——————— 'White Swan.' Pure white rays. 1.5′–2′ in height.

ECHINOPS, Compositae. (100)   Globe Thistle

The stately Globe Thistles form erect stands of sturdy stems, branched and leafy. The Thistle-like leaves are basal or alternate, pinnatifid to several times pinnately cut, often white-woolly beneath; lobes and teeth usually armed with prickles. The individual flower heads—each a single floret surrounded by an involucre of bracts—are tightly grouped into large, spherical compound heads. Easy, undemanding plants for a sunny location. Only rarely need division. Excellent for cutting and drying. The taller species,

Echinacea purpurea

Echinops bannaticus

which may need staking, are appropriate for the back of the border; the smaller combine well with yellow Heleniums or Daylilies. Propagate cultivars and hybrids by division and root cuttings only. The species are much confused in gardens and in the trade.

| *bannaticus* | BLUE | SU-EF | 4′–6′/2′ |
| | ○ | Z10-3 | DRS *** |

The lower leaves are pinnately parted, the upper pinnatifid; rough-hairy above, white-downy beneath. Gray blue 2″ compound heads. Southeastern Europe.

| *exaltatus* | BLUE | SU-EF | 4′–6′/2′ |
| | ○ | Z10-3 | DRS ** |

[*E. commutatus*]. Similar to *E. bannaticus*. Its stems are white-woolly. The leaves are pinnatifid, green and bristly above, white-tomentose underneath. The heads often exceed 2″, with gray blue or sometimes white florets. Russia.

| *humilis* | BLUE | SU-EF | 3′–4′/2′ |
| | ○ | Z10-3 | DRS **** |

Lyrate lower leaves, with sinuate, almost spineless margins; pinnatifid and spined stem leaves. The foliage is cobwebby above, white-hairy beneath. The inflorescence, 1½″–2″ across, has steel blue florets. Plants sold as *E. ritro* usually belong here. Western Asia.
————— 'Taplow Blue' has bright metallic blue flowers. Free blooming.

| *ritro* | BLUE | SU-EF | 2′–3′/1.5′ |
| | ○ | Z10-3 | DRS ✳✳ |

Plants sold under this name are usually *E. humilis* or hybrids. The true species is smaller than the other more familiar Globe Thistles. White-woolly stems. Oblong leaves, to 8″ in length, pinnately dissected into lanceolate lobes; green above, white-woolly below. Metallic blue 1½″ heads. Eastern Europe, western Asia.

——————— *ruthenicus* [*E. r. tenuifolius, E. ruthenicus*]. The true subspecies has leaves cut into linear lobes. The plant grown in gardens under the name *E. ruthenicus* is probably a hybrid. It reaches 3′–4.5′ in height and has dark green leaves, silvery white beneath. Bright blue flowers. This superior plant unfortunately does not seem to be available in the trade here.

——————— 'Veitch's Blue' is about 3′–3.5′ tall, with gray green leaves and numerous heads. Probably a hybrid. Readily available.

| *sphaerocephalus* | WHITE | SU-EF | 5′–7′/3′ |
| | ○ | Z10-3 | DRS ✳✳ |

Gray-woolly to glandular-hairy stems. The leaves are pinnatifid, to 14″ long, with rounded lobes and revolute margins; glandular-hairy above, white or gray-woolly beneath. The lower leaves are clasping. The silvery heads may exceed 2″ in diameter. *E. nivalis* Hort. and *E. niveus* Hort. are probably just forms with grayer foliage. Central Europe, western Asia.

ECHIOIDES, Boraginaceae. (1)

| *longiflorum* | YELLOW | LSP | 1′/10″ |
| | ○ ◑ | Z9-5/H | DRS ✳✳ |

Prophet Flower. [*Arnebia echioides*]. Hairy, oblanceolate to oblong leaves, in a basal tuft. The stems, clothed in smaller, alternate leaves, end in scorpioid cymes typical of the Borage family. The primrose yellow 1″ corolla is funnel shaped and 5 lobed, marked with a purple spot at the base of each sinus between the lobes. The spots, prominent in young flowers, fade with age. Well-drained light soil. Mulch well in colder areas. Dislikes hot and humid conditions, otherwise quite easy. Long flowering. Near East.

ECHIUM, Boraginaceae. (40)

These are very impressive plants indeed; some are of monumental dimensions. They are useful as accent plants or for a bold, shrubby effect. All have narrow, gray green, hairy leaves, alternate or in dense, basal rosettes. The complex inflorescences are composed of simple or branched scorpioid cymes, typical of the Borage family, aggregated into large, even massive, crowded panicles. The small, tubular to funnel-shaped

Echioides longiflorum

flowers have 5 unequal lobes and often prominent, exserted stamens. Echiums need well-drained soil, and should not be overwatered lest they make excessive foliage at the expense of flower production. Tolerant of drought and salt. All are tender and withstand only slight frosts. Self-sow readily to the point of becoming a nuisance, but as most are short-lived, this ensures a continuous supply of new plants.

| *decaisnei* | WHITE | SP/LSP | 3′–6′/3′–4′ |
| | ○ | ZI0-9/H | CS * |

Shrubby, with several ascending to erect stems. Leaves lanceolate; foliar surfaces spiny or scaly. Large, broadly conical panicles of white flowers. Corolla funnelform, lightly striped with blue; with equal lobes. Of similar habit, *E. giganteum* has ovoid panicles of white flowers. The corolla is laterally compressed, with unequal lobes and exserted stamens. *E. leucophaeum* has linear-lanceolate leaves and a domed panicle of white flowers. Canary Islands.

| *fastuosum* | BLUE | SP/LSP | 3′–6′/3′–4′ |
| | ○ | ZI0-9/H | CS **** |

Pride of Madeira. Dense stands of upright stems, becoming woody with age, clothed in lanceolate 6″ leaves which stand out from the stems to bristling effect. Dense, foot-long, conical panicles taper to a point. Blue to purplish blue flowers. Remove spent flower spikes and prune to encourage compactness. Common in southern California. Combines well with *Romneya* or white *Cistus*. Canary Islands.

Echium fastuosum

| *pininana* | BLUE | SP/LSP | 8'–12'/3'–4' |
| | ○ | Z10-9/H | CS ** |

The giant of the genus is a biennial or short-lived perennial; it dies after flowering. It forms a dense, basal rosette of coarse, lanceolate to elliptic leaves, 2' or more long, and a single, erect flowering stem, often bare of leaves above. The huge, cylindrical or narrowly conical panicle is several feet long; the flowers are pale blue. Canary Islands.

| *simplex* | WHITE | SP/LSP | 6'–8'/2'–3' |
| | ○ | Z10-9/H | CS ** |

Also a monocarpic biennial or short-lived perennial. Single stemmed, erect. It makes a full rosette of hairy, lanceolate to elliptic leaves, some 1.5' long; stem leaves are smaller. The very large, dense panicle of small white flowers is narrowly conical. Canary Islands.

| *wildpretii* | RED | SP/LSP | 4'–6/2'–3' |
| | ○ | Z10-9/H | CS *** |

Tower of Jewels. [*E. bourgaeanum*]. Monocarpic biennial or short-lived perennial, with a single, erect stem. The linear to lanceolate leaves, larger and more numerous at the base than above, are clothed in long, silvery hairs. Does not form a well-defined rosette as in *E. pininana* and *E. simplex*. The massive, tapering panicle of rose red flowers is mixed throughout with prominent, slender, leaflike bracts. May be hardier than indicated. A statuesque and very beautiful plant, far superior to the 2 other single-stemmed species. Canary Islands.

Epilobium angustifolium

EOMECON, Papaveraceae. (1)

chionantha	WHITE	SP	1′–1.5′/1′
	◐ ●	Z9-6	DRS **

Snow Poppy, Poppy-of-the-Dawn. A charming and rarely grown Asian relative of our native Bloodroot, with the same reddish orange sap. Slender, spreading rhizomes give rise to tufts of glaucous, rather fleshy, long-petioled leaves; cordate to reniform with wavy margins, to 4″ across. The pure white 2″ Poppy flowers face upward and are arranged in few-flowered, terminal panicles. Each bloom has 2 joined, early-deciduous sepals and 4 rounded petals, set off by a central boss of golden stamens. May become invasive, particularly in deep, humusy soil. An unusual plant for difficult, shady places. By late summer or fall the foliage starts to look scruffy; plant with ferns or other shade lovers. Propagate in spring. Tolerates sun in northern zones. Possibly hardier than Z6. Eastern China.

EPILOBIUM, Onagraceae. (200)   **Fireweed**

These graceful plants all dislike hot, humid summers. The New Zealand species are somewhat tender.

angustifolium	PINK	SU/F	3′–5′/2′
	○	Z9-3/H	DS ****

Fireweed, Great Willow Herb. [*Chamaenerion angustifolium*]. Erect, branching stems with alternate, lanceolate 2″–6″ leaves, at times small-toothed. Many rose pink, 4-petaled ¾″–1″ flowers in long, spiky, terminal racemes. The capsules open to reveal seeds with glossy, feathery hairs, to charming effect. Likes moist soils. A highly invasive plant. *E. latifolium* is more compact, with larger but fewer flowers. North America, Europe, Asia.

———— 'Album.' White flowered and less invasive.

chloraefolium kaikourense	WHITE	SU	6″–1.5′/1′
	○	Z10-8/H	DS **

Several stems branch from a somewhat woody base. The opposite leaves are small, ovate, toothed, and variably tinted reddish brown. Cream white, axillary 1½″ flowers, with 4 deeply notched petals. New Zealand.

dodonaei	PINK	SU	2′–3′/1.5′
	○	Z9-3/H	DS **

[*E. rosmarinifolium*]. Many erect stems clothed in alternate, linear 1″–2½″ leaves. The gray foliage contrasts beautifully with the crowded terminal spikes of mauve pink 1″ flowers. *E. fleischeri* is similar but smaller. Europe, western Asia.

glabellum	WHITE	SU	I′/I′
	○	ZIO-8/H	DS ✳✳

The numerous dark, wiry, erect stems bear small, opposite, ovate leaves, sometimes sparsely and irregularly toothed. White, cream, or rarely pink, the I″ flowers have deeply notched petals. A charming and quite long-flowering plant for the front of the border. New Zealand.

***EPIMEDIUM**, Berberidaceae. (25)*	**Barrenwort**

Long-lived and adaptable, Barrenworts or Bishop's Hats have elegant, often evergreen foliage, and unusual flowers held in airy sprays. Several make excellent, dense, ground covers, although increase is seldom rapid. Sunny or shady locations, with rich, moist soil, are most suitable, but they will tolerate dry shade and even competition from tree roots. On strong, wiry stems, the leaves are mostly basal and compound, pinnately divided into angel wing or triangular leaflets; usually light green, some with rosy veining or mottling, often turning bronzy in cold weather. The curious, mostly cup-shaped flowers are 4-parted. Their sepals are in 2 rows, the outer early deciduous, the inner petaloid, flat or reflexed. The petals are frequently modified into showy spurs or pouches. Propagate by division before flowering time or after the foliage matures. In late winter cut back the dead foliage of deciduous and semievergreen species to expose the new young growth. The nomenclature, particularly of the hybrids, is confused in the trade.

grandiflorum	RED	SP	I′–I.5′/I′
	◑●	Z8-4	D ✳✳✳✳

Longspur Epimedium. [*E. macranthum*]. A deciduous clump-former, with basal foliage 2 or 3 times divided. The spiny, toothed leaflets, to I″ across, may be edged in red. Flower stalks bearing a single stem leaf end in loose spikes of spidery, violet crimson I″–I½″ flowers held well above the foliage. The conspicuous, white I″ spurs are elegantly reflexed. A parent of several of the popular hybrids. Japan. The cultivars are larger flowered than the species. Best grown as specimens.

———— 'Rose Queen' has deep pink flowers, the spurs tipped with white. Very showy.

———— 'White Queen' ['Album'] is white flowered. Possibly the same as 'Snow Queen.'

perralderianum	YELLOW	ESP	I′/I.5′
	◑●	Z9-5	D ✳✳

Evergreen in the south, semievergreen in colder climates, this plant forms compact clumps of basal foliage. When young, the ternate leaves are bronzy, marbled with light green; leaf margins gently scalloped and distinctly spined. The bright yellow ½″ flowers are almost flat, except for tiny brown spurs, held away from the inner sepals. They are supported by slender stems, barely above the foliage. Algeria.

———— 'Frohnleiten' is superior to the species, with the flowers held well above the leaves. Perhaps a selection of *E.* x *perralchicum (E. perralderianum* x *E. pinnatum colchicum).* The hybrids resulting from this cross are much more floriferous than either parent.

| *pinnatum* | YELLOW | SP | 8″–1′/1′ |
| | ◐● | Z9-4 | D *** |

Persian Epimedium. With flowers similar to *E. perralderianum,* this vigorous, rhizomatous plant forms a dense mat of almost evergreen, all-basal foliage. The slightly hairy leaves are variable, mostly biternate, bronzy along the margins, and not spined. Scapes to 1.5′ tall end in many-flowered clusters. The flat, minutely brown-spurred ¾″ flowers are bright yellow. Northern Iran, Caucasus. *E. p. colchicum* is most often grown for its larger, more conspicuously spurred flowers. Leaflets barely spined. An excellent ground cover.

| x *rubrum* | RED | SP | 6″–1′/1′–1.5′ |
| | ◐● | Z8-4 | D *** |

[*E. alpinum* 'Rubrum,' *E.* x *coccineum*]. *E. alpinum* x *E. grandiflorum.* This variable, semievergreen forms thick clumps of fresh green, spiny-edged foliage, beautifully margined and veined with red. Long flower stems, with one or more leaves, bear many-flowered racemes of dainty ¾″–1″ flowers; crimson inner sepals surround the white or cream spurs. Best as a specimen to show off the clouds of lovely flowers. Often recommended as a ground cover, but since crowding impairs flower production, it is better grown as a specimen. Planted on 15″–18″ centers, it blooms abundantly.

| x *versicolor* | YELLOW | ESP | 1′/1′ |
| | ◐● | Z9-5 | D *** |

E. grandiflorum x *E. pinnatum colchicum.* Several clones of this hybrid are available, of which 'Sulphureum' [*E. pinnatum* 'Sulphureum,' *E. sulphureum*] is the most widely grown. Spreading by rhizomes, this robust plant is similar in most respects to *E. pinnatum.* Its foliage is more refined, but stands up well throughout the season. The flowers have light yellow inner sepals and conspicuous deep yellow spurs. An excellent ground cover with good fall color. Cut back in late winter.

| x *warleyense* | BICOLOR | ESP | 1′/1′ |
| | ◐● | Z8-4 | D ** |

E. alpinum x *E. pinnatum colchicum.* Rhizomatous. The rather coarse basal foliage, with 5–9 leaflets, matures after flowering time. Flowers smaller but similar to those of *E. pinnatum,* with striking, coppery red inner sepals and small bright yellow spurred petals. Rather sparse as a ground cover, but splendid in the wild garden.

| x *youngianum* | WHITE | LSP | 8″/1′ |
| | ◐● | Z8-4 | D *** |

E. diphyllum x *E. grandiflorum.* The best-known clone is 'Niveum' [*E. grandiflorum* var. *niveum, E. macranthum* var. *niveum, E. niveum*]. Clump forming, with attractive, pale green deciduous foliage. The pure white ¾″ flowers are variable, spurred or

Epimedium x *youngianum* 'Roseum'

spurless, in dainty inflorescences just above the foliage. It is the last of the genus to bloom.

———— 'Roseum' [*E. lilacinum* Hort.] has white flowers flushed with purple.

EPIPACTIS, Orchidaceae. (24)

Commonly known as Helleborines—not to be confused with Hellebores—these terrestrial orchids, more interesting than showy, are perhaps most appropriate in native and wild gardens. Their vertical, unbranched, leafy stems end in loose racemes of flowers, each subtended by a leafy bract. The leaves, broadly ovate to lanceolate, are conspicuously ribbed along their length and reminiscent of *Veratrum,* the False Helleborine. The Orchid flowers are small, mostly greenish and flushed with pinkish purple, brown, or maroon. The 3 spreading sepals and 2 slightly larger petals are all similar; the 3-lobed, fleshy lip is somewhat inflated and saclike. Plant the short, creeping rhizomes no more than 1″ deep, in rich, moist, humusy soil. Divide when overcrowded or to propagate, and then very carefully.

gigantea	GREEN	SU	2′–5′/2′
	○ ◑	Z10-4	D **

Giant Helleborine, Stream Orchid, Chatterbox. Variable both in height and size, and eventually forming large clumps. Their leaves are normally ovate, 2″–8″ long. The

Epipactis gigantea

strong stems bear few to many, slightly nodding, greenish ¾"–1" flowers; marked and veined, mostly on the lip, with maroon or purple. Best in damp areas, especially along stream banks, even in boggy ground. Shade from strong sun in hot climates. Montana to British Columbia, south to California, Mexico. European *H. helleborine* [*H. latifolia*], Broad-Leaved or Bastard Helleborine, is sometimes grown in wild gardens. It reaches 3'–4' and has pointed, broadly ovate leaves to 7" long, clasping the stem at their bases. The solitary ½" flowers, subtended by long narrow bracts, are greenish, tinged with pink or purple, and with purple lips. They bloom from early summer until early fall. Naturalized in northeast North America and Canada.

EREMOSTACHYS, Labiatae. (60)

laciniata	WHITE	ESU	3'/2'
	○	Z9-6/H	DS **

[*Phlomis laciniata*]. The stiffly erect inflorescence rises from a basal mound of coarsely hairy, deeply pinnately divided and lobed, 6"–10" leaves; short-petioled or sessile stem leaves reduced. Many-flowered verticillasters are spaced along the woolly, elongating spike. Their cream white 1" flowers are 2 lipped; the upper lip hooded, the lower 3 lobed, splashed with yellow and at times tipped with brown. Easy under average conditions. More useful as a filler than as a specimen plant. Asia Minor. *E. labiosa* has larger yellow flowers in dense 1.5' spikes. Siberia.

Known as Desert Candles, Foxtail Lilies, or King's Spears, these imposing plants make basal rosettes of fleshy, broadly strap-shaped leaves. In summer they produce tall scapes topped with long, often tapering, terminal racemes of small white, pink, yellow, or orange flowers. These open from the bottom up, ensuring a long period of bloom. Held at right angles to the stem, each bell-shaped flower has 6 perianth segments joined at the base and 6 usually protruding stamens. Desert Candles are valuable at the back of the border and among shrubs, where their height is an asset; planted against a background of dark foliage, they are most dramatic. Superb as cut flowers. The foliage dies down after flowering time, leaving a gap in the border; plant with later-blooming plants to fill in. Even by blooming time, their leaves may become shabby and brown tipped, and a contrasting foliage plant such as *Ferula* planted in front serves as an attractive foil. Most are root hardy, at least to Z6, but they must be protected from late spring frosts as their shoots emerge. Shelter from drying winds. Deep, rich, well-drained soil is essential. The fibrous roots are thick and cordlike, but very brittle; plant them at least 4"–6" deep in the fall, preferably on a bed of sand. Mulch generously with porous material. Once established, do not disturb. The plants may be increased by dividing the crowns carefully in the fall or early spring. Seed-grown plants take up to 6 years to reach flowering size. Usually listed by bulb merchants.

himalaicus	WHITE	LSP/ESU	3'–8'/3'
	○	Z8-5	DS ***

Himalayan Desert Candle. The most often grown and probably the easiest species. The basal rosette has glabrous leaves, to 2' long, slightly hairy along the margins. Its massive, tapering racemes of white 1" flowers may reach 2' or even more in length by 4" in diameter. Himalayas.

x *isabellinus*	VARIOUS	ESU	6'/2'
	○	Z9-6	DS ***

Shelford Hybrids, Shelford Foxtails. [*E.* x *shelfordii* Hort., *E.* x *warei* Hort]. *E. olgae* x *E. stenophyllus.* This lovely strain of hybrids has the habit of *E. stenophyllus* and combines the color range of both parents. Trade offerings are usually of mixtures of plants with white, yellow, pink, and orange flowers, although named cultivars are available sometimes.

robustus	PINK	SU	6'–9'/3'
	○	Z9-6	DS ***

The Giant Desert Candle needs plenty of room for its wide-spreading roots. Its smooth, glaucous green leaves are 2'–4' long by about 2" wide. Hundreds of peach-colored 1½" flowers crowd into 2'–3' columnar racemes on ramrodlike scapes. They are showstoppers for several weeks. Tolerant of heavy soils as long as drainage is adequate. Turkestan.

Eremurus himalaicus

stenophyllus	YELLOW	SU	3′–5′/2′
	○	Z9-6	DS ✱✱✱

[*E. aurantiacus, E. bungei*]. More in scale with modern gardens, this species makes much smaller clumps of narrow, grassy leaves, about 1′ long. The narrow spires are closely set with bright yellow ¾″ flowers, which age to burnt orange. Demands excellent drainage. May be offered as *E. stenophyllus bungei* or *E. stenophyllus* var. *bungei*. Iran, Russia. *E. x tubergenii (E. stenophyllus x E. himalaicus)* is an attractive hybrid with pale yellow flowers. It may be hard to find.

ERIGERON, Compositae. (200)   Fleabane

This large, mostly American genus contains many gardenworthy species, as well as a number of fine hybrids. Their Daisy-like flower heads have at least 2 rows of very narrow rays, usually in the white and pink through purple color range, and yellow disk florets. The heads are backed by a bell-shaped involucre of 2 or 3 rows of narrow bracts. Basal leaves petioled, stem leaves alternate, sessile and sometimes clasping. The sun-loving Fleabanes grow best where the soil is well drained and not too rich. The taller ones are excellent for cutting, the smaller are charming in the rock garden. Maintenance is minimal. Colorful over a long period. Spring propagation is recommended.

aurantiacus	ORANGE	SU	1′/1′
	○	Z10-4	DS ✱✱✱

Double Orange Daisy, Orange Fleabane. Velvety, spatulate 3″–4″ leaves in a basal rosette; oblong stem leaves, clasping at the base. The slender, erect stalks carry solitary, bright orange, semidouble 1½″–2″ daisies. Prefers thin soil and light shading from intense sun. Turkestan.

glaucus	MAUVE	SP-SU	1′–1.5′/1.5′
	○ ◑	Z10-6/H	DS ✱✱✱

Beach Fleabane, Seaside Daisy. [*E. hispidus*]. This Pacific coast evergreen carpets the ground with basal tufts of clammy-hairy, glaucous foliage. Broad, spoon-shaped leaves, to 6″ long, on winged petioles. Its numerous lavender 1″–2″ flower heads rise on strong, hairy stems. Particularly tolerant of seaside conditions, but not of strong sun. Propagate cultivars by division. Oregon, California.
———— 'Elstead Pink' has light pinkish mauve flowers.
———— 'Roger Raiche.' Dark purple flowers.

x *hybridus*	VARIOUS	SP-F	9″–2.5′/2′
	○	Z10-6	CD ✱✱✱✱

The parentage of this group is obscure, but includes at least *E. speciosus macranthus, E. glaucus,* and *E. aurantiacus.* These robust and easy hybrids resemble the fall-blooming hardy Asters, but flower in early summer and rebloom sporadically throughout the season. They form neat clumps of basal foliage. The strong, leafy stems bear

Erigeron x *hybridus* 'Quakeress'

clusters of 1″–2″ flower heads with several rows of pink to violet and purple rays. Best in regions with cool summers; shade from hot sun. Cut back between flushes to encourage more bloom and the new basal growth necessary to overwinter well. The taller cultivars often need a light support of twiggy brush.

————— 'Azure Fairy.' Lavender flowers. 1′–2.5′ tall.

————— 'Darkest of All' has deep violet flowers on 2′ stems.

————— 'Double Beauty.' Deep violet double flower heads. 1.5′.

————— 'Foerster's Darling' [Foerster's Liebling]. Bright pink semidouble heads. 1.5′–2′ in height.

————— 'Pink Jewel.' Pale pink flowers on 2′ stems.

————— 'Prosperity' has almost double mauve blue flower heads. 1.5′ tall.

————— 'Quakeress,' pale lilac pink flowers on 2′ stems, which tend to flop.

| *karvinskianus* | WHITE | SP-F | 6″–1.5′/2′ |
| | O | Z10-9 | DS **** |

Bonytip Fleabane, Mexican Daisy, Vittadinia. [*E. mucronatus*]. A trailing plant, sometimes woody at the base, with much-branched, wiry stems. The slightly hairy 1″ leaves are linear to ovate, tipped with several teeth. White ¾″ daisies, aging to pink, bloom abundantly throughout the season. Flowers the same season if seeded in early spring. Tolerant of dry soils. Charming in walls and between paving. Mexico, Panama.

| *speciosus* | LILAC | SU | 1′–2.5′/2′ |
| | O ◑ | Z10-2 | CDS *** |

Oregon Fleabane. Clump forming, with ciliate, spatulate 3″–6″ basal leaves; numerous

Erigeron karvinskianus

smaller, lanceolate stem leaves, often clasping at the base. The loosely branched stems are topped by 1½″ daisies, each with countless narrow light purple rays. Self-seeds readily. *E. s. macranthus* [*E. macranthus, E. grandiflorus*], Aspen Daisy, has broader leaves and clusters of 3–5 flower heads. Important as a parent of the large hybrid group, by which it has generally been replaced in gardens. Western United States.

***ERIOGONUM*, Polygonaceae. (150)**			**Wild Buckwheat**

crocatum	YELLOW	ESP-SU	8″–1′/1′–1.5′
	○	Z10-9/H	S ***

Saffron Buckwheat. This compact, shrubby little plant has white-woolly stems and foliage. Persistent, ovate to elliptic 1″–1½″ leaves. The stiff, angular branches of the inflorescence end in flat 1″–3″ clusters of durable, apetalous flowers consisting of 6 tiny, sulfur yellow, petaloid sepals which age to rust brown. All the species described must have a sunny, dry location in very well-drained, sandy or gritty soil. Established plants need occasional watering only in hot, dry weather. They have long taproots and should be transplanted only when small. Prune to keep plants compact. Southern California.

grande **var.** *rubescens*	RED	LSP-LSU	1′/1′–1.5′
	○	Z10-9/H	S ***

Red Buckwheat. [*E. rubescens*]. Woody-based, decumbent stems, clothed in basal

Eriogonum crocatum

foliage. The oblong-ovate 1″–3½″ leaves have wavy margins and are green above, white-woolly beneath. Branching flower stems bear dense, rounded cymes of small, red-sepaled flowers. Prune young plants regularly to control their sprawling nature. Southern California.

umbellatum var. *polyanthum*	YELLOW	LSP-SU	1.5′–3′/1.5′–3′
	○	Z10-6/H	CS ***

Sulfur Buckwheat is a rounded subshrub with woody-based stems, branching and leafy toward the ends. Obovate to elliptic 1″–1½″ leaves, green above, white-woolly below. Dense umbels of small flowers with lemon yellow sepals. Very free flowering. This is the most commonly available variety; some others are low growing or even mat forming. California to Oregon.

ERIOPHYLLUM, Compositae. (13)

lanatum	YELLOW	SP/SU	1′–2′/1′–1.5′
	○	Z10-6/H	DS ***

[*E. caespitosum*]. This charming plant rewards gardeners for many months with a profusion of small yellow daisies against a background of delicate, gray-woolly herbage. Erect to spreading stems. Variable leaves, from the more usual pinnatifid to nearly entire, to 2″ long. The flower heads, ¾″ to more than 1″ wide, are borne singly or in loose corymbs on slender stalks. Summer flowering in colder zones, earlier in warm areas. This western native does not usually thrive in climates with hot, humid summers, but with good garden practice it can succeed; plant in full sun in an open, airy location in poor, gritty, very well-drained soil. There are several variants; most appealing are those plants with the finest, grayest foliage. Western North America.

ERODIUM, Geraniaceae. (60)   Heronsbill

The majority of Heronsbills are small, low-growing plants mostly suitable for rock gardens. The following, larger and more vigorous, provide attractive, durable foliage and charming flowers for the front of the border. All prefer a sunny position, but will tolerate some shade. Sandy, well-drained soils. A light winter mulch is beneficial in cold areas. The small flowers, borne in loose, long-stalked, axillary umbels, are 5 petaled, either regular, or slightly asymmetrical, the 2 upper petals differing in size from the lower 3, and often streaked or blotched in a darker color. The slender, beaklike fruits split at the base at maturity and twist into 2 tight spirals.

| *absinthoides* | PINK | SU | 8″/1′–1.5′ |
| | ○ | Z10-6 | CDS ** |

[*E. olympicum*]. Of graceful, sprawling habit. The feathery, gray green, hairy 2″ leaves are oblong in outline, bipinnately cut into slender segments. Regular ¾″ flowers,

Erodium absinthoides

varying in color from violet to pink or white. The petals may be veined in a darker color. There are several geographical variants. Southeastern Europe, Asia Minor.

| *carvifolium* | PURPLE | SP/SU | 1′–1.5′/1.5′–2′ |
| | ○ | Z10-7 | CDS ** |

Feathery, bipinnately divided leaves. Purple red ½″ flowers; the upper 2 petals with a dark, basal blotch. Central Spain.

| *manescavii* | PURPLE | SU | 1.5′–2′/2′ |
| | ○ | Z10-7 | CDS ** |

Slender, pinnate, basal leaves, 6″–1′ long, with ovate, toothed or lobed leaflets. Purple red 1½″ flowers on long stalks; dark basal spots mark the 2 upper petals. Pyrenees. *E.* x *hybridum* [*E. daucoides* x *E. manescavii*] resembles *E. manescavii,* but has more delicate foliage and smaller, paler-colored flowers.

| *pelargoniflorum* | WHITE | SU | 1′/1.5′ |
| | ○ | Z10-7 | CDS ** |

A shrubby, branching plant, with mounded, basal foliage. The heart-shaped, woolly leaves have scalloped and round-toothed margins. White or pale pink flowers, lightly veined in purple; the 2 upper petals are purple spotted at the base. Asia Minor.

ERYNGIUM, Umbelliferae. (230)

Unaccountably neglected by American gardeners, these handsome, long-flowering plants bear tight, conical or round flower heads of tiny white, green, or blue florets usually subtended by a ruff of decorative, spiny bracts. Many of the most ornamental have silvery, steel blue or metallic purple flowers, bracts, and stems. Stiff and leathery, the alternate leaves are sometimes entire but usually lobed or divided, even Thistle-like in the Old World species. The American species have sword-shaped, toothed or spine-edged, mostly basal, evergreen foliage. This confused and confusing genus needs complete reworking by a competent botanist; many of the plants in gardens and commerce are misidentified, particularly the New World species. All thrive in full sun and well-drained soil. Some of the larger species tend to flop unless grown in poor soil. All resent winter wetness and benefit from a gravel mulch around the crown. Dislike root disturbance. Excellent as cut or dried flowers. Most are long-lived. Biennial *E. giganteum,* 3′–4′ tall or more, usually dies after blooming, but self-sows readily. It is a superb plant with ovate, basal leaves, many large flower heads, and broad silvery white-veined bracts. Cultivar 'Miss Willmott's Ghost' has nearly white bracts.

| *agavifolium* | GREEN | SU/LSU | 4′–5′/1.5′–2′ |
| | ○ | Z10-8 | DS ** |

Stout, sword-shaped leaves in a basal rosette; leaf margins armed with large, spiny teeth. The tall, sturdy stems bear a compact, terminal inflorescence of several small-bracted, green 2″ flower heads, with others solitary and well-spaced below. Argentina. *E. serra* from Brazil and Argentina is smaller and has double-toothed leaves.

| *alpinum* | BLUE | SU/LSU | 2′–2.5′/1.5′ |
| | ○ | ZI0-3 | DRS *** |

Perhaps the most beautiful species. Its lower leaves are heart shaped and spiny toothed, to 6″ long; the upper leaves, palmately lobed or divided and tinged with blue, as are the upper stems. The blue 1½″ heads are subtended by several ruffs of delicate, pinnately cut, steel blue bracts, unusually soft to the touch. Will tolerate very light shade and heavier soils than the other species. Europe.
———— 'Improved Form' has larger inflorescences.

| *bourgatii* | GREEN | SU | 1′–1.5′/1.5′ |
| | ○ | ZI0-5 | DRS ** |

Beautiful, white-veined, gray green 2″ leaves, dissected into narrow segments. Greenish ¾″ flower heads, with long, linear, silvery bracts. Southwestern Europe. Also low-growing *E. variifolium* forms a basal mound of glossy, heart-shaped leaves prettily veined in white. Its short, erect stems bear discreet, green ½″ heads with pale, slender, sharp-pointed bracts. Morocco.

| *eburneum* | WHITE | SU | 4′–6′/2′–3′ |
| | ○ | ZI0-8 | DS ** |

[*E. paniculatum, E. balsanae*]. Arching linear leaves, to 1.5′ long, armed with small spines. The tall, stout, many-branched flower stems bear a constellation of round,

Eryngium bourgatii

greenish white ½" flower heads with inconspicuous bracts. Sold under many incorrect names. South America. *E. descaisneana* [*E. pandanifolium*] is a much larger plant, with 4'–6' leaves. It reaches 8' in height and is topped with clouds of tiny purple heads in late summer. Likes evenly moist soil. South America.

maritimum	BLUE	SU	1'–2'/1'
	○	Z10-5	DRS **

Sea Holly. The glaucous, blue gray foliage is stiff and leathery. Leaves 2"–4" long, broadly ovate and 3 lobed, with large, spiny teeth. The many rounded, pale blue 1" flower heads are each surrounded by a few broad, spiny, silvery bracts. Salt tolerant. Europe.

x *oliveranum*	BLUE	SU	3'/2'
	○	Z10-5	DR **

An old hybrid of obscure derivation; one parent is probably *E. alpinum* which it most resembles, the other possibly *E. planum*. Ovate-cordate lower leaves, palmately divided stem leaves, both spiny toothed. Large blue 1½" heads with a ruff of stiff, spiny bracts. Often needs staking.

proteiflorum	BLUE	SU	2.5'/1.5'
	○	Z10-8	DS **

Substantial, sword-shaped leaves, armed with strong spines. Each large, steel blue flower head is surrounded at its base by several subordinate heads and a showy collar of broad, sea green, toothed bracts. High mountains of Mexico.

x *tripartitum*	BLUE	SU	2'–2.5'/2'
	○	Z10-5	DR ***

[*E. tripartitum* Hort.]. Most probably a hybrid, with *E. planum* as one of its parents. Long-stalked, spine-toothed leaves in a basal rosette. The branching, wiry stems end in rounded, steel blue ½" flower heads, with narrow, spiny, blue bracts. Free blooming and the best of the "small-flowered" type. *E. planum* of eastern Europe grows to 3' tall with long-stalked, ovate to oblong, small-toothed 6" leaves. Many rounded ½" heads of a paler blue with blue green bracts. 'Blue Dwarf' is a smaller cultivar. Rarely found in gardens, true *E. amethystinum* from southeastern Europe reaches 2' in height and is much branched. The entire plant is silvery gray; upper stems, bracts, and heads are tinged with purple. Its heads are slightly larger than those of *E. planum,* with long, slender, spiny-toothed bracts. Plants labeled *E. amethystinum* in gardens are most probably hybrids with *E. planum*. To compound the confusion, the name is also occasionally misapplied to some plants with much larger flower heads.

yuccifolium	WHITE	SU	4'/1'
	○	Z10-3/T	DS **

Rattlesnake-Master, Button Snake-Root. This erect, sparsely leaved native has long, strap-shaped leaves reaching 3' and armed with small marginal teeth. Several rounded 1" flower heads in a branched terminal inflorescence. Eastern and central United States.

x *zabelii*	BLUE	SU/LSU	2′–2.5′/1.5′
	○	Z10-5	DR ***

In the strictest sense, these are hybrids between *E. alpinum* and *E. bourgatii.* The name is also applied now to a miscellaneous group of hybrids of unknown parentage; all have large blue flower heads and fancy bracts, suggesting their derivation from *E. alpinum.*
———————— 'Donard Variety' has steel blue heads and bracts.
———————— 'Violetta,' with violet blue heads, bracts, and upper stems.

ERYSIMUM, Cruciferae. (100)   Blister-Cress

The Blister-Cresses are often confused with closely related *Cheiranthus,* from which they differ in details of their flowers and fruits. The leafy stems branch freely into loose, evergreen mounds, topped with elongating racemes of cruciform flowers. All prefer limy soils. Some will tolerate dry conditions.

allionii **Hort.**	ORANGE	LSP-ESU	1.5′/1′
	○	Z10-3/H	CS ***

Siberian Wallflower. [*Cheiranthus allionii, E. asperum, E. perofskianum* Hort.]. Short-lived. Bushy, sometimes woody at the base, with erect, leafy, branching stems. The lanceolate leaves may reach 3″ long; the lower are scallop toothed. Its fragrant ½″–¾″ flowers are luminous orange. Often grown as a biennial and used for bedding, under-planting spring bulbs. Nomenclature is confused. *E. allionii* Hort. is thought to be a hybrid by some experts, or it may be an American form of European *E. hieraciifolium.* *E. alpinum* [*Cheiranthus alpinus*] from Norway may also belong here. It is noted for its fragrant pale yellow flowers and silky-haired foliage. Its cultivar 'Moonlight' has dark crimson buds and flowers the color of grapefruit.

linifolium	LAVENDER	ESU-LSU	1′/1′
	○	Z10-5/H	C **

Alpine Wallflower. [*Cheiranthus linifolius*]. Wide, loose mounds of often decumbent, wiry stems and narrowly lanceolate, gray green leaves. The flowers are lavender or lilac purple. Spain, Portugal. *Cheiranthus* 'Bowles Mauve' often is listed here erroneously.
———————— 'Variegatum' has foliage edged in cream. Particularly striking in winter.

ESCHSCHOLZIA, Papaveraceae. (10)

californica	ORANGE	SP-SU	8″–2′/1′
	○	Z10-8	S ****

California-Poppy. Although it can be a short-lived perennial in warmer areas, *E. californica* is usually grown as an annual. Its many slender, branching, erect to

Eschscholzia californica

decumbent stems bear blue green, finely dissected, alternate leaves. The conical calyces are deciduous. The brilliant orange, Poppy-like 2″–3″ flowers have 4, or sometimes more, petals. Well-drained, sandy, poor soil is required for maximum bloom. Very long flowering if deadheaded and watered. Flowers the first year from seed. Resents transplanting. Best in informal areas. California. Named cultivars and strains will not come true from self-sown seed. Cultivars are available with cream, yellow, light to dark orange, pink, and red flowers. Named strains include 'Ballerina' with semidouble fluted flowers, 'Mission Bells' with semidouble or double flowers, and 'Sunset' with single flowers, all in separate or mixed colors.

EUPATORIUM, Compositae. (1200)   **Boneset**

Very few plants of this mostly American genus are considered gardenworthy; the best are not only suitable for wild gardens, but deserve a place in borders and flowerbeds as well. They have straight, erect stems and mostly opposite or whorled leaves. The small, fluffy heads, crowded with minute, tubular, disk flowers, are grouped into flat or domed corymbs or corymbose panicles. In some species, the inflorescences are very large and showy. They like fertile, moist soils; some even thrive in damp ground. *E. sordidum* from Mexico, a sizable subshrub with large corymbs of violet flower heads, is one of several excellent Central or South American species, sometimes grown in Z10-9 gardens.

Eupatorium purpureum

| *coelestinum* | BLUE | SU-EF | 1′–3′/1′–1.5′ |
| | ○ ◑ | Z10-6/T | DS **** |

Mist Flower, Hardy Ageratum, Blue Boneset. [*Conoclinium coelestinum*]. This scantily hairy plant with erect, branching stems is a taller version of related *Ageratum.* The ovate-triangular 1½″–3″ leaves are coarsely toothed. Light blue to violet ½″ flower heads are clustered into corymbs. The white-flowered form is less common. Southeastern and south central United States, West Indies.

| *purpureum* | PURPLE | SU/EF | 4′–6′/2′–4′ |
| | ○ ◑ | Z10-3 | DS **** |

Joe-Pye Weed. Eventually forms a massive clump of robust, canelike stems, sometimes purple at the nodes. The sharp-toothed, lanceolate to ovate leaves, to 1′ long, are in whorls of 3–5. Very large, terminal, domed, corymbose panicles of rose pink to purplish flower heads. An effective plant for naturalizing in the landscape, beside water, or for the back of wide borders. Eastern and central United States.
———— 'Atropurpureum.' Stems and leaf veins purple.
Similar plants occurring naturally on wet soils are *E. maculatum,* whose stems are speckled with purple, and *E. fistulosum,* with purple, hollow stems. *E. dubium* is altogether smaller. Double-flowered *E. cannabinum* 'Plenum' from Europe is a poor relation of its American cousins.

| *rugosum* | WHITE | LSU-EF | 2′–4′/1′–2′ |
| | ○ ● | Z10-3 | DS **** |

White Snakeroot. [*E. ageratoides, E. fraseri* Hort., *E. frasieri, E. urticifolium*]. Slender, branching stems. The pointed, Nettle-like 3″–6″ leaves are sharply and coarsely toothed. Brilliant white ¼″ flower heads are grouped into flat-topped corymbs. This useful, long-blooming plant flowers late in the season, at a time when whites are rare in the garden. Unfortunately the foliage is often disfigured by leaf miners. Poisonous to cows, and will render their milk toxic to humans. Eastern and central North America. This is the most attractive and widely grown of several white-flowered species of similar habit such as *E. perfoliatum*.

EUPHORBIA, Euphorbiaceae. (1600)　　　　　　　　　　　**Spurge**

In this large and very diverse genus, the hardy, herbaceous Spurges which concern us here have a strong family likeness. The leaves, either opposite or alternate, are mostly long, narrow, and crowded along the stems. The individual flowers are apetalous and insignificant. The units of inflorescence, or cyathia, are surrounded by showy, colored bracts, often grouped into large, attractive heads. All species have a white, milky sap which is poisonous and may cause severe skin reactions; it is wise to wear gloves when handling Euphorbias. In most, the colored bracts are long lasting, and the attractive foliage is persistent. Long-lived, and free of both pests and diseases. Most prefer well-drained, poor to medium soils. Transplant when small or from containers, because of the usually long taproots.

amygdaloides **var.** *robbiae*	GREEN	ESP/SP	2′/1.5′
	○ ●	ZI0-8/H	D ∗∗

Mrs Robb's-Bonnet. [*E. robbiae*]. An erect plant, with deep green foliage. Broad, spatulate leaves in dense rosettes. The flowers have contrasting pale green bracts. Tolerant of dry shade and poor soils. Turkey.

characias characias	GREEN	ESP/SP	3′–4′/3′
	○ ◑	ZI0-8/H	CS ∗∗

[*E. characias*]. Strong, erect stems, crowded with blue green, glaucous, narrow leaves, to 5″ long. The very large, yellow green inflorescences are cylindrical or rounded. The cyathia bear dark reddish brown glands. A noble plant. Dislikes clay soils. Remove old stems. Western Mediterranean.

characias wulfenii	GREEN	ESP/SP	4′–5′/3′
	○ ◑	ZI0-8/H	CS ∗∗∗

[*E. wulfenii, E. veneta*]. This magnificent plant is similar to *E. characias characias,* but has larger leaves and huge heads of a yellower green. Its glands, which are yellow green, are less conspicuous. Gertrude Jekyll called it "one of the grandest and most pictorial of plants." Eastern Mediterranean.

corollata	WHITE	LSP/ESU	3′/2′
	○	ZI0-3	S ∗∗∗

Flowering Spurge is the only native species of horticultural interest. A slender, erect,

Euphorbia characias wulfenii

and branching plant with whorls of oblong 1″–2″ leaves, which turn red in the fall. Flowers in umbel-like cymes with delicate white bracts. North America.

cyparissias	YELLOW	ESU/SU	1′/1′
	○	Z9-3	DR ✳✳✳

Cypress Spurge is erect and branching, crowded with linear, blue green ½″–1″ leaves. Long-lasting, umbel-like cymes. The yellowish bracts mature to red. A good ground cover for a sunny bank. Spreads viciously. Europe.

griffithii	RED	LSP	2′–3′/2′
	○ ◐	Z9-5/H	DS ✳✳✳

This superior species has slender, erect stems and lanceolate leaves with pink midribs. Loose heads of small flowers with conspicuous orange red bracts. Spreads by creeping rhizomes, but is not invasive. Prefers well-drained soil. Eastern Himalayas.

——————— 'Fireglow,' an Alan Bloom cultivar with brighter red bracts, is more commonly grown than the species.

x *martini*	GREEN	LSP	2′/2′
	○ ◐	Z10-8/H	C ✳✳

This natural hybrid between *E. amygdaloides* and *E. characias* is variable and may favor either of its parents. An attractive refined plant, recently available to American gardeners. France.

Euphorbia griffithii 'Fireglow'

myrsinites	YELLOW	SP/LSP	6″–8″/1′
	○	Z10-5/H	CDS ***

Trailing, foot-long stems, with persistent, blue green, glaucous foliage. The short, fleshy leaves, to ¾″ long, are obovate and arranged in close spirals. Flowers in umbels of 5–10 rays, with showy yellow bracts. An excellent plant for the edge of the border, wall, or rock garden. Needs good drainage. Southern Europe.

nicaeensis	GREEN	SU/F	1.5′/1.5′
	○	Z10-6/H	S **

Bushy and erect, with blue green, glaucous foliage. Fleshy, oblong to lanceolate leaves. Domed flower clusters with persistent yellow green bracts. Southern Europe, Mediterranean.

palustris	YELLOW	LSP	3′/3′
	○ ●	Z9-7/H	CD **

Similar to *E. polychroma,* but taller and of a more graceful habit. Elliptic 1″–3″ leaves. Its 4″–6″ inflorescences are larger and more rounded. Tolerant of both dry and wet conditions, even suitable for the bog garden. Europe.

polychroma	YELLOW	SP/LSP	1.5′–2′/2′
	○ ◑	Z9-3	DS ****

Cushion Spurge. [*E. epithymoides*]. Forms a compact, domed clump of sturdy stems, with numerous dark green, oblong leaves, to 2″ long. Densely covered with long-

Evolvulus nuttallianus

lasting, umbel-like cymes of small flowers with chartreuse bracts. The foliage turns red in the fall. Long-lived, and one of the best of all border plants. Does not spread. Free of diseases and pests. Eastern Europe.

rigida	YELLOW	ESP	**1.5′/1.5′**
	○ ●	Z10-8/H	S ∗∗

[*E. biglandulosa*]. Erect to decumbent, with gray green, lanceolate 1½″–2½″ leaves. Domed, umbel-like cymes, with showy yellow bracts. Reminiscent of *E. myrsinites*. Needs good drainage. Mediterranean.

seguierana niciciana	YELLOW	SU/LSU	**1.5′/1.5′**
	○	Z10-6/H	S ∗∗

This subspecies forms a compact, many-stemmed plant, with linear, blue green, glaucous leaves and large, many-flowered flat umbels. The tiny flowers are brightened by yellow green bracts. Long flowering. Southern Europe.

EVOLVULUS, Convolvulaceae. (100)

nuttallianus	BLUE	LW-EF	**1′/1′-1.5′**
	○	Z10-4	CS ∗∗∗

The only commonly cultivated species is this spreading, hairy subshrub, which has branching stems and attractive gray green foliage. The alternate, lanceolate to oblong leaves are only some ¾″ long. The pretty blue or lavender blue ½″–¾″ flowers are borne, most often singly, in the axils of the upper leaves. Corolla broadly funnelform, sometimes with a white throat. Very long flowering, throughout the year in frost-free areas. Grow in a sandy, well-drained soil. Southwestern and south central United States, north to Montana and South Dakota. The plants in the trade are relatively tender, hardy out of doors only in Zones 10 and 9, and undoubtedly propagated from material collected in the southern part of this range; it is to be hoped that hardier selections will become available soon. The plant sold as *E. glomeratus* is suspiciously similar.

FELICIA, Compositae. (83)

amelloides	BLUE	SP-SU	**1.5′/1′**
	○	Z10-9	CDS ∗∗∗∗

Blue-Daisy, Blue-Marguerite. [*Felicia capensis, Agathaea coelestis*]. An erect, spreading subshrub, with small, rough, oval leaves, about 1″ long. The Daisy-like 1″–1¼″ flower heads, borne on long stalks, have blue ray flowers and yellow disks. One of the best perennials for warm, dry areas; will flower constantly if regularly deadheaded. Shear

Felicia amelloides 'Variegata'

back hard at the end of the season. There are many named cultivars, as well as a variegated form. Often grown as an annual for bedding in colder climates. South Africa.

FERULA, Umbelliferae. (100)

communis	YELLOW	SU	8′–12′/3′–4′
	○	Z9-6	S **

Giant Fennel. This handsome plant makes huge mounds of delicate light green foliage, pinnately divided several times, into threadlike segments. The leaves have conspicuously sheathing petioles. As thick as a broom handle, the stiff flower stalk supports large, domed, compound umbels of tiny greenish yellow flowers high above the foliage. The lower umbels are long stalked. Takes some years to flower from seed. Its long, thick roots require deep, moist soil for good growth. Needs plenty of space to display its striking architectural form. Southern Europe. *F. tingitana,* from northern Africa, is similar but smaller. *F. asafoetida* has less finely divided foliage and numerous smaller umbels of flowers. Iran.

FILIPENDULA, Rosaceae. (10)   **Meadowsweet**

The fluffy, flattened or plumelike inflorescences of the Meadowsweets comprise a

Ferula asafoetida

multitude of tiny, 5-parted flowers with a tuft of stamens, which are sometimes exserted. Strong, leafy stems hold these terminal panicles above the folige. The alternate, compound leaves are pinnate; the terminal leaflet much enlarged, palmately cleft or cut, the laterals toothed or cut. These plants are much confused in the trade since several species are quite similar, separated chiefly by flowering time and minor leaf characteristics. All, save *F. vulgaris,* prefer damp or even wet soils and make magnificent displays beside ponds and streams. Excellent for cutting. A winter mulch is necessary in cold zones, unless there is snow cover, since their woody rootstocks lie so close to the surface. Mildew may need controlling in dry soils; otherwise little maintenance is required. The genus was formerly included in *Spiraea.*

palmata	PINK	SU	3'/2'
	○ ◑	Z9-2	DS **

Siberian Meadowsweet. [*Spiraea digitata, S. palmata*]. Closely similar to *F. purpurea* and *F. rubra.* Its leaves differ in having a terminal 3″–8″ leaflet, palmately lobed into 7–9 segments, covered with white woolly hairs underneath. The lateral 1″–3″ leaflets, lobed and cut, are usually in 2 pairs. Heart-shaped, leafy stipules. The pale pink flowers fade to white with age. Plants offered under this name are often, in fact, *F. purpurea.* Siberia, Kamchatka.

————— 'Elegans' has pink flowers on 15″ stems.

————— 'Nana' [*Spiraea digitata nana* Hort.]. Mounds of dissected foliage covered with pink flowers, throughout the summer. 6″–1′ tall.

purpurea	PINK	LSU-F	1'–4'/2'
	○ ◑	Z9-6	DS **

Japanese Meadowsweet. [*Spiraea palmata*]. Probably of hybrid origin, this oriental is a superior perennial for the back of the border. The leaves have pointed 4″–8″ terminal leaflets, with 4–7 lobes, doubly serrate along the margins; laterals are often absent. Fragrant, deep pink or carmine flowers in flattened clusters on red stems. Tolerates full sun if the soil is kept moist. Divide in spring. Japan.

————— 'Alba' has white flowers.

————— 'Elegans' [*F. palmata* 'Elegans'] has white flowers with conspicuous red stamens. 2′–4′ tall.

rubra	PINK	SU	6'–8'/4'
	○ ◑	Z9-3	DS ****

Queen-of-the-Prairie. [*F. lobata, Spiraea lobata, S. palmata, S. venusta, Ulmaria lobata*]. This statuesque native forms massive stands. The interruptedly compound, dark green, jagged leaves have 4″–8″ terminal leaflets, each 7 to 9 lobed, and 2–5 pairs of incised laterals; hairy underneath, only along the veins. The generous panicles of peach pink flowers are spectacular, particularly when massed in the distance. Best in cool, moist climates. New York to Minnesota, North Carolina, Kentucky. Russian *F. camtschatica* [*Spiraea camtschatica, S. gigantea* Hort.] is even taller, to 10′ when well grown. The foliage is less cut, often without lateral leaflets. Huge panicles of fragrant white flowers. Needs space!

Filipendula purpurea

——— 'Venusta' ['Magnificum,' *Spiraea venusta* Hort.]. Martha Washington's Plume has deeper pink flowers. The species often masquerades under this name. There is also a white form. 4'–6'.

ulmaria	WHITE	SU-LSU	3'–6'/2'
	◑	Z9-3	DS ✱✱✱

Queen-of-the-Meadow, European Meadowsweet. [*Spiraea ulmaria*]. Similar to *F. rubra,* but its foliage is white-tomentose beneath. Each long-petioled 1'–2' basal leaf has its terminal leaflet cut 3–5 times and as many as 5 lateral pairs of ovate 1"–3" leaflets, each only double toothed or shallowly lobed; stem leaves reduced, the uppermost simple. Fragrant, cream white flowers in plumy, irregular 10" panicles. This variable species has become naturalized in North America. Europe, Asia.
——— 'Aurea' is grown for its golden yellow foliage. Cut down in midsummer for fresh fall growth. Provide shelter from direct sun.
——— 'Flore-Plena' is a snow white, double-flowered cultivar. 4'–6' in height.
——— 'Variegata.' The leaves are yellow variegated. 4' tall.

vulgaris	WHITE	SU	1'–3'/1.5'
	○ ◑	Z10-3/H	DS ✱✱✱✱

Dropwort. [*F. hexapetala, Spiraea filipendula*]. Its tuberous roots underlie low mounds of dark green, ferny, mostly basal foliage. The leaves, to 1.5' long, have many pairs of pinnately lobed, toothed 1" leaflets; the terminal 3 times cleft. Slender but strong, unbranched stems support flattened, dainty 4" wide sprays of cream white ¾" flowers,

Foeniculum vulgare purpureum

which may be red tinged on the outside. Best in full sun, in fairly dry soils. Europe, Siberia.

——— 'Flore-Pleno', Double Dropwort, has larger, pure white double flowers, which last longer than those of the species. 1' tall.

FOENICULUM, Umbelliferae. (5)

vulgare	FOLIAGE	SU	3'–6'/2'
	O	ZI0-4/H	S ****

Fennel. Erect and branching, with smooth, stout stems. Aromatic, billowy masses of yellowish green, finely dissected, filamentous foliage. The countless tiny, greenish yellow, 5-petaled flowers congregate in large, flat umbels. If allowed to flower, it will seed abundantly. Often treated as an annual. Useful in front of bare-stemmed plants, such as *Eremurus*. Southern Europe.

——— *purpureum*, Copper Fennel, has deep purple foliage when young, which matures to bronze.

FRANCOA, Saxifragaceae. (1)

appendiculata	PINK	SU	2'–3'/2'
	O	ZI0-8/H	DS **

Bridal Wreath. [*F. ramosa* [*F. glabrata*], *F. sonchifolia*]. This variable species sends up leafy clumps of essentially basal, evergreen foliage; slightly viscid, lyrate 6"–12" leaves, with an enlarged, lobed and undulate terminal segment. Pink or white ½" flowers, with 4–5 petals feathered with crimson inside, crowd into wandlike, simple or branched, terminal racemes. An easy, long-flowering perennial, most suitable for areas with equitable climates; will tolerate hot, but not torrid summers. Sometimes overwintered under glass in colder zones. A good cut flower. Variability has led some experts to split the genus into 4 or 5 species. Chile.

GAILLARDIA, Compositae. (28)   Blanket Flower

These easy-to-grow, New World natives brighten the border, cutting garden, or meadow garden for many weeks. Blanket Flowers have showy, solitary flower heads with dark, hairy disks and brightly colored, often banded rays, 3 toothed at the tip. Drought tolerant. Best in lean, free-draining soils.

Francoa appendiculata

aristata	YELLOW	SU	2′–3′/1.5′
	○	Z9-3	S ***

Of sprawling habit with lobed, lanceolate, basal leaves, to 10″ long; stem leaves entire and sessile. Its colorful 3″–4″ flower heads have yellow rays, purplish at the base, and normally purple disk flowers. Very tolerant of drought. For the meadow or wild garden. Northwestern and north central United States.

x *grandiflora*	VARIOUS	ESU-F	2′–3′/1.5′
	○	Z10-3/H	DRS ****

G. aristata x *G. pulchella.* Erect or spreading plants, with soft, hairy, dark green foliage. The basal leaves are lanceolate, with lobed margins; stem leaves sessile and entire. Large 3″–4″ flower heads. Short-lived, particularly in heavy soils. In late summer, cut back untidy growth to encourage fall bloom. Strains are raised from seed, but as is usual, to retain uniformity in the named cultivars, it is essential to propagate them vegetatively.

————— 'Baby Cole.' Rays red with yellow tips. The most dwarf cultivar, only 6″–8″ tall.

————— 'Burgundy.' Wine red 3″ flowers. 2′–5′ in height.

————— 'Goblin' has large, dark red flowers, with a wide, irregular, yellow border. 1′ high.

————— 'Yellow Queen.' Bright yellow throughout. 2′–5′ tall.

STRAINS:

'Monarch.' Vigorous plants in a wide range of colors: yellow and orange to dark red. 2′–5′ in height.

Gaillardia x *grandiflora*

Galax urceolata

Galega x *hartlandii* 'Her Majesty'

GALAX, Diapensiaceae. (1)

urceolata	WHITE	LSP-ESU	1.5′/1′
	●	Z8-3	DS ***

Beetleweed, Wand-Flower. [*G. aphylla*]. This choice native woodlander forms rosettes of evergreen basal foliage, bronzing in winter. The shiny, leathery leaves are cordate, to 5″ across, on long petioles; margins round toothed. The erect scapes are topped with narrow 3″ racemes of tiny white flowers. Excellent as a specimen plant or as a ground cover, among shrubs or under deciduous trees. Virginia to Georgia.

GALEGA, Leguminosae. (6)

officinalis	BLUE	SU	3′–5′/3′
	○	Z9-3	DS **

Goat's Rue. A bushy plant, forming large stands of erect stems. The odd-pinnate leaves have 5–8 pairs of narrow, oblong 1″–2″ leaflets. Vertical racemes of Pea-like 2″ flowers; white (*G. o.* 'Alba') and in shades of blue to purple. The best selections are hybrids of *G. officinalis* x *G. patula,* known as *G.* x *hartlandii;* these include 'Her Majesty' with lilac flowers and 'Lady Wilson' with cream and mauve pink flowers. *G. orientale* has large, erect spikes of violet blue flowers earlier in the season, but has a spreading habit and may be invasive. Once popular in cottage gardens, Galegas make good fillers in sunny or lightly shaded borders. Usually need staking. Central Europe to southwestern Asia.

GALIUM, Rubiaceae. (300)

odoratum	WHITE	LSP	6″–1′/1′
	◑●	Z9-3/H	D ****

Sweet Woodruff. [*Asperula odorata*]. A fragrant, sprawling plant with many weak, slender, 4-angled stems, along which are spaced whorls of 6–8 sessile, linear 1″ leaves. Its tiny, pure white, salverform flowers cluster into loose, branched cymes. Prefers moist, slightly acid conditions. Excellent as a ground cover, particularly under Rhododendrons or in damp crevices. May become invasive. Europe, northern Africa, Asia. European *G. verum*, Lady's Bedstraw, has become a widespread weed on drier soils, but can be useful as a ground cover on difficult banks, where it does not need to be confined. Sweet-smelling yellow flowers massed in dense panicles.

GAURA, Onagraceae. (18)

lindheimeri	WHITE	ESU-F	3′–4′/1′–2′
	○	Z10-6/T	CS ****

Forms a crowded stand of erect, slender stems, with gray green, hairy, Willow-like foliage. The sessile, lanceolate to spatulate 1½″–3½″ leaves are recurved, somewhat

Galium odoratum

Gaura lindheimeri

wavy and toothed. Wiry stalks bear loose, elongating spikes or panicles of white 1″ flowers, which open, a few at a time, from pink buds. The 4 unequal, clawed petals darken to pink with age. A well-drained soil is essential. Cut back to 8″ in midseason of the second year to encourage fuller growth. This graceful, very long-blooming native thrives even in our most southern states, tolerating both drought and extreme heat and humidity. Louisiana, Texas.

GAZANIA, Compositae. (50)

These popular South African natives hybridize readily in the wild, and also have been much crossed by growers. Few plants now found in gardens and in the trade are pure species. Modern selections are not only available in a dazzling array of colors, but appear to be better behaved, forming more compact clumps than their parents. All bloom most heavily in spring or early summer; in mild areas, they continue to flower periodically throughout the year. In Z10-9 and even into Z8 they are perennial; in colder areas, treat as annuals. Well-drained, average soils. Water established plants only infrequently. A light annual fertilizing is recommended. To obtain uniform plants, vegetative propagation is essential. Most of the species have short, lightly branched, prostrate or decumbent stems, which produce tufts of leaves so that the plants appear to make clumps of basal foliage. The leaves are variable, entire to pinnatifid,

Gazania ringens 'Gold Sun'

usually densely hairy on their undersides and often on their upper surfaces as well. The large, colorful, Daisy-like flowers are borne above the foliage on bare scapes. The ray florets are often elaborately patterned at the base.

krebsiana	RED	SP-ESU	6″–8″/1′
	O	Z10-9/H	CS **

[*G. pavonia*]. Short stemmed, it makes a compact tuft of usually pinnately lobed, oblong leaves, to 9″ long; dark green and rough above, white-hairy beneath. Red or brownish red 3″ flower heads, with a dark yellow or orange disk. The ray florets are marked at the base with a brown or black spot, often with a white eye. South Africa. Involved in many hybrids; yellow, orange, and red flowered, some with striped petals. Similar *G. pectinata* [*G. pinnata*] has pointed rather than blunt involucral bracts.

linearis	YELLOW	SP-ESU	6″–8″/1′
	O	Z10-9/H	CS ***

[*G. longiscapa*]. A compact clump-former. The variable leaves are lanceolate, entire to pinnatifid, and white-woolly below; revolute and hair-fringed margins. The golden yellow 3″ flower heads are carried on long scapes above the foliage. The ray florets often have a dark basal spot. South Africa. Also much implicated in hybrids; among them *G. x hybrida (G. linearis x G. nivea).*

ringens	YELLOW	SP-ESU	6″–8″/1′
	O	Z10-9/H	CS ****

Treasure Flower. [*G. splendens* Hort.]. Short stems with upright branches. Lanceolate to spatulate leaves, entire or pinnatifid, to 5″ long, and densely white-woolly beneath. Yellow or orange 3″ flower heads; ray florets with a dark, white-eyed, basal spot. Again a parent of many hybrids. Origin unknown, but presumably from South Africa.
——————— var. *leucolaena* [*G. leucolaena, G. ringens* var. *uniflora, G. uniflora*] is a trailing plant, rapidly spreading to 1.5′ or wider. It has variably hairy leaves and 1½″ flower heads. South Africa. 'Gold Sun,' bred by the Los Angeles State and County Arboretum, has small, narrowly spatulate leaves, densely felted on both sides. Both the ray and disk florets are yellow. 'Sunburst' has orange flowers with a black basal spot. 'Sunglow' is yellow flowered. 'Sunrise Yellow' has yellow, black-spotted flowers and green leaves.

Hybrids	VARIOUS	SP-ESU	6″–1′/1′
	O	Z10-9/H	CS ****

There are numerous hybrids of complex and uncertain ancestry; many are said to involve more than 2 parents. Some are listed under *G. x splendens;* others incorrectly as cultivars of *G. ringens.* Named hybrids are uniform only when propagated from cuttings. Named hybrid seed strains usually produce variable results. In any event, it is best to buy plants in flower.
'Copper King.' Copper red flowers, gray green leaves.
'Gold Rush' has orange yellow flowers with brown basal spots.
'Royal Gold' has bright yellow double flowers.

Seed strains include 'Colorama' and 'Fire Emerald,' offered in mixed colors. The 'Mini-Star' strain is available in separate colors.

GENTIANA, Gentianaceae. (400)   Gentian

Most of the Gentians are small and temperamental, best suited to the rock or alpine garden. However, those discussed here are suitable for more general use and require only little extra care. Erect to decumbent stems, seldom branched, bear opposite, usually sessile leaves. The blue, yellow, or white flowers are solitary, or in terminal or axillary clusters. Campanulate or funnel-shaped, the corollas are 4 or 5 lobed, each lobe erect to flaring, often toothed or fringed. In some species, between the corolla lobes there are pleated membranes, which may also be fringed or toothed. Gentians prefer well-drained, rich soils and cool conditions, such as are found in the Pacific Northwest. However, that should not deter enthusiasts willing to provide minimal extra care. Some will not tolerate lime. Several species are now classified in the genera *Gentianopsis* and *Gentianella,* but their only gardenworthy species are annuals or biennials.

andrewsii	BLUE	LSU-EF	1'–2'/1'
	○ ●	Z9-3/H	DS ***

Bottle Gentian, Closed Gentian. Unbranched stems with horizontal pairs of sessile, lanceolate 6" leaves. Several dark blue or rarely white flask-shaped 1½" flowers, which never open, cluster in the axils of the upper leaves and bracts. Sepals reflexed; petals joined and barely exceeded by a whitish, fringed membrane. *G. clausa* and less hardy *G. saponaria* are similar, but the slightly shorter membrane leaves the petals free at the tips. Easy in wet woodland or streamside gardens. Northeastern and north central North America.

asclepiadea	BLUE	SU/EF	1'–3'/2'
	◐ ●	Z9-5/H	DS **

Willow Gentian. A gracefully arching plant with strong, slender, leafy stems, along which are spaced pairs of conspicuously 5-veined, Willow-like 3" leaves in ranks of 2 or 4. The stalkless, campanulate 1½"–2" flowers are solitary, or 2 or 3 are grouped in the upper leaf axils. Various shades of dark rich blue, their deep throats are usually purple spotted inside. The beautiful white form, *G. a.* 'Alba,' is marked with green in the throat. Less demanding than many, they prefer a cool position with deep, neutral to acid soil, kept rich and moist with plenty of humus. Resent disturbance. Choice for the shady garden. Central Europe, Caucasus.

dahurica	BLUE	LSU	1'/1'
	○ ◐	Z9-5/H	DS **

Sprawling, branched stems, with lanceolate 6"–8" lower leaves; smaller upper leaves. Solitary, axillary, and tubular, the 1½" flowers are deep purplish blue, often spotted with white. Tolerates sun, except in hot areas. Northeast Asia.

Gentiana lutea

lutea	YELLOW	SU	3′–4.5′/2′
	○	Z9-6/H	S **

Great Yellow Gentian, Felwort, Bitterwort. In the border, this handsome plant is striking in its erect bearing. Glaucous, stalked, ovate-elliptic 6″–12″ leaves, ribbed with 5–7 prominent veins; smaller and sessile above. Axillary clusters of 20 or more golden flowers form tiered spires on the upper stem. The atypical, starry flowers have short-tubed corollas, cleft 5–9 times almost to the base, with pointed 1″ lobes. Tan fruiting heads follow. Best sown in containers, since it does not transplant readily. Culture as for *G. asclepiadea.* Europe, western Asia. Not as tall, but somewhat similar, *G. punctata,* the Spotted Gentian, has yellow flowers speckled with maroon. Europe.

scabra	BLUE	F	1′/1′
	◐ ●	Z9-5/H	S **

Rough Gentian. Stiff, erect or sometimes sprawling, with pairs of ovate 1½″ leaves, rough along their margins, with 3 prominent veins. Rich sapphire blue flowers, convolute in bud, face upward, in terminal clusters of 4–5 or in axillary pairs. Each bell-shaped flower is about 1¼″ long; the membrane comes to a point between the corolla lobes. Well-drained, rich, acid soil. Topdress with cinders or grit to improve surface drainage. Best in the rock garden. Northern China. Japanese *G. s. buergeri,* to 3′ tall, has larger, deeper blue flowers. *G. makinoi,* from the mountains of central Japan, is 1′–1.5′ tall, with paler blue flowers; those of 'Royal Blue' are of a deeper color.

septemfida	BLUE	LSU	1′/1′
	◐ ●	Z9-3/H	DS ***

Crested Gentian. [*G. cordifolia*]. The square, erect or flopping stems are well-clothed in ovate 1½″ leaves. Small, terminal clusters of dark blue, narrowly campanulate 1½″–2″ flowers, their whitish throats speckled with light purple. Between the corolla lobes, the membrane is conspicuously pleated and fringed. Western Asia. *G. lagodechiana* [*G. s. lagodechiana*] from the Caucasus mountains is more prostrate and has smaller flowers. It favors a sunnier position. The two species are often confused, and there are also hybrids between them.

triflora	BLUE	F	1′–2′/1′
	○ ◑	Z9-6/H	S **

Upright stems bear narrowly lanceolate 5″ leaves, the lower with sheathing bases. The bright purplish blue tubular flowers, about 1½″ long, are solitary or in small terminal or axillary groups. Needs good light, but requires shade from hot sun. Moist, humusy soils. Japan.

GERANIUM, Geraniaceae. (400)   Cranesbill

The Cranesbills must not be confused with the popular bedding and pot plants, known under the common name Geranium, but actually belonging in the genus *Pelargonium.*

Geranium pratense 'Plenum Violaceum'

Often they are called Hardy Geraniums, although a few of the species are in fact quite tender. Cranesbills form low mats or mounds, or erect to sprawling clumps, sometimes needing the support of neighboring plants or a few well-placed pea sticks. Their long-stalked basal leaves combined with leafy, branched flowering stems form substantial masses of attractive and durable foliage. The leaves, mostly rounded in outline, are palmately divided, and lobed and toothed, usually quite coarsely, sometimes into very fine segments. The upper leaves become progressively smaller up the stem. The flowers, in pairs or loose clusters, have 5 petals, occasionally notched at the apex. The beaklike fruits, from which the Cranesbills derive their common name, rupture at maturity to discharge their seed. Most of the Cranesbills are remarkably easy plants, satisfied with quite ordinary, but well-drained soil. Most thrive in full sun, except in our warmest climates, as well as in light shade. All are essentially free of pests and diseases. Many are long flowering and will even rebloom if deadheaded. New species, cultivars, and hybrids are being introduced every year as gardeners come to recognize the fine qualities of these plants. In addition to those listed, there are several excellent smaller species suitable for rock gardens, such as *G. cinereum* and its varieties and *G. dalmaticum*. Enthusiasts are referred to what is perhaps the best book on a single genus of perennials: Peter Yeo's *Hardy Geraniums*.

| **x** *cantabrigiense* | PINK | LSP-ESU | 1′/1.5′ |
| | ○ ◑ | Z10-5/H | D ✳✳✳ |

G. dalmaticum x *G. macrorrhizum*. Trailing stems; attractive, light green leaves,

1"–3½" wide, with 7 divisions and rounded lobes. Bright pink or white, flat 1" flowers. A sterile hybrid.

——————— 'Biokovo' is more diffuse in habit. Its white flowers are flushed with pink at the center.

endressii	PINK	LSP-LSU	1'–1.5'/2'
	○ ◑	Z9-4/H	DS **

The species, uncommon in gardens, forms low mounds of light green foliage. Its basal leaves, 2"–4" wide, are deeply divided into 5 jaggedly lobed segments. Bright to salmon pink, funnel-shaped 1¼"–1½" flowers; petals notched, dark veined at the tip. Pyrenees.

——————— 'Wargrave Pink' is a more vigorous cultivar, reaching 2' in height and spreading to 3'. It has pale salmon pink flowers. Quite readily available.

himalayense	BLUE	LSP-SU	1'–1.5'/2'
	○ ◑	Z10-4/H	D ***

[*G. grandiflorum, G. grandiflorum alpinum* Hort.]. Spreading mounds of bold foliage; the basal leaves, 2"–8" wide, are divided into 7 broad, rather bluntly lobed segments. The violet blue 1½"–2¼" flowers, with a pinkish center, are larger than those of any other Cranesbill. Central Asia.

——————— 'Plenum' ['Birch's Double'] is less vigorous. Its double, purple violet flowers only reach 1¼" in diameter.

incanum	PINK	SP-F	6"–8"/1'–1.5'
	○	Z10-9/H	CS ****

This tender species forms bushy mounds or mats of delicate leaves, each about 2" in width, and divided into 5 linear, lobed and toothed segments. Deep magenta pink flowers, 1" or more across, with notched, dark-veined petals. Trim after each flush of bloom. Cut to the ground in early spring every second year for neatness. South Africa.

'Johnson's Blue'	BLUE	LSP-ESU	1'–2'/2'
	○ ◑	Z10-5/H	D ****

G. himalayense x *G. pratense.* One of the best, in spite of its sprawling habit. The basal leaves, 2"–8" wide, are divided into 7 narrow segments, and delicately lobed. The flat 2" flowers, of a difficult violet blue, are borne profusely over a long season. Does not set seed.

macrorrhizum	PINK	SP-LSP	1'–1.5'/1.5'–2'
	○ ◑	Z10-3/H	CD ***

This aromatic plant spreads as a dense ground cover. Its basal leaves, 4"–8" wide, are divided into 7 blunt, lobed segments. Dense clusters of pink, purplish pink, or white ¾"–1" flowers. Sometimes reblooms. Southern Europe.

——————— 'Album' is white flowered.
——————— 'Bevan's Variety' has deep magenta flowers with red sepals.
——————— 'Ingwersen's Variety' has pale pink flowers over light green foliage.
——————— 'Spessart' is pink flowered.

maculatum	PINK	SP-ESU	1.5'–2'/1'–1.5'
	○ ◑	Z10-3/H	DS ***

Our only commonly cultivated native species has a loose habit. While pretty enough, it is not of the first rank and is best confined to wild gardens. Its basal leaves, 2"–8" across, are deeply divided into 5 or 7 widely spaced segments, each sharply lobed and toothed. Clusters of pale to deep pink 1¼" flowers. Eastern and central North America. ———— forma *albiflorum* [var. *album*] has white flowers.

maderense	PINK	SP-LSP	3'–4.5'/2'–3'
	○ ◑	Z10-9/H	S **

This astonishing plant develops a stout stem, 2' tall by 2" or more in diameter, topped by a rosette of very large, ferny leaves. The leaf blade, to 2' across, is deeply divided into 5 segments, each twice-lobed and toothed. The massive inflorescence arises from the center of the rosette, its many branches densely covered in purplish glandular hairs, as are the sepals. Purplish pink 1½" flowers, dark veined at the center and veined in white toward the tips of the petals. Often dies after flowering, but may survive by producing lateral branches. Madeira. *G. palmatum* [*G. anemonifolium*], also from Madeira, and *G. canariense,* from the Canary Islands, are somewhat smaller plants with less finely dissected foliage. Both are well worth growing when obtainable.

x *magnificum*	VIOLET	LSP	1.5'–2'/2'
	○ ◑	Z10-3/H	D ***

G. ibericum ibericum x *G. platypetalum.* Superior to both of its parents. The basal leaves, 2"–6" wide, are usually divided into 9 overlapping segments, each lobed and toothed nearly to the base. Intense violet blue flowers, about 1½" in diameter, with darker veins. Blooms profusely. A sterile hybrid.

x *oxonianum* 'Claridge Druce'	PINK	ESU-EF	1.5'–2'/2'–3'
	○ ◑	Z9-4/H	DS ***

G. endressii x *G. versicolor.* Vigorous and free flowering, this is one of the best of the Cranesbills, forming broad mounds of attractive foliage. Its gray green 2"–8" leaves are divided into 5 segments with rather coarse lobes. The funnel-shaped 1½" flowers are rose pink, the petals darker veined and slightly notched. This hybrid comes fairly true from seed. Less commonly available, *G.* x *oxonianum* 'A. T. Johnson' [*G. endressii* 'A. T. Johnson'] is 1'–1.5' tall, with silvery pink flowers.

phaeum	VARIOUS	LSP-ESU	1.5'–2.5'/1'–1.5'
	◑●	Z10-5/H	DS ***

Mourning Widow is a variable plant, appealing more to collectors of the unusual than to the average gardener. It has tall, branching stems. Its basal leaves, 4"–8" wide, are divided little more than halfway into 7 or 9 lobed and toothed segments. The small ¾"–1" flowers, with pointed, reflexed petals, range in color from nearly black through maroon, purple, violet, pink, lilac, and white. Europe. There are numerous regional variants, as well as cultivars.

| *pratense* | | BLUE | LSP-ESU | 2'–3'/2' |
| | | ○ ◑ | ZIO-4/H | DS *** |

Substantial clumps of upright, branching stems. The leaves are deeply divided into 7 or 9 segments, jaggedly lobed and toothed; the largest basal ones often exceed 8″ in width. Crowded inflorescences of saucer-shaped 1¼″–1¾″ flowers, violet blue, blue, varying to white. Europe, Asia. A variable species. Numerous cultivars.

———— forma *albiflorum* [var. *album*] covers white-flowered forms. 'Galactic' has white flowers with translucent veins.

———— 'Plenum Album' is a small-flowered, white double.

———— 'Plenum Caeruleum' has small double flowers of a pale lavender blue tinged with lilac.

———— 'Plenum Violaceum' is a superior plant with small but perfect double flowers, deep violet blue, tinged with purple. 'Kashmir Purple,' with purplish violet flowers, and 'Kashmir White,' with white, pink-veined flowers, now belong under *G. clarkei,* a species from Kashmir. Both reach 1.5' in height. Their basal leaves, 2″–6″ wide, have 7 divisions, each pinnately cut into slender lobes. Loose inflorescences of open 1½″ flowers.

| *psilostemon* | | PINK | LSP-SU | 2.5'–4'/3'–4' |
| | | ○ ◑ | ZIO-5/H | DS ** |

[*G. armenum*]. The tall, upright stems, crowded into a broad clump, need the support of a few discreetly placed pea sticks. The large basal leaves, often more than 8″ wide, are divided into 7 broad segments, each lobed and toothed; the smaller stem leaves have 5 divisions. Brilliant magenta 1¼″ flowers with a black eye and black veins. Turkey, Caucasus. *G.* 'Ann Folkard,' a hybrid of *G. psilostemon* and *G. procurrens,* reaches 1.5' in height. Its yellow green leaves are similar in shape and size to those of *G. psilostemon*. Purplish magenta 1¼″–1½″ flowers, with a black center and veins. Propagate by division.

| *renardii* | | WHITE | LSP-ESU | I'/I' |
| | | ○ ◑ | ZIO-4/H | D ** |

A superb foliage plant, with velvety, Sage-like, gray green leaves, to 4″ across. The blades are divided only halfway into 5 or 7 blunt, barely lobed segments. Crowded clusters of small, flat whitish flowers, with narrow, notched petals, boldly veined in violet. Caucasus.

| x *riversleaianum* | | PINK | LSP-EF | 9″/2'–3' |
| | | ○ ◑ | Z9-8/H | D *** |

G. endressii x *G. traversii.* Trailing stems and hairy, gray green 2″–4″ basal leaves rather coarsely divided into 7 lobed segments. Makes up for its rather diffuse inflorescences by blooming continuously. Light pink to deep magenta, broadly funnelform ¾″–1¼″ flowers, with slightly notched petals.

———— 'Mavis Simpson' has shiny, light pink flowers, with purple veining.

———— 'Russell Pritchard' has magenta pink 1¼″ flowers.

Geranium sanguineum var. *striatum*

| *sanguineum* | PINK | LSP-SU | I′/I.5′ |
| | ○ ◑ | ZI0-4/H | DS **** |

Bloody Cranesbill is a variable species, forming low mounds of deeply divided leaves, up to 4″ wide; each of the 5 or 7 segments is usually 3 lobed. The saucer-shaped I″–I½″ flowers range from magenta to pink or white, mostly with darker veins; the petals are often shallowly notched. Europe, western Asia.
———— 'Album,' with pure white flowers, has a loose habit.
———— 'Shepherd's Warning' has reddish pink flowers.
———— var. *striatum* [*G. s. lancastriense, G. s.* var. *lancastrense, G. s.* var. *prostratum*] has pale pink flowers with darker veins. Long blooming.

| *sylvaticum* | VIOLET | SP-LSP | I′–2′/I.5′–2′ |
| | ○ ◑ | ZI0-5/H | DS *** |

Erect stems. Basal leaves, 4″–8″ wide, divided into 7 or 9 deeply lobed and toothed divisions. Dense inflorescences of I″ flowers, usually violet blue, with a white center, also in various shades of pink, or white. Europe, Asia Minor. There are numerous regional variants, as well as cultivars.

| *wallichianum* | PINK | ESU-EF | I′/3′ |
| | ○ ◑ | ZI0-6/H | S ** |

This variable species lacks basal leaves; its trailing stems are clothed in pairs of somewhat wrinkled and marbled 2″–6″ leaves, each divided into 3 or 5 parts, with rather coarse lobes. Freely borne, flat 1″–1½″ flowers, in deep to purplish pink, or blue, with a white eye and darker veining. Himalayas.

———— 'Buxton's Variety' ['Buxton's Blue'] is superior to the species, more compact in habit. Its blue flowers have large white centers.

GERBERA, Compositae. (70)

jamesonii	ORANGE	LSP-SU	1.5′–2′/1′–1.5′
	○	Z10-8/T	DS ****

African Daisy, Barberton Daisy, Transvaal Daisy. This, the only commonly cultivated species, forms substantial rosettes of hairy, runcinate leaves to 10″ long, variably lobed or pinnatifid. The elegant and showy, solitary 3″–4″ flower heads are carried on slender scapes, well above the mass of foliage. In the species, the flowers range from yellow, to orange and scarlet. Numerous cultivars, as well as hybrids with the unprepossessing *G. viridifolia,* display a range of radiant colors: white, cream, yellow, orange, pink, and several shades of red. The hybrids are grouped under the name *G.* x *cantabrigiensis.* These lovely daisies are most appealing in their single or semidouble forms; the over-blown doubles have an artificial look. Nature can be improved upon, but here breeders have shown a remarkable lack of restraint and good taste. Gerberas flower over a long

Gerbera jamesonii

period, in warm areas nearly all year long. Deadhead regularly for the sake of appearance. They need a very well-drained soil, enriched with plenty of organic matter. Never plant deeply, as they are susceptible to crown rot. Water well during hot weather, but allow to dry out between waterings. Apply dilute fertilizer several times during active growth and flowering. These deep-rooted plants resent disturbance, and should only be divided when flower production diminishes. Easy and rewarding once their special needs are met. Fresh seed germinates readily, but seedlings are quite variable. Beware of slugs and snails. Superb and long lasting as cut flowers. South Africa.

GEUM, Rosaceae. (40)   Avens

Commonly called Avens, this genus is valued for its handsome, hairy foliage, cheerful flowers, and long blooming time. The predominantly basal leaves are pinnate or lyrate, often with a large terminal segment. Red, orange, or yellow saucer-shaped, 5-petaled flowers on long, erect, usually branching stems bloom well above the mound of foliage. Geums require sharp drainage, particularly in winter, and good, fertile soil. Most require division every 3–4 years but are otherwise carefree. Shade from full sun in hot areas.

'Borisii'	ORANGE	ESU	1'/1'
	○ ◑	Z10-5/H	D ***

This garden hybrid probably includes *G. reptans, G. bulgaricum,* and *G. coccineum* in its parentage. Different from yellow-flowered *G.* x *borisii (G. reptans* x *G. bulgaricum).* Dense tufts of bright green, wedge-shaped, toothed 6″–8″ leaves. The brilliant orange ½″ flowers are carried on leafy stems. Also a hybrid, similar 'Georgenberg' has bright yellow flowers and pinkish buff fruiting heads. Excellent drainage is essential. A good ground cover.

quellyon	RED	ESU-SU	1'–2'/1'
	○ ◑	Z10-5/H	DS ****

[*G. chilense, G. chiloense, G. coccineum* Hort.]. Thick rhizomes underlie clumps of hairy, pinnate, coarsely toothed leaves to 1′ long. The terminal leaflet may be twice as long as the laterals; stem leaves much reduced. Loose panicles of scarlet 1½″ flowers. Chile. Many cultivars are available, of which the following is a selection. Hardier than the species.

———— 'Fire Opal.' Single, flame red to orange 2½″–3″ flowers.

———— 'Lady Stratheden' has semidouble, clear yellow ½″ flowers. This and the next are old cultivars; both come true from seed.

———— 'Mrs. Bradshaw.' Semidouble, scarlet ½″ flowers.

———— 'Red Wings' has semidouble, bright scarlet flowers on 2′ stems. Long blooming.

———— 'Starkers Magnificent' has double apricot orange flowers on 15″ stems.

Geum quellyon 'Red Wings'

---

rivale PINK LSP-SU $1'/1'$

○ ◑ Z8-3 DS ✳✳✳

Water Avens, Chocolate Root. Robust, basal clumps of dark green, hairy, pinnate foliage, with as many as 6 pairs of ¼"–¾" laterals and a broad 1"–2" terminal leaflet. The nodding ½" flowers, often in 3s, are bell shaped, with a brownish purple calyx surrounding the pink petals. Excellent for damp areas. Eurasia, north central United States.

———— 'Leonard's Variety' has double coppery rose flowers with dark calyces on 15" stems. A charming plant. Probably a hybrid with *G. urbanum*.

Gillenia trifoliata

GILLENIA, Rosaceae. (2)

trifoliata	WHITE	SU	2′–3.5′/2′
	○ ◑	Z8-4/T	DS ***

Indian Physic, Bowman's Root. [*Porteranthus trifoliatus*]. This charming native is an erect, branching plant with wiry, reddish stems. The trifoliate leaves are composed of sharply toothed, lanceolate to oblong 1½″–4″ leaflets. Loose, terminal panicles of starry, white to pinkish 1″–1½″ flowers. The decorative red calyces persist after the petals drop. Prefers a somewhat acid soil. Partial shade in hot areas. Eastern North America.

GLAUCIDIUM, Ranunculaceae. (1)

palmatum	MAUVE	LSP	2′–4′/2′
	●	Z9-6	DS *

Each of several thick, unbranched stems, arising from the tuberous rootstock, bears 1 or 2 bold, light green, handsome leaves. Kidney shaped, deeply palmately lobed, and with sharply dentate margins, they may reach 1′ across. Terminal and solitary, barely above the foliage, the apetalous Poppy-like 3″–4″ flowers have 4 pale pinkish lavender, petaloid sepals surrounding a central boss of yellow stamens, through which the divided style protrudes. Prefers an acid, humusy soil, well enriched with leaf mold, in a position where it is sheltered from sun and wind. This choice woodlander is seldom grown in

Glaucium flavum

American gardens; it can be difficult but is worth any extra effort. Its hardiness has not been positively established. There is a white-flowered form, 'Leucanthum.' Japan.

GLAUCIUM, Papaveraceae. (25)

| *flavum* | YELLOW | SU/LSU | 2′–3′/1.5′ |
| | ○ | ZI0-5 | S *** |

Horned Poppy, Sea Poppy. [*G. luteum*]. This disorderly, short-lived plant, with many unruly stems, is redeemed by its beautiful, glaucous foliage. The somewhat wavy leaves are pinnately lobed below, clasping and deeply cut above. The long-stemmed, yellow or more rarely orange, Poppy-like 2″ flowers have 4 delicate petals, surrounding a tuft of stamens. Unusually long seedpods. Earlier flowering in very warm areas. Unfortunately quite ephemeral. Grow in poor, very well-drained soil, in full sun. Sow in place or in containers, as it resents root disturbance. Often grown as an annual or biennial. Has become naturalized in parts of eastern North America. Mediterranean.

GONIOLIMON, Plumbaginaceae. (20)

| *tataricum* | PINK | SU/LSU | 1′–1.5′/2′ |
| | ○ | ZI0-4 | DS *** |

[*Limonium tataricum, Statice tatarica*]. Airy masses of tiny flowers create an effect similar to *Gypsophila*. The leathery, lanceolate 4″–6″ leaves taper to long petioles and are grouped in a loose basal rosette. Slender scapes end in compound panicles of many winged branches, divided into 2- to 6-flowered spikelets. A persistent, papery white calyx surrounds the rose pink petals. For culture, see *Limonium*. Southeastern Europe, Russia.

————— var. *angustifolium* [*G. t.* 'Angustifolium,' *Limonium dumosum* Hort.] has narrower leaves and silvery lavender flowers.

————— 'Nanum' is a 9″ dwarf.

GUNNERA, Gunneraceae. (35)

manicata	GREENISH	ESU	6′–8′/8′
	○ ◗	ZI0-7	DS ***

An elephantine plant, forming huge, domed mounds of coarse, toothed, palmately lobed, rounded leaves up to 6′ wide. All basal, the peltate leaves are borne on thick, hairy, rust-colored stalks. Massive, club-shaped panicles, with long, flexuous side branches of dull green flowers, hide among the foliage. Southern Brazil. *G. chilensis* [*G. tinctoria*] is slightly smaller, with more erect, coarsely toothed leaves. Its dense panicles have stiff, short side branches with often reddish flowers. These dramatic plants are at their best alone, or with a low ground cover, on stream banks and pond edges. They are heavy feeders and need deep, moist, fertile soil. In cold winter areas protect the crowns with a heavy mulch of their own leaves and other organic matter.

Gunnera manicata

Baby's Breath, with its clouds of tiny white or pink flowers, provides an airy contrast to more substantial plants in the garden. Slender, wiry, branched stems, enlarged at the nodes, bear opposite linear leaves. The 5-parted flowers have rounded or notched petals and toothed or cleft calyces. They thrive in free-draining, sweet soils. Too small for inclusion here, *G. cerastioides, G. aretioides, C. bungeana,* and *C. tenuifolia* are low, mounding plants, excellent for the rock garden. Korean *G. oldhamiana,* seldom offered, has dense heads of pale pink flowers on 2.5′–3′ stems. It is tolerant of heat and humidity, but hardy only to Z5.

paniculata	WHITE	SU	1.5′–4′/4′
	○	ZI0-3/H	S ****

Baby's Breath, Chalk Plant. Deep, thick, and rather fleshy roots underlie billowy mounds of brittle, branched, and tangled stems with gray green, narrowly lanceolate 3″ leaves, smaller above. A multitude of pure white ¼″ flowers are borne in wide panicles. Excellent for cutting, it also dries admirably if gathered in full bloom. The large sprays of flowers cause the plants to become top-heavy; staking is essential and must be sufficiently robust to provide support in bad weather. A strong corset of heavy brush, bamboos and twine around the plant, or one of the specially designed wire rings should be installed when growth is only a few inches high. The plant will grow through, mound over, and hide the structure. In regions with long seasons, cut back after flowering to encourage a second flush of bloom. Spring planting is recommended in most areas. Its deep taproot resents disturbance, making transplanting difficult. Winter

Gypsophila paniculata 'Compacta Plena'

protection is necessary in the coldest zones. The double-flowered cultivars are often root grafted onto species stock. Stem cuttings may succeed, but seed propagation in containers is the usual method, in spite of variable results. Europe, Siberia.

——————— 'Bristol Fairy.' The best-known cultivar and the standard by which all others are judged. It has double white flowers on 3′ stems.

——————— 'Compacta Plena' is a longer-lived and more reliable dwarf version of 'Bristol Fairy.' 'Compacta Plena Rosea' is pink flowered. Both 1.5′ tall.

——————— 'Dantziger,' a selection from Israel, is reputed to be tolerant of low light conditions. Similar to 'Bristol Fairy.'

——————— 'Flamingo' has large, double, mauve pink flowers. 3′.

——————— 'Flore-Pleno,' a natural, double form of the species, has been largely replaced by superior cultivars.

——————— 'Perfecta.' An improved form of 'Bristol Fairy,' with much larger blooms. 4′ in height.

——————— 'Pink Fairy' has large, double, light pink flowers. 1.5′.

——————— 'Pink Star' has large, double pink flowers on 1′–2′ stems. More dependable than 'Flamingo.'

——————— 'Snowflake' blooms earlier than most. The best for hot climates. Double white flowers on 3′ stems.

——————— 'Rosy Veil' ['Rosenschleier'] may be a hybrid. Semidouble, soft pale pink flowers on sprawling, tangled 15″ stems.

repens	WHITE	ESU-LSU	4″–1′/1.5′
	○	Z10-3/H	C ****

Creeping Gypsophila. [*G.dubia*]. Similar to *G. paniculata,* but a much smaller and more resilient plant. Its extensive mats of trailing 18″ stems are clothed in narrow, bluish green 1″ leaves and covered by masses of pink-tinged, white ¼″ flowers. Mostly too low for flower beds, it excels in the rock garden and is particularly effective tumbling over boulders and walls. Pyrenees, European Alps. *G.* x *bodgeri* is probably a hybrid between *G. r.* 'Rosea' and *G. paniculata.* It is about 15″ tall with prostrate lower branches. Mounding, loose panicles of double pink-tinged white flowers.

——————— 'Rosea' is pink flowered.

HEDYCHIUM, Zingiberaceae. (50)   Ginger Lily

The Ginger Lilies are unsurpassed for creating tropical effects in our warmest zones. Evergreen in frost-free areas, they die down to the ground when subjected to cooler temperatures. Some species are root hardy; these will survive into z8 with winter protection. A few cultivars of the more tender species are similarly root hardy, no doubt because the stock was originally collected from the coldest part of their natural range. Stout, canelike stems bear large, lanceolate, elliptic or oblong leaves, in 2 ranks. The showy inflorescence is composed of a spike of large, overlapping or spreading bracts, from the axils of which emerge beautiful flowers of complex structure. The long,

narrow, tubular corolla expands into 3 slender lobes, surrounding 3 petaloid staminodes, the central one usually 2-lobed and much larger. The single, often colorful,
tubular, exserted stamen encloses a slender style and stigma. Most of the species vary
considerably in height, leaf shape, flower size, and color. Grow in organically rich,
moisture-retentive soil; water well during active growth, less when dormant. Remove
spent flower stems down to the ground. Propagate by dividing the fleshy rhizomes in
spring.

coccineum	RED	SU-EF	4'–6'/2'–3'
	○ ◑	ZI0-9/T	D ***

Red Ginger Lily. Slender, glaucous leaves, to 2' long by 2" wide. Broad spikes, to 10",
of scarlet to dark red 2" flowers. India.
——————— var. *angustifolium* has narrower leaves and longer spikes of salmon to brick
red flowers.
——————— 'Tara' has orange flowers. Hardier than the species. Unfortunately not presently available.

coronarium	WHITE	LSU-EF	4'–6'/2'–3'
	○ ◑	ZI0-9/T	D ****

Butterfly Ginger, Garland Flower, White Ginger Lily. Lanceolate to elliptic leaves, to
2' long by 5" wide, downy beneath. The large floral bracts form a tight, elliptic spike,
from which emerge large white or rarely yellow 4"–5" flowers with a long, weak corolla
tube. The staminodal lip is large and broad, sometimes blotched with yellow at the base.
Very fragrant. India.
——————— var. *maximum* [*H. maximum*]. The all-white flowers are larger than those
of the species.
Yellow Ginger, *H. flavescens* [*H. coronarium* var. *flavescens*], is a similar, but more
tender plant. Its yellow flowers are marked with red at the base of the lip. India.

densiflorum	ORANGE	SU-LSU	4'–5'/2'
	○ ◑	ZI0-8/T	D **

Elliptic leaves, to 14" long by 4" wide. Dense, cylindrical 6"–8" spikes of sometimes
fragrant, small, orange to yellow orange flowers. Eastern Himalayas.

gardneranum	YELLOW	LSU-EF	5'–6'/2'–3'
	○ ◑	ZI0-9/T	D ****

Kahili Ginger. [*H. gardnerianum*]. Lanceolate to oblong-lanceolate leaves, to 1.5' long
by 6" wide. Clear yellow 3½" flowers, with narrow corolla lobes and staminodes, in
a broad 1'–1.5' spike. The long red stamen is prominently exserted. Invasive. Nepal to
Assam.

greenei	RED	SU-LSU	4'–5'/2'–3'
	○ ◑	ZI0/T	D ***

Dark green, oblong 6"–8" leaves, purplish beneath. Large, ovate floral bracts. Short,
dense spikes of red 3" flowers, with a darker staminodal lip. Assam, Bhutan, India.

spicatum	WHITE	LSU-EF	3′–5′/2′
	○ ◑	ZI0-8/T	D ∗∗

The lanceolate to oblong-lanceolate leaves, to 1.5′ by 4″, are glossy above, hairy beneath. Long floral bracts in a loose 8″ spike. White, sometimes cream 4″ flowers, with a yellow to orange basal spot and a long, weak corolla tube; broad, lateral staminodes and a white, obovate staminodal lip. The filament of the stamen is reddish. China, India.
———— var. *acuminatum* [*H. acuminatum*], the most commonly cultivated form, has petiolate leaves, distinctly hairy beneath. Its cream flowers, with an orange basal spot, have purple corolla lobes and staminodes, and a lanceolate staminodal lip.

HEDYSARUM, Leguminosae. (150)

coronarium	RED	SU	2′–4′/2′
	○	Z9-5	DS ∗∗

French Honeysuckle, Sukka Sweetvetch. A vigorous plant, with lax, branching stems. The alternate, glaucous leaves are odd pinnate, composed of 3–7 pairs of oval 1½″ leaflets. Small, deep red Pea-like flowers crowd into short, dense, long-stemmed racemes; fragrant and excellent for cutting. *H. c.* 'Alba' is a white-flowered form. Prefers a light, well-drained soil; plant in a sheltered position, particularly in cold zones. May be treated as a biennial. Protect from slugs. Mediterranean. A pretty native of the

Hedysarum coronarium

Pacific Northwest, *H. occidentale* has dense racemes of deep pink ¾″ flowers. *H. multijugum* is a summer-flowering Asian shrub. It is best treated as an herbaceous perennial and cut down each fall. Its long racemes of crimson purple flowers bloom over a long period after most other shrubs are past. Plant with gray or silver-foliaged plants.

HELENIUM, Compositae. (40)   Sneezeweed

Sneezeweeds are indispensable in late summer and early fall borders, and for cutting gardens. Their abundant flowers, in a glorious array of yellows and bronzes, bloom over a long season. They have strong, erect stems and alternate, often prematurely deciduous leaves that may extend down the stem as wings. Solitary or clustered, the Daisy-like flower heads have a prominent, raised and rounded knob of disk florets, surrounded by somewhat reflexed, triangular, 3-notched rays. The disk varies from yellow to chestnut and brownish purple, while the ray flowers are mostly yellow. The heads are surrounded by 2 or 3 rows of leafy involucral bracts. All do best in full sun in soil that does not dry out; tolerant of wet soils. The taller cultivars will need to be staked; pinching in late spring promotes bushiness and reduces height, but delays flowering. Division in spring or fall every 2–3 years discourages foliage loss and promotes strong growth.

Helenium autumnale 'Moerheim Beauty'

autumnale	YELLOW	LSU-EF	4′–5′/1.5′
	o	Z10-3/T	D ****

Common Sneezeweed, Helen's Flower. This vigorous, essentially glabrous clump-former has stout, branched stems, winged by its decurrent leaf bases. Its numerous toothed 2″–6″ leaves are ovate to lanceolate. The all-yellow 2″ flower heads, with high, hemispherical disks and drooping, 3-toothed rays, are displayed in leafy cymes. The species is seldom grown except in the wild garden, but has contributed its hardiness and late-blooming time to a host of cultivars and hybrids, frequently with *H. bigelovii* as the other parent. Eastern and north central North America.

—————— 'Brilliant' has chestnut-colored rays and dark brown disks. Late summer to fall. 3′ tall.

—————— 'Bruno' has red and bronze flowers on 2′–4′ stems. Fall.

—————— 'Butterpat.' Long blooming, with all-yellow flowers. 3′.

—————— 'Copper Spray' has wide clusters of coppery red flowers.

—————— 'Gartensonne' is all-yellow. 4′–5′ in height.

—————— 'Moerheim Beauty' is an old cultivar with rich brownish red flowers fading to burnt orange. Summer to fall. About 3′.

—————— 'Riverton Beauty' and the following are old, well-tried cultivars. Yellow, with a purplish brown disk. 4′–5′.

—————— 'Riverton Gem' has mahogany brown flower heads on 4′ stems.

—————— 'Waldtraud' has large, tawny orange flowers.

bigelovii	YELLOW	SU	2′–3′/1.5′
	o	Z10-7	D **

Bigelow Sneezeweed. Similar to *H. autumnale,* but with mostly unbranched stems. Its glossy, lanceolate leaves are also decurrent, to 10″ long, becoming progressively smaller up the stem. The slightly larger flower heads are usually solitary, and with a dark yellow or brownish eye. Some of the hybrids have inherited its early-flowering trait and larger flowers. California, Oregon.

hoopesii	ORANGE	ESU-LSU	3′/1.5′
	o ◑	Z9-3	D ***

Orange Sneezeweed. Robust clumps of gray green foliage, from woody rootstocks. Leaves, not decurrent at the base, oblanceolate, to 1′ long below; narrowly lanceolate and reduced above. The large, yellowish orange or deep gold flower heads, with narrow, only slightly reflexed rays, are mostly in clusters of 3–8. Widely used as a cut flower. Rocky Mountains to California, Oregon.

HELIANTHEMUM, Cistaceae. (110)   Sun Rose

The Sun Roses are spreading, evergreen subshrubs, with ascending to erect branches and small, opposite, green or gray green, sometimes hairy, leaves. Terminal racemes of few to many white, yellow, orange, pink, or red flowers. The rotate corolla, of 5 silky

Helianthemum nummularium

petals, surrounds a tuft of yellow stamens. The luminous flowers contrast splendidly with the attractive, matte foliage. They bloom from late spring to early summer, earlier in mild areas, but the individual flowers last for only one day. Sun Roses must be grown in full sun. They require a neutral to alkaline soil; add lime where necessary. The soil must also drain sharply; this is particularly important in cold winter areas where "wet feet" is the main cause of failure. Mulch after the ground has frozen with evergreen boughs or salt hay. Shear back to encourage late-season reblooming. *H. scoparium* var. *aldersonii*, a charming California native, forms a low mound of wiry stems with linear 1″ leaves and loose, terminal panicles of clear yellow ¾″ flowers in spring.

| *apenninum* | WHITE | LSP-ESU | 1′–1.5′/1.5′–2′ |
| | ○ | Z10-5/H | CS *** |

[*H. poliifolium, H. pulverulentum, H. velutinum*]. Oblong leaves, to 1¼″ long, gray-hairy beneath or on both sides, with more or less revolute margins. Each leaf is subtended by a short linear stipule. White 1″ flowers. Europe, Asia Minor.
———— var. *roseum* [*H. rhodanthum*] has rose pink flowers. Sometimes confused with the hybrid 'Wisley Pink.'

| *croceum* | YELLOW | LSP-ESU | 1′/1′–1.5′ |
| | ○ | Z10-6/H | CS ** |

[*H. glaucum*]. Variable. Narrowly lanceolate to rounded ¾″–1″ leaves, white-hairy on both sides, often with revolute margins; each subtended by a large, leaflike stipule. Yellow, sometimes white, 1″ flowers. Western Mediterranean.

nummularium	YELLOW	LSP-ESU	8″–1′/2′–3′
	O	ZI0-5/H	CS ****

[*H. chamaecistus, H. variabile, H. vulgare*]. This variable species is the most commonly grown. The leaves, lanceolate to ovate, to 2″ long, are variably hairy beneath or on both sides; each has a long leaflike stipule. Flowers yellow, sometimes white, pink, or orange, 1″ across. *H. n. grandiflorum* [*H. grandiflorum*] has larger flowers. Europe. Plants sold as *H. nummularium* may be cultivars, or hybrids with one of the 2 preceding species. A wide range of colors is available, as well as double-flowered forms.

——————— 'Buttercup.' Golden yellow flowers.
——————— 'Fire Dragon.' Orange red flowers, gray foliage.
——————— 'Henfield Brilliant.' Orange red flowers.
——————— 'Jubilee.' Double yellow flowers.
——————— 'Raspberry Ripple.' Pink and white striped flowers.
——————— 'St. Mary's.' White flowers, dark green leaves.
——————— 'Wisley Pink' has soft pink flowers and gray foliage.

HELIANTHUS, Compositae. (150) — Sunflower

Related to the common, annual Sunflower and to Jerusalem Artichoke, these robust plants are suitable for the back of the border or for naturalizing in less formal areas. They are rather coarse and garish, and should be used with discretion if they are not to overpower their neighbors. A little goes a long way—which is exactly what happens, as most are highly invasive! They have large, often toothed, opposite leaves, sometimes alternate above. The large, long-stalked flower heads are either solitary or carried in loose corymbose clusters. A single row of ray flowers surrounds the disk. Many of the horticultural forms are semidouble or double. Grow in full sun, in ordinary not overly rich soil. Fertilize annually with care; they need fertilizing to flower well, but too much will cause excessive vegetative growth. Tall plants may need staking. Divide every 2–3 years to control invasiveness and stimulate flower production. Mildew may be a problem.

atrorubens	YELLOW	SU-LSU	4′–5′/2′
	O	ZI0-8	DS ***

Dark-Eye Sunflower has lanceolate-ovate to ovate, toothed, hairy leaves, to 6″ long, with winged petioles. Flower heads to 2″ across; disk flowers purple. Southeastern and south central United States.

——————— 'Monarch' has semidouble flowers.

decapetalus	YELLOW	SU-LSU	4′–5′/2′
	O	ZI0-5	DS ***

Thin-Leaf Sunflower. Narrowly ovate to ovate, toothed leaves, to 8″ long. The flower heads may reach 3″ wide. Both disk and ray flowers are yellow. Double-flowered plants sold under this name probably should be assigned to *H.* x *multiflorus.* Eastern and central United States.

| x *multiflorus* | YELLOW | SU-LSU | 4'–6'/2' |
| | ○ | ZI0-3 | D **** |

H. annuus x *H. decapetalus.* Mostly alternate, ovate leaves, to 10″ long. Single, semidouble, or double flower heads, 3½″–5″ across. *H. decapetalus,* a parent of this hybrid, also may be involved in another hybrid, *H.* x *laetiflorus (H. decapetalus* x *H. tuberosus),* but some authorities consider this to be a cross between *H. rigidus* and *H. tuberosus; H. annuus* and other species may be involved also. Perhaps some cultivars of *H. decapetalus* belong here as well. Numerous cultivars are attributed to one or the other hybrid. Buy named cultivars for your garden.

——— 'Flore Pleno' has bright yellow double flowers.

——— 'Loddon Gold,' golden yellow, double flowered.

——— 'Miss Mellish,' semidouble. Very invasive.

| rigidus | YELLOW | LSU-EF | 5'–6'/2' |
| | ○ | ZI0-3 | DS *** |

Stiff Sunflower. [*H. scaberrimus*]. Erect, often red stems. The rough, sometimes toothed leaves are lanceolate to narrowly ovate, to 10″ long. Its flower heads reach 4″ across; yellow to red disk flowers. Central United States.

Helianthus rigidus

salicifolius	YELLOW	LSU-EF	6'–8'/2'
	○	Z10-4	DS ***

[*H. orgyalis*]. Stout stems, with gracefully drooping, Willow-like foliage. Alternate, linear to lanceolate leaves, to 8″ long. The numerous flower heads, with purplish brown disks, may reach 2″ in width. Usually needs staking. Central United States.

HELICHRYSUM, Compositae. (500)

angustifolium	FOLIAGE	LSP-SU	1'–1.5'/1'–1.5'
	○	Z10-8/H	C ***

Curry Plant. Numerous slender stems rise erect from the woody base. Both these and the crowded, linear 1½″ leaves are densely white-woolly. Terminal 1″–2″ clusters of diminutive flower heads with yellow bracts. Well-drained, dry situations. The foliage has a spicy, currylike scent. Southern Europe.

bracteatum 'Dargan Hill Monarch'	YELLOW	SP-F	1.5'–3'/2'–3'
	○	Z10-9	CS ***

If you thought that the Strawflower, *H. bracteatum,* was an annual, you were right— and wrong. There are regional variants which are fully perennial; this particular one eventually may receive specific status of its own. Erect and bushy, it spreads to form a large clump. The alternate, lanceolate to elliptic leaves are gray green and woolly, as are the branching stems. The terminal, solitary, golden yellow 1½″–3″ diskoid flower heads are surrounded by several overlapping rows of shiny, petal-like bracts. Blooms heavily all year long in warm climates. Likes moist but well-drained soils. Australia. *H. bracteatum* 'Diamond Head' is an altogether smaller plant, only 6″–8″ tall, and spreading to 1.5′ across. Its small, dark green leaves are linear-oblong. Flower heads about 1½″ wide.

petiolare	FOLIAGE	SU	2'–3'/3'–4'
	○	Z10-9/H	C ****

Licorice Plant. [*H. petiolatum, Gnaphalium lanatum*]. Sprawling and subshrubby. The silvery gray, branched stems and foliage are densely felted with soft, woolly hairs. Crowded, heart-shaped ¾″–1″ leaves. Tiny flower heads with cream bracts in 1″–2″ corymbose cymes. Does not always produce flowers. Well-drained soils. Tolerant of drought. Often grown as a bedding plant in colder areas. A superb foliage plant. South Africa.

———— 'Limelight' has pale, chartreuse yellow foliage.
———— 'Microphyllum' has tiny ¼″ leaves.
———— 'Variegatum' is faintly variegated in cream.
Both 'Limelight' and 'Variegatum' combine beautifully with the variegated form of *Felicia amelloides.*

Helichrysum 'Sulfur Light'

'Sulfur Light' YELLOW SU/LSU **1.5'/1.5'**

○ **Z10-5** C **

['Schwefel Licht']. This recent introduction may be a hybrid, possibly involving *H. arenarium, H. graveolens,* or *H. orientale.* A dead ringer for *Anaphalis margaritacea,* but with sulfur yellow flowers. Its clumps of stems, lanceolate leaves, and flower buds are all densely white-woolly. Tiny flower heads in crowded 1"–2" terminal clusters. Well-drained soil.

HELIOPSIS, Compositae. (12)

This North American native is commonly known as False Sunflower, and indeed is closely related and similar to *Helianthus.* While somewhat coarse in the wild, the cultivars are more refined and deserving of their place in the garden. Fine border plants, they are also striking among shrubs and in less formal areas. Their long stems make them superior as cut flowers. They have large, Daisy-like flower heads, mostly brassy yellow with a darker disk, surrounded by a leafy involucre. All species are tolerant of drought and poor soil; the cultivars respond favorably to well-drained but fertile soils

Heliopsis helianthoides 'Light of Loddon'

and additional water during times of drought. Relatively free of pests and diseases. Seldom in need of staking.

helianthoides	YELLOW	SU-EF	**5′/2′**
○		**Z9-4**	CDS ✳✳✳✳

[*H. laevis*]. Variable in the wild; usually erect and branching, with opposite, coarsely toothed, ovate leaves. Subspecies *scabra* [*H. scabra*] has rough-hairy leaves. Both are included in the pedigree of many fine cultivars. The single, semidouble, or double 3″–4″ flower heads bloom throughout the summer. Regular deadheading extends the season. Most cultivars must be propagated vegetatively. Ontario to Florida.

———— 'Golden Greenheart' has fully double, yellow 3″ heads, bright green at the center when they first open. 2′–3′ tall.

———— 'Golden Plume' has almost double, deep yellow 2½″ flowers on 4′ stems. A German introduction.

———— 'Incomparabilis' has semidouble, deep golden yellow heads on 2′–3′ stems.

———— 'Karat' is a European cultivar, with very large, single, deep yellow flowers. 4′ tall.

———— 'Light of Lodden.' Semidouble, bright yellow flower heads.

———— 'Patula' has semidouble, orange yellow flowers. 2′–3′.

———— 'Summer Sun' has orange 3″–4″ daisies on 2.5′–4′ stems.

Heliotropium arborescens

HELIOTROPIUM, Boraginaceae. (250)

arborescens	PURPLE	SP-F	1.5′–4′/1′–2.5′
	○ ◑	Z10-9	CS ✴✴✴✴

Heliotrope, Cherry Pie. [*H. corymbosum, H. peruvianum*]. This erect, branching, hairy perennial becomes large and shrublike in warm climates. In colder areas, it is grown annually as a bedding plant and does not attain its full size. It can also be trained successfully into a standard. Alternate, coarsely veined, ovate to oblong-lanceolate 1″–3″ leaves, often tinged with purple. Close examination reveals that the clustered inflorescences are composed of broad, branched, scorpioid cymes. The fragrant flowers are purple, violet, or white. The tubular ¼″ corollas are 5 lobed. Well-drained soil; do not over water once plants are established. Pinch to encourage compact growth; dead-head for continuous bloom. Peru. Numerous cultivars display variation in size, flower, and foliage color. Most should be propagated from cuttings; seed-grown plants tend to be very variable.

———— 'Alba' has white flowers.

———— 'Black Beauty.' Deep purple flowers.

———— 'Iowa' has deep purple blue flowers.

———— 'Marine.' Violet purple flowers. The best cultivar to raise from seed. Compact.

Discreetly charming, the Hellebores are welcome harbingers of spring. Their flowers are mostly nodding, bell- or cup-shaped, with a conspicuous central boss of stamens, ringed by rounded, petaloid sepals. The true petals are reduced to nectaries. The sepals often persist for several weeks after the stamens are shed, and range from green through white to pink and dark purple. Yellow-flowered forms are currently being developed. For convenience, Hellebores may be divided into 2 groups according to their growth habits: those that are truly herbaceous with all basal foliage and flowers, and those that are evergreen, with leafy stems ending in clusters of flowers, in their second year. Both groups have leathery, often handsome, palmately divided leaves. They generally prefer some shade and deep, rich, neutral or alkaline soils. The thick, tough roots resent disturbance; buy young or pot-grown plants. Propagate by division in fall. Very long-lived. Poisonous.

| *argutifolius* | GREEN | SP | I'–2'/3' |
| | ○ ◑ | ZI0-6/H | D *** |

Corsican Hellebore. [*H. corsicus, H. lividus corsicus*]. Bushy clumps of thick, leafy stems. The light, blue green, trifoliate leaves are conspicuously veined and coarsely sharp-toothed along the margins. In the second year, the stems put forth leafy clusters of 10–20 apple green, nodding, cup-shaped 1″ flowers, which persist well into the summer. In hot areas, the foliage will burn in full sun, but plants become leggy if they are too shaded. Drought tolerant once established. In mild climates blooming may begin in winter. Self-seeds readily. Corsica. Less hardy *H. lividus* from the Balearic Islands has similar foliage, but its leaf margins are entire or nearly so. It is a smaller plant, with pale purple flowers. Fertile hybrids between the two are most variable, and are grouped under the name *H.* x *sternii*.

| *foetidus* | GREEN | ESP | 1.5'/1.5' |
| | ◑● | ZI0-3/H | S ** |

Setterwort, Stinking Hellebore. It has bottle green stem leaves with 7–11 toothed, lanceolate leaflets arranged in a fan. The stout stems are topped with leafy clusters of pale green, bell-shaped 1″ flowers, which become rimmed in purple with age. Tolerant of most growing conditions, but avoid intense sun. Some forms are more floriferous than others. Self-seeds freely. Western Europe.

| *niger* | WHITE | LW | 8″–I'/I.5' |
| | ◑● | Z9-3/H | DS **** |

Christmas Rose. Somewhat variable, with dark, evergreen, basal foliage. The leaves are divided into 7–9 sparsely toothed, ovate leaflets. Its charming, cup-shaped flowers, 1–3 per stem, are semierect or nodding, to 4″ across. Opening a pristine white, they mature to blush pink. 'Potter's Wheel' is a large-flowered cultivar with a green eye. Considered to be a subspecies or variant by some experts, *H. niger macranthus* [*H. alnifolius, H. n. alnifolius*] has narrower, toothed leaflets and several larger pink-flushed flowers

Helleborus orientalis

per stem. Christmas Roses benefit from topdressings of limestone chips to sweeten the soil and improve surface drainage. They can be very temperamental. Cut flowers last well if stems are slit. Causes dermatitis in some people. Southern Europe. The progeny of *H.* x *nigericors* (*H. niger* x *H. corsicus* or *H. lividus*) bear clusters of cup-shaped flowers on thick, leafy stems. Several clones appear to be promising, but are not readily available. They are sterile and must be increased vegetatively—a lengthy process.

orientalis	WHITE	ESP	2′/2′
◐●	ZI0-3/H	DS ****

Lenten Rose. The long-stemmed, basal leaves are glossy, to 1′ across, with 5–11 leaflets edged with numerous fine teeth. The branched flower stems bear conspicuous leafy bracts and small clusters of commonly nodding, cup-shaped 2″ flowers. *H. orientalis* hybridizes readily, and most plants offered under this name are hybrids with *H. guttatus, H. abschasicus, H. atrorubens, H. cyclophyllus,* or *H. purpurascens.* Flower color ranges from pale green through white, pink to maroon, often with beautiful speckling inside. The 'Millet' strain is particularly fine, with white, pink, or maroon flowers, streaked with red. Excellent under shrubs or foundation plantings, as a low-maintenance ground cover. Asia Minor. *H. atrorubens* Hort. has dark purple flowers, similar to those of the *H. orientalis* hybrids, but blooms at the same time as *H. niger. H. viridis* is also part of this complex, and has brilliant green flowers.

Few perennials have earned the widespread popularity enjoyed by Daylilies in this country. These easy and accommodating plants are seen in formal and informal gardens from the Deep South to the frigid northern states, contributing color and elegance through the season. Their robust clumps of predominantly basal foliage may be evergreen or partially so, or fully deciduous. The strap-shaped and usually arching, 2-ranked leaves are grooved along the midrib on their upper surface, and keeled beneath. Above, the smooth, tough, vertical or inclined, mostly branched scapes support several upturned, Lily-like flowers in loose clusters, generally subtended by a leaflike bract. Established plants may produce as many as a dozen scapes, providing a long succession of flowers, each lasting only a day. The large funnelform or bell-shaped perianth consists of 6 recurved, flaring, or straight tepals, mostly elliptic to ovate in shape; these join into a tube at their base and encircle 6 long, upward-curving stamens and an even longer, slender style. All colors are represented, excepting only pure white and blue. Flowering times vary from spring until frost; in subtropical regions, bloom is possible all year round by careful selection. Since the late 1800s, breeding programs in Europe and the United States have resulted in a multitude of named hybrid cultivars; hundreds of new ones are added annually. Detailed information on all aspects of Daylilies may be obtained from The American Hemerocallis Society and from specialist nurseries around the country. Most Daylilies thrive, in sun or light shade, in a wide range of soils, as long as drainage is adequate, but favor deep, fertile loam. Thorough watering every week during hot weather ensures better and more abundant bloom. A light application of a complete fertilizer when growth begins is usually adequate for the season; overfeeding, particularly with high-nitrogen fertilizers, results in excessive and weak vegetative growth at the expense of flowers. Pests and diseases are seldom a problem, but be alert for aphids, thrips, and red spider mites, as well as slugs. Deadhead daily for neatness except in natural settings. Division of the fleshy, rhizomatous roots is the usual method of increasing stock, best done during cool seasons; when, after several years, the clumps become overcrowded, they should be lifted and divided.

aurantiaca	ORANGE	SU	3'/2'
	○ ◑	Z10-6	DS **

Orange Daylily. Widely spreading rhizomes underlie the clumps of rather coarse, evergreen leaves, 2'–3' long by 1"–1½" wide, and strongly keeled beneath. The fragrant, bright orange 3"–4" flowers, often flushed with brown or purple, only open to about 4" across, on scapes as long or barely longer than the foliage. Most often grown 'Major' [var. *major*] has larger flowers, which open to about 6" across. Its rootstock is more compact. Probably not hardy outside of Z10-9. China. *H. littorea* [*H. a. littorea*] from Japan postpones blooming until late summer and has more reddish flowers, flushed with dark yellow at the throat. All are involved in breeding programs.

citrina	YELLOW	SU	4'/2'
	○ ◑	Z10-3	DS **

Citron Daylily. Vigorous, fountainlike clumps of coarse, dark green leaves, 3'–3.5' long by 1" or more wide. The scapes, longer than the leaves, bear a number of fragrant, grapefruit-colored 6" flowers, which open during the late afternoon and remain so overnight. Their flaring ½" wide tepals unite into a long 1½" perianth tube. China.

| *dumortieri* | ORANGE | SP | 1.5′–2′/1.5′ |
| | ○ ◑ | Z10-3 | DS ✱✱✱ |

Early Daylily. [*H. graminea, H. sieboldii*]. Thick, arching clumps of narrow, grassy leaves, to 1.5′ long. The unbranched scapes, almost as long as the foliage, are topped with clusters of several almost sessile flowers; the subtending bract is short and leaflike. Brown in bud, they open into pale orange or gold, funnel-shaped 2½"–2¾" blooms, with reflexed and tapering outer tepals and a very short perianth tube. Most attractive in front of yellow Azaleas. Japan. Siberian *H. middendorffii* has somewhat taller, compact clumps of leaves, to 2′ long. Subtended by a broad bract, its clusters of slightly later-blooming, almost sessile, golden orange 4" flowers open from brown buds. It too has unbranched scapes.

| *fulva* | ORANGE | SU | 3′–6′/3′ |
| | ○ ◑ | Z10-3/T | D ✱✱✱✱ |

Tawny Daylily, Orange Daylily. This, the best colonizer of the genus, has become naturalized all across the country. Its spreading, fleshy rhizomes are superbly efficient for holding banks and controlling erosion. Arching and strongly keeled, the bright green leaves are 1.5′–2′ long by almost 1½" wide. The taller scapes are strong and erect; each cluster of 6–12 unscented, flaring 5" flowers is subtended by a linear, leaflike bract, which may be twisted. Rusty or tawny orange, often with a darker zone or stripe along the midrib, the outer tepals are about ¾" wide, the inner, somewhat broader and undulate along their margins. The most common form is 'Europa,' which does not set seed but has fertile pollen. Double-flowered 'Kwanso' ['Flore Pleno,' *H. kwanso* Hort.] is larger throughout and blooms a little later. 'Rosea' [*H. f.* var. *rosea*] has rose red flowers. All are involved in the parentage of most of the modern garden hybrids. Europe, Asia.

| x *hybrida* | VARIOUS | SP-F | 1′–4′/2′–3′ |
| | ○ ◑ | Z10-3/T | D ✱✱✱✱ |

Hybrid Daylily. [*H. hybrida*]. This vast complex of Daylilies involves all of the species listed here, as well as *H. minor, H. altissima,* and no doubt others. The color range is broad, from cream white to yellows and pinks, oranges to reds, burgundy and mahogany, orchid to lavenders and purples, frequently with contrasting stripes, edging, or throats. Some are fragrant. Many of the most recent introductions are tetraploids, with enlarged, often ruffled and frilled flowers. Most of the species are seldom seen in gardens today, being overshadowed by these extremely popular hybrids. They assort attractively with other perennials and shrubs, in addition to naturalizing admirably in wild or meadow gardens. The smaller are suited to rock gardens, or may be used as edging and front-of-the-border plants. While most tolerate a wide range of climatic and soil conditions, some adapt better than others. It may be wise therefore to select plants in flower locally unless a particular cultivar is desired. In the Deep South and along the

Hemerocallis x *hybrida* 'Golden Chimes'

Gulf Coast, evergreen cultivars are the most satisfactory. At the end of each year, The American Hemerocallis Society polls its membership and publishes a list of the most popular cultivars. The following list is only a sampling, including a range of heights, colors, and flowering times:

'Betty Woods.' Chinese yellow 5½″ flowers on 26″ stems. Early blooming; repeats. Evergreen foliage.

'Becky Lynn' has large rose-colored flowers early in the season. 20″ tall. Evergreen.

'Cherry Cheeks.' Raspberry pink 6″ flowers. 2′–2.5′ in height. Midseason to late.

'Chicago Thistle' has mildly fragrant, deep lavender 5¼″ blooms, chartreuse at the throat. 26″ tall. Semievergreen. Early midseason.

'Double Cutie' has chartreuse 4″ flowers, green at the throat. 1′. Evergreen; early midseason.

'Eenie Weenie.' Miniature, light yellow 2½″ flowers, green at the throat. 14″ tall. Early midseason; reblooms. Semievergreen.

'Fairy Tale Pink.' Pink 5½″ blooms on 2′ scapes above semievergreen leaves. Midseason; repeats.

'Golden Chimes' has miniature, chrome yellow 2″ flowers, mahogany in bud, on 3.5′ stems. Very floriferous. Early midseason.

'Heavenly Harp.' Fragrant, ruffled, apricot 6½″ flowers, overlaid with gold. 2.5′ tall. Midseason; reblooms.

'Hyperion.' A popular old standard, against which the modern hybrids are judged. Fragrant, lemon yellow 5″ flowers on 3′ stems. Early midseason.

'Ice Carnival.' Fragrant, almost white 6″ flowers with green throats. 2.5′ tall. Midseason.

'Joan Senior' has almost white flowers, green at the throat. Early midseason. 2′ tall. Semievergreen.

'Mary Todd' has ruffled yellow flowers, 6″ across. 2′ scapes. Early.

'Midnight Magic.' Very dark, blackish red 5½″ flowers above evergreen foliage. 28″ tall. Midseason.

'Ruffled Apricot' has ruffled, golden apricot 7″ blooms, darker at the throat. 28″ tall. Early midseason. A vigorous grower.

'Stella d'Oro.' This popular, recent introduction has dainty, canary yellow 2¾″ bells, with golden throats, on 1′–2′ scapes. Slightly fragrant. Early midseason, but repeats until fall.

'Tick Tock.' Small, golden yellow flowers, 4″ across, on 18″ stems. Late blooming.

| *lilioasphodelus* | YELLOW | SP-ESU | 2′–3′/1.5′ |
| | ○ ◑ | Z10-4 | DS ✱✱✱✱ |

Lemon Daylily, Lemon Lily. [*H. flava*]. Its spreading rhizomes make this species a good colonizer, especially useful on awkward banks. Fountainlike clumps of dark green, broad, arching 1.5′–2′ leaves, overtopped by weak, leaning scapes, each with 6–9 fragrant flowers. Their reflexed, lemon yellow perianths, to about 4″ in length, have tubes to 1″ long. Blooming a little later, *H. l.* var. *major* ['Major'] is taller, with larger, deeper yellow flowers, which are more reflexed at the tips. May be a hybrid. Southeastern Europe to Japan.

| *multiflora* | YELLOW | LSU-F | 3′–4′/2′ |
| | ○ ◑ | ZI0-5 | DS ** |

Mayflower Daylily. Compact clumps of dark green, strongly arching leaves, about 2.5′ long by ¾″ wide. Well above them rise tall, slender, well-branched scapes, bearing numerous yellow orange 2½″ flowers, tinged with red in the bud. Very free flowering. Its late blooming time and lovely habit have been passed on to several hybrids. China.

HERACLEUM, Umbelliferae. (60)   Cow Parsnip

These giants among perennials are suitable only as accent plants in the landscape, or near large ponds and streams where they can enjoy the moisture they prefer; not for the small garden or border. Short-lived, they often die after setting seed, but self-sow prolifically. Deadhead before seed formation to avoid an invasion of unwanted off-spring.

| *mantegazzianum* | WHITE | SU | 8′–I0′/3′ |
| | ○ ◑ | Z9-3 | S ** |

Giant Hogweed has stiffly erect, ribbed, and red-spotted stems. The stout leafstalks, also spotted, bear large leaves to 3′ long, divided into 3 deeply lobed and toothed leaflets. Huge compound umbels of tiny, white, rarely pale clear pink flowers. Causes a severe

Heracleum mantegazzianum

dermatitis in susceptible individuals; wear gloves and long sleeves when handling. Caucasus.

| *sphondylium montanum* | WHITE | SU | 3′–9′/2′–3′ |
| | ○ ◐ | Z9-3 | S * |

Masterwort, American Cow Parsley. [*H. lanatum*]. Strong, erect stems. The sheathing leafstalks bear variably hairy leaves; the lower, to 1′ long, are divided into 3 deeply lobed and toothed, ovate leaflets; the upper are smaller. Large, compound umbels, looser than those of *H. mantegazzianum*. North America, Europe, eastern Asia.

HERMODACTYLUS, Iridaceae. (1)

| *tuberosus* | GREEN | ESP | 1′–2′/1′ |
| | ○ | Z9-6 | DS ** |

Widow Iris, Snake's Head Iris. [*Iris tuberosa*]. Evergreen clumps of 2-ranked, linear, glaucous, bluish green leaves. The leaf blade is square in cross section, narrowly winged at the corners. A single, fragrant Iris-like 2″ flower tops each hollow 6″–12″ scape, sheathed by the leaf bases. The 3 spatulate, glassy yellow green falls are each marked with a large, round, purple blotch; the 3 erect standards, barely 1″ long, are bright pea green. A conspicuous, greenish yellow, 3-forked style stands erect at the center of the flower. Light, well-drained soils are preferred; add lime where it is acid. The smooth, fingerlike 1″ tubers may be planted in early fall or spring, with division at the same time if the plants have become crowded. A most unusual plant for the sunny rock garden or border. Easily forced for winter bloom in the conservatory or plant room. Mediterranean region.

HESPERALOE, Agavaceae. (3)

| *parviflora* | RED | LSP/ESU | 5′–8′/3′–4′ |
| | ○ | Z10-8 | DS *** |

Red Yucca. [*H. yuccifolia*]. This elegant evergreen can be grown as a specimen in the border or as an accent plant in the landscape. It forms a dense clump of narrow, leathery, arching, gray green leaves, 3′–4′ long by 1¼″ wide, edged with loose, fibrous threads. The slender, often branched flower spikes rise on long erect scapes to more than twice the height of the foliage, to 8′–9′ in older plants. Each clump bears several spikes of many nodding, orange red to red flowers, with narrowly campanulate, 6-tepaled 1¼″ perianths. Reblooms in mild areas. Drought resistant and tolerant of a wide range of soil conditions. Texas.

———— var. *engelmannii* has more broadly campanulate flowers, to 1″ long. Hardier than the species, to Z7.

Hesperis matronalis

HESPERIS, Cruciferae. (24)

matronalis	PURPLE	LSP/SU	I′–3′/I.5′
	○ ◑	Z9-3	S ***

Dame's Rocket, Sweet Rocket, Dame's Violet, Rogue's Gilliflower. This collection of common names suggests that it has been grown in gardens for centuries; indeed it has. Variable, it is usually much branched and often subshrubby at the base, with alternate, lanceolate 4″ leaves, toothed a long the margins. Many cruciform ½″ flowers, arranged in loose but showy terminal racemes, in purple, lilac, or white. The double-flowered form has become scarce. Deliciously fragrant, particularly in the evening. Deadhead to force a second flush of bloom. Self-seeds prolifically. Raise new plants from a spring seeding every few years, as the older ones deteriorate. Seed is available mixed or by color. The sometimes temperamental, double-flowered form must be propagated from cuttings; efforts to increase it by tissue culture are currently on going. The singles are easy to grow in well-drained, moisture-retentive, sweet soils, but will tolerate less than favorable conditions. Protect from strong sun. Mediterranean, temperate Asia.

HETEROCENTRON, Melastomataceae. (27)

[*Heeria*]. In the wild, this genus is confined to mountain regions of Mexico and Central America. Good border plants in frost-free areas, they may be raised under glass for late summer bedding in colder zones. The wheel-shaped flowers, solitary or arranged in terminal panicles, are 4-parted, with 8 uneven stamens, 4 of them split at the ends. The opposite leaves, with conspicuous, parallel veins, are typical of the family. Propagate by cuttings or division in early summer, or from seed. Best in free-draining, sandy loam, enriched with humus. Spanish Shawl, *H. elegans* [*Heeria elegans, Schizocentron elegans*], is a prostrate species, commonly used as a ground cover in the tropics.

macrostachyum		PINK	F-EW	1′–3′/1.5′
		○	Z10/T	CS ∗∗

[*H. roseum, Heeria rosea*]. Erect, somewhat branched stems, subshrubby at the base, and thick with fine hairs. The elliptic to ovate 2″–3″ leaves taper toward the petiole and are covered with coarse hairs, red along the involute margins. The deep rose pink or cerise ¾″–1″ flowers are arranged in generous, terminal panicles. Mexico.

subtriplinervium		WHITE	F-EW	4′–6′/3′
		○	Z10/T	CS ∗∗

Similar, but much larger, with often winged stems, covered with reddish brown hairs. Its short-petioled leaves may reach 4″ long. The slightly smaller white flowers are displayed in terminal panicles. A pink-flowered form is sometimes listed erroneously as *H. roseum.* Mexico.

———— 'Pink Bouquet' has pink flowers.

———— 'White Bouquet' is a superior cultivar.

HEUCHERA, Saxifragaceae. (50)   Alumroot

These North American natives are distinguished by their durability. The plants are long-lived, their handsome foliage is evergreen except in the most severe climates, and their sprays of dainty flowers are enduring. Alumroots form dense, spreading mounds of long-stalked, rounded or kidney-shaped leaves, variously lobed and toothed, often zoned or mottled, usually hairy as well. Wiry stems bear racemes or panicles of many tiny flowers, well above the mass of foliage. The campanulate, urceolate or saucer-shaped, 5-lobed calyx usually exceeds the 5 short petals. Heucheras thrive in full sun or partial shade in areas with hot summers. Soils must be well drained, liberally enriched with organic matter. In cold climates mulch after the ground has frozen to control heaving. Divide usually every 4–5 years when the crown becomes excessively woody and bloom is reduced. Propagate by division, preferably in spring, or by seed. Much admired as cut flowers. (See X *Heucherella.*)

| x *brizoides* | VARIOUS | SP-SU | 1′–2.5′/1′–1.5′ |
| | ○ ◑ | Z10-3 | D **** |

These hybrids of *H. sanguinea, H. micrantha,* and perhaps *H. americana* have supplanted red-flowered *H. sanguinea* and even the best of its cultivars in modern gardens. Their mounds of scalloped foliage are overtopped by numerous slender panicles of red, pink, or more rarely white flowers. Many of the best forms have been developed at Alan Bloom's Bressingham Gardens.

———————— 'Bressingham Hybrids.' Mixed colors.
———————— 'Chatterbox' has large pink flowers.
———————— 'Coral Cloud' is coral pink.
———————— 'Firebird.' Deep scarlet.
———————— 'June Bride' has pure white flowers.
———————— 'Oakington Jewel.' Bronze-mottled foliage. Coral red flowers.
———————— 'Pluie de Feu' is scarlet.
———————— 'Pretty Polly' is pink flowered.
———————— 'Queen of Hearts' has bright salmon flowers.
———————— 'Scarlet Sentinel' is scarlet red.
———————— 'Scintillation.' Bright pink flowers tipped with red.
———————— 'Snowflake' is white.
———————— 'Spitfire' has rose red flowers.
———————— 'White Cloud' is white flowered.

Heuchera x *brizoides* cv.

cylindrica	CREAM	LSP-SU	2′–3′/1′
	○ ◑	Z10-3	DS ***

Ovate to rounded 1½″–2½″ leaves, with 5–7 deep, blunt, toothed lobes. Small cream to greenish flowers in tall, slender panicles. Northwestern North America.
——————— 'Greenfinch' has greenish yellow flowers, prized for flower arranging.
——————— 'Green Ivory,' selected by Alan Bloom as a seedling of 'Greenfinch,' has whitish flowers with a green base.
——————— 'Hyperion' has deep pink flowers.

maxima	WHITE	LW-ESP	1.5′–3′/1′–2′
	◑	Z10-9/H	DS ***

Island Alumroot has rounded 2½″–7″ leaves, deeply 7 to 9 lobed, and toothed. Its stout flower stalks bear long, cylindrical panicles of tiny whitish flowers. Southern California and Channel Islands. 'Santa Ana Cardinal' is a hybrid with *H. sanguinea,* from the Rancho Santa Ana Botanic Garden. A vigorous, free-flowering, long-blooming plant, with rose red flowers.

micrantha	WHITE	LSP-ESU	1′–2.5′/1′–1.5′
	○ ◑	Z10-4	DS **

Maple-like 1″–3″ leaves, with 5–7 obtuse lobes, and rounded teeth. Minuscule flowers; their whitish petals, longer than the green to purple-tinged calyx. British Columbia to central California.
——————— *diversifolia* 'Palace Purple' has bronze red leaves, beet red beneath, with a wrinkled surface. A superb foliage plant selected by the Royal Botanic Gardens, Kew. Readily available.

sanguinea	RED	SP-SU	1′–1.5′/1′
	○ ◑	Z10-3	DS **

Coral Bells. This, the only red-flowered species, is a parent of most of the hybrids found in gardens today. Plants listed under this name in the trade most often belong under *H.* x *brizoides.* Rounded to kidney-shaped leaves. 1″–2″ across, with blunt lobes and teeth. Panicles of bell-shaped ¼″–½″ flowers, red, or more rarely pink or white. Arizona, Mexico.

X HEUCHERELLA, Saxifragaceae. (2)

These intergeneric hybrids between *Heuchera* x *brizoides* and 2 species of *Tiarella* are intermediate between their parents. They have similar cultural requirements to *Heuchera.* (See *Heuchera* and *Tiarella.*)

alba 'Bridget Bloom'	PINK	LSP-ESU	1.5′/1′
	○ ◑	Z10-3	D ***

Heuchera x *brizoides* x *Tiarella wherryi.* It resembles the latter parent in foliage.

X *Heucherella alba* 'Bridget Bloom'

Delicate panicles of tiny pale pink flowers rise on wiry stalks, well above the mound of leaves.

tiarelloides	PINK	LSP-ESU	1.5′/1′–1.5′
	○ ◑	Z10-3	D **

Heuchera x *brizoides* x *Tiarella cordifolia*. Broadly ovate to suborbicular leaves, to 3½″ long, with 7 lobes and rounded teeth. Narrow panicles of tiny flowers; pale pink petals longer than the dark pink calyx.

HIBISCUS, Malvaceae. (300)   Rose Mallow

The Rose Mallows have the largest flowers of any perennial, at times attaining 1′ in diameter. These are sturdy, tall plants, forming stands of substantial, erect stems. Large, alternate leaves, most often palmately lobed or sometimes divided, but rarely entire. The showy flowers, white, or in many shades of pink, or red, are borne in the upper leaf axils; they have 5 broadly ovate, silky, pleated petals. As is typical of the Mallow family, the stamens are fused into a prominent tubular column around the pistil; the stigma is 5 lobed. Most of the following species are native to North American wetlands and thrive in moist, rich soils. Full sun or very light shade.

coccineus	RED	ESU-F	3'–6'/3'
	○	Z9-6/T	S ***

[*H. speciosus*]. The leaves are palmately parted into 3–7 slender, toothed segments; sometimes palmately compound. Red 6"–8" flowers. Southeastern United States.

lasiocarpus	VARIOUS	ESU-F	3'–7'/3'
	○	Z9-5/T	S ***

[*H. californicus, H. incanus, H. lasiocarpus* var. *californicus*]. Its hairy, ovate leaves, to 6" long, are usually sharp toothed, but seldom lobed. The flowers, white, pink, rarely pale yellow, with a maroon center, may reach 8" across. Densely hairy fruit capsules. Southern United States.

militaris	PINK	ESU-F	3'–7'/3'
	○	Z9-4/T	S ***

Soldier Rose Mallow, Halberd-Leaved Rose Mallow. The lower leaves are ovate, to 6" long; the upper leaves, 3 to 5 lobed, with a longer central lobe. Pale pink flowers with a crimson center, to 6" across. Eastern and central United States.

moscheutos	VARIOUS	ESU-F	3'–8'/3'
	○	Z9-4/T	S ****

Common Rose Mallow, Swamp Rose Mallow, Mallow Rose. The lanceolate to ovate leaves are toothed, unlobed or shallowly 3 to 5 lobed, to 8" long; densely white-woolly

Hibiscus moscheutos 'Southern Belle'

underneath. Flowers white, pink, or rose, usually with a crimson center, to 8″ wide. Eastern and central United States.

——————— *moscheutos.* Lanceolate to narrowly ovate leaves; the upper unlobed, the lower 3 lobed. White flowers. Southeastern and south central United States.

——————— *palustris.* Marsh Mallow, Sea Hollyhock. Ovate to rounded leaves, mostly 3 lobed. White, pink, or rose pink flowers. Hairy fruits. Eastern and central United States.

These are variable plants, the species and subspecies intergrading and overlapping geographically. Southeastern *H. grandiflorus* is similar, with broader, 3- to 5-lobed, hairy leaves and white, pink, or rose flowers, sometimes crimson at the center. The popular hybrids between *H. moscheutos, H. coccineus,* and *H. militaris* are more frequently grown than the species. They are often listed as cultivars of *H. moscheutos,* incorrectly as *H. meehanii,* or as *H. grandiflorus* of gardens, not the species. Superior new hybrids are: 'Lord Baltimore,' 5′ tall with bright red flowers and descriptively named 'New Blood Red' and 'Ruffled Cerise.' 'Southern Belle,' with white, pink, or red flowers on 4′ stems, is available as seed or as plants. The dwarf 'Disco Belle' strain produces 1.5′–2′ plants and is available in mixed or separate colors.

HIERACIUM, Compositae. (1000)			Hawkweed

The Hawkweeds are widespread in temperate regions, but only a few have ornamental value. They are particularly useful in hot, dry gardens, with poor or gravelly soil. Their foliage is mostly in basal rosettes, above which their milky-sapped stems bear small, Dandelion-like flower heads. Their nomenclature is confused, due to their ability to produce seed apomictically.

aurantiacum	ORANGE	ESU-F	9″–2′/1′
	○	Z9-3	DS **

Devil's Paintbrush, Grim-the-Collier. [*H. brunneocroceum*]. Underground stolons give rise to rosettes of hirsute, lanceolate leaves to 8″ long. Its erect, hairy stems support clusters of vivid, burnt orange ¾″–1″ flowers. Seeds itself to the point of being invasive, but valuable for its unusual flower color over a long season. Europe.

lanatum	YELLOW	SU-F	1′–2′/1′
	○	Z10-3/H	DS **

[*H. tomentosum, H. waldsteinii* Hort., *H. welwitschii* Hort.]. Its attractive basal rosettes of gray, felted, ovate leaves, about 1′ long, make this an interesting foliage plant. The clusters of bright yellow 1″ flowers may be removed unless seed is required. Southern Europe.

maculatum	YELLOW	SU-F	1′–2′/1′
	○	Z9-3	DS **

Tufts of hairy, oblong to lanceolate, toothed leaves, blotched with chocolate. The rather

Hieracium lanatum

dull yellow flower heads are in loose panicles on hairy stems. Grown for its interesting foliage. Central Europe.

| *villosum* | YELLOW | SU | I'–$2'/\mathrm{I}'$ |
| | ○ | Z9-3 | DS ** |

Shaggy Hawkweed. Neat clumps of softly woolly silver foliage. Its oval, toothed leaves are covered with silky hairs. The fragrant, bright yellow flower heads may reach 2″ across. Europe.

***HOSTA*, Liliaceae. (40)**	**Plantain Lily**

[*Funkia*]. These natives of Eastern Asian woodlands have endeared themselves to the North American gardening public, as have only a handful of other perennials. Their diverse foliage, handsome throughout the season, and often elegant flowers, coupled with their ease of culture and affinity for shaded sites, have contributed to their popularity for both large and small gardens across the country. Very long-lived rhizomatous crowns with tough roots underlie heavy clumps of mostly basal foliage. Often long-stalked, the narrowly lanceolate to heart-shaped to almost round leaves are conspicuously veined in most species, and display a broad range of textures and colors. Some are puckered, others are smooth; some lustrous, others glaucous with a waxy bloom. From deep greens to light greens, to yellow greens and blues, all colors are represented and may be enhanced with white, yellow, or cream variegations. Of secondary importance, their mostly one-sided racemes of white, lavender, or violet flowers rise above the lush foliage mass on vertical, unbranched, often bracted scapes. The funnelform or campanulate perianths, with a long tubular base, open into 6 rounded or pointed lobes; the 6 upcurved stamens and the slender style are conspicuous, sometimes protruding. Plantain Lilies are at their best in moisture-retentive, humusy soils under dappled shade. However, they will endure a wide range of conditions; some thrive in bright sun, some even in deep shade. Slugs are their most serious problem, particularly damaging early in the season when the leaves are still tightly furled; as the buds expand, the holes become apparent, marring the beautiful new growth. Propagation is usually by division of the crowns before growth begins in spring; do not disturb unless stock increase is required. Millions of plants are raised commercially, using tissue culture techniques. Although not a large genus in number of species, its nomenclature is very confused. This situation has arisen over many years for several reasons. Hostas mutate freely, displaying a wide range of natural variation in the wild. Moreover, they interbreed promiscuously; some even produce seed apomictically. Foliage shapes and patterns vary on the same plant in response to culture, and juvenile leaves may differ from mature ones. The forms now found in gardens include: *(a)* some collected from the wild, *(b)* others no longer found in the wild which came long ago from Japanese and Chinese gardens, and *(c)* more recent sorts raised through breeding and selection in the United States and Europe as well as in Japan. The last are mostly well documented, and new cultivars are now registered with the American Hosta Society and the University of Minnesota Landscape Arboretum, which maintain the national register of over 600 forms. This joint organization supports the ongoing work of several leading Hosta authorities in their attempt to unravel the genus. Only a small proportion of those available are included in the following listings. Specialist nurseries and the American Hosta Society can supply further information on hundreds of others. Heights given in the Rapid Reference Lines refer to the foliage mounds rather than to the length of the flower scape.

crispula	LAVENDER	ESU	1'–1.5'/2.5'
	◑	Z9-3	D **

Flattened domes of long-petioled, dull, deep green 5"–7" leaves; ovate, with extended tapering and drooping tips. The irregular white margins are wavy, which sometimes causes the leaf to twist slightly. The racemes, with as many as 35–40 pale lavender 1¾" flowers, bloom on 3' scapes. Best as a ground cover. The white leaf margin is subject to windburn. Often confused with *H. fortunei marginato-alba* [*H. f.* 'Albomarginata'], which has wider white margins and blooms later. Japan.

decorata	LILAC	SU	9"–1'/1.5'
	◑●	Z9-3	D ***

Usually listed under the name 'Thomas Hogg' in this country, this plant has smaller, blunter leaves than the last, with a narrower white edge extending down the winged petioles. Its racemes of about a dozen deep lilac, bell-shaped flowers rise on 2' scapes,

Hosta sieboldiana

which are clasped in the middle by a leaflike bract. Somewhat stoloniferous; best as a ground cover. Japan. *H.* 'Butter Rim,' *(H. decorata* x *H. sieboldii)* has the same mounded habit, with yellow-margined leaves.

fortunei	LILAC	SU	I′–I.5′/2′
	◐●	Z9-3	D ✶✶✶✶

This extremely variable, widely grown species is perhaps only a variety of *H. sieboldiana,* or may indeed be an old hybrid. In its normal form, the slightly glaucous, gray green, ovate to elliptic 6″–12″ leaves form 2′-wide mounds. Aloft, the 3′–4′ scapes support racemes of flaring, pale lilac 1″–1½″ flowers. It has given rise to several important cultivars, all good as ground covers. Late to emerge in the spring. Japan. *H. f. obscura* has shiny, very deep green, oval 8″ leaves, with 9–11 pairs of deeply impressed veins.

———— 'Albo-picta.' ['Golden Spring,' *Funkia ovata aurea, F. o. albopicta, H. fortunei viridis-marginata*]. The young growth is pale yellow, with irregular, dark green margins. The leaves change to solid dark green by summer.

———— 'Aurea.' ['Twinkles']. Smaller than the last, with pale yellow young leaves bordered in cream. Pale green in summer. Very late to start into growth.

———— 'Gloriosa' [*H.* 'Gloriosa'] has oval green leaves with a narrow white margin.

———— var. *hyacinthina.* [*H. f.* 'Hyacinthina,' *H.* 'Hyacinthina']. Blue gray green leaves, very glaucous beneath, with a pencil-thin, gray rim.

———— 'Francee' has dark green, heart-shaped leaves, rimmed with a persistent white band. 15″–18″ high. Tolerates some sun. Superior to the next.

———————— *marginato-alba* ['Albo-marginata,' 'Silver Crown'] has large, irregularly and broadly white-rimmed leaves of a thin texture. Its pale lilac flowers bloom in early fall. Abundantly grown in borders and as a ground cover. Possibly a white-margined form of *H. f. obscura.* Less prone to windburn than *H. crispula.*

| *lancifolia* | LILAC | LSU | I'/1.5' |
| | ◑● | Z9-3 | D ✶✶✶✶ |

Narrow-leaved Plantain Lily. [*H. japonica, Funkia lanceolata*]. It makes 1.5' wide mounds of long-petioled, glossy, deep green 2"–6" leaves, lanceolate and pointed at the tip, with 4–5 pairs of veins. Almost 2' in length, the numerous slender scapes are spotted in purple below. They support 8- to 10-flowered racemes of almost horizontal, flaring, lilac 1½"–2" flowers, flushed with purple and with purplish anthers. The somewhat stoloniferous rootstock breaks dormancy early. Excellent for edging. Japan.
———————— 'Louisa' is very small. Its white flowers bloom over mounds of white-variegated leaves.

| *nakaiana* | VIOLET | SU | 6"–9"/I'–1.5' |
| | ◑● | Z9-3 | D ✶✶✶ |

[*H.* 'Makaimo Minor']. Suitable for edgings, this species forms low, foot-wide mounds of undulate, dark green, heart-shaped 2" leaves on long, purple-spotted petioles. Many graceful 1.5' scapes, also purple spotted below, support headlike racemes of light purple to violet, bell-shaped 2" flowers. An ancestor of several collector's items such as *H. venusta.* Japan.

| *plantaginea* | WHITE | SU | 2'/3' |
| | ◑● | Z9-3 | D ✶✶✶✶ |

August Lily, Fragrant Plantain Lily. [*Funkia subcordata, H.* or *F. japonica, H. spathulata, H. subcordata*]. This robust, somewhat heat-resistant Chinese species has long been cultivated in the West, and was a favorite in cottage gardens. It makes mounds, 3' across, of lustrous, medium green foliage, sometimes with a yellowish cast. The heart-shaped to orbicular leaves, on long, winged petioles, are about 10" long, with 9 pairs of deeply impressed veins. Short racemes, on 2.5' scapes, of sweetly scented, waxy, pure white flowers, trumpet shaped and to 4" long. Frequently offered *H. p.* var. *grandiflora* [*F. grandiflora, H. p. japonica*] has even longer flowers.
x 'Honey Bells.' This hybrid with *H. sieboldii,* has green 1' leaves and slightly fragrant, pale mauve flowers on 3' scapes.
x 'Royal Standard' has more numerous but smaller white flowers over rich green, deeply veined foliage. Tolerates full sun, except in the hottest zones, as well as deep shade. Z10-6. A Wayside Gardens hybrid.

| *sieboldiana* | LAVENDER | SP-ESU | 2.5'/2.5'–4' |
| | ◑● | Z9-3 | D ✶✶✶✶ |

[*H. glauca, Funkia sieboldii, F. glauca, H.* or *F. fortunei robusta*]. Dramatic, 4'-wide clumps of magnificent dark gray green foliage, covered with a waxy blue bloom. Long petioled, the heavily seersuckered, heart-shaped 1'–1.25' leaves may reach 1' across and

Hosta fortunei 'Albo-Picta'

have 12–14 pairs of deeply impressed veins. Scarcely above rise 6- to 10-flowered scapes of purple-tinged, flaring 1″–1½″ blooms. The foliage turns gold in the fall. Variable, but all forms make superior accent plants. Japan.

—————— 'Elegans.' Its lavender flowers are borne just above the mass of immense, blue gray, puckered leaves. Its sun-tolerant, natural sport 'Color Glory' has yellowish green, heart-shaped leaves, irregularly and broadly banded in deep olive green.

—————— 'Frances Williams' remains as popular as ever. The substantial, crinkled and cupped leaves are blue green, with a bold, uneven golden edge. A striking specimen plant.

—————— 'Ryan's Big One' has very large, bluish green leaves.

sieboldii	LILAC	LSU	1′/1′
	◑●	Z9-3	D ****

[*H. albomarginata, H. lancifolia marginata*]. Similar to *H. lancifolia*. Its undulate, spear-shaped 4″–5″ leaves, with 4–5 pairs of veins, are a matte dark green, shiny beneath. The scapes, about 1.5′ in height, bear 2–3 leaflike bracts and are topped with racemes of nodding, bell-shaped, white 1½″–2″ flowers, veined in deep purple.

—————— 'Kabitan.' Its ruffled, lanceolate 4½″ leaves are pale yellow green with green margins. Violet flowers. A parent of several golden hyrids.

tardiflora	LAVENDER	F	1′/1.5′
	○ ●	Z9-3	D ****

[*H. lancifolia tardiflora, H. sparsa*]. Valued also for its very late blooms, this species makes neat, rounded 1'-wide clumps; glossy, dark green, lanceolate 6" leaves, on petioles spotted with purple below. The erect scapes, as tall as the leaves, support crowded racemes of funnel-shaped, pale 1½" flowers, flushed with purple or blue, and with yellow anthers. Japan, but not from the wild. *H. x tardiana* (*H. tardiflora* x *H. sieboldiana* 'Elegans') developed by Eric Smith is a race with small bluish leaves and pale lavender pink flowers. Among its cultivars are 'Hadspen Blue,' 'Dorset Blue,' and 'Halcyon.' All are excellent as edging plants.

tokudama	WHITE	ESU	1'/1.5'
	◗●	Z9-3	D ***

[*H. sieboldiana glauca, H. glauca, Funkia sieboldiana condensata*]. Similar to but slower growing than *H. sieboldiana,* this may be the same plant as *H. sieboldiana fortunei.* Its domed mounds of foliage spread about 1.5' wide. The heavily puckered, blue 9" leaves may reach 8" across, and are rounded and cupped, with 11–13 pairs of veins. Short dense racemes of urn-shaped, milky white flowers rise on 1.5' scapes. Japan.

———— 'Aureo-nebulosa' has cupped, rounded leaves, flushed with yellow in the center, and irregularly and broadly edged in blue green. A choice specimen plant. Slow growing.

———— 'Flavo-circinalis.' ['Golden Circles']. Blue green, quilted leaves with creamy yellow margins.

undulata	LILAC	ESU	1.5'/1'–1.5'
	◗●	Z9-3	D ****

Wavy-Leaf Plantain Lily. [*Funkia undulata, H. lancifolia* var. *undulata, H. media-picta*]. Often sold under the name *H. variegata.* Probably of hybrid origin, this sterile type comes in many forms. Normally, its sometimes contorted, wavy leaves have a broad cream stripe in the center, surrounded by a wide band in 2 shades of green, darker around the edge. Elliptic to ovate 5"–6" blades, pointed at the drooping tip, with 10 pairs of veins. Spotted with purple below, the 2'–3.5' scapes support 8- to 10-flowered, one-sided racemes of recurved, funnelform, pale lilac 2" flowers with purple anthers. Setting no seed, they drop quickly and neatly. Then a second crop of foliage unfurls, seldom so boldly variegated. Often sports to other forms. Japan, but not in the wild. The cultivars are best bought locally in full leaf, since their names are often confused.

———— 'Albo-marginata' ['Silver Rim'] has wavy, tapering, elliptic leaves, heart shaped at their bases. Their centers are green and gray green, their margins irregularly edged in cream. Fast growing and spreads well; a fine ground cover in sun or shade.

———— 'Erromena' [*H.* var. *erromena, H. erromena, H. lancifolia* var. *fortis*] makes more vigorous 2'-wide mounds of solid, medium green leaves, on channeled 1.5' petioles. Endures deep shade.

———— 'Univittata.' [*H.* var. *univittata*]. Rounded 2'-wide mounds of pointed, cordate, green leaves painted in white down their centers. Often reverts to all-green.

———— 'Variegata.' ['Undulata']. Foliage mounds only to 10" high, with smaller leaves irregularly streaked with white in the center, with an undulating green margin; the elongated, pointed tips of the leaves are spiraled.

ventricosa	VIOLET	SU	2'/3'
	◑ ●	Z9-3	DS ****

[*H. caerulea, H. ovata*]. Lush, rich green mounds, about 3' across, of heart-shaped 5"–7" leaves which taper to a point; margins slightly undulate, 8–9 pairs of veins. The petioles are narrowly winged and channeled. Many rigidly erect, round 2'–3' scapes, red flushed at the base and with a single bract, support loose racemes of 20–30 nodding, violet 1½"–2" flowers, darkly striped in blue. Above the perianth tube, the lobes balloon into a bell shape; violet anthers. Sets seed freely. Resistant to slugs. China.

————— 'Aureo-Marginata.' ['Variegata']. Its substantial green leaves are bordered in yellow, which bleaches to cream but holds through the season.

venusta	VIOLET	ESU	4"/1'
	◑ ●	Z9-3	D ****

The smallest of the Hostas, this stoloniferous little charmer has soft green, wedge-shaped to elliptic 1"–2" leaves with 3–4 pairs of veins. Both the long petioles and the hollow 10"–1' scapes are parallel grooved. Few-flowered racemes of darkly veined, violet, funnelform 1"–1½" flowers. China, Korea.

————— 'Variegated' has leaves with a cream center and wavy margins in 2 shades of green.

Cultivars/Hybrids:
'Antioch' has large, medium green leaves, broadly edged in cream. Fast growing. Best in shade, although tolerant of sun.

'August Moon.' Crinkled gold leaves; white flowers on 2' scapes.

'Big Mama' has very large, puckered and cupped, intense blue leaves. Superb architectural quality for backgrounds or screening. White flowers in summer.

'Blue Cadet.' Small, neat clumps of blue foliage; lavender flowers in late summer.

'Ginko Craig' is a rapid grower, with frosted, lanceolate leaves edged in white. Lavender flowers. Good for edging.

'Gold Edger.' Chartreuse to gold heart-shaped leaves; abundant lavender flowers in midsummer. Endures full sun well.

'Gold Standard' makes upright mounds of strongly ribbed, light yellowish green, heart-shaped leaves, edged in dark green. When grown in partial shade, the leaves become more golden.

'Krossa Regal' [*H. nigrescens elatior*]. Very large, upright, domed mounds of frosty blue pointed leaves. Scapes of lavender flowers to 5' tall.

'Love Pat.' An improved and popular form of *H. tokudama*. Neat clumps of intensely blue, cupped and puckered, rounded leaves. Very shade tolerant. Cream white flowers in late summer.

'Piedmont Gold' is a fine background or accent plant with curved, heart-shaped, golden leaves. White flowers in midsummer. Fast growing.

'Sum and Substance.' Increasingly popular as an accent plant, it makes upright mounds of glossy, ribbed, heart-shaped leaves in chartreuse to gold. Tolerates full sun. Late blooming, lavender flowers.

x 'Wogon Gold.' This hybrid of unknown parentage is only suitable for shade. Its golden leaves are similar in shape to those of *H. lancifolia* but smaller.

HOUTTUYNIA, Saururaceae. (I)

cordata	WHITE	SU	6"–2'/1.5'
	○ ●	ZI0-6	CD **

This spreading plant forms a dense ground cover of alternate, heart-shaped leaves. The substantial, dark green leaves are edged with a fine red line. The dense 1"–2" spike of minute flowers is subtended by 4 showy white bracts. Each flower is itself underlaid

Houttuynia cordata 'Variegata'

Hunnemannia fumariifolia

by a tiny bract. Thrives and may become invasive in damp or wet soils. Eastern Asia. The following cultivars are more readily available than the species:

———— 'Flore Pleno.' More ornamental than the species. The white bracts of the individual flowers are enlarged and petaloid.

———— 'Variegata' ['Chameleon'] has leaves irregularly variegated in green, cream, and red.

HUNNEMANNIA, Papaveraceae. (1)

| *fumariifolia* | YELLOW | SU/F | 1'–2'/1'–1.5' |
| | ○ | Z10-9 | S *** |

Mexican Tulip Poppy has erect stems, bushy with blue green, glaucous leaves, ternately dissected into narrow segments. The 4-petaled, Poppy-like 3″ flowers are long stemmed. The clear yellow of the flowers combines exquisitely with the graceful bluish foliage. Very long flowering. Likes a warm, well-drained situation. Take care not to overwater. Resents root disturbance; buy container-grown plants or sow in place. Self-seeds prolifically. Frequently grown as an annual. In the warmest areas, it may flower early. Mexico.

HYLOMECON, Papaveraceae. (1)

| *japonicum* | YELLOW | SP | 1'/1' |
| | ○● | Z9-6 | DS ** |

[*H. vernalis*]. This summer dormant, shallow-rooted plant increases slowly to form large, low clumps of light green foliage. The odd-pinnate leaves, to 1' long, have 2–3 pairs of ovate, toothed leaflets. Bright yellow 2″ Poppy flowers are held in the upper leaf axils, singly or in pairs. Pretty in informal, woodland areas, where the soil is moist and humusy. Sometimes included in *Chelidonium*. Asia.

HYPOESTES, Acanthaceae. (40)

| *aristata* | PINK | LF-ESP | 3'–5'/2'–3' |
| | ○ ◑ | Z10 | CDS *** |

This bushy evergreen has erect, branching stems, bearing widely spaced pairs of softly downy, ovate 2″–3″ leaves. Spikelets of pale to dark rose pink flowers cluster in the axils of the upper leaves. The tubular 1″ corolla opens into 2 recurved lips. The upper lip is 3 lobed; the central one purple-spotted, the 2 laterals white striped. The smaller lower lip is 2 lobed, striped with white. Withstands only very light frost. In frost-free areas it blooms throughout the winter. Cut back hard in springtime; pinch new growth

Hylomecon japonicum

to stimulate branching. Needs a light, fertile soil and water during summer drought. Excellent for cutting. South Africa.

HYSSOPUS, Labiatae. (5)

officinalis	BLUE	SU	1.5′–2′/1′–1.5′
	○	Z10-3/H	CDS ****

Hyssop. [*H. aristata, H. vulgaris*]. An aromatic, variably hairy herb, with branching, square stems, woody at the base. Opposite, linear to oblong leaves, to 1½″ long. The whorls of violet blue ½″ flowers, with prominent stamens, form loose, slender, terminal spikes. Corolla asymmetrical; upper lip 2 lobed, lower lip 3 lobed. There are white, pink, and red variants. Some garden forms have broader, lanceolate-ovate leaves, and dense, uninterrupted flower spikes. Southern and eastern Europe.

IBERIS, Cruciferae. (30)   Candytuft

Candytufts are popular plants for the front of the border as well as for rock gardens and walls. Of easy culture, they do best in sunny positions, although they will usually bloom well enough with only a few hours of sunlight each day. A well-drained soil is essential, preferably with some added lime. Shear hard after flowering to promote compact growth. *I. pruitti* and *I. saxatilis,* both lovely in the rock garden, are too small for consideration here.

gibraltarica	LILAC	LSP	1'/2'
	◑	Z10-7	CDS *

Gibraltar Candytuft. This compact clump-former has fleshy evergreen leaves about 1" long. Its lilac pink flowers, often white toward the center, are arranged in flattish clusters which do not elongate. Gibraltar.

sempervirens	WHITE	SP-ESU	1'/3'
	○ ◑	Z10-3/T	CDS ****

Perennial Candytuft, Edging Candytuft. [*I. garrexiana*]. Procumbent and spreading, subshrubby below, and crowded with more or less evergreen foliage. Its dark green, leathery 1"–2" leaves are narrowly oblong, blunt at the tip. The pure white flowers, which become pinkish with age, cluster into dense, pyramidal racemes that elongate as the lower flowers fade. The corolla has 4 petals, the outer pair much larger than the inner. Numerous cultivars abound, most with a more compact habit. Mediterranean.

———————— 'Alexander's White' has sparkling white flowers in very dense racemes.
———————— 'Autumn Beauty' reblooms in fall. 8" tall.
———————— 'Little Gem' is a compact form. 6" in height.
———————— 'Purity' has larger flowers over a longer period. 8"–10" tall.
———————— 'Pygmaea.' A very dwarf, heavy bloomer. 4" tall.
———————— 'Snowflake' has brilliant white flowers on 8" stems.

Iberis sempervirens

Impatiens balfourii

IBOZA, Labiatae. (12)

riparia	WHITE	LF-W	3'–6'/2'–3'
	○ ◑	Z10-9	CS ***

Misty Plume Bush. [*Moschosma riparium*]. This aromatic subshrub has strong, erect, branching stems and opposite, broadly ovate 2"–3" leaves with blunt teeth. Dense 1' panicles of tiny white, pale pink, or lilac flowers with exserted stamens create a soft, misty effect. The corolla is tubular, with 4–5 unequal lobes. Long blooming. Likes fertile and moist but well-drained soils. Withhold water in winter. Fast growing. Cut back very hard before new growth begins. Best propagated from cuttings which will flower within the year. South Africa.

IMPATIENS, Balsaminaceae. (600)   Touch-Me-Not

The perennial species of *Impatiens* are tender and are usually treated as "summer-flowering" annuals even in frost-free areas, where they will flower almost constantly. Foliage and stems are cut down to the ground even by a light frost, after which only a few of the species will grow back from the roots. All thrive in semishade or shade, even in sun in gentle climates, in moist, porous, organically rich soils. Propagation by seed is easy in some species, trickier in others; the seed requires light to germinate—scatter it on the surface of the growing medium. Cuttings root with great ease. Erect to spreading, the succulent stems are often branched; the thin foliage is rather lax. The alternate, opposite, or whorled leaves are nearly always edged with small teeth. Solitary or in small clusters or racemes, the flowers arise from the upper leaf axils. The individual flower is asymmetrical and has an extremely complex structure. From a normal position as a young bud, the maturing flower twists 180° on its stalk until completely inverted or resupinate. The parts are named as positioned in the mature flower. Of the 3–5 sepals, the lowest is petaloid, enlarged, and forms a sac or spur called the lip. There are 3 deeply 2-lobed petals, the upper known as the standard, the 2 lower as the wings. When touched, the capsules scatter their seed explosively in all directions. One species, *I. wallerana,* is so common that it is recognized even by nongardeners; the New Guinea hybrids are well on their way to a similar popularity, but most of the others are less well-known.

balfourii	PINK	SU	2'–3'/1'
	◑ ●	Z10	CS ***

Erect, branching stems. The alternate, lanceolate to ovate 3"–5" leaves are edged with small, sharp teeth. Delicate, short, terminal racemes. Lip, pink tinged and short; standard, white and hooded; wings, purplish pink and unevenly lobed. Self-seeds very freely; can be invasive. Western Himalayas.

New Guinea Hybrids   VARIOUS   SU   8″–3′/1′–1.5′

○ ◑   Z10/T   CS ✶✶✶✶

The so-called New Guinea Hybrids are of recent introduction and uncertain botanical status; they are probably not hybrids at all, but variants and selections of *I. hawkeri* [*I. herzogii, I. mooreana, I. schlechteri*]. This highly variable species has branching, erect to decumbent stems, often colored red or purple. The lanceolate, ovate, or elliptic leaves are 1½″–9″ long; green, bronze, or purple, or variegated centrally in yellow, or yellow and red. The long-spurred 1½″–2½″ flowers may be white, lilac, pink, orange, or one of several shades of red. Pinch to force branching. Mostly propagated from cuttings; seed strains are becoming available. New Guinea area.

niamniamensis   RED   SU   1′–2.5′/1′–1.5′

◑ ●   Z10/T   CS ✶✶✶

The robust stem bears alternate, long-stalked, ovate to elliptic leaves to 8″ long, concentrated in the upper part of the plant. Slender-stalked flowers arise from crowded, terminal axils or form axillary clusters along the stem. The red lip is swollen and recurved; the white or greenish standard and wings are much reduced. Tropical Africa.
———— 'Congo Cockatoo.' The flower, shaped like a flattened cornucopia, has a yellow lip ending in a recurved red spur and pale green, laterally compressed petals. Children find it entrancing.

oliveri   PINK   SP-F   4′–8′/2′–3′

◑ ●   Z10-9/T   CS ✶✶✶

Of shrublike stature, this plant makes large stands of erect, lightly branched stems. Whorls of 4–8 sharp-toothed, oblanceolate leaves to 8″ long. Long-spurred, pink, lavender, or lilac 2″–2½″ flowers are borne on slender stalks from the leaf axils. Very free flowering, all year in frost-free climates. Tolerates sun in mild coastal areas. Grows back from the roots if cut down by frost. Plant in a location sheltered from strong winds. East Africa. *I. tinctoria* of eastern Africa has stout, erect 3′–6′ stems and small-toothed, elliptic 4″–9″ leaves. Fragrant, white 1½″–2½″ flowers in loose racemes. Each flower has a long, slender spur and a small standard. The wings are 2 lobed; the upper lobes small, the lower large and streaked with pink or purple.

wallerana   VARIOUS   SU   6″–2′/6″–1.5′

◑ ●   Z10/T   CS ✶✶✶✶

Busy Lizzy. [*I. holstii, I. sultanii*]. Erect to spreading, with branching stems. Mostly alternate, the crenulate 1″–3″ leaves are lanceolate to ovate or elliptic. The foliage is concentrated in leafy rosettes in the upper part of the plant. Clustered or solitary 1″–2″ flowers with long, slender spurs are borne continuously. They range from white to pinks, oranges, and various shades of red, as well as bicolors, in single, semidouble, and double-flowered forms, some with variegated foliage. Breeders have developed dwarfs, semidwarfs, and early-flowering forms. The variety of cultivars and strains is bewildering. To be assured of your color preference, buy flats of plants in bloom; they reach flowering size very early. Seeds are best selected from catalog descriptions. Pinch to encourage fullness. East Africa.

Incarvillea delavayi

INCARVILLEA, Bignoniaceae. (14) **Hardy Gloxinia**

The Hardy Gloxinias contribute an exotic splash of color to the early summer border. Their odd-pinnate leaves appear late, often at the same time as the purplish pink, trumpet-shaped flowers. The deep, well-drained soils they favor must be kept moist during flowering time. In hot climates, avoid full sun. Protect from slugs.

---

delavayi	PINK	LSP/ESU	2′–3′/1′
	○	ZI0-5/H	DS ***

Hardy Gloxinia. Handsome clumps of essentially basal, arching, dark green foliage. The compressed stem bears alternate leaves to 1′ long, with 8 or more pairs of toothed, ovate leaflets; the terminal one is obovate and lobed. Loose clusters of showy 2″ flowers on strong stems; the corollas are flaring 5-lobed trumpets, bright purplish pink with yellow throats. Their fleshy, fanglike roots are best divided in spring. Winter protection is recommended in colder zones. China.

---

mairei	PINK	LSP/ESU	1′/1′
	○	ZI0-4/H	DS **

Very similar to *I. delavayi.* Its leaves have fewer pairs of lateral leaflets. The more commonly grown *I. m. grandiflora* [*I. grandiflora*] has even fewer leaflets and spectacular flowers reaching 3″ or 4″ in diameter. China.

The yellow Daisy-like flower heads of Inulas brighten sunny borders and cutting gardens throughout the summer. Solitary or in clusters, the flower heads are usually large, composed of slender, 3-toothed rays, surrounding a disk of yellow, tubular florets. The hemispherical or bell-shaped involucre consists of several rows of bracts, sometimes conspicuously leafy or hairy. All are of strictly erect habit. Some, such as *I. racemosa,* are so coarse as to be suitable only for spacious, naturalistic plantings, where they make massive stands. These generally low-maintenance plants require only a well-drained soil.

| *ensifolia* | YELLOW | SU | 1′–2′/1′ |
| | ○ ◑ | Z9-3 | DS **** |

Swordleaf Inula. This dense, clump-former bristles with sessile, pointed, linear 4″ leaves, hairy along the margins. Its stiff, unbranched stems are topped with solitary, bright yellow 1″–2″ flower heads, backed by softly downy involucral bracts. Mildew may be a problem. Blooms the first season from an early spring seeding. Caucasus. *Buphthalmum salicifolium,* sometimes listed as *I.* 'Golden Beauty,' may be of hybrid origin. It is taller and earlier blooming than *I. ensifolia.*

| *helenium* | YELLOW | SU-F | 6′–7′/3′ |
| | ○ | Z9-3 | DRS *** |

Elecampane. The robust, branched stems are ridged and hairy, clothed in coarse foliage, bristly above, softly velvety beneath. Its oblong lower leaves, to 2′ in length,

Inula ensifolia

narrow toward the petiole; the pointed, ovate stem leaves, cordate at the base, are sessile. Fine-rayed, bright yellow flower heads, surrounded by leafy involucral bracts and clustered loosely on long stalks, are a full 3″ across, but are dwarfed by this massive plant. Widely naturalized but probably endemic to central Asia. Showier *I. magnifica* [*I. afghanica* Hort.] is even larger, with hairy stems and broad, rough foliage. Large clusters of deep yellow 5″–6″ daisies, brown in bud, bloom in late summer. Caucasus. Both are seen to best advantage grouped informally in an open setting or backed by dark-leaved shrubs, such as *Cotinus coggygria* 'Purpureus.'

hookeri	YELLOW	LSU-F	1.5′–2.5′/2′
	○	Z9-4	DS **

Hooker Inula. Broad clumps of branching stems, well clothed in softly pubescent, broadly linear 4″ leaves, denticulate along the margins. Its pale greenish yellow 3″ flower heads have slender rays. Prefers damp soils, where it will spread into substantial colonies. Usually needs staking. Himalayas.

orientalis	YELLOW	LSU	1.5′–2′/1.5′
	○	Z9-3	DS **

Caucasian Inula. [*I. glandulosa*]. Similar to *I. ensifolia,* with oblong 6″ leaves, clasping at the base. The woolly buds open into showy, orange yellow 3″ flower heads, with a raised central disk and narrow, rather shaggy rays. Useful for the front of the border. Caucasus.

royleana	YELLOW	SU	1′–2′/1.5′
	○	Z9-3	DS ***

Himalayan Elecampane. One of the best. A hairy plant with stout, unbranched stems and clasping, ovate leaves to 1′ long below. The solitary, terminal, orange yellow 3″–5″ daisies are black in the bud. Will not tolerate dry soils. Himalayas.

IRIS, Iridaceae. (300)

Named for the Greek messenger of the gods whose rainbow spanned the gap between heaven and earth, the Iris is sometimes known as the Rainbow Flower. Irises have been cultivated for centuries and feature prominently in literature, particularly for their herbal and medicinal properties, but also as a heraldic symbol. Extremely diverse, their natural habitats range from sea-level swamps to alpine meadows; in cultivation, they tend to be quite specific in their cultural requirements. Their underground storage organs, including bulbs, rhizomes, and rhizomatous rootstocks, give rise to linear leaves of various widths and textures, often grassy or in 2-ranked fans. Some species, such as *I. unguicularis,* are almost stemless, while some of the tall bearded sorts may have scapes reaching 3.5′ or more, which branch widely. Their elegant flowers are enclosed in the bud stage by 2 to several persistent bracts, usually termed spathes. These may be leaflike or papery; some are keeled, others linear or even expanded into a boat shape. Solitary or in few-flowered clusters, the unique blooms are so complex in structure that they require a terminology of their own. Their 6-parted perianths, tubular below, are composed of an outer row of segments or "falls," which narrow at their bases to a "haft." The falls are frequently darker in color than the rest of the flower, and may be decorated with a patch or "signal," contrasting veins, or a "beard," "crest," or ridge. The inner segments are known as the "standards," and narrow to a haft or claw below. Forming a cover or hood, the style branches protect the stamens and stigma, which are further protected by a stigma flap. As a whole, the genus can be divided into bulbous and nonbulbous types. Our concern is with the latter, which may be split into: *(a)* the broad-leaved, fleshy rhizomed, bearded or pogon types, such as *I.* x *germanica, (b)* the more narrow leaved, thick-rhizomed, beardless or apogon types, sometimes called Sibirica or Grass Iris, such as *I. sibirica,* and *(c)* the slender-rhizomed, crested types, such as *I. cristata.* These groups are further subdivided into numerous sections, subsections, and series. The American Iris Society concerns itself with all aspects of the genus *Iris* and has several branches, which concentrate on the different classes. The American Rock Garden Society has a strong interest in the smaller types of Iris, and has a seed exchange. In addition, specialist nurseries have large listings of the various types and offer information on their culture.

| **Bearded Iris** | VARIOUS | SP-ESU | 6″–4.5′/1′–2′ |
| | ○ | Z10-3/H | D **** |

This huge, hybrid complex of Pogon Irises encompasses innumerable selections. For convenience, the American Iris Society has subdivided them by height. Earliest to bloom are the Miniature Dwarfs or the Dwarf Iris group (MDB), to 8″ tall. The Standard Dwarfs or Barbata Nana group (SDB), 8″–15″ tall, bloom slightly later. The Medians, all 15″–28″ tall, cover (1) the Intermedias, known as the Iris-Barbata Median group (IB), (2) the Table Iris or Miniature Tall Bearded group (MTB), and (3) the Border Iris (BB). The Medians and the Standard Talls, Tall Bearded Iris, or Barbata Elatior group (TB), which top 28″, bloom more or less together in late spring. All arise from fleshy rhizomes, and their sometimes voluptuous flowers are characterized by bearded falls. Best in sunny positions, but some light shading is necessary in the hottest zones. They require free-draining soils, particularly during the winter. Water deeply during drought. Except in hot regions, where they should be set just below the surface, plant the horizontal rhizomes so that ½ to ⅓ of their diameter is exposed, to ripen in the sun after flowering. Traditionally, in cool climates, the foliage of the median and taller types is cut into a fan shape after flowering, at about 1′, in order to expose the rhizomes to more sun. Divide every 3–4 years, as the clumps die out in the center due to overcrowding. Many growers advocate dusting cut surfaces of the rhizome with a fungicide and allowing them to dry for a day or so before replanting. Iris borer, which is followed by bacterial or fungal infections of the rhizomes, is the most serious pest. The rhizomes must be destroyed to prevent the spread of borers; contaminated soil should also be removed. Aphids and thrips cause damage to the flowers and spread virus diseases; control with insecticides. Large numbers of named selections are available. Each year the American Iris Society publishes a list of the most popular, and gardeners should consult this, as well as the catalogs of specialist nurseries.

chrysographes	VIOLET	SU	1′–2′/1′
	○ ◑	Z9-7	DS ***

Of the Apogon types, this is one of the most beautiful. Its stout rhizomes give rise to light green, linear leaves about 1.5′ long by ½″ wide. The hollow, unbranched flower stems end in 1 or 2 fragrant, beardless 2¼″–2¾″ flowers. Their deeply drooping, oblong 2¼″ falls are dark reddish violet, with golden yellow veining, flecks, and hafts; the oblanceolate standards are deep violet. Cultivars include 'Rubella,' with deep wine red flowers, and 'Black Knight,' which has close to black, very dark blue flowers. Yunnan, Szechuan, northeastern Burma. From the same region, *I. bulleyana* may be a natural hybrid between *I. forrestii* and *I. chrysographes.* Its slightly larger flowers have obovate, cream falls, flecked and tipped with purplish blue, and spreading, light purplish blue standards. *I. forrestii,* is 1′–1.5′ tall. Its slender, lustrous leaves are gray green on one side. Above them the unbranched flower stems end in 1–2 fragrant yellow 2″ flowers; their falls are traced and dotted with brownish purple, their standards are erect. From wet areas of Yunnan and Szechuan Provinces, vigorous and later-blooming *I. delavayi* has gray green leaves, 2′–3′ long by 1″ wide. Pairs of 2½″–3½″ flowers grace each branch of the 2′–4.5′ scape. The almost circular falls range in color from light to dark purplish blue, emblazoned with a white signal down the center; the smaller, paler standards are oblique. Another late bloomer, *I. clarkei,* also belongs in this group. Its lustrous leaves, glaucous beneath, are 1½″–1¾″ wide. The solid, 1- to 3-branched stems may reach 2′ in length, each branch ending in a pair of 2¾″–3″ flowers. Their obovate falls range from medium blue violet to dark blue or purple, with a sizable white signal, veined in purple, and a yellowish haft; the violet standards are almost horizontal. All these species require moist, lime-free soil.

cristata	BLUE	SP	6″–10″/1′
	○ ◑	Z9-6	DS ***

Crested Iris, Dwarf Crested Iris. This woodlander's slender, creeping rhizomes spread widely, but not rapidly. The sword-shaped leaves, 4″–8″ in length by ⅓″–⅔″ wide, are arranged in fans and elongate after flowering time. Single or paired in each spathe, the sweetly fragrant, almost stalkless 1″–1½″ flowers are raised barely above the foliage by their 1½″–2″ perianth tubes. Colors range from pale lavender and lilac through blue, violet, and purple. The spreading, obovate 1½″ falls, crested in cream or yellow, have a large central white blotch rimmed in purple or violet; the monochrome standards are essentially upright. A useful, native ground cover for partly shaded places. Best in neutral, humus-rich soil. Water in sunny locations. A favorite of slugs. Maryland to Oklahoma and Georgia.

———— 'Alba' has pure white flowers, with a yellow crest.

———— 'Shenandoah Sky.' Pale lavender blue flowers.

———— 'Summer Storm' has deep blue flowers.

———— 'Vein Mountain.' This recent introduction from We-Du Nursery has very pale blue flowers with orange crests outlined in deep purple. Broad foliage.

| *douglasiana* | VARIOUS | LSP | 1'-2'/2' |
| | ◑ | Z9-8/H | DS ** |

[*I. douglasiana* var. *watsoniana* Hort., *I. watsoniana*]. One of the Pacific Coast Irises, this beardless type grows well in acid soils in light shade. Its evergreen, conspicuously veined, dark leaves, about ¾" wide, are somewhat coarse, taller than the flower stems and red flushed at the base near the reddish rhizomes. The variable flowers, in shades of mostly blue and purple, sometimes yellow or white, are borne on branched stalks in 2- to 3-flowered spathes; oblanceolate to obovate falls, about 3½" long, oblanceolate standards. Coastal Oregon, California. Some others in this group include *I. innominata* and *I. tenuissima,* also evergreen, and deciduous *I. tenax.* Seed is sometimes available but seldom offered in the trade. All are lime haters. Sun-loving *I. innominata* has been crossed with *I. douglasiana* resulting in the 'Pacific Coast Hybrids,' which are becoming well-known. Hardy in colder climates, probably to Z7, and tolerant of the hot, humid conditions of the East. None should be allowed to dry out. They prefer acid, humusy soils. Their flowers come in a splendid array of colors, in blues and yellows, with intricate patterns of veining.

| *ensata* | VARIOUS | SU | 2'-3'/1.5' |
| | ○ ◑ | Z10-5 | DS **** |

Japanese Iris, Japanese Water Iris. [*I. kaempferi* Hort]. Usually the last of the Irises to bloom, this Apogon type has stout rhizomes and broad, sword-shaped foliage. The leaves may reach 2' in length by 1½"-4¾" wide, with a conspicuous, raised midrib. Seldom branched, the longer flower stalks support 2-4 flowers, which range from white to reddish violet, blue, or purple. The size of the individual, rather flattish blooms varies from 4"-6" across, to 10" in some modern cultivars. The arching falls, about 3" long, are elliptic to ovate, often darkly veined, and blotched with yellow toward the base with yellow hafts; the almost horizontal, plain standards are a little smaller. At home in shallow standing water or very moisture-retentive soils free of lime. These beauties do not adapt well to hot, dry conditions. Divide and replant without delay, about 2" deep, after flowering or in fall. This is usually necessary every 3-4 years, as the plants become crowded. Northern China, Japan. Breeding programs have resulted in a wide range of cultivars, many of which are tetraploids. Yellow-flowered 'Rising Sun' and 'Aichi-No-Kagayaki' are hybrids between *I. ensata* and *I. pseudacorus.*
——————— 'Eleanor Parry' has deep lilac flowers, traced in purple.
——————— 'Favorite.' Medium blue flowers.
——————— 'Great White Heron' has semidouble, pure white flowers.
——————— 'Pink Lady is pink flowered.
——————— 'Royal Banner' has deep wine falls blotched in yellow.
Earlier blooming but closely related, *I. laevigata* is also water loving, but will tolerate lime. Its broader leaves lack the prominent midrib of *I. ensata;* the standards are more upright, the falls, pointed ovate. Cultivars include 'Alba,' a white-flowered form, and 'Regal,' a British introduction with rosy purple flowers. 'Variegata,' known as the Variegated Rabbitear Iris, has leaves bordered in cream and dark bluish purple flowers. Eastern Asia, China, Japan.

'Florentina'	BLUE	LSP	15″–2.5′/2′
	○	Z10-3	D **

Orris Root. [*I. florentina, I.* x *germanica* var. *florentina*]. This, the source of the orris root of perfumery, is now considered to be a variety of *I.* x *germanica* rather than a species in its own right. It belongs to the intermediate bearded (IB) group, and is probably of ancient origin. Its slightly glaucous green, ribbed leaves may reach 2′ tall by 1½″–2″ wide, and are arranged in spreading fans. Well branched, the stout stems support 4–5 very delicately fragrant, pale bluish white flowers, subtended by bracts, which become papery by flowering time. The lateral flowers are stemmed. The deeply recurved falls, to 3½″ long, have dark yellow beards and greenish yellow hafts; the erect standards, about 3¼″ tall, are wavy along the margins. Culture as for Bearded Iris. Naturalized in southern France, northwestern Africa, and southern Spain, but thought to originate in western and central Italy and some of the Mediterranean islands. 'Albicans,' also now reduced in status to *I.* x *germanica* var. *albicans,* is similar, and often the two are confused. However, its stems are largely unbranched, and any lateral flowers are sessile, lying close to the stem. They are subtended by blunt, purple-flushed bracts, papery only at their tips. The beard is white, tipped with yellow. There is a blue-flowered form, 'Madonna.' Saudi Arabia, Yemen.

foetidissima	MAUVE	SP/SU	1.5′–2.5′/2′
	○ ●	Z10-7	DS ***

Stinking Iris, Gladdon Iris, Gladwyn Iris, Scarlet-Seeded Iris. Basal tufts of tough, glossy, evergreen foliage rise from slow-spreading, compact rhizomes. The dark green, lanceolate leaves are 2′–4′ long by ¾″ wide, malodorous when crushed. Flattened on one side, the shorter flower stalks branch 2 or 3 times, each branch ending in 1–3 flowers, which open consecutively. There may be as many as a dozen flowers per spike. Beardless, the discreet 2″–2½″ flowers have dull yellow falls, darkly veined in purple, creating a mauve brown effect; their hafts, almost as wide as the falls, are winged. The outward curving, bronzy yellow standards are shorter than the falls. In early autumn, the club-shaped seed capsules split widely into 3 sections, each with 2 rows of scarlet, sometimes yellow or white, round seeds, which remain decorative throughout the winter. These germinate readily if sown as soon as ripe, but the seedlings take 4–5 years to reach flowering size. White and yellow seeds germinate into scarlet-seeded offspring. Tolerant of dry to damp but not waterlogged soils. A little added lime and humus is beneficial. For the best display, fertilize lightly in spring and water deeply during dry spells. The foliage browns at the tips and becomes ragged in windy sites. Control leaf miners and be alert for virus-infected plants, which must be destroyed. Poisonous to cattle. Western Europe, northwestern Africa. Superior 'Citrina' is larger throughout. Its pale yellow flowers are veined in purple. There are also forms with white flowers, heavily veined in purple. Rarely a true blue-flowered form is available, occasionally a double. 'Variegata' has attractive green and gold variegated foliage well into the winter, but is essentially sterile and seldom sets seed. The excellent hybrid 'Holden Clough' is probably *I. foetidissima* x *I. chrysographes.* Its golden yellow flowers, overlaid with purple veining, appear to be brown, with a yellow blotch on the falls. Vigorous and free blooming, especially in its preferred moist soil.

| x *germanica* | VARIOUS | LSP | 1.5'–2.5'/2' |
| | ○ | Z10-3/H | D **** |

German Iris, Flag Iris. Of unknown origin, this old hybrid of cottage gardens is similar in habit to the Intermediate (IB) and Tall Bearded (TB) types, of which it is a parent. It is a very tough, easy-to-grow plant, tolerant of a wide range of conditions, although regrettably these attributes have not been passed along to its modern offspring. It makes upright clumps of glaucous, 2-ranked leaves, about 1½″ wide, above which rise taller, branched scapes. Each branch is about 2″ long, and ends in a 2- to 3-flowered, short, boat-shaped spathe, green or purplish below, brownish and papery above. The pendent, obovate, deep violet falls may reach 3″ long, with yellow-tipped white beards and yellow-flushed hafts; the paler standards are arching and obovate. Flower color is variable. Probably from the Mediterranean region. The countless hybrids that have resulted from its crosses have spawned an entire industry. (See entry for Bearded Iris.)

| **Louisiana Iris** | VARIOUS | SP/SU | 6″–4'/1'–1.5' |
| | ○ ◑ | Z9-4/T | D ** |

The Louisiana Iris group, botanically termed the Hexagonae series of the Apogon type, is comprised of several species and their hybrids. These include *I. fulva* [*I. cuprea*] with brick-colored flowers, *I. brevicaulis* [*I. foliosa, I. lamancei*] with blue flowers, *I. giganticaerulea* with blue violet flowers, *I. hexagona* with white and purple flowers, and reddish purple or yellow-flowered *I. nelsonii.* All are native to the wetlands of the South, especially to the Mississippi basin. Where their ranges cross, they interbreed readily and natural hybrids abound. Breeding programs have also resulted in several notable hybrids, such as *I.* x *fulvala (I. fulva* x *I. brevicaulis).* These are known as the 'Louisiana Hybrids' or sometimes *I.* x 'Louisiana.' Detailed information may be obtained from the Society for Louisiana Irises. Their elegant flowers, without crests or beards, come in an extremely wide range of colors. Well adapted to moist borders, the taller sorts make fine cut flowers. They do not demand very wet soils, and tolerate but do not require lime. Plant about 2″ deep in late fall and mulch heavily. Propagation is by division of the slender rhizomes.

| *pallida* | LAVENDER | LSP | 3'–4'/2' |
| | ○ | Z10-3/H | D ** |

Orris. [*I. glauca, I. odorissima, I. pallido-coerulea*]. Also grown for the production of orris for the perfumery trade. This is one of the original ancestors of the modern Tall Bearded Iris (TB). Extremely variable, and split into subspecies and varieties by most authorities. Its almost evergreen, beautiful, silvery gray green 2' leaves are about 1½″ wide. Rigid and robust, the few-branched scapes rise well above and bear several fragrant flowers in each conspicuous, papery, silver spathe. The laterals lie almost vertically close to the main stem on short pedicels. Larger *I. p. dalmatica* is superior to the species and has clear lavender blue flowers, bearded in yellow. *I. p. d.* 'Variegata' ['Argenteo-variegata,' *I. p.* 'Variegata'] has leaves striped in cream; it may be listed as 'Zebra.' 'Alba-variegata' has white-striped leaves, those of 'Aurea-variegata' are yellow striped.

Iris pallida dalmatica 'Variegata'

| *pseudacorus* | YELLOW | ESU | 2.5′–6′/1.5′ |
| | ◗ | Z9-4 | DS ✱✱✱✱ |

Yellow Iris, Yellow Flag, Water Flag. [*I. bastardii, I. lutea*]. One of the Laevigatae series, of the Apogon type. In time, the vigorous rhizomes colonize large patches, particularly in damp soil, alongside streams and lakes. Rather coarse, glaucous green, sword-shaped leaves to 5′ long or more by ½″–1¼″ wide. The slender, branching stems, as long as the leaves, bear 3–5 beardless flowers to 4″ across in each leafy, lanceolate spathe. The pale to deep yellow, ovate 2″ falls have a darker yellow, central zone with brown or violet veining radiating from it; some forms lack both. Narrowly oblong to elliptic, the ¾″–1″ standards are horizontal, ascending at their tips; the stigma flaps are bilobed. Self-seeds readily; remove the attractive, lustrous, green seed capsules before they split. Generally considered to be the "Fleur de lis" of the kings of France and possibly the biblical "lilies of the field." At their best in large, landscape settings in shallow water or close to it; they adapt well to border conditions if the soil is moist. Cut flowers last well. Naturalized in damp areas of eastern North America. Native to Western Europe, North Africa.

———— 'Alba.' Not really white, but very pale, cream yellow flowers.

———— 'Bastardii' has pale yellow flowers without dark veining.

———— 'Flora Plena' is an unusual, double-flowered form.

———— 'Variegata' has very attractive yellow- and cream-striped leaves, which regrettably age to green before summer's end. Striking in a foliage combination with *Hosta sieboldiana* 'Elegans.'

| *pumila* | VARIOUS | SP | 9″/1′ |
| | ○ | ZI0-3 | D *** |

[*I. aequiloba, I. taurica*]. This ancestor of the modern Dwarf Iris (MDB) rises from rhizomatous roots. Its gray green, sword-shaped leaves, in tufted fans of 3–5, reach only 4″ long by flowering time, but elongate to twice that length afterward. Usually a single flower rises on a very short stalk and is elevated by its 2″–3″ perianth tube, enclosed by 2 long bracts. The fragrant 2″ flowers are variable in color. The oblong standards and reflexed falls may be yellow to blue or purple, the latter with a white, yellow, or bluish beard. There are numerous color forms. Possibly of hybrid origin. Good at the front of the border or in rock gardens in well-drained, limy soil. Avoid fertilizers high in nitrogen. Not always easy; division increases its longevity. Central Europe to southern Russia, Asia Minor.

| *sibirica* | VARIOUS | LSP/ESU | 2′-4′/3′ |
| | ○ ◑ | ZI0-4 | DS **** |

Siberian Irises form elegant, upright clumps of slightly arching, narrow, linear foliage. Their bright green leaves in slender sheaves are about ½″–¾″ wide, ribbed and

Iris sibirica 'Mountain Lake'

thickened along the midrib. Above rise strong, hollow, sparsely branched stems; 1 or 2 typically blue or violet 2″–3″ flowers, subtended by a long, leaflike or papery bract, top each branch. The reflexed, obovate or rounded falls, ¾″–1½″ across, have a large central blotch, white or heavily veined in purple, which spreads down the narrowing haft. The shorter, broadly linear to ovate standards are erect. Its dark brown, elliptical pods, which follow the flowers, are 1″–2″ long, triangular in cross section; useful for dried winter arrangements. Central Europe, Russia. Oriental *I. sanguinea* [*I. sibirica* var. *orientalis, I. orientalis*] is similar, and both are involved in the parentage of the many Siberian Iris selections currently available. All are fine border plants, combining well with other perennials as well as shrubs. As cut flowers, they last only 1 or 2 days. They bloom just after the bulk of the Bearded Iris and before the Japanese types. Tolerant of a broad range of soils, they do best where it is neutral or slightly acid, well enriched with moisture-retentive humus. Water deeply during dry spells. They thrive in full sun, except in the hottest zones, but bloom well in lightly dappled shade such as is found under high-pruned deciduous trees. Divide to propagate or when clumps become crowded in late summer or fall. These very tough, easy, and reliable plants are essentially free of pests and diseases.

———————— 'Caesar's Brother.' Very erect, with velvety, deep purple flowers on 3′ stems.

———————— 'Dreaming Spires' has large, deep lavender flowers with bright blue falls. 2.5′ tall.

———————— 'Eric the Red.' Purplish wine flowers. 3′ in height.

———————— 'Flight of Butterflies' has intricately patterned, delicate, violet blue flowers.

———————— 'Little White' is a diminuitive white cultivar. 15″.

———————— 'Mountain Lake.' Clear blue flowers on strong 2′–2.5′ stems.

———————— 'Orville Fay.' This tetraploid has medium blue 4″–5″ flowers with darker veining. 3′ tall.

———————— 'Perry's Pygmy' has dainty blue flowers on slender 2.5′–3′ stems. A British introduction.

———————— 'Sky Wings.' Pale blue with a yellow blaze. 2.5′–3′.

———————— 'White Swirl' is gently ruffled, pure white, the throat barely splashed with yellow. 2.5′–3′.

tectorum	VARIOUS	ESU	8″–1′/1′
	○ ◑	Z10-4	DS ***

Japanese Roof Iris. This crested Iris, of the Evansia group, has stout, greenish rhizomes, unusually similar to those of the Bearded Iris. Almost evergreen, its pale, rather lax, thin-textured leaves are broadly lanceolate, 1.5′ long by 1″–1½″ wide, arranged in fans. Branched flower stalks as long as the foliage have 2–3 flowers subtended by each spathe. Appearing almost star shaped, the flattish 3″–4″ blooms have purplish blue or lilac, slightly deflexed, obovate 2″ falls, marked with darker streaks toward their tips; the lilac 1½″ standards spread widely. The undulating margins and very dissected, white crest of the falls, as well as the irregularly toothed margins of the 2-lobed-style branches, present a frilly effect. The rhizomes tend to push themselves out of the ground and benefit from a heavy mulch each spring and fall. Soil should be rich, moist, and slightly acid. Protect from slugs. Divide after flowering time. For best effect, plant in drifts at the front of the border or in the rock garden. Central and southwestern China. ———————— 'Album' has delicate white flowers with yellow hafts.

| *unguicularis* | LILAC | LF/ESP | 1′–1.5′/2′ |
| | ○ ◑ | Z10-8/H | DS ** |

Winter Iris. [*I. stylosa*]. This small, tuft-forming Iris unfurls its exquisite flowers during the dark days of winter. Its rhizomes produce evergreen, grassy ½″ leaves, which may reach 2′ long and often obscure the emerging flowers. Almost stemless, the solitary, fragrant 2″–3″ flowers are raised up on 2″–9″ perianth tubes. Their wedge-shaped, spreading, deep lavender or lilac falls are darkly veined around the central yellow signal; the uniform lavender standards are oblong and more or less erect. Variable in color; several forms, such as 'Marginata' and 'Walter Butt' have been named, but all are beautiful and worth seeking. Divide in early fall or after flowering, but only when the clumps become crowded or for propagation, since they resent disturbance. Rather temperamental and often shy to flower. Well-drained but moisture-retentive, slightly acid to alkaline soils in light shade are recommended in hot zones; in gentler climates, a warm position in full sun is favored. Traditionally, the addition of mortar rubble to the soil was suggested, no doubt both to improve drainage and to sweeten overly acid soils. The flowers are frequently marred by slug damage. Algeria, eastern Mediterranean.

| *versicolor* | BLUE | SP-SU | 1′–3′/2′ |
| | ○ ◑ | Z9-3 | DS ** |

Blue Flag, Wild Iris, Poison Flag. Of the Laevigatae series. This native, water-loving Iris is best suited to wet or boggy positions in informal areas, although border conditions are satisfactory if the soil is well supplied with humus. It forms vigorous clumps of upright or arching, rather glaucous, sword-shaped ½″–1″ leaves, 2′ or more in length, above which rise slightly longer, branched flower stalks. Each short green spathe encloses 2 or 3 lavender, blue, violet, or purple 2½″–3″ flowers; their widely spreading, ovate to kidney-shaped 2″ falls are often blotched in yellow and purple veined; their erect standards are smaller, usually paler in color. Good as a cut flower. Eastern Canada, northeastern and north central United States.

ISOPLEXIS, Scrophulariaceae. (3)

| *canariensis* | ORANGE | LSP/ESU | 3′–4′/2′ |
| | ○ | Z10-9 | CS ** |

[*Digitalis canariensis*]. This stiffly erect, evergreen subshrub with hairy, reddish stems becomes woody at the base with age. Its opposite leaves are lanceolate, to 6″ long, thick, shiny, and lightly toothed. Dense, terminal 1′ spikes of dark orange, 2-lipped flowers. The corolla is 5 lobed; the larger upper lip curves down over the lower. Needs a well-drained soil. Spectacular against a background of variegated *Phormium*. Canary Islands.

Isoplexis canariensis

Isotoma axillaris

ISOTOMA, Campanulaceae. (11)

axillaris	BLUE	SP	1'/1'–1.5'
	○	Z10-9	CDS ✱✱

[*Laurentia axillaris*]. Many-branched, slender stems with narrow 2″–3″ leaves, deeply and irregularly pinnately lobed. Light blue to lavender, axillary 1″ flowers. The nearly symmetrical corolla has a slender tube and 5 flaring, pointed lobes. Well-drained but fertile soils. Usually grown as an annual. Australia.

JASIONE, Campanulaceae. (10)

Not often grown, Jasiones deserve a wider audience. Lovely in the rock garden or at the front of the border, they furnish a succession of blue Scabious-like flowers on wiry stems for most of the summer. Excellent for cutting. They prefer a lean, sandy soil in full sun, but will tolerate shade for part of the day. Propagate in the fall.

laevis	BLUE	SU	9″–1.5'/1'
	○ ◐	Z9-6	DS ✱✱

Shepherd's Scabious, Sheep's-Bit. [*J. perennis, J. pyrenaica*]. The lower leaves, narrowly obovate and about 4″ long, form a grayish basal rosette; alternate, reduced stem

Jasione heldreichii

leaves. Numerous leafy, nonflowering shoots. The erect, hairy flower stems, sometimes branched, leafless above, are topped with 2″ globes of tiny, misty blue flowers. A stiff collar of bracts surrounds each head. Southern Europe. *J. jankae* is an extremely variable, taxonomically confused species, with smaller, spherical heads of pale to deep blue flowers. Now it is usually included in *J. heldreichii*.

————— 'Blue Light' has azure blue flowers on 2′ stems in mid to late summer.

JUSTICIA, Acanthaceae. (300)

brandegeana	WHITE	ALL YEAR	1′–3′/1.5′–3′
	○ ◗	Z10/T	CS ****

Shrimp Plant. [*Beloperone guttata, Drejerella guttata*]. This odd subshrub has weak, branching stems and opposite, softly hairy, ovate 1″–3″ leaves. Its small flowers, borne in arching, terminal spikes to 6″ long are nearly hidden by prominent, overlapping, bronze 1″ bracts. The corolla is white and 2 lipped, with reddish spots on the lower lip. Grows well in sun, but even better in very light shade. Well-drained soil. Pinch young plants to encourage fullness; cut back spent flowering stems. Also popular as a house-plant. Mexico.

————— 'Chartreuse' has yellow green bracts.
————— 'Jambalaya' has reddish bronze bracts.
————— 'Variegata,' leaves marked with cream.
————— 'Yellow Queen' has yellow bracts.

Justicia brandegeana 'Jambalaya'

KALANCHOE, Crassulaceae. (200)

Although most are grown as pot or greenhouse plants by collectors, a few species will serve outdoors in essentially frost-free southern gardens. They look best when combined with other succulents and need to be grown in the very free-draining but not infertile soil which such plants favor. Easily propagated from seed and by stem or leaf cuttings. Kalanchoes are extremely varied; some are grown for their flowers, others for their attractive foliage. Generally, these plants have branching stems, sometimes woody at the base, and opposite, fleshy leaves, entire, toothed, or more rarely pinnatifid. The numerous flowers in cymes are clustered into terminal panicles. The perianth is 4 parted; the corolla salverform or urceolate. The genus is taxonomically confused; as a result, many plants in the trade are sold under incorrect names.

beharensis	FOLIAGE	LW/F	4'–5'/3'
	○ ◑	Z10/T	CS ***

Feltbush, Felt Plant, Velvet Elephant-Ear, Velvetleaf. This curious plant at times exceeds its usual 4'–5' height, which is unfortunate, as its bare stems are most unattractive. The handsome 4"–15" leaves, clustered at the end of the stems, are roughly triangular, lobed and undulate, thickly felted with brown to gray hairs. Insignificant, yellowish, urn-shaped flowers in long-stalked, axillary inflorescences; blooms unpredictably. Try it behind a bronze-leaved *Phormium* or a clump of *Puya*. Madagascar.

| *blossfeldiana* | RED | W-ESP | $1'/1'$ |
| | ○ | Z10/T | CS **** |

[*K. globulifera* var. *coccinea*]. This popular, long-blooming species has branching stems and glossy, obovate 1″–3″ leaves, round toothed at their outer end. Dense cymes of tiny, scarlet, salverform flowers on stems of varying length above the compact mass of foliage. A large selection of cultivars and hybrids is available in yellow, orange, salmon, and shades of red, ranging in size from dwarf to vigorous forms. Extensively grown as a pot plant. Madagascar. *K. flammea*, 1.5′–2′ tall, has a looser habit and gray green leaves. Large, long-stemmed clusters of yellow to orange red 1″ flowers. Tropical Africa.

| *fedtschenkoi* | PINK | W-ESP | $1'-2'/1.5'$ |
| | ○ | Z10/T | CDS *** |

[*Bryophyllum fedtschenkoi*]. Branching and erect, except for the sterile stems which are decumbent and root along their length. Its glaucous, purple-tinged, obovate 1″–2″ leaves are tipped with rounded teeth. Long flower stalks, adorned with pairs of leaflike bracts and loose, terminal clusters of pendent, brownish pink ¾″ flowers. The calyx is inflated; the corolla lobes are short and spreading. Madagascar.
————— 'Marginata' has leaves edged with a cream band.

| *grandiflora* | YELLOW | ESP | $1.5'-2'/1.5'$ |
| | ○ | Z10/T | CS ** |

Erect stems crowded toward the end with round-toothed, broadly ovate to obovate 2″–3″ leaves, glaucous, gray green, and suffused with purple. Panicled cymes of lemon yellow, salverform ¾″ flowers. East Africa, India.

Kalanchoe grandiflora

Kensitia pillansii

Kirengeshoma palmata koreana

tomentosa	FOLIAGE	SU-LSU	1'–1.5'/1'
	○	Z10/T	CS ***

Panda Plant, Pussy-Ears. Both the branching stems and the close, fleshy foliage are velvety with soft grayish or silvery hairs. The alternate 1½"–3" leaves are oblong-obovate; their blades edged with coarse, blunt, brown teeth. Rather insignificant purple and yellow flowers on exceedingly long stalks. Madagascar.

KENSITIA, Aizoaceae. (1)

pillansii	PINK	ESP-SP	1'–2'/1.5'
	○	Z10/H	CS *

[*Piquetia pillansii*]. This shrubby succulent has erect, branching, reddish stems, and glaucous, 3-angled 1¼" leaves, opposite and just joined at the base. The solitary, terminal, pinwheel-shaped 2" flowers have purplish rose, spatulate petals, with long white claws and a domed center crowded with brilliant white stamens and staminodes. The spent flowers are persistent and unattractive; deadhead regularly. Needs well-drained soil. Drought tolerant. South Africa.

KIRENGESHOMA, Saxifragaceae. (1)

palmata	YELLOW	LSU/EF	3'–4'/2'–3'
	◐	Z9-5	DS ***

This elegant, shrublike plant has erect, purple stems, arching at the top. The opposite, Maple-like leaves are palmately lobed and toothed; the lower leaves are stalked. Pendent terminal or axillary cymes of pale yellow 1½" flowers. The corolla is campanulate and 5 petaled. Thrives in moist rich soils. Japan.
——— *koreana* [*K. p. erecta*] is slightly taller, with more erect inflorescences and more open flowers. Hardier than the species. Korea.

KNAUTIA, Dipsacaceae. (40)

macedonica	RED	SU	2'/2'
	○	Z10-5/H	DS **

[*Scabiosa macedonica, S. rumelica*]. A loosely erect, rather straggling plant, with many branched stems. The clumping, basal leaves are lyrate, the stem leaves entire to pinnately cut. Intense wine red, domed 2" heads, similar in shape to those of *Scabiosa columbaria*. Cultural requirements also as for *Scabiosa*. Rarely grown in this country, its hardiness is somewhat uncertain. For best effect, it needs a strong background, such as a stand of *Miscanthus sinensis* 'Variegatus.' Eastern and southeastern Europe.

Knautia macedonica

KNIPHOFIA, Liliaceae. (75)   Torch Lily

[*Tritoma*]. These old-fashioned favorites are found in the wild in tropical and southern Africa and in Madagascar. The genus is confused taxonomically, and most available plants are probably hybrids. Torch Lilies have undergone extensive breeding, resulting in plants with cream, yellow, and coral flowers, as well as the familiar two-toned yellow and red forms. Many of the newer kinds are more compact and better suited to small gardens. Along the way, their hardiness has been increased. They are valuable in borders or among shrubs, as well as in the cutting garden. The larger species are also useful for their bold foliage, frequently evergreen in mild climates. Dense mats of cordlike, fibrous roots underlie tufted clumps of arching, grassy leaves, above which rise strong, erect scapes topped with crowded, tapering racemes or "pokers" of drooping, tubular flowers. In most, the lower buds open first, the upper ones in succession over a long period. The perianth tubes are more or less cylindrical and expand into 6 short lobes; the stamens may or may not be exserted. Torch Lilies need protection from intense sun, but generally thrive in sunny positions. They should have a good, well-drained soil, amply supplied with humus. If the plants are allowed to dry out while buds are setting, flowers will be sparse. Once established, they resent disturbance, and require division only infrequently. Both planting and division should be done in spring; avoid setting more than 2″–3″ deep. In colder areas, tie the foliage over the crowns or protect with a heavy winter mulch of salt hay or leaves. Where they are not hardy, the plants must be lifted and stored. Blooming time varies and may be earlier in the warmest climates.

| *caulescens* | RED | EF | 3′–4′/2′ |
| | ○ | Z10-7 | D * |

Grown as much for its distinctive evergreen foliage as for its flowers, this species has very thick, trunklike stems which bear rosettes of overlapping, bluish green leaves, keeled and to 3′ long by about 3″ wide, with purplish blue bases. The dense 6″ spikes are carried aloft on thick, strong scapes. Coral red in bud, the flowers open to pale yellow, with conspicuously exserted stamens. Requires very well-drained soils or the crowns will rot. Eastern Cape Province, Lesotho.

| *triangularis* | RED | EF | 1′–2′/1.5′ |
| | ○ | Z10-7 | D * |

[*K. macowanii, K. nelsonii*]. This species is so variable that recent revisions have split it into 2 subspecies. Ssp. *triangularis* now includes the two species named as synonyms, as well as *K. galpinii* Hort. It makes thick, grassy clumps of strongly keeled leaves, triangular in cross section. Slender, wiry stems bear elegant pokers of well-spaced, flame, orange, or orange red flowers with flaring perianth lobes. Its blooming period extends well into the fall. Ssp. *obtusiloba* has wider, less grassy leaves and small spikes of only orange flowers. The species has contributed its small stature to many of the modern forms.

| *uvaria* | RED | SP-F | 3′–4′/3′ |
| | ○ | Z10-6 | D *** |

Red Hot Poker, Common Torch Lily, Poker Plant. [*K. alooides, Tritoma uvaria*]. One of the parents of most of the modern hybrids, it has largely been replaced by them. It is a variable species, forming heavy clumps of gray green foliage. The sword-shaped leaves are about 3′ long by 1″ wide, often keeled and abrasive along the margins. Tall, stiff scapes bear cylindrical 8″–10″ pokers of 1″–2″ flowers, bright red in bud, maturing to bright yellow or orange. Cape Peninsula. *K. praecox* is a splendid, more robust version, attaining 6′ in height. It was formerly known as *K. u.* 'Nobilis,' *K. u.* 'Grandiflora,' or *K. alooides* 'Maxima.' Spikes to 7″ or so long of scarlet flowers, aging to orange.

Hybrids

Over the years, numerous hybrids and cultivars have been named. Some have stood the test of time, but others have been lost. There is some overlapping of names, in spite of recent attempts to untangle them. A sampling of the range of *Kniphofia* selections follows; new ones are being added every year.

'Ada.' Deep tawny gold spikes on 3′–3.5′ stems. Summer.

'Earliest of All' has long, soft coral red pokers on 2.5′ scapes. Early summer.

'Gold Mine,' an American cultivar, has deep yellow flowers on 2.5′–3′ stems in late summer.

Kniphofia 'Ada'

'Little Maid.' Very long, narrow, creamy white spikes in late summer. 2' tall. A Beth Chatto introduction.

'Pfitzeri' has deep orange flowers on 2'–2.5' stems. Plants sold under this name may vary in height and color.

'Primrose Beauty' has graceful, soft yellow flowers in early summer. 2.5' tall.

'Royal Standard' is an old Pritchard (Christchurch, New Zealand) cultivar for midsummer bloom. Vermilion and acid yellow pokers on 3' stems.

'Springtime' is another midsummer bloomer, despite its name. Yellow and coral two-toned flowers on 3.5' stems.

'Vanilla' is small and elegant, with early, pale yellow flowers. 2' tall.

LACTUCA, Compositae. (100)

[*Cicerbita, Mulgedium*]. This genus is represented in the flower garden by just a few species. All have small, pale blue or lavender, ligulate flower heads, surrounded by several rows of involucral bracts and arranged in loose panicles, on tall, milky-sapped stems. Any well-drained soil is suitable; water deeply during dry periods. Shade from scorching sun. Some are highly invasive, particularly *L. bourgaei;* once established, it is impossible to eradicate! Admire from afar.

Lactuca bourgaei

alpina	BLUE	SU	3'–6'/3'
	○	Z9-2/H	DS **

Mountain Thistle, Blue Sow Thistle. [*Cicerbita alpina, Mulgedium alpinum*]. Stout, erect stems, the upper parts covered with reddish hairs, rise from a basal rosette of lyrate 8″ leaves, with a large terminal lobe; stem leaves alternate and much reduced. The pale blue ¾″ flower heads are encircled by a double row of purplish green involucral bracts. Suitable for smaller gardens; it seldom reaches its full height, especially in cold climates. Arctic and alpine Europe. *L. plumieri* is similar, with hairless 4' stems and loose clusters of deep blue or violet flower heads. Central Europe.

bourgaei	BLUE	SU-F	4'–8'/3'
	○	Z9-6/H	DS **

Blue Sow Thistle. [*Mulgedium bourgaei*]. The thick but brittle invasive roots give rise to rosettes of hirsute, fiddle-shaped, basal leaves. Leafy, well-branched, wandlike stems carry large, loose panicles of lavender flower heads, with pink involucral bracts. Self-seeds very freely. Asia Minor.

LAMIASTRUM, Labiatae. (1)

Formerly included under *Lamium, Lamiastrum* [*Galeobdolon*] now has a genus of its own. It has been segregated because of its yellow flowers, as well as minor differences

Lamiastrum galeobdolon 'Variegatum'

in floral structure. Yellow Archangel is a valuable plant for woodland or shady gardens, either in groups or closely planted as a ground cover. Evergreen except where winters are severe. The variegated form is grown for its silver-splashed foliage, which stands out so well, especially in dark corners. Average, well-drained but moisture-retentive soils. Slugs and snails need control.

| *galeobdolon* | YELLOW | SU | 1′–2′/2′ |
| | ☽● | Z9-3 | CDS **** |

Yellow Archangel. [*L. luteum, Lamium galeobdolon, Galeobdolon luteum*]. A vigorous, often hairy plant with surface runners, which root at the nodes. Their slender, square stems have long internodes and are erect or trailing. The opposite and decussate 1½″–3″ leaves are ovate to heart shaped, with round-toothed margins. A whorl of hairy, 2-lipped flowers is borne in the axils of each pair of upper leaves, forming a loose spike. The bright yellow ½″–1″ corollas are marked with brown; the upper lip forms a hood over the lower, which is evenly 3 lobed and drooping. Cut back after flowering for neatness. Spreads rapidly. Europe.

———— 'Herman's Pride' has smaller, dark green, metallic leaves, flecked with silver. Makes neat mounds about 8″ tall.

———— 'Variegatum' ['Florentinum']. Its foliage is broadly marked with silver, leaving only green midribs and margins. Sometimes reverts to solid green.

LAMIUM, Labiatae. (40) Dead Nettle

Dead Nettles are easy plants for shady places, with much the same uses as *Lamiastrum*. They differ in the shape of their pink or white, 2-lipped flowers. The lower lip of the corolla is divided into a large, central lobe and 2 minute laterals. As is typical of the Mint family, the stems are square; well clothed in more or less evergreen, opposite and decussate leaves. Shear in midsummer after the first flush of bloom to promote compact growth. Tolerates dry shade. In some parts of the country, Dead Nettles have escaped from gardens and become naturalized, proof of their invasive tendencies. Be alert for slugs.

| *album* | WHITE | SP-LSU | 1′–2′/1′ |
| | ☽● | Z10-3 | CD *** |

White Dead Nettle, Snowflake, Archangel. Its leafy, decumbent stems are usually unbranched. The softly hairy 3″ leaves are ovate and pointed, with round-toothed margins. Pure white, hairy 1″ flowers arranged in verticillasters, in the upper leaf axils. Europe, Asia.

| *maculatum* | PINK | SP-LSU | 1′–1.5′/1′ |
| | ☽● | Z10-3 | CD **** |

Spotted Dead Nettle. Similar to *L. album,* but more compact, with blunt leaves, painted

Lamium maculatum 'Album'

with greenish white along the midrib. Pink or purplish 1″ flowers. Europe, Asia. The cultivars are superior to the species and less invasive.

————— 'Album' has cream white flowers and paler green and white leaves.

————— 'Aureum.' Pink flowers and golden leaves with a broad white midrib.

————— 'Beacon Silver' has rosy pink flowers. The silver leaves are edged in green. Requires shade. Less hardy than the species. Popular for hanging baskets. 6″–8″ tall.

————— 'Chequers.' Deep mauve pink flowers. Leaves with a central, silver flash. 8″–1′ in height.

————— 'White Nancy' is a lovely sparkling, white-flowered version of 'Beacon Silver.' Tolerates sun where soil is moist. Hardy to Z3. 6″–8″.

LAMPRANTHUS, Aizoaceae. (178)

These succulent, South African subshrubs are not subtle plants; they are closely covered with flowers in season. Gardeners who are unafraid of brilliant colors will be rewarded by electrifying displays of bloom. Ranging from erect to sprawling, with branching stems, they bear many slender, curved, 3-angled or cylindrical leaves in opposite pairs, often joined at the base. Terminal or axillary flowers, solitary or in cymes. The individual flower is Daisy-shaped, with several rows of narrow petals. Drought resistant. Well-drained soils. Renew tired plantings when necessary from easily rooted cuttings. A large genus; the species are difficult of identification except by a specialist. Often mislabeled in the trade; buy plants in flower to obtain desired colors. In addition to the

Lampranthus spectabilis

common species described, several others are worth growing when available: *L. blandus* has very pale pink flowers; *L. eximius, L. roseus,* and *L. watermeyeri* are various shades of brighter pink; *L. coccineus* is a brilliant red; *L. vernalis* and *L. zeyheri* are purple flowered. (See *Carpobrotus.*)

| *aurantiacus* | ORANGE | W-SP | 1′–1.5′/1.5′–2′ |
| | ○ | Z10-9/H | CS **** |

Erect to spreading stems. Gray green, 3-angled leaves, about 1″ long, rough with small papillae. Solitary, bright orange 1½″–2″ flowers. South Africa.
———— 'Glaucus' has brilliant yellow flowers.
———— 'Sunman' is golden yellow.
Similar *L. aureus* has red-tipped, smooth 2″ leaves with a waxy bloom. Orange 2″ flowers.

| *productus* | PURPLE | EW-ESP | 1′–1.5′/1.5′–2′ |
| | ○ | Z10-9/H | CS **** |

Much-branched stems. Gray green, nearly cylindrical 1″–1½″ leaves with bronze tips. Purple 1″ flowers. South Africa.

| *spectabilis* | VARIOUS | LW-SP | 1′/1.5′–2′ |
| | ○ | Z10-9/H | CS **** |

Prostrate to decumbent stems, with leaves crowded on short branches. Glaucous, gray green, 3-angled leaves, 2″–3″ long, with red tips. Purple, red, rose, or pink 2″–3″ flowers. South Africa.

Lathyrus vernus

LATHYRUS, Leguminosae. (130)

While climbing species, notably *L. odoratus,* the annual Sweet Pea, dominate this genus, it also includes some worthwhile, nonclimbing perennials. All have conspicuous racemes of Pea-like flowers and alternate, odd-pinnate leaves. The terminal leaflet sometimes ends in a tendril.

| *japonicus* | | PURPLE | ESU-LSU | 1.5′/2′ |
| | | ○ | Z9-3 | S ** |

Beach Pea, Sea Pea. [*L. maritimus, L. maritimus japonicus*]. A rather sprawling plant, with weak, angled stems. The thick, glaucous, blue leaves bear 3–6 pairs of pointed, oval 1″–2″ leaflets, and end in a branched tendril. A pair of large, leafy, sagittate stipules girds each node. Racemes of 5–10 showy flowers; the standard or banner is bright purple, the wings and keel paler. Best planted in spring. The creeping rootstock spreads freely. Well suited to sandy soils; salt tolerant. Northern United States, Asia.

| *luteus* | | YELLOW | ESU | 1′–2′/1′ |
| | | ○ | Z9-3 | DS ** |

[*L. gmelinii, Orobus luteus*]. Erect, unbranched stems, with 3″–4½″ leaves, each consisting of 3–5 pairs of oval leaflets, green above, but attractively glaucous beneath. Tendrils absent. Axillary racemes of bright yellow 1″ flowers on long stems. Suitable for the front of the border or rock garden. Europe.
——— *aureus* [*O. aurantiacus*] has branched stems and fresh green leaves. Loose racemes of unusual fawn flowers. Turkey.

| *vernus* | | PURPLE | LSP-ESU | 6″–12″/1′ |
| | | ○ | Z9-4 | DS *** |

Spring Vetchling. [*Orobus vernus*]. Neat clumps of many erect stems, some branched. The leaves are composed of 2–3 pairs of shiny, pointed, ovate leaflets. Racemes of 4–8 nodding ¾″ flowers on 15″ stems; corolla reddish purple, changing to blue with age. Prefers a deep, moist soil. Europe.
——— 'Roseus.' Early flowering with pink flowers on 1′ stems.
——— 'Spring Delight.' Creamy pink flowers. 15″ tall.
——— 'Spring Melody' has violet blue flowers. 12″–15″.
——— 'Variegatus' [*L. v. albo-roseus*]. Pink and white flowers on 15″ stems.

LAURENTIA, Campanulaceae. (25)

| *petraea* | | WHITE | SP-F | 1′–1.5′/2′ |
| | | ○ | Z10-9 | CDS ** |

[*Isotoma petraea*]. This spreading plant has erect stems, and alternate, ovate-lanceolate leaves, to 2½″ long, with large, jagged, irregular teeth. Solitary white or lilac 1½″ flowers. The long-tubed, asymmetrical corolla has 5 nearly equal lobes; the upper lip

Laurentia fluviatilis

is 2 lobed, the lower, 3 lobed. Well-drained but fertile soil. Very long blooming. Australia. Hardier, blue-flowered *Laurentia fluviatilis* is a charming, prostrate ground cover.

LAVATERA, Malvaceae. (25)

cachemiriana	PINK	SU	4'–8'/3'–4'
	○	Z9-4	S ***

An elegant, erect, long-blooming subject for the back of the border. Its softly hairy, crenate 2"–3" leaves are heart shaped to rounded, 5 lobed below and 3–5 lobed above. The large, clear pink, Mallow-like 2"–3" flowers are borne in the upper leaf axils. Each corolla has 5 silky, deeply notched petals. This sturdy plant does not need staking. Sow seeds in place. Kashmir. Similar *L. thuringiaca* from southern Europe is less tall and has rose pink flowers.

LEONOTIS, Labiatae. (30)

leonurus	ORANGE	SU-F	4'–7'/3'
	○	Z10-8	CDS ***

Lion's-Ear. [*Phlomis leonurus*]. An imposing, long-flowering subshrub, branching at

Lavatera cachemiriana

the base into strong, square stems, very leafy below. The opposite leaves, hairy, toothed, and 2½ " long, are oblong-lanceolate to oblanceolate. It produces many tiers of crowded, axillary whorls of large bright orange flowers; new whorls develop as the stem grows. The corolla is velvety; the upper lip concave to 2½ " long, the lower lip short and 3 lobed. Cut back hard at the end of winter; in colder areas cut down in fall and mulch for protection. Likes a well-drained soil, but water well. Fertilize at the start of the growing season. *L. l.* var. *albiflora* has cream-colored flowers. *L. dysophylla* and *L. dubia* are smaller plants. South Africa.

LEONTOPODIUM, Compositae. (30)

This genus, best known for the celebrated Edelweiss of the Swiss Alps, is native mainly to mountain regions. Difficult taxonomically; the species are all quite similar and vary so much in response to growing conditions that numerous subspecies are recognized. From basal rosettes of foliage the stems rise, bearing alternate leaves and small, diskoid flower heads in terminal clusters, subtended by a decorative, flattened collar or ruff of large, intensely woolly, bractlike leaves. The overlapping, involucral bracts of the flower heads are also woolly, but papery along their margins. Soils should be gritty, lean, and well limed, with good surface runoff; a gravel mulch is beneficial. Short-lived, and often best treated as biennials; easily raised from seed. Other species scarce in cultivation but worth seeking include strongly lemon-scented *L. haplophylloides* [*L. aloysiodorum*

Leonotis leonurus

Leontopodium alpinum

Hort.], which has 2″ inflorescences on leafy 1′ stems, and *L. palibinianum,* to 15″ tall, with narrow, sharply pointed, and almost upright, bractlike leaves. Other smaller species are of interest only to rock garden enthusiasts.

alpinum	YELLOW	SU	6″–1′/1′
	○	Z9-4/H	DS ***

Edelweiss. [*Gnaphalium leontopodium*]. This popular alpine is highly variable, and several subspecies are recognized. Creeping rhizomes underlie the tufts of gray-woolly, narrowly linear 1″–4″ basal leaves. Unbranched, leafy stems, also covered in white hairs, bear crowded, terminal cymes of 7–9 flower heads, each ¼″ wide. The showy, starfish-shaped collar below the inflorescence, 2″ or more across, is composed of broadly linear, bractlike leaves, recurving at the tips and thickly flanneled with short, silvery gray or white hairs. The ruff becomes dingy and loses much of its appeal in polluted environments. European Alps. The Russian species *L. leontopodioides* [*L. sibiricum*] is slightly taller, with narrower, erect leaves and larger flower heads.

LEONURUS, Labiatae. (4)

cardiaca	PURPLE	SU-F	3′–5′/3′
	○ ◑	Z9-3	DS **

Motherwort. Considered by some to be weedy and coarse, for its foliage alone it merits a place in the large garden. The vertical, square stems are often purplish brown and

Leonurus cardiaca

form robust clumps, with pairs of opposite, softly pubescent leaves, prominently purple veined. The lower leaves are long petioled, deeply palmately lobed and incised; the small, woolly upper leaves are usually 3 parted, each lobed 3 times. Dense verticillasters of pinkish purple, hairy, 2-lipped flowers crowd the upper leaf axils. An attractive foil for *Anthemis tinctoria*. This tough, spreading plant can become invasive, particularly in fertile soil. Europe, Mediterranean.

LEWISIA, Portulacaceae. (20)

These western American natives are highly prized, particularly by specialists in alpines, as much for their challenging, temperamental habits as for the striking beauty of their flowers. Evergreen or deciduous, all have fleshy, succulent foliage, usually arranged in a basal rosette. In the deciduous species, this shrivels and falls at flowering time or just afterward. The white, pinkish yellow, or red flowers may be solitary or in panicles, atop sturdy stems. Lewisias demand perfect drainage. Gritty loam with coarse leaf mold added and a light dressing of bonemeal is often used when plants are grown in pots; a similar mixture, rammed between vertical rocks, is suitable in the garden. To provide for the difficult, dry period essential after flowering, protect from overhead moisture and mulch around the collar with gravel or crushed stone to a depth of 1″–2″ to speed surface drainage. Sometimes they are grown as annuals to avoid this awkward time. Propagation is easy from seed, sown as soon as it is ripe, or from cuttings (pups) taken

Lewisia cotyledon

prior to flowering. Lewisias hybridize freely. Excellent for scree gardens or alpine houses. Other choice species include *L. rediviva, L. tweedyi,* and *L. brachycalyx,* too small for inclusion here. All are native to mountain regions of the West.

columbiana	PINK	SP	6″–1′/6″
	◑	Z9-3/H	CS **

Perhaps the easiest to grow. Evergreen rosettes of dark green, flat, spatulate 1″–3″ leaves. Upright sprays of many starry, pink-veined, white or pale pink ½″ flowers. Washington, Oregon.
———— 'Edithiae.' Salmon pink. Flowers in spring and early summer.
———— 'George Henley' has small, dark green leaves. Wine red flowers in spring, repeating in late summer.
———— *rosea.* Deep pink flowers.

cotyledon	PINK	SP-ESU	9″–1′/8″
	◑	Z9-3/H	CS ***

[*L. finchae, L. purdyi*]. The most widely grown. Evergreen spatulate to obovate leaves to 4″ long, often with crinkled or wavy margins, form the basal rosette. Thick, branching stems carry 8- to 10-petaled flowers, about 1″ wide, in varying shades of pink or candy striped on white. Requires a slightly richer soil than other Lewisias. Variable. California, Oregon.
———— var. *heckneri* has broad, toothed leaves.
———— var. *howellii.* The narrow leaves have wavy to crisped margins.

LIATRIS, Compositae. (40)   Blazing Star

The Blazing Stars, or Gayfeathers, are native American wildflowers, excellent for the border, meadow, or wild garden. Their unbranched, vertical, leafy stems rise from a more or less tuberous rootstock and end in a dense, long-lasting spike of small flower heads, which generally open from the top down. Each consists only of tubular, disk florets, surrounded by a cuff of papery or leafy, involucral bracts. An exceptionally good cut flower, both fresh or dried. All prefer moderately fertile, sandy soils. While they will tolerate excess soil moisture during active growth, they will not endure winter wetness; some will withstand drought. Divide in early spring. Attractive to butterflies.

aspera	PURPLE	SU-F	4′–6′/1.5′
	○	Z10-3/T	DS ***

[*L. scariosa* Hort.]. Stiff stems, crowded with linear to lanceolate leaves, to 16″ long, smaller and almost sessile above. The inflorescence is composed of many well-spaced ¾″–1″ flower heads; sessile or on short pedicels, each consists of 25–40 florets and is ringed by rounded, papery bracts. The flowers open more or less at the same time, making it a superior cut flower. Drought tolerant, but particularly demanding of good winter drainage. May need staking. Central and southeastern North America.

Liatris spicata 'Kobold'

———————— 'September Glory.' Rosy purple flowers on 2'–4' stems.
———————— 'White Spires' has clean white flower heads. 3' tall.

pycnostachya	PURPLE	SU-EF	3'–5'/1.5'
	○	ZI0-3/T	DS ***

Cattail Gayfeather, Kansas Gayfeather. Its erect, pubescent stems are very leafy. The narrow, lower leaves reach 1' long by ½" wide; the upper are much reduced. The slender, dense flower spikes to 1.5' long bear many sessile, fluffy, purplish pink, sometimes white, flower heads, each of 5–10 florets; sharply pointed, recurved involucral bracts. Winter mulching is recommended in cold climates. May need staking. Central United States.

spicata	PURPLE	SU-F	2'–5'/1.5'
	○	ZI0-3/T	DS ***

Spike Gayfeather, Dense Blazing Star. [*L. callilepis* Hort.]. Similar to both preceding species. Spikes to 2.5' long on glabrous stems; sessile flower heads of 5–14 rosy purple florets, ruffed with a few blunt, erect, mostly purple, involucral bracts. Drought resistant. The following cultivars are more commonly grown than the species. Eastern and central United States.
———————— 'Kobold.' A compact plant, with heavy, dark purple wands on 1.5' stems.
———————— 'Silver Tip' has lavender flower spikes. 3' tall.

LIBERTIA, Iridaceae. (20)

Libertias are attractive for informal plantings in warmer zones. They make large clumps of evergreen, grassy foliage, above which rise sprays of white flowers, subtended by sheathing bracts. Each flower has 2 sets of 3 perianth segments, the inner usually much longer and showier. Attractive pods with yellow or orange seeds follow. All require only average, well-drained soils, but resent drying out, which aggravates the browning of the leaf tips. May be hardy to Z8, especially if sheltered from the wind. Propagate in spring. A rare species from Chile, *L. caerulescens,* has pale blue flowers on 1'–1.5' stems.

formosa	WHITE	ESU	2'–4.5'/2'
	○ ◑	ZI0-9/T	DS **

Close tufts of stiff, swordlike leaves, to 1.5' long. Strong scapes hold crowded, terminal panicles well above the foliage. Each ivory flower is about ¾" across on a pedicel shorter than the bract; the outer perianth segments are greenish brown. Chile.

grandiflora	WHITE	SU	2'–3'/2'
	◑ ○	ZI0-9/T	DS **

Stiff, Iris-like foliage, to 3' long by ¼"–½" wide. Larger than those of *L. ixioides,*

Libertia ixioides

the waxy, white flowers are arranged in loose panicles, on pedicels longer than the bracts. Bright orange seeds. New Zealand.

| *ixioides* | WHITE | SU | 1′–2′/2′ |
| | ○ ◑ | ZI0-9/T | DS *** |

Its slender, arching leaves are paler along the midrib. The spreading panicles of large, pure white flowers dance just above the foliage. Their showy, inner perianth segments may reach almost ½″ long; the greenish outer ones are much shorter. Attractive orange ½″ seeds in the fall. New Zealand.

LIGULARIA, Compositae. (150)

These noble plants, all quite similar in habit, form large, domed masses of leathery, dark green, basal leaves. The erect inflorescences rise well above the foliage. These impressive but undemanding plants flourish in deep, rich, moist soils, as well as in the bog garden, and can also be grown in ordinary garden soil if they are not allowed to dry out. All benefit from soil amendment, mulching, and fertilizing. Water deeply during dry spells, and in hot areas grow in partial shade. Unfortunately attractive to snails and slugs.

| *dentata* | ORANGE | SU/LSU | 3′–4′/2′–3′ |
| | ○ ◑ | ZI0-4/H | DS **** |

Golden Groundsel. [*Ligularia clivorum, Senecio clivorum*]. The foot-long, kidney-shaped, sharp-toothed leaves rise on 1′ stalks in a loose basal rosette. Tall, sparsely leaved flower stalks bear loose, flat corymbs of ragged, orange, Daisy-like flower heads, some 4″ across. China, Japan. *L. hodgsonii* from Japan is altogether smaller, differing only in having 2 narrow bractlets on each peduncle.
——————— 'Desdemona' is more compact than the species. Its lower leaf surfaces, stems, and petioles are dark purple. Darker orange flower heads.
——————— 'Orange Queen.' Vigorous, with large flower heads.
——————— 'Othello.' A slightly smaller version of 'Desdemona.'

| **'Gregynog Gold'** | ORANGE | SU/LSU | 5′–6′/2′–3′ |
| | ○ ◑ | ZI0-4/H | D ** |

Substantial, sharp-toothed, heart-shaped leaves. Dense, broadly conical, disheveled spikes of orange, Daisy-like flower heads. Often listed as a cultivar of *L. dentata* or *L.* x *hessei*, it is a 1950 hybrid of *L. dentata* and *L. veitchiana* from Gregynog Hall, Newtown, Powys, Wales.

| **x** *hessei* | ORANGE | SU/LSU | 5′–6′/2′–3′ |
| | ○ ◑ | ZI0-4/H | D ** |

[*Senecio* x *hessei*]. *L. dentata* x *L. veitchiana* x *L. wilsoniana*. Large, leathery, kidney-shaped leaves, with small, sharp teeth. Short panicles of large orange yellow flower heads.

Ligularia macrophylla

| *macrophylla* | YELLOW | SU/LSU | 4'–6'/2'–3' |
| | ○ ◑ | ZIo-4/H | DS * |

[*Senecio ledebourii*]. This majestic species has toothed, elliptic to oblong-ovate 2' leaves, reminiscent of those of Horse-Radish. Massive, long conical panicles of small yellow ½"–¾" flower heads. Altai Mountains.

| **x** *palmatiloba* | YELLOW | SU | 3'–4'/2'–3' |
| | ○ ◑ | ZIo-4/H | D ** |

L. dentata x *L. japonica.* An impressive hybrid, superior to either of its parents. Substantial, rounded to heart-shaped, gently lobed and toothed leaves. Loose corymbs of several large flower heads.

| *pzrewalskii* | YELLOW | SU/LSU | 5'–6'/2'–3' |
| | ○ ◑ | ZIo-4/H | DS *** |

[*Senecio pzrewalskii*]. The leaves, triangular in outline and up to 1' long, are deeply palmately lobed, the lobes further lobed and toothed. Slender, loose racemes of small yellow flower heads on dark stems. Northern China.

| *stenocephala* | YELLOW | ESU | 4'–5'/2'–3' |
| | ○ ◑ | ZIo-4/H | DS *** |

Heart-shaped to triangular, sharp-toothed 1' leaves, of finer texture than those of most of the other species. Long, slender, dark-stemmed racemes of 1¼" flower heads. China, Japan, Taiwan.

———— 'The Rocket.' A superior and popular cultivar from Alan Bloom. Sometimes listed under *L. pzrewalskii.* It is perhaps a hybrid. Propagate by division only.

Limonium perezii

| *tussilaginea* | YELLOW | LSU/F | 2'/1' |
| | ○ ◑ | ZIO-7/T | DS *** |

[*L. kaempferi, Senecio kaempferi, Farfugium grande*]. Large, round to kidney-shaped, long-stalked leaves, with angled and sometimes toothed margins. The leafless stems bear loose corymbs of large, light yellow heads to 2″ wide. China, Korea, Japan, Taiwan.
————— 'Argentea.' An irregularly variegated form with green, gray green, and white foliage.
————— 'Aureo-maculata.' Leopard Plant has leaves splattered with small, rounded yellow spots. Often grown in greenhouses.
————— 'Crispata.' Parsley Ligularia has green leaves with crisped margins.

| *veitchiana* | YELLOW | SU/LSU | 5'-6'/2'-3' |
| | ○ ◑ | ZIO-4/H | DS ** |

[*Senecio veitchianus*]. Large, heart-shaped, dentate leaves. Very long, slender racemes of small, bright yellow flower heads. China.

LIMONIUM, Plumbaginaceae. (150)   Sea Lavender

This large genus includes many species of horticultural merit, though none superior to those recommended. All are easy, requiring only good drainage. Most are salt tolerant and drought resistant. The common *L. sinuatum,* usually grown as an annual, has cultivars in various colors.

| *latifolium* | BLUE | SU/LSU | 2'/1.5' |
| | ○ | ZIO-3 | DS **** |

Sea Lavender, Statice. [*Statice latifolia*]. Leathery, evergreen foliage in a sprawling rosette. The elliptic or spatulate leaves, to 10″ long, taper into long petioles. Long, wiry scapes end in many-branched panicles, which form a rounded, airy mass of tiny flowers. A white calyx surrounds the lavender blue corolla. Southern Russia, central Europe.
————— 'Violetta' is 1.5' tall, with violet blue flowers.
————— 'Collier's Pink' has pink flowers.

| *perezii* | PURPLE | SP-SU | 3'/2' |
| | ○ | ZIO-9 | S **** |

[*Statice perezii*]. This handsome plant forms a loppy clump of large, leathery, gray green, basal leaves to 1' long, the ovate blades as long as the tapering petioles. Sturdy, many-branched, flower stalks rise above the foliage, ending in dense panicles of 2-flowered spikelets. The vivid purple, papery, funnelform calyx encloses a small white corolla. Canary Islands.

LINARIA, Scrophulariaceae. (100)   Toadflax

Toadflaxes have asymmetrical, 2-lipped flowers with a long, basal spur, the throat closed by a prominent palate. The Snapdragon-like flowers are borne in terminal racemes or spikes. The leaves, opposite or whorled at the base but often alternate above, are sometimes toothed or lobed. Linarias are of easy culture, needing only full sun and a moderately well-drained soil. Susceptible to root and stem rot.

| *genistifolia dalmatica* | YELLOW | SU | 3'/1' |
| | ○ | Z10-4 | DS *** |

[*L. dalmatica*]. Many erect, branching stems, with sessile, gray green, ovate-lanceolate 1½" leaves. Racemes of yellow 1"–2" flowers with orange throats. Long flowering. Eastern Europe.

| *purpurea* | PURPLE | SU | 3'/1' |
| | ○ | Z10-4 | DS *** |

Numerous slender, vertical stems, with narrow, gray green leaves. Graceful, pointed racemes of lilac to purple ⅓" flowers. This charming, long-blooming plant should be much more popular. Southern Europe.
——— 'Canon J. Went' has light pink flowers.

| *triornithophora* | PURPLE | SU | 3'–4'/1'–1.5' |
| | ○ | Z10-8 | CS ** |

Three-Birds-Flying. The sturdy, erect stems, with brilliant green, lanceolate leaves in whorls, bear racemes of showy, long-spurred, lilac and purple 1½" flowers. Grown as an annual in colder areas. Spain, Portugal.

| *vulgaris* | YELLOW | SU | 2'/1' |
| | ○ | Z10-3 | DS *** |

Butter-and-Eggs has stiff stems, clothed in narrow, gray green 1½" leaves. Racemes of lemon yellow 1"–1½" flowers with bearded orange palates. It self-seeds readily and has become naturalized as a weed in North America. An appealing plant for cottage gardens. Europe, Asia.

LINDELOFIA, Boraginaceae. (14)

| *longiflora* | BLUE | SP | 1.5'–2'/1.5' |
| | ○ | Z9-6 | DS ** |

[*L. spectabilis, Cynoglossum longiflorum*]. Without the superb gentian blue of its flowers, this would be just one more of many, rather ordinary, Boraginaceous plants. Characteristically hairy throughout, with lanceolate to oblong-lanceolate 3"–4" basal leaves. The leafy, branching stems end in scorpioid cymes of small blue flowers; the

Linaria genistifolia dalmatica

corolla is funnelform and 5 lobed. Beware of inferior color forms. Needs good drainage; winter-mulch in cold areas. Reblooms lightly throughout the summer. Himalayas.

LINUM, Linaceae. (230) — Flax

The Flaxes are dainty, short-lived perennials, pretty in the border but unfortunately not suitable as cut flowers. Twisted in bud, the open, funnel-shaped flowers have 5 rounded petals with a silky sheen; each lasts only 1 or 2 days. The plants are generally drought resistant and prefer well-drained, sunny positions. Mulch in winter in cold areas.

flavum	YELLOW	SP-SU	1′–2′/1′
	○	Z9-5	CS ✱✱✱

Golden Flax. Robust, upright stems, often woody at the base, crowded with dark green, alternate leaves; spoon shaped below, lanceolate above. The bright yellow, waxy 1″ flowers are arranged in large cymes. Europe.
———— 'Compactum' is a dwarf form, only 6″ tall.
———— 'Cloth of Gold' is slightly taller. 9″ in height.

narbonense	BLUE	LSP-ESU	1.5′–2′/1.5′
	○	Z10-5/H	CS ✱✱✱

Narbonne Flax. Still delicate, but with more erect, stronger stems than *L. perenne*. The lanceolate ¾″–1½″ leaves are glaucous and stiff. Silky flowers of a clear, azure blue

Linum narbonense

with a white eye are borne in great profusion over a long season. The slightly larger flowers are longer lasting than those of Blue Flax. Mediterranean.
——————— 'Album.' A white-flowered form.
——————— 'Heavenly Blue' has copious, darker blue flowers.
——————— 'Six Hills' is an excellent form with sky blue flowers.

| *perenne* | BLUE | LSP-SU | 1'–2'/1.5' |
| | ○ | Z10-5/H | CS **** |

Blue Flax, Perennial Flax. Variable. Delicate and slender, the wiry, arching stems are mostly bare of foliage below. The bluish green leaves, about 1″ long, are narrower than those of *L. narbonense*. Free blooming, with large panicles of pale blue 1″ flowers, which open on sunny days but usually close by the afternoon. Self-sows abundantly. Good for informal or meadow gardens. Europe.
——————— 'Album' has white flowers.
——————— *alpinum* [*L. alpinum, L. julicum*] has small, Heather-like leaves and clear blue ¾″ flowers on 9″–12″ stems.
——————— *lewisii* [*L. lewisii*]. Prairie Flax. A robust, western native with sky blue flowers. Tolerant of partial shade. 2'–3'.
——————— 'Nanum Sapphire.' Sapphire blue flowers. Very free blooming. 10″–12″ tall.

LIRIOPE, Liliaceae. (5)   Lilyturf

The evergreen Lilyturfs excel as edging plants or massed as ground covers, especially in shady places. They are used extensively in large-scale, public landscape projects, particularly in the South and West. Their foliage is grasslike and should be cut back in early spring to encourage new growth. Tiny flowers cluster into narrow spikes reminiscent of Grape Hyacinths *(Muscari),* and may be followed by black fruits. Closely related to similar *Ophiopogon, Liriope* differs in minute, botanical details. Easily propagated by division in spring. Slugs and snails must be controlled.

| *muscari* | PURPLE | F | 1.5'–2'/1.5' |
| | ○ ● | Z10-5/T | D **** |

Big Blue Lilyturf. [*L. graminifolia densiflora, L. m. densiflora* Hort., *L. platyphylla, Ophiopogon muscari*]. Tufted clumps of stiffly arching, shiny, dark green leaves to 2' long by ½″–¾″ wide. Its dense whorls of violet purple flowers are spaced along the 4″–5″ spikes, held just clear of the foliage. Tolerant of dry soils even in shade. Useful for flower arrangements. Many cultivars. China, Japan.
——————— 'Christmas Tree' ['Monroe #2']. The robust, pointed spikes of lavender flowers bloom late. 8″ tall.
——————— 'John Burch.' Crested, lavender flower spikes. Variegated foliage. 1' in height.
——————— 'Majestic' [*L. majestica* Hort.]. The larger spikes of deep lilac flowers are often distorted by fasciation. 1'–2'.

———— 'Monroi's White' ['Monroe White,' 'Monroe #1,' *L. m.* var. *munroei* Hort.]. White flowers above narrower leaves. 1′ tall.

———— 'Silvery Midget.' Leaves banded with yellow. Violet spikes. 6″ high.

———— 'Silvery Sunproof' has leaves striped in white and yellow. 12″–15″ tall. Endures intense sun better than most of the variegated cultivars.

———— 'Variegata.' The foliage is cream, striped with green; it bleaches in direct sun. 8″–12″ tall. Not as hardy as the species. Striking with *Ajuga reptans* 'Purpurea.'

spicata	LAVENDER	LSU-EF	8″–1′/1.5′
◖●		Z10-4/T	D ***

Creeping Lilyturf. [*L. graminifolia*]. Rather invasive, rhizomatous roots give rise to mounds of narrow, grassy leaves. The flowers are pale lavender or almost white in 3″ spikes, held more or less at foliage level. Not as showy as *L. muscari.* Tolerates deeper shade and moister soil. China, Japan.

LISIANTHUS, Gentianaceae. (50)

nigrescens	BLACK	SU	2′–6′/2′
○ ●		Z10-9/T	S *

This funereal curiosity has erect, branching stems and lanceolate-ovate leaves, opposite and joined at the base. Loose clusters of nodding, deep purple black 2″–3″ flowers; corolla narrowly funnelform, cleft into 5 slender, spreading lobes. Known to thrive in well-drained, alkaline soils, but may well be less particular. Height varies greatly with cultural conditions. Southern Mexico, Central America.

LITHOSPERMUM, Boraginaceae. (44)   Puccoon

These native Americans are not widely grown, although they are hardy and well-suited for flower beds or rock gardens. Puccoons, or Gromwells, are generally erect, with simple, alternate leaves and yellow or orange, 5-lobed, rotate flowers. They thrive in acid, poor, sandy to gravelly soils; rich soil fosters soft, vegetative growth at the expense of flowers. Free of pests and diseases.

canescens	YELLOW	LSP	9″–15″/9″
○		Z9-3	RS **

Hoary Gromwell, Yellow Puccoon, Indian Paint. Hoary-pubescent, with several branched stems, bearing almost sessile, oblong 1½″ leaves. Numerous orange or yellow ½″ flowers, crested at their throats, are arranged in loose, arching cymes. A red dye is obtained from the roots. Southeastern Canada, eastern United States. *L. multiflorum* and *L. rudicale* are both western species, about 2′ tall. Their corolla tubes are longer, but lack the crested throats.

Liriope muscari 'Variegata'

Lithospermum sp.

Lobelia cardinalis

carolinense	YELLOW	LSP	1.5′–2.5′/1′
	○	Z9-2	RS **

Caroline Gromwell, Hairy Puccoon. [*L. caroliniensis, L. croceum*]. Rather coarse, with pubescent stems crowded with rough-hairy, lanceolate leaves. Helicoid cymes of showy, flat 1″ flowers, hairy at the base of the corolla. Central North America. Narrow-Leaved Puccoon, *L. incisum* [*L. angustifolium, L. linearifolium, L. mandanense*], has slender 2″ leaves and 2 types of flowers in leafy clusters: sterile, showy, yellow 1″ flowers, with fringed corolla lobes and crested throats, followed by smaller, fertile flowers, which never open. Southern Canada, central United States, Mexico.

LOBELIA, Lobeliaceae. (375)

This varied genus is included by some authorities in the Campanulaceae or Bellflower family. However, in the asymmetrical flowers of Lobelia, the tubular corolla opens into 2 distinct lips; the upper 2 lobed, the lower 3 lobed. Sturdy, erect stems support the leafy racemes high above basal clumps of foliage. Most prefer a rich, moist soil and are particularly effective naturalized beside streams or ponds, where they may self-sow. They are also suitable for the border, although they are generally short-lived. Mulch during the growing season and provide winter protection in cold climates. Much breeding work is in progress; the nomenclature of the hybrids is rather confused.

cardinalis	RED	LSU	3′–4′/1′
	○ ●	Z9-2/H	DS ****

Cardinal Flower. The dark green or reddish, unbranched, leafy stems rise above a deep green basal rosette. The alternate leaves are lanceolate, pointed and toothed, to 6″ long. Brilliant scarlet 1½″ flowers with exserted stamens cluster in slender, erect racemes. Forms with white, *L. c.* 'Alba,' and pink, *L. c.* 'Rosea,' flowers are available. Eastern and central United States. Similar plants with bronze or reddish basal foliage are probably hybrids with *L. splendens.*

——————— 'Angel Song.' Salmon and cream bicolored flowers.

——————— 'Arabella's Vision.' Brilliant red flowers.

——————— 'Twilight Zone' has shell pink flowers. These 3 American cultivars were bred by Thurman Maness.

x *gerardii*	PURPLE	SU-F	2.5′–3′/1′
	◑●	Z8-4/H	DS **

[*L.* x *vedrariensis, L.* x *hybrida, L.* x *milleri*]. *L. cardinalis* x *L. siphilitica,* and *L. siphilitica* x *L. splendens. L.* x *gerardii* includes hybrids resulting from both these crosses and their progeny. Since *L. cardinalis* and *L. splendens* were confused during the early part of this century, there is no way of determining the precise ancestry of these plants. Moreover, these hybrids have been backcrossed. In general, they are stout and robust with leafy stems. Their striking, purple or violet flowers are in terminal racemes to 1.5′ long, with later-blooming, axillary branches. Superb for cutting. Heavy winter mulching is essential. Comes true from seed. The 'Surprise' series developed by Thurman Maness has fuchsia-colored flowers.

siphilitica	BLUE	LSU	2′–3′/1′
	○ ◑	Z9-4	DS ****

Great Blue Lobelia. A stately plant, with more or less glabrous, unbranched, stiffly vertical stems. Lanceolate to oblong-elliptic 3½″–6″ leaves with toothed margins. Its slender, leafy racemes of 1″ flowers, each with a small, purplish upper lip and a much larger, blue lower lip, are often striped in white. *L. s.* 'Alba' is white flowered; *L. s.* 'Nana' is dwarf. Eastern United States.
——— 'Blue Peter.' A superior selection from Alan Bloom.

x *speciosa*	RED	SU	1.5′–5′/2′
	○ ◑	Z9-3	D ***

Canadian Tetraploid Group: the result of a complex breeding program by Wray Bowden, these tetraploid hybrids are vigorous, hardy plants. Their racemes are long and heavy, with large individual flowers. They require division every 2 years in early spring and a heavy winter mulch in Z5-3. A sheltered position out of the wind is recommended.
——— 'Oakes Ames' has scarlet flowers and dark green foliage. 2.5′–3′ tall.
——— 'Wisley.' Lighter scarlet flowers with medium green leaves on 2.5′ stems.

Lunaria annua 'Variegata'

splendens	RED	LSU	3′/1′
	○ ◑	Z9-7	DS ∗∗

[*L. fulgens*]. Similar to *L. cardinalis,* but with somewhat downy, linear to lanceolate 2″–7″ leaves and slightly larger flowers. Not as hardy, this species is sometimes forced under glass for spring floral displays. Mexico.

———— 'Bees Flame.' Long racemes of blazing red flowers and reddish leaves.

———— 'Queen Victoria.' Spires of bright red flowers and maroon foliage. A parent in the Canadian Tetraploid breeding program. Both these cultivars may be hybrids. They are hardy in Z9-4, with winter mulching in cold areas.

tupa	RED	LSU	5′–7′/3′
	○ ◑	Z10-8	CS ∗∗

A spectacular, tender subshrub, with thick, dark stems and substantial, pale green foliage. Its softly pubescent leaves are oblong-elliptic and pointed, with finely toothed margins. Large, tapering racemes of long-stalked 2″ flowers. The curious, jasper red corollas are swollen at the base; the clawlike lower lip curls under, the stamens are exserted upward. Shelter from the wind, even in very mild climates. Resents disturbance. Chile.

LUNARIA, Cruciferae. (3)

rediva	WHITE	LSP-ESU	2′–3′/2′
	○ ●	Z9-6	DS ∗∗

Perennial Honesty. Bold clumps of rough-hairy stems, with broadly ovate, toothed 2″–5″ leaves, the upper on conspicuous petioles. Terminal racemes of very fragrant, white to lavender ¾″–1″ cruciform flowers rise above the foliage. The flat, narrowly elliptical 2″–3″ seedpods are invaluable for dried arrangements. Easy to grow in moderately fertile, moist soils. Europe. Closely related *L. annua* [*L. biennis*], Silver Dollar Plant, frequently survives as a short-lived perennial. Its purple flowers are followed by flat, almost round, silvery pods. *L. a.* 'Alba' is white flowered; the showy foliage of *L. a.* 'Variegata' is splashed with cream. Both come true from seed if grown alone. Europe.

LUPINUS, Leguminosae. (200)   Lupine

It is surprising that so large a genus of exquisite wildflowers has given us so few gardenworthy plants. Only a small number of Lupines have proved amenable to cultivation. Two Californian shrubs of exceptional beauty, *L. albifrons* (Z10-9/H) and *L. arboreus* (Z10-8/H), are useful in the mixed border and for naturalizing. Crossing the latter with the herbaceous perennial *L. polyphyllus* and perhaps some annual species

Lupinus 'Russell Hybrid'

resulted in the famous Russell Hybrids. These and their descendants are the only Lupines commonly grown in gardens. Collectors may have favorite species which they consider eminently gardenworthy, but even the best of these should be relegated to wildflower and native plant gardens. Among them are *L. polyphyllus* of northwest North America, *L. latifolius,* native to the West Coast, and eastern *L. perennis.* Lupines have palmately compound leaves with narrow leaflets, often enhanced with silky or silvery hairs, which trap pearls of water after a shower. The asymmetrical Pea-like flowers, borne in slender spikes or racemes, consist of an erect standard or banner, 2 wing petals, and an incurved keel. The fruit is a flat pod.

| **Russell Hybrids** | VARIOUS | LSP-ESU | 3'–4'/1.5'–2' |
| | ○ ◑ | Z9-4/H | CS ✱✱✱✱ |

The plants of this hybrid group and other similar strains form clumps of erect stems, bushy with long-stalked, palmately compound leaves of exceptional beauty and grace. Above the mass of foliage, they bear long, dense racemes, crowded with papilionaceous flowers in a great variety of colors, both selfs and bicolors: white, cream, yellow, orange, shades of pink through red, pale to dark blue, and purple. They are usually available as plants or as seed in strains of related colors or in mixtures. 'Little Lulu' ['Dwarf Lulu,' 'Lulu'] and 'Minarette' are dwarf strains, only about 1.5' tall. Individual named cultivars, as offered in England, are not known here. Hybrid Lupines will not succeed in climates with hot summers, either dry or humid. Unlike most of the species, which thrive under rather poor conditions, the hybrids prefer a richer soil, neutral to slightly acid, and well drained. Water deeply in dry weather and mulch to conserve moisture. Supply winter protection in cold areas. Remove spent flower spikes to encourage reblooming, to prevent plants from exhausting themselves in seed production, and to avert prolific self-seeding. Easily propagated from seed, which must be scarified or otherwise treated to speed germination, or from basal cuttings. Root disturbance is resented; sow in place or grow in containers. Tall plants may need staking. Hybrid Lupines are short-lived and need frequent replacing. Aphids may be a nuisance, as well as slugs and snails. Virus-infected plants must be destroyed.

LYCHNIS, Caryophyllaceae. (12)			**Campion**

| *chalcedonica* | RED | SU | **3′–5′/1′** |
| | ○ | Z10-3/H | DS **** |

Maltese Cross, Jerusalem Cross, Scarlet Lightning. The upright stems are rather hairy and coarse, with opposite, ovate and toothed 2″–4″ leaves clasping the stem. Its intense scarlet ¾″ flowers, with deeply notched petals, are arranged in dense, terminal, domed clusters. Light, well-drained soil. Staking is often necessary. The leaves tend to brown and drop during dry spells; site behind lower-growing, bushy plants. Combines well with silver-leaved plants. Russia, Siberia.

——————— 'Alba' has white flowers.

——————— 'Plena.' Double scarlet flowers.

——————— 'Rosea.' Dark peach flowers, with an even darker eye. The very showy hybrid *L.* x *arkwrightii* (*L. chalcedonica* x *L.* x *haageana*) has clusters of fewer but larger scarlet flowers. Its foliage is bronzy purple. 1′ tall. Not as hardy.

| *coronaria* | PINK | SU | **1.5′–2.5′/1.5′** |
| | ○ | Z10-3/H | DS **** |

Rose Campion, Mullein Pink. [*Agrostemma coronaria*]. Spreading basal rosettes of silvery, woolly, ovate 4″ leaves on short petioles. The branched stems bear pairs of smaller, sessile leaves; and solitary and terminal, wheel-shaped, luminous cerise 1″ flowers. These may be removed to create a gray ground cover. Does well in dry, poor soils. Short-lived, but self-seeds abundantly. Southeastern Europe.

——————— 'Abbotswood Rose' has brilliant magenta flowers.

——————— 'Alba' is white flowered. 2′–5′ tall.

——————— *oculata.* White flowers with a conspicuous, bright pink eye.

| x *haageana* | VARIOUS | SU | **1′–1.5′/1′** |
| | ○ | Z9-4 | S *** |

L. coronata x *L. fulgens.* Clumps of dark green, lanceolate 2″–4″ leaves. Its flashy, white, red, or orange 2″ flowers are grouped in 2s and 3s on hairy, often weak stems. Must be well mulched, particularly in climates colder than Z6. Short-lived. Often comes true from seed. A favorite of slugs. Keep moist and mulch in hot weather.

Lychnis chalcedonica

viscaria	PINK	LSP-ESU	$1'-1.5'/1'$
	○	Z9-3	DS ✶✶✶✶

German Catchfly. [*L. vulgaris* Hort., *Viscaria viscosa, V. vulgaris*]. This neat, often evergreen plant makes grassy tufts of narrowly lanceolate 5″ leaves. The strong stems, sticky along the internodes, support loose clusters of 3–6 vivid, purplish pink ½″ flowers. A very easy, low-maintenance species. Europe, northern Asia.
———— 'Alba.' White flowers, on 9″ stems.
———— 'Splendens.' Bright magenta flowers. 1′ tall.
———— 'Splendens Flore Pleno.' Double magenta flowers. The basal foliage colors in the fall. A good cut flower. 10″–12″.
———— 'Zulu.' Deep salmon pink flowers on 2′ stems.

LYSIMACHIA, Primulaceae. (165)   Loosestrife

Loosestrifes are well adapted to damp, informal areas or watersides. They thrive in moist soils and are easy to grow. The white or yellow flowers are bell or wheel shaped, grouped into usually many-flowered inflorescences.

ciliata	YELLOW	SU	$3'-3.5'/2'$
	○ ◑	Z10-3	DS ✶✶

Fringed Loosestrife. [*Steironema ciliatum*]. Slender and erect clumps, with opposite, Willow-like leaves, about 6″ long; both petioles and leaves fringed with hairs. The nodding, light yellow 1″ flowers are solitary or in very loose panicles in the leaf axils. Not as invasive as some. Northeastern United States. Southeastern *L. fraseri* is similar, but has branched clusters of numerous flowers. It does not spread.

clethroides	WHITE	LSU	$2'-3'/3'$
	○ ◑	Z10-3/H	DS ✶✶✶

Gooseneck Loosestrife, Shepherd's Crook. An elegant, upright plant, with vigorous, running roots. The alternate 3″–6″ leaves are ovate to lanceolate, tapered at both ends, revolute along the margins. Its starry ½″ flowers crowd into slender, arching, terminal racemes. Invasive, particularly in moist soils. China, Japan.

ephemerum	WHITE	SU-EF	$3'/1'$
	○ ◑	Z9-6/H	DS ✶✶✶

Tight, vertical stands, with glaucous gray foliage. The lanceolate 4″–6″ leaves are opposite and joined at their bases. Pearly white, the small flowers are in dense, narrow spires. An unusual cut flower. Noninvasive. Dislikes hot, dry conditions. Europe.

punctata	YELLOW	SU	$1.5'-3'/2'$
	○ ◑	Z9-4	DS ✶✶✶✶

Yellow Loosestrife, Circle Flower. [*L. verticillata*]. The stiff, erect stems form large, bushy colonies with lanceolate leaves to 4″ long, opposite or in whorls of 3–4. Their

Lysimachia punctata

bright yellow 1″ flowers nestle in the leaf axils. Tolerates drier soil conditions than the other species, particularly in partial shade. Especially lovely in large sweeps alongside water, where its invasive roots have sufficient space to spread. East central and southern Europe.

LYTHRUM, Lythraceae. (35)				Loosestrife

Lythrums have become widely naturalized in wet areas, and their invasiveness has given them a bad reputation. However, the modern cultivars are less aggressive than the species and are valuable garden plants. They bloom over an extended period, at a time when there is often a shortage of color in the garden. Some of the popular cultivars may in fact be hybrids. Not related to *Lysimachia* in spite of their common names.

---

salicaria	PINK	SU-F	2′–6′/2′
	○ ◑	ZI0-3/H	CD ✳✳✳✳

European Purple Loosestrife. Vigorous, crowded stands of upright, branching stems, well clothed in sessile, opposite and decussate, or whorled foliage. Its grayish green Willow-like leaves may reach 4″ long. The straight, narrow, terminal 6″–12″ spikes of clustered flowers are interrupted by leafy bracts. A vibrant magenta pink, the ¾″

Lythrum salicaria 'Robert'

corolla has 6 thin, crumpled petals. Prefers damp soil, but also does well under border conditions. Self-seeds freely. The cultivars are preferable, except in large, natural areas. Eurasia.

———— 'Dropmore Purple' has rich violet flowers on 3' stems.

———— 'Firecandle.' Intense rosy red flowers. 2'–3' tall.

———— 'Happy.' A dwarf, dark pink cultivar. 15"–18".

———— 'Morden's Gleam.' Carmine rose flowers. 3'–4'.

———— 'Morden's Pink' has pink flowers. Free blooming. 3.5' in height. Noninvasive.

———— 'Purple Spires.' Fuchsia purple. 3'–5'.

———— 'Robert.' Bright fuchsia flowers. Fall foliage color. 1.5'–2' tall. Tolerates wetter soil conditions than the other cultivars, particularly in sun.

virgatum	PINK	SU	2'–3'/2'
	○ ◑	ZI0-3/H	CD ***

Wand Loosestrife. Similar, but more refined. Its slender wands of deep pink flowers are excellent for cutting. Europe.

———— 'Rose Queen.' A superior, clear pink cultivar. 2' tall. Resents drying out.

MACLEAYA, Papaveraceae. (2)

These stately plants need plenty of room to display their wide stands of strong, vertical, unbranched stems. The beautiful, pinnately lobed leaves alternate on the stems throughout their length; the undersides are felted with silvery hairs. Large panicles of apetalous flowers create a light, fluffy effect. Distinctive as a specimen plant, alone or backed by shrubs. Give some shade in hot areas.

cordata	WHITE	SU	8'/2'–3'
	○ ◑	ZI0-4/H	CDR ***

Plume Poppy, Tree Celandine. [*Bocconia cordata, B. japonica*]. The light green 8"–12" leaves, with lobes sinuate along their margins, are densely white-pubescent beneath. Countless small white flowers, each with 24–30 conspicuous stamens, cluster into feathery plumes to 1' long. Seldom needs staking in spite of its height. Less invasive than *M. microcarpa*. China, Japan.

microcarpa	BUFF	SU	8'/3'–4'
	○ ◑	ZI0-4/H	CDR ****

[*Bocconia microcarpa*]. Very similar, but with invasive running roots. The flowers have only 8–12 stamens. Division is necessary at least every 3–4 years. A well-drained, lean soil helps to control spreading. Central China.

———— 'Coral Plume' is a lovely pink-flowered cultivar.

Macleaya cordata

Malephora sp.

MALEPHORA, Aizoaceae. (15)

These low-growing, succulent, South African subshrubs are useful for edging and as ground covers in warm, dry climates. They display their Daisy-shaped flowers over a long period, but not as profusely as *Lampranthus* and some of the other Ice Plants. Drought resistant, but should be given some water during hot, dry spells. They become rather shabby with age and should be replaced about every fourth year. This can be done from cuttings which root easily or from flats of small plants purchased at little expense. Well-drained soils. (See *Carpobrotus.*)

| *crocea* | ORANGE | SP-ESU | 6"–9"/1'–1.5' |
| | ○ | ZI0-8/H | CS ✱✱✱✱ |

[*Hymenocyclus croceus*]. Trailing, woody stems. Stubby, 3-angled, glaucous leaves about 1¾" long. Solitary, terminal, dark coppery orange 1½" flowers with yellow centers. These tough plants are commonly used along roadsides and for erosion control on slopes. Hardier than most Ice Plants. South Africa.
———— var. *purpureocrocea* [*Hymenocyclus purpureocroceus*] has redder flowers and blue green, glaucous foliage.

| *lutea* | YELLOW | SP | 6"–9"/1'–1.5' |
| | ○ | ZI0-9/H | CS ✱✱✱ |

[*Hymenocyclus luteus*]. With much the same habit as *M. crocea,* but slimmer leaves.

Bright yellow flowers to 2″ wide, with slender petals. South Africa. *M. luteola,* slightly taller, with light green, glaucous foliage and smaller, yellow flowers, as well as *M. englerana, M. herrei,* and *M. thunbergii* are occasionally found in cultivation.

MALVA, Malvaceae. (40)   Mallow

Closely related to both *Lavatera* and *Sidalcea.* The Mallows have alternate leaves, lobed or cleft, with toothed margins. Their Hollyhock-like flowers have 5 broad, squared, notched or 2-lobed petals and a central, staminal column. These easy plants bloom over a long season and make a colorful display in sunny borders. Tend to self-sow freely. Prefer a little shade and deep soil where summers are hot.

---

alcea	PINK	SU-F	3′–4′/1′–1.5′
	○	Z9-4	CDS ✻✻✻

Mallow, Hollyhock Mallow. Upright and well branched, with rather downy, light green, rounded leaves, shallowly 5 lobed. The pink to light rosy purple 2″–3″ flowers are borne in great profusion, both along the stems and in terminal spikes. Drought tolerant. Europe.

——— 'Fastigiata.' Darker-colored flowers on neater, more vertical plants. Superior to the species.

Malva moschata

| *moschata* | PINK | SU-F | 2′–3′/2′ |
| | ○ | ZI0-3/H | CDS *** |

Musk Mallow. Bushy, with numerous, branched stems. Dark green, palmately lobed 2″–4″ lower leaves; stem leaves deeply divided, each segment pinnately cleft and dissected. The satiny, bright rose pink 2″ flowers have 2-lobed petals. They are both solitary, in the leaf axils on long pedicels, and in terminal clusters. North Africa, Europe.

——— 'Alba.' A form with pure white flowers. Comes true from seed.

| *sylvestris* | PINK | SU-F | 2′–3′/2′ |
| | ○ | Z9-3 | DS *** |

High Mallow, Cheeses. Variously described as a self-seeding annual, biennial, or short-lived perennial, its longevity depends upon its culture and climatic growing conditions. It makes sturdy bushes, covered with dark green, palmately lobed foliage. Long-petioled, rounded to kidney-shaped 2″–4″ basal leaves, with 5–7 shallow, blunt lobes; upper leaves with 5–7 deep, triangular lobes. The long-stalked, rose purple 2″ flowers cluster thickly in the upper leaf axils; the petals are 3–4 times as long as the sepals and feathered with darker stripes. Very long blooming, even after light frost in fall. An old favorite in European herb and dooryard gardens. Europe.

——— *mauritiana* [*M. mauritiana*] has lightly veined, rich, dark purplish pink flowers, semidouble or ruffled. 3′–6′ tall.

——— 'Primley Blue.' A blue-flowered dwarf form.

Meconopsis grandis

——————— 'Zebrina' [*Althaea zebrina, M. zebrina*] has white to deep pink flowers, the petals conspicuously feathered with purple or dark red. 3′ tall.

MARRUBIUM, Labiatae. (30)

incanum	FOLIAGE	SU	2′–3′/2′
	○	ZIO-3	CS **

[*M. candidissimum*]. Its cool, silver gray herbage is useful as a foil to strong colors in the garden. Woolly throughout, this bushy, aromatic plant has erect, square stems and wrinkled, Sage-like foliage. The opposite leaves, to 2″ long, are ovate, with small, rounded teeth. Distant, axillary whorls of insignificant, small whitish flowers. The corolla is 2 lipped; the upper notched, the lower broad and 3 lobed. Best in rather poor, free-draining soils. Southeastern Europe. *M. cylleneum* is a smaller, attractive, Greek species. *M. vulgare,* the common Horehound, has little ornamental value.

MARSHALLIA, Compositae. (10)

grandiflora	PINK	SU	1′–2′/1′
	○ ◐	Z9-5	DS **

Barbara's Buttons. Though seldom grown, this native merits a place in the wild garden or even the border. Neat basal rosettes of ribbed, lanceolate leaves to 7″ long. Its solitary 1″–1¼″ flower heads, surrounded by a chaffy involucre and somewhat reminiscent of *Centaurea,* are composed of tubular, pink florets with bluish purple anthers. Prefers damp soil. Southeastern United States.

MECONOPSIS, Papaveraceae. (45)   Asiatic Poppy

These much-prized Poppies, with one exception native to the mountains of eastern Asia, succeed only in limited areas of North America. They demand cool, moist summers and relatively mild winters, conditions seldom found outside of the Pacific Northwest. Even then, some of the species are so temperamental as to try the patience of the most ardent and expert gardener; fortunately others are less demanding. Since some of the species hybridize freely, the genus is taxonomically confused. Several, including *M. paniculata* and *M. integrifolia,* are monocarpic and not true perennials, but their basal rosettes are handsome, however brief their floral contribution. The foliage varies from entire, to dissected or lobed. Nodding or outward-facing, the Poppy-like flowers may be solitary, or in large racemes or panicles; the topmost flowers open first. Each flower has 2 early-deciduous sepals and 4–9 lustrous, tissue paper-crumpled petals, surrounding a central boss of yellow stamens. An acid to neutral, humusy soil, moist but free-draining in winter, seems to suit them best. Only *M. cambrica* tolerates lime and thrives in a wide range of soils. All need shade from midday sun, particularly in dry climates. Sow seed as soon as it is gathered, since it rapidly loses its viability. The following are a few of the most commonly grown species; gardeners who fall under the spell of *Meconopsis* should seek the help of specialists.

betonicifolia	BLUE	ESU	3'–5'/1.5'
	◐ ○	Z9-7	DS **

Himalayan Blue Poppy. [*M. baileyi*]. The elusive Blue Poppy is usually a short-lived perennial, though sometimes monocarpic. Grayish green and covered with coarse, reddish brown hairs, the oblong 6"–8" leaves have heart-shaped bases and coarsely serrated margins; petioled below, sessile above. Its strong stem ends in a loose cyme of several nodding 2" Poppies. From a glorious clear sky blue, they vary to a rather muddy lavender, possibly a result of lime in the soil or water. Seedlings should be prevented from blooming until a large enough crown has developed, to increase the longevity of the plant. The white-flowered form *M. b.* 'Alba' is usually monocarpic. A well-grown stand under high trees or among yellow Rhododendrons is an unforgettable sight. Mountains of Tibet, Yunnan, and Burma. *M. grandis* is a similar, though somewhat larger plant. Seed offered under this name may be of hybrid origin. Hybrids between the two have clear blue flowers, and are known as *M.* x *sheldonii*. *M.* x *sarsonii* *(M. betonicifolia* x *M. integrifolia)* has yellow or cream-colored flowers.

Melianthus major

cambrica	YELLOW	LSP	1'–2'/1'
	◑ ●	Z9-6	S **

Welsh Poppy. This, the least demanding of the genus, forms neat, upright clumps of bright green, hairy foliage, sometimes whitish beneath. The bipinnately dissected leaves, to 8″ in length, are on long petioles below, shorter ones above. Taller than the foliage, slender, hairy stems carry solitary, swan-necked, bristly buds, which open into lemon yellow 2½″ flowers. Self-seeds freely to the point of becoming a nuisance if conditions are favorable. Only fresh seed germinates readily. Western Europe.

——————— 'Aurantiaca' has orange flowers.

——————— 'Flore Pleno' is a double-flowered form.

quintuplinervia	LAVENDER	SP	1'–1.5'/1'
	◑ ●	Z9-7	D *

Harebell Poppy. The hairy, obovate 8″–10″ leaves are all basal and form thick mats of foliage. Each rosette gives rise to a slender, bristly scape, which bears a solitary, nodding, bell-shaped ½″ flower, delicate lavender, often flushed with purple at the base of the petals. Tolerates drier soils than most species. More reliably perennial. Mountains of Tibet.

MELIANTHUS, Melianthaceae. (6)

major	BROWN	ESP/LSU	8'–12'/4'
	○	Z10-8/T	CDS ***

Honeybush is an erect to spreading subshrub, mostly grown for its superb foliage. Alternate, odd-pinnate 1' leaves, with winged stalks, each with an enlarged, leaflike stipule. The elliptic leaflets are blue green, glaucous, and coarsely but regularly toothed. Terminal, slender and erect 1' racemes of reddish brown 1″ flowers, with 5 petals, one of them reduced. Decorative, papery, persistent seedpods follow. Evergreen in warm areas; in colder climates, where it flowers late or not at all, cut to the ground after it dies back at the end of the season and mulch heavily. Possibly hardy to Z7 with winter protection. Invasive, it should never be grown in the border with other perennials, but is a striking accent plant in the landscape. Best raised from seed. Southern Africa, India. Rare *M. minor* is similar, 3'–5' tall, and less hardy. Southern Africa.

MENTHA, Labiatae. (25) — Mint

Most of the Mints are more appropriate in the herb garden than in the border. However, some of the variegated forms make attractive foliage plants if their invasiveness can be contained. This can be accomplished by planting in a plastic container with a few holes punched in the bottom to allow for drainage. The damp soil in which they thrive is thus assured.

x *gentilis* 'Variegata'	FOLIAGE	SU	1'–2'/2'
	○ ◐	Z10-5	CD ✳✳✳

Variegated Ginger Mint, Scotch Mint, Golden Apple Mint. [*M. gentilis*]. *M. arvensis* x *M. spicata*. Its wiry, upright stems have crowded pairs of irregularly toothed, ovate 2″ leaves on short petioles; bright green and conspicuously veined in yellow. Widely spaced verticillasters of tiny, pale purple flowers in the upper leaf axils.

suaveolens 'Variegata'	FOLIAGE	SU	1'–1.5'/2'
	○ ◐	Z10-5	CDS ✳✳✳✳

Pineapple Mint. [*M. rotundifolia* 'Variegata']. Somewhat weedy, with slender, erect stems, well clothed in hairy, grayish green, rounded leaves of wrinkled texture. The crenate leaf margins are banded irregularly in white and cream. Mauve, 2-lipped flowers, clustered in dense verticillasters, crowd into narrow spikes. The whole plant is faintly pineapple scented. Southern Europe. *M.* x *rotundifolia* 'Variegata' is very similar, but has larger leaves more irregularly variegated. Plants offered under this name are usually *M. suaveolens* 'Variegata.'

MERTENSIA, Boraginaceae. (50)   Bluebells

This genus is sadly neglected in gardens; only *M. virginica* is widely grown, the other species are scarce. Those listed are well worth seeking. Bluebells grow from thick, fleshy roots; their leafy stems have alternate, gray green or bluish foliage. The appealing flowers, in loosely branched, one-sided clusters or terminal racemes, often nod. The calyx is 5 lobed, as is the trumpet- or bell-shaped corolla. Most prefer a moist, rich soil and are easy to grow. Propagate from seed sown as soon as it is ripe.

asiatica	BLUE	ESU	1'/1'
	○	Z9-6	DS ✳✳

This Oriental species has trailing, glaucous stems covered in distinctly blue gray 1¼″–3¼″ leaves. The tubular, pale blue flowers are in terminal clusters. Tolerant of seaside conditions. Japan.

ciliata	BLUE	SP-SU	1'–2'/1.5'
	◐ ●	Z9-4	DS ✳✳

Chiming Bells, Mountain Bluebell, Languid Ladies. A graceful plant, with arching stems and strongly blue green, lanceolate to oval 6″ leaves, the lower on 4″ petioles. The purplish pink buds open into intense blue, tubular ¾″ flowers with flaring lobes; the calyces are fringed. Long blooming. Moist soil will delay summer dieback. Rocky Mountains. *M. sibirica* has deeper blue flowers; calyx not fringed.

maritima	BLUE	SU	1'/3'
	○	Z9-5	DS ✳✳

Northern Shorewort, Oysterleaf, Sea Mertensia. [*Pulmonaria maritima*]. Low mounds

Mentha suaveolens 'Variegata'

Mertensia asiatica

Mimulus cardinalis

of fleshy, glaucous leaves, sometimes used in salads. The pink buds open into lavender blue bells. A charming seaside plant, which demands gritty, free-draining soil, and an open position. Coastal areas of northern Europe and eastern United States.

| *virginica* | BLUE | LSP/ESU | 1′–2′/1.5′ |
| | ◖● | Z10-3/H | DS **** |

Virginia Bluebells, Virginia Cowslip. This handsome, glabrous plant is one of our best-loved natives. Its upright, ridged stems bear elliptic to obovate leaves to 6″ in length, the lower ones narrowed at the base. Leafy stalks support loose, nodding clusters of fragrant, trumpet-shaped 1″ flowers, pink in bud, opening to a clear porcelain blue. Most attractive with *Dicentra spectabilis,* and ferns to fill in after both die back in midsummer. This woodlander needs an acid, humus-rich soil. Self-seeds under favorable conditions. In warm regions, avoid full sun. New York to Minnesota, south to Alabama and Tennessee.

——————— 'Alba' is a white-flowered form.
——————— 'Rubra.' Pink flowers. Both are scarce.

MEUM, Umbelliferae. (1)

| *athamanticum* | WHITE | ESU | 1′–2′/1.5′ |
| | ○ | Z9-6 | DS ** |

Dense tufts of fresh green, aromatic, threadlike foliage. The 3–4 times pinnately divided leaves are mostly basal; their petioles, as long as the leaf blades, persist and form a fibrous crown over the rootstock. The tiny, pinkish white or purplish flowers are 5 petaled, borne in compound 1″–3″ umbels. Seldom grown, but useful for its attractive foliage and ease of culture. Europe.

MIMULUS, Scrophulariaceae. (150)   Monkey Flower

Monkey Flowers are best adapted to damp places. They thrive in full sun, but several also tolerate partial shade. In colder zones some are grown as annuals. They have opposite, often toothed leaves and showy flowers, axillary or in terminal racemes. A conspicuously 5-ribbed calyx surrounds the tubular, 2-lipped corolla. Its upper lip is usually 2 lobed and sometimes reflexed; the lower has 3 spreading lobes, exposing the throat, which may be closed by a palate.

| *cardinalis* | RED | SP-F | 4′/2′ |
| | ○ ◗ | Z10-7/H | CDS ** |

Scarlet Monkey Flower. A handsome, clump-forming plant, with rather weak, branched stems and sessile, downy, obovate leaves to 4½″ long. The scarlet to pinkish yellow, long-stalked 2″ flowers have exserted stamens. Prune in late summer to encourage good fall reblooming. Requires plenty of water, particularly in hot weather. Western and southwestern United States.

guttatus	YELLOW	ESU-F	1′–2′/2′
	○ ◑	Z10-6/H	CDS ***

Common Monkey Flower. [*M. grandiflorus, M. luteus* Hort., *M. langsdorfii*]. This variable, fleshy plant has watery, erect or sprawling stems which may become stoloniferous. The toothed, ovate 1″–6″ leaves are long petioled below, sessile above. Bright yellow ½″–2½″ flowers, usually red speckled in the throat, cluster into short, terminal racemes. This long bloomer enjoys moist or even wet conditions, and is valuable on stream banks or in bog gardens. Often grown as an annual; self-sows very freely. Alaska to Mexico.

x *hybridus*	VARIOUS	ESU-F	1′–2′/2′
	○ ◑	Z10-6/H	CDS ****

[*M. tigrinus*]. *M. guttatus* x *M. luteus*. Similar to *M. guttatus,* but with even larger flowers. Breeding has produced several strains; their flower colors range from pale yellows through gold and bronze to red tones, often with unusual blotching and speckling. In full sun the soil must be kept constantly damp. Frequently grown as annuals for summer bedding and hanging baskets, particularly in cold zones.

STRAINS:

'Calypso.' Available separately or in a mixture of yellows and reds, as well as deeper colors, with speckles and spots of different colors on the throat or overall. These F1 hybrids are 14″ tall.
'Malibu.' Yellow and orange, with paler, often speckled throats. Available in separate colors. F1 hybrids. 10″–12″.

lewisii	PINK	SU	3′/1.5′
	○ ◑	Z9-5	CDS **

[*M. bartonianus* Hort.]. An erect, bushy plant, clammy with soft hairs. Its gray green, ovate leaves with toothed margins are about 3″ long. The flowers are borne in pairs, on long stalks, in the leaf axils. The deep rose to pink 2″ corolla has a yellow throat, often peppered with crimson. Grows under drier conditions than the other species. Long blooming. A parent of *M.* x *bartonianus.* Western United States.

luteus	YELLOW	SP-SU	1′/1′
	○ ◑	Z9-6/H	CDS **

Golden Monkey Flower. Low mats of creeping or decumbent stems, often rooting at the nodes. Its toothed, oval 1″ leaves have 5–7 prominent veins radiating from the base. The long-stalked flowers are in leafy racemes; the bright yellow 1½″ corolla has red or brown spots, similar to those of *M. guttatus,* on its open throat. This excellent ground cover can become rampant in damp places. Chile.

| *ringens* | PURPLE | SU-F | 2′–3′/1′ |
| | ◗ | Z9-3 | CDS *** |

Allegheny Monkey Flower. A handsome native, with erect, watery, square and ridged stems and sessile, toothed, lanceolate 4″ leaves. Axillary pairs of long-stemmed, light purplish lavender flowers. Their corollas are marked in violet on the lower lobe; a yellow palate almost closes the throat. Tolerates full sun if the soil never dries out. Valuable for its long period of bloom in damp or boggy places, or even in shallow water. Seeds itself freely. Eastern and southeastern United States.

MIRABILIS, Nyctaginaceae. (60)

Four-O'Clocks, or Umbrella Worts, are used as border plants or even hedges in warmer regions. Where it is colder, they are usually treated as annuals, planted out after the danger of frost has passed. Their tuberous roots send up numerous branching stems, often swollen at the nodes of the opposite leaves, which are petioled below, sessile above. The showy flowers, long and tubular, flare at the mouth; lacking petals, they are composed of a petaloid calyx, surrounded at the base by a calyxlike, 5-lobed involucre. This may hold one or several flowers. Trouble-free in average soil.

Mirabilis jalapa

| *jalapa* | VARIOUS | SU | 2′–3′/3′ |
| | ○ | Z10-8/T | DS *** |

Four-O'Clock, Marvel-of-Peru, Beauty-of-the-Night. Wide, leafy clumps of erect, well-branched stems. The ovate 2″–6″ leaves are pointed, cordate at the base. Each involucre surrounds a solitary 1″–2″ flower. Extremely floriferous, with fragrant red, pink, white, or yellow blooms, sometimes striped or patterned. Opening in the late afternoon, they will remain so until the next morning if it is cloudy. The tubers may be lifted and overwintered in cold regions or seedlings may be started in spring. Self-sows freely; it has become naturalized in the South. South America. This species has been hybridized with Mexican *M. longiflora,* producing a wider range of colors. These should correctly be called *M.* x *hybrida.*

| *multiflora* | PINK | SU | 1′–3′/3′ |
| | ○ | Z10-7/H | DS ** |

Widely spreading, bushy mounds of sticky herbage. The heart-shaped leaves may reach 3″ in length. Opening in the late morning, the numerous magenta or rose pink flowers are 1″–2″ long by 2″ wide, 5 or more in each involucre. Very drought tolerant; suitable for wild and native plant gardens. Southwestern United States.

MOLTKIA, Boraginaceae. (6)

| *doerfleri* | VIOLET | ESU | 1.5′/1.5′ |
| | ○ ◑ | Z9-6/H | DS ** |

[*Lithospermum doerfleri*]. An erect plant, well clothed in hairy, lanceolate 2″–4″ leaves. The vivid blue to violet tubular flowers, about 1″ long, are borne in drooping, terminal clusters. Avoid full sun in warm zones. Seldom grown here, but deserves a wider audience. Albania.

| *petraea* | VIOLET | SU | 1′/1′ |
| | ○ ◑ | Z9-6/H | DS ** |

[*Lithospermum petraeum*]. This bushy subshrub is covered throughout with rough hairs. The alternate 2″ leaves are linear-oblong. Compact, terminal clusters of blue ½″ flowers, tinged with pink and maturing to deep violet; exserted stamens with conspicuous blue anthers. Albania.

MONARDA, Labiatae. (12)   Wild Bergamot

The Wild Bergamots are among the best native plants for meadow gardens, and are also handsome in the border. Their running rootstocks make large clumps of strong, erect, square stems, well clothed in aromatic, dark green, opposite leaves. Curved,

Moltkia petraea

tubular, and 2 lipped, the flowers crowd into terminal or axillary verticillasters, often subtended by a collar of colorful, leafy bracts. Useful for cutting. Easy to grow in sunny or lightly shaded sites; short-lived where summers are long and hot. Very susceptible to mildew, particularly in dry soils; best where soil is rich and moisture retentive. May become invasive; divide in spring every 2–3 seasons. Cut back hard in fall. Attractive to hummingbirds.

| *didyma* | RED | SU | 2.5′–3′/1.5′ |
| | ○ ◑ | ZIO-4/H | D **** |

Beebalm, Oswego Tea. Toothed, ovate 3″–5″ leaves, strongly mint scented. The scarlet 2″ flowers, closely set in 2-layered, terminal clusters, are ringed by red-tinged bracts. Spreads rapidly, particularly in dry shade. A large number of hybrids and selections has resulted from crossing this species with *M. fistulosa* and other species. Eastern United States.

'Adam.' Bright, clear red flowers; free blooming. 2′–3′ in height.

'Cambridge Scarlet' has bright red to crimson flowers. 2.5′–3′.

'Croftway Pink' is a soft rose pink. 2.5′–4′ tall.

'Mahogany' has deep Indian red flowers on 2′–3′ stems.

'Prairie Night.' Rich, purplish violet flowers. 3′.

'Snow White' is a good creamy white. 2′ tall.

'Violet Queen' has lavender to violet flowers and grayish foliage. 2′–3′ tall.

Monarda didyma cv.

---

fistulosa	PURPLE	SU	3'–4'/1.5'
	○ ◑	Z10-3	D ***

Pubescent, ovate-lanceolate 3"–4" leaves. The solitary, terminal heads of rather drab lavender flowers are surrounded by whitish bracts. Their calyx and upper corolla lip are distinctly hairy. Tolerates drier soils than *M. didyma,* but is seldom appropriate outside the wild garden. Eastern United States to the Rocky Mountains.

---

punctata	YELLOW	SU	1.5'–2'/1'
	○ ◑	Z10-5	DS ****

Horsemint, Spotted Beebalm. The branched stems bear oblong leaves to 3" in length. Terminal and axillary, the tiers of dense whorls of purple-spotted, yellow 1" flowers are ringed with large, showy pink bracts. Extremely variable. Prefers sandy soil. New York to Florida, Texas.

MORINA, Dipsacaceae. (10)

longifolia	WHITE	ESU/SU	2'–3'/1'–1.5'
	○ ◑	Z9-6/H	DS **

Whorlflower. This appealing but temperamental plant forms a rosette of Thistle-like, basal foliage; spiny, double-toothed, linear 1' leaves. The strict stem bears whorls or pairs of smaller leaves at intervals. The white 1" flowers, subtended by spiny bracts, are

Morina longifolia

whorled in an erect, terminal spike. The corolla, a long, slender tube flaring into 5 lobes, changes to pink then crimson with age. Needs well-drained but moist soil. Will not tolerate high heat and humidity. Most effective planted in groups of 3–5. Himalayas.

MYRRHIS, Umbelliferae. (1)

odorata	WHITE	ESU	3'–5'/2'
	○ ◑	Z9-4	DS ✶✶✶

Myrrh, Sweet Cicely, Anise, Sweet Chervil. This bushy, anise-scented plant has upright, grooved, branching stems, thick with deeply cut, ferny foliage. The 2–3 times pinnate leaves may reach 1' long on sheathing petioles. Numerous minute white flowers crowd into compound 2" umbels and are followed by attractive, dark brown, ribbed, licorice-flavored seeds. Deadhead only to prevent self-seeding. Useful in front of shrubs, or tall perennials with unsightly stems. The foliage persists until the cold weather. Both seeds and leaves are used for seasoning. Europe.

NEPETA, Labiatae. (250)   **Catmint**

These aromatic plants, with attractive, usually gray foliage, are effective foils for many brighter-hued herbaceous plants and small shrubs. *N. cataria*, Catnip, should be confined to the herb garden, but those recommended here are perennials of quality. Catmints thrive in hot, sunny areas in well-drained soil and will tolerate drought. However, few will succeed in a combination of heat and high humidity. The small, tubular flowers are blue, lavender, white, or yellow, arranged in whorls in long, terminal and axillary racemes. Their calyces are toothed; the corollas, 2 lipped, the upper 2 lobed, the lower 3 lobed, with a larger central lobe. Insert some thorny twigs among the stems to prevent cats from rolling on the plants. Rare *N. tuberosa* from Spain and Portugal has cylindrical, spikelike inflorescences of purple flowers with deep rose calyces on 2.5' stems. From Kashmir, *N. clarkei* is also scarce. Its small, bright blue flowers, blotched with white on the lower lip, crowd into long but close terminal racemes on 3'–4' stems. Both deserve to be more widely grown.

x *faassenii*	LAVENDER	ESU-LSU	1'–2'/1.5'
	○	Z10-3/H	CD ✶✶✶✶

[*N. mussinii* Hort.]. *N. mussinii* x *N. nepetella*. Variable in habit, but usually upright and billowy. The soft gray, crenate 1½" leaves are narrowly ovate, wedge shaped at the base. A great profusion of soft lavender ½" flowers are borne on branched stems well above the foliage. After flowering, cut back by half to encourage a second flush of bloom. This hybrid is sterile; best propagated by division in spring. Select a good clone. Seedlings of *N. mussinii* are sometimes offered under this name. Use as a low hedge or edging plant; a fitting underplanting for roses.

Nepeta goverumma

governiana	YELLOW	SU	2′–3′/2′
○ ◑		Z8-4/H	CDS ∗∗

[*Dracocephalum govianum, N. govaniana*]. Bushy with vertical stems and yellow green foliage. The pointed and ovate 3″–4″ leaves are cordate at the base, with toothed margins. Loose racemes of cream yellow ¾″ flowers, blotched with brighter yellow on the lower lip, dance on branched stems to graceful effect. Kashmir.

mussinii	LAVENDER	SU	1′/1′
○		Z10-3/H	CDS ∗∗∗

A loose, sprawling plant with pubescent, toothed, gray leaves about 1″ long, broadly ovate or cordate. The lavender blue ⅓″ flowers in terminal racemes bloom only briefly. Self-seeds freely. Much less desirable than *N.* x *faassenii,* although good selections have their place. Iran, Caucasus.

——————— 'Blue Wonder.' Compact and uniform. 1′ tall.

——————— 'White Wonder.' A white-flowered form of the preceding cultivar.

nervosa	BLUE	SU	1′–2′/1′
○		Z9-4/H	CDS ∗∗

This handsome, bushy plant has green, conspicuously veined, lanceolate 2″–4″ leaves, serrate along the margins. The eye-catching flowers are bright blue, sometimes yellow, crowded into dense, cylindrical 1″–3″ racemes. Kashmir.

sibirica	BLUE	SU-LSU	2′–3′/1.5′
○		Z10-3/H	CDS ∗∗

[*Dracocephalum sibiricum, N. macrantha*]. Upright, foliose stems. The toothed, lanceolate leaves to 3½″ long are almost glabrous above, covered with tiny hairs beneath. Its tiered racemes of deep blue 1½″ flowers last for several weeks. Intolerant of wet soils. Siberia, China.

——————— 'Blue Beauty.' ['Souvenir d'Andre Chaudron']. Similar to the species, but only 1.5′ tall. Probably a hybrid.

'Six Hills Giant'	LAVENDER	ESU-LSU	3′/3′
○		Z10-3/H	CD ∗∗∗

[*N. gigantea* Hort.]. May be a hybrid or a large selection of *N.* x *faassenii.* It forms waves of aromatic, gray foliage under a mist of blue flower spikes. Cut back by half after flowering for neatness and to force a second flush of bloom. More tolerant of damp climates than the other species.

NICOTIANA, Solanaceae. (70)

Flowering Tobaccos are hardy only in frost-free climates and are treated as annuals elsewhere. Sticky with glandular hairs throughout, their vertical stems carry frequently large, alternate leaves, which are usually sessile and may be decurrent. Their often deliciously fragrant flowers, borne in terminal panicles or long, one-sided racemes, open in the evening; during the day, particularly in sunny weather, the blooms close partially. In color they range from white, often tinged or flushed with yellow or green, to red and purple. The persistent, short calyx is 5 lobed and tubular; the long-tubed, salver-form corolla flares widely at the mouth into 5 unequal lobes, causing the limb or "face" of the flower to be slightly irregular or oblique. All prefer light shade and must be protected from intense sun. Water regularly during hot weather. They are easy to propagate from seed, which requires light to germinate; self-sows freely. Best-known Brazilian *N. alata* [*N. affinis*], Jasmine Tobacco or Flowering Tobacco, is widely grown as an annual bedding plant. Its stems may reach 3'–4.5' in height, with decurrent, ovate 4"–10" leaves below and clasping, smaller leaves above. Very fragrant white flowers, greenish on the outside, in loose, short racemes, bloom over a long season, but open fully only in the evening. The slender 2"–4" corolla tube expands at the throat and spreads into an irregular 1" limb of 5 broadly ovate lobes. *N. a. grandiflora* is larger throughout and is more often grown. Red Flowering Tobacco, *N.* x *sanderae (N. alata* x *N. forgetiana),* is a very similar annual. Extensive breeding has resulted in numerous strains and hybrids in a broad range of heights and colors; white, lime, yellows, reds, and maroons. The flowers of some, including the dwarf 'Domino' hybrids available in mixed or separate colors, and the 2.5'–3' tall 'Sensation' strain, usually sold as a mixture, remain open during the day. Also popular are the 'Nicki' hybrids, which are weather-resistant 1'–1.5' plants, available in separate or mixed colors. Regrettably, much of their fragrance has been lost. *N. langsdorffii* from Chile and Brazil has unusual, nodding, green flowers on 2.5' stems. Their short, stubby corolla tubes balloon at the throat and gently spread into ½" bell-shaped "skirts"; the anthers are turquoise blue.

sylvestris	WHITE	SU-F	4'–6'/1'
	○ ◑	Z10-9	S ***

This vertical, branching plant has strong, stout stems clothed in sessile, rough-textured, lyrate leaves, which may reach a foot or more in length. Dense panicles of pendulous, pure white flowers, which open on cloudy days but save their sweet scent to attract night-flying moths. The spindle-shaped 3½" corolla tube flares widely at the mouth to 1"–1½" across. A fine specimen or dot plant for partly shaded borders. Argentina.

NIEREMBERGIA, Solanaceae. (30)   Cupflower

Commonly grown as summer-flowering annuals wherever they are not hardy, these South American plants are popular for their long and profuse displays of bloom. They have slender, ascending to erect, branching stems and alternate, small, linear leaves. Their solitary white, blue, or violet flowers are borne in the upper leaf axils. The tubular corolla opens into a broad bell with 5 flaring lobes. Grow in a fertile, well-drained but moderately moist soil. Shade lightly in very hot areas. Deadhead to encourage continuous bloom. Cut back hard at the end of the season to promote compact growth.

Nierembergia hippomanica var. *violacea*

Reduced flowering indicates the need for division, but better results are obtained from new young plants.

hippomanica **var.** *violacea*	VIOLET	ESU-F	6″–1′/6″–1′
	○	ZI0-7/T	CS ★★★★

Cupflower. [*N. caerulea, N. hippomanica* Hort., *N. hippomanica* var. *caerulea*]. This neat little mounded plant has erect to ascending branched stems and linear to narrowly lanceolate ¾″–1″ leaves. The violet to violet blue 1″ flowers have yellow throats. Argentina.

———— 'Purple Robe' has darker, purplish flowers.

N. gracilis has a more reclining habit. White 1″ flowers marked inside with violet and a yellow throat. Whitecup, *N. repens* [*N. rivularis*], is a small, creeping plant suitable for the rock garden. It has spatulate leaves and larger white flowers with a yellow throat. Less tolerant of heat than the other species.

scoparia	VIOLET	ESU-F	2′–3′/1′–1.5′
	○	ZI0-7/T	CS ★★★★

Tall Cupflower. [*N. frutescens*]. Less well behaved than the Cupflower; trim occasionally to maintain an attractive shape. Erect, branching stems clothed in linear to narrowly spatulate leaves. Violet blue 1″ flowers with yellow throats. There are also forms with white or purple flowers. Argentina, Uruguay.

Nolana acuminata

NOLANA, Nolanaceae. (60)

These seashore plants have prostrate to decumbent branching stems. Their leaves are fleshy and hairy, as those of coastal plants so often are; alternate, becoming opposite toward the ends of the stems. The solitary, axillary flowers have broadly funnel-shaped corollas with shallow lobes. All need a sandy soil and full sun. Frequently grown as summer-flowering annuals. They are useful for edging paths and flower beds.

| *acuminata* | BLUE | SP/SU | 4″/1′ |
| | ○ | ZI0-9 | S ** |

[*N. lanceolata*]. Lanceolate leaves to 3½″ long. The blue or lavender blue 1½″ corollas have white or yellow throats. Chile.

| *humifusa* | BLUE | SP/SU | 6″–8″/1′ |
| | ○ | ZI0-9 | S ** |

[*N. prostrata*]. Ovate to rhombic leaves to 1″ long. Blue 1″ flowers, prettily veined with purple in the throat. Peru.

| *paradoxa* | BLUE | SP/SU | 6″–8″/1′ |
| | ○ | ZI0-9 | S *** |

[*N. atriplicifolia, N. grandiflora*]. Ovate leaves to 2¼″ long. This most commonly grown species has 2″ flowers which vary from sky blue to a rather poor, lavender blue; the throat of the corolla is banded with white, yellow inside. There is also a white-flowered form. Chile.

OENOTHERA, Onagraceae. (80)   Evening Primrose

Exclusively a New World genus. Species that flower during the day are known as Sundrops or Suncups; those that open late in the day and close the following morning are called Evening Primroses. The more colorful make fine additions to the border or rock garden, flowering over a long season; the less ornamental species may be used in native plant and wild gardens. Generally tinged with red, the erect or trailing stems bear alternate, sometimes pinnately lobed leaves. Solitary or clustered, the cup-shaped or funnelform flowers are borne in the upper leaf axils. Yellow, sometimes white or pink flowers, with parts in 4s. Their sepals are strongly reflexed; their petals, oblanceolate to obovate, with a silky sheen. Easy to grow in full sun, even in thin, dry soils; avoid overly rich or poorly drained soils. Divide in spring or start from seed.

| *missouriensis* | YELLOW | SU | 9″–2′/2′ |
| | ○ | Z10-4/H | S **** |

Ozark Sundrop, Missouri Primrose. [*O. macrocarpa, Megapterium missouriensis*]. Sprawling, with prostrate to decumbent stems and dark green, lanceolate 4″–6″ leaves, covered with velvety hairs. Toward the end of the day, enormous, fragrant, lemon yellow goblets open from reddish buds. Persistent, decorative, winged 2″–3″ seedpods follow. Blooming may stop temporarily during very hot spells. Prefers a deep, fertile soil with free drainage. An excellent front-of-the-border or rock garden plant. Missouri, Kansas to Texas.

| *odorata* | YELLOW | SU | 3′/1′ |
| | ○ | Z10-5/H | S ** |

[*O. sulphurea* Hort.]. This night bloomer forms a narrowly erect plant from a basal rosette of glaucous, lanceolate leaves, crisped along their margins. Its red buds open into fragrant, pale yellow 3″ flowers, which fade to a pinkish red. Self-seeds freely. Chile.

| *speciosa* | PINK | SU | 6″–2′/2′ |
| | ○ | Z10-5/H | DS *** |

Showy Primrose. This charming day bloomer has aggressive running roots under loose mounds of grayish herbage. The linear-lanceolate leaves to 3″ long are pinnately lobed below, gently toothed or undulate above. Solitary in the upper leaf axils, the attractive, bowl-shaped 2″ flowers are a delicate pink or white aging to pink. Plant only where the roots can spread or confine to a container. Kansas to Texas. *O. berlandieri* [*O. s. childsii, O. tetraptera childsii*], Mexican Evening Primrose, is similar but not as hardy.

Oenothera berlandieri

It forms compact rosettes of gray foliage; deep rose flowers on slender, ascending to erect 6″–10″ stems. Ideal for the front of hot, dry borders. Invasive. Texas, Mexico.

tetragona	YELLOW	SU	2′–3′/1′
	○	ZIO-4/H	DS ****

Sundrops. [*O. fruticosa youngii, O. glauca, O. youngii* Hort.]. This variable species is often confused in the trade with similar *O. fruticosa*. Its loose, leafy clumps of reddish, upright and branched stems bear dark green, ovate 8″ leaves. The numerous spare spikes of bright yellow, cup-shaped ½″ flowers bloom in succession throughout the summer. Thrives in good soil, but will produce too much foliage if overfertilized. May need support. Eastern United States.

——— *fraseri* [*O. cinaeus, O. fruticosa fraseri, O. glauca*] has broader leaves, glaucous only on their undersides. Dark purplish new growth. 1′–1.5′ tall.

——— ———'Fyrverkeri' ['Fireworks,' 'Illumination'] has bright red buds and leathery, purplish brown leaves. 1.5′.

——— 'Highlight' has red 1′–2′ stems with large yellow flowers.

——— 'Yellow River.' Flowers to 2″ across on green 1.5′ stems.

OMPHALODES, Boraginaceae. (29)   **Navelwort**

Navelworts are not widely grown in this country, but are useful early-blooming perennials. Their basal leaves are long-petioled; the few smaller, alternate, stem leaves, more

Omphalodes verna

Ononis rotundifolia

or less sessile. Loose racemes of Forget-Me-Not-like flowers. Best in woodsy soil in partial shade, but tolerant of dry shade. Excellent under shrubs.

| *cappadocica* | BLUE | ESP | 9″/9″ |
| | ☾ | Z10-6/H | DS ** |

Thick clumps of rather hairy, heart-shaped leaves to 4″ long. The airy sprays of intensely bright blue ⅓″ flowers rise on upright stems. An excellent noninvasive ground cover. Asia Minor.
——————— 'Anthea Bloom' has pure blue flowers.

| *verna* | BLUE | ESP | 6″–8″/12″ |
| | ☾ | Z9-5 | DS *** |

Blue-Eyed Mary. This trailing plant spreads by underground stolons. Its fine-textured basal leaves are ovate to 3″ long; evergreen in mild zones. The gentian blue ½″ flowers are larger than Forget-Me-Nots. Not very floriferous, but charming. Europe.
——————— 'Alba' has white flowers.

ONONIS, Leguminosae. (75)

| *rotundifolia* | PINK | SU | 1′–1.5′/1′ |
| | ○ | Z9-5/H | S ** |

Rest Harrow makes rounded bushes, subshrubby at the base, with hairy, branched stems which bear stipulate, trifoliate leaves. Their softly hairy, rounded leaflets are dentate to 1″ long. Pea-like ½″ flowers vary from pale pink to cerise in axillary clusters on 2″–3″ peduncles; persistent 1″ seedpods follow. Thrives in dry, free-draining soils and is tolerant of drought. Difficult to transplant; best raised in pots. Mountains of southern Europe.

ONOSMA, Boraginaceae. (150)

Onosmas are bristly hairy plants, with alternate, gray green leaves and drooping, scorpioid cymes of long-blooming flowers. The calyx is deeply 5 lobed; the mouth of the tubular corolla is rimmed with 5 tiny lobes. Best suited to sunny rock gardens. Needs very sharp drainage, particularly in winter.

| *echioides* | YELLOW | SP-SU | 1′–1.5′/1.5′ |
| | ○ | Z9-5/H | CS ** |

Golden Drop is covered throughout with stiff, yellow hairs. Heavy clumps of erect, sometimes branching stems. The dark gray green leaves are linear to 3½″ below; lanceolate and smaller above. Its pale lemon yellow ½″–¾″ flowers crowd into curved racemes. Spain to Greece.

Onosma echioides

OPHIOPOGON, Liliaceae. (10)   **Lilyturf**

Mondo Grass is often confused with *Liriope,* to which it is closely related. Both make excellent evergreen ground covers. *Ophiopogon* is used predominantly in warmer zones, while *Liriope* is hardier. Easy, but slugs and snails readily mar the foliage. In mild climates divide in fall, but where winters are cold, in spring.

---

jaburan	WHITE	SU	2′/1′–1.5′
	●	Z10-7/T	DS **

White Lilyturf. [*Mondo jaburan*]. The dense clumps of foliage only increase slowly, limiting its use as a ground cover. Its arching, dark green, linear leaves may reach 3′ or more in length. The clusters of white ¼″ flowers are borne in short racemes, often hidden by the foliage; oblong, metallic blue fruits follow. Good for cutting. There are many cultivars, with foliage variegated in white or yellow. Japan.

---

japonicus	LAVENDER	SU	1′/6″–9″
	◑●	Z10-7/T	DS ****

Mondo Grass, Dwarf Lilyturf. [*Mondo japonicum*]. Thick turflike clumps develop from its tuberous roots and spread into an incomparable ground cover. Dark green, curving, narrow leaves about 1′ long. The sparsely flowered racemes of pale lavender flowers may be hidden by the foliage. Iridescent blue fruits. In coastal areas it tolerates full sun, but

Ophiopogon planiscapus 'Arabicus'

requires shade in hot, dry locations. Dwarf cultivars are available for rock gardens. Japan, Korea.

---

planiscapus 'Arabicus'	WHITE	SU	6″–1′/2′
	○ ◑	ZI0-6/T	D ***

[*O. arabicus* Hort., *O. p.* 'Nigrescens,' *O. p.* 'Nigricans']. Similar to the preceding species, but with 10″ leaves that emerge green and shortly turn almost black. Its spikes of pink-flushed flowers rise slightly above the foliage on black stems. Slow to increase. Excellent as a specimen plant contrasted with small, yellow-leaved Hostas and delicate ferns or underplanted with *Lysimachia nummularia* 'Aurea.' Any mulch should contrast, not blend with the foliage.

ORIGANUM, Labiatae. (20)   Marjoram

Most of these aromatic plants are confined to the herb garden, but a few have greater ornamental possibilities. They have the usual square stems of the Mints, wiry and lightly branched, and opposite, ovate to heart-shaped or rounded leaves. The small whorled flowers, often subtended by attractive overlapping bracts, are borne in slender to rounded spikes, one or more at the end of each branch. The asymmetrical flowers are 2 lipped; the upper lip is shallowly notched, the lower, 3 lobed. They adapt readily to a variety of soils, provided the drainage is good, and seldom need watering. Some appealing English hybrids currently not available in this country deserve a place in collectors' gardens.

dictamnus	PINK	SU-F	I′/I′
	○	ZI0-8	CS ***

Dittany-of-Crete. [*Amaracus dictamnus*]. This subshrub has wiry, ascending stems and densely white-woolly, ovate to rounded I″ leaves, sometimes mottled with purple. The pink to purplish ½″ flowers, subtended by leafy bracts, are borne in drooping spikelets, reminiscent of the catkins of Hops *(Humulus),* and clustered into loose panicles. The bracts age to purplish pink after the flowers have passed. Greece, Crete.

rotundifolium	PINK	SU	8″/I′
	○	ZI0-8	CDS **

Spreads to make a dense clump of wiry stems, clothed in clasping, heart-shaped, gray green ½″–¾″ leaves. Each stem ends in a nodding Hops-like spike. The large apple green bracts all but hide the insignificant pink flowers. This splendid little plant should be treasured by any gardener fortunate enough to own it. Turkey.

vulgare var. *aureum*	FOLIAGE	SU	1.5′–2.5′/I′–1.5′
	○	ZI0-3	DS ***

[*O. vulgare* 'Aureum']. The golden-leaved form of Marjoram puts on a show from spring to midsummer, when its leaves turn green like those of the common herb. Enjoy it while it lasts, then remember the pleasure it gave you earlier. It makes a compact clump of erect stems, well clothed in slightly hairy, ovate to ovate-lanceolate 1½″

Origanum rotundifolium

leaves, sometimes toothed. The clusters of purple or white small-bracted flowers are aggregated into loose, paniculate inflorescences. The flowers only detract from the effect of the foliage; shear them off. The species is native to Europe.

ORTHROSANTHUS, Iridaceae. (8)   Morning Flag

[*Elvetria*]. The Morning Flags or Morning Stars differ from closely related *Sisyrinchium* only in minute botanical details. Tufts of stiff, linear, 2-ranked leaves rise from the short, woody rootstocks. Long scapes support loose, terminal clusters of short spikes, each sheathed by a spathe. The flowers are composed of 6 spreading, ovate or oblong tepals, united into a short tube below. Each blooms lasts for only a day. Tolerant of a few degrees of frost, but unsuitable out of doors, except in the most favored climates; elsewhere they are elegant subjects for the cool greenhouse or conservatory. Best in moist, humus-laden soil out of direct sun. Propagate from seed or divide established plants.

| *chimboracensis* | BLUE | ESP | 1′–3.5′/1.5′ |
| | ◑ | Z10-9/H | DS * |

[*Moraea chimboracensis, Sisyrinchium moritzianum*]. The leaves, about 15″ long by ¼″ wide, are finely toothed along their margins. Rigidly erect scapes bear 2- to 3-flowered clusters of almost sessile blooms above the foliage. The dark lavender blue 1¼″–1½″ flowers have obovate segments of nearly equal size; the outer sharply pointed, the inner rounded. Mountains of Mexico and Peru.

| *multiflorus* | BLUE | ESU | 1′–2′/1′ |
| | ◑ | Z10-9/H | DS * |

Purple Morning Flag. [*Sisyrinchium cyaneum*]. Dense clumps of glabrous 1.5′–2′ leaves. Sky blue 1″–1½″ flowers, similar to those of *O. chimboracensis;* the inflorescence consists of one sessile bloom and a 4″–8″ spike of several-flowered clusters, all borne at foliage level. Prefers light, dry soil. Southern and western Australia, Victoria.

| *polystachys* | BLUE | LSP-ESU | 1.5′–2.5′/1′ |
| | ◑ | Z10-9/H | DS ** |

[*Sisyrinchium polystachys*]. Glaucous leaves, sometimes with rough margins. The lengthy inflorescences are composed of several, long-peduncled flowers, with 3–6 sessile ones in a 6″–8″ spike above. Western Australia.

OSCULARIA, Aizoaceae. (3)

Succulent, erect to spreading, and much-branched subshrubs. Their fleshy, 3-angled leaves, broader at the tip than at the base, are armed with blunt teeth, often touched

Orthrosanthus polystachys

Oscularia deltoides

with red. The Daisy-shaped pink flowers are small and short petaled but very freely borne. The plants of this genus are unusual for their fragrant, almond-scented flowers. Like other Ice Plants, these should be renewed about every fourth year from cuttings which root with great ease. Well-drained soil. Drought tolerant, but water lightly during dry spells. (See *Carpobrotus.*)

| *caulescens* | PINK | LSP/ESU | 1′/1′–1.5′ |
| | ○ ◑ | Z10-9/H | CS *** |

Reddish stems with glaucous, gray leaves about ¾″ long. Rose pink ½″ flowers. Exceptional among Ice Plants for its tolerance of shade. South Africa.

| *deltoides* | PINK | LSP/ESU | 1′/1′–1.5′ |
| | ○ | Z10-9/H | CS **** |

Reddish stems with glaucous, blue gray leaves less than ½″ long. Purplish pink ½″ flowers. South Africa.

| *pedunculata* | PINK | LSP/ESU | 1′–1.5′/1′–1.5′ |
| | ○ | Z10-9/H | CS *** |

Glaucous, gray leaves to ¾″ long. Pink ½″ flowers. South Africa.

Osteospermum hybrid

OSTEOSPERMUM, Compositae. (70)

These South African herbaceous perennials and subshrubs are so floriferous that they well deserve their great popularity. Their mostly alternate leaves are entire or toothed in all the following species; their surfaces, glandular hairy. Terminal and solitary, or more rarely in loose corymbs, the Daisy-like flower heads are borne on long, wiry peduncles. Only a single row of ray florets surrounds the disk. These easy plants thrive in full sun, in well-drained, moderately fertile soil. They are drought resistant once established, but look better for an occasional watering. Pinch early in the season to promote bushiness; cut back straggling plants. Easily propagated by seed or from cuttings. There are many cultivars and hybrids; in most cases their origins appear to be poorly documented. *O.* 'Buttersweet' has the habit of *O. barberae* and pale yellow flower heads. It may be a hybrid between *Osteospermum* and *Dimorphotheca*. The amusing flower heads of *O.* 'Whirligig' have white, spoon-shaped ray florets with a blue reverse.

barberae		PURPLE	F-SP	2′-3′/3′
	○		Z10-9/H	CS ✱✱✱

[*Dimorphotheca barberae*]. This straggling subshrub is clothed in entire or lightly toothed, oblong to spatulate leaves to 3″ long; the upper leaves are smaller and sessile. The purple 2½″ flower heads, dull purple beneath, have darker disks. South Africa. Often confused with *O. jucundum*, which has smaller flower heads and a more upright form.

| *ecklonis* | WHITE | ESU-F | 2′–4′/2′–4′ |
| | O | ZIO-9/H | CS **** |

[*Dimorphotheca ecklonis*]. A bushy, branching subshrub with oblanceolate to obovate 2″–4″ leaves, variably toothed. The 2″–3″ flower heads, solitary or in loose corymbs, arise from the ends of the branches. White ray florets, violet or blue and sometimes edged with white beneath, surround an azure blue disk. South Africa.

| *fruticosum* | WHITE | F-ESP | 6″–1′/3′ |
| | O | ZIO-9/H | CS **** |

Freeway Daisy, Trailing African Daisy. [*Dimorphotheca fruticosa*]. Prostrate to decumbent stems to 2′ long cover extensive areas in short order, rooting as they go. Obovate to spatulate, sessile leaves to 4″ long. Short-stalked white or lilac 1¾″ flower heads, violet, lilac, or purplish pink beneath; purple disks. Easily propagated from rooted stem cuttings. South Africa.

———— 'African Queen' has purplish flowers fading to white.

———— 'Burgundy Mound.' Light wine red flowers. Selected by the Los Angeles State and County Arboretum.

———— 'Hybrid White' ['Snow White,' 'White Cloud'] has a more upright habit, which suggests that it is a hybrid with one of the shrubby species. White flowered.

OSTROWSKIA, Campanulaceae. (I)

| *magnifica* | LILAC | ESU | 4′–6′/1.5′ |
| | O | Z9-8/H | RS * |

Giant Bellflower. This rare and temperamental beauty has stout, erect stems with remote whorls of 4–5 leaves. The silvery 6″ leaves are ovate, with small, irregular teeth. Huge, bell-shaped 4″–6″ flowers, pale lilac with darker veins, usually with 6 short, broad lobes, are arranged in loose, terminal racemes. Dies back after setting seed. Demands very deep, well-drained, alkaline soil and a warm, sunny position. The long, tuberous roots make it difficult to transplant or divide. Propagated from seed, it will bloom in 3–4 years; from root cuttings, in one year. Mulch well to protect from winter wetness and from late frosts. This mountain plant may be hardier than indicated, given proper cultural conditions. Turkestan.

OXYPETALUM, Asclepiadaceae. (I50)

| *caeruleum* | BLUE | LSP-LSU | 1′–2.5′/9″ |
| | O | ZIO-9/H | CS **** |

Southern Star. [*Tweedia caerulea*]. Only its glorious blue flowers redeem this ungainly plant. Softly downy, even clammy, its weakly twining or sprawling stems are woody below. The opposite, short-petioled 2″–4″ leaves are oblong to lanceolate, heart shaped

Oxypetalum caeruleum

at the base. Sparse clusters of starry 1″ flowers bloom in the upper leaf axils. A unique silvery blue, the deeply 5-parted corolla darkens as it matures; the corona forms a central, dark blue eye. Pinch to force branching. In colder areas, it may be grown as a greenhouse plant or as an annual for bedding. White flies can be a serious problem. South America.

PAEONIA, Ranunculaceae. (30)   Peony

Beloved by gardeners and nongardeners alike for centuries, Peonies have been called the "Queen of Garden Flowers." Assorting well with other perennials and with shrubs, they are ideal for gardens where low maintenance is important. They are also superior as cut flowers. Mostly clump forming, their strong stems are abundantly clothed in large, alternate leaves, often biternate below, ternate above. The foliage frequently remains in good condition throughout the season, sometimes coloring in the fall. Solitary or clustered, the showy flowers range in color from white to yellows, pinks, reds, and purples. Their 5 persistent sepals surround 5–10 or more broad petals; the yellow stamens form a central boss encircling 2–8 often decorative carpels. Peonies demand good drainage. The soil should be deep and very well enriched with thoroughly rotted manure or compost. Plant preferably in the fall during dormancy; in the south before new growth begins. Care must be taken to set the stout, fleshy roots so that their "eyes" are no deeper than 1″–2″; deep planting is a common cause of lack of flowers. Most thrive in full sun, although they should be shaded from intense summer sun in our hotter zones. Avoid sites with overhanging trees or shrubs; do not plant too close to a south-facing wall, where they will be subjected to undue thawing and freezing during the winter. Best where winters are long and cold and summers are not excessively hot. In Z10-8, select early-blooming species and cultivars, which will complete flowering before hot weather sets in. Staking is usually necessary, particularly for those with large, heavy blooms. Gray mold, *Botrytis cinerea,* and leaf blotch, *Cladisporium paeoniae,* may become problems, but are effectively controlled with fungicidal sprays. Detailed information on all phases of Peony culture, cultivars, and exhibition is available from the American Peony Society.

anomala	CRIMSON	LSP	1.5′–2′/2′
	○	Z10-2	DS *

The glabrous, biternate leaves, similar to those of *P. emodi,* differ in their leaflets being pinnatisect with pointed, narrow, oblong 3″–3½″ segments. The solitary, deep red 3″–3½″ flowers have obovate petals, yellow stamens, and 3–5 smooth pistils, with red or yellow stigmas. Eastern Russia to central Asia. More commonly grown, *P. a.* var. *intermedia* has carpels covered with hairs. The purplish red flowers, several per stem, of closely related but less robust *P. veitchii* from China, also have hairy carpels. All are involved in the modern hybrids.

brownii	MAROON	ESU	1′–1.5′/1′
	○	Z10-4	DS *

Seldom-branched stems, with few glaucous, dark green, biternate leaves; the fleshy, deeply 3- or 4-lobed leaflets are short stalked. The solitary, globose 1″ flowers have rounded, deep maroon or brownish petals and 5 glabrous carpels. California to Wyoming, Nevada, British Columbia. Our other native, *P. californica,* is closely related. A little taller, it has essentially sessile, deeply cut leaflets. The purplish 1¼″ flowers have purple-rimmed petals, and 3 carpels. California. Both are suitable for native plant gardens.

daurica	RED	LSP	1.5′–2′/2′
	○	Z10-3	DS **

[*P. triternata*]. The broadly oblong or obovate, round-tipped leaflets of the biternate lower leaves are wavy, slightly cupped along their margins, and may be somewhat hairy beneath. Solitary, the single 3″–4″ flowers have rose red, rounded petals and 2–3 white-hairy carpels. Northwest Yugoslavia to Caucasus.

emodi	WHITE	SP	1′–2.5′/2′
	◑	Z10-3	DS **

Its bright green leaves, biternate below, ternate above, have mostly decurrent, elliptic leaflets, with smooth margins and conspicuous, puberulent veins. Several very fragrant, pure white 3″–5″ flowers are borne on each of the elegant, curving stems. Their obovate petals surround countless golden stamens and 1 or 2 spreading carpels, thickly covered in yellow hairs. *P. e.* var. *glabrata* has smooth carpels. The foliage remains attractive throughout the season. Important in breeding. Kashmir.

| *lactiflora* | WHITE | LSP/ESU | 1.5′–3.5′/2′–3′ |
| | ○ | Z10-2 | D **** |

Common Garden Peony, Chinese Peony. [*P. albiflora*, *P. chinensis* Hort., *P. edulis*, *P. fragrans*, *P. sinensis* Hort.]. Substantial, upright clumps of reddish brown stems branched above. On long petioles, the dark green, biternate 4″–12″ leaves have elliptic to lanceolate leaflets. The foliage remains handsome throughout the season and often colors well in the fall. Several per stem, the fragrant, open or cup-shaped 3″–4″ blooms have 8 or more petals around a large boss of yellow stamens and 4–5 usually glabrous red pistils. Northeastern Asia. *P. lactiflora* is the major source of most of the large-flowered, so-called Chinese hybrids, which have been developed over centuries in France, Great Britain, and the United States, as well as China and Japan. The group includes not only single forms, but also doubles and semidoubles, Japanese and anemone forms, in which parts of the flower, usually the stamens, are absent or become petaloid or staminodal. There are variations within the types, and all are documented precisely by the American Peony Society. Thousands of names are registered; below are listed a few of the most widely grown:

'Alice Harding' has double, light pink flowers. Midseason. Good fall color.

'Claire de Lune' has very early, single yellow flowers.

'Coral Charm' is a recent breakthrough in color. Its semidouble peach flowers open from coral buds. Early.

Paeonia 'Cytherea'

'Cytherea.' Faintly scented, semidouble, deep cherry blooms fade to pale peach. Strong stems. Midseason.

'Festiva Maxima' is an old reliable type with strong stems. Fragrant, fully double white flowers flecked with dark red. Early.

'Gay Paree.' A Japanese type with cherry outer petals and a shell pink petaloid center. Midseason.

'Miss America.' Semidouble, with snowy white petals and golden yellow stamens. Early.

'Monsieur Jules Elie' has huge double flowers of silvery rose pink. Fragrant and early flowering. One of the best for cutting.

'Nippon Gold.' Anemone-centered, dark pink flowers with bright yellow staminodes.

'Sarah Bernhardt' has large, apple blossom pink double flowers late in the season. Free blooming.

'Seashell.' A clear light pink single. Midseason.

mlokosewitschii	YELLOW	SP	1.5'–2.5'/2'
	○	Z10-3	DS **

Molly-the-Witch. This superb, early-blooming species makes neat clumps of thick, glabrous stems. Its soft gray green, biternate leaves, covered with short hairs beneath, are rimmed and veined in red. Their 3"–4" leaflets are broadly oblong, the laterals pointed at the apex. Solitary, lemon yellow 4"–5" flowers, with about 8 concave petals; numerous yellow stamens encircle 2–4 very hairy and decorative carpels. Caucasus. From the same region, similar *P. wittmaniana* has larger, more sharply pointed leaflets, with long hairs underneath. Its solitary, yellowish 4"–5" flowers also have hairy carpels; those of the more commonly grown *P. w.* var. *nudicarpa* lack hairs.

officinalis	RED	LSP/ESU	2.5'–3.5'/3'
	○	Z10-2	D ***

Common Peony. Spreading tuberous roots underlie the seldom branched, slightly hairy stems. The dark green, biternate lower leaves are deeply cleft into many pointed, narrowly oblong 3"–4" leaflets; the upper leaves are less cut. Both are paler and pubescent beneath. The solitary, crimson 4"–5" flowers are saucer shaped with obovate petals, surrounding a boss of yellow stamens with red filaments and 2–3 densely white-woolly carpels. Southern Europe, Asia.

———— 'Alba Plena' has double white flowers.

———— 'Rubra Plena.' Double, deep red flowers.

tenuifolia	CRIMSON	SP	1'–2.5'/1.5'
	○ ◑	Z10-4	D **

Fernleaf Peony. Unbranched stems, heavily clothed in elegant, finely cut foliage, rise from spreading, thick, tuberous roots. The bipinnatifid or tripinnatifid leaves are dissected into narrowly linear segments, dark green and glabrous above, hairy beneath. Solitary and terminal, the deep crimson or purplish cupped 2¼"–3¼" flowers appear to sit on a ruff of leaves; 8–10 obovate to oblanceolate petals surround a tuft of yellow stamens and 2–3 tomentose carpels. A longer-blooming double form, 'Rubra Plena,' is sometimes available; pale pink-flowered 'Rosea' has become rare. Divide with care, since the roots are brittle; they often take 2–3 years to become established. The foliage dies down by midsummer. Southeastern Europe, Caucasus. *P. tenuifolia* has passed on its delicate foliage to several fine hybrids. These include 'Early Bird,' which has olive green leaves and early, single crimson flowers on 1.5′–2′ stems. *P.* x *smouthii* (*P. tenuifolia* x *P. lactiflora*) is sometimes incorrectly called *P. anomala, P. anomala smouthii,* or *P. laciniata.* It is an old hybrid with deeply cut foliage and fragrant, single red flowers very early in the season.

PAPAVER, Papaveraceae. (100)   Poppy

Poppies are showy, often flamboyant plants for sunny borders. Most are covered throughout with coarse hairs; their stems exude a milky sap when cut. The pinnately divided leaves are largely basal. Nodding in bud, their upturned, solitary flowers shed their sepals to expand 4 or more tissue paper-crumpled petals in a glorious array of colors, excepting only blue. Numerous stamens form a conspicuous, central boss, which surrounds a seed capsule decorated with a wheel-like pattern. Planting is best in the fall, but most do not transplant readily. If used as a cut flower, Poppies are best gathered in the cool of the morning in bud; sear the base of the stems with a flame or dip into hot water to prevent the sap from "bleeding."

| *alpinum* | VARIOUS | SP-ESU | 6″–1′/1′ |
| | ○ | Z10-5/H | S *** |

Alpine Poppy. This extremely variable group includes *P. burseri, P. kerneri, P. pyrenaicum, P. rhaeticum, P. sendtneri,* and *P. suaveolens,* all considered to be legitimate, individual species by some taxonomists. Short-lived and often treated as biennials, Alpine Poppies form low tufts of gray or bluish green, finely pinnatifid 1″–2″ basal leaves. Above, on slender 1′ scapes, dance fragrant 1″–1½″ flowers in white and various shades of pink and yellow. The seed capsules are ovoid. Must have very porous, rather poor soil, preferably with added lime chips. Mountain regions of Europe.

| *atlanticum* | RED | LSP-SU | 6″–2′/1.5′ |
| | ○ | Z10-5/H | DS *** |

Short-lived clumps of silvery green, basal foliage with silky hairs on the upper surfaces. The coarsely crenate or pinnately lobed, oblong-oblanceolate leaves may reach 10″ in length on long petioles below; reduced and sessile above. The hairy buds open into delicate 1¼″–1½″ flowers in various shades of red and orange on low-branching 1.5′ scapes. The green or brown seed capsules taper sharply at the base. Self-seeds profusely. Morocco. Similar and closely related Spanish *P. rupifragum* is 1′–1.5′ tall. It is hairy only along the veins, on the undersides of its blue gray, basal leaves. Brick red to orange flowers open from hairless buds and bloom from late spring well into summer. Plants offered as *P. californicum* are often in fact *P. atlanticum.* The true *P. californicum,* Mission Poppy, is an annual species, native to California.

| *nudicaule* | VARIOUS | SU-F | 1′–2′/1.5′ |
| | ○ | Z10-3/H | S **** |

Iceland Poppy, Arctic Poppy. [*P. macounii, P. miyabeanum*]. This variable, short-lived perennial is nearly stemless and makes close tufts of rather glaucous, pale green, basal foliage. Long-petioled, pinnately lobed or cleft 1″–3″ leaves. The fragrant, silky flowers, 1″–3″ or more across, bloom in a full range of colors from white through yellows and oranges to reds; their inner petals are smaller than the outer. Several strains have been developed, particularly for the cut flower trade. Blooms the first year from an early seeding and is often grown as an annual. Mountains of Asia, Arctic, and subarctic regions.

STRAINS:

'Champagne Bubbles.' Large, long-stemmed flowers in a mixture of pastel colors. 1.5′ tall.
'Sparkling Bubbles' has a wider range of colors, including deep rose and scarlet, as well as pastels. 15″ tall.

| *orientale* | RED | LSP/ESU | 2′–4′/2′–3′ |
| | ○ | Z9-3/H | DR **** |

Oriental Poppy. [*P. bracteatum*]. Large, robust clumps of coarse, bristly-hairy 10″–12″ leaves, pinnately dissected, with oblong, toothed or lobed segments. Stout, hispid stems support the solitary, brilliant vermilion, goblet-shaped 4″–6″ flowers, subtended by large, leafy bracts. The crepey petals, usually 4 or 6 in number, are boldly blotched at their bases, with deep purple or maroon, and surround a boss of dark purple stamens and a conspicuous, velvety black, wheel-patterned capsule. Provide a well-drained, deep, rich soil. Once established, do not disturb, except for propagation by root cuttings in mid to late summer. Plant when dormant or from containers. Best alone or in groups of no more than 3. Since their foliage dies down by midsummer, combine with Gypsophila (Gertrude Jekyll's choice), Limonium, Dahlias, or some other leafy, later-blooming species to fill in the gap. Will not tolerate hot, humid conditions; best where summers are cool. Closely related *P. bracteatum,* Great Scarlet Poppy, is now considered to be a variety of *P. orientale* and is certainly involved in the parentage of some of the modern hybrids. Turkey, southwestern Asia. Popular and undemanding, Oriental Poppies have been bred extensively, resulting in a vast number of selections with larger, sometimes double flowes in a wide range of colors. A sunny location with well-drained, fertile soil is satisfactory. Staking is frequently necessary.
———— 'Beauty of Livermore.' Bright, fire engine red flowers on 2.5′ stems.
———— 'Bonfire' has flame red flowers with black centers.
———— 'China Boy.' Soft orange flowers, white at the base of the ruffled petals.
———— 'Glowing Rose.' Large, brilliant watermelon pink flowers. Early blooming.
———— 'Lavender Glory.' Deep lavender flowers, black at the base of the petals.
———— 'Mrs Perry' has baby pink flowers. One of the earliest selections from Perry's Hardy Plant Farm, which later contributed several other enduring cultivars.
———— 'Pinnacle' has large white flowers edged in scarlet.
———— 'Queen Alexandra.' Salmon pink flowers.

Papaver orientale cv.

———— 'Raspberry Queen.' Raspberry pink flowers, black at the center. Midseason to late.

———— 'Warlord' has deep crimson flowers.

STRAINS:

Unfortunately, the Oriental Poppies have several undesirable traits. They bloom over a short season with only a few flowers; these have a persistent seed capsule, sometimes considered to be unsightly. James DeWelt of Mohn's Inc., California, has conducted an intensive breeding program over many years to minimize these drawbacks. He has bred a hybrid strain of Poppies, which he calls the 'Minicap' series. These sterile plants bloom over 2–4 months, with as many as 50–100 flowers each. The large seed capsule has been reduced and is almost hidden by the stamens. Heat tolerance has also been bred in, making them better suited to hot climates; their resistance to high humidity is doubtful.

'Angelface.' Large, soft pink flowers on 2'–4' stems. Very free blooming.

'Cardinal' has scarlet red flowers. 2'–4' tall.

'Downtown.' Soft orange flowers on 1.5' stems.

'Sprite.' White, almost ruffled petals, with a wide pink border. Soft blue, ferny foliage. Very floriferous. 2'–4'.

'Sundance' has large, light orange flowers. 4'–6' tall. Very tolerant of heat.

'Tara' has clear pink 8″ flowers on 4'–6' stems.

PARADISIA, Liliaceae. (2)

liliastrum	WHITE	LSP/ESU	1'–2'/1'
	○ ◑	Z9-5	DS ✳✳

St. Bruno's Lily, Paradise Lily. [*Anthericum liliastrum*]. More refined, but similar to *Anthericum liliago*. Its broadly linear, basal foliage to 2' long forms handsome clumps. Erect scapes as long as or shorter than the leaves support loose, one-sided, terminal racemes of fragrant, delicate white funnelform flowers. The 6 free 1″–2″ tepals are accented by a green spot at their pointed tips. Culture as for *Anthericum*. Southern Europe. *P. l.* 'Major' is taller with larger, less delicate flowers. Not as hardy. *P. lusitanica,* a Portuguese species, is more vigorous and may reach 5' in height.

PARIS, Liliaceae. (20)

polyphylla	GREEN	SU	2'–3'/1.5'
	◑●	Z8-4	DS ✳

Rhizomatous roots underlie several unbranched, erect, smooth stems, each topped with a whorl of 4–9 dark green leaves, pointed, ovate, and net veined, to 6″ long. The unique, solitary flowers held on a short stalk just above the collar have 4–6 green, lanceolate,

Paradisea lusitanica

Paris polyphylla

leaflike sepals and the same number of spidery, threadlike yellow petals. The stamens, yellow edged with maroon, surround a conspicuous, knoblike maroon stigma. If fertilized, the capsule splits to reveal bright orange-red seeds, which should be sown at once. Plant deeply in acid, woodsy soil. More a curiosity than a display plant, but it has a subdued elegance that appeals to collectors of the unusual. The flowers may last for as long as 3 months. Himalayas.

PATERSONIA, Iridaceae. (18)

Fans of stiff, Iris-like leaves surround numerous scapes, which end in close spikes of purplish blue or yellow flowers. Each has 3 broadly spreading outer tepals and 3 much smaller, inner ones, all joined at the base into a long, slender perianth tube. The flowers open in succession over a long season, but each lasts only a few hours. Plant in a sunny position with good drainage. All deserve a wider popularity.

glauca	PURPLE	SP-SU	1'–1.5'/1'
	O	Z10-9/H	S *

Short Purple Flag. [*P. fragilis*]. Its glaucous, narrowly linear leaves, almost circular in cross section, may reach 1.5' in height. Shorter than the leaves, the erect scapes bear purple 1" flowers in clusters of 2–4. More tolerant of poorly drained soils than the other species. The Long Purple Flag, *P. longiscapa,* is similar, but its flower spikes rise above the foliage. Both are from southeastern Australia.

Patersonia drummondii

| *sericea* | VIOLET | SP-SU | I′/I′ |
| | ○ | ZIO-9/H | S * |

The foliage is clothed in long, silky hairs. The large, deep violet flowers are slightly cupped. Southeastern Australia. Western Australian *P. drummondii* is hairy only at the base of its leaves.

| *umbrosa* | PURPLE | SP-SU | I.5′–2′/I′ |
| | ○ | ZIO-9/H | S * |

An erect and very stiff plant with violet flowers about I″ across. *P. xanthina* is similar, but has yellow flowers. Both need shading from intense sun. Western Australia.

PATRINIA, Valerianaceae. (15)

Seldom grown in American gardens, Patrinias are at their best in lightly shaded woodlands, where the soil is peaty and moist. Valuable for their very long blooming time. Easy to grow.

| *gibbosa* | YELLOW | SU/LSU | I′–2′/I′ |
| | ○ ◑ | Z9-5 | DS *** |

The shiny, broadly ovate leaves are pinnately cut and jaggedly toothed to 6″ long.

Patrinia gibbosa

Loose, branching 3"–4" clusters of acid yellow flowers, less than ¼" across, each 5 lobed with one longer, straplike lobe. Japan.

triloba	YELLOW	SU	1′–2′/1′
	○ ◑	Z9-5	DS ✳✳✳

[*P. palmata*]. Of erect habit. Their fresh green, opposite leaves are palmately cleft and irregularly, coarsely toothed on 2"–3" petioles. Wiry, brownish stems hold airy, axillary clusters of light yellow flowers well above the foliage. Each panicle-like cluster, 3"–4" across, is composed of many ¼" flowers. Tolerant of some sun, but the soil must be kept cool and moist, especially in warm areas. Spreads slowly. Japan.

PELARGONIUM, Geraniaceae. (280)   **Geranium**

This large and complex genus is known in the vernacular confusingly as Geranium or Storksbill. Predominantly South African, Pelargoniums are hardy only in dry, essentially frost-free climates, but are grown elsewhere for summer bedding and as easy-to-grow pot plants for conservatories, garden rooms, and window sills. Their widespread popularity over the last 150 years or so has led to extensive breeding, resulting in countless horticultural varieties and hybrids. Their flowers, in white, pinks, reds, and maroons, often bicolored, are borne in umbels or trusses in the upper leaf axils on long, stiff stalks, swollen at the base. Strongly reflexed in bud, the florets assume a more or less erect position by the time they open. The individual, asymmetrical, 5-parted flowers are characterized by the fusion of the spurred calyx to the pedicel, evidenced by a slight bump at the point of junction. There are usually 10 stamens, some of which are nonfunctional staminodes. The flowers are followed by 5-valved, beaklike fruits, which dehisce spirally. Petioled and subtended by conspicuous leafy stipules, the often strongly aromatic leaves range from entire to finely dissected; many are attractively variegated. Most Geraniums thrive in full sun, but resent the intense heat of the day. Excellent in coastal regions and where the daytime heat is relieved at night. Variegated sorts should be protected from direct sun and reveal their strongest colors in less exposed positions. Fertile, slightly acid to neutral soil is ideal if it drains freely. Water deeply during times of drought, but avoid overwatering. Pinch to maintain bushiness, and prune lightly to shape throughout the season. Damp, stagnant air encourages the spread of *Botrytis,* to which the flower trusses are susceptible; keep spent heads removed and spray with a fungicide as necessary. Aphids, mealybugs, and red spider mites are probably the most common pests, particularly on pot-grown plants. A regular spray program will usually provide good control. Oedema (edema) is a problem which most seriously affects the Ivy-leaved group, although Zonals may suffer as well. It manifests itself as raised, corky areas on the undersides of the leaves; remove the most unsightly. Once thought to be a viral condition, it is now accepted as physiological, caused by a sudden increase in sap pressure. Well-grown plants, adequately fed and watered, are seldom at risk. Avoid severe drying out. Decreasing the humidity is helpful to plants under glass; increasing air circulation by thinning helps out of doors. Propagation is by seed or by soft cuttings taken from young shoots. These should be about 2″–4″ in length and allowed to dry out for a few hours prior to sticking in sand. Many commercial nurseries root and ship in Jiffy-7 peat pellets. The use of hormones hastens rooting. Be alert for black leg caused by the *Pythium* fungus. Virus-free, indexed stock is available, raised by tissue culture. Be sure that your supplier offers clean material, propagated from an indexed source. Specialized information can be obtained from the International Geranium Society, which publishes a quarterly bulletin and has a seed exchange. For convenience, the genus may be loosely divided into 4 groups: (1) the Common, Zonal or Bedding Geraniums, *P.* x *hortorum,* (2) the Trailing or Ivy-Leaved Geraniums, *P. peltatum,* (3) the Lady Washington or Martha Washington Geraniums or Pelargoniums, *P.* x *domesticum,* and (4) the species, many of which have scented leaves. These last are popularly grown in herb gardens. The species with unscented leaves are largely grown by collectors. Unfortunately the nomenclature is badly confused in the trade, with much overlapping.

| *capitatum* **Hort.** | **PINK** | **SP-SU** | **1′–2′/2′** |
| | ○ | **Z10/H** | **CS ✳✳✳** |

Rose-Scented Pelargonium. Plants offered in the trade as *P. capitatum* are usually derived from *P. graveolens.* They make sprawling, weak growth with thick, fleshy stems, woody below. Soft velvety with long hairs, their long-petioled, lightly rose-scented 1″–2″ leaves are 3–5 lobed, cordate at the base, and toothed and ruffled along the margins. The rosy lavender flowers, their longer, upper petals veined in red, are almost sessile and crowd into 9- to 20-flowered heads. Hybridizes readily. The true species is involved in the parentage of the *P.* x *domesticum* group. South Africa.

'Attar of Roses' is most widely available. It is probably a hybrid, often listed under *P. graveolens.* Compact, with strongly rose-scented, ruffled leaves. Popular for pot-pourri.

'Shotesham Pet' ['Concolor Lace'] has deeply lobed, pointed leaves and rosy flowers. Smells of filbert nuts!

crispum	PINK	SP-SU	I′–3′/I′
	○	ZIO/H	CS ****

Finger Bowl Geranium, Lemon-Scented Geranium. [*P.* 'Lemon Crispum']. Subshrubby, with many stiff, upright stems, characteristically clothed in 2 ranks of grayish foliage, strongly fragrant of lemons. The very small, 3-lobed leaves are rounded with crisped margins. Pale lavender pink ¾″–1″ flowers with dark-veined upper petals, top short peduncles, in 1- to 3-flowered umbels. South Africa. The numerous cultivars and hybrids of this species are frequently listed by herb specialists.

———— 'Minor' ['Crispum Minor'] smells of citronella. Its very small leaves are traditionally used in finger bowls.

'Prince Rupert' ['Prince Rupert Lemon'] is strongly lemon scented. Its leaves are the largest of the group. A variegated form with cream-edged leaves is known as 'French Lace' ['Prince Rupert Variegated'].

x *domesticum*	VARIOUS	SP-SU	I.5′–3′/I.5′
	○	ZIO/H	CS ****

Lady Washington Geranium, Martha Washington Geranium, Pansy-Flowered Geranium, Regal Pelargonium, Show Pelargonium. This extensive group is considered to include at least *P. cucullatum* [*P. angulosum*], *P. grandiflorum, P. capitatum,* and *P. fulgidum* in its parentage. Subshrubby, sometimes woody at the base; the tough, hairy stems are erect, clothed in dark green foliage, which lacks the zoning of the *P.* x *hortorum* group and has only a slight odor. The ovate 2″–4″ leaves are heart shaped or kidney shaped at the base, mostly angled or lobed, and serrated along the margin. Loose trusses of 5 or more, very asymmetrical, flat or bell-shaped 1″–2½″ flowers top the stiff, downy flower stalks. The petals are commonly blotched or veined in a darker color, especially the upper ones; mostly 5–9 in number, they are arranged in the same plane so that the flowers are never fully double. Plants with more or less flat flowers are often called Pansy-Flowered Geraniums; others with ruffled petals appear to be double and are sometimes known as Azalea-Flowered Geraniums. Confusingly, Angel Pelargoniums are also offered as Miniature Regals, although their parentage is different. This strain resulted from crossing 'The Shah,' a Regal cultivar, with *P. crispum.* All are best where daytime heat is relieved by cool nights. Although blooming time is at its peak from spring through summer, many of the recent introductions continue to flower into the autumn. Prune hard afterward for best late winter and spring flower production.

'Candy.' This introduction from Fischers has variegated purple and lavender upper petals and baby pink lower ones.

'Grand Slam' is one of the best red-flowered cultivars. Its deep red flowers are overlaid with salmon, with dark brown spots on each petal. An American introduction from W. Schmidt. Its sports include 'Lavender Grand Slam,' with orchid flowers, and 'Harewood Slam,' with flowers variegated in brown and red.

'Miss Australia' has grayish green leaves rimmed with white. Its small flowers are pink.

'Mrs. Layal' ['Madame Layal']. An old-fashioned French cultivar of the Angel group, with small Pansy-like flowers. Upper petals plum colored, rimmed in white; the lower petals white with a central purple blotch.

'Rogue' has deep red flowers blotched with black or maroon. Bushy in habit; seldom needs pinching.

'Voodoo.' Its deep velvety red flowers are blotched in black. Taller than most and with more triangular leaves.

'White Champion.' Large, Azalea-like flowers of pure white.

echinatum	BICOLORED	LF-SP	1'–1.5'/1'
	○	Z10/H	CS **

Cactus Geranium or Sweetheart Geranium makes compact, upright subshrubs with branched, fleshy gray stems, armed with brown, hooked, thornlike stipules. The ends of the short branches bear tufts of long-petioled foliage. Silky with white hairs beneath, the gray green, ovate to heart-shaped 1"–1½" leaves have 3–7 shallow, crenate lobes. The slender, branching flower stems bear only a few leaves, mostly on the lower part, but may support 10 or more 3- to 6-flowered umbels of delicate 1½" flowers. These are white, each petal notched, the upper pair marked conspicuously with a heart-shaped reddish crimson blotch. After flowering, the plants need a period of rest, preferably out of sight, since they are far from attractive. Water sparingly. South Africa.

graveolens	PINK	SU	1'–2'/2'
	○	Z10-9/H	CS ***

Rose-Scented Geranium, Sweet-Scented Geranium. [*P. terebinthinaceum*]. Softly pubescent throughout, this vigorous grower becomes woody below. The opposite, almost heart-shaped 1"–4" leaves are deeply palmately cleft into 3–5 lobes, each further lobed and round toothed. Axillary umbels of 2–7 small, almost sessile flowers; rose pink, the upper pair of petals with a central purple spot. This widely grown species interbreeds freely and many of the cultivars are probably hybrids. Cape Province.

'Grey Lady Plymouth.' Not as strongly rose scented as the species, but just as robust. Grayish foliage edged in white.

'Lady Plymouth' ['Silver Leaf Rose'] is dwarfer than the species. Its leaves are grayish with white blotches.

'Little Gem' [*P. terebinthinaceum*] is strongly lemon rose scented. Its fine, pale green leaves are deeply 3 cleft and cleft again; low, compact plants. Lavender rose flowers veined in purple.

'Red-flowered Rose' ['Vandesiae']. Dwarf and somewhat trailing, with deeply fingered leaves, crinkled along the edges when young. Slightly rose scented. Cerise flowers with black-spotted, dark upper petals.

'Rober's Lemon Rose' may possibly have the strongest fragrance of the rose-scented types, with a touch of lemon. Bushy with soft, deeply cut, gray green leaves and lavender flowers. Probably a hybrid of the species with *P. tomentosum*.

'Variegatum' may be confused in the trade with 'Lady Plymouth.' Rose mint-scented, gray green, deeply lobed leaves edged in cream.

| **x *hortorum*** | VARIOUS | SP-F | 6″–3′/1.5′ |
| | ○ | ZIO/H | CS **** |

Bedding Geranium, Fish Geranium, Horseshoe Geranium, Zonal Pelargonium. This huge, hybrid complex is considered to be largely derived from *P. zonale* x *P. inquinans*, although over the years blood from other species, particularly *P. hybridum* and *P. frutetorum*, has been introduced. Their stout, often succulent stems branch widely and become shrubby with age or in response to drought. The softly hairy foliage is strongly aromatic, emitting a somewhat fishlike odor when bruised. In varying shades of green and gray green, the leaves are highlighted by an irregularly broad band of darker green, bronze, or brown, parallel to the margin. There are numerous cultivars with variegated foliage commonly known as Fancy-Leaved Geraniums. Mostly alternate, the 1″–5″ leaves are round to kidney shaped, often deeply cordate at their bases, with irregularly crenate and scalloped, wavy margins. Axillary and terminal, the long, stiff flower stems are downy and end in showy, rounded umbels of many single, semidouble, or double flowers. In color, these range from white to assorted pinks and salmon, oranges, and reds, sometimes bicolored. The petals are usually of equal size, although sometimes the upper pair is significantly smaller than the lower 3. Novelty forms are common: Cactus-flowered types have long, very narrow, pointed petals; Rosebud or Noisette Geraniums have small, very tightly double flowers like tiny rosebuds; the Carnation-flowered have serrate petals; the flowers of Bird's Egg Geraniums are speckled with darker dots; the Phlox-flowered type always has single flowers with flattened, broad petals accented by a darker central band or eye. Stellar Geraniums have narrow, cleft upper petals and broad, triangular lower petals, with serrate edges; their small leaves are deeply cut or fringed. Dwarf and Miniature types are also available. Recently, seed strains of F1 hybrids have been developed. All may be listed by specialist nurseries in their own categories or lumped under Zonal Geraniums. The following are just a few of the most popular cultivars:

'Aurora' has large umbels of brilliant magenta, semidouble flowers, white at the center.

'Blues.' Large, semidouble pink flowers with a white eye. Vigorous but compact.

'Chinese Cactus.' One of the Stellar types, with fringed leaves and white-throated coral flowers.

'Damon's Gold Leaf' has fuzzy gold leaves with a rust-colored zone. Its single flowers are reddish salmon.

'Mars' blooms freely with weather-resistant, bright red, semidouble flowers on compact plants.

'Irene.' This strong, free-branching, American cultivar was the first of a group of hybrids carrying the 'Irene' name. Large umbels of bright cerise, semidouble flowers. Once widely used for bedding, but largely replaced by more modern cultivars.

'Medley.' A double, white-flowered hybrid with petals edged in pink. This small-leaved dwarf is well suited to window box and houseplant culture.

'Mrs H. Cox' has pale salmon single flowers, but is grown more for its strikingly tricolored leaves of pale green broadly banded in reddish brown and edged in cream yellow.

'Pink Camellia' is one of the most widely grown pink Zonals. Its semidouble flowers are light salmon pink, paler around the edges.

'Sincerity' blooms freely, with intensely bright red, semidouble flowers.

'Snowmass.' Semidouble white flowers. A prolific bloomer.

'Sunbelt Dark Red' ['Toreador']. Bright crimson, semidouble flowers held well above the large plants. The 'Sunbelt' group of cultivars was developed by Dr. Griffith Buck to tolerate the nighttime heat and humidity of midwestern summers.

'Yours Truly' has semidouble scarlet flowers.

SERIES:

'Orbit.' Early to mature from seed, they make neat, compact plants, with large, distinctively zoned leaves. Usually available in mixed or separate colors of white through pinks and lavenders, to red and violet. A free-blooming F1 hybrid series.

'Ringo.' This almost dwarf series has strongly zoned leaves. Blooms early and freely. Available in pinks, lilac, and reds. The white-flowered selection has unzoned leaves.

peltatum	VARIOUS	SP-F	1'–1.5'/1'
	○ ◑	Z10/H	CS ****

Ivy-Leaved Geranium, Trailing Geranium. Mostly trailing and several feet in length when well grown, the smooth stems bear alternate, long-petioled, peltate leaves, 2"–3" across. These are Ivy-shaped, very broadly ovate, with 5 angled lobes, glossy and of a leathery texture. The long, slender flower stems end in elegant, 5- to 7-flowered umbels. The pink to white flowers, on short, hairy pedicels, are asymmetrical, with the upper pair of petals longer than the lower 3. Excellent tumbling over walls and in hanging baskets. Ivy-Leaved Geraniums enjoy enormous popularity and have been bred extensively. The range of cultivars, and hybrids usually with the Zonal types, includes some with variegated foliage, as well as single, semidouble, and double flowers, in white, through salmons, pinks, and lavenders, to deep reds and violets. Not as tolerant of strong sun as the Zonals; provide shade during the heat of the day or grow in partly shaded places. Top growth is damaged when the temperature drops to 25°F. The species is from South Africa.

'Apricot Queen' has small, double, salmon pink flowers, which fade through pink to almost white. Pinch to keep bushy.

'Beauty of Eastbourne.' Double cerise flowers. A profuse bloomer.

'Double Lilac White' ['Cliff House'] has double white flowers, tinged and veined in lilac.

'Mexican Beauty.' Semidouble flowers of a striking, deep rosy red.

'Rouletta' is a sport of the last. Its semidouble white flowers are edged in cerise. Keep pinched.

'Sugar Baby.' This dwarf cultivar is compact and bushy. Its small, bright baby pink flowers are double.

'Sybil Holmes.' Tightly double, bright pink "rosebuds" on compact plants. Free blooming.

'White Mesh.' The thick, deep green leaves of this exciting hybrid are crisply veined in cream, the result of a nonspreading virus. Large, double pink flowers.

tomentosum	WHITE	SP	1′–3′/2′
	○ ◑	Z10/H	CS ✱✱

Peppermint-scented Geranium is considered by some to be the best of the mint-scented group. Its shrubby, more or less prostrate stems are thickly covered in soft hairs. Opposite or alternate, on long petioles, the dentate 3″–5″ leaves are shaped like Grape leaves; velvety above, white-woolly beneath. Umbels of 4–20 tiny white flowers on abbreviated pedicels top the short, slender flower stalks. The upper petals are marked in purplish red, the lower slightly longer and narrower. Keep pruned to shape. Very frost tender. Excellent in potpourri. Cape Province.

'Joy Lucille.' Probably *P. tomentosum* x *P. graveolens.* This vigorous grower is popular for its pale green, triangular leaves, strongly peppermint scented. Its whitish pink flowers are not notable. 'Joy Lucille Variegated' has ivory-marbled leaves.

tricolor	BICOLORED SP		8″–1′/1.5′
	○	Z10/H	CS ✱✱

[*P. violareum*]. This low, spreading subshrub has many-branched stems, clothed in densely velvety, gray green, silvery foliage. Its variable, lanceolate to narrowly ovate leaves are unevenly cut and toothed. Most branches bear several flower stalks toward their tips, each with usually 3, sometimes as many as 6 flowers, with obovate, clawed petals. The upper pair are deep red, veined and blotched at their bases in very dark red to black; the lower petals are almost pure white, traced in red. Sandy soil is preferred. Cape Province.

Pelargonium tricolor

Peltiphyllum peltatum

PELTIPHYLLUM, Saxifragaceae. (1)

peltatum	WHITE	SP	2′–4′/2′–3′
	○ ◑	Z9-6	D ***

Umbrella Plant. [*Saxifraga peltata*]. This native of western stream banks blooms in spring on leafless, hairy, and ruddy flower stalks which bear large corymbose cymes of white flowers, aging to pink. The rotate ½″ corolla is composed of 5 petals. The magnificent, mostly taller foliage develops later; large, peltate, basal leaves on long, hairy petioles arise from the thick, horizontal rhizomes. The lobed and toothed 1′–2′ leaf blades cup in the center. Fiery fall color. Likes deep, moist, organically rich soils; also thrives in the bog garden. Northern California, Oregon. Dwarf *P. peltatum* 'Nanum' is only 1′ tall.

PENSTEMON, Scrophulariaceae. (250)   Beard-Tongue

North American with only one exception, this genus includes some of our most beautiful wildflowers. Unfortunately many of the species do not adapt readily to conditions much different from those of their native environments. Penstemons generally are erect, but some are spreading or even prostrate. Their leaves are opposite or sometimes whorled; the basal or lower ones are stalked, the upper sessile. Their showy flowers are borne in terminal panicles, less often in racemes. The asymmetrical corolla is tubular, opening to a 2-lobed upper lip and a 3-lobed lower lip. One of the 5 stamens is modified into a usually bearded staminode, from which the common name Beard-Tongue is derived. Penstemons thrive in full sun; shade lightly in torrid climates. Even the easiest must have good drainage. Many are extremely temperamental and must be grown in a mixture of sand and gravel. Never mulch with organic matter, only with gravel to discourage crown rot. Resist the temptation to fertilize these short-lived plants, as they will exhaust themselves rapidly. The ancestry of the popular hybrids is confused, and much in need of clarification. The American Penstemon Society has an extensive seed list and is an excellent source of expert information.

| *barbatus* | RED | ESU/SU | 2'–3'/1'–1.5' |
| | O | Z9-3 | DS *** |

[*Chelone barbata*]. Erect to ascending stems rise from a basal tuft of oblong to ovate leaves to 6″ long; the stem leaves are smaller and much narrower. Loose panicles of slender, bright scarlet flowers about 1″ long, with a yellow-bearded lower lip. Not recommended for the Pacific Coast. Southwestern North America. Its selections and hybrids have a better habit.
——— 'Rose Elf' has rose pink flowers on 1.5' stems. Long blooming.
P. x *johnsoniae* [*P.* 'Flathead Lake'], a very promiscuous natural hybrid of *P. barbatus,* has been used in a number of crosses with other species by the North Platte Experiment Station of the University of Nebraska. 'Prairie Dusk' has rose purple flowers on 1'–1.5' stems. 'Prairie Fire' has vermilion flowers on stems nearly 2' tall. Seedlings of hybrids are extremely variable both in height and flower color.

| *campanulatus* **hybrids** | VARIOUS | LSP-SU | 1.5'–2.5'/1.5'–2' |
| | O | Z10-8 | CD ** |

The hybrids in this group, said to have resulted from crossing the Mexican species *P. campanulatus* and *P. hartwegii,* are often confused with those of the *P. gloxinioides* Hort. group. They form bushy plants with narrower leaves and smaller flowers about 1¼″ long in various shades of pink, violet, and purple. They are also somewhat hardier.
——— 'Evelyn' has rose pink flowers. Very free blooming.
——— 'Garnet' has wine red flowers. Slightly taller than the preceding.

| *digitalis* | WHITE | LSP-ESU | 2'–4'/2'–3' |
| | O | Z9-3 | DS *** |

Erect to ascending stems. Elliptic to oblanceolate basal leaves, lanceolate to oblong-ovate stem leaves to 7″ long and usually toothed. Broad, open panicles of 1″–1¼″ flowers, all white or sometimes flushed with purple. Only the pure white form is worth growing. Eastern and central United States.

| *gloxinioides* **Hort.** | VARIOUS | SU | 2'–3'/1.5' |
| | O | Z10-9 | CD *** |

[*P.* x *gloxinioides, P.* x *hybridus*]. This botanically invalid name covers a group of tender or barely hardy plants, which are considered to be either variants of Mexican

Penstemon campanulatus 'Garnet'

P. hartwegii or hybrids of *P. cobaea* and *P. hartwegii*. Perennial in mild climates and grown as annuals elsewhere, these popular plants form bushy clumps of erect stems well clothed in broad, smooth leaves. In summer (earlier in frost-free areas), they produce showy panicles of large flowers to 2″ long in a wide range of colors: white and many shades of pink, red, and purple. Mixed seed strains are available, as well as many cultivars in individual colors.

————— 'Firebird' ['Ruby,' 'Schönholzeri'] is bright red.
————— 'Holly's White' has white flowers, flushed with pink.
————— 'Lady Alice Hindley' ['Gentianoides'] has pale mauve and white flowers.
————— 'Midnight' is deep purple.
————— 'Sour Grapes' has purple flowers with a touch of white.

heterophyllus purdyi	BLUE	SP/ESU	1′–2′/1.5′
	○	Z10-5	CS ***

Shrubby, with erect to spreading stems and linear to lanceolate 1″–3″ leaves. Short panicles of lavender to blue 1″–1½″ flowers. California. 'Blue Bedder' and 'Blue Spring' are good blue-flowered selections.

hirsutus	VARIOUS	SU	1′–2′/1′–1.5′
	○	Z9-3	CS ***

[*P. pubescens*]. A mound-forming plant, hairy throughout, with toothed, lanceolate to oblong leaves to 4½″ in length. Loose, short panicles of pink, violet, or rarely white 1″ flowers. Usually quite short-lived, but self-sows freely. Eastern and central North America.

————— 'Pygmaeus' has violet flowers on 6″ stems. It is not reliably dwarf from seed.

ovatus	BLUE	LSP	2′–3′/2′
	○	Z9-3	CS **

Stiff, erect stems above a basal rosette. Toothed, lanceolate to ovate leaves to 6″ long. Loose panicles of blue or purple ¾″ flowers. Difficult to germinate. Northwestern North America.

palmeri	PINK	SP-ESU	2′–4′/2′
	○	Z10-5/H	CS **

Erect stems, with glaucous, oblong-ovate basal leaves and lanceolate-ovate stem leaves to 6″ long. The upper leaves are clasping to perfoliate. Long, elegant panicles of pink 1¼″ flowers; the throat of the corolla is inflated, the prominent lower lip is reflexed. Perhaps the most beautiful of all Penstemons. Unfortunately only suited to the dry situations and lean, sandy soils of our southwestern gardens. Southwestern United States.

serrulatus	PURPLE	LSP-ESU	1.5′–2′/1.5′–2′
	○	Z9-3	CS **

Bushy clumps of stiff stems, with elliptic to lanceolate or ovate leaves to 3″ long, rather crinkled and variably toothed. Short, leafy panicles of purplish blue to purple 1″ flowers, with a yellow-bearded staminode. Easy from seed. Northwestern North America.

smallii	PINK	LSP-ESU	1.5′–2′/1′–2′
	○	Z10-4	CS **

Bushy in habit, with lanceolate to ovate, sharply toothed leaves to 5″ long. Rose pink 1″ flowers in varying shades striped with white inside. Free blooming. Usually short-lived, but self-seeds prolifically. North Carolina, Tennessee.

spectabilis	BLUE	SP	3′–4′/1.5′–2′
	○	Z10-8/H	CS **

One of the most beautiful Penstemons, but unfortunately suited only to southwestern gardens. Stiff, erect stems with glaucous, toothed, oblanceolate to ovate leaves to 4″ long. The upper leaves are perfoliate. Long, slender panicles of lavender blue 1″–1¼″ flowers. Short-lived. Southern California, northern Baja California.

PENTAS, Rubiaceae. (34)

lanceolata	RED	SU	1′–4′/1.5′
	○	Z10	CS ***

Star Cluster, Egyptian Star. [*P. carnea*]. Upright bushes, becoming subshrubby at the base. Evergreen and opposite, the hairy, short-petioled 3½″–6″ leaves are mostly broadly ovate, pointed at the tip. Showy, compact, domed clusters of numerous flowers in shades of red, pink, and purple or sometimes white. The slender corolla tube, about 1″ long, flares into 5 spreading, pointed lobes; conspicuously exserted, branched styles.

Pentas lanceolata

These easy plants bloom almost continuously. While hardy only in frost-free areas, elsewhere they are used extensively for bedding and as greenhouse plants. Mealybugs may be a nuisance under glass. Tropical East Africa.

PEROVSKIA, Labiatae. (7)

atriplicifolia	BLUE	SU/LSU	3′–5′/1.5′–2′
	○	Z10-5/H	CS ✱✱✱

Russian Sage. This graceful, aromatic subshrub, clothed in silvery gray hairs throughout, has stiff, erect, square stems and opposite, weakly toothed, lanceolate to lanceolate-ovate 1½″–2″ leaves. Airily branching 1′ panicles of small, whorled, lavender blue flowers. The asymmetrical ⅜″ corolla is 2 lipped, the upper lip 4 lobed. Needs well-drained soil. Cut back to the ground before new growth starts. Western Pakistan. Rare in cultivation, *P. abrotanoides* is 3′–4′ tall with bipinnately cut 2″ leaves and narrower panicles of purplish blue flowers. Turkestan to northeast Iran. Most common in gardens are 2 presumed hybrids of these species:
'Blue Haze,' with paler blue flowers and nearly entire leaves.
'Blue Spire' has finely dissected leaves.

PETASITES, Compositae. (15)   Butterbur

Butterburs should be planted in gardens only after much careful consideration. Their far-reaching, thick rhizomes make them highly invasive and difficult to eradicate. However, they are invaluable as almost impenetrable ground covers in such places as lakesides or on steep banks. Tolerant of heavy, rocky, or otherwise poor soils, but best under moist conditions.

fragrans	FOLIAGE	LW	8″–1′/1′
	○ ◐	Z10-5/H	DS ✱✱

Sweet Coltsfoot, Winter Heliotrope. The light green, toothed 8″ basal leaves are almost round, strongly cordate at their bases. The new leaves are felted beneath and appear at the same time as the almond-scented flower heads. Sturdy, pinkish 1′–1.5′ stems support the Groundsel-like clusters of pink or white flower heads; buds and calyces are reddish purple. The rather shaggy, female flower heads have erect rays, streaked with purple. Western Mediterranean.

x *hybridus*	FOLIAGE	ESP	1′–2′/2′
	○ ◐	Z8-4	DS ✱✱✱

Butterbur, Bog Rhubarb, Butterfly Dock. [*P. vulgaris*]. The long-petioled, heart-shaped or reniform, basal leaves appear after the flowers. They may reach 2.5′–3′ across, with

Perovskia 'Blue Spire'

Petasites japonicus

hairy undersides and lightly toothed margins. Clublike spikes of diskoid purple flower heads rise on thick, hollow stems. Naturalized in some eastern states. Europe, Asia.

| *japonicus* | FOLIAGE | LW/ESP | 3′/2′ |
| | ○ ◑ | Z9-4/H | DS ** |

Japanese Butterbur has bold, handsome basal leaves to 16″ across on long petioles. They are rounded or kidney shaped, lightly toothed, and woolly underneath. The flowers, which precede the foliage, are almost enclosed in bud by several large green bracts. This and the following are cultivated for their edible petioles. Japan, China, Korea.

———— *giganteus.* Giant Butterbur. With leaves to 4′ across on 6′ petioles, this is certainly not for small gardens. It forms enormous, overlapping mounds of deciduous foliage. In late winter, baseball-sized flower buds erupt from bare soil, opening to reveal a tight cluster of greenish white flower heads, surrounded by light green bracts. Japan.

PHLOMIS, Labiatae. (100)

These variably hairy plants have square stems and opposite leaves. Their hooded flowers are borne in widely spaced, axillary whorls. The upper lip of the corolla curves over the spreading, 3-lobed lower lip. Well-drained soil.

| *fruticosa* | YELLOW | SP-SU | 3′–4′/3′ |
| | ○ | ZI0-8/H | CDS **** |

Jerusalem Sage. The branching stems of this bushy subshrub become quite woody with age. Its gray-woolly, ovate to elliptic 2″–4″ leaves are scarcely toothed. Crowded, globose whorls of strong yellow 1″ flowers. Drought resistant. Cut back at the end of the season to control its shape. Invaluable in the mixed border as a foil to plants of vivid coloration. Mediterranean.

| *italica* | PINK | SU | 1′–1.5′/1′ |
| | ○ | ZI0-8/H | CDS ** |

An erect subshrub with oblong leaves about 2″ in length. Both the light silver gray stems and leaves are densely woolly. Whorls of small, hooded flowers of an exquisite pale dusty pink. The colors of the flowers and foliage combine to superb effect. Balearic Islands.

| *russeliana* | YELLOW | SU | 3′–4′/2′ |
| | ○ | ZI0-4/H | CDS *** |

[*P. viscosa* Hort.]. This substantial plant, with stout, erect stems is woolly throughout. Its coarsely wrinkled 6″–8″ leaves, white-woolly beneath, are broadly ovate with crenate margins. Dense whorls of large, yellow, hooded flowers. Much hardier than was once thought. Asia Minor.

Phlomis russeliana

| *tuberosa* | PINK | SU | 4′–6′/2′–3′ |
| | ○ | Z10-3/H | CDS ** |

Bushy, with stout, erect stems arising from tuberous roots. Variably hairy and wrinkled, the long-ovate, coarsely toothed leaves reach 8″–10″ in length, but are smaller above. Dense whorls of purplish pink flowers; the upper lip of the corolla, fringed with long hairs, is erect, not hooded as in most of the species. Central and southeastern Europe to central Asia.

PHLOX, Polemoniaceae. (60)

This predominantly North American genus has given us some of our most cherished plants for the border, wild, and rock garden. Most have opposite leaves, sometimes alternate above, sessile or on short stalks, and often with a conspicuous midrib. Their flowers, in shades of pink, red, lavender to purple, yellow and orange, as well as white, may be solitary, but more often are arranged in showy, terminal cymes or panicles. The slender, persistent calyx is 5 lobed or cleft, sometimes only toothed. Twisted in bud, the salverform corolla is composed of a narrow, cylindrical tube, which flares into 5 spreading lobes, each rounded or wedge shaped and frequently notched or cleft. The Border or Garden Phlox make attractive cut flowers, but tend to be rather short-lived in water. Spring-blooming *P. nivalis, P. subulata,* and *P. bifida* and their hybrids are low-growing, showy plants suitable for walls and rock gardens.

| *adsurgens* | PINK | SP | 1′/1′ |
| | ◑● | Z9-7/H | CDS ** |

Periwinkle Phlox. Lax, decumbent or trailing stems produce evergreen mats of shiny, dark green foliage. Their sessile 1″–1¼″ leaves are broadly ovate or elliptic. Hairy, wiry stems, formed the previous season, bear the sparse clusters of ½″–1″ flowers in various shades of pink, sometimes lavender, purple, or white. Their obovate petals, often with a darker stripe, usually pale toward the center. Thrives in acid, moisture-retentive soil. Protect from slugs. Not for areas with severe winters or hot summers, where closely related *P. stolonifera* may be used in its stead. California, Oregon.
———— 'Wagon Wheels' has very narrow salmon pink petals.

| *caroliniana* | VARIOUS | ESU | 2′–4′/2′ |
| | ○◑ | Z9-4/H | CD *** |

Thick-Leaved Phlox, Carolina Phlox. [*P. suffruticosa* Hort.]. While resembling the better-known *P. paniculata* and often confused with *P. maculata,* this species differs from both on several counts. It makes tidy clumps of strong, erect stems, clothed in thick, shiny, deep green, lanceolate 4″–5″ leaves more resistant to both mildew and red spider mite. The earlier-flowering, flattish panicles of pink to purple ¾″ flowers bloom over several weeks. Tolerant of light shade. Soil should be moist, well enriched with humus; dry soils encourage mildew. Southeastern United States.

divaricata	BLUE	SP	I′/I′
◐●	Z9-4	DS ****

Wild Blue Phlox, Wild Sweet William. [*P. canadensis*]. This semievergreen woodlander with spreading stems forms loose, creeping mats. Ovate to oblong leaves to 2″ long by about ¾″ wide. The slender flower stems, sticky with glandular hairs, are topped with loose clusters of light blue or lavender I″ flowers; petals scarcely notched. An attractive ground cover with late-blooming spring bulbs or under later-blooming perennials. Moist, humus-rich soil in light or dappled shade; cut back after flowering. Mildew is sometimes a problem. Northeastern and north central United States.

———— 'Fuller's White' has clean white flowers with deeply notched petals. Strong stems.

———— *laphamii* has deeper blue flowers with entire petals. More tolerant of sun. It is probably a parent, along with *P. pilosa,* of *P.* x 'Chattahoochee,' a fine hybrid about 10″ tall which has bluish lavender flowers with a maroon eye.

The Downy Phlox *P. pilosa* [*P. aristata*] flowers at the same time as *P. divaricata* with similar but larger usually pink to lavender flowers. Its stiff, pubescent stems to 1.5′ long sprawl but do not creep. The leaves are linear and pointed, about 3″ long. An excellent plant for dry, sunny positions in acid, sandy loam. Northeastern and central United States. *P.* x *arendsii* (*P. divaricata* x *P. paniculata*) has the showy flowers of Border Phlox and the dwarf stature of its other parent. Its cultivars include 'Hilda,' a pure lavender, 'Suzanne,' with red-eyed white flowers, and 'Lisbeth,' a lavender blue. Presently these German selections are scarce in the trade.

maculata	PURPLE	ESU	2′-4′/2′
○ ◐	Z9-3	CDS ****

Wild Sweet William or Meadow Phlox has strong, erect stems, usually purple spotted and well clothed in whorls of glossy, linear to lanceolate 2″-4″ leaves. Elegant, cylindrical clusters of very fragrant ½″ flowers with a long corolla tube in shades of purple or pink, sometimes white. Resistant to mildew. Seldom requires staking. Cut back to encourage a second flush of bloom. Culture as for *P. caroliniana,* but adapts better to damp soils. Mid-Atlantic to Midwestern states.

———— 'Alpha' has lilac pink flowers with a darker eye on sturdy 3′ stems.

———— 'Miss Lingard,' familiarly known as the Wedding Phlox, is often listed under *P. caroliniana.* Its elegant 6″ panicles of pure white flowers are on 2′-4′ stems. Can be temperamental.

———— 'Omega' is also white, but its flowers are lightly flushed with violet and have a violet eye. Unspotted 2.5′ stems.

———— 'Rosalinde.' Purplish pink flowers on vigorous 3′-4′ stems.

mesoleuca	VARIOUS	ESU-F	6″-I′/1.5′
○	Z9-7	DS **

Chihuahuan Phlox. Recently rediscovered in the wild by the late Dr. Paul Maslin, these plants are now increasingly available to gardeners. They form sprawling mounds with linear 3″ leaves. Above rise slender, wiry stems topped with vividly colored 1½″ flowers, which bloom until heavy frost. All require deep, well-drained soil in sun, with

Phlox maculata 'Miss Lingard'

plenty of water during flowering time, but they must be kept dry during the winter. With snow cover, they will withstand temperatures to o°F. Excellent in walls and scree gardens. Northern Mexico. Cultivars include 'Tangelo,' a free bloomer with flowers the color of orange peel, 'Mary Maslin,' a brilliant red, and 'Vanilla,' a rich cream.

paniculata	VARIOUS	SU-EF	2′–5′/2′
	○	Z9-3/H	CDR ✳✳✳✳

Border Phlox, Garden Phlox, Summer-Blooming Phlox. [*P. decussata*]. This old-fashioned, clump-forming perennial has largely been replaced in gardens by its showy cultivars, many of which may be hybrids with *P. maculata.* The species has strong, leafy stems, which bear pairs of minutely toothed, lanceolate to ovate 3″–6″ leaves. The sweet-smelling, purplish magenta ¾″ flowers are carried in pyramidal, terminal panicles. Northeastern and north central United States. The garden selections of Border Phlox are legion. Flower color ranges from pure white through all shades of pink, red, lavender, and purple, often with a contrasting eye; only pure blue and yellow are absent. The individual flowers, mostly larger than in the species, are massed in heavy, triangular trusses. These handsome plants require high maintenance to perform at their best, and when neglected mar even the most beautifully designed garden. To maintain vigor, divide plants every 2–3 years, preferably in early fall, and replant only the small, strong, outer divisions. Soil must be deep, porous, and fertile, well enriched with organic material to retain moisture. Water deeply at the roots during dry periods; avoid wetting the foliage. Thin the new shoots when growth begins in the spring; most plants can support only 4–6 strong stems at best, although many more are produced. As well as ensuring high-quality flowers, thinning also helps to increase air circulation among the stems, thereby discouraging the spread of powdery mildew. This last, as well as red spider mites are the 2 most serious problems for Border Phlox; gardeners must be diligent in controlling both. Nematodes may be troublesome, but for the most part have been eliminated by the use of clean stock. Deadhead to maintain vigor and curtail self-seeding; seedlings usually have muddy magenta flowers. Propagate by division or cuttings; propagated commercially by root cuttings where a rapid buildup of stock is required. The following sampling indicates the vast range of colors, heights, and flowering times. The 'Symons-Jeune' strain was bred in England and is very long blooming. It is reputedly less susceptible to powdery mildew.

'Blue Ice' has pinkish blue flowers which age to white, except for the corolla tube. To 3.5′ tall. This and the next 2 are 'Symons-Jeune' selections.

'Bright Eyes.' Pale pink flowers with a cerise eye. 2′ stems.

'Dodo Hanbury Forbes' is a clear, light pink, with enormous panicles of large, weather-resistant florets. 3′ tall.

'Harlequin' is an Alan Bloom selection, with bold, white-variegated foliage. Purplish flowers on 3′ stems.

'Mt. Fuji' ['Mt. Fujiyama'] may be the best white, with weather-resistant trusses of large florets. A strong grower. 3′–3.5′ tall.

'Orange Perfection' has large, luminous, salmon orange flowers, the closest to true orange in a Border Phlox. Vigorous 2′–3′ stems.

'Pinafore Pink' is low growing. Leafy 6″–8″ stems topped with panicles of bright pink florets, accented by cerise centers.

'Sir John Falstaff' makes vigorous clumps, topped by trusses of wide, intense salmon pink 2″ florets with darker eyes. 3′ tall.

'Starfire' blooms early, with cherry red flowers on 2′–3′ stems.

'The King' has large, deep violet flowers. 2′–2.5′ in height.

'World Peace' opens its pure white flowers at the beginning of fall. 3.5′ tall.

stolonifera	PINK	LSP	6″–1′/1′
◐ ●		Z9-3	CDS ****

Creeping Phlox. [*P. reptans*]. Its slender, hairy stolons produce low mats of evergreen foliage; short-stalked, elliptic to broadly ovate ¾″–2½″ leaves. In the spring, erect, sparsely foliaged flower stems rise above the leaves and end in loose, few-flowered clusters. The deep rose purple 1″–1½″ flowers have obovate petals and conspicuous yellow stamens. Tolerant of sunny positions in cool climates, but otherwise prefers dappled or light shade. An attractive woodland ground cover. Culture as for *P. divaricata*. Appalachian Mountains, southeastern United States.

———— 'Blue Ridge' has large, clear, pale blue flowers with broadly rounded, overlapping petals. 1′ stems.

———— 'Bruce's White' ['Ariane'] has pure white flowers with very conspicuous yellow stamens. 6″ tall. Blooms slightly earlier than the species.

———— 'Pink Ridge' is a pink-flowered version of 'Blue Ridge.' Selections of *P.* x *procumbens* [*P. amoena* Hort.] *(P. stolonifera* x *P. subulata)* make attractive evergreen clumps. 'Millstream' is an excellent 6″–1′ form from Lincoln Foster. It has narrow, dark green leaves and loose heads of mauve pink ¾″ flowers, with a central, cerise star surrounded by a white ring.

PHORMIUM, Agavaceae. (2)   **Flax Lily**

These popular, evergreen accent plants make stiff stands of sword-shaped basal leaves. Their open panicles of curved, tubular flowers are carried aloft on long scapes. The 6-parted flowers flare at the tip, displaying prominent stamens. The numerous cultivars and hybrids show much variation in leaf color and plant size; both should be propagated by division. All prefer well-drained, moist, fertile soils. Very adaptable, they resist drought, salt, and urban pollution.

---

colensoi		YELLOW	LSP/SU	5′–7′/3′
		○ ◑	ZIo-8/T	DS ✳✳✳

Mountain Flax. [*P. cookianum*]. The inflorescence rises well above the 3′–5′ leaves, less rigid than those of *P. tenax.* The yellow 1½″ flowers are followed by long capsules. New Zealand.

———— 'Cream Delight.' 1′–1.5′ leaves with a cream margin and green center.
———— 'Dwarf Form' has 2′ leaves.
———— 'Emerald Green.' Like the species, but with stiffer, bright green leaves.

Phormium colensoi 'Tricolor'

———— 'Tricolor.' Somewhat smaller than the species, with a red edge, cream stripe, and green center.

———— 'Variegatum.' The name is applied to several variegated cultivars of different size.

tenax	**RED**	**LSP/SU**	**6'–12'/4'**
	○ ◑	**Z10-8/T**	**DS ******

New Zealand Flax has stiff, gray green leaves to 6'–10' long, splitting at the ends and often edged with red. The inflorescence usually towers over the foliage; rust red 2" flowers. The capsules are shorter than those of *P. colensoi.* New Zealand. There is a bewildering range of cultivars and hybrids.

———— 'Atropurpureum' has purple leaves.

———— 'Aureum' has leaves broadly striped with yellow.

———— 'Goliath' is even larger than the species.

———— 'Nanum.' Variable in size; dwarf or semidwarf.

———— 'Purple Giant.' Like 'Goliath,' but with purple leaves.

———— 'Purpureum' is purple leaved.

———— 'Rubrum' is a bronze-leaved semidwarf.

———— 'Sundowner.' Compact. Purple-tinged leaves with pinkish stripes.

———— 'Tiny Tim.' Semidwarf. Bronze leaves with a yellow stripe.

———— 'Tricolor' has leaves with a reddish margin and a cream-white edge.

———— 'Variegatum' is variable with cream-white variegation.

———— 'Veitchii' ['Veitchianum']. Leaves striped with yellow.

———— 'Williamsii Variegatum' has a broad yellow stripe down the center of each leaf.

'Bronze Baby.' Bronze-leaved semidwarf.

'Coffee.' Semidwarf, with a bronze cast to the foliage.

'Dazzler.' Semidwarf to dwarf. Purplish leaves.

'Gold Sword.' A yellow-variegated semidwarf.

'Thumbelina.' Miniature. Purplish bronze leaves.

'Yellow Wave.' Yellow-variegated leaves. Semidwarf.

PHUOPSIS, Rubiaceae. (30)

stylosa	**PINK**	**SU**	**9"–12"/2'**
	○ ◑	**Z10-6/H**	**DS ****

Crosswort. [*Crucianella stylosa*]. A delicate, sprawling plant with lax, square stems and clammy, lanceolate ¾" leaves in whorls of 8–9. Its small, purplish pink flowers are arranged in dense, globose heads to 1½" across. The styles protrude well beyond the tubular corollas to a pins-in-a-pincushion effect. Tolerant of dry soil. Suitable as an edging or ground cover. Surprisingly, it smells of garlic! Easy from seed; often grown as an annual. Caucasus.

———— 'Purpurea' has larger, rich purple flowers.

Phuopsis stylosa

PHYGELIUS, Scrophulariaceae. (2)

These erect, subshrubby, South African plants have many slender, angled or winged stems and opposite, ovate to ovate-lanceolate leaves with small rounded teeth. Their tubular flowers, with 5 short lobes, nod in long, terminal panicles. Evergreen in warm climates. In cold areas, grow against a south-facing wall; cut back and mulch heavily in early winter. Prune to keep plants compact. Need a well-drained, light soil, moist during the growing season. Hybrids between the 2 species are known as *P.* x *rectus.* 'African Queen' (*P. aequalis* x *P. capensis* 'Coccineus') has deep salmon flowers.

aequalis	RED	SU-F	3'/1.5'
	○	Z10-7	CDS ✱✱✱

Leaves 1"–4" long. Slender, crowded panicles of pinkish red 2" flowers with yellow throats on short pedicels; corolla tubular and straight with spreading lobes. South Africa.

———— 'Yellow Trumpet' has pale butter yellow flowers.

capensis	RED	SU-F	3'–4'/2'–3'
	○	Z10-6	CDS ✱✱✱

Cape Fuchsia has 2"–5" leaves. Very long, loose panicles of orange to red 2" flowers borne on long pedicels; corolla tubular and slightly curved, with flaring to reflexed lobes. South Africa.

———— 'Coccineus,' the most commonly grown form, has large orange red flowers.

Phygelius aequalis 'Yellow Trumpet'

Physalis alkekengi

PHYSALIS, Solanaceae. (80)

alkekengi	ORANGE	LSU/F	1′–2′/2′
	○ ◑	ZI0-3/T	CDS ****

Chinese Lantern Plant. [*P. franchetii*]. Grown for its orange red, inflated, papery calyces, this unaccountably popular plant has all the subtlety of a neon sign. The crooked stems bear alternate, rather limp, ovate 2″–3″ leaves. Inconspicuous white ¾″ flowers with rotate, 5-lobed corollas. The showy mature calyx, 2″ long, resembles a small paper lantern; it encloses a round, edible, but insipid fruit. Easy, even invasive. Often grown as an annual. Dried for winter arrangements. A good plant for a child's garden, but an adult's sense of aesthetics should be mature enough to avoid it. Southeastern Europe to Japan.

———— 'Gigantea' is altogether larger than the species.

———— 'Pygmaea' ['Pygmy']. Dwarf to about 8″ tall.

PHYSOSTEGIA, Labiatae. (15)

virginiana	PINK	SU-F	3′/1.5′
	○ ◑	ZI0-3/H	CDS ****

False Dragonhead, Obedient Plant, or Virginia Lion's Heart is clump forming from a stoloniferous rootstock. Its stiff, square stems bear pairs of sharp-toothed, lanceolate

Physostegia virginiana 'Rosy Spire'

3″–5″ leaves, the upper ones reduced. Rigidly erect, the terminal and axillary 8–10″ spikes of close-set, pale pink to purplish pink flowers are subtended by small, leafy bracts. The irregular, tubular 1½″ corollas are 2 lipped, the upper lip entire, the lower 3 lobed. Useful in the flower border, wild garden, or as a cut flower. Long blooming and easy to grow. Thrives in moist, slightly acid soil, but tends to spread rapidly and needs division every 2–3 years. Vegetative propagation of good selections is recommended. Eastern and central United States.

———— 'Alba.' White flowers followed by attractive, green, fruiting spikes.

———— 'Rosy Spire' has rosy crimson flowers in late summer to fall. 3′ tall.

———— *speciosa* 'Rose Bouquet.' ['Rose Bouquet,' 'Bouquet Rose']. Larger throughout, with lilac pink flowers in late summer to fall. 3′–3.5′.

———— 'Summer Snow' is a popular cultivar with pure white flowers and dark green foliage. Spreads less than 'Alba.' Mid to late summer. 2′ tall.

———— 'Variegata' has beautiful foliage, marked with gray and irregularly banded with cream. In bud, the spikes are vertically striped in green and cream. Lilac flowers. 1.5′.

———— 'Vivid.' Bright rose flowers. Excellent for cutting. Later than 'Summer Snow' by 2–3 weeks. 1.5′–2′ stems.

PHYTEUMA, Campanulaceae. (40)	Horned Rampion

A temperamental, little alpine, *P. comosum,* is the best-known species. Others, more easily grown, are suitable for the front of the border or for informal cottage gardens. These graceful plants make loose tufts of long-petioled, basal foliage; their narrow, sessile, stem leaves are alternate. The erect flower stalks are so slender that they may topple over but then sprawl gracefully. The strange flowers are crowded into domed or rounded heads or short spikes. Horned Rampions are well named, as their delicate corollas are horn shaped. Five linear petals, which bulge at the base, taper to a point at the tip, where they join; later they may separate and expand. Well-drained, preferably alkaline soils. Afford slight protection from the sun in hot summer areas.

betonicifolium	BLUE	LSP-ESU	1′–1.5′/1′
	○	Z9-5	DS ****

Blue-Spiked Rampion has toothed, lanceolate-ovate basal leaves to 2″ long; the smaller, linear stem leaves are subsessile. Its ovoid 1½″ spikes of blue to lilac flowers elongate with age. Southern Europe.

spicatum	WHITE	ESU	1′–2.5′/1′
	○	Z9-5	DS **

Spiked Rampion. Double-toothed, ovate to heart-shaped 1½″–2″ basal leaves; smaller, lanceolate stem leaves. White, cream, or rarely, blue flowers in 1½″–3″ cylindrical spikes. Europe.

Phyteuma tenerum

---

tenerum	BLUE	ESU	6″–1.5′/1′
	○	Z9-5	DS **

Lanceolate-ovate, finely toothed basal leaves; narrowly lanceolate stem leaves. Domed 2″ heads of deep purplish blue flowers. Western Europe. *P. orbiculare* is similar.

PHYTOLACCA, Phytolaccaceae. (25)   Pokeweed

The Pokeweeds are coarse, loosely erect plants, with thick, succulent stems and large lax, alternate leaves. Not for the small garden—they may grow even larger than usual, under favorable conditions.

americana	WHITE	SU/LSU	4′–6′/2′–3′
	○ ◑	Z9-3	CDS ****

Pokeweed, Poke, Pokeberry, Scoke. [*P. decandra*]. This common weed has oblong to ovate-lanceolate leaves. The loose 8″ racemes of small, whitish, apetalous flowers become pendulous as the fruits develop. The stems, darkening to purplish pink with age, contrast beautifully with the shiny black berries. All parts of the mature plant are poisonous. Eastern North America to Texas and Mexico.

clavigera	PINK	SU	4′–8′/2′–3′
	○ ◑	Z9-6	CDS **

Elliptic to ovate-lanceolate leaves. Erect, densely crowded racemes of tiny pink flowers.

Stems, aging to pink, with brilliant black berries. Perhaps hardier than Z6. More ornamental than *P. americana*. China.

PIMPINELLA, Umbelliferae. (140)

major 'Rubra'	PINK	SU	2'–3'/1'
	○	Z9-5	D **

[*P. magna* 'Rubra,' *P. magna* 'Rosea']. This graceful plant, like a pink Queen Anne's Lace, has erect, thick but rather brittle ribbed stems. Its pinnate leaves have 7–13 coarsely toothed 1½" leaflets. The small dusty pink flowers are in umbels about 1½" wide. Plant in groups of 3 for best effect; charming in combination with blue Campanulas or Platycodons. Europe.

PLANTAGO, Plantaginaceae. (200) Plantain

lanceolata	FOLIAGE	SU	6"/1'–1.5'
	○	Z10-3/T	DS **

The species is a common weed, but the cultivars are quite elegant. Lanceolate, ribbed

Phytolacca clavigera

Pimpinella major 'Rubra'

leaves to 1' long in a low, basal rosette. Wiry scrapes bear slim spikes of minute green flowers of no account. Europe. Propagate the variegated forms by division.
———— *marginata.* Leaves edged and blotched with white.
———— 'Streaker.' Leaves with broad white margins.

major	FOLIAGE	LSP/SU	1'–1.5'/1'
	○	ZI0-3/T	DS ✳✳✳

Plantain. Only the horticultural forms of this pernicious weed are grown for ornament. Most often they come true from seed. The species is Eurasian.
———— 'Atropurpurea' forms a loose, basal rosette of ribbed, elliptic to ovate 6″ leaves on long, winged petioles. The foliage is bronze purple above, bronze green below. Tiny, 4-lobed green flowers in dense, pencil-thin spikes on long scapes. Sometimes listed as 'Rubrifolia.'
———— 'Rosularis' is about 8″ tall, with short scapes ending in a tight rosette of leaflike bracts subtending the minute flowers. Its foliage is green.
———— 'Rosularis Rubrifolia' has reddish purple foliage.

PLATYCODON, Campanulaceae. (I)

grandiflorus	BLUE	SU/LSU	1.5'–2.5'/1'
	○ ◑	ZI0-3	CDS ✳✳✳✳

Balloon Flower. Sheaves of erect stems, branching above. Gray green, sharp-toothed, ovate to ovate-lanceolate 3″ leaves. Solitary and terminal flowers. Balloon shaped in

Plantago lanceolata 'Streaker'

Platycodon grandiflorus

the bud, the purplish blue 2″ corolla opens into a cup with 5 pointed lobes. Long blooming. An easy and tolerant plant, although not adaptable to Southern Florida and the Gulf Coast. Slow to begin growth in the spring. Division of the fleshy roots is tricky. An excellent cut flower if the base of the stem is seared. Eastern Asia. Innumerable named cultivars.

——— 'Albus,' white flowered.
——— 'Apoyama,' dwarf to about 9″ tall.
——— 'Autumnalis,' late flowering.
——— 'Japonicus' has 10-lobed flowers.
——— 'Mariesii' [var. *mariesii* Hort.], has expanded corolla. Also in white and pink.
——— 'Mother of Pearl' ['Perlmutterschal'] has pale pink flowers.
——— 'Roseus,' pink flowered.
——— 'Roseus Plenus' has pink semidouble flowers.
——— 'Shell Pink' has delicate pale pink flowers.
——— 'Snowflake,' white flowered.

PODOPHYLLUM, Podophyllaceae. (2)

peltatum	WHITE	SP	1.5′/1′
	◗	Z9-3	DRS ****

Mayapple. This handsome ground cover for lightly shaded areas produces 2 different types of leaves on its erect stems. The sterile stems bear 1 rounded, peltate leaf; the forked flowering stems 2 roughly half-round leaves. Both types, to 1′ wide, are deeply lobed and toothed. Almost hidden by the foliage in the fork between the 2 branches, the solitary, nodding 1½″–2″ flower is cup shaped, with 6–9 petals. It is followed by an edible, yellow, ovoid 2″ fruit. Likes the deep, humus-rich, moist soil of open woodlands. Not a plant for small gardens, as its shallow rhizomes spread freely. Eastern and southern North America. Probably less hardy than the American species, Himalayan *P. hexandrum* [*P. emodi*] has purplish brown spotted leaves with fewer lobes. Its fruits are red. *P. h.* 'Majus' is a large form; *P. h. chinense* has pink flowers.

POLEMONIUM, Polemoniaceae. (50)   Jacob's Ladder

Jacob's Ladder has alternate, odd-pinnate leaves, with leaflets arranged like the rungs of a ladder in pairs, decreasing in size toward the separate larger terminal leaflet. Erect or nodding, the blue, white, or pink flowers are loosely clustered; their campanulate or wheel-shaped corollas are 5 lobed. Best in partial shade in cool, moist conditions; will tolerate full sun only where summers are moderate. Divide carefully in spring, avoiding damage to the brittle stems.

Podophyllum peltatum

caeruleum	BLUE	LSP-ESU	1'–3'/2'
	◐●	Z9-3	DS ****

Jacob's Ladder is generally of upright habit. The basal leaves have as many as 13 pairs of lanceolate 1"–1½" leaflets. Long, terminal clusters of nodding, pale blue 1" flowers, with corolla lobes twice as long as the tube and conspicuously exserted, orange stamens. Blooming time extends well into summer if the weather remains cool. Split into several subspecies by some authorities. Europe, Asia.

———— *lacteum* ['Album' Hort.]. An elegant, white-flowered form.

carneum	PINK	ESU	1'–1.5'/1'
	◐●	Z9-5/H	DS **

[*P. amoenum*]. Similar to *P. caeruleum*, though smaller and more sprawling. The attractive, flesh-colored flowers are flushed with deeper pink. Requires a sandy soil enriched with peat or leaf mold. Can be temperamental. Cascade Mountains.

foliosissimum	BLUE	SU	2.5'/2'
	◐●	Z9-4/H	DS **

[*P. filicinum*]. Long blooming and possibly the best species. Its erect stems bear leaves with 5–12 pairs of narrowly lanceolate leaflets, the apical ones often joined. Crowded clusters of deep lavender or lilac blue, occasionally white or cream, cup-shaped ½" flowers with bright orange stamens. Variable. Idaho, Wyoming south to Arizona, New Mexico.

pulcherrimum	BLUE	LSP-SU	1'/1'
	○ ◑	Z9-3/H	DS **

Skunkleaf Polemonium. [*P. haydenii, P. lindleyi*]. Dense tufts of basal leaves, each with 5–11 pairs of ovate ¾" leaflets. The sky blue, bell-shaped ¼"–⅓" flowers, often with yellowish throats, are arranged in loose clusters. Mountains of Alaska to California.

reptans	BLUE	SP-SU	1'–2'/1'
	◑ ●	Z9-3/H	DS ****

Jacob's Ladder, Greek Valerian, or Creeping Polemonium has weak, often sprawling stems; the leaves have 3–9 pairs of ovate leaflets to 2" long. Loose, terminal sprays of pale lavender blue, bell-shaped ¾" flowers with white stamens. Self-sows readily. Lovely in the wild garden. New York to Kansas and Alabama.

———— 'Blue Pearl' probably belongs here, but is frequently listed under *P. caeruleum*. An excellent, clump-forming cultivar with medium blue flowers on strong 1' stems.

Polemonium reptans

Polygonatum biflorum

POLYGONATUM, Liliaceae. (30)   Solomon's Seal

These elegant natives of temperate woodlands are mostly quite similar, resulting in some confusion in nomenclature. Their strong, unbranched stems rise from fleshy, jointed rhizomes, and are clothed in alternate parallel-veined leaves. From the leaf axils hang clusters, or pairs, of pendulous, greenish white, sometimes fragrant flowers; the bell-shaped perianths are 6 lobed. Solomon's Seals prefer moist, woodland-type soils. Fine low-maintenance perennials for informal use in the garden; they combine well with ferns and Astilbes. Attractive autumn color. Good for cutting.

| *biflorum* | GREEN | LSP | 1'–3'/1' |
| | ◑● | Z9-4/H | DS *** |

Small Solomon's Seal. [*P. canaliculatum*]. Somewhat variable, but generally a reduced version of *P. commutatum.* Its yellow green flowers, usually in pairs, are on short pedicels; blue black berries follow. Eastern and central North America. Hairy Solomon's Seal, *P. pubescens,* has hairs on the undersides of the leaves along the veins. Southern Canada, north central and northeastern United States.

| *commutatum* | WHITE | LSP | 3'–6'/2'–3' |
| | ◑● | Z9-4/H | DS *** |

Giant Solomon's Seal, Great Solomon's Seal, True Solomon's Seal. [*P. giganteum* Hort.]. Frequently offered in the trade as *P. canaliculatum,* this bold, handsome plant has tall, arching stems, leafy above. The broadly elliptic, sessile leaves to 7″ long have conspicuous veins. Clusters of 2–10 lightly fragrant flowers on 1″ peduncles; corolla ¾″–1″ long, white, tinged with green at the mouth. Large, blue black berries later. Eastern United States.

x *hybridum*	WHITE	LSP	**3'–4'/2'**
◐ ●	Z10-4/H	D ****

[*P. multiflorum* Hort.]. *P. multiflorum* x *P. odoratum*. A wide-spreading plant with gracefully arching, ribbed stems. The elliptic 2"–6" leaves are prominently veined. Ivory ½" flowers, tipped with green, hang in 4- to 5-flowered clusters. Variable; choose a good selection. The true *P. multiflorum* is a less substantial plant, with waisted flowers in clusters of 2–5. Europe, Asia.

———— 'Flore Pleno' [*P. m.* 'Flore-Pleno']. Double flowered; rare.

———— 'Variegatum' [*P. m. striatum*] has leaves striped in cream.

odoratum	WHITE	LSP	**1.5'–2'/1'**
◐ ●	Z9-5/H	DS ***

[*P. officinale*]. Its arching stems are distinctly angular or ridged and bear elliptic to ovate 4" leaves. Solitary or paired, fragrant 1" flowers. Europe, Asia.

———— *thunbergii*. [*P. japonicum, P. thunbergii*]. Larger and more robust throughout. 3.5' tall. Japan.

———— *thunbergii* 'Variegatum.' [*P. japonicum* 'Variegatum,' *P. falcatum* 'Variegatum']. Beautifully variegated leaves with cream white edges and tips. Maroon-tinged 2'–3' stems. Japan.

POLYGONUM, Polygonaceae. (150)   Knotweed

Called Knotweeds because of their conspicuously swollen nodes. The joints of the stems are sheathed by leafy stipules; the leaves are alternate. In England, they are grown extensively, and occupy a prominent place in late summer and fall gardens. In America, they are not as popular, perhaps because of the infamous reputation of 1 or 2 dangerously invasive species. *P. cuspidatum* [*P. sieboldii, Reynoutria japonica*], the Mexican Bamboo or Japanese Knotweed, which grows to 8' tall, and *P. sachalinense* [*Reynoutria sachalinensis*], the Sakhalin Knotweed, which may reach 12', are pernicious weeds and should never be planted as ornamentals. The gardenworthy species have showy, attractive racemes or clusters of pink, white, or red, apetalous flowers. Individually tiny, they have 5 petal-like perianth lobes. Most are easy in damp, fertile soil. Himalayan *P. capitatum* is hardy only in mild zones, but is grown elsewhere as an annual for bedding or containers. It makes a useful 3"–6" ground cover, with dark green foliage marked with a brown chevron. Its pink flowers cluster into small, dense heads, which bloom throughout the summer.

affine	PINK	SU-EF	**10"–12"/12**
○ ◐	Z9-3	D ***

Himalayan Fleece-Flower. Mat forming. Its broadly lanceolate 2"–4" leaves, tapering at the base, are erect; they turn red and copper in cold weather and persist through the winter. Cylindrical 2"–3" spikes of closely packed, mixed pink and white flowers rise stiffly above the foliage. Long blooming. Must not dry out. Attractive at the front of the border. Himalayas.

————— 'Darjeeling Red,' an old cultivar with deep pink flowers, which mature to crimson.

————— 'Dimity' has spikes of pale pink and crimson flowers.

————— 'Donald Lowndes' has salmon pink flowers.

————— 'Superba.' A new cultivar, reputed to have superior vigor. White flowers flushed with pink, aging to crimson.

| *amplexicaule* | RED | SU-LF | 2'–5'/4' |
| | ○ | Z9-6 | DS *** |

Mountain Fleece. [*P. oxyphyllum*]. This fine border plant makes stout, bushy clumps of leafy stems. The pointed, ovate 5"–7" leaves are wavy margined, cordate at the base. Its pencil-thin 6" spikes of rosy red ¼" flowers start to bloom early in the season on still immature growth. As the plant reaches its full height and girth, it becomes covered with dense spikes of bloom. The white form, *P. amplexicaule* 'Album,' is often listed as *P. oxyphyllum*. Noninvasive. Himalayas.

————— 'Atrosanguineum' has crimson flowers.

————— 'Firetail.' Larger, crimson scarlet spikes on 4' stems.

| *bistorta* **'Superbum'** | PINK | ESU | 2'–3'/2' |
| | ○ ◑ | Z9-3 | D ** |

One of the best of all Polygonums, this excellent selection eventually makes wide stands. Its Dock-like leaves, with slightly wavy, serrate margins, may attain 1' long by about half as wide. Erect, branched stems hold the dense, robust 3½"–4" pokers of pale pink flowers well above the foliage. One of the showiest and longest blooming, particularly under damp conditions. Shade from strong sun. A compact plant, Himalayan *P. sphaerostachyum* [*P. macrophyllum*], also in the 'Bistort' group, blooms a little later, with spikes of waxy, deep rose flowers. *P. milettii,* from Western China, displays its dark red spikes of bloom later still. It requires a very moist soil.

| *campanulatum* | PINK | SU-F | 3'–4'/3' |
| | ○ ◑ | Z9-6 | D ** |

Extends into large clumps of slender, upright, well-branched stems covered with foliage throughout their length. The hairy, lanceolate 3"–4" leaves are prominently veined, pinkish along the midrib. Loose, terminal panicles of deep rose buds, which open into pale pink ½" bells. Very long blooming. Tends to spread, but is shallow rooted and easy to control. Excellent for massing. Provide shade from intense sun and a cool, moist root run. Himalayas. Fall-blooming *P. polystachyum* from the same region is similar, but has white, feathery flowers. Invasive, it should be confined to the wild garden.

| *cuspidatum* **'Compactum'** | PINK | LSU | 3'/3' |
| | ○ | Z10-4/H | D **** |

[*P. compactum, P. reynoutria* Hort.]. Invasive, but not rampant. The arching, canelike stems, with rounded 1"–2" leaves, are topped by loose panicles. Their pink flowers

Polygonum bistorta 'Superbum'

mature to deep rose red and are followed by crimson seeds. This plant, usually listed as *P. reynoutria* in catalogs, is much more variable in height than the descriptions would indicate. There may in fact be dwarf forms, but those generally available are seldom reliably compact. All require close attention to keep them within bounds. Appropriate for massing on difficult banks. 'Spectabilis' has leaves marbled with red, white, and green, and is less vigorous. The true species *P. reynoutria* is a 4″–6″ creeper.

POTENTILLA, Rosaceae. (500)	Cinquefoil

The Cinquefoils are easy and reliable plants for the border or rock garden. Some low-growing species such as *P. tridentata,* Wineleaf Cinquefoil, *P. cinerea,* Rusty Cinquefoil, and *P. tabernaemontani* [*P. verna*], Spring Cinquefoil, make excellent ground covers. *P. fruticosa,* Bush Cinquefoil, is a small shrub with a host of cultivars, which are attractive companions for herbaceous perennials. Potentillas have Strawberry-like leaves, toothed, usually palmately compound, and much larger at the base than on the stem. Their small flowers, seldom solitary, are mostly borne in clusters or sprays on branching stems just above the foliage. Colors range from white, yellow, and orange to pink and red. The Rose-like flowers are wheel shaped. Five spreading sepals alternate with bractlets; 5 broad, frequently notched petals surround a tuft of stamens. Tolerant of a wide range of soils, most thrive on a rather lean diet and tend to produce

Potentilla 'William Rollison'

soft, leafy growth if the soil is rich. Plant the taller kinds close together to support each other. Where summers are hot, shade from direct sun. Easily propagated from seed sown in the spring; divide the hybrids in spring or early fall.

atrosanguinea	RED	SU	1.5'–2'/1'–2'
	○	Z9-5/H	DS **

Ruby Cinquefoil. [*P. argyrophylla atrosanguinea*]. Clumps of widely branching, leafy stems. The long-petioled leaves are silvery gray, covered with silky hairs on the upper surface, white hairy beneath. Sprays of blood red 1″ flowers bloom for many weeks. Tolerant of drought. This species was formerly included under yellow-flowered *P. argyrophylla.* Both, together with *P. nepalensis,* have been crossed to produce a wide range of superb cultivars. Regrettably many of these have been lost over the years, but those that remain are common and fine additions to the front or middle of the border. Himalayas.

'Firedance.' Free flowering; small, salmon orange blooms with a large red center. 10″–15″ tall.

'Gibson's Scarlet' has red flowers throughout the summer. Green foliage and rather lax stems.

'William Rollison.' Flame orange semidouble flowers with a yellow reverse. 1.5' stems. 'Yellow Queen' has silvery foliage and bright yellow flowers with a red eye. Early summer. 1' tall.

nepalensis	RED	SU	1.5'/2'
	○	Z10-5/H	DS ***

Nepal Cinquefoil. [*P. coccinea, P. formosa*]. Tufts of erect stems, abundantly covered in hairy leaves. Long-stemmed clusters of 1″ flowers in various shades of deep pink and red. A good cut flower. Nepal.

———— 'Miss Willmott' [*P. willmottiae*] is a superb, free-blooming selection, with cherry red, crimson-centered flowers. 1' tall, spreading to 1.5'. This and the next come true from seed.

———— 'Roxana' has deep salmon pink 1″ flowers with a red center. 1.5' tall.

recta 'Warrenii'	YELLOW	SU	2'/2'
	○	Z10-3	S ****

Sulfur Cinquefoil. [*P. warrenii* Hort.]. Usually offered as 'Warrensii.' This is a garden-worthy form, although the species tends to be weedy. Strong, upright clumps, with very dark green, coarsely hairy, palmately compound leaves, each with 5–7 toothed leaflets. Numerous brilliant yellow flowers the size of a quarter cover the plants throughout the summer; blooms sporadically into the fall. Self-sows readily. *P. recta* 'Macrantha' is very similar and indeed may be the same plant. Pale yellow *P. recta* 'Sulfurea' is worth seeking. The species is European.

x *tonguei*	ORANGE	LSP-SU	8″–1'/2'
	○ ◑	Z10-5/H	D ***

Staghorn Cinquefoil. [*P. tonguei, P. tormentilla-formosa*]. *P. anglica* x *P. nepalensis.*

This hybrid has trailing, almost prostrate stems about 1' in length and evergreen foliage. Soft apricot flowers, deep red at the center, about 1" across. Effective at the front of the border or trailing over a bank or wall.

PRIMULA, Primulaceae. (500)	Primrose

Primroses include some of our most charming and familiar spring flowers. Many are temperamental, better suited to alpine houses and specialized collections than to gardens. Others with a little extra care are reliable, though generally short-lived perennials. They are predominantly native to the higher altitudes of temperate Asia, where summers are moderate to cool. In cultivation, they resent hot, dry conditions, and are most successful in semishaded positions in moist soil, amended with copious amounts of humus and mulched in the summer. Never must they be allowed to dry out, particularly during the growing season; also, most will fail if waterlogged during the winter. Mulch lightly to avoid heaving and subsequent drying out of the short, rhizomatous rootstock and roots during very cold weather. Most can be divided after blooming time; seed germinates readily if sown as soon as it is ripe. Slugs and snails are their most serious pests, but gardeners must be alert for infestations of aphids, flea beetles, and red spider mites, the latter particularly during hot, dry weather. Their entire, toothed or lobed leaves are all basal, forming neat rosettes. Above rises either a pedunculate solitary flower or an umbellate or tiered inflorescence, supported by an often hairy scape. The pentamerous flowers have a persistent, cylindrical or campanulate calyx, often ribbed or angled. The corolla may be tubular, bell-shaped, salverform, or funnelform; its long corolla tube opens into erect or flaring lobes, which are often 2 notched. All colors of the rainbow are represented, often with a contrasting margin or eye. In several species, the leaves, scapes, and umbels are covered with a mealy or granular substance known as "farina." Botanists have divided this large and varied genus into 30 sections, grouped according to their probable relationships. Species in the same section generally have similar cultural needs. Additional information, as well as seed, is available from the American Primrose Society and the American Rock Garden Society. Primroses are popularly grown in and best adapted to the Pacific northwest, although some of the hardier ones listed here flourish elsewhere.

auricula	YELLOW	ESP	6"–8"/1'
	◐	Z9-3	DS ✱✱

[*P. alpina, P. lutea*]. Section Auricula. The evergreen rosettes of thick and rather fleshy or leathery, obovate to oblanceolate 2"–4" leaves are frequently gray-farinose on both sides. Their margins, variably toothed toward the apex, have an unusually tough, wavy edge. The stout 2"–6" scape ends in a 3- to 20-flowered umbel of mostly fragrant ½"–1" flowers on ½"–¾" pedicels. Typically, the bright yellow funnelform corollas have overlapping, obovate, 2-notched lobes. This variable species has been divided into several subspecies and varieties by the experts. European Alps. Closely related *P. rubra* [*P. hirta*] and *P. viscosa* have been hybridized extensively with *P. auricula,* resulting in *P.* x *pubescens,* more often referred to as "Auriculas." These hybrids display a very wide range of flower colors and combinations, predominantly yellows, reds, and purples, often with a large, paler eye and contrasting rim. Many have flowers with zones covered in a mealy "paste" prized by collectors. *P. marginata,* also in this section, is a diminutive alpine under 6″ tall with umbels of mostly lavender flowers. All need very fast-draining but moist soil.

| *beesiana* | PINK | LSP/ESU | 1.5′–2′/1′ |
| | ◑ | Z9-5 | DS *** |

Bee's Primrose. Section Candelabra. Its mostly blunt, rounded, ovate to lanceolate 6″–10″ leaves taper toward their bases and winged petioles; margins irregularly and finely toothed. The strong scapes support 2–8 tiers of 8–16 flowers on short pedicels, each tier subtended by grassy 1″ bracts. The upper part of the scapes and the inflorescences are mealy. The showy, salverform, rosy purple flowers, ½″–1″ across, are yellow eyed and have an orange tube; the campanulate calyx has lanceolate lobes. Mulch in winter without fail. Red spider mites need to be controlled in hot, dry weather. Yunnan, Szechwan. *P. bulleyana,* Bulley's Primrose, is also from China. Its deep yellow or reddish orange flowers bloom until midsummer in dense 5- to 7-flowered tiers on scapes to 2.5′ tall; their calyces are cup shaped. The thin-textured 5″–14″ leaves, reddish along the midribs, taper to a winged petiole. These 2 species have been crossed, resulting in *P.* x *bullesiana,* or Bulle's Primrose. Blooming in late spring and early summer, its flowers range from cream to rose and deep reds, lavender, to mauve and purples. All prefer to have their deep roots in cool, moist, even wet soils; they thrive alongside lakes or streams. All are deciduous.

| *denticulata* | LILAC | ESP | 10″–15″/9″ |
| | ◑ | Z8-3 | DS *** |

Section Denticulata. Himalayan Primrose [*P. cachemiriana*], frequently sold under its synonym, is an endearing little plant, grown to best advantage in rocky places alongside streams, in woodlands, or at the front of moist borders. Its wavy and irregularly fine-toothed, crinkled, spatulate or oblong-ovate leaves are 3″–4″ long at blooming time, but elongate later to 1′ or more on broad-winged petioles. Sturdily erect, the 4″–12″ scape is topped with a crowded 2″ globe of funnelform ½″ flowers, lavenders, lilacs, or pale purples, sometimes white, all with a yellow eye. The overlapping corolla lobes are 2 notched; the brownish calyces are bell shaped. Himalayas. *P. denticulata* var. *cachemiriana* is a later-blooming variety from Kashmir with violet, yellow-eyed flowers. Many named cultivars are available, including white-flowered 'Snowball' and red-flowered 'Ruby.' The 'Ronsdorf Hybrid' strain has flowers in shades of blue, pink, and mauve, as well as white.

| *florindae* | YELLOW | SU | 2′–3′/2′ |
| | ◑ | Z9-6 | S *** |

Tibetan Primrose. Section Sikkimensis. This vigorous species appears late in the season. Its glabrous, toothed, broadly ovate to heart-shaped leaves may reach 9″ long by 6″ wide. Their red petioles, sometimes a foot in length, are channeled. Established plants

Primula japonica

have several sturdy 1′–3′ or even longer scapes, each topped with a large umbel of 30–40 or more fragrant, drooping ½″ flowers, all dusted with white farina. The bright yellow long-tubed corollas are bell shaped. Tibet. This species is preferred to smaller Himalayan *P. sikkimensis,* as it is easier to grow. Both enjoy very damp soil, even shallow running water, but the former adapts readily to moist border conditions and woodlands.

| *japonica* | VARIOUS | LSP | 1′–2.5′/1′ |
| | ❶ | Z9-5 | DS ✳✳✳ |

The deciduous Japanese Primroses, in the Candelabra Section, are among the easiest to grow. Their blunt, broadly spatulate 8″–10″ or even 12″ leaves are slightly wrinkled, with fine, irregular teeth along the margins; the petioles are winged. High above the foliage, 2–5 many-flowered whorls of ½″–1″ flowers with dark or yellow eyes rise on sturdy 1.5′–2.5′ scapes. Colors range from white and pale pink to crimsons and purplish reds. The small, tubular calyx is slightly farinose inside, as are the ¾″ pedicels. Self-seed freely and gradually make large colonies, particularly in wet places; the resulting swarm will flower in the full range of colors. Tolerant of sunnier positions, as long as the soil is very well enriched with moisture-retentive humus. 'Miller's Crimson' is a good red cultivar; 'Postford's White,' an excellent pure white. Japan.

| *malacoides* | VARIOUS | LW-SP | 8″–12″/1′ |
| | ❶ | Z10-8 | S ✳✳✳ |

Fairy Primrose, Baby Primrose. Section Malacoides. This short-lived perennial is only for warm zone gardens; elsewhere it is grown as an annual for bedding or as a conservatory pot plant. Its pale green, hairy, ovate to elliptic 3″ leaves are shallow-lobed and toothed on long petioles. The erect scapes, a foot or more in height, bear several loose, superimposed umbels of dainty ½″–1½″ flowers in white, pinks, and lavenders. Several horticultural strains, such as 'Bright Eyes,' are on the market, some with double flowers. China.

| *obconica* | VARIOUS | LW-ESP | 1′/1′ |
| | ◗ | Z10-8 | S *** |

Poison Primula or German Primula, of the Section Obconica, is the only species of horticultural importance in its section. Hardy only in our warmer zones, where it is useful under the shade of trees; elsewhere treated as a bedding annual or as a houseplant. Its hairy, ovate or elliptic leaves are long petioled, to 10″ in length; the hairs cause an unpleasant skin rash in some people. The flowers cluster into many-flowered, loose umbels atop an upright, stout, hairy scape; their 2″ corollas, in white or shades of pink, lavender, or red, have conspicuously 2-notched lobes. Several strains, mostly with larger flowers, some of them hybrids, are available. Best in cool positions. China.

| **x** *polyantha* | VARIOUS | SP | 10″–15″/9″ |
| | ○ ◗ | Z9-3 | DS **** |

Polyanthus Primroses, sometimes called English Primroses or Polyanthus, are among the earliest of the spring flowers to bloom in northern regions. They are frequently used as an underplanting for tulips and other bulbs, and large numbers are grown as potted plants to be enjoyed during dark, late winter days. Widely grown since the seventeenth century, they are considered to include *P. vulgaris, P. veris,* and *P. elatior* in their parentage. These perky plants make vigorous rosettes of persistent, almost puckered, round-toothed, dark green 4″–6″ leaves on short, narrow-winged petioles. The obovate blades are blunted at the apex, tapered at the base. Several-flowered, rather flat umbels of fragrant 1″–2″ flowers rise on scapes from an inch or so to 1′ in length. Colors range from pure white to pinks, reds and maroon, lavender, mauve and purple, and even brilliant purplish blue, all with a yellow eye. Separate colors are available as such. Numerous strains, many of them F1 hybrids, are listed. The 'Pacific Giant' strain, developed on the West Coast, is a large-flowered strain, but is somewhat less cold hardy. The 'Regal' strain from Tasmania is reputed to be more tolerant of a wide range of conditions than others. It offers several unusual forms, including "Jack in the Green" types, which have leafy ruffs at the base of each flower. Other forms include the ostensibly double-flowered "hose-in-hose" types, often difficult to find today. All flourish in well-prepared, humus-enriched soils in light shade; in climates where summers are moderate, they will endure full sun. Their vibrant colors brighten the front of the border and rock gardens.

| *sieboldii* | VARIOUS | LSP | 9″–15″/1′ |
| | ○ ◗ | Z9-4 | DS *** |

Japanese Star Primrose, or Siebold Primrose, of the Section Cortusoides, makes light green rosettes of long-petioled, wrinkled, ovate to oblong 4″ leaves, which are scalloped and toothed, hairy on both sides. The white, mauve, or pink, white-eyed 1½″ flowers, often with deeply notched or frilled corolla lobes, are arranged in 6- to 10-flowered umbels on slender scapes. More tolerant of hot conditions than some, since the plants die down by midsummer. 'Alba' is a fine white-flowered cultivar; there are several strains, including the superior 'Barnhaven' strain. Possibly the best species for northeastern gardens. Japan.

| *veris* | YELLOW | SP | 4″–12″/9″ |
| | ○ ◑ | Z9-5 | DS ** |

Cowslip. [*P. officinalis*]. Section Vernales. This variable species, split into several subspecies by some authorities, is found in the wild in damp meadows of the British Isles, central Europe, and western Asia. Its wrinkled, pubescent, ovate to oblong 2″–3″ leaves narrow abruptly into slender-winged petioles as long as the blades; white with hairs beneath. The downy 4″–8″ scape rises vertically above the rosette and bears a one-sided, many-flowered umbel of delicately fragrant, nodding, bright yellow blooms. Their bell-shaped ½″–¾″ corollas, each lobe 2 notched, are constricted at the mouth and encircled below by a pale green, puffy, 5-angled calyx. Horticultural forms in other colors are sometimes available, but lack the quaint charm of the original. Cowslip Primrose, *P.* x *tomasinii* [*P.* x *variabilis*], is an essentially sterile hybrid between this species and *P. vulgaris.* It is rarely available commercially, although found in colonial and cottage gardens. Its flowers are bright yellow with a darker eye; its leaves do not narrow abruptly into petioles. Similar *P. elatior,* Oxslip, thought by some to be an old, natural hybrid between *P. veris* and *P. vulgaris,* is not as hairy as the last. Its smaller, flatter, less bell-shaped flowers are paler in color. They all face the same way and lack the constrictions at the mouth. Their long seed capsules are the same length as the calyx; the leaves are similar to those of *P. veris.* Interbreeding is common when they are grown together. Culture of all as for *P.* x *polyantha.*

| *vialii* | LILAC | LSP | 1′–2′/1′ |
| | ◑ | Z9-5/H | DS ** |

[*P. littoniana*]. Section Muscarioides. This short-lived plant, arresting in flower, has downy, pointed, lanceolate to oblong 1′ leaves, which taper to a winged petiole; the margins are irregularly dentate. Its strict scape, mealy above, supports a dense, conical 3″–6″ spike of fragrant, slightly nodding, tubular ½″ flowers; their pointed corolla lobes are lilac blue, the tube violet. The tiny, bell-shaped calyces, bright red when the flowers are in bud, later turn pink. Dramatic in a drift, under dappled shade, where the soil is moist. Northwest Yunnan, southwest Szechwan.

| *vulgaris* | YELLOW | SP | 6″/9″ |
| | ◑ | Z9-5 | DS ** |

English Primrose, Common Primrose. [*P. acaulis, P. hybrida*]. Section Vernales. This lightly fragrant native of country hedges conjures up thoughts of rural Britain as does no other flower, although its range spreads beyond, throughout western and southern Europe. Its crenate and recurved, wrinkled 1″–3″ leaves elongate after flowering time to about 6″. Their blunted, elliptic to ovate blades, soft with hairs beneath, taper to a short, broad-winged petiole. Essentially scapeless, the solitary, primrose yellow salver-form 1″–1½″ flowers, blotched in the center with a darker eye, are borne on long, slender, downy pedicels, reddish toward the base; their soft yellowish green ½″ calyces are also fuzzy. The unusual occurrence of uneven stigma and style lengths, common in Primroses, is most apparent in this species. Where the stamens are short and the style, appearing as a pinhead, is as long as the corolla tube, the condition is called "pin-eyed"; when the reverse occurs, the longer stamens are conspicuous and the flowers are said to be "thrum-eyed." Subspecies *sibthorpii* has very attractive lavender pink flowers. Differently colored, named cultivars are on the market, as well as the charming 'Barnhaven Doubles' strain. Closely related *P. juliae* from the Caucasus Mountains, smaller than *P. vulgaris,* spreads slowly by creeping rhizomes. Its dark green mats of roundish, glabrous 1″ leaves on red petioles serve as an attractive background for the profusion of solitary magenta flowers. The best-known cultivar is 'Wanda,' which has cerise to purple yellow-eyed flowers. The 'Juliana Hybrids,' resulting from crosses with other members of the Vernales section, occur with flowers in a range of white, pinks, and reds. A 'Barnhaven' strain of these, too, is available. Best in heavy clay soils, which they favor in the wild.

PRUNELLA, Labiatae. (7)	Self-Heal

Self-Heal makes low mats of evergreen foliage, which remains attractive throughout the season. The dark green 1″–2″ leaves are ovate, often cordate below; the smaller stem leaves are paired. In early summer, the rough-hairy square stems carry dense, conical flower spikes composed of bracted tiers of 6-flowered verticillasters. The corollas are strongly 2 lipped; the upper 2 lobed and forming a hood over the lower, which is 3 lobed. A front-of-the-border or rock garden plant, as well as a good ground cover under shrubs. Seeds itself readily; the cultivars must be divided. Self-Heal thrives in average, well-drained soils and even tolerates dry conditions in partial shade. In hot climates, shade lightly and add plenty of moisture-retaining humus. *P. vulgaris* [*P. incisa*] is a weedy species, seldom worthy of garden space. It frequently becomes a nuisance in lawns.

grandiflora	VIOLET	ESU-LSU	1′/1.5′
○ ◑		Z9-4	DS ****

Bigflower Self-Heal is so variable that it is split into subspecies by some authorities on the basis of minor leaf characters. The showy 3″ spikes of 1″–1½″ flowers are held well above the foliage. Europe.
————— 'Alba' is white flowered.
————— 'Rosea' has pinkish red flowers.

webbiana Hort.	PURPLE	SU	1′/1.5′
○ ◑		Z9-4	D ****

[*P. grandiflora webbiana*]. Considered to be a cross between *P. g. grandiflora* and

Prunella webbiana Hort.

P. g. pyrenaica [*P. g. hastifolia*], this hybrid is similar to *P. grandiflora,* but has smaller, blunted leaves. The widely grown 'Loveliness' series is generally superior to either parent.

———— 'Loveliness' has deep lavender ¾″–1″ flowers.

———— 'Pink Loveliness.' Very large, rose pink flowers.

———— 'White Loveliness' has pure white blooms, which unfortunately tend to brown at the tips before the whole inflorescence opens.

PTILOTUS, Amaranthaceae. (100)

exaltatus	PINK	SP	2′–3′/2′
	○	Z10-9	RS **

Mulla Mulla, Pussy-Tails, Woolly-Bears. [*Trichinium exaltatum*]. From "down under" comes this bushy little plant with sturdy, erect, reddish stems and alternate, stiff, gray green leaves. The upper leaves are ovate and sessile; the lower ovate to lanceolate, to 5″ long. The dense, pink to reddish flower spikes, like large, woolly heads of Clover, are ovoid to conical, elongating to 6″ with age. Fragrant. Likes a well-drained but fertile soil; water early in the growing season. Tolerant of drought and heat. *P. manglesii* and *P. spathulatus* are smaller species. Australia.

Ptilotus manglesii

PULMONARIA, Boraginaceae. (12)   Lungwort

These European natives go by numerous common names such as Lungwort, Cowslip, Bethlehem Sage, and Jerusalem Sage. The mostly basal leaves are long petioled and rather hairy, sometimes even coarse. Their handsome foliage, dappled with silver in several species, is evergreen in mild climates. The flower stems, sparsely clothed in alternate, usually sessile leaves, end in branched cymes of funnelform flowers. The calyx is 5 lobed; the tubular corolla flares into 5 rounded lobes. Although not very showy, the purplish red or blue flowers are valued as a foil for spring-flowering bulbs and shrubs. Lungworts are superb as ground covers, at their best under deciduous trees, as they are intolerant of strong sun. Prefer cool, moist soil. Usually propagated by division of the creeping rootstock in fall. Seed produces extremely variable plants because *Pulmonaria* hybridizes freely. Seldom bothered by diseases or pests other than slugs. *P. lutea* Hort. is correctly *Symphytum grandiflorum.*

angustifolia	BLUE	ESP	9″–1′/1.5′
	◐●	Z9-3/H	DS ***

Blue Lungwort, Cowslip Lungwort. [*P. azurea*]. Bristling with hairs, the dark green 1′ leaves are narrowly lanceolate and taper to the base; the smaller stem leaves are elliptic and clasping. Small sprays of intense blue flowers open from pink buds. Eastern Europe.

————— 'Azurea' is a selection with pure blue flowers on 10″ stems.

————— 'Johnson's Blue' has deep, clear blue flowers. 8″ tall.

longifolia	BLUE	ESU	1′/1.5′
	◑●	Z9-5	DS ***

Joseph and Mary, Spotted Dog. Narrowly upright in habit over a star-shaped, basal rosette of white-spotted, pointed leaves to 1.5′ in length and 6 times longer than wide; erect, lanceolate stem leaves. Its crowded inflorescences of violet blue flowers do not elongate like those of *P. saccharata.* Portugal, Spain, France.

officinalis	BLUE	SP	1′/1.5′
	◑●	Z10-3/H	DS ****

Jerusalem Cowslip, Common Lungwort. [*P. maculata*]. Bold silver-spotted foliage, rough with bristly hairs. The short-petioled, ovate 2″–4″ leaves are distinctly cordate at the base; stem leaves sessile. The violet blue, bell-shaped ½″–¾″ flowers open from purplish pink buds. Europe.

————— 'Sissinghurst White' is an albino form with clean white flowers. The leaves are well marked with silver spots.

rubra	RED	ESP	1′–2′/1.5′
	◑●	Z10-3/H	DS ***

[*P. montana*]. Its clumps of pale green foliage develop after the flowers. The oblong 5″–6″ leaves are covered with long, soft hairs. Brick red ¾″ flowers open in very early spring on sparsely leaved stems. Mountains of southeastern Europe.

Pulmonaria saccharata 'Mrs. Moon'

——————— 'Bowles Red' may be a hybrid. Reddish pink flowers.

——————— 'Redstart' is a superior selection of the species.

——————— 'Salmon Glow' has large heads of bright salmon pink flowers.

saccharata	BLUE	SP	1′–1.5′/2′
	◗●	Z9-3	DS ****

Bethlehem Sage. Similar to *P. officinalis,* but its basal leaves reach 1′ in length by half as wide and are elegantly dappled with silver and gray. Rosy buds open into violet blue flowers arranged in elongating, lax clusters. A lovely underplanting for Doronicums. Southeastern France, Italy.

——————— 'Alba' has large white flowers and well-marbled foliage.

——————— 'Argentea.' Blue flowers and silver-frosted green leaves. 1′ tall.

——————— 'Margery Fish' has more uniform leaf markings than the next. A British selection.

——————— 'Mrs Moon' may be a hybrid. Leaves well marked with large silvery spots. Pink flowers fading to blue. One of the best for use as a ground cover. 10″ tall.

——————— 'Pink Dawn' has pink flowers.

——————— 'Roy Davidson' has sky blue flowers in early spring. Foliage evenly blotched with silver. An American selection by Jerry Flintoff.

PUYA, Bromeliaceae. (168)

These uncommon terrestrial Bromeliads make striking accent plants for warmer regions. The foliage is attractive enough to hold its own while awaiting the rare flowering event. Best propagated from offsets, which also keeps mature plants from spreading too much. Plants grown from seed will take several years to flower. All need a well-drained but fairly rich soil and occasional fertilizing. Related *Fascicularia bicolor* and *F. pitcairniifolia* are Chilean terrestrial Bromeliads, which form dense rosettes of narrow, spiny leaves to 1.5′ tall. Their red-tinted, inner leaves set off the tight, stemless clusters of blue flowers. Z10-9/H.

alpestris	BLUE	SP/LSP	3′–4.5′/2′–3′
	○	Z10-9/H	DS ***

[*P. whytei*]. Forms one to several large rosettes of arching, very narrow, spine-edged leaves. The sturdy flower stalks rise well above the foliage and carry huge, stiff, many-branched panicles. Flowers are borne only on the lower half of the branchlets, the lower or innermost flowers opening first. Each of the 2″ flowers, subtended by a reddish bract, has 3 thick petals of an intense, dark blue green, and prominent, bright orange anthers. Chile.

berteroniana	BLUE	SP/LSP	7′–8′/3′–4′
	○	Z10-9/H	DS ***

Often confused with *P. alpestris,* this species is altogether larger. Its gray green leaves

Puya spathacea

may reach 4′ in length and 2″ in width at the base, and bear larger, stiffer spines. The tall inflorescences are more densely branched. The petals are a vivid electric blue green. It is also somewhat hardier. Chile.

spathacea	BLUE	ESU	2′–3′/3′
	○	ZI0-9/H	DS ✳✳✳

Crowded rosettes of arching, sword-shaped, toothed leaves. The red flower stalks bear large, loose panicles of small blue green flowers, nearly hidden by red bracts and sepals. Argentina.

venusta	PURPLE	SP/LSP	4′–5′/2′–3′
	○	ZI0-9/H	DS ✳✳

Stiff rosettes of narrow, gray green 1′ leaves. The red flower stalks end in tight, conical spikes of purple flowers; bracts and sepals also red. The 3 narrow petals are crowded into a slender, tubular corolla. Similar but larger *P. coerulea* has longer leaves and dark blue flowers. Chile.

RANUNCULUS, Ranunculaceae. (400)   Buttercup

Buttercups are well-known and widely distributed wildflowers, but the genus also includes several species of garden merit. They have alternate, often palmately compound leaves and yellow, white, or sometimes red flowers. The floral parts, in 5s, surround a central boss of stamens. Most grow best in damp soil, but adapt well to borders, meadows, or wild gardens. *R. asiaticus,* Turban Flower, grows from tuberous roots and is suitable only for Z10-8 gardens, and then shaded from hot sun. *R. montanus* and other alpine species will appeal to rock garden enthusiasts. *R. repens,* Creeping Buttercup, is a weedy nuisance, although in its double-flowered form, *R. r.* 'Pleniflorus' ['Flore Pleno'], it deserves a place in the garden. In spring, the mats of lustrous, dark green, heart-shaped foliage of *R. ficaria,* Lesser Celandine, make an attractive ground cover in the wild garden. Its brilliant yellow 1″ flowers have numerous shiny petals. Also available with double, white or orange flowers or purple leaves.

| *aconitifolius* | WHITE | SP-SU | 2′-3′/3′ |
| | ○ ◑ | Z9-4/H | DS ** |

Strong clumps of branched, leafy stems. Its dark green leaves are deeply cleft almost to the base, with each ovate segment lobed and notched. The wiry flower stems branch widely and are topped with dainty panicles of pure white ¾″-1″ Buttercups. Slow growing. Self-seeds readily. Mildew may be a problem. Central Europe.
———— 'Flore Pleno.' Fair-Maids-of-Kent (or France). The very dark foliage of this elegant plant contrasts well with the clean white, fully double, button flowers. Rich, moist soil. Mulch well after the foliage dies back in late summer.
———— 'Luteus Plenus' has double yellow flowers.

| *acris* | YELLOW | LSP-ESU | 2.5′-3.5′/1′ |
| | ○ | Z9-5/H | D *** |

———— 'Flore Pleno.' Bachelor's Buttons. [*R. a. multiplex, R. a. plenus*]. A tidy, clump-forming plant with hairy, branched, hollow stems and deeply palmately cleft and lobed leaves. Fully double, bright yellow ¾″-1″ button flowers in profusion. It should not be allowed to dry out. Divide and replant every 3-4 years for the best display of flowers. The species is Eurasian.
———— 'Stevenii.' A large-flowered form of the Common Buttercup, available with single or double flowers.

| *insignis* | YELLOW | ESU | 1′-3′/1.5′ |
| | ○ | Z9-8/H | D * |

A choice, handsome species with dark green foliage, hairy beneath. Rounded 4″-6″ leaves with crenate margins; upper leaves smaller and deeply toothed. It has large panicles of cup-shaped, glistening yellow 2″ flowers. The Mountain-Lily, *R. lyallii,* is similar, but has erect panicles of white flowers on 1′-5′ stems. Both species are rare and difficult to grow. Probably only for the Pacific northwest. New Zealand.

| *lingua* | YELLOW | SU | 2′-4′/2′ |
| | ○ | Z9-4/H | D ** |

Greater Spearwort is vigorous and bold, with creeping stoloniferous roots. Its leaves are broadly lanceolate to 1′ long, clasping above. The glabrous, branched, hollow stems

Ranunculus acris 'Stevenii'

end in bright yellow 1″–2″ Buttercups. Only for the waterside or bog garden, where its invasive tendencies will not intrude. Europe, Siberia.

speciosus plenus **Hort.**	YELLOW	ESU-LSU	1′–1.5′/1.5′
	○	Z9-3/H	D **

[*R. gouanii* 'Plenus,' *R. bulbosus* 'Speciosus Plenus']. Noninvasive. Its attractively gray-flecked and spotted foliage is deeply cleft and lobed. Tightly double, the glossy yellow 1½″–2″ flowers with green centers are very long lasting, particularly when grown in moist soil.

REHMANNIA, Scrophulariaceae. (10)

There is considerable confusion between the 2 most ornamental species of this genus. The plant once grown as *R. angulata* appears to be *R. elata,* although plants grown in American gardens do not always match the published descriptions in all particulars. Some of these plants exhibit features ascribed in the literature to the true *R. angulata.* Granted that both are very variable, the confusion remains. Is it possible that the plants in commerce are hybrids? The entire genus needs to be reworked. Both grow well in sun or shade, but in areas with hot summers should have some protection. Well-drained, fertile soils. Moderately hardy; failures are more likely due to winter wetness

Rehmannia elata 'Beverly Bells'

than to cold. Very long blooming in mild climates, where they are also evergreen. These plants have mostly basal, obovate to oblong leaves; the stem leaves are smaller and alternate. The flowers, in loose racemes, are each subtended by a leaflike bract. The asymmetrical, tubular, ventricose corolla is 2 lipped; the upper lip 2 lobed, the lower 3 lobed.

angulata	RED	SP-F	1′–3′/1′
	○ ●	Z10-8/H	CS *

Deeply lobed and toothed or just toothed leaves to 6″ long. Purplish red 2″ flowers; the upper lip of the corolla is edged in scarlet, the lower decorated with orange spots. China.

elata	PINK	SP-F	2′–3′/1′–2′
	○ ●	Z10-8/H	CS ***

Spreads to form substantial clumps. The leaves are coarsely but not deeply lobed and not toothed to 10″ long. Purplish pink 2″–3″ flowers; the throat of the corolla is yellow with dark red spots. A rarer, white-flowered form has a pale yellow throat; propagate it only from cuttings. The species is often described as being much larger than *R. angulata,* with stems reaching 6′ and flowers 3″–4″ long; plants of this size remain elusive in gardens. China. *R. glutinosa* is occasionally grown.

REINWARDTIA, Linaceae. (2)

indica	YELLOW	LF/EW	3′/3′
	○ ◑	Z10-9/T	CD ***

Yellow Flax. [*R. tetragyna, R. trigyna*]. This erect, evergreen subshrub has alternate, elliptic 1″–3″ leaves. Its bright yellow 2″ flowers are solitary or in small, mostly terminal clusters. The 5 flaring petals are united at the base into a long tube. Likes well-drained but fertile and moist soils. Pinch frequently to force branching; cut back hard in late winter. Flowers profusely over a long season. Northern India, China.

RHAZYA, Apocynaceae. (2)

orientalis	BLUE	ESU	1.5′–3′/1′
	○ ◑	Z9-6	CS **

Strong, wiry, upright stems. Its alternate, sessile 1″–2″ leaves are lanceolate; their pale midribs stand out against the darker green of the blades. The starry, salverform ¾″ flowers are grayish lavender blue but deeper in bud, and arranged in terminal clusters. Similar to *Amsonia,* but less hardy. A good container plant for conservatories and sun rooms in colder climates. Slow, but trouble-free once established. Southern Europe to Asia.

Reinwardtia indica

Rhazya orientalis

RHEUM, Polygonaceae. (50) Rhubarb

These ornamental relatives of the edible Rhubarb, *R. rhabarbarum,* are useful both for their bold foliage effects and for their tall, branched spires of tiny, 6-tepaled flowers, which are followed by attractive fruits. Their domed mounds of large, long-stalked, basal leaves make a strong display in the border or as accents in the landscape and at watersides. They like deep, organically rich soils. Mulch to keep the roots cool and moist. Fertilize these hungry plants each spring. Mostly very cold hardy; they seldom succeed in warmer zones, except where summers are cool, as in northern California and the northwest coast.

| *alexandrae* | CREAM | ESU | 3′–4′/2′ |
| | ○ ◑ | Z9-5/H | DS * |

This unusual and extremely temperamental plant has ovate, prominently veined 1′ leaves, with a deep sinus at the base. The long inflorescence is completely draped with large cream to yellow green ovate bracts, which nearly conceal the short, flowering branches. The bracts become red tinged with age. Only for cool, moist climates. Himalayas.

| *officinale* | WHITE | ESU | 6′–10′/4′ |
| | ○ ◑ | Z9-5/H | DS ** |

Huge, shallow-lobed 3′ leaves, rounded in outline. Spreading, short-branched panicles of minute white or greenish flowers. Western China, Tibet.

Rheum palmatum 'Atrosanguineum'

| *palmatum* | RED | ESU | 6'–10'/4'–6' |
| | ○ ◑ | Z9-5/H | DS *** |

This, the best known of the ornamental Rhubarbs, has large, rounded, deeply palmately lobed and toothed 2'–3' leaves; its foliage is highly variable. Branched panicles of tiny pink or reddish flowers.

————— *tanguticum* [*R. p.* 'Atropurpureum'] is a coarser plant, with less-cut, purple-tinged foliage. White, pink, or red flowers.

————— 'Atrosanguineum' [*R. p.* 'Rubrum']. Its young leaves are red, its mature leaves only red beneath. Crimson red flowers. 'Bowles Variety' and 'Bowles Crimson' are similar cultivars. Featured in the famous Red Borders at Hidcote Manor, England. 'Ace of Hearts' [*R. kialense* x *R. palmatum*]. This 4' hybrid has pale pink flowers.

RHEXIA, Melastomaceae. (11)

| *virginica* | PINK | SU-EF | 1'–1.5'/1' |
| | ○ | Z9-4 | DS ** |

Virginia Meadow Beauty, Deer Grass. This handsome, swampland native has straight, ridged stems bearing pairs of sessile, ovate to lanceolate 2"–3" leaves, each with 3–5 conspicuous longitudinal veins and hairy, serrulate margins. Loose clusters of dark rose purple 1½" flowers with 4 oblique petals and 8 curved bright yellow stamens. Soil

Rhexia virginica

Rodgersia pinnata 'Superba'

should be acid and sandy but moisture retentive. Lovely in drifts, particularly in damp areas or bog gardens. Eastern United States. *R. mariana* is similar, with narrower leaves and white or pale pink flowers. Not as cold hardy. Eastern coastal plain, south central United States.

RODGERSIA, Saxifragaceae. (6)

Too rarely grown in American gardens, these handsome plants, spreading by thick rhizomes, form bold clumps of large, long-petioled leaves. They are even more esteemed for their beautiful foliage than for their long-stemmed, plumy panicles, reminiscent of *Astilbe*. The tiny flowers usually lack petals, but the ornamental calyx has 5 petal-like lobes. All like moist, rich soil and thrive in bog gardens and at watersides. In drier situations, keep well watered to prevent leaf scorch. They hybridize freely in gardens.

| *aesculifolia* | CREAM | SU | 3'–5'/2'–2.5' |
| | ○ ◑ | Z9-4/H | DS ** |

Resembling those of the Horse-Chestnut, the palmately compound 1.5' leaves are coarsely veined, toothed, and bronze tinged; the 10" leaflets, usually 7 in number, are obovate. Tiny cream to pink flowers in broad, pyramidal panicles are followed by reddish fruits. China.

| *pinnata* | PINK | SU | 3'–4'/2' |
| | ○ ◑ | Z9-4/H | DS *** |

Pinnately compound leaves with 5–9 oblanceolate, toothed 8" leaflets. Red-stalked panicles of tiny pale pink flowers, followed by reddish fruits. China.
——— 'Alba' is white flowered.

———— 'Superba.' A superior and larger cultivar with bronze-flushed leaves and long panicles of bright pink flowers.

podophylla	CREAM	SU	3'–4'/3'
	○ ◑	Z9-4/H	DS ✳✳

The palmately compound leaves have 5 broadly ovate, jaggedly lobed and toothed leaflets to 10″ long. The foliage, bronze when young, matures to green and ages to bronze again. Loose panicles of yellowish white flowers. China, Japan.

sambucifolia	WHITE	SU	2'–3'/2'
	○ ◑	Z9-4/H	DS ✳✳

This compact plant has pinnately compound leaves with 3–11 leaflets. Flat-topped panicles of white flowers. China.

tabularis	WHITE	SU	3'/3'
	○ ◑	Z9-4/H	DS ✳✳

Huge, pale green, round, peltate leaves, 2'–3' wide, with shallow lobes. Astilbe-like panicles of white flowers. Northern China, Korea.

ROMNEYA, Papaveraceae. (1)

coulteri	WHITE	LSP/ESU	3'–8'/3'–4'
	○	Z10-6/H	RS ✳✳✳✳

Matilija-Poppy. These magnificent plants have strong, erect, branching stems, partly woody below. Both stems and foliage are glaucous and blue green. The leaves are pinnately divided, somewhat toothed, and edged with hairs. The smooth, beaked flower buds open into fragrant, 6″-wide terminal flowers. Six, often less, brilliantly white, thin, crinkled petals surround a yellow globe of stamens. Site with care, as this is an extremely invasive plant. Needs deep, gravelly, well-drained soil. Drought tolerant once established. Cut back to 6″ in the fall. In cold areas, plant in a warm, sheltered spot and mulch heavily. Propagate by root cuttings in fall. Seeds are difficult to germinate: cover planted seeds with an inch of hay or pine needles and burn. Southern California, Baja California. Hybrid *R.* x *hybrida* and the cultivar 'White Cloud' are even superior to the species.
———— var. *trichocalyx* differs in having narrower leaf lobes and rounded, bristly buds; its petals are pleated rather than crinkled. Reputed to be slightly hardier.

ROSCOEA, Zingiberaceae. (17)

Adapted to regions with cool summers and mild winters, these exotic-looking plants may also be grown under glass. Along their length the stems are sheathed by alternate,

Romneya coulteri

glossy, lanceolate leaves, smaller but reminiscent of those of *Cautleya*. Shortly after the foliage emerges, the Orchid-like flowers, which may be solitary or clustered in short spikes, appear. Each has a tubular calyx, split down one side, from which protrudes the long-tubed, 3-lobed corolla. The upper lobe is upright or hooded and much wider than the 2 laterals, a feature which distinguishes this genus from related *Cautleya*. The showy, petaloid, staminal lip is large and broad, sometimes wrinkled. Divide the clumps of fleshy roots when growth begins in early summer. Plant at least 5″ deep in moist, humusy soil.

cautleoides	YELLOW	ESU	1′/6″
	○ ◑	Z9-8/H	DS **

This elegant plant produces short spikes of 2–5 cream yellow 3″ flowers just above the 5″ leaves. A choice addition to the rock garden or front of the border. China. Similar *R. humeana* has rich purple flowers. Western China. *R. alpina* from the Himalayas is about 6″ tall with purple flowers and is suitable for the rock garden. *R. capitata* is sometimes offered as *R. alpina*.

purpurea	PURPLE	SU	1′–1.5′/6″
	○ ◑	Z9-8	DS **

Variable, but generally a taller, narrower plant than *R. cautleoides*. Its erect stems are clothed in 5–6 narrowly lanceolate 6″ leaves, undulate along their margins and partially

Roscoea cautleoides

folded along their length. Short, terminal spikes of bright purple flowers; often white throated and veined, staminal lip longer than wide. Himalayas. *R. p. procera* [*R. superba*] is even taller with much larger flowers. Its broad 2″ lip is a strong purple; lateral lobes white.

RUDBECKIA, Compositae. (25)   Coneflower

These native North Americans adorn the garden with flamboyant color from summer till frost. Coneflowers have large, Daisy-like flower heads, with usually drooping yellow or orange rays around a central, cone-shaped disk; some cultivars are double flowered. All are easy to grow and thrive in sun or light shade in moderately fertile soils. Suitable for the border or meadow garden and excellent as cut flowers. Divide in spring every 4 years or so. Control leaf miners and mildew. *R. hirta,* Black-Eyed Susan, common as a roadside plant, is a free-seeding annual or biennial with many named cultivars, among them the tetraploid Gloriosa Daisies. A similar and closely related genus, *Ratibida* [*Lepachys*], was formerly included with *Rudbeckia. Ratibida pinnata* [*L. pinnata, Rudbeckia pinnata*], Gray-Headed Coneflower, has deeply cleft leaves and branching stems bearing gay flower heads, with tan to gray, ovoid disks and deeply reflexed, yellow 1″–2″ rays.

Rudbeckia fulgida sullivantii 'Goldsturm'

fulgida	YELLOW	SU-F	2′/1.5′
	○	Z10-3/T	DS ****

Orange Coneflower has rhizomatous rootstocks which give rise to robust, hairy plants. The dark green, dentate 3″–6″ leaves are lanceolate to ovate on long petioles below; the smaller stem leaves are sessile. Its erect, branching flower stems bear a long succession of 1½″–3″ flower heads with bright orange yellow rays, deep orange at their bases, and brownish purple blunt disks. A variable plant with several named forms. New Jersey to Florida, Missouri, Michigan.

————— *deamii*. [*R. deamii*]. Leafier, with broader, coarsely toothed foliage.

————— *speciosa*. [*R. newmanii, R. speciosa* Hort.]. To 5′ tall, with almost toothless basal leaves but very coarsely toothed stem leaves.

————— *sullivantii*. [*R. speciosa sullivantii*]. The stem leaves are bractlike above. 'Goldsturm,' possibly the best cultivar, is a selection of this. It has 3″–4″ heads on strong, branched 1.5′–2′ stems. Must be propagated vegetatively, although seed-grown stock is often offered, sometimes as 'Goldstrum Strain.' These plants do not have the quality and uniformity of the selection.

laciniata	YELLOW	SU-F	6′–7′/2′
	○	Z10-3/T	D ***

Cutleaf Coneflower is a coarse, robust, clump-former. Its dark green leaves are deeply cleft and wide toothed. Smooth, branched stems support large flower heads with olive green, raised disks and drooping, golden yellow 1″–2″ rays. Needs moist soil. Southern Canada to Florida, west to the Rocky Mountains.

————— 'Hortensia.' ['Golden Glow']. Very invasive. Double, with ray flowers only, on branched 6′–8′ stems. Largely replaced in gardens by superior *L. nitida* 'Goldquelle.'

maxima	YELLOW	SU	4′–5′/2′
	○	Z9-6/T	D **

Valued for its grayish leaves, to 1′ long. Its Black-Eyed Susan flowers have drooping, yellow rays, and elongated, black disks. Prefers moist soil. Missouri to Louisiana and Mississippi.

nitida	YELLOW	LSU-F	3′–4′/2′
	○	Z10-7/T	D ***

Similar to *R. laciniata,* but with lobeless, toothed, ovate leaves. Its conical disks are greenish. Georgia, Florida to Texas.

————— 'Herbstsonne' ['Autumn Sun']. Much showier, with 3″–4″ flower heads on 5′–6′ stems. Rays yellow, disks green. Z10-5/T.

————— 'Goldquelle' is probably a hybrid between 'Herbstsonne' and *R. laciniata* 'Hortensia.' Fully double, brash yellow 3″–4″ flower heads on strong stems to 6′ tall. Not an aggressive spreader. Z10-3/T.

RUELLIA, Acanthaceae. (250)

Hardy only in our warmest gardens, these tropical subshrubs can withstand only a few degrees of frost. Their large and showy flowers make them worth the risk of loss in an exceptionally cold spell. Branching stems, woody toward the base, and opposite leaves. The flowers, either solitary or in clusters, originate from the upper leaf axils. The slightly irregular corolla is tubular, with 5 more or less equal flaring lobes. All bloom profusely, particularly in spring and fall. A porous, moist soil, well enriched with organic matter, suits them best. Shade from full sun. Sometimes offered and suitable for the wild garden, hardy *R. ciliosa* is 1′ tall and has 2″ lavender blue flowers. There are several other unexciting native species.

brittoniana	BLUE	SP-F	2′–3′/2′
	○●	Z10/T	CS ***

Erect with branching stems. The leaves are linear to 1′ long, sometimes with wavy edges. Leafy, axillary clusters of flowers. The lavender to violet blue 1″–2″ corolla has spreading, broad, rounded lobes. Mexico.

graecizans	RED	SP-F	1′–2′/1′–1.5′
	○●	Z10/T	CS ***

[*R. amoena, R. longifolia*]. The pointed 2″–5″ leaves are ovate to oblong. Bright red flowers are clustered on long, axillary stalks; the corolla to 1″ long has a swollen tube and short, erect to spreading lobes. There is a white-flowered form. South America.

macrantha	PINK	SP-F	2′–3′/2′–3′
	◑●	ZIO/T	CS ****

This erect, branching subshrub at times may exceed its usual height. Wrinkled, ovate-lanceolate leaves to 5″ long. Showy 2″–3″ flowers crowd into the upper leaf axils; the purplish pink corolla is funnelform, with rounded, flaring lobes, veined in purple, and lightly brushed with gold in the throat. Brazil.

makoyana	RED	SP-F	1′–1.5′/2′–3′
	◑●	ZIO/T	CS ***

Monkey Plant, Trailing Velvet Plant. Spreading, with decumbent, branched stems. Velvety, ovate to elliptic 1½″–3″ leaves, green, flushed with violet above, purple beneath, and prominently white veined. Axillary, crimson red 2″ flowers. Brazil.

RUTA, Rutaceae. (40)

As an ornamental, Rue is grown for its blue green herbage. It may be used effectively as a contrast or specimen plant in the flower border, particularly where a cool effect is desired. Wear gloves when pruning, as it may cause dermatitis. Some people find its pungent odor objectionable. The leaves are a favorite food of the caterpillars of Monarch butterflies; they can defoliate a plant rapidly.

Ruellia macrantha

Ruta graveolens

graveolens	YELLOW	SU	2'–3'/1.5'
	○	ZI0-4/H	CDS ****

Herb of Grace, Rue. This glaucous, evergreen subshrub forms clumps of erect stems. The alternate, smooth, soft blue green leaves are 2–3 times pinnately divided, the segments oblong or spoon shaped. Loose corymbs of dirty yellow ½" flowers rise just above the foliage. Prune back in spring to force bushiness. Tolerates dry conditions well. Southern Europe. Cultivars have been selected for their improved foliage color.
——— 'Blue Beauty.' Blue Mount Rue is bushy and compact with steel blue leaves. 1.5'–3' tall.
——— 'Blue Mound.' Deep blue, larger leaves. 2'.
——— 'Jackman's Blue.' Blue, deeply divided, waxy foliage. 1.5'–2' in height.
——— 'Variegata.' Leaves abundantly splashed with cream or white, especially when young. Keep pruned to force new growth. Excellent for foliage arrangements, but not one of the best variegated foliage plants for the garden. Comes true from seed. 1.5'.

SALVIA, Labiatae. (750)   Sage

Among the most popular of garden plants, the Sages combine beautiful flowers with attractive and often aromatic foliage. Most have the square stems typical of the Mint family. The opposite leaves may be toothed or entire, but are only rarely lobed or divided. Most often they are thick, wrinkled, somewhat woolly, and edged with small, usually rounded teeth; this pattern is so characteristic that the phrase "Sage-like leaves" is commonly used in describing other plants. Upper leaves frequently differ from the lower or are reduced to bracts. The flowers, sometimes subtended by large, showy bracts, are borne in verticillasters of 2 to many, arranged in spikes, racemes, or panicles. The tubular corolla opens into a 2-lipped limb; the upper lip is erect to arching, the lower spreading and 3 lobed. All Sages need a sunny site in well-drained, fertile soil. Division is necessary only when the center of the plant starts to look thin. *Salvia officinalis,* the common culinary Sage, is a compact, leafy shrub about 1.5'–2' tall. Either the ordinary gray-leaved form or one of the cultivars with golden, purple, variegated, or tricolored foliage makes a splendid background for many front-of-the-border flowers. A biennial or short-lived perennial, Mediterranean *S. argentea* makes a low rosette of large, ovate leaves, densely furred with silver hairs. It is grown principally for its superb foliage, and its life will be prolonged if the flowering stems are removed. Also biennial or briefly perennial, handsome *S. sclarea* var. *turkestanica* has sturdy 3' stems and broadly ovate, hairy, wrinkled 6"–9" leaves. Its flowers are nearly concealed by showy pinkish bracts. Turkestan. The following species are among the best, but in a genus so large, there are many others of merit.

azurea	BLUE	SU-F	3'–6'/2'
	○	Z10-4/T	CDS ***

Blue Sage makes a tall stand of erect, branched stems. Lanceolate to oblong, toothed, gray green leaves, 2"–3" long; linear and entire upper leaves. Whorls of many clear blue ¾" flowers in long spikes; the white form is inferior. Unfortunately needs staking. Eastern to central United States.

——— var. *grandiflora* [*S. a. pitcheri, S. pitcheri*] has hairy stems, larger and more numerous flowers. A better garden subject. Central United States.

coccinea	RED	SP-SU	1'–2'/1'
	○	Z10-8/T	CDS ***

Texas Sage. Ovate to heart-shaped 1"–2" leaves, variably hairy, with small, rounded teeth. Slender racemes of scarlet red 1" flowers; purplish calyces and upper stems. Often grown as an annual. Southern United States, Mexico. Cultivars include a white-flowered form, a bicolor with red and white flowers, and both dwarf and more robust variants. Pineapple Sage, *S. elegans* [*S. rutilans*], is hardy only to Z9. It is a taller plant, to 3' or 4', with fragrant, pointed, ovate 2"–4" leaves and slender racemes of scarlet 1½" flowers. *S. fulgens* has branching 2'–3' stems, pointed, ovate 1½"–2" leaves, hairy above and white-woolly beneath, and hairy, scarlet 2" flowers. Both are Mexican. Although usually grown as an annual, popular *S. splendens,* Scarlet Sage, is a perennial and cannot escape mention here. Its limp, grass green foliage is ordinary and its flowers are strident in color. Not only ugly in its own right, it is often used in bedding schemes in insensitive and inappropriate combinations with such plants as Wax Begonias and Cannas. The purple, rose, or white cultivars are less objectionable, but their foliage is also undistinguished.

| *farinacea* | BLUE | SP-F | 2′–3′/1′–1.5′ |
| | ○ | Z10-7/T | CS **** |

Mealy-Cup Sage. Mostly grown as an annual. Hairy, branching stems and gray green, lanceolate to ovate 1½″–3″ leaves, edged with small teeth. Many slender spikes held above the foliage; calyx thickly felted, corolla violet blue about ½″ long. Good for drying. Southwestern United States.

———— 'Blue Bedder.' A widely available, superior cultivar.

———— 'Victoria.' Only 1.5′ tall.

———— 'White Porcelaine' has silvery white flower spikes.

| *forskahlei* | PURPLE | LSP-SU | 2′–3′/1′–1.5′ |
| | ○ | Z10-8 | S ** |

(Also spelled *S. forskaohlei*). Mostly basal foliage, with a few branched, leafy stems. Variable in size, the large, ovate, wrinkled leaves are irregularly toothed. Tall panicles of purplish blue 1″ flowers. The lower lip of the corolla is marked with white and yellow. An ungainly plant, but nevertheless a favorite of collectors. Southeastern Europe, Asia Minor.

| *greggii* | RED | LSP-SU | 2′–3′/1′–1.5′ |
| | ○ | Z10-9 | CS *** |

A much-branched subshrub with oblong to spatulate ½″–1″ leaves. Many short racemes of crimson 1″ flowers with a broad lower lip. Texas, Mexico. Available in both white and pink cultivars.

| *guaranitica* | BLUE | LSU-F | 3′–5′/2′–3′ |
| | ○ | Z10-9/T | CS *** |

[*S. ambigens, S. coerulea*]. This subshrubby plant, with thin, erect stems, has rough, round-toothed, ovate 2″–5″ leaves. Long, slender racemes of 1½″–2″ flowers; corolla indigo blue. Often grown as an annual. South America. *S.* 'Purple Majesty,' a hybrid available in California nurseries, has a similar habit and long spikes of royal purple 2½″ flowers.

| *haematodes* | BLUE | LSP-LSU | 2′–3′/1.5′ |
| | ○ | Z10-4 | CDS *** |

Mostly basal foliage in a rosette; wrinkled and crenate, ovate to oblong leaves to 6″ in length. It bears several large panicles of whorled flowers well above the foliage. The lavender blue 1″ corolla has a hooded upper lip much larger than the lower. Probably only a superior variant of *S. pratensis*. A short-lived perennial or biennial. Self-seeds readily. Greece.

———— 'Indigo' has deep purplish blue flowers.

| *hians* | BLUE | LSP-ESU | 2′–3′/1.5′ |
| | ○ | Z9-6/H | DS ** |

Erect, branching stems. The rough-hairy and toothed 3″–5″ leaves are triangular-ovate.

Panicles of purplish blue flowers in 2- to 6-flowered whorls; corolla tube broad with spreading lips, the lower marked with white. Kashmir.

| *jurisicii* | BLUE | ESU | 1.5′–2′/1.5′ |
| | ○ | ZIO-5/H | DS ** |

A spreading and much-branched plant, white-hairy throughout. The lower leaves are ovate-oblong and toothed; the upper pinnately divided into narrow lobes. Slender spikes of resupinate flowers in a branched inflorescence; corolla purplish blue, sometimes pink or white, to ½″ long. Southern Yugoslavia.

| *leucantha* | WHITE | LSP-F | 2′–3′/2′–3′ |
| | ○ | ZIO-9/H | CDS *** |

Mexican Bush Sage. This subshrub spreads to form large clumps of gracefully arching, white-woolly stems, well clothed in linear-lanceolate 2″–6″ leaves, edged with small round teeth, rough and hairy beneath. Long, slender spikes of white or rarely lavender flowers. The showy calyces, thickly covered with bright purplish pink hairs, outdo the modest flowers. Drought tolerant. Pinch young plants to promote fullness. Cut out old stems after flowering. A perfect background for *Erigeron karvinskianus*. Mexico.

| *patens* | BLUE | SU-F | 1.5′–2.5′/1′–1.5′ |
| | ○ ◑ | ZIO-9 | CDS **** |

Gentian Sage. The entire plant, erect stems, foliage, and flowers, is covered in glandular hairs. Ovate to triangular leaves, at times hastate, 2″–5″ long, with crenate margins. Loose spikes of 2-flowered verticillasters; the azure blue 2″–2½″ corolla has a markedly hooded upper lip. Often grown as an annual. Mexico.
———— 'Alba' is white flowered.

Salvia x *superba* 'Lubeca'

———— 'Cambridge Blue' has flowers of a lighter blue than the species. Try it with one of the lime green *Nicotiana* cultivars.

x *superba*	PURPLE	LSP-SU	1.5′–3′/1.5′–2.5′
	○	Z10-5	D ****

[*S. nemorosa* Hort., *S. virgata* Hort., *S. virgata nemorosa* Hort.]. *S. nemorosa* x *S. pratensis* x *S. villicaulis.* This catchall includes a number of sterile, hybrid cultivars, assumed to be the results of crossing the foregoing species, and by extension, cultivars of *S. x sylvestris (S. nemorosa* x *S. pratensis)*. These plants were, and often still are, sold under many names, including *S. nemorosa, S. virgata, S. virgata nemorosa, S. haematodes, S. pratensis,* and *S. x sylvestris.* Woody at the base, they form clumps of erect, branched stems, well clothed in rough, gray green foliage. The ovate to oblong 1″–3″ leaves are edged with small, round teeth. Numerous, slender, crowded spikes of violet purple ½″ flowers with reddish purple bracts. Well named, these are indeed superb garden plants. Lovely with one of the compact Yarrows such as *Achillea* 'Moonshine.'
———— 'East Friesland' ['Ostfriesland'] has purple flowers. 1.5′–2′ tall.
———— 'May Night' ['Mainacht']. Dark violet blue flowers on 1.5′–2′ stems.

uliginosa	BLUE	SU-F	4′–6′/1.5′–2′
	○	Z10-8	CDS ***

Slender, erect, branching stems. Oblong-lanceolate leaves to 3½″ in length, with large sharp teeth. Long, paniculate inflorescences of many azure blue ⅔″ flowers. Needs a moister soil than most Salvias. South America.

SAMBUCUS, Caprifoliaceae. (20)

ebulus	WHITE	SU	3′–4′/3′
	○	Z9-3	CDS **

Dwarf Elder, Danewort. Dying to the ground in winter, it is the only herbaceous ornamental in its genus. An erect, many-stemmed plant of shrublike appearance. The odd-pinnate leaves are opposite; the 4″–6″ leaflets are lanceolate, with numerous sharp teeth. The broad, flat 3″–4″ cymes bear many tiny white or pinkish flowers with 5-lobed corollas. Small shiny black fruits follow. Undemanding. Europe, western Asia, northern Africa.

SANDERSONIA, Liliaceae. (1)

aurantiaca	ORANGE	ESU/SU	1′–2′/1′
	○ ◑	Z10-9	S **

Chinese-Lantern Lily, Christmas Bells. From the tuberous roots rise slender stems clothed in alternate, linear to lanceolate 2″–4″ leaves. The nodding flowers, borne on

Sambucus ebulus

Sanguinaria canadensis 'Multiplex'

wiry pedicels in the upper leaf axils, resemble small Chinese lanterns. The orange perianth, like a swollen bell, is constricted at the mouth and has 6 minute lobes. Likes organically rich soil. Dies down after flowering until the following spring. Self-sows readily. South Africa.

SANGUINARIA, Papaveraceae. (1)

canadensis	WHITE	ESP	6″–9″/1′
	◗●	Z9-3	DS ****

Bloodroot, Red Puccoon. In its usual form, this charming American wildflower is best suited to the native plant garden, but the double-flowered *S. c.* 'Multiplex' ['Flore Pleno,' *S. c. plena*] is worthy of the rock garden or even the front of the border. Its common names allude to its red sap. A single-petioled leaf rises from each rhizome bud. The gray green leaves are variable, usually deeply palmately lobed, cordate at the base, with wavy, sometimes lobed margins, 8″–12″ across at maturity. A pristine white 1½″–2″ flower emerges from within each tightly rolled leaf on a scape about 8″ long. Eight or more narrowly elliptic petals surround a tuft of yellow stamens. In the longer-blooming, double form, these are replaced by additional petals. Bloodroot thrives in shade, beneath trees or shrubs, in moist, humusy soil, but tolerates drier conditions if well-shaded. Mulch in the spring. Propagate by dividing the fleshy rhizomes in late summer or fall after the foliage has died down; the species can be grown from seed. Spreads slowly and establishes large colonies in time. The handsome foliage makes a dense ground cover, but becomes shabby by late summer. Combines well with ferns. Southern Canada, eastern United States.

SANGUISORBA, Rosaceae. (3)   Burnet

The bottlebrushes of Burnet grace summer and early fall gardens. In erect or arching spires, they rise above the strong clumps of alternate, saw-toothed, odd-pinnate foliage. Usually lacking petals, each of the small individual flowers has 4 petaloid sepals and 4 protruding stamens, to fluffy effect. Tolerates most conditions, but best where soil does not dry out. Plant in full sun, or light shade where summers are hot. Staking is usually necessary.

canadensis	WHITE	LSU/F	4′–6′/2′
	○ ◑	Z9-3	DS ***

Canadian Burnet. [*Poterium canadense*]. It has long-petioled, bright green 1.5′ leaves with oblong 2″–3″ leaflets. Its branching stems end in erect, cylindrical 3″–8″ spikes of white flowers. This vigorous native thrives in damp or even boggy conditions. Northeastern United States. Similar *S. officinalis,* European Great Burnet, has spatulate leaflets and spikes of purplish flowers. Its foliage is sometimes used in a salad.

Sanguisorba obtusa

obtusa	PINK	SU	2'–4'/2'
	○ ◑	Z9-4	DS **

Japanese Burnet. [*Poterium obtusum*]. The rather gray green foliage serves as an attractive foil for the rosy purple, arching flower spikes, which mature to pale pink. Japan. *S. tenuifolia* [*Poterium tenuifolium*] is more delicate, with slender, graceful spires of pink to red flowers. *S. t.* var. *purpurea* has purple flowers.

SAPONARIA, Caryophyllaceae. (30)   Soapwort

Few of the Soapworts deserve a place in the border, although some are good rock garden subjects. Their leaves are paired along the stem at the swollen nodes. The flowers are arranged in showy clusters; the calyx is 5 lobed, the 5 clawed petals often notched at the end. Lean, well-drained soil.

ocymoides	PINK	LSP-SU	9"/3'
	○	Z10-2	CDS ****

Rock Soapwort is more or less evergreen. Its long, branched, trailing stems are well clothed in softly hairy, paddle-shaped ½" leaves. In late spring, the spreading mats are blanketed with loose, terminal clusters of bright pink, starry ¼" flowers with purple anthers. 'Alba' is white flowered. Shear hard after bloom for neatness and to encourage new vegetative growth. Effective in a frontal position or draped over rocks or walls. European Alps.

officinalis	PINK	SU	1'–3'/2.5'
	○	Z10-3	CDS ***

Bouncing Bet has strong, upright, unbranched stems, which bear glabrous, 3-veined, ovate leaves to 4" long. Terminal and axillary clusters of fragrant, pale pink 1" flowers. The species is only worth growing in wild or very informal gardens, but the less vigorous, double-flowered cultivars listed below are charming in the border. They have sterile, rather shaggy flowers. Europe, Asia.

———— 'Alba Plena' is white flowered.
———— 'Rosea Plena' is a pale mauve pink.
———— 'Rubra Plena' has purple crimson flowers.

SAXIFRAGA, Saxifragaceae. (370)   Saxifrage

Most of the Saxifrages are small, temperamental plants, suitable only for rock gardens and collections of alpines. The following are sometimes grown in temperate climates as edging plants or small-scale ground covers, but even these will not survive in areas with hot, humid summers. They form rosettes or tufts of evergreen, basal foliage, above

Saponaria officinalis 'Rosea Plena'

which rise slender stems, branching into airy panicles of many small flowers. The corolla is 5 parted and varies from regular to distinctly asymmetrical.

cortusifolia	WHITE	LSU-EF	1′/1′
	◑●	Z9-5/H	DS **

Handsome, leathery foliage in a basal mound. Rounded to kidney-shaped 2″–6″ leaves, with 5–11 toothed lobes. Slender-stalked, loose panicles of white ¾″ flowers, 1 or sometimes 2 of the lower petals much longer than the others. Likes a moisture-retentive, humusy soil, free of lime. Eastern Asia.
———— var. *fortunei*. [*S. fortunei*]. Hardy only to Z7, it has brownish green, 7-lobed leaves and tall panicles of white flowers. Later blooming than the species. Japan. Cultivars of this variety include 'Rubrifolia,' with reddish brown leaves and red flower stems, blooming in late summer, and 'Wada' ['Wada's Form,' 'Wada's Variety'], with purplish foliage.

stolonifera	WHITE	SU	1′–2′/1′
	◑●	Z10-6/H	DS ****

Strawberry Begonia, Strawberry Geranium, Mother-of-Thousands. [*S. sarmentosa*]. This familiar houseplant is surprisingly hardy out of doors. From a loose tuft of hairy, basal foliage it sends out wiry, pink runners, ending in tiny plantlets. The convex, rounded to kidney-shaped 2″–4″ leaves are gently lobed, attractively veined in silver gray and purplish red beneath. Airy panicles of small, asymmetrical white flowers dotted with yellow and red. The 2 lower petals are much longer than the upper three. Less exigent than *S. cortusifolia;* will tolerate drier and more alkaline soils. Tolerates city conditions. Propagated by seed, division, or most easily from runners. Eastern Asia. 'Cuscutiformis' is a more robust form.

x *urbium*	WHITE	SP-ESU	1′–1.5′/1′
	◑●	Z9-6/H	DS ***

London Pride. [*S. umbrosa* Hort.]. *S. spathularis* x *S. umbrosa*. This hybrid forms rosettes of leathery foliage. The spatulate to obovate, round-toothed 1″–2½″ leaves are reddish on their undersides and taper into slightly winged petioles. Loose panicles on wiry stems of tiny, starry white flowers, pink at the center. There are several excellent but mostly smaller cultivars. *S. umbrosa,* the true species, is infrequently grown.

SCABIOSA, Dipsacaceae. (80)   **Scabious**

These charming, old-fashioned plants have a laxly erect habit and opposite leaves, which are mostly basal or borne low. The flat to domed heads, subtended by leafy bracts, are composed of many small flowers, the outer ones larger and radiating. The individual florets have a tubular, 4- or 5-lobed corolla, which varies from nearly

Saxifraga x urbium

symmetrical to 2 lipped. Bristly, persistent calyces make the seed heads highly decorative. Scabiosas are long flowering if conscientiously deadheaded. None thrive in hot, humid climates. All need a well-drained, neutral to alkaline soil; add lime if the soil is acid. Divide occasionally to encourage prolific flowering. Excellent for cutting. The old-fashioned annual *S. atropurpurea* is one of the loveliest of flowers and combines well with many perennials.

africana		BLUE	SP/ESU	3′–4′/1.5′
	○ ◗		Z10-9/H	S *

Quite different in appearance and culture from the other species, this rare plant is suited only to West Coast gardens. The erect stem is woolly, as is the evergreen foliage. Up to 8″ in length, the obovate to oblong, basal leaves, borne in a low rosette, are coarsely and irregularly blunt toothed. The smaller, opposite or whorled upper leaves have narrow, pointed lobes. The stem ends in a loose, widely branched inflorescence of several lavender blue 2″ heads. Ordinary soil; water deeply throughout the year. Cut back after flowering to just above the basal rosette. Plant in groups for best effect. South Africa.

caucasica		BLUE	SU/LSU	1.5′–2.5′/1′–2′
	○		Z10-3/H	DS ****

Scabious, Pincushion Flower. The best of the perennial species. Long-stalked, oblong, basal leaves, entire to pinnately lobed; stem leaves pinnately divided into linear segments. The flat 2″–3″ heads, with large marginal florets, are held on long peduncles. Caucasus. Numerous excellent cultivars.

————— 'Clive Greaves' has lavender blue flowers.
————— 'Miss Willmott' is white flowered.

columbaria		BLUE	SU/LSU	1.5′–2′/1.5′–2′
	○		Z10-5/H	DS ***

Obovate, basal leaves, occasionally pinnately lobed; upper leaves pinnately cut into linear segments. Both foliage and stems are variably hairy. The long-stalked, domed 1½″ heads are lilac blue, rarely pink or white. Mulch for winter protection. Will flower continuously in frost-free areas if deadheaded. Europe, western Asia, northern Africa.

graminifolia		BLUE	SU/LSU	1′–1.5′/1′–1.5′
	○		Z10-5/H	DS **

Forms a low mound of mostly basal, silvery pubescent, linear leaves. The flat, blue or lavender 2″ heads are similar to those of *S. caucasica.* An excellent subject for the front of the border or the rock garden. Southern Europe.

————— 'Pinkushion' is a pink-flowered cultivar from Alan Bloom.

ochroleuca		YELLOW	SU/LSU	1.5′–2′/1.5′–2′
	○		Z10-5/H	DS ***

Similar to *S. columbaria,* but with soft yellow flowers. Southern Europe, Asia Minor.

Scaevola 'Mauve Clusters'

SCAEVOLA, Goodeniaceae. (80)

| 'Mauve Clusters' | PINK | SP-F | 6″–1′/1.5′ |
| | ○ | Z10-9 | C *** |

This attractive hybrid forms a dense mat of alternate, ovate 1″ leaves with small, sharp teeth. In spring and fall, it is covered with asymmetrical, mauve pink 1″ flowers. The tubular corolla is split to the base on its upper side and fans out into 5 lobes in the shape of an open hand. Needs a well-drained soil. Shear at the end of the season to promote new growth. There are several ornamental species of similar habit, but none appears to be in cultivation in this country. Australia.

SCHIZOSTYLIS, Iridaceae. (2)

Kaffir Lilies are valued for their late season burst of color. Their light green, sword-shaped leaves make compact tufts, above which rise airy wands of lustrous, starry flowers. The fleshy, rhizomatous roots demand adequate moisture for good growth and bloom; provide a humus-rich, well-drained soil and a summer mulch. Shade lightly in hot climates; shelter from the wind. Winter protection is necessary in cold zones.

| *coccinea* | RED | LSU-F | 1′–2′/6″–9″ |
| | ○ | Z10-6/H | DS *** |

Kaffir Lily or Crimson Flag has basal leaves to 1′ long, with prominent midribs; the sheathing stem leaves are shorter. Spikelike racemes of as many as 8 brilliant red,

Schizostylis coccinea

upfacing 2″–2½″ flowers, each subtended by a leafy bract. Good for cutting. When growing vigorously, division is required every 3 years. Southern Africa.

————— 'Major' ['Gigantea,' 'Grandiflora'] has larger flowers than the species.

————— 'Mrs. Hegarty.' The pale pink flowers open a little later than those of 'Major.'

————— 'Sunrise' has large, bright salmon pink flowers. An Eric Smith introduction.

————— 'Viscountess Byng' has light pink flowers; usually the last to bloom.

SCROPHULARIA, Scrophulariaceae. (200)

auriculata 'Variegata'	FOLIAGE	ESU/SU	2′–3′/1′
	○ ◑	Z9-6	CD *

Water Figwort. [*S. aquatica* 'Variegata', *S. nodosa* 'Variegata']. This variegated form of the common wildflower is prized by British plantsmen for its beautiful foliage. Erect, square, branching stems. Opposite, ovate to ovate-lanceolate 3″–6″ leaves, toothed, wrinkled, and marginally variegated in cream white. Tiny, asymmetrical, 2-lipped brown flowers in loose, paniculate inflorescences. The flowers are often removed to prevent free seeding. Thrives in moist or wet rich soils. Perhaps hardier than Z6. Great Britain. Most Scrophularias have small and uninteresting flowers. Perhaps one day, *S. calliantha* from the Canary Islands will be introduced into California gardens; it has showy red and yellow ½″ flowers in long panicles.

SCUTELLARIA, Labiatae. (300)   Skullcap

The Skullcaps have the square stems and opposite leaves typical of the Mint family. Their flowers are asymmetrical; the long corolla tube curves upward and expands into a hooded, 2-lobed upper lip and a dilated, 3-lobed lower lip, with spreading laterals. In addition to the plants described below, the genus boasts several charming, more or less prostrate ornamentals suitable for the rock garden, including *S. alpina* and *S. orientalis*.

baicalensis	BLUE	SU	1′/1′–1.5′
	○	Z10-6	CDS **

Stems procumbent at the base, then ascending or erect. Lanceolate leaves with ciliate margins. One-sided racemes of blue to purple blue 1″ flowers; corolla tube upturned and dilated. Light, well-drained soil. Eastern Asia.

————— var. *coelestina* has bright blue flowers.

costaricana	ORANGE	LSP/ESU	1.5′–3′/1′–1.5′
	○ ◑	Z10/T	CS **

This tender perennial has slender, erect, purple stems to 3′ or more. Ovate to elliptic 3″–5½″ leaves with a puckered surface. The bright, orange red flowers are erect,

Scrophularia auriculata 'Variegata'

Scutellaria costaricana

crowded into short, compact, one-sided racemes. Corolla tube slender and straight, to 2½" long, with a yellow lower lip. Likes a moist, organically rich soil. Costa Rica.

| *incana* | BLUE | LSP-SU | 2′–3′/1.5′–2′ |
| | ○ | Z9-3/T | CDS ** |

[*S. canescens*]. A robust, erect, hairy plant, with gray green, round-toothed, ovate 2"–4" leaves. The stems branch above into several racemes of blue ¾"–1" flowers. Eastern and central United States.

| **SEDUM**, Crassulaceae. (600) | | | **Stonecrop** |

This very large genus of succulents includes only a handful of plants tall enough for beds and borders, and a small number of intermediate height suitable for edging. The majority are low-growing ground cover and rock garden plants. Most of the Stonecrops have simple stems and alternate, rather small, fleshy, sessile leaves. The clustered, starry little flowers are 5 parted, the petals, free or united at the base. Very easy in lean, fast-draining soil. Water sparingly. Best in full sun, but will tolerate some shade.

| *aizoon* | YELLOW | ESU-SU | 1.5′/1.5′ |
| | ○ ◑ | Z10-4 | CDS *** |

[*S. maximowiczii, S. woodwardii*]. Dense stands of sturdy, vertical stems, clothed in light green foliage. The narrowly elliptic 2"–3" leaves are toothed, except at their bases. Flat, terminal cymes of bright yellow ½" flowers. Eastern Asia.
———— 'Aurantiacum' has dark red stems and orange flowers.

| *alboroseum* | WHITE | LSU | 1.5′/1.5′ |
| | ○ ◑ | Z10-4 | CDS ** |

Strong, upright, clustered stems, with opposite and decussate 2"–3" leaves on short petioles. The pale green, glaucous leaf blades are elliptic, slightly toothed along the outer half. Several terminal clusters of small white flowers tinged with green. Eastern Asia.
———— 'Medio-variegatus.' Leaves centrally variegated in yellow. More common in the trade than the species.
Also white flowered, *S. telephoides* is a slighter plant, with alternate, coarsely toothed, obovate to rhomboid 1½" leaves. Eastern United States.

| *kamtschaticum* | YELLOW | LSP-LSU | 6"–1′/1′ |
| | ○ ◑ | Z10-4 | CDS **** |

Slender, sprawling stems. The oblanceolate to spatulate ½"–2" leaves are coarsely toothed along their outer half. Loose, flat, 4-branched terminal cymes of dark yellow ½" flowers. Eastern Asia.
———— 'Variegatum.' This flashy cultivar has leaves banded with cream.

maximum 'Atropurpureum'	PINK	SU-LSU	1.5′–2′/2′
	○ ◑	Z10-4	CD ***

[*S. telephium maximum* 'Atropurpureum']. Purple or maroon weakly erect herbage. The clasping, lightly toothed, ovate 2″–5″ leaves are usually in whorls of 3. Small pink flowers in terminal or axillary clusters forming a large, paniculate inflorescence. The species is Asian and European.

purpureum	PINK	SU-LSU	1.5′–2′/1.5′
	○ ◑	Z10-4	CDS ***

[*S. telephium purpureum*]. Clumps of sturdy, straight stems. The crowded, elliptic to obovate 2″–3″ leaves are coarsely and irregularly toothed, except at their bases. Dense clusters of small pink or purplish pink flowers in domed, terminal inflorescences. Asia, Europe.

———— 'Autumn Joy' ['Herbstfreude']. This superior, late-blooming cultivar, common in the trade, has gray green leaves and 3″–4″ domes of pink flowers, aging to copper, persistent and rust colored in winter. Although deserving of its fine reputation, it is a difficult plant to place because of the changing color of its flowers. Combines well with ornamental grasses. Propagate vegetatively. 'Indian Chief' is very similar and possibly the same.

rosea	YELLOW	SP-LSP	1′/1′
	○ ◑	Z10-3	CDS ***

Roseroot. [*S. rhodiola, Rhodiola rosea*]. Variable. Dense clumps of upright stems crowded with glaucous, lanceolate to obovate ½″–1½″ leaves tipped with small teeth. Compact, terminal corymbose inflorescences. Yellow or sometimes purplish 4-petaled ¼″ flowers. Arctic to temperate Northern Hemisphere.

———— *integrifolium*. Compact. Pink to reddish purple flowers. Western North America.

'Ruby Glow'	RED	LSU	8″–10″/1′
	○ ◑	Z10-4	CD ***

Red, rather sprawling stems with obovate, lightly toothed 1″–1½″ leaves, edged and tinged with dark red. Loose, flat heads of small, deep pink to ruby red flowers. Slightly larger 'Vera Jameson' has purplish or bronzy foliage and magenta pink flowers. Excellent for the front of the border. Both are hybrids of questionable parentage.

spectabile	PINK	LSU-EF	1.5′–2′/1.5′–2′
	○ ◑	Z10-4	CDS ***

Showy Stonecrop. Numerous strict stems. Opposite and decussate, the pale green, ovate 2″–3″ leaves are only weakly toothed. Flat, terminal 3″–4″ inflorescences of crowded, pale pink ½″ flowers. Eastern Asia.

———— 'Brilliant' has flowers of a stronger pink.
———— 'Meteor.' More vivid pink flowers.
———— 'Star Dust' has white to very pale pink flowers.
———— 'Variegatum.' Of neat habit, with variegated foliage.

Sedum kamtschaticum 'Variegatum'

Sedum spectabile 'Brilliant'

Selinum candollei

SELINUM, Umbelliferae. (4)

candollei	WHITE	ESU	3′–5′/2′
	○ ◐	Z8-4/H	DS *

[*S. tenuifolium, Oreocome candollei*]. Erect, branching stems and light green, ferny, tripinnate leaves. Many flat-topped, compound umbels of tiny white flowers with black anthers. This charming, graceful plant, a favorite of William Robinson and E. A. Bowles, is treasured in English gardens but practically unknown here. Native to high altitudes, it should be quite cold hardy, but likely to suffer from summer heat and humidity. Prefers a well-drained soil. Himalayas.

Sempervivum tectorum

SEMPERVIVUM, Crassulaceae. (40)

This confused and confusing genus is of interest principally to collectors of succulents. The species exhibit great variability in the wild and also hybridize freely. They are found listed under a bewildering array of often outdated and invalid names. Most are very small plants, limited in use to rock gardens, walls, and containers, the larger ones for edging. Hens-and-Chickens form dense, stemless or short-stemmed rosettes of succulent, evergreen foliage. They spread by offsets into large clumps or mats. Mostly the alternate, fleshy leaves are oblong to obovate, with often colored, pointed tips and marginal hairs. The stiff, leafy flower stalks end in compact cymes of starry flowers with fleshy sepals. After blooming, the individual rosette dies. Easy to grow in well-drained, rather poor soil. Do not neglect watering; these are not particularly drought-tolerant plants. Propagate by offsets or from seeds which germinate readily but with unpredictable results.

| *tectorum* | PINK | SU | 1′–1.5′/1′–1.5′ |
| | ○ | Z10–5 | DS **** |

Common Houseleek, Hens-and-Chickens, Old-Man-and-Woman. Rosettes, 3″–4″ to even 6″ wide, of many glabrous, obovate 1½″–3″ leaves with dark tips. The white-hairy, leafy flower stalks bear cymes of purplish or reddish pink, many-petaled ¾″–1″ flowers. This most commonly grown species is extremely variable; a great many cultivars and hybrids are available under a variety of names. Most nurseries have their own selections. Propagate favorites yourself from offsets. Europe.

———— var. *calcareum* has glaucous leaves tipped with purple.

———— var. *glaucum* is also glaucous, with white leaf bases. Cobweb Houseleek, *S. arachnoideum,* the next most common species, is a smaller, equally varied plant. Its leaf tips are connected by cobwebby hairs. Sparse clusters of reddish flowers. Southern Europe.

SENECIO, Compositae. (3000)   Groundsel

This vast genus encompasses species from the world over and from very different habitats. Among them, many are especially adapted to survive drought: some are very deep rooted, some are fleshy and store water within the plant, others are covered with wax or hairs, and still others have very finely dissected foliage to reduce transpiration. Nearly all produce abundant seeds. Their leaves are basal or alternate on the stem. The solitary or clustered flower heads may be diskoid or radiate, and are usually surrounded by a single row of involucral bracts. Yellow, red, orange, blue, or purple ray florets are common. *C. x hybridus* [*C. cruentus* Hort.], the showy Florists Cineraria, is perhaps the best known. A perennial in warm climates, it is mostly grown as an annual for bedding or containers. Its enormous clusters of daisy flowers come in a wide range of brilliant colors. Many of the succulent species, mostly from southern Africa, are popular additions to the collections of specialists or are grown as houseplants. Several Canary Island species such as *S. populifolius* and *S. webbii* have potential as ornamentals and are worth seeking. This genus also includes some excellent, gray-foliaged shrubs, such as *S. laxifolius, S. monroi,* and *S. compactus,* often misidentified as *S. greyii,* all from New Zealand. They are admirable subjects for our warm western gardens, particularly near the coast. Their leathery, evergreen foliage, heavily felted beneath, is crowned with masses of bright yellow daisies in summer and fall.

| *adonidifolius* | YELLOW | ESU | 8″–1.5′/1′ |
| | ○ | Z9-5 | DS ** |

[*S. artemisiifolius*]. Glabrous throughout, with upright, unbranched stems and deep green foliage. The short-petioled, Parsley-like leaves are deeply pinnately dissected into pointed, linear segments. Its small, yellow or orange, Daisy-like flower heads cluster in terminal, compound corymbs. Southern France, Spain. Plants offered under this name may be *S. abrotanifolius* [*S. carpathicus, S. tiroliensis*], a similar plant with somewhat larger, reddish orange flowers.

| *aureus* | YELLOW | LSP | 1′–2′/1.5′ |
| | ○ | Z9-5 | D ** |

Golden Groundsel makes bushy clumps of fresh green, cordate to broadly ovate, toothed basal leaves on long petioles. Above rise numerous erect, dark, smooth stems, sparsely clothed in essentially sessile, narrow, pinnately cleft leaves. Corymbs of brilliant deep yellow ½″–1″ flower heads, with 8–10 notched ray flowers surrounding the yellow disk. Thrives in damp, even wet soils. Suitable for the bog garden. Eastern and central United States.

| *cinerea* | FOLIAGE | SU | 1′–2′/1.5′ |
| | ○ | Z10-8 | CS **** |

Sea Ragwort, Silver Groundsel, Dusty Miller. [*Centaurea maritima, S. maritima*]. Known as Dusty Miller, a name unfortunately also applied to several species of *Centaurea* and *Artemisia* and with which it is frequently confused. It is chiefly grown for its attractive and durable, woolly silver herbage, which is extremely tolerant of seaside conditions. Its tough, upright stems are subshrubby below. The thickly felted 2″–6″ leaves are deeply pinnately cut, each segment about ¼″ wide, ending in 3 or more short, blunt lobes. Terminal compound corymbs of pale yellow or cream ½″ daisies bloom throughout the summer, but are of secondary ornamental value. Selections include 'Cirrhus,' a dwarf, 'Colchester White,' a particularly white form, and 'Silver Dust,' which has very deeply cut, silvery leaves. Prune regularly to shape. Demands free-draining soil; succumbs readily to "wet feet." Easily propagated from seed; the selections, from cuttings. Grown as an annual in unfavorable climates. A splendid foil for brightly colored annuals and perennials; particularly effective in evening light. Mediterranean region. Argentinian *S. vira-vira* [*S. leucostachys, Cineraria candidissima* Hort., *C. maritima* var. *candidissima* Hort.] is a similar, though larger and less compact plant. Its white-woolly foliage is more finely dissected into pointed segments.

| *mandraliscae* | FOLIAGE | LSU-F | 1'-1.5'/1' |
| | ○ | Z10-9/H | CDS ** |

[*Kleinia mandraliscae*]. The succulent, sprawling or procumbent stems, woody at the base, are densely clothed in fleshy blue gray foliage. Their pointed, curving 3"–4" leaves are semicylindrical, flattened and sometimes grooved along their upper surface. Above the foliage, inconsequential grubby white flower heads cluster into loose cymes. Although the bulk of their flowers appear in late summer and fall, a few may be in bloom at any time. A valuable ground cover plant for warm gardens. Reputedly from southern Africa, but not known there in the wild. *S. aizoides* [*K. aizoides*] is similar.

| *pulcher* | PURPLE | F | 1.5'-2.5'/1.5' |
| | ○ | Z10-8 | DS * |

Showy Groundsel. The herbage is cobwebby with silver hairs, particularly when young. Petioled below, reduced and clasping above, the leathery, dark green 4"–10" leaves are oblong to broadly lanceolate, with irregularly round-toothed margins. The showy 2"–3" flower heads are solitary or in few-flowered terminal clusters. Up to 20 crimson magenta ray florets surround the yellow central disk; woolly, blunt, involucral bracts. Requires deep, well-drained soil and a cool root run. Very late blooming. Possibly hardy in Z7 if protected from cold winds. Uruguay, Argentina.

| *smithii* | WHITE | SU | 3'-5'/2' |
| | ○ ◑ | Z9-7 | DS ** |

Bold, robust clumps of large, coarse, basal foliage, slightly grayed with loose woolly hairs when young. The broadly paddle-shaped 8"–10" leaves are puckered and rather lax, crisped and undulate at the margins; petioles 4" or more long. Barely above the

Senecio smithii

foliage, numerous white 1½″ daisies crowd into terminal panicles, each 4″–6″ across, on stiff erect stems; fluffy white seed heads follow. Soil should be deep, rich, and damp. Be alert for slugs and snails. Excellent beside streams and lakes, where it combines well with Astilbes and late-blooming Primulas. Only for gardens where winters are mild and summers moderate. Southern Chile, Falkland Islands.

tanguticus	YELLOW	EF	4′–6′/2′
	○ ◑	Z9-6	D ∗∗

Chinese Ragwort. [*Ligularia tangutica*]. A rampant grower with invasive, rhizomatous roots and thick, erect, leafy stems branching above. Up to 8″ long and as wide below, the glabrous, broadly ovate, petioled leaves are deeply pinnately cut, each lobe spear shaped and toothed. Hundreds of small, 3-rayed yellow daisies less than ½″ across crowd into elegant 6″–12″ plumes, followed by attractive straw-colored seed heads. Avoid fertile, moisture-retentive soil unless there is plenty of space! China.

SETCREASEA, Commelinaceae. (6)

pallida	PURPLE	SP-F	1′–1.5′/1.5′
	○	Z10-9/T	C ∗∗∗∗

Grown for its green to purple, glaucous foliage, this plant has succulent, decumbent to ascending stems. The fleshy, lanceolate to oblong leaves to 7″ in length are fringed with hairs. Terminal or sometimes axillary clusters of small 3-petaled flowers are each subtended by a pair of large, leafy bracts. Purple-tinged white, pink, or rose flowers

Setcreasea pallida 'Purple Heart'

Shortia galacifolia

bloom consistently in warm weather. Thrives in rather poor, well-drained soil; do not overwater. Evergreen in frost-free areas, the foliage is damaged even by a light frost, but the plant will recover from the roots. In colder climates root cuttings annually; they root with astonishing ease. Mexico.

———————— 'Purple Heart.' Purple Heart. [*S. purpurea, S. tampicana*]. This most commonly grown form has purple herbage and purplish rose flowers. Use with discretion; best combined with gray or silver-leaved plants.

SHORTIA, Diapensiaceae. (8)

These charming evergreen plants of compact habit are suitable for woodlands, rock gardens or as a ground cover under Rhododendrons. The long-stalked, all-basal leaves are rounded to heart shaped. Leafless stems bear solitary or a few nodding, bell-like flowers; corollas 5 lobed, white or pink. Shortias require an acid, richly organic soil which never dries out, and benefit from mulching with partially decomposed leaf mold or compost. They will spread slowly, but only under favorable conditions. Divide the creeping roots in early spring; absolutely fresh seed is essential for germination.

galacifolia	WHITE	SP	8″/1′
	●	Z8-4	DS ✱✱✱

Oconee-Bells. The shiny, leathery, bright green foliage overwinters to reddish bronze.

Leaves almost circular and toothed to 2″ wide. The beautiful, pink-tinged ¾″ flowers have irregularly toothed lobes. A little gem. North Carolina, South Carolina.

soldanelloides	PINK	SP	6″–8″/1′
	●	Z8-4	DS **

Fringe-Bell, Fringe Galax. [*Schizocodon soldanelloides*]. Not as compact as *S. galacifolia*. Its rounded 2″ leaves have heart-shaped bases and deeply toothed margins. Several deeply fringed 1″ flowers are borne in a loose raceme on a 4″–12″ scape above the foliage. The color varies from rosy pink to almost white. Japan.
——— *ilicifolia* [*S. ilicifolia*]. Leaves sharply and more coarsely toothed.
——— *magna* [*S. macrophylla*] is larger throughout.

uniflora	WHITE	SP	8″/1′
	●	Z8-4	DS **

Nippon-Bells. [*Schizocodon uniflorus*]. Its slightly larger, cordate leaves with wavy margins distinguish it from related *S. galacifolia*. White or very pale pink ¾″ flowers, semipendulous and gently fringed. *S. u.* var. *grandiflora* has larger flowers. Japan.

SIDALCEA, Malvaceae. (22)

The elegant spikes of silky, Mallow-like flowers and the handsome, usually palmately lobed foliage of our native Prairie Mallow or Checkerbloom are distinctive in the perennial or cutting garden. Terminal racemes of 5-petaled flowers, each petal squared or indented at the tip. Easy to grow in sunny or lightly shaded positions in deep, fertile, loamy soil. Cut back after flowering to encourage a second flush of bloom and the new basal growth needed for overwintering. Usually requires little maintenance, although tall cultivars will need support. Plant in groups for best effect.

malviflora	PINK	SU	2′–4′/1′–1.5′
	○ ◑	Z10-5	DS ****

Prairie Mallow or Miniature Hollyhock makes narrowly erect clumps. The long-petioled basal leaves are rounded and shallow lobed to 3″ across; the alternate stem leaves become progressively smaller and more deeply fingered up the branching stems. Loose racemes of long-blooming 1″ flowers. The species is seldom cultivated, being largely replaced by superior cultivars and hybrids. California.
——— 'Brilliant' has deep rose flowers on 2.5′ stems.
——— 'Elsie Heugh' is a soft shell pink with fringed petals. 2.5′ tall.
——— 'Rose Queen.' Rosy pink flowers. 4′ in height.
——— 'Sussex Beauty.' A fine, clear pink cultivar. 2.5′ tall.
——— 'William Smith' has bright salmon flowers on 3′ stems.

Sidalcea malviflora 'Sussex Beauty'

Sideritis hyssopifolia

SIDERITIS, Labiatae. (100)

| *hyssopifolia* | YELLOW | SU | I′/I′–I.5′ |
| | ○ | ZI0-7/H | CDS ** |

This compact and neat subshrub has the quiet charm of so many members of the Mint family. It makes a dense stand of erect, straight stems to 16″ tall, although in the wild it is often a much smaller plant. The opposite leaves, to 1½″ long, vary from linear to elliptic and are sometimes coarsely toothed. Dense spikes of serried, 6-flowered whorls with spine-tipped bracts. The small yellow flowers, often spotted with purple, are 2 lipped, the lower, larger and 3 lobed. For well-drained soils. Southern Europe.

SILENE, Caryophyllaceae. (500)   **Campion**

Only a few members of this large genus, closely related to *Lychnis,* have ornamental value, and are best displayed in the rock garden. Solitary or in sprays, their flattened, white, pink, or red flowers are sometimes large and showy. The tubular, 5-toothed calyx balloons out in some species; the 5 clawed petals are often notched or lobed at the apex. Their leaves are basal or opposite on the stems.

Silene caroliniana

| *caroliniana* | PINK | ESU | 8″–1′/1′ |
| | ○ | **Z8-5** | DS ✶✶✶✶ |

Wild Pink. A neat mound of slightly hairy, bluish green, broadly to narrowly oblanceolate 3″–5″ leaves. Slender and unbranched, the jointed, glabrous stems support loose clusters of pale to deep pink ¾″–1″ flowers with wedge-shaped, notched petals. Some authorities separate the subspecies *pensylvanica* [*S. pensylvanica*] and *wherryi* [*S. wherryi*] on the basis of details of the calyx. Tolerant of dry soils. Short-lived, but easy from seed. New Hampshire to Ohio, North Carolina, Tennessee.

| *virginica* | RED | LSP-SU | 1′–2′/1′ |
| | ○ ◑ | **Z9-3** | DS ✶✶✶ |

Fire-Pink has basal clumps of almost glabrous, oblanceolate 3″–4″ leaves. The glandular sticky stems carry several pairs of much longer, sessile leaves. Axillary and terminal clusters of crimson 2″ flowers; their narrow calyces may reach 1″ long, the petals are often deeply notched. Plant more closely when used as a ground cover. Short-lived. New Jersey to Minnesota, south to Georgia, Oklahoma.

| *vulgaris* | WHITE | SU | 1′–2′/1′ |
| | ○ | **Z9-4** | DS ✶✶✶ |

Bladder Campion, Maiden's Tears. [*S. cucubalus, S. glauca, S. inflata, S. latifolia, S. wallichiana*]. This most variable species may be glabrous or pubescent. It has erect, branched stems and ovate to linear 1″–2″ leaves. The large white, sometimes red flowers, solitary or clustered, have conspicuously inflated and veined calyces and deeply notched petals. Europe, northwest Africa, temperate Asia. Subspecies *maritima* [*S. maritima*], Sea Campion, from the coasts of northern Europe, has glaucous, trailing stems, which form a light green mat. Its white ¾″ flowers rise on erect stems. Attractive 'Flora Plena' ['Plena'] is fully double and is usually preferred to the species.

SILPHIUM, Compositae. (20)   Rosinweed

The Rosinweeds are coarse, gangling natives, with sturdy, erect stems and bold, rough, hairy foliage. Usually, their lower leaves are opposite, the upper alternate. The large, Sunflower-like heads, with yellow disk and ray florets, are loosely clustered. These undemanding plants can be used at the back of the border and for naturalizing.

laciniatum	YELLOW	SU/LSU	5′–9′/3′
	○	Z10-3/T	S ***

Compass Plant has rough, hairy stems. Its leaves, to 1.5′ long, are pinnately parted into narrow or pinnatifid segments; the stem leaves are smaller. The flower heads may reach 5″ in width. The common name alludes to the tendency of the lower leaves to align themselves in a north-south direction. Central and southeastern United States.

perfoliatum	YELLOW	SU/LSU	4′–8′/2′–3′
	○	Z10-3/T	DS ***

Cup Plant has smooth stems, square in cross section, and entirely opposite foliage. The deltoid to ovate leaves, to 1′ long, are coarsely toothed; the upper leaves join at the base to form a cup. Flower heads to 3″ across. Central and southeastern North America.

terebinthinaceum	YELLOW	SU/LSU	3′–9′/3′
	○	Z10-3/T	S ***

Prairie Dock. Smooth, practically leafless stems. The basal, long-stalked leaves, to 1.5′ in length, are ovate, oblong or elliptic, and coarsely toothed to lobed. Flower heads to 3″ wide. Central and southeastern North America.

SISYRINCHIUM, Iridaceae. (75)

The clusters of usually yellow or blue, very short-lived flowers are subtended by a leaflike spathe. Wheel-shaped, or in other species bell-shaped, the perianths have 6 spreading segments, which spiral tightly as they fade. They should not be allowed to dry out during the growing season. Self-sow freely. Plant in groups for best effect.

Silphium perfoliatum

Sisyrinchium striatum

bellum	BLUE	SP	1′–1.5′/1′
	○	Z10-8	DS ***

Blue-Eyed Grass. [*S. angustifolium bellum, S. eastwoodiae*]. Sparse tufts of grassy, bluish green 8″–10″ leaves. The loose clusters of violet blue ¾″–1″ flowers are borne well above the foliage on branched and winged flower stalks. Coastal California. Later-flowering *S. californicum,* Golden-Eyed Grass, has yellow 1″–1½″ flowers. California, Oregon.

striatum	YELLOW	SU	2′–2.5′/1′
	○	Z10-7	DS **

Erect clumps of gray green, Iris-like leaves to 1.5′ long by ½″–1″ wide; stem leaves smaller. Their unbranched, narrowly winged stems bear clusters of ½″ flowers along their upper third, arranged in a dense, narrow spike. The short-pediceled, pale yellow flowers are veined in purple. Southern Chile.
————— 'Variegatum' ['Aunt May'] has beautifully variegated leaves, longitudinally striped with cream. Shade lightly from intense sun.

| *racemosa* | WHITE | ESP/SP | 1.5′–3′/1′–1.5′ |
| | ◑ | Z9-3 | DS *** |

False Solomon's-Seal, False Spikenard, Treacleberry. [*Vagnera racemosa*]. So called because it resembles *Polygonatum,* the true Solomon's-Seal, in habit and foliage. It forms clumps of arching stems, with essentially stalkless, alternate leaves, borne flat, nearly in one plane. The parallel-veined, elliptic 3″–6″ leaf blades are hairy on their undersides. A feathery 6″ panicle of tiny, cream white, 6-tepaled flowers terminates each stem, followed by attractive red berries spotted with purple. Likes moist, organically rich, slightly acid soils. Widespread in North America.

———— var. *amplexicaulis,* Fat Solomon, the West Coast form, has ovate, clasping leaves.

S. stellata, Starflower, is a modest plant, better suited to gardens of native wildflowers.

Smilacina racemosa

SOLIDAGO, Compositae. (130)   **Goldenrod**

American gardeners disdain the familiar Goldenrods and blame them unjustly for
causing hay fever; in Europe they are prized both in the garden and as cut flowers. In
time, these variable plants form broad clumps of tall, erect stems, branching only in
the inflorescence. The alternate leaves, much longer than wide, may be toothed. The
tiny, yellow, or very rarely white flower heads are composed of disk florets surrounded
by a single row of rays. Vast numbers of flower heads crowd into showy inflorescences
of various types: corymbs, panicles, racemes, or thyrses. Goldenrods bloom from
midsummer well into fall and combine most attractively with Michaelmas Daisies and
other Asters. They thrive in sun or light shade in soils of average fertility. Many are
aggressive, even invasive plants and need regular division, usually every 2–3 years. Few
of the species are grown, and those more often in wild gardens than in formal situations.
Among the best are: *S. altissima, S. canadensis, S. graminifolia, S. rigida, S. rugosa,
S. sempervirens,* and *S. speciosa.* All are very hardy. Try any locally available. The
numerous hybrids (hardy in Z10-3) are more suited to garden use than the species, due
to their better and more predictable performance. They are often incorrectly listed as
S. x *hybrida,* or as cultivars of *S. canadensis.* In fact, the exact parentage of most is
unknown. *S. canadensis* and European *S. virgaurea* are involved in many of the crosses.
'Cloth of Gold' has deep yellow flower heads on 1.5′ stems.
'Crown of Rays.' Bright yellow heads in large panicles. 2′ tall.
'Gold Dwarf' is only 1′ tall.
'Goldenmosa' is a bright yellow early bloomer. 2.5′–3′ in height.
'Golden Thumb' is a 1′ dwarf.
'Peter Pan' flowers late on 2′–2.5′ stems.

X *SOLIDASTER*, Compositae. (1)

luteus	**YELLOW**	**SU-EF**	**2′–2.5′/1.5′–2′**
	○ ◑	**Z10-4**	**D ✳✳✳**

[X *S. hybridus, Aster hybridus luteus, A. luteus,* X *Asterago lutea*]. *Aster ptarmicoides*
x *Solidago* sp.. Erect but sprawling when heavy with flowers. Sparsely toothed leaves,
to 6″ long, oblanceolate below, linear-elliptic above. Pale yellow, Daisy-like ½″ flower
heads in a large, branched, corymbose panicle. The flowers age to cream. Culture as
for *Solidago.* Not for southern Florida or the Gulf Coast.

SONCHUS, Compositae. (50)

The Canary Islands have given us a number of fine ornamentals, well suited to California climates, but the temperate zone species are too weedy to serve in gardens.

Solidago 'Goldenmosa'

X *Solidaster* 'Lemore'

Sonchus congestus

congestus	YELLOW	SP/LSP	1′–3′/2′–3′
	○	ZI0-9/H	CS **

[*S. jacquinii*]. This handsome subshrub makes one or more rosettes of dark green, lanceolate to oblanceolate, pinnatifid 1′–2′ leaves; the lobes are pointed and edged with small, sharp teeth. In young plants, the rosettes are essentially stemless and appear to arise directly from the ground; with age, woody stems develop, bearing the rosettes terminally. From each of these emerges a short, woolly scape supporting an umbel-like cluster of bright yellow, Dandelion-like 2″–3″ flower heads. Needs a well-drained soil. Canary Islands. This is the best-known species, but others worth trying include *S. acaulis* which makes a single, basal rosette, to 3′ across, of pinnately lobed leaves. Its long, stout scape is topped by a large umbel of yellow flower heads. *S. radicatus* is smaller, with gray green, lyrate leaves. Graceful *S. tectifolius* has pale green, slender, arching, pinnate leaves, with overlapping, ovate to rounded leaflets, silver gray beneath.

SPHAERALCEA, Malvaceae. (50)   Globe Mallow

The long-blooming Desert Mallows are drought tolerant. Most are covered with short, grayish, star-shaped hairs, some to the point of being felted. The alternate, palmate leaves are lanceolate to rounded in outline; their deep to shallow lobes are further lobed

Sphaeralcea munroana

or only saw toothed. In terminal spikes, axillary clusters, or solitary, the pink, reddish, or orange flowers resemble small Hollyhocks, to which they are related. A warm, sheltered position is preferable. Demand excellent drainage.

ambigua	**PINK**	**LSU-F**	**2′–3′/2′**
	○	**Z10-7/H**	**CS ✳✳**

Desert Mallow, Desert Hollyhock, Wild Hollyhock. This southwestern native, variable in habit, generally makes a thin, vase-shaped clump of sturdy, sparsely foliaged stems, subshrubby at the base. The broadly ovate or rounded, 3-lobed ¾″–2½″ leaves are thick and pubescent. Open panicles of 2″ flowers, in various shades of pink and orange. Effective in desert gardens; showy for many weeks. If watered, the plants may reach 4′ or 5′ in height. Southwestern United States, Mexico. Also southwestern *S. fendleri* is smaller and has mostly orange flowers. Where their ranges overlap in the wild, these 2 species hybridize freely.

munroana	**RED**	**SU/F**	**1′–3′/1′**
	○	**Z10-7/H**	**CS ✳✳✳**

Its woody rootstock gives rise to several hairy, slender, trailing stems. The sparse, rough-hairy, shallowly 3-lobed 1″–2″ leaves are wider than long; the lobes, toothed or cut again. The Mallow-like 1″ flowers, arranged in clusters both terminally and in the upper leaf axils, vary from bright red to orange pink and apricot. Tolerant of poor soils. Western and northwestern North America.

SPIGELIA, Loganiaceae. (30)

| *marilandica* | RED | LSP/ESU | 1′–2′/1′ |
| | ○ ◐ | Z10-5/T | DS ** |

Indian Pink, Pinkroot. This striking, southeastern native forms a sheaf of unbranched, erect stems, bearing widely spaced pairs of ovate 2″–4″ leaves. Terminal, one-sided cymes of showy 2″ flowers; corolla funnelform, scarlet outside, yellow inside, with 5 flaring, pointed lobes. This woodlander welcomes some shade in hot areas, but will grow in full sun in gentler climates. Southeastern and south central United States.

STACHYS, Labiatae. (300)   Betony

Several of the Betonies or Woundworts are well-nigh indispensable plants for the garden. They have the square stems and opposite leaves common to most members of the Mint family. The small, asymmetrical flowers, in whorls of 2 or more, often interspersed with small leaves or bracts, are borne in compact to loosely arranged spikes. The tubular corolla expands into 2 lips; the lower 3-lobed. All like well-drained, fertile soils and moderate watering. Divide only as necessary.

| *byzantina* | PINK | LSP/SU | 1′–1.5′/1′ |
| | ○ ◐ | Z10-4/H | DS **** |

Lamb's-Ears. [*S. lanata, S. olympica*]. Spreads to form a thick mat of densely white-woolly, oblong to elliptic 3″–4″ leaves. The silvery foliage is soft and velvety to the touch and is very appealing to small children. The leafy flower spikes, also white-woolly throughout, detract from the effect of the superb foliage and may be removed. Corolla pink to purplish pink, ½″ long. One of the best edging plants; let it sprawl, to soften hard paving lines. Tends to rot in hot, humid summers. Self-seeds freely. Turkey, southwestern Asia.

———— 'Silver Carpet.' This sterile cultivar does not produce flowering stems; propagate by division.

| *citrina* | YELLOW | SP/SU | 1′–1.5′/1′–1.5′ |
| | ○ | Z10-8/H | DS ** |

A low, bushy subshrub with hairy, gray green, crenulate 1″–1½″ leaves, blunt and broadly elliptic in outline. Short, broad spikes of whorled sulfur yellow flowers. Greece.

| *coccinea* | RED | SP/SU | 1′–2′/1′ |
| | ○ | Z10-9/H | DS ** |

Stiff, erect stems, rather sparsely clothed, in gray green, Sage-like foliage. The round-toothed, wrinkled 1″–1½″ leaves are ovate to triangular. The stems end in loosely tiered whorls of scarlet 1″ flowers. Southwestern United States, Mexico.

Stachys byzantina

Stachys grandiflora

| *grandiflora* | PINK | LSP/SU | 1'–2'/1'–1.5' |
| | ○ ◑ | Z10-3 | DS *** |

Big Betony. [*Betonica grandiflora, B. macrantha, S. macrantha*]. Round-toothed, wrinkled, hairy foliage in a lush mound, much bolder in effect than that of *S. officinalis*. Ovate to heart-shaped leaves. Erect spikes of purplish pink flowers in well-spaced verticillasters; corolla 1"–1½" long. Asia Minor.

———— 'Alba' has white flowers.

———— 'Robusta' is a larger plant with purplish pink flowers.

———— 'Rosea' is pink flowered.

———— 'Superba.' A vigorous plant with purplish pink flowers.

———— 'Violacea' has violet-colored flowers.

| *officinalis* | PURPLE | SP/SU | 1'–2'/1'–1.5' |
| | ○ ◑ | Z10-4 | DS *** |

Betony. [*S. betonica, Betonica officinalis*]. Makes a bushy little clump of attractive, round-toothed, wrinkled foliage; the blunt, oblong 1"–4" leaves may be hairy. Erect, leafy flower stalks bear compact 1"–3" spikes of small purplish red to purplish pink flowers. Europe, Asia Minor. Plants in the trade variously labeled as *S. officinalis, S. densiflora,* and *S. spicata,* or as cultivars of one of these, may be garden forms of *S. officinalis,* or of the true *S. densiflora* [*S. hirsuta*], or even hybrids. This needs to be expertly clarified.

———— 'Alba.' White flowered.

———— 'Rosea' has clear pink flowers.

STANLEYA, Cruciferae. (8)

| *pinnata* | YELLOW | SU | 1'–3'/1.5' |
| | ○ | Z10-3 | DS ** |

Prince's Plume. This stately plant produces tall, stout stems from a subshrubby base. The alternate, grayish leaves, to 6" long, are pinnately divided below, entire and almost linear above. Their elongating, plumelike racemes display over an extended period; the lemon yellow, cruciform 1" flowers open from the bottom. Conspicuous seedpods. Tolerant of drought. Western United States.

STOKESIA, Compositae. (1)

| *laevis* | BLUE | SU-F | 1'–2'/1'–1.5' |
| | ○ | Z10-5/T | DRS **** |

Stokes' Aster. [*S. cyanea*]. The cluster of stiff, branching, decumbent stems bears coarse, long and narrow, alternate leaves, sometimes toothed toward the base; the upper leaves are small, often clasping. Large, terminal flower heads to 4" across. The small

Stanleya pinnata

Stokesia laevis

inner florets are tubular, the outer strap shaped and 5 lobed. Evergreen in the south. Long flowering, commencing earlier in warm climates. Needs good drainage, especially in winter, and a light mulch in cold areas. Southeastern United States. Numerous cultivars.

——————— 'Alba' has white flower heads.
——————— 'Blue Danube' is deep blue and early flowering.
——————— 'Blue Moon'. Silvery blue to lilac heads.
——————— 'Blue Star' is large flowered.
——————— 'Lilacina.' Lilac flower heads.
——————— 'Lutea' has pale yellow flower heads.
——————— 'Rosea' is pink flowered.
——————— 'Silver Moon' has pure white flower heads.

STRELITZIA, Strelitziaceae. (4)

reginae	ORANGE	F-SP	3′–5′/3′–5′
○ ◑	ZIO/T	DS ****	

Bird-of-Paradise. [*S. parvifolia*]. Erect clumps of substantial, Banana-like leaves on long stalks; flowering stems equally tall and straight. The unique flowers rise out of almost horizontal, greenish 6″–8″ spathes. Each 3″ flower consists of 3 orange sepals and 3 blue petals, 2 of which are fused into a pointed tongue. Needs a rich, deep, but well-drained soil. Fertilize and water copiously. A useful, long-lived plant for frost-free areas, it blooms all year, but most abundantly in cool weather. Long lasting as a cut

Strelitzia reginae var. *juncea*

Symphyandra hoffmannii

flower. Best propagated by rooted suckers, or buy container-grown plants. Dwarf cultivars are available. South Africa.

———————— var. *juncea* has narrow, reedlike leaves, less tropical in appearance. Not as readily available.

STROBILANTHES, Acanthaceae. (250)

atropurpureus	PURPLE	LSU-F	4′–5′/2′
	○	Z10-6/T	D **

Large, bushy clumps of strong, well-branched, leafy stems. The Nettle-like leaves are opposite, broadly ovate and coarsely toothed, with conspicuous veins. The flowers, in numerous loose, terminal and axillary panicles, have deeply 5-cleft calyces; their arching, tubular 1¼″ corollas have 5 spreading lobes. Blackish purple in bud, the violet blue flowers change to a violet purple by noon. Not very showy, but a useful contrast to the predominantly warm colors of fall. Drought tolerant. Spring division is recommended. Northern India, Kashmir.

SYMPHYANDRA, Campanulaceae. (8)

hoffmannii	WHITE	SU	1′–2′/1′–1.5′
	○ ◑	Z9-5/H	S **

Has erect but rather weak, branching stems and softly hairy foliage. The lanceolate to oblanceolate leaves are coarsely and irregularly toothed. Basal leaves, to 7″ long, with winged stalks; smaller and sessile upper leaves. The white or cream, broadly bell-shaped, pendulous 1½″ flowers are borne in leafy panicles. This graceful relative of Campanulas is rarely grown in American gardens and has the undeserved reputation of being temperamental. It is nevertheless not a plant for climates with hot and humid summers. Short-lived, it tends to exhaust itself in seed production; deadhead conscientiously, leaving only enough for propagation. The other species, all charming plants, are well worth growing, but even rarer in the trade. Yugoslavia. The biennial *S. wanneri* from the European Alps is particularly beautiful.

SYMPHYTUM, Boraginaceae. (25)   Comfrey

Like many other Borages, Comfreys tend to be rather coarse and hairy. They have simple, alternate leaves, often large at the base, almost opposite and smaller above. The nodding, funnelform flowers are in clusters of scorpioid racemes. *S. officinale* has been grown for its medicinal properties for centuries, but is too coarse for use except in herb or wild gardens.

caucasicum	BLUE	SP	1′–2′/2′
	○ ◗	Z9-3	DRS ***

A freely spreading plant, which makes large mounds of grayish green, ovate to lanceolate leaves to 8″ long. Arching sprays of flowers, opening reddish purple and aging to deep sky blue. Lovely under Magnolias. Very invasive. Caucasus Mountains.

grandiflorum	YELLOW	ESP	1′/1′
	○ ◗	Z9-3	DRS ****

[*Pulmonaria lutea* Hort.]. A neat, carpeting plant with dark green, rather crinkled, ovate 4″ leaves. The cream yellow flowers are orange tipped in bud. Will rebloom if cut back. An excellent weed-controlling ground cover under shrubs, even in dry shade. Caucasus.

———— 'Hidcote Blue.' Red in bud, changing to blue, then white. 1.5′ tall.

———— 'Hidcote Pink.' Pink flowers fading to white. 1.5′.

———— 'Variegatum.' An Eric Smith selection from England, with cream and yellow variegated foliage.

Also useful as a ground cover, *S.* x *rubrum* Hort. is considered a hybrid between *S. officinale* and *S. grandiflorum.* In early summer, its sprays of crimson flowers bloom on 1.5′ stems. Cut back after flowering. In partial shade, if soil is moist, it spreads slowly, but it also tolerates dry shade well.

x *uplandicum*	BLUE	SU	3′–5′/3′
	○	Z9-3	CDR ***

Russian Comfrey. [*S. peregrinum*]. *S. asperum* x *S. officinale.* Variable and vigorous, with branching stems well clothed in hairy, ovate to lanceolate leaves. Free blooming, with many sprays of pale violet flowers, pinkish in bud. Ideal for sunny meadows, but too coarse elsewhere.

———— 'Variegatum.' Striking, grayish green leaves, bordered with wide bands of cream. Lilac blue flowers. Needs some shade in hot areas and deep, moisture-retentive soil. 2′–5′ tall.

TANACETUM, Compositae. (60)   Tansy

Tansys have attractive, strongly aromatic foliage, and need not be confined to the herb garden. Their alternate leaves are entire or more commonly pinnately compound, often finely dissected. Yellow flower heads, of tubular disk or disk and ray flowers, are arranged in terminal corymbs. They prefer dryish soils. May be invasive.

douglasii	YELLOW	SU	1′–2′/1′
	○	Z10-8/H	DS **

Sturdy, rather hairy stems with finely dissected, grayish 4″–8″ leaves, hairy beneath. The button-shaped flower heads, to ¾″ across, are fringed with minute ray flowers. Coastal California to British Columbia. Similar *T. camphoratum* has coarser, more hairy leaves. Coastal California.

Symphytum officinale 'Variegatum'

Tanacetum douglasii

Telekia speciosa

herderi	YELLOW	SU	9″–1′/9″
	○	Z10-8/H	CD ***

This mat-former has silvery gray, very finely dissected foliage. It produces few small rayless flower heads. Tolerant of most well-drained soils. Turkestan. Subshrubby *T. densum* 'Amanum' [*Chrysanthemum densum amanum*] forms low 6″–15″ mounds of soft, feathery, silver 1″ leaves. Likes limy soils. For the front of dry, sunny borders. Turkey.

vulgare	YELLOW	SU	2′–3′/1.5′
	○	Z9-3	DS ****

Common Tansy, Golden Buttons. [*Chrysanthemum vulgare*]. An upright, vigorous plant, forming large clumps of bright green, ferny foliage. The finely dissected and toothed 8″ leaves are petiolate below, sessile above. Rayless, studlike ⅓″–½″ flower heads crowd into flat, terminal clusters. The more ornamental *T. v.* 'Crispum' is valued for its crisped leaves, a welcome contrast in foliage combinations. Europe.

TELEKIA, Compositae. (2)

speciosa	YELLOW	SU	3′–6′/3′
	○	Z9-3	DS ***

Oxeye Daisy. [*Buphthalmum speciosum*]. Handsome clumps of stiff, erect stems, branching above, and bold alternate foliage. The large lower leaves, to 10″ long, are heart shaped and coarsely double toothed; the smaller sessile upper leaves are ovate and edged with sharp teeth. Each stem bears several 2½″–4″ flower heads; both disk and ray florets are yellow. This easy plant blooms for several weeks. Needs space, as it is quite invasive. Southeastern Europe, Asia Minor, southern Russia.

TELLIMA, Saxifragaceae. (1)

grandiflora	WHITE	LSP/ESU	1′–1.5′/1′–1.5′
	◑●	Z9-4	DS **

False Alum Root, Fringe Cups. [*T. odorata*]. Dense hummocks of dark green, hairy foliage, similar to that of *Heuchera,* grow from thick horizontal rhizomes. The long-petioled 2″–4″ leaves are rounded, cordate to reniform, and shallowly 5 to 7 lobed; evergreen in mild climates. Above the foliage, erect, wiry stems support long racemes of small, greenish white bells, which age to pink. Each ¼″ flower has 5 reflexed, lightly fringed petals. Moist, humusy soil. A good ground cover plant, but also useful in the shaded border or rock garden, where it acts as a foil for more gaudy neighbors. *T. g.* 'Purpurea' has red-flushed leaves, which turn almost maroon in winter, and pinkish flowers. Alaska to California.

Tellima grandiflora

These discreet plants clearly show their affinity to the Sages. Variably hairy, they have mostly erect square stems and small opposite leaves, toothed in all the following species. The whorls of 2 to several flowers are borne in heads or racemose spikes; the corolla is asymmetrical, 5 lobed, with a large lower lip and a small, deeply cleft upper lip. All, save *T. canadense,* favor well-drained soils.

canadense	PINK	SU/LSU	$2'-3'/1'$
	○ ◑	ZI0-3/T	CDS ***

American Germander, Wood Sage. Erect, usually unbranched, hairy stems. The ovate-lanceolate, Sage-like 3″ leaves are pubescent beneath. Whorls of 6 purplish pink ¾″ flowers in a long, racemose spike. Adapted to moist or wet soils. Eastern and central North America.

chamaedrys	PURPLE	SU/LSU	$1'-2'/1'-2'$
	○	ZI0-5	CDS ****

Many decumbent to ascending, somewhat woody stems, crowded with dark green, leathery, oblong ¾″ leaves. The whorls of 6–10 purplish or sometimes white ¾″ flowers are in loose, racemose clusters. Shear to force side branching; can be clipped as a low hedge. Europe, southwestern Asia. Similar *T. lucidum* is more erect, with larger, ovate-oblong leaves and flowers in whorls of only 2–4. Europe.

Teucrium scorodonia

| *hircanicum* | PURPLE | LSU | 2.5'/2'–3' |
| | ○ | Z10-7 | CDS ** |

Erect and bushy, with gray green Sage-like ovate leaves to 1″ or longer. Slender, dense, racemose spikes of pale purple ¾″ flowers. Probably hardier than indicated. Caucasus, Iran.

| *scorodonia* | YELLOW | SU/LSU | 1'–1.5'/1' |
| | ○ ◑ | Z10-5 | CDS ** |

Wood Germander, Wood Sage. This erect little subshrub has wrinkled, Sage-like, ovate to heart-shaped 1″–2½″ leaves. Pairs of tiny yellow green flowers are borne in loose, spiky, branched inflorescences. Dislikes limy soils. The plain species is rarely grown, but the listed cultivars are quite pleasing. Europe.

———— 'Crispum' has crisped leaves.

———— 'Crispum Marginatum' has crisped leaves with a white edge.

Thalictrum rochebrunianum

With their elegant stately habit, ferny foliage, and delicate flowers, the Meadow Rues boast some of the most graceful of all border plants. The predominantly basal foliage is usually 2 to 3 times ternately or pinnately compound, the leaflets most often toothed or lobed. Panicles or racemes of small flowers are held well above the mass of foliage; each apetalous flower has 4–5 sepals and numerous stamens. The most decorative species follow one of two patterns: either they have large, persistent, petaloid sepals, with clusters of short, pendent stamens, or they have small, early-deciduous sepals and large, colorful stamens in conspicuous, fluffy tufts. Afford some shade and mulch well in hot climates. Ordinary soil is adequate if loosened with moisture-retentive organic matter. Overfertilizing promotes weak growth. The taller species often need staking. Related *Trautvetteria carolinensis* has stout 2′–3′ stems, branching above. Its rounded leaves, to 16″ wide, are palmately divided into 5–11 toothed lobes, stem leaves smaller. Corymbs of white, apetalous ½″ flowers with 3–5 early-deciduous sepals and a tuft of stamens. North America, Japan.

aquilegifolium	PURPLE	LSP/ESU	2′–3′/1′
	○ ◑	Z10-5/H	DS ****

The tight clump of hollow stems may exceed 3′ in height. Glaucous leaves, 2 to 3 times pinnate; orbicular to oblong leaflets, to 1½″ wide, tipped with 3–6 broad, rounded teeth or lobes. As the specific epithet suggests, the leaflets are reminiscent of those of Columbine. Crowded corymbose panicles of light purple, sometimes dark purple, pink, or white flowers. Small, early-deciduous, green or white sepals; erect, club-shaped stamens in fluffy tufts. Europe, northern Asia.

delavayi	PURPLE	SU/LSU	4′–5′/1.5′–2′
	○ ◑	Z10-5/H	DS ***

[*T. dipterocarpum* Hort.]. Only this species is long-lived in warm climates. Slender stems, with 2 to 3 times ternately or pinnately compound leaves; leaflets usually 3 lobed. Large, loose, wiry-branched panicles of nodding ½″–1″ flowers, with persistent, pale purple sepals and pendent pale yellow stamens. All of the large purple-flowered species combine dramatically with tall orange lilies. Western China.

———— 'Album' is white flowered.

———— 'Hewitt's Double' has long-lasting, double flowers. *T. delavayi* is often listed as *T. dipterocarpum,* which is a similar but less hardy species. It has ternately compound leaves, mauve ½″ flowers, and distinctly 2-winged fruits. Himalayan *T. chelidonii* is also similar to *T. delavayi,* but has much-toothed leaflets. Rather temperamental, it thrives only in areas with cool summers.

flavum	YELLOW	SU	3′–5′/1.5′–2′
	○ ◑	Z10-5/H	DS ***

Sturdy, furrowed stems. The leaves are 2 to 3 times pinnate; the obovate to elliptic leaflets, less than 1″ wide, are entire or 3 lobed, dark green above and paler below. Erect panicles of clustered, fuzzy flowers. The small yellow sepals are early-deciduous; the stamens, bright yellow in large tufts. Europe, Asia.

———— *glaucum* [*T. f. speciosum, T. glaucum, T. speciosissimum*] is more robust, with glaucous, blue green foliage and larger inflorescences.

minus	FOLIAGE	SU	1′–3′/1′
	○ ◑	ZI0-3/H	DS ****

[*T. adiantifolium* Hort.]. Branching stems, extremely variable in height. The leaves, triangular in outline, are 3 to 4 times pinnate; the leaflets, usually glaucous and 3 lobed, to 1″ wide. Loose panicles of insignificant, greenish flowers with small, early-deciduous sepals. Invasive. Europe, northern Asia.

rochebrunianum	PURPLE	SU/EF	4′–6′/1.5′–2′
	○ ◑	ZI0-5/H	DS ***

This clump-former resembles *T. delavayi* and *T. dipterocarpum*. Glaucous, blue green foliage with rounded, entire, or 3-lobed leaflets. Large, airy, wiry-branched panicles of light purple flowers, with persistent sepals and pale yellow stamens. Japan.

THERMOPSIS, Leguminosae. (20)			False Lupine

The False Lupines are cheerful, low-maintenance plants for the border, meadow, or wild garden. They bloom only over a short season, but their foliage remains attractive. The alternate leaves are trifoliate, often with paired, leafy stipules. Bright yellow, Pea-like flowers in terminal racemes. Their fruiting pods are narrow and flattened, unlike those of closely related *Baptisia*. Free of pests and diseases. Drought resistant. Sow fresh seed in the fall in pots or in place; difficult to transplant.

montana	YELLOW	LSP-ESU	1.5′–2.5′/2′
	○ ◑	ZI0-3/T	S ***

Mountain Thermopsis, Golden Banner. This mountain species has a running rootstock and may become invasive. Obovate to linear-lanceolate 2″–4″ leaflets. The stout, branched stems are topped with loose 6″–8″ racemes of ½″ flowers. Rocky Mountains to Washington. Similar *T. lupinoides* [*T. lanceolata*] is clump forming and blooms a little later. Alaska, Siberia. Southeastern *T. mollis* has slightly smaller flowers and is covered with soft hairs.

villosa	YELLOW	SU	3′–5′/2′
	○	ZI0-3/T	S ***

Carolina Lupine. [*T. caroliniana* Hort.]. A similar species, but with rigidly erect, unbranched stems, well clothed in gray green leaves. Its ovate 2″–3″ leaflets are silky with hairs beneath; conspicuous leafy stipules. Canary yellow ½″ flowers crowd into slender 10″ racemes, which are in bloom for only 1–2 weeks. Southeastern United States.

Thermopsis montana

Thymus x *citriodorus* 'Silver Posie'

Tiarella trifoliata

THYMUS, Labiatae. (300-400) — Thyme

Several of these aromatic, sun-loving herbs are valued as prostrate or mat-forming ground covers or are suitable for low edgings. Essentially evergreen, the leaves are opposite and entire, about ¼" long. Whorls of tiny, asymmetrical flowers in axillary or terminal clusters; the corollas are 2 lipped, the upper lip notched, the lower cleft into 3 lobes. Thymes prefer light, free-draining soils of moderate fertility. Shear to keep shapely and prune out winter damage. *T. herba-barona, T. pseudolanuginosus,* and *T. serpyllum* are common ornamentals, too low for inclusion here.

x *citriodorus*	PINK	SU	8"–1'/1'
	○	Z10-4	C ****

Lemon Thyme. *T. pulegioides* x *T. vulgaris.* Bushy, with upright, branched stems, subshrubby below. The short-petioled, narrowly ovate ½" leaves are strongly lemon scented. The rosy flowers are in oblong clusters. Needs winter protection in cold climates.
———— 'Gold Edge.' Green leaves bordered with gold. 6"–8" tall.
———— 'Silver Posie' has silver-edged leaves. 6"–8" in height.
———— 'Silver Queen.' Grayish green leaves bordered with white. 8"–12".

vulgaris	PINK	SU	6"–1'/1'
	○	Z10-5	CS ****

Highly variable Common Thyme makes bushy plants, which are subshrubby at the base. The fragrant, gray green ¼" leaves are oval and slightly woolly. Its pale lilac flowers are arranged in dense, terminal clusters. Valuable as an edging or low hedge, particularly in herb gardens. Attractive to bees. Named variegated cultivars belong under *T.* x *citriodorus.* Mediterranean.

TIARELLA, Saxifragaceae. (6) — False Miterwort

These charming woodlanders form mounds of neat, basal foliage, evergreen in mild climates, often coloring attractively in winter. The long-stalked leaves are palmately lobed or divided. Wiry stems with only a few small leaves carry delicate racemes or panicles of starry, mostly white, ¼" flowers well above the foliage. The flowers have 5 petals and long, exserted stamens. They need moist, humusy soil and thrive in cool, shaded positions. All are undemanding, easily grown plants. (See X *Heucherella.*)

cordifolia	WHITE	LSP/ESU	1'/1.5'–2'
	◑	Z9-3	DS ****

Foamflower, Allegheny Foamflower. Clusters of broadly ovate to heart-shaped leaves, to 4" wide, rise from spreading stolons. The downy leaves are 3–5 lobed and round toothed. Airy racemes of white, sometimes pink, or red flowers, with oblong petals. Eastern North America. There are cultivars with foliage marbled in bronze or purple.

Rare East Asian *T. polyphylla* has 3-lobed leaves, to 2½" across. Its racemes reach 1.5'–2' in height; its petals are filiform and inconspicuous, or absent. Probably hardy to Z5.

laciniata	WHITE	SU	1'/1'–1.5'
	◗	Z9-4	DS ✳✳✳

Has leaves palmately divided into 3 leaflets, each very deeply lobed and toothed. Loose panicles of white flowers with filiform petals. Northwestern North America. The leaflets of related *T. trifoliata* are less deeply lobed. The Sugar-Scoop, *T. unifoliata,* resembles *T. cordifolia,* but bears its inconspicuous flowers in panicles rather than racemes. None of these western species is likely to take kindly to hot, humid, eastern summers.

wherryi	WHITE	SU	1'/1'–1.5'
	◗	Z9-3	DS ✳✳✳✳

[*T. cordifolia* var. *collina*]. Much resembles *T. cordifolia,* but is more compact and lacks stolons. Its leaves, to 3½" wide, are more sharply lobed and toothed; the foliage turns red in cold weather. Slender racemes of white or pink flowers with narrow petals. Southeastern United States.

Tovara virginiana filiformis 'Painter's Palette'

TOVARA, Polygonaceae. (1)

virginiana	FOLIAGE	SU-EF	$2'-3'/2'$
	○ ◑	Z9-7	CD **

[*Polygonum virginianum*]. The species is rarely grown, but the cultivars are prized for their attractive foliage. This rhizomatous plant makes sizable stands of upright, leafy stems with swollen nodes. It has alternate, elliptic to oblong 4″–8″ leaves. Plant the cultivars in moisture-retentive soil in a sheltered position where their delicate leaves are protected from wind and sunburn. Botanists include this species under *Polygonum,* but horticulturists retain the name *Tovara.* Eastern and central United States, eastern Canada, Japan.

———— filiformis [*P. filiforme*] 'Painter's Palette' has leaves strongly marked with a chocolate chevron; the young foliage is splashed with cream yellow and a touch of pink overlays the chevron.

———— 'Variegata.' A variegated form. Leaves splashed and marbled with cream. Largely replaced in gardens by the preceding. Interesting in combination with Zebra Grass, *Miscanthus sinensis* 'Zebrinus'.

TRACHELIUM, Campanulaceae. (10)

caeruleum	BLUE	SU	$2'-3'/1'-1.5'$
	○ ●	Z10-8	CS ***

Throatwort has slender, erect stems, clothed below with alternate, ovate 3″ leaves, sharply pointed and double toothed. Its dense, branching, flat-topped clusters are crowded with numerous blue or lavender blue flowers; the corolla, only ¼″ across, is tubular, with 5 minute spreading lobes. Likes well-drained but evenly moist soil and a bit of lime. Often treated as an annual or biennial. The dingy white-flowered form is not worth growing. The other species in cultivation are rock garden plants. Southern Europe.

TRACHYSTEMON, Boraginaceae. (2)

orientale	BLUE	SP	$1'-2'/2'$
	◑ ●	Z9-7	DS **

[*Nordmannia cordifolia*]. Rapidly makes large, handsome patches of coarsely hairy, dark green foliage, which reaches its mature size only after flowering time. The bold, chiefly basal and long-petioled leaves are heart shaped, with wavy margins, to 1′ long; smaller, oval stem leaves. Scorpioid cymes of white-throated, bluish purple ½″ flowers on branched, hairy pink stems; tubular corollas, with 5 reflexed lobes. The black-tipped stamens are joined into a conspicuous, pointed beak. Tolerant of most soils. It makes a thick ground cover and is particularly useful for rough, shaded, transition areas,

Trachelium caeruleum

where its invasiveness is an asset. Plant with delicate ferns for contrast. Eastern Mediterranean, Caucasus Mountains.

TRADESCANTIA, Commelinaceae. (60)			**Spiderwort**

albiflora	WHITE	SP-F	6″–1′/1′–2′
	◐ ●	Z10-9/T	CD ✶✶✶✶

Wandering Jew. [*T. tricolor* Hort., *T. viridis* Hort.]. This useful ground cover or pot plant has decumbent to erect stems, rooting at the nodes. The alternate, oblong 2″–3″ leaves, green on both sides, have ciliate margins, and sheath the fleshy stems. White, 3-petaled, ¼″ flowers cluster in the axils of leaflike bracts. Well-drained but moisture-retentive soils. Cut back hard if plants become rangy. Very easy to propagate from cuttings. South America.

————— 'Albovittata,' Giant White Inch Plant, has leaves striped with white.

————— 'Aurea' has greenish yellow leaves.

————— 'Laekenensis' ['Rainbow,' *T. laekenensis* Hort.] has pale green leaves striped in white and light purple.

————— 'Variegata' [*T. striata* Hort.] has leaves striped with yellow and white.

Two other species are commonly cultivated under similar conditions: Argentine *T. blossfeldiana*, Flowering Inch Plant, has trailing to ascending, hairy, purple stems. Its elliptic leaves, to 4″ long, are densely hairy, purple on their undersides. The woolly

Tradescantia x *andersoniana*

clusters of ½" flowers emerge between pairs of unequal, leaflike bracts; the white petals are tipped with pink. *T. b.* 'Variegata' has leaves with pale green, cream, and yellow stripes. Of similar habit, South American *T. fluminensis* is also known as Wandering Jew. It has ovate leaves to 1½" long, purple beneath, and clusters of white ¼" flowers, subtended by a pair of unequal, leafy bracts. Its variegated form has leaves striped with cream and yellow.

| x *andersoniana* | VARIOUS | LSP-F | 1.5′–3′/2′ |
| | ○ | Z10-5 | D **** |

[*T. virginiana* Hort.]. *T. ohiensis* x *T. subaspera* x *T. virginiana*. Most of the hardy Spiderworts seen in gardens belong under this heading. The parents of these hybrids and other native species are best relegated to wildflower gardens. Dense clumps of erect, rather fleshy stems, with clasping, linear to lanceolate, parallel-veined leaves to 1′ long or more. Pretty 1"–1½" flowers with 3 broadly ovate petals are borne in mostly terminal umbels in the axils of leaflike bracts. The filaments of the stamens are conspicuously hairy. Long blooming. By midseason, the foliage tends to sprawl untidily. Starve to control excessive vegetative growth; rather poor soil, minimal watering and feeding. If cut back hard, they will make new growth and reflower with the advent of cooler, end-of-season weather. In hot, dry climates, they need more water and even light shading. Spiderworts should not be planted in a foreground where the unattractive foliage is readily visible. Their shortcomings have not detracted from their popularity; there are innumerable cultivars in a great range of flower colors.
———— 'Blue Stone.' Lavender blue.

———— 'Innocence.' White.

———— 'Iris Pritchard.' White tinged with violet.

———— 'Isis.' Deep blue.

———— 'James Stratton.' Deep blue.

———— 'Leonora.' Violet blue.

———— 'Osprey.' White with a blue center.

———— 'Pauline.' Mauve pink.

———— 'Purewell Giant.' Red purple.

———— 'Purple Dome.' Purple.

———— 'Red Cloud.' Deep magenta pink.

———— 'Snowcap.' White.

———— 'J. C. Weguelin.' China blue.

———— 'Zwanenburg Blue.' Royal blue.

TRICHOSTEMA, Labiatae. (16)

lanatum	BLUE	SP/ESU	2′–5′/3′
	○	ZI0-9/H	S ****

Woolly Blue-Curls, Romero. This bushy evergreen, with many branching stems, becomes woody at the base with age. Its opposite leaves are narrow and shiny, woolly beneath. The long, spiky inflorescences, composed of numerous verticillasters, are

Trichostema lanatum

densely covered in blue, white, or pink hairs. The woolly, blue ½″ corollas are tubular, with 5 nearly equal lobes, the lowest slightly enlarged; very long, arching, exserted stamens. Thrives in full sun in freely draining soils. Withhold water during the summer. Cut back to encourage compact new growth. Long flowering; will rebloom if dead-headed. Delightfully mint scented. Southern and central California.

TRICYRTIS, Liliaceae. (10) — Toad-Lily

Presently enjoying a boom in popularity, these natives of shaded eastern Asian and Himalayan woodlands are welcome additions to our fall gardens. Their long, arching or erect stems bear numerous alternate, ovate, sometimes clasping leaves. Solitary or clustered, both axillary and terminal, the peculiar white or yellow flowers are spotted inside with purple. Each campanulate or saucer-shaped flower has 6 free perianth parts, the outer 3 with bulbous, basal pouches. The 6 stamens and 3 Y-shaped styles are joined into a central column or crown. Site the plants close to a path or where the flowers can be admired at close quarters. In time, Toad-Lilies form large colonies. Best in light shade in slightly acid, deep, humusy soil. Their rhizomatous roots should never dry out; mulch well and water during hot weather. Where the season is short, plant in a sunnier spot to insure blooming. They resent disturbance; divide only when necessary. Slugs may be a problem.

| *flava* | YELLOW | F | 1′–1.5′/1.5′ |
| | ◐● | Z9-7 | DS *** |

Yellow Toad-Lily. The slightly hairy, broadly elliptic 5″–6″ leaves are deep green, lightly spotted with purple. Terminal and axillary, upward-facing lemon yellow 2″ flowers, heavily purple spotted within. Japan.

| *formosana* | MAUVE | F | 2′–3′/1.5′ |
| | ◐● | Z9-5 | DS *** |

Its freely branching stems are clothed along their length in clasping, glossy, dark green leaves. Branched, axillary clusters of erect flowers; mauve in overall effect, each is yellow throated, heavily spotted with purple, on a white ground. *T. f. stolonifera* [*T. stolonifera*] is generally offered. It is a taller plant which spreads more rapidly. Taiwan.

| *hirta* | WHITE | EF-LF | 1′–3′/1.5′ |
| | ◐● | Z9-5 | DS *** |

Hairy Toad-Lily, the most commonly grown of the Toad-Lilies, is fuzzy with soft hairs. Erect, unbranched stems bear clasping, broadly oblong 5″–6″ leaves. Several upright 1″ flowers, variously spotted and speckled with dark purple, cluster in the upper leaf axils; each bloom lasts as long as 3 weeks. Self-sows readily, especially in moist, rich soil. Japan.

———— 'Alba' is a choice, white-flowered form.

———— 'Variegata' has leaves edged with gold.

latifolia	YELLOW	LSU-EF	2′/1′
	◑ ●	Z9-6	DS **

[*T. bakeri* Hort.]. More or less glabrous, with clasping, sharply pointed, heart-shaped leaves to 6″ long. The yellow 1″ flowers, densely dotted with purple inside, are carried on branched pedicels in terminal and axillary cymes. Japan, China. *T. macropoda* is similar, but has flowers of a creamier yellow.

macranthopsis	YELLOW	LSU	2.5′/1.5′
	●	Z9-6	DS *

The arching stems are clasped by ribbed, lanceolate 3″–3½″ leaves. Solitary, bell-shaped flowers hang from the upper leaf axils. The bright yellow, waxy perianth parts, reflexed at the tips, are brightly speckled inside with red. Japan. *T. macrantha* is similar.

TRIFOLIUM, Leguminosae. (300)

The Clovers or Shamrocks are better known as agricultural crops or tokens of good luck than as ornamentals. *T. repens* 'Atropurpureum' has leaves of 4 chocolate-colored, rounded leaflets, each rimmed with bright green. It is an unusual low foliage plant for the rock garden.

pannonicum	YELLOW	SU	2′–3′/3′
	○	Z9-6	DS **

Hungarian Clover forms upright, bushy clumps of leafy, branched stems, with stipulate, ternately compound leaves. Below, the leaflets are small and rounded; above, they reach 2″ or more across, oblong to lanceolate, slightly reflexed and softly hairy. The elongated, pale yellow florets crowd into conical 2″ heads, large for a Clover. A variable species from eastern Europe.

TRILLIUM, Liliaceae. (30)   Wake-Robin

Among the showiest of woodland plants, the Trilliums are familiar to lovers of wild-flowers and to anyone frequenting wooded areas in springtime. These unusual plants are aptly named, as their leaves, sepals, and petals all come in 3s. From a thick rhizome, a single or several straight stems rise to a whorl of 3 ovate to rhombic or rounded leaves, net-veined and often somewhat wrinkled. The flower, stalkless or short stalked, consists of 3 narrow sepals and 3 usually much broader erect or spreading petals. In this genus, aberrant plants are common, occurring with parts in greater number than the usual 3, or abnormally streaked or colored. All need a moist, humus-rich soil in a cool, semi-shaded location. These are not difficult plants, although the western species do not adapt readily to eastern gardens. Propagation from seed is a lengthy process, as germi-

Tricyrtis latifolia

Trifolium pannonicum

nation is slow and plants take several years to reach flowering size. The rhizomes are usually divided, or are induced to produce offsets by judicious wounding. Trilliums are not at their best in a border. They naturalize elegantly among shrubs or under the light shade of deep-rooted trees; they will not compete successfully with surface roots. All the species described are North American; those from eastern Asia have little ornamental value.

| *cernuum* | WHITE | SP/LSP | 1′–1.5′/1′ |
| | ◑ | Z9-3 | DS ✳✳✳ |

Nodding Trillium has rhombic-ovate leaves to 4″ long. Small, nodding, white to pinkish flowers on short stalks. Eastern North America.

| *chloropetalum* | GREEN | ESP/SP | 1′–1.5′/1′ |
| | ◑ | Z9-6 | DS ✳✳✳ |

[*T. sessile* var. *californicum*]. Sessile, rhombic-ovate leaves to 6″ long, often mottled with dark blotches. The stalkless 5″–6″ flowers are green, yellow green, sometimes whitish, or touched with purple, with erect petals. Central California to Washington.
———— var. *giganteum* has reddish flowers.

| *erectum* | PURPLE | ESP/SP | 1′–2′/1′ |
| | ◑ | Z9-3 | DS ✳✳✳ |

Brown Beth, Purple Trillium, Squawroot, Stinking Benjamin. [*T. flavum*]. Sessile, broadly rhombic leaves to 7″ long. The stalked, purple brown 2″–3″ flowers vary

Trillium grandiflorum pumilum

sometimes to yellow or green; the petals are spreading. Ill scented. Central and eastern North America.

——————— forma *albiflorum* [*T. e.* 'Album,' *T. e.* var. *album*] has white flowers.

T. vaseyi reaches 2' or more in height. Purplish brown 4"–6" flowers with recurved petals. South Carolina to Tennessee.

grandiflorum	WHITE	SP	1'–1.5'/1'
	◑	Z9-3	DS ****

Snow Trillium, White Wake-Robin. The showiest and most easily grown species. Ovate, rhombic or rounded leaves to 5" long. The stalked, white 3" flowers fade to pink and nod with age; the petals are spreading. Central and eastern North America. *T. g. pumilum* is a dwarf form; *T. g.* 'Flore Pleno' is double flowered.

ovatum	WHITE	LW/ESP	1'–1.5'/1'
	◑	Z9-5	DS ***

Coast Trillium. [*T. californicum*]. Rhombic-ovate leaves to 6" long, nearly sessile. The stalked 2" flowers, white aging to pink, have narrow petals. Essentially a western version of *T. grandiflorum*. Northwestern North America.

recurvatum	PURPLE	ESP/SP	1'–1.5'/1'
	◑	Z9-3	DS ***

Bloody-Butcher, Purple Trillium, Purple Wake-Robin. The elliptic to ovate leaves, to 4" long, are spotted with purple. The brownish purple 1¾" flowers have erect, clawed petals. Central and eastern United States.

undulatum	WHITE	LSP	1'–1.5'/1'
	◑	Z9-3	DS ***

Painted Trillium. This temperamental plant has ovate leaves reaching 7" in length. Erect to nodding white 1½" flowers, purple veined at the base, with spreading to recurved petals. Scarlet fruits follow. Central and eastern North America.

viride	GREEN	ESP/SP	1'–1.5'/1'
	◑	Z9-5	DS ***

Wood Trillium. The sessile, often mottled 2½"–4" leaves vary from lanceolate to rounded. Stalkless, greenish 2" flowers with erect petals. Central United States.

——————— var. *luteum* [*T. luteum, T. sessile* var. *luteum*] has yellow flowers. Southeastern United States.

TROLLIUS, Ranunculaceae. (20)	Globeflower

Globeflowers are splendid, low-maintenance subjects for watersides or bog gardens, but also make fine border plants, given moisture-retentive soil. Their clumps of dark green, deeply palmately cleft and toothed leaves remain handsome throughout the season. The

Trollius ledebourii Hort.

Buttercup-like flowers on erect stems are long blooming if deadheaded regularly, and are also good for cutting. Slow to increase and best planted in groups of 3–5. Shade from intense sun. Both planting and division in the fall are recommended. Free of pests and diseases.

| **x *cultorum*** | YELLOW | LSP-SU | 2′–3′/1′ |
| | ○ ◑ | ZIO-3/H | D **** |

[*T.* x *hybridus*]. *T. asiaticus* x *T. chinensis* x *T. europeus.* Many of the best-known cultivars fall into this group. Most have the larger flowers and good foliage of *T. europeus.*

————— 'Etna.' Strong orange blooms on 2′–5′ stems. Early.
————— 'Goldquelle.' Yellowish orange flowers. 2′ tall.
————— 'Lemon Queen.' Lemon yellow. 1.5′–2′.
————— 'Orange Princess.' Deep orange flowers. 2.5′ in height.

| *europeus* | YELLOW | SP-ESU | 1′–2.5′/1′ |
| | ○ ◑ | ZIO-3/H | DS **** |

Common Globeflower. Clump forming, with dark green foliage, paler beneath. Pentagonal in outline, the long-petioled 4″–6″ basal leaves have 3–5 ovate or wedge-shaped lobes, each irregularly and sometimes deeply toothed; the few sessile stem leaves are smaller and 3 lobed. Usually solitary, globe-shaped 1″–2″ flowers with delicate pale yellow, incurving petaloid sepals. Europe. The cultivars have superior substance.

————— 'Superbus.' True butter yellow flowers.
————— 'Verdus' has light lemon yellow flowers, greenish in the bud.

| *ledebourii* **Hort.** | ORANGE | SU | 3'/1.5' |
| | ○ ◑ | ZI0-3/H | DS *** |

Ledebour Globeflower. Its leaves are cleft to the base and further cut and toothed. The showy, bright orange flowers, 2″ or more across, consist of an outer ring of cupped, petaloid sepals around 12–15 narrow, vertical petals. Siberia. The true species *T. ledebourii,* is not in cultivation.

——————— 'Golden Queen.' Bright orange yellow 3″–4″ flowers on stems to 4' tall. Probably a hybrid and sometimes listed under *T.* x *cultorum.*

TULBAGHIA, Amaryllidaceae. (24)

These long-flowering, South African relatives of *Agapanthus* have narrow, gray green basal leaves forming broad clumps, evergreen in mild areas. The small, starry violet flowers are borne in umbels on long scapes. The perianth consists of a short tube with 6 flaring lobes surrounding a small corona. Of easy culture; rarely need dividing. Fertile, porous but moist soils. Water well during the growing season, less when plants are dormant. They recover well from frost damage.

| *fragrans* | LILAC | W | 1.5'/1'–1.5' |
| | ○ ◑ | ZI0-9 | DS *** |

Its fleshy leaves often exceed 1' in length by ¾″ wide. The long scape ends in a 3″ umbel of 20–30 deep lilac ½″ flowers, with a cup-shaped corona. An excellent, sweet-scented cut flower. South Africa.

| *violacea* | LILAC | SP-SU | 1'–2'/1'–1.5' |
| | ○ ◑ | ZI0-9 | DS **** |

Society Garlic. [*T. cepacea*]. Very slender leaves to 1' long. The slight 1'–2' scape is topped by a loose 2½″ umbel of 8–20 dark lilac ¾″ flowers; the corona is composed of scales. The whole plant smells strongly of garlic or onion when cut or bruised. South Africa.

——————— 'Silver Lace' has white-margined leaves. Less vigorous than the species.

UVULARIA, Liliaceae. (5)

| *grandiflora* | YELLOW | ESP/SP | 1.5'–2.5'/1' |
| | ○ ◑ | Z9-3 | DS *** |

Bellwort, Merrybells. From its slender rhizomes, this graceful woodlander sends up clusters of wiry, erect, branching stems. Its alternate, oblong to lanceolate-ovate leaves, to 4½″ long, are perfoliate. Solitary and terminal, the nodding flowers appear before the plant attains its full summer height. Each pale yellow, narrowly bell-shaped flower is composed of 6 twisted, lanceolate tepals about 1½″ long. Prefers an open, moist,

Tulbaghia violacea

Uvularia grandiflora

humus-rich, sweet soil. In full sun mulch to conserve moisture and water well. Eastern and central North America. Similar *U. perfoliata* is slightly smaller throughout. Its flowers are covered inside with minute, glandular projections. Acid soil. *U. caroliniana* [*U. puberula, U. pudica, Oakesiella puberula*] and *U. sessilifolia* [*Oakesiella sessilifolia*] are smaller, infrequently cultivated natives. *Disporum,* Fairy-Bells, is a closely related and similar genus.

VALERIANA, Valerianaceae. (200)	Valerian

Valerian is often confused with related *Centranthus.* Opposite and decussate, its entire or divided leaves are sometimes aromatic. Numerous tiny 5-lobed tubular flowers crowd into terminal panicles or clusters. Easy to grow in sun or partial shade in average, well-drained soil. Staking is usually necessary.

alliariifolia	PINK	SU	1.5′–2.5′/2′
	○ ◐	Z10-5/H	DS *

This woodlander's strong stems are clothed below in heart-shaped leaves, toothed along their margins, to 8″ across; the smaller stem leaves are ovate. Dense, rounded panicles of pink flowers are followed by fluffy seed heads. Greece, Caucasus. The Pyrenean species *V. pyrenaica* differs in having divided upper leaves.

Valeriana officinalis

officinalis	PINK	SU	2'–5'/3'
	○ ◑	ZI0-5/H	DS ✳✳✳

Cat's Valerian, Common Valerian, Garden Heliotrope. This scented herb, a favorite of cats, can be an agreeable addition to the border. Its thick rootstocks give rise to substantial clumps of deeply lobed, basal foliage. The stems bear odd-pinnate leaves, with 7–10 pairs of toothed leaflets, ovate on the lower leaves, lanceolate above. Fragrant pinkish or sometimes lavender flowers in long-stalked, compact, rounded 2″–4″ panicles, which expand and relax with age. *V. o.* 'Alba' has white flowers; those of 'Coccinea' and 'Rubra' are red. Europe, Asia.

phu 'Aurea'	FOLIAGE	SU	2'–3'/2'
	○	ZI0-5/H	DS ✳✳

Grown for its clumps of striking, bright yellow spring foliage, which regrettably ages to quite an ordinary green by summer. Otherwise similar to a white-flowered *V. officinalis*. The basal leaves are long petioled and toothed but not cleft; the 5″–7″ stem leaves have 3–4 pairs of rounded oblong leaflets. Caucasus.

VANCOUVERIA, Berberidaceae. (3)

Native to woodlands of the Pacific coast, these plants can be used as delicate and ornamental ground covers in shaded places, particularly under shrubs. Clumps of ternate or biternate leaves rise at intervals along the length of the slender, creeping rhizomes. The pale green undulate leaflets may be gently lobed. Usually leafless, the erect, wiry stems hold delicate panicles just above the foliage. The long-stalked, drooping flowers, similar to those of related *Epimedium,* have their parts in multiples of 3. The outer sepals, 6 or 9 in number, drop early, revealing 6 inner petaloid sepals and 6 true petals, all strongly reflexed, exposing the stamens and a beaklike style. Moist, acid soil, well enriched and mulched with leaf mold or humus. Divide in spring or fall.

hexandra	WHITE	LSP	6″–1.5′/1′
	◑ ●	Z9-5/H	D ***

Vancouver Fern. [*Epimedium hexandrum*]. Aggressively creeping roots rapidly produce large patches of dainty, foot-high foliage, reminiscent of that of Maidenhair Fern. The 3-lobed, broadly ovate ¾″–2″ leaflets are a fresh green, often glaucous beneath. Above dance loose panicles of as many as 30 white ½″ flowers. This tough, deciduous ground cover even tolerates dry shade. Washington to California.

planipetala	WHITE	LSP	6″–1′/1′
	◑ ●	Z9-6/H	D **

Inside-Out Flower, Redwood Ivy. [*V. parviflora*]. Less hardy and much slower to colonize than the preceding species. The leathery foliage is mostly evergreen, except in exposed sites. Usually the leaves are several times ternately divided; the glossy, dark green or sometimes grayish 1″–2″ leaflets have thickened, wavy margins. Many-flowered panicles of violet-tinged white ½″ flowers. Oregon, California. From the same region another evergreen species, yellow-flowered *V. chrysantha,* has leaflets which are both thickened and crisped along the margins. It increases very slowly and must be planted closely when used as a ground cover.

X VENIDIO-ARCTOTIS, Compositae.

Hybrids	VARIOUS	SP-SU	1′–1.5′/1.5′–3′
	○	Z10-9/H	C ***

The results of crossing *Arctotis stoechadifolia* var. *grandis, A. breviscapa,* and the annual *A. fastuosa* [*Venidium fastuosum*], these excellent plants form mounds of extremely variable foliage. Their slender leaves range from deeply pinnatifid to barely sinuate, from rough-hairy to nearly glabrous. The solitary, Daisy-like 2½″–3″ flower heads come in cream, yellow, orange, rose, red, purple, and bronze, and in combinations of these colors. There are numerous selections, named and unnamed. These sterile plants can only be propagated from cuttings. Similar in culture to *Arctotis.*

X *Venidio-arctotis* 'Rosita'

VENIDIUM, Compositae. (20)

The Namaqualand Daisies differ from *Arctotis* only in minute botanical details. Annual *V. fastuosum,* the Cape Daisy, is now correctly *Arctotis fastuosa;* it is one of the parents of the superb X *Venidio-arctotis* hybrids. (For culture, see *Arctotis.*)

decurrens	YELLOW	SP	1′–1.5′/1.5′
	○	ZI0-9/H	CS **

[*V. calendulaceum*]. Softly hairy throughout; the loosely branching stems are clothed in alternate, lyrate 4″–6″ leaves, with enlarged terminal lobes and earlike basal lobes. The solitary 2½″ flower heads have golden yellow ray florets, darker disks, and an involucre of several rows of bracts. South Africa.

VERATRUM, Liliaceae. (45)   **False Hellebore**

Esteemed by English gardeners, the False Hellebores are rarely grown here, although several species are native to North America. These noble plants make bold clumps of parallel-veined, pleated foliage. The alternate, clasping leaves are elliptic to lanceolate, usually 1′ long by half as wide, smaller above. The imposing vertical woolly panicles, crowded with starry, 6-tepaled flowers, rise above the foliage on stiff, stout stems. Of easy culture, all thrive in moist to wet situations. The foliage eventually becomes shabby; protect from intense sun and wind, and site behind other plants to conceal the damage. Slow to reach flowering size from seed. Poisonous.

| *album* | WHITE | SU/LSU | 3'–4'/2' |
| | ○ ◑ | Z9-3/H | DS ✽✽ |

European White Hellebore. The entire plant is hairy, save the upper leaf surfaces. Very long panicles of white to green ¾" flowers, green on the outside. Europe, northern Asia.

| *californicum* | WHITE | SU | 4'–6'/2' |
| | ○ ◑ | Z10-4/H | DS ✽✽ |

Corn Lily, Skunk Cabbage. Similar to *V. viride*. Its leaves may attain 16" in length by 8" wide. The lower branches of the panicles are erect; white ¾" flowers. Western United States.

| *nigrum* | BROWN | SU | 3'–5'/2' |
| | ○ ◑ | Z9-3/H | DS ✽ |

Small, dark brown to purplish black ⅓" flowers, in narrow, woolly 1'–3' panicles. An astonishing plant. Europe, Asia.

| *viride* | GREEN | SU | 4'–7'/2' |
| | ○ ◑ | Z9-3/H | DS ✽✽ |

American White Hellebore, Indian Poke. The stems are leafy along their entire length. Hairy 1.5' panicles, with drooping lower branches; yellow green 1" flowers. North America (except southern states).

VERBASCUM, Scrophulariaceae. (360)   Mullein

The best known of the Mulleins are the stately biennial species, such as *V. bombyciferum* [*V. broussa* Hort., *V.* 'Broussa'], *V. olympicum*, *V. phlomoides*, and *V. thapsiforme*. All of these form large rosettes of bold, felted foliage, above which in their second year rise tall, woolly spikes of clear yellow flowers. So useful are they as accent plants or as contrasts to stronger-colored flowers that they must be mentioned along with their more subdued perennial relatives. In fact, not all are intruders here, as some are, at times, short-lived perennials. *V. vernale* Hort., which belongs in this group, is definitely perennial. All of these plants hybridize with abandon, as do all Verbascums. They are much confused in gardens and in the trade. The genus as a whole appears to need revision. The erect Verbascums have alternate, generally ovate leaves, either entire or toothed, only rarely lobed; they are large at the base and decrease in size up the stem. Most are moderately to very hairy or woolly. The flowers are in narrow spikes or racemes, sometimes compounded into panicles; the corolla is rotate, deeply 5 lobed. The stamens may be prominently bearded. A well-drained soil is essential; wetness is not tolerated.

Veratrum viride

Verbascum bombyciferum

| *chaixii* | YELLOW | LSP/SU | 3′/1.5′ |
| | ○ | Z10-5 | DRS *** |

Its vertical stems bear woolly, gray green leaves to 6″ or longer; the blades are crenate and conspicuously net-veined. Narrow spires of crowded, pale yellow 1″ flowers with purplish red, bearded stamens. Southern and central Europe.

———— var. *album* ['Album']. This superb, white-flowered form combines well with blue Campanulas.

| *dumulosum* | YELLOW | SU | 1′/1′ |
| | ○ | Z10-8/H | RS ** |

This compact, branched subshrub has densely felted foliage; its leaves, usually some-what round toothed, are elliptic to oblong-elliptic. The lemon yellow 1″ flowers, in short, branched spikes, have a red eye and purple-haired stamens. Turkey. *V.* 'Letitia' *(V. dumulosum* x *V. spinosum),* only 8″ tall, has a looser habit and smaller leaves, scalloped along the edge. Its primrose yellow flowers bloom throughout the summer.

| x *hybridum* | VARIOUS | LSP/ESU | 3′-4′/1.5′ |
| | ○ ◑ | Z10-6 | R ** |

This group of hybrids of *V. phoeniceum* and other species, known as Cotswold Hybrids, is extremely variable. 'Pink Domino,' with spires of deep rose pink flowers on 3.5′ stems, is the most readily available. Other selections, popular in England, deserve to be introduced here. All are short-lived.

————— 'Cotswold Gem' has terracotta-colored flowers.

————— 'Cotswold Queen' is golden yellow.

————— 'Gainsborough' has primrose yellow flowers and gray green foliage.

————— 'Mont Blanc' is white with grayish leaves.

| *nigrum* | YELLOW | SU | 2′–3.5′/1′–1.5′ |
| | ○ | Z10-5 | RS ** |

Dark Mullein has deep green leaves, slightly hairy above, conspicuously so beneath. Its clusters of yellow ¾″ flowers are displayed in a slender, sometimes branched raceme. The long stamens are prominently bearded, with red hairs. Europe, Asia.

| *phoeniceum* | VARIOUS | LSP/ESU | 2′–4′/1′–1.5′ |
| | ○ ◑ | Z10-6 | RS *** |

Purple Mullein forms a basal rosette of ovate to oblong leaves, usually toothed, glabrous above and hairy beneath; the few stem leaves are smaller. Narrow racemes of solitary 1″ flowers on slender pedicels. They range in color from white, pink, and red, to most commonly purple. A superb rose form is well worth seeking. Short-lived. Southeastern Europe, Asia.

Verbena rigida

[*Glandularia*]. This predominantly tropical or subtropical genus is best known for its gaudy hybrids, so frequently grown as bedding plants. Most Verbenas are rough-hairy, with 4-angled, erect or trailing stems. The leaves are commonly opposite and coarse toothed, often spaced widely on the stem. Spikes of small flowers, subtended by bracts, are terminal or sometimes grouped into panicles or flattened clusters. The salverform to funnel-shaped corolla is irregularly 5 lobed and appears to be 2 lipped. The low-growing sorts are excellent for bedding or as ground cover plants in warm zones; the taller species, attractive additions to the border. Several have become naturalized in the warmer states. Most tolerate drought and heat well, but resent wet conditions.

bonariensis	PURPLE	SU-EF	3′–6′/2′
	○	Z10-7/H	S ✱✱

[*V. patagonica*]. Strict, self-supporting, wiry stems, branching above, are bare except for a few pairs of widely spaced, clasping 4″ leaves. The tiny lilac purple flowers are fragrant, crowded into dense ½″ spikes, which are often clustered. Group for effect, since the individual plants are spare. Self-seeds freely. Effective when underplanted with silver-foliaged plants. South America.

canadensis	PINK	SU-F	6″–1.5′/2′
	○	Z10-5/H	DS ✱✱✱✱

Rose Verbena, Creeping Vervain. [*V. aubletia, Glandularia canadensis*]. Normally grown as an annual, this rough-hairy plant has decumbent stems and pinnatifid, ovate leaves with toothed lobes. Dark purplish pink ½″–¾″ flowers in large, showy clusters; cultivars in various shades of lilac, red, and white. It is effective tumbling over a wall or in a stone container. Pennsylvania to Florida, Colorado to Mexico. Hardier *V. bipinnatifida,* the Dakota Verbena, is usually shorter and has light purple flowers.

hastata	PURPLE	SU-F	4′–5′/2′
	○	Z10-3/H	DS ✱✱

Blue Vervain, Simpler's Joy. This native clump-former has stiffly erect stems and pairs of pointed, broadly lanceolate 6″–8″ leaves. The narrow, candelabralike inflorescences consist of slender, close spikes of small purplish or pink flowers and dark purple bracts, which give an attractive bicolored effect. Long blooming in fertile soil. North America.

x *hybrida*	VARIOUS	SU-F	6″–1.5′/2′
	○	Z10/H	CS ✱✱✱✱

Garden Verbena. [*V.* x *hortensis*]. The parentage of this hybrid is not reliably documented, but probably includes *V. peruviana* and *V. platensis*. It is popularly grown as an annual, but is a short-lived perennial in frost-free regions. The bristly, much-branched, trailing stems often root at the nodes and rapidly spread into wide patches. The grayish or bright green 2″–4″ leaves are oblong, bristly hairy and toothed. Salver-form ½″–1″ flowers, in brilliant reds, pinks, white, and purples, often white centered, crowd into compact, flattened clusters. The numerous strains and cultivars include 'Dwarf Jewels,' a short, early-flowering strain in mixed colors, 'Amethyst,' which has vivid, purplish blue, white-eyed flowers, and 'Trinidad,' a compact grower, with large, deep rosy pink flowers with a white eye. In early spring, prune ground cover plants hard to promote bushy growth. Powdery mildew may be a problem.

rigida	PURPLE	SU/F	1′–2′/1′
	○	Z10-8/H	DS **

Vervain. [*V. venosa*]. Spreading plants with mostly upright stems, widely branched above. Clasping, the rough-hairy, dark green 3″–4″ leaves are oblong, pointed at the tip and irregularly toothed. The showy cylindrical spikes of violet purple ¼″ flowers are often grouped in 3s. *V. r.* 'Alba' has white flowers; those of 'Lilacina' are lavender. Drought tolerant and carefree. Naturalized in the southeast. Southern Brazil, Argentina. Larger *V. corymbosa* has panicles of reddish purple flowers. The bases of its leaves are lobed. Spreads readily, particularly in moist soils. Chile.

VERNONIA, Compositae. (1,000)

While not in the first rank of ornamentals, the rich violet to purple flowers of Ironweeds are most welcome in informal late summer and autumn gardens. They make substantial clumps of erect stems, abundantly clothed in alternate leaves and topped by broad clusters of diskoid flower heads. Species of lesser ornamental value include *V. acaulis,* native to dry woodlands from North Carolina to Florida. It has flat, basal rosettes of foliage, and blooms on 1′–4′ stems in midsummer. Texan *V. lindheimeri* has attractive, white-hairy stems and leaves. Both are appropriate for meadow or native plant gardens.

noveboracensis	VIOLET	LSU-F	4′–6′/3′
	○	Z9-5	DS **

New York Ironweed. Somewhat coarse, with strong stems and sessile, rough-textured, lanceolate 6″–8″ leaves, serrate along their margins. Leafy, terminal clusters of deep purple ½″ flower heads. Easy in rich, moist soils. New England to Missouri, Ohio. *V. crinita* and *V. altissima* are similar; both reach 10′ in height.

VERONICA, Scrophulariaceae. (300)   Speedwell

Many of the Speedwells are superb, long-blooming border plants, important components of late spring and summer gardens, assorting particularly well with other perennials. The prostrate species such as *V. prostrata* [*V. rupestris*], *V. repens,* and *V. pectinata* are suitable only for the rock garden or perhaps as ground covers. Extensive selection and breeding, not always accurately documented, has improved the taller sorts; their cultivars and hybrids are grouped below according to their probable origin. Generally

Vernonia altissima

Veronicas have opposite leaves, sometimes whorled or alternate above. Usually the small flowers are arranged in long, terminal or axillary spikes. The calyx is cleft into 4–5 lobes; the short-tubed corolla has 4–5 spreading lobes. The exserted stamens are conspicuous. Easy to grow, thriving in average, well-drained soil that does not dry out; overly rich soil causes weak, sprawling growth. Divide every 3–4 years.

gentianoides	BLUE	LSP	1'–2'/1.5'
	○ ◑	Z9-4/H	D ✱✱✱✱

Gentian Speedwell. Tufted basal rosettes of rather fleshy, glossy, dark green, oblong 2"–3" leaves, lightly toothed. The stems are topped with loose racemes of ice blue ½"–¾" flowers with darker veining. White-flowered and variegated forms are sometimes available. A lovely companion for *Viola cornuta.* Caucasus.

incana	BLUE	SU	1'–2'/1.5'
	○ ◑	Z10-3/H	DS ✱✱✱✱

Woolly Speedwell. Low clumps of silvery gray herbage; short-petioled, Sage-like 1"–3" leaves. The violet ¼" flowers are crowded into 8" spikes. Not as free flowering as some species, but its foliage remains attractive throughout the season. A parent, along with *V. longifolia,* of several fine hybrids. Northern Asia.
————— 'Barcarolle' has dusty gray foliage and rose pink flowers on 10" stems.
————— 'Minuet.' Pink flowers, grayish leaves. 15" tall. Both are Alan Bloom selections.

latifolia	BLUE	LSP/SU	1.5'–3'/1'
	○ ◑	Z10-3/H	D ✱✱✱✱

Hungarian Speedwell. [*V. teucrium, V. austriaca teucrium*]. A variable, hairy plant, with erect or sprawling stems and deeply toothed, ovate ½"–1" leaves. The bright blue ½" flowers cluster in loose, axillary and terminal 2"–4" racemes. Usually needs brush staking. Southern Europe.
————— 'Crater Lake Blue' is compact with gentian blue flowers. 1' tall. One of the best.
————— 'Royal Blue' has medium blue flowers on 1'–1.5' stems.

longifolia	BLUE	ESU-LSU	2'–4'/1'
	○ ◑	Z10-4/H	D ✱✱✱✱

[*V. maritima*]. Clumps of strong stems, with toothed, pointed-ovate 3" leaves in pairs or whorls of 3. Long, dense racemes of violet blue ¼" flowers. A parent, probably with *V. spicata,* of many superior plants. Northern Europe, Asia.
————— 'Alba' is white flowered.
————— 'Blue Giant' has pale blue spires throughout the summer on 4' stems.
————— 'Foerster's Blue.' Dark blue flowers. Long blooming. 1.5' tall.
————— 'Romiley Purple.' Deep purple. 1.5' in height.
————— *subsessilis.* Superior to the species, with larger flowers on 2.5'–3' stems. 'Sunny Border Blue' is long blooming, with spires of dark violet flowers on compact 1.5'–2' plants. Introduced by Robert Bennerup.

Veronica spicata 'Red Fox'

---

perfoliata	BLUE	LSU	2'/1.5'
	○	Z10-8/H	CS ✱✱

Digger's Speedwell. [*Parahebe perfoliata*]. An unusual subshrub, with long, arching stems, clothed in pairs of fleshy, glaucous blue, ovate 1"–2½" leaves. The blades sometimes join at their bases, surrounding the stems completely. Branching sprays of small, violet blue ½" flowers. Good for trailing over walls. Australia.

---

spicata	BLUE	SU	1'–1.5'/1'
	○ ◑	Z10-3/H	D ✱✱✱✱

Spike Speedwell is extremely variable. Compact and pubescent, with oblong 1"–2" leaves with crenate margins. The numerous dense, tapering racemes of ¼" flowers are mostly terminal. Europe, Asia.

———— 'Blue Charm' has lavender blue flowers. 2' tall.

———— 'Blue Peter' is a good medium blue. 1.5' in height.

———— 'Icicle.' The vertical racemes of clean white flowers contrast well with the dark foliage. Probably a hybrid with *V. incana* or *V. longifolia*. 1.5'–2' tall.

———— 'Red Fox.' Deep rosy pink flowers on 10" stems.

Veronicastrum virginicum 'Album'

VERONICASTRUM, Scrophulariaceae. (2)

Bowman's Root, native to northeastern woodlands and meadows, is an elegant plant for the late summer garden, particularly in combination with tall Anemones or Asters. Distinctive at the back of the border or in native plant or wild gardens; especially effective near water. Easy to grow.

virginicum	BLUE	LSU-F	4'–7'/1.5'
	○ ◑	ZI0-3/H	CDS ***

Bowman's Root, Culver's Root, Blackroot. [*Veronica virginica, Leptandra virginica*]. Strong, vertical stems branching above support numerous horizontal whorls of 3–5 short-petioled leaves, their 3"–5" blades lanceolate and sharply toothed. Each branch ends in a close-set 6"–9" raceme of tiny, very pale blue or white flowers. The salverform 4- to 5-lobed corolla has conspicuously exserted stamens. Seldom needs staking in spite of its height. Takes 3 years to show its best form. Eastern United States.

———— 'Album' has clean white flowers, set off by very dark green foliage. The most popular cultivar.

———— 'Roseum' has pale lavender pink flowers.

VICIA, Leguminosae. (150)   Vetch

Many of the Legumes are rather unruly; the Vetches are certainly no exception, and few are gardenworthy. They have scrambling, rarely erect, branching stems and even-pinnate leaves. The papilionaceous or Pea-like flowers are borne in racemes. Well-drained soils in full sun or very light shade.

canescens	BLUE	LSP/ESU	1'–1.5'/1.5'
	○	ZI0-8	S *

The erect to sprawling stems are densely woolly, as are the compound leaves; linear-elliptic leaflets in 8–12 pairs. Lavender to blue flowers in compact racemes. An attractive gray foliage plant to let sprawl over stones or the edge of a path. Lebanon.

tenuifolia	VIOLET	ESU/SU	3'–5'/2'–3'
	○ ◑	ZI0-3	DS **

And *V. t.* var. *stenophylla*. The somewhat scrambling habit of these freely branching plants is easily overcome with a few well-placed pea sticks. Slightly hairy compound leaves, ending in a tendril, usually with 9–10 pairs of linear to linear-oblong leaflets. Long, slender racemes of lavender to violet blue ¾" flowers, with paler or whitish wings. Europe.

unijuga	VIOLET	LSP/SU	2'–3'/1'–1.5'
	○	ZI0-3	S *

[*Ervum gracile, Orobus lathyroides*]. Wiry, erect stems. The leaves are compound, with

Vicia tenuifolia var. *stenophylla*

only one pair of ovate 1½″–3″ leaflets. Short, crowded racemes of lavender to violet or purple flowers. Northeastern Asia.

VIOLA, Violaceae. (500)	Violet

Violets, Pansies, and Violas are found throughout the temperate regions. Mostly small in stature, they form either tufts of long-petioled, basal foliage or have stems well clothed in alternate leaves. Most have essentially heart-shaped, round-toothed leaves, often subtended by leafy stipules. The solitary, nodding spring flowers are most often white, yellow, or violet, frequently traced with darker markings in the throat. The calyx consists of 5 sepals; the 5 petals of the corolla are arranged in 2 unequal pairs above a larger lower petal, which is usually spurred. Some have 2 types of flowers. The familiar, showy, spring-blooming kind is sterile, but the plants also produce inconspicuous, apetalous, fertile flowers later. These never open and are often buried in the soil, where they self-pollinate within the unopened bud and produce copious amounts of seed. Most Violas thrive under partial shade in fertile, well-drained soil. The species hybridize freely both in the wild and in gardens. Be alert for red spider mites, particularly during hot, dry weather; slugs and snails mar the leaves especially where it is cool and moist. The ever-popular Pansies, *V.* x *wittrockiana* [*V. tricolor hortensis*], and Violas, *V.* x *williamsii,* both of which have been hybridized extensively, are usually

Viola cornuta

grown as annuals or biennials. Less showy, lower-growing species such as *V. blanda,* Sweet White Violet, and yellow-flowered *V. rotundifolia,* Roundleaf Violet, are fine ground cover plants. *V. labradorica,* considered by some authorities to be correctly *V. adunca minor,* makes a choice 6″ ground cover. Its glabrous, very dark green leaves, flushed with purple, clothe elongating, prostrate to ascending stems; light purple ½″ flowers. *V. pedata* and *V. sulfurea,* as well as other low species, are charming in the rock garden. A host of natives is available for wild gardens. The plants described below are suitable for the front of the border or for edgings along paths and walkways.

---

canadensis	WHITE	SP-ESU	1′–1.5′/1′
	◑●	Z8-3	DS ***

The Canada Violet is a neat clump-former arising from short, thick rhizomes. Its purplish, rather hairy stems are well clothed in cordate 2″–4″ leaves. Borne in the leaf axils, the short-spurred, white ¾″ flowers are flushed with purplish brown on the outside and have yellow throats. Southern Canada, northern United States. *V. canadensis rugulosa* [*V. rugulosa*] is similar, though slightly larger. Its widely spreading, stoloniferous rhizomes may become invasive.

---

cornuta	VIOLET	SP-LSU	6″–1′/9″–1′
	○◑	Z10-6/H	CDS ****

Horned Violet, Tufted Violet, Tufted Pansy. More or less glabrous, neat, tufted plants with round-toothed, ovate leaves, subtended by large, leafy, dissected stipules. Each violet 1″ flower has a slender spur a little shorter than the petals. Tolerant of full sun only where summers are cool. Cut back after the first flush of bloom. Well-drained, humusy soil; mulch in summer. Blooms the first year from early seeding. Spain. Breeding has resulted in numerous cultivars, usually with shorter-spurred flowers, in a wide range of colors.

———— 'Arkwright Ruby.' Bright ruby maroon flowers with a darker blotch and small yellow eye. Fragrant.

———— 'Chantreyland' has very large apricot flowers.

———— 'Jersey Gem' has long-stemmed, large, deep purple flowers.

———— 'Scottish Yellow.' Lemon yellow flowers, sometimes shaded to orange at the center.

———— 'White Perfection' is pure white.

| *cucullata* | VIOLET | LSP-ESU | 10″–1′/1′ |
| ◑ | | Z8-4 | DS ∗∗∗ |

Marsh Blue Violet has scaly, branched rhizomes, which spread slowly and form large colonies. All basal, its long-petioled, dark green leaves are round toothed, triangular to reniform, to 3″ or more across. Above, dark lavender or pale violet ½″ flowers, deeper in color toward the throat, nod on very long pedicels. The short, lower petal is traced in purple; the laterals are bearded. Prefers damp soil. Eastern and central North America.

———— 'Freckles' has large very pale blue flowers variously speckled with purple.

| *odorata* | VIOLET | SP | 8″–1′/1′ |
| ◑ | | Z10-6/H | DS ∗∗∗ |

Sweet Violet, Garden Violet, Florists' Violet. The Violet of literature and romance. Its rosettes of dark green foliage arise from long stolons; the cordate to reniform 2″ leaves have crenate margins. Very fragrant, short-spurred, violet ½″–¾″ flowers top slender 8″ pedicels. Europe, Africa, Asia. Over the years, many hybrids have been bred, some with *V. alba* and other European species in their parentage. Their larger flowers have not always retained their fragrance, but all those listed below are sweetly scented. All thrive in organically rich soil which does not dry out. Fertilize in very early spring. Best in part shade, but will tolerate full sun where summers are cool. May be hardy in even colder zones.

———— 'Rosina.' Very free blooming, with deep, old rose flowers flushed darker and blotched with maroon at the throat.

———— 'Royal Robe' has vibrant purple flowers, with a tiny white eye, on 6″ stems.

———— 'White Czar.' White flowers, cream at the throat; the large lower petal is veined in deep purple.

The Parma violets are thought to have been derived from either *V. odorata* or *V. alba*. At one time, several cultivars were available, but today they are scarce. Their large double flowers, carried on long stems, are very fragrant. 'Lady Hume Campbell' has mauve flowers; 'Swanley White' is a pure white. Both have narrow, glossy leaves. Hardy only to Z9; grow elsewhere with the protection of a cold frame.

WACHENDORFIA, Haemodoraceae. (25)

Wachendorfias make large stands of handsome, ribbed foliage, above which rise long, narrow panicles of usually yellow, 6-tepaled funnelform flowers. Although each lasts only a day, the whole inflorescence is showy for several weeks. Suitable for sheltered flower borders, particularly where the soil can be kept damp; most effective alongside ponds or streams. Tolerant of full sun in coastal regions. Propagation is best in spring by division of the bright red, tuberous roots; seedlings takes 3 years to reach flowering size.

| *thyrsiflora* | YELLOW | SP/ESU | 2'–4'/1.5' |
| | ○ ● | Z10-8 | DS ** |

Red Root. Two upright ranks of bright green, deeply pleated, sword-shaped leaves, which may reach 3' long by 3" wide. The thick, stiffly erect stems are topped with crowded, cylindrical 1.5' wands of mustard-colored 1¼" flowers. Easy to grow in damp soil, but tolerates drier conditions if well-shaded; the leaves brown and fray at the tips in exposed positions or if the roots dry out. South Africa. Shorter *W. paniculata* has larger, bright yellow flowers marked with brown.

XEROPHYLLUM, Liliaceae. (2)

| *asphodeloides* | WHITE | LSP-SU | 2'–5'/2' |
| | ◗ | Z8-6 | DS ** |

Turkeybeard, Mountain Asphodel. This elegant plant makes 2' tussocks of grassy, gray green foliage. The basal leaves are serrate to 1' long; the stem leaves diminish in size above. Starry cream white flowers crowd into showy, terminal 6"–12" racemes on stout, erect stems. As the fragrant ¼"–½" flowers open, the inflorescence elongates, creating a striking cylinder of bloom. Acid peaty or sandy soils are recommended for this native of pine barrens and mountain woods. Lovely in the wild garden. Divide the thick rhizomes carefully in the spring, only when necessary for propagation. Can be difficult. New Jersey to North Carolina, west to Tennessee. The Western species *X. tenax*, Bear Grass, Indian Squaw Grass, is similar, but may reach 6' tall, with 1'–3' long, basal leaves. Its large racemes form pyramids of flowers. Found on dry, exposed ridges in the wild, but prefers a damp, peaty soil in cultivation. British Columbia to Wyoming, central California.

YUCCA, Agavaceae. (40)

These noble evergreen plants have an architectural quality rare among perennials that makes them invaluable as accent plants in borders and elsewhere in the garden. Our

Wachendorfia thyrsiflora

concern is with those species that are stemless or nearly so, although some will develop a stem with age or in response to climate. Yuccas form close rosettes of long, linear or sword-shaped leaves. Stout, leafless stalks rise above the foliage, lofting massive panicles or racemes of pendent white or cream flowers, often flushed with pink or purple on the outside. The bell-shaped or open flowers consist of 6 waxy tepals. In some species, the rosette of leaves dies after flowering, but survival is ensured by offsets. All need a sunny location and sharply drained soils. Drought resistant and mostly quite tolerant of hot, humid conditions. Flowering time and plant size vary; expect plants to flower early and grow to larger sizes in mild climates. Propagate by root cuttings, division of the offsets, or seed. Yuccas were great favorites of Gertrude Jekyll, who combined them with *Euphorbia characias wulfenii, Acanthus,* and *Kniphofia.*

| *baccata* | WHITE | SP/ESU | 4'–7'/3'–4' |
| | O | Z10-4 | DRS *** |

Banana Yucca, Blue Yucca, Datil, Spanish-Bayonet. Clump forming; stemless, or with a short, prostrate stem. The leaves, 2.5' long by 2¼" wide, have coarse, marginal fibers and an apical spine. The dense 2'–2.5' panicle is carried on a short, stout stalk. Large, bell-shaped white or cream flowers sometimes tinged with reddish or purplish brown. Southwestern United States.

| *filamentosa* | WHITE | SU/LSU | 4'–6'/2'–3' |
| | O | Z10-4/T | DRS **** |

Adam's-Needle is clump forming and essentially stemless. Spine-tipped, gray green leaves, 1.5'–2.5' long by 1" wide, broaden toward the end and are edged with curling, marginal fibers. The long, diffuse panicle rarely reaches its maximum height of 15'. White, bell-shaped 2" flowers sometimes flushed with reddish brown. Southeastern United States. There are several forms with variegated foliage:
———— 'Bright Edge' has cream-colored marginal variegation.
———— 'Golden Sword.' Foliage edged in yellow.
———— 'Variegata.' Leaves striped in cream.

| *flaccida* | WHITE | LSU | 4'–7'/2'–3' |
| | O | Z10-4/T | DRS *** |

The leaves, to 2.5' by 1", with straight marginal threads, narrow from base to tip and often bend over at the top. Bell-shaped, cream white flowers in a tall open panicle. Southeastern United States.
———— 'Variegata' has leaves with cream white margins.

| *glauca* | WHITE | SU | 3'–6'/2'–3' |
| | O | Z10-3/T | DRS **** |

Soapweed, Soapwell. [*Y. angustifolia*]. Short, sometimes prostrate stems. The sharp-pointed, linear leaves, 1'–2.5' long by ½" wide, are gray green with paler edges and marginal threads. The inflorescence is a slender raceme, to 3' long, of greenish white 2½" flowers flushed with red. Central United States.
———— 'Rosea' has pink-tinged flowers.

| *gloriosa* | WHITE | LSU/F | 6'–8'/3'–4' |
| | O | Z10-7/T | DRS *** |

Lord's-Candlestick, Palm Lily, Roman Candle, Spanish-Dagger. This species may form a trunk, but at the northern end of its natural range and in equally cool climates, it is essentially stemless. Its leaves, 2.5' long by 2″ wide, end in a stiff point. The short, dense panicle of large greenish white to reddish bell-shaped flowers is short stemmed. Southeastern United States.

———— 'Variegata.' Yellow-striped leaves.

| *smalliana* | WHITE | SU/LSU | 4'–8'/2'–3' |
| | O | Z10-5/T | DRS *** |

Adam's-Needle, Bear Grass. Tapering at both ends, the leaves, to 2' long, have curling marginal threads and a slender apical spine. The tall, dense panicle of cream white 1½″–2″ flowers occasionally reaches an extreme of 15' in height. Southeastern and south central United States.

———— 'Maxima' is larger than the species. Its scape bears leafy bracts.
———— 'Rosea' has flowers flushed with pink.
———— 'Variegata' has variegated leaves.

| *whipplei* | WHITE | LSP/ESU | 6'–12'/2'–3' |
| | O | Z10-5 | DRS *** |

Our-Lord's-Candle. [*Hesperoyucca whipplei*]. Stemless to short stemmed. The crowded, stiff, gray green linear leaves, to nearly 2' long by ¾″ wide, end in a sharp spine; finely toothed leaf margins. The long panicle may reach a height of 12'; cream white 2″ flowers, at times purple tinged. California, Baja California.

———— var. *whipplei* dies after flowering. Other varieties form several to many offsets.

ZANTEDESCHIA, Araceae. (6)   Calla Lily

Callas have long-petioled, basal leaves arising from a thick rhizome; their large, shiny blades are usually sagittate. The inflorescence, on a leafless flower stalk, consists of a spathe and spadix. The spathe, a large, flaring, trumpet-shaped bract, surrounds the spadix which is crowded with tiny flowers. All need moisture in summer and a well-drained soil in winter during their dormant season, except for *Z. aethiopica,* which will grow in mud. All, save *Z. aethiopica,* are best propagated by seed. Numerous new hybrids are being developed.

| *aethiopica* | WHITE | SP/SU | 3'–4'/1'–2' |
| | O ◑ | Z10-8 | DRS **** |

Common Calla, Calla Lily. [*Z. africana* Hort., *Richardia africana, R. aethiopica* Hort.]. Leaf blades to 1.5' long. The white or cream-colored spathe reaches 10″ in length; the yellow spadix is fragrant. Grow in rich, moist soil, even in mud at water's edge.

Yucca glauca

Zantedeschia aethiopica 'Crowborough'

Zauschneria californica

Fertilize early in the season. Propagate by division or root cuttings. South Africa. 'Childsiana,' 'Godfreyana,' 'Little Gem,' and 'Minor' are dwarf cultivars.

——————— 'Crowborough' is reputed to be hardier than the species.

——————— 'Green Goddess' has white spathes brushed with green.

| *albomaculata* | YELLOW | SP/SU | 2'/1.5' |
| | ○ | Z10-8 | DRS ** |

Black-Throated Calla, Spotted Calla. [*Z. melanoleuca*]. The leaves are marked with clear unpigmented spots. Spathe to 5″ long, variably white, cream, lemon, or darker yellow, with a purple blotch deep in the throat. South Africa.

——————— 'Helen O'Connor' has an apricot pink spathe. Comes true from seed.

| *elliottiana* | YELLOW | LSP/SU | 2'/1.5' |
| | ○ | Z10-8 | DRS *** |

Golden Calla, Yellow Calla. Spotted leaves. The yellow spathe reaches 5″ in length. Very heat tolerant. Probably of garden origin.

| *pentlandii* | YELLOW | SP/SU | 2.5'/1.5' |
| | ○ | Z10-8 | DRS ** |

The yellow spathe, to 7″ long, has a black patch deep in the throat. South Africa.

| *rehmannii* | PINK | SP | 1'–1.5'/1' |
| | ○ | Z10-8 | DRS ** |

Pink Calla, Red Calla. Long, narrow, lanceolate leaves. The spathes, to 4″ long, come in various shades of pink. South Africa.

——————— 'Superba' has dark pink spathes.

ZAUSCHNERIA, Onagraceae. (4)   California Fuchsia

These California natives are spreading, much-branched, leafy plants, usually somewhat woody at the base. The gray green leaves, sessile or nearly so, are alternate or often opposite below. Loose racemes of striking, scarlet, funnel-shaped, Fuchsia-like flowers. The red calyx is elongated; its 4 lobes as long as the 4 red petals. Well-drained soils. Drought tolerant. Unruly and somewhat invasive; pinch to encourage compactness. A recent botanical revision has placed this genus under *Epilobium*.

| *californica* | RED | LSU/EF | 1'–3'/1.5' |
| | ○ | Z10-8 | CDS **** |

California Fuchsia. This variable plant, often split into several subspecies, has hairy lanceolate to oblong 1½″ leaves. The scarlet flowers are 1″–2″ in length. There is a rare white-flowered form. Evergreen in mild climates. California, Baja California.

——————— 'Glasnevin' has dark green leaves and intensely red flowers.

——————— *latifolia* is shorter stemmed, with ovate to ovate-lanceolate leaves. This fully

Zigadenus elegans

herbaceous subspecies is the hardiest form, probably to Z5. According to Lester Rountree, "It ought to enjoy the cold winters and hot summers of the northeastern states." Oregon to California.

cana	RED	LSU/EF	1′–2′/1.5′
	○	Z10-8	CDS ***

[*Z. californica* var. *microphylla*]. The crowded, very narrow gray leaves are hairier than those of *Z. californica.* Scarlet 1″–2″ flowers. Evergreen in mild climates. Central and southern California.

ZIGADENUS, Liliaceae. (15)

These unusual and seldom grown natives arise from rhizomatous or bulbous rootstocks. The best species, listed below, are bulbous. Propagate by dividing the offsets or from seed.

elegans	WHITE	SU	2′–3′/1′
	○ ◑	Z9-3	DS **

Mountain Death Camas, White Camas, Alkali Grass. Dense tussocks of glaucous, grassy leaves to 1′ long. The strong, erect stems are topped with loose racemes of greenish white, starry ½″ flowers, ringed at the center with bright green glands. An elegant, specimen plant. Soil must be moist, but well drained. Poisonous to man and livestock. Minnesota to Missouri, west to Alaska and Arizona. *Z. glaucus* is similar, but has longer leaves; its flowers are in panicles. Western *Z. fremontii,* Star Lily, has long-stalked flowers in panicles on 1′–3′ stems.

GARDENING WITH PERENNIALS

While this book focuses on the plants themselves rather than on the techniques of gardening with perennials, the less experienced reader may benefit from a review of some of the general aspects of culture. Study of more basic texts together with indispensable personal experience will provide the necessary foundation for success.

SOIL

Soil is composed of clay, sand and silt, and organic matter in varying proportions. Its composition is one of the most important factors affecting plant growth. Heavy clay soils are difficult to work, tend to drain poorly, and are slow to warm up after the winter. In contrast, light, sandy soils are easy to cultivate, drain too freely, and warm up quickly after cold weather. Most soils fall somewhere in between these extremes, but it is essential for the gardener to understand his own soil type and thus know its assets and limitations. In all cases, adequate preparation is essential. Soils in poor condition will never support good plants; thorough groundwork will pay dividends for many years. While annuals occupy a space for only a single season, perennials, like shrubs, do so for several years, and it is a false economy to expect them to perform well without readying their site properly. Clear the ground of all perennial weeds and their roots, such as Dandelions, Poison Ivy, Quack Grass, and Thistles, even Ivy and Pachysandra if you are reclaiming a bed from these ubiquitous ground covers. Their most minute pieces of root will sprout and become a nuisance after new plantings are established. In severe cases, treatments such as a suffocating mulch of black plastic or several thicknesses of newspaper, or the application of an herbicide usually does the trick, although it may take quite some time, perhaps more than one year. Avoid planting too soon after applying herbicides and be certain to follow the manufacturer's directions to the letter. Annual weeds can be removed or dug under to decompose; complete this task before the plants have gone to seed, or a bumper crop of weeds will spring up the following year. While working the soil, remove as many rocks and stones as possible. The smallest help to improve drainage, but large ones hinder cultivation and are unsightly, unless of sufficient size to be used as a design feature. Traditionally, ground earmarked for perennials was prepared by double digging. This method is still considered the ideal, but involves heavy work. The ground is dug to a single spade depth, 10"–12" and put aside. The next spit down is then forked thoroughly, incorporating as much organic material as possible. The top layer of soil from the next trench is placed in the first. Repeat over the whole area to be cultivated. Of course, this assumes that an entire bed is being prepared, but the basic method is the same if only for one or two plants. If double digging is not practicable, dig or rototill the ground as deeply as possible and then go over it again, incorporating organic matter. Either method may be carried out in fall or spring. Where winters are cold, fall preparation is preferable so that the exposed soil may be subjected to the crumbling action of frost. Particularly beneficial for heavy clay soils, it makes them easier to work the following spring. If necessary, lime or gypsum may be applied at this time. In the fall, organic additives do not need to be thoroughly decomposed, as planting is usually delayed until spring. It is unwise, however, to incorporate fresh manure or undecomposed material during spring preparation if planting is to follow at once. Fresh manure will burn new young roots. During decomposition, the soil is depleted temporarily of available nutrients, particularly nitrogen; compensate with an application of a nitrogen-rich fertilizer.

Drainage is of paramount importance to most perennials; this cannot be stressed too strongly. True, a few thrive under damp or even boggy conditions, as noted in the text, but the majority prefer to grow in free-draining but moisture-retentive soil. After planting, it is almost impossible to remedy a serious drainage condition; corrective measures must be taken at the outset. In extreme cases, the proposed site will need a major professional operation, with the installation of drainage tile. Perhaps there is an underlying bed of compacted and impervious soil known as "hardpan"; if so, it must be broken up. In most cases, nothing as serious is required. An alternative to these expensive operations is to build raised beds, filling them with imported soil. Both heavy clay soils and very porous sandy soils are improved by the addition of organic material. Many forms are available, including stable manure, compost, leaves, green manure, spoiled hay, spent hops, seaweed, or almost any vegetable matter. Over time, this breaks down, and when fully decomposed is known as "humus." In different parts of the country, various materials are available, often at very low cost, sometimes for free. For example, it is worth inquiring if your community is one of many that collects its leaves in the fall, recycling them as rich black compost in the spring. Sewage compost—sewage sludge decomposed with wood chips—is a valuable additive available in some areas. Humus added to clay soils causes their very small particles to flocculate into clumps. The resulting larger interparticular spaces enable air and water to pass through more freely. On the other hand, free-draining, large-particled, sandy soils, when enriched with humus, retain additional moisture and provide a more stable environment for plant growth. As well as improving structure and drainage, each application of humus adds some nutrients to the soil. Humus is seldom a major source of plant food, which most often is applied in the form of chemical fertilizers. At the time of initial preparation, the soil should be tested to alert the gardener to what nutrients are required, and in what quantities. Soil tests also should include a reading of acidity or alkalinity, known as the "pH level" of the soil. The bulk of perennials grow satisfactorily in moderately acid soils, with a pH level of about 5.5–6.6. It is wise to repeat-test every few years, more often if you suspect a problem. Most communities have a cooperative extension, county agent, college, university, botanical garden, or arboretum that conducts soil tests at low cost. They will give you a detailed analysis, and also offer advice on other horticultural problems.

PLANTING

Planting may be done either in spring or fall, although some perennials establish more readily in one season or the other. Those with brittle, early-emerging buds, such as

Peonies, are best planted in the fall. Both seasons have their advantages. Spring planting, usually favored in cold winter climates, ensures a cool rooting period prior to the arrival of hot summer weather. However, the soil is still cold and new root growth may not be as rapid as one would like. Moreover, since spring is such a busy time in the garden, it is easy to overlook essential follow-up watering, allowing the plants to dry out at their most vulnerable. On the other hand, fall planting enables the plants to establish readily in warm soil. Follow-up watering is just as important at this time of the year, particularly if the weather is dry and windy. It is essential to set the plants out early in order to allow sufficient time for a good root system to develop before the onset of cold weather. Without firm anchoring and especially during the first winter, particular attention must be paid to heaving in cold winter climates. This is caused by alternate freezing and thawing of the soil, particularly during the sunny days of late winter. Some shallow-rooted perennials, such as *Heuchera,* are especially susceptible. In favorable climates, the planting season is much longer, even throughout the winter. However, since hot weather begins early there, fall planting is usually recommended. Container-grown stock may be set out at any time, except when the ground is frozen, or too wet and sticky after thawing or heavy or prolonged rain. As with bare-root plants, close attention must be paid to keeping the ground moist after planting. It is easy to forget that these apparently well-established plants have been transplanted recently, and have yet to extend an active new root system into the surrounding soil. Often container-grown stock is found to be pot bound; if so, the old root ball should be carefully split or broken up prior to planting to encourage new root growth. Always soak containerized stock before planting so that the roots and stems are turgid. At whatever time of year you choose to plant, it is important to provide as good a start as possible. A cool, overcast day is ideal, especially if it precedes a mild, drizzly period, difficult to predict at best. Make sure that the hole is sufficiently deep and wide to allow the roots to spread out. Set plants no deeper than they were in the nursery bed or container, and firm thoroughly. New gardeners are often afraid to do this, thinking that they will cause damage. Loose plants are susceptible to rocking by winds and to winter heaving. Always water deeply after planting and be conscientious about follow-ups, unless adequate rain falls.

SELECTION

One of the time-honored pleasures of gardening is exchanging plants, cuttings, or seeds with friends and neighbors. Few of us who have gardened for more than a season are unable to point to at least one or two plants as gifts from other enthusiasts. These are special because of their associated memories. However, most plants will be purchased, either as seeds or as plants. Both are offered by local nurseries as well as mail-order houses. The latter usually carry a much larger variety, including the most recent introductions. Some specialize in only one or a few genera, such as Hostas, Pelargoniums, or Daylilies, and offer the newest and most exotic cultivars. It is a pleasant winter occupation to thumb through the latest, often enticingly illustrated catalogs, dreaming of the "paradise" that your property will become the following season! Many local nurseries also have catalogs, and if your favorite is reliable and has healthy, pest-free plants of the type you want, there is no advantage to buying by mail. However, it is foolish to settle for locally available plants of poor quality or an inferior cultivar in spite of the savings on shipping costs. Mail-order plants are mostly sold bare root or are small, pot-grown specimens to facilitate shipping. They will take some time to become established and must endure the added stress of shipment. If they are dried out on arrival, soak in a very weak solution of fertilizer for an hour or two prior to planting. An extensive list of nurseries is included in the Appendix. There are several advantages to buying locally. The material is usually sold in 4″ pots, quart-, or larger-sized containers, or is dug immediately prior to sale, providing the customer with the opportunity to select a particular specimen. The plants are probably larger and will make an instant display in your garden. If pot grown, there is less urgency to plant immediately if it is not convenient or if the growing site is not ready.

MAINTENANCE

Many of the perennials listed here thrive with a regimen of low maintenance. This definitely does not mean no maintenance. Even the most carefree require attention from time to time and will repay the gardener with more floriferous, healthy, and beautiful growth.

1. Watering

Watering is required at some time of the year in most places, although only minimally in a few fortunate climates. Where dry conditions are normal year after year, it is prudent to select plants for their tolerance to drought. Where soil has been properly prepared, the roots will grow deeply, reducing the need for frequent applications of water. It is of prime importance to apply enough water so that the roots will reach down for it rather than congregate near the surface. A light sprinkling every day or so will do more harm than good, making the plants more vulnerable to the scorching rays of the sun. An hour or so after watering, make a test to see how far the water has penetrated. If only the top surface soil is moist, more is required. Overwatering is not only wasteful but also detrimental. It results in soft, lush growth, which is more susceptible to pests and diseases, and increases the need for staking. Today, many gardens are equipped with sprinklers, soaker hoses, or either drip or trickle irrigation systems, often controlled by a clock. However effective these are, there are still usually a few spots in the garden that must be watered by hand. Large quantities of water are wasted by overhead watering because so much is lost through evaporation. Moisture is needed at the roots, and ideally should be applied at or near ground level. Many gardeners have strong opinions about what time of day is best for watering. If early in the morning, the plants benefit from cool, moist roots, but much of the water will soon evaporate in the heat of the day. Alternatively, watering in the evening ensures the plants time to soak up the moisture and become turgid before sunrise. However, foliage still wet at dusk remains damp overnight and is more susceptible to disease, particularly mildew. Ideally, late afternoon seems to be best, but ultimately, the timing is of far less importance than the quantity.

2. Fertilizing

Most soils, if properly prepared and mulched, do not require heavy applications of fertilizer to support strong growth of ornamental perennials. Except for those that are gross feeders, as noted in the text, most are well satisfied with a light annual application of a balanced fertilizer, such as 10-10-10, at the beginning of the growing season. Some, notably those that are sustained by underground storage organs, such as Bearded Iris and Dahlias, benefit from an application of fertilizer after flowering, when the plants are storing food. Long bloomers may require an additional light dressing of fertilizer in the middle of the flowering season. Be alert to the condition of your plants; with experience, you will recognize when a plant is starved. Always apply chemical fertilizers to damp soil and water them in well. The foliage must be dry; leaf burn results from dry fertilizer sticking to damp foliage. A specialized text on soils and fertilizers should be consulted for additional information. See the Bibliography.

3. Mulching

There are several sound reasons for mulching. It helps to reduce the evaporation of soil moisture, keeps the roots cool, discourages the germination of weed seeds, and reduces the spreading of diseases. As if these reasons were not enough, organic mulches gradually decompose, enriching the soil. Some, such as pine needles, can help to keep the soil from becoming too alkaline. Many are aesthetically pleasing, giving the bed or border a neat, cared-for appearance. Almost any organic material can be used; some of the most popular include shredded bark or leaves, pine needles, buckwheat hulls, and compost. Save expensive peat moss for adding to the soil, since as a mulch, it forms a crust which effectively prevents water from penetrating the soil. Grass clippings are also a poor choice, best added to the compost pile; seaweed is usually confined to vegetable gardens. Bark nuggets decompose very slowly, and may be more pleasing among evergreen trees and shrubs than among perennials. Sometimes gravels or colored pebbles are used as an inorganic mulch. Many are attractive, but should be saved for places such as desert or rock gardens or in tree wells. They are effective spread over a plastic cover to suppress weeds, under the eaves of houses, or other difficult spots in the garden where no rain falls. Elsewhere they may be a nuisance since they are difficult to remove. Mulch is applied after planting or after spring cleanup, to a depth of about 2″–3″, and replenished through the season. Avoid mulching too close to the crowns of the plants as this tends to encourage pests and diseases, particularly crown rot. Weed and water the area prior to applying the mulch.

4. Winter Protection

Where winters are cold, many plants, especially those newly installed or of questionable hardiness, benefit from some protection in the form of winter mulches. These are usually applied as soon as the ground has frozen, and serve to maintain an even soil temperature throughout the winter. Evergreen boughs and salt hay are favorite materials, as well as pine needles. Avoid anything, such as Maple leaves, that will mat down and retain moisture around the crowns. Delay the operation until the surface of the soil is frozen, because mulch readily becomes a perfect winter home for destructive small rodents.

5. Staking

Many perennials require staking, especially in exposed or windy sites. However, support also may be necessary in other situations: where plants are overcrowded, grown too closely together, drawn up toward the light, placed too close to a wall or hedge, overly shaded by buildings or trees, or planted in excessively rich soil. All of these factors can be corrected. Divide as soon as plants become overcrowded and plant far enough apart to accommodate their eventual girth. Well-grown, lean plants are less susceptible to wind damage. Shorter plants often may be used to provide natural support for those of greater stature. Unfortunately some of the taller perennials, such as Dahlias and Delphiniums, are naturally weak stemmed or weak at the base and will always require staking or support of some kind to look their best. If a relatively maintenance-free garden is desired, avoid these types and select lower-growing species or cultivars. Naturally, plant them out of the wind or protect with a windbreak.

Staking must be as unobtrusive as possible while providing sufficient support. This is an art. Little is as unsightly as plants poorly staked, often strangled by string, or standing stiffly like a company of soldiers at attention. Always insert the stakes early, while growth is still low. The plants will then hide their support by flowering time.

Many materials are available for staking, some more locally popular than others. The methods may be divided roughly into three categories: (a) Brush staking makes use of twiggy brush often called "pea sticks." Though sometimes difficult to find, they are inexpensive or even free, and are ideal for supporting bushy plants such as Coreopsis, Hardy Asters, Chrysanthemums, and other Daisies. Brush stakes should be about ⅔ as tall as the ultimate height of the plants. Sharpen the bottoms of the sticks, and insert several around and within each plant. Bend over the topmost 8″–12″ toward the center, creating a tangle of brush. As the plants grow through this, they are firmly supported. Some gardeners use coarse chicken wire securely staked into the ground and slide this upward as the plants grow. Initially, this is not very attractive, but it is an efficient method for some, such as hardy Geraniums, that tend to flop badly in rainy weather. (b) Bamboo canes and metal or wooden stakes are used for tall plants with only a few individual stems, such as Dahlias and Delphiniums. Bamboos are offered in different thicknesses, from very thin, split canes to those of ¾″ and 1″ diameter. Metal stakes, often coated in green plastic, are stronger and more durable but are much more expensive. If wooden stakes are selected, those made of redwood, cedar, or other water-resistant woods are best, and can be reused year after year. Sharpen their lower tip and extend their life with a nontoxic wood preservative. Bamboos and wooden stakes are often dyed green so that they blend with foliage; some preservatives contain a green dye. Obviously, the girth of the stake should be in proportion to the diameter of the plant stem; a thick Dahlia stem will need stronger support than a bamboo or slender metal stake can provide, but the fine spikes of the taller Monkshoods are overpowered by heavy wooden stakes. Tie each stem loosely at intervals, using soft, natural-colored string, twine, or a plastic-covered twist; use a figure 8 tie, which allows for flexibility in the wind. Cut off overly long stakes for the sake of appearance. Because it is easy to lean onto a stake and thus cause eye or facial injuries, always use caution when working. Some gardeners affix a knob to the end for safety. Bamboo canes may be combined with twine or string, providing some of the support. Several canes are inserted deeply around a clump, with string looped around each, encircling the entire plant. Beware of tying the string too tightly, which produces a strangled effect. This type of corset works well, even with Gypsophila, although for this plant the stakes must be deeply and firmly set into the ground. Alternatively, the string may be crisscrossed over the young stems, which then grow through it, a good method to use with Garden Phlox and other multistemmed species. Still another method is to insert a heavier stake in the center of the clump and tie each stem to it with a long string. This is rather time-consuming, but the mechanics are well camouflaged. (c) Wire circles or squares on legs are readily available in garden centers and in catalogs. Expensive initially, they last indefinitely. They serve well for such plants as Peonies and medium-height Chrysanthemums that need support only along their lower stems and have sufficient foliage to overhang the structure.

6. Deadheading

After their blooms have faded, many perennials become unsightly. To remedy this condition, spent flowers are removed. How far to cut back depends on the growth habit of the particular plant: Should the entire stem be cut at ground level or just cut off at the next lowest leaf node? It is important to look closely at the plant to determine if the flowers are borne on new stems arising from the base, as in Kniphofia and Dicentra, or if they are borne in the leaf axils over much of the plant, as in most of the Daisy family. Some, Linaria, Delphiniums, Monkshood, and Lobelias, for example, carry their flowers in the upper leaf axils and should be deadheaded to the next lowest node, thereby stimulating the growth of lateral spikes. The flowers of some perennials, notably Tradescantia and Perennial Flax, among others, wither neatly and drop afterward; by contrast, most Daylily flowers curl up but remain unsightly on the plant for several days unless removed by hand. Conscientious deadheading not only improves the appearance of the garden but also assures a longer blooming time. As noted in the text, some plants, such as Perennial Candytuft, will rebloom later in the season if cut back just after the primary flush has faded. Blackberry Lily and Gladwyn Iris are examples of perennials which should not be deadheaded, as their decorative berries provide prolonged interest. Late bloomers, such as Sedum 'Autumn Joy' and many of the ornamental grasses have long-lived and attractive seed heads, valuable in winter gardens.

7. Division

At some time or other, most perennials need division to rejuvenate the plants, to curtail their spread, or to increase stock. This is not a difficult task and may be undertaken in either spring or fall. As long as the plants are kept well watered afterward, many are not particular as to the season, although some may reestablish slowly in hot weather. The need for division is evident when the center of a plant begins to die out and all the robust, young growth is concentrated around the edges of the clump. Anthemis, Shasta Daisies, and Chrysanthemums are some which demand frequent division in order to retain their vigor. If the clumps are reasonably small, they are easily lifted and pulled apart by hand; save only the strongest, outer divisions for replanting. If the center has declined, but the plant is to remain in the same place, one can avoid lifting the whole plant by digging out the old middle, adding fresh soil, and inserting a piece of young growth cut from the edge. Wide, spreading plants can be troublesome, particularly those such as Siberian Iris and Daylilies, which make thick, tough clumps. Water deeply the night before, and unless only a few inches high, cut down the top growth to about 6". Then lift the clump carefully with a spading fork, damaging the roots as little as possible. Insert two spading forks back to back and pry apart the roots. This sometimes requires a good deal of strength, and may be accomplished more easily by two people. In all cases, be sure that the new pieces are large enough to make a good display of flowers the following season; if too small, blooms will be forfeited, although further division may be delayed a year or so. Discard any woody pieces.

8. Pests and Diseases

In common with most plants, perennials are subject to attack by various pests and diseases, and many entries in the text contain warnings of particular susceptibilities. The most common pests include aphids, white flies, leaf miners, spider mites, slugs and snails, and small mammals such as mice, moles, gophers, and rabbits. In many parts of the country, deer have recently proved to be an almost unsurmountable problem, and remedies range from high electric fences to hanging balls of human hair from shrubs and small trees. Common diseases include mildews and rusts, as well as viruses, such as mosaic. Conscientious soil husbandry and good growing practices, particularly sanitation, go a long way toward controlling the spread of both pests and diseases. General as well as specialized gardening texts provide detailed information on all aspects of identification and control. See the Bibliography.

9. Propagation

As noted, all entries include the usual methods of propagation. While the experienced gardener will find these commonplace, beginners should consult one of the encyclopedias or specialized texts listed in the Bibliography. Even longtime gardeners find that certain species are temperamental and difficult to propagate, so the less experienced should not be discouraged if success is less than total.

SOURCES OF PLANT MATERIAL: NURSERIES AND SEEDSMEN

Abbey Garden Cacti and Succulents
4620 Carpinteria Avenue
Carpinteria, CA 93013
805–684–5112/1595

Bay View Gardens
1201 Bay Street
Santa Cruz, CA 95060
408–423–3656
Iris

Bernardo Beach Native Plant Farm
Star Route 7, Box 145
Veguita, NM 87062
505–345–6248
Southwestern natives

Blooming Nursery
Rte. 4, Box 9
Cornelius, OR 97113
503–359–0317
Does not ship

Kurt Bluemel, Inc.
2740 Greene Lane
Baldwin, MD 21013
301–557–7229
Ornamental grasses

Bluestone Perennials, Inc.
7211 Middle Ridge Road
Madison, OH 44057
216–428–7535
Liners

Borbeleta Gardens, Inc.
15974 Canby Avenue, Rte. 5
Faribault, MN 55021
507–334–2807
Daylilies, Siberian Iris,
  Median Bearded Iris

W. Atlee Burpee Co.
Warminster, PA 18974
1–800–327–3049
Seeds and plants

Busse Gardens
635 East 7th Street, Rte. 2,
  Box 13
Cokato, MN 55321
612–286–2654
Hosta, Daylilies, Peonies,
  Siberian Iris

California Flora Nursery
P.O. Box 3
Fulton, CA 95439
707–528–8813

Canyon Creek Nursery
3527 Dry Creek Road
Oroville, CA 95965
916–533–2166
Uncommon perennials

Carroll Gardens, Inc.
Box 310, 444 East Main
  Street
Westminster, MD 21157
301–848–5422

Color Farm
2710 Thornhill Road
Auburndale, FL 33823
813–967–9895
Coleus

Conley's Garden Center
Boothbay Harbor, ME 04538
207–633–5020
Wild flowers, ferns

Cooley's Gardens
11553 Silverton Road N.E.

P.O. Box 126
Silverton, OR 97381
503–873–5463
Bearded Iris

The Country Garden
Rte. 2, Box 455A
Crivitz, WI 54114
715–757–2045
Seeds and plants for cutting
  gardens

Country Gardens
74 South Road
Pepperell, MA 01463
617–433–6236

The Crownsville Nursery
1241 Generals Highway
Crownsville, MD 21032
301–923–2212

Daystar
Rte. #2, Box 250
Litchfield, ME 04350
207–724–3369
Rock garden plants,
  Primulas, Ericaceae

Far North Gardens
16785 Harrison
Livonia, MI 48154
313–422–0747
Barnhaven Primulas,
  Alpines, Iris species

Garden Import
P.O. Box 760
Thornhill, Ontario L37 4A5
  Canada
416–731–1950
Imported bulbs, seeds, and
  rare plants

Garden Place
6780 Heisley Road
P.O. Box 388
Mentor, OH 44061
216–255–3705

Gardens of the Blue Ridge
P.O. Box 10
Pineola, NC 28662
704–733–2417
Wild flowers

Geraniaceae—Robin Parer
122 Hillcrest Avenue
Kentfield, CA 94904
415–461–4168
Hardy Geranium species

**Gladside Gardens—Corys
    M. Heselton**
61 Main Street
Northfield, MA 01360
413–498–2657
Gladiolus, Dahlias, Cannas

Russell Graham
4030 Eagle Crest Road N.W.
Salem, OR 97304
503–362–1135
Cyclamen, natives and
    ferns, specialty bulbs

Greenwood Nursery
P.O. Box 1610
Goleta, CA 93116
805–964–2420
Daylilies

High Altitude Gardens
P.O. Box 4238
Ketchum, ID 83340
208–726–3221
Wild flowers, herbs,
    natives

Hillside Gardens
Litchfield Rd.
P.O. Box 614
Norfolk, CT 06058

203–542–5345
Does not ship

Holbrook Farm and Nursery
Rte. 2, Box 223B
Fletcher, NC 28732
704–891–7790

J. L. Hudson, Seedsman
P.O. Box 1058
Redwood City, CA 94064
Seeds

Joyce's Garden
Bill & Joyce Glimm
64640 Old Bend Redmond
    Highway
Bend, OR 97701
503–388–4680

Klehm Nursery
Rte. 5, 197 Penny Road
South Barrington, IL 60010
312–551–3715
Peonies, Hostas, Daylilies,
    Iris

Lamb Nurseries
E. 101 Sharp Avenue
Spokane, WA 99202
509–328–7956/328–1505
Uncommon perennials,
    rock garden plants

Logee's Greenhouses
55 North Street
Danielson, CT 06239
203–774–8038
Begonias, rare plants,
    Geraniums, herbs

Maver Nursery—Rare Seeds
Rte. 2, Box 265 B
Asheville, NC 28805
704–298–4751
Seeds

Merry Gardens
Camden, ME 04843

207–236–9064
Herbs

Mid-America Iris Garden
P.O. Box 12982
Oklahoma City, OK 73157
405–946–5743
Bearded Iris

Mileager's Gardens
4838 Douglas Avenue
Racine, WI 53402–2498
414–639–2040

Mission Bell Gardens
2778 West 5600 South
Roy, UT 84067
Bearded Iris

Mohn's, Inc.
P.O. Box 2301
Atascadera, CA 93423
805–466–4362
'Minicap' strain of Oriental
    Poppies

Native Plants, Inc.
Nursery Division
417 Wakara Way
Salt Lake City, UT 84108
801–533–8498
Natives

Native Sons
Wholesale Nursery, Inc.
379 West El Campo Road
Arroyo Grande, CA 93420
Natives

Orchid Gardens
6700 Splitland Road
Grand Rapids, MN 55744
218–326–6975
Wild flowers

The Plant Group, Inc.
Rte. 207, Box 465
North Franklin,
    CT 06254

203–642–6030
Micropropagators

Plants of the Southwest
1812 Second Street
Santa Fe, NM 87501
505–983–1548
Southwestern wild flowers.
Ship seed only

Prairie Nursery
P.O. Box 365
Westfield, WI 53964
608–296–3679
Prairie wild flowers

Putney Nursery, Inc.
Putney, VT 05346
802–387–5577
Wild flowers

Savory's Greenhouses and Gardens
5300 Whiting Avenue
Edina, MN 55435
612–941–8755
Hostas

Shady Hill Gardens
821 Walnut Street
Batavia, IL 60510–2999
312–879–5665
Pelargoniums

Siskiyou Rare Plant Nursery
2825 Cummings Road
Medford, OR 97501–1524
503–772–6846
Woodland and rock garden plants

Anthony J. Skittone
2271 31st Avenue
San Francisco,
CA 94116
415–753–3332
Unusual bulbs, plants, and seeds

Stallings Nursery
910 Encinitas Blvd.
Encinitas, CA 92024
619–753–3079
Subtropical and tropical plants

Sunny Border Nurseries, Inc.
1709 Kensington Road
P.O. Box 86
Kensington, CT 06037
203–828–0321
Wholesale only

Sunnybrook Farms Nursery
P.O. Box 6
9448 Mayfield Road
Chesterland, OH 44026
216–729–7232
Herbs, Scented Geraniums.
Homestead Division:
Hostas

Sunnyslope Gardens
8638 Huntington Drive
San Gabriel, CA 91775
818–287–4071
Chrysanthemums

Swan Island Dahlias
P.O. Box 800
Canby, OR 97013
503–266–7711
Dahlias

Thompson and Morgan
P.O. Box 1308
Jackson, NJ 08527
201–363–2225
Seeds

TyTy Plantation Bulb Co.
Box 159
TyTy, GA 31795
912–382–0404
Tender and unusual bulbs

Vick's Wildgardens, Inc.
Conshohocken State Road

Box 115
Gladwyne, PA 19035
215–525–6773
Wild flowers

Andre Viette Farm and Nursery
Rte. 1, Box 16
Fishersville, VA 22939
703–943–2315

Mary Walker Bulb Co.
P.O. Box 256
Omega, GA 31775
912–386–1919
Tender bulbs

Walters Gardens, Inc.
P.O. Box 137
Zeeland, MI 49464
616–772–4697

Wayside Gardens
Hodges, SC 29695–0001
1–800–845–1124

We-Du Nurseries
Route 5, Box 724
Marion, NC 28752
704–738–8300
Natives of southeastern United States

Well-Sweep Herb Farm
317 Mt. Bethel Road
Port Murray, NJ 07865
201–852–5390
Herbs

Western Hills Nursery
16250 Coleman Valley Road
Occidental, CA 95465
707–874–3731
Does not ship

Weston Nurseries, Inc.
E. Main Street (Rte. 135)
P.O. Box 186
Hopkinton, MA 01748-0186

617-435-3414
Does not ship

White Flower Farm
Litchfield, CT 06759-0050
203-567-4565

Gilbert H. Wild and Son, Inc.
HPB-84
1112 Joplin Street

Sarcoxie, MO 64862-0338
Peonies, Daylilies, Iris

Wildwood Farm
10300 Hwy. 12
Kenwood, CA 95452
707-833-1161

Woodlanders, Inc.
1128 Colleton Avenue

Aiken, SC 29801
803-648-7522
Natives

Young's Mesa Nursery
2755 Fowler Lane
Arroyo Grande,
    CA 93420
805-489-0548
Pelargoniums

Many nurseries require payment for their catalogs. Most carry a wide range of perennials; some have specialties as noted.

SPECIALIST SOCIETIES

Alpine Garden Society
E. Michael Upward
Lye End Link, St John's
Woking, Surrey GU 21 1SW
England

American Dahlia Society
Michael L. Martinolich
159 Pine St.
New Hyde Park,
NY 11040

**American Hemerocallis
Society**
Elly Launius
1454 Rebel Dr.
Jackson, MS 39211

American Hosta Society
Jack A. Freedman
3103 Heatherhill Dr. S.E.
Huntsville, AL 35802

American Iris Society
Carol Ramsey
6518 Beachy Ave.
Wichita, KS 67206

**American Penstemon
Society**
Ann W. Bartlett
1569 S. Holland Ct.
Lakewood, CO 80226

American Peony Society
Greta Kessenich
250 Interlaken Rd.
Hopkins, MN 55343

American Primrose Society
Brian Skidmore, Treasurer
6730 W. Mercer Way
Mercer Island, WA 98040

**American Rock Garden
Society**
Buffy Parker
15 Fairmead Rd.
Darien, CT 06820

**Cactus and Succulent
Society of America**
Louise Lippold
P.O. Box 3010
Santa Barbara, CA 93130

**Canadian Chrysanthemum
and Dahlia Society**
G. H. Lawrence
83 Aramaman Dr.
Agincourt, ONT M1T 2PM
Canada

The Delphinium Society
Mrs Shirley E. Bassett
"Takakkaw"
Ice House Wood
Oxted, Surrey RH8 9DW
England

Hardy Plant Society (UK)
Simon Wills
The Manor House
Walton-in-Gordano,
Clevedon
Avon BS21 7AN
England

**Hardy Plant Society
(USA)**
Connie Hanni
33530 S.E. Bluff Rd.
Boring, OR 97009

Herb Society of America
2 Independence Ct.
Concord, MA 01742

**International Geranium
Society**
Betty Tufenkian
4610 Druid Street
Los Angeles, CA 90032

**National Chrysanthemum
Society, Inc.**
Galen L. Goss
5012 Kingston Dr.
Annandale, VA 22003

**New England Wild Flower
Society**
Garden in the Woods
Hemenway Rd.
Framingham, MA 01701

**The Perennial Plant
Association**
Steven Still, Secretary
Dept. of Horticulture
Ohio State University
2001 Fyffe Court
Columbus, OH 43210

**The Royal Horticultural
Society**
80 Vincent Square
London SW1P 2PE England

**Sempervivum Fanciers
Association**
Dr. C. William Nixon
37 Oxbow Lane
Randolph, MA 02368

**The Society for Growing
Australian Plants**
Glen Harvey
5 Ellesmere Rd.
Crymea Bay, NSW 2227
Australia

DISPLAY GARDENS

ALABAMA

**Bellingrath Gardens &
    Home**
Route 1, Box 60
Theodore, AL 36582
205–973–2217

**Birmingham Botanical
    Garden**
2612 Lane Park Rd.
Birmingham, AL 35223
205–879–1227

ARIZONA

**Boyce Thompson
    Southwestern Arboretum**
Box AB
Superior, AZ 85273
602–689–2811

Desert Botanical Garden
1201 North Galvin Parkway
Phoenix, AZ 85008
602–941–1225

CALIFORNIA

Blake Garden
70 Ricon Rd.
Kensington, CA 94707
Mailing Address:
    2 Norwood Place
Kensington, CA 94707
415–524–2449

Filoli Center
Canada Rd.

Woodside, CA 94062
415–364–2880

**Huntington Botanical
    Gardens**
1151 Oxford Rd.
San Marino, CA 91108
818–405–2100

**Los Angeles State and
    County Arboretum**
310 N. Baldwin Ave.
Arcadia, CA 91006
213–446–8251

**Mildred E. Mathias
    Botanical Garden**
University of California
Los Angeles, CA 90045
213–825–2714

Quail Botanical Gardens
230 Quail Gardens Dr.
Encinitas, CA 92024
714–753–4432/436–3036

**Rancho Santa Ana Botanic
    Garden**
1500 North College Ave.
Claremont, CA 91711
714–625–8767

**Regional Parks Botanic
    Garden**
Tilden Regional Park
Berkeley, CA 94708
415–841–8732

**Santa Barbara Botanic
    Garden**
1212 Mission Canyon Rd.
Santa Barbara, CA 93105
805–682–4726

**Strybing Arboretum
    & Botanical Gardens**
Ninth Avenue at Lincoln
    Way
San Francisco, CA 94122
415–559–3622

UCSC Arboretum
University of California
Santa Cruz, CA 95064

**University of California
    Arboretum, Davis**
Dept. of Botany
University of California
Davis, CA 95616
916–752–2498

**University of California
    Botanical Garden**
Centennial Dr.
Berkeley, CA 94720
415–642–3343

**University of California,
    Irvine**
Biological Sciences UCI
Irvine, CA 92717
714–856–5011

**University of California
    Botanic Gardens,
    Riverside**
Dept. of Botany and Plant
    Science
Riverside, CA 92521
718–787–4650

Western Hills Nursery
16250 Coleman Valley Rd.
Occidental, CA 95465
707–874–3731

COLORADO

Denver Botanic Gardens
909 York Street
Denver, CO 80206
303–575–2547

CONNECTICUT

Hillside Gardens
Litchfield Rd.
P.O. Box 614
Norfolk, CT 06058
203–542–5345

**Olive W. Lee Memorial
    Garden**
89 Chichester Rd.
New Canaan, CT 06840

University of Connecticut
Dept. of Plant Science
U-67, 1376 Storrs Rd.
Storrs, CT 06268

White Flower Farm
Litchfield, CT 06759-0050
203–496–9600

DELAWARE

Nemours
Rockland Rd.
Wilmington, DE 19899
Mailing Address:
    Reservations Office
P.O. Box 109, Wilmington,
    DE 19899
302–651–6912

**Winterthur Museum and
    Gardens**
Winterthur, DE 19735
302–654–1548

DISTRICT OF COLUMBIA

Dumbarton Oaks
1703 32nd St. N.W.
Washington, DC 20007
202–338–8278

**United States National
    Arboretum**
Agricultural Research
    Service
U.S. Dept. of Agriculture
3501 New York Ave. N.E.
Washington, DC 20002
202–472–9279

FLORIDA

Busch Gardens
3000 Tampa Blvd.
Tampa, FL 33612
813–971–8282

Fairchild Tropical Garden
10901 Old Cutler Rd.
Miami, FL 33156
305–667–1651

**Marie Selby Botanical
    Garden**
800 S. Palm Ave.
Sarasota, FL 33577
813–366–5730

**Vizcaya Museum and
    Gardens**
3251 South Miami Ave.
Miami, FL 33129
305–579–2708

GEORGIA

Atlanta Botanical Garden
P.O. Box 77246
Atlanta, GA 30357
404–876–5858

Callaway Gardens
Pine Mountain, GA 31822
404–663–2281

**The State Botanical
    Garden of Georgia**
2450 South Milledge Ave.
Athens, GA 30605

IDAHO

University of Idaho
Plant Science Dept.
Moscow, ID 83843

ILLINOIS

Cantigny
15151 Winfield Rd.
Wheaton, IL 60187

Chicago Botanic Garden
Lake Cook Rd.
Glencoe, IL 60022
312–835–5440

Glen Oak Botanical Garden
Peoria Park District
2218 N. Prospect Rd.
Peoria, IL 61603
309–685–4321

Morton Arboretum
Route 53
Lisle, IL 60532
312–968–0074

INDIANA

Eli Lilly Botan
Gardens of the Indianapolis
    Museum of Art
1200 W. 38th St.
Indianapolis, IN

Purdue University
Dept. of Horticulture
West Lafayette, IN 47907

KANSAS

The Bartlett Arboretum
Box 39
Belle Plaine, KS 67013
316–488–3451

KENTUCKY

University of Kentucky
Horticulture and
    Landscape Arch. Dept.
Lexington, KY 40506

LOUISIANA

**Longue Vue House and
    Gardens**
7 Bamboo Rd.
New Orleans, LA 70124
504–488–5488

**Rosedown Plantation and
    Gardens**
Hwy. 10–61
P.O. Box 1816
St. Francisville, LA 70775
504–635–3332

MAINE

**The Abby Aldrich
    Rockefeller Garden**
Seal Harbor, ME

MARYLAND

Brookside Gardens
1500 Glenallen Ave.

Wheaton, MD 20902
301–949–8230

**William Paca House and
    Garden**
1 Martin St.
Annapolis, MD 21401
301–269–0601/267–6656

MASSACHUSETTS

Berkshire Garden Center
Box 826, Rtes. 102 and 183
Stockbridge, MA 10262
413–298–3926

**Garden in the Woods of
    the New England Wild
    Flower Society**
Hemenway Rd.
Framingham, MA 01701
617–877–6574

**Heritage Plantation of
    Sandwich**
Box 566, Grove St.
Sandwich, MA 02563
617–888–3300

**Newberry Perennial
    Gardens**
65 Orchard St. RR 2
Byfield, MA 01922

**The Botanic Garden
    of Smith College**
Lyman Plant House
Northampton, MA 01063
413–584–2700, ext. 2748

**The Case Estates of the
    Arnold Arboretum**
135 Wellesley St.
Weston, MA 02193
Mailing Address: The
    Arnold Arboretum
Jamaica Plain, MA 02130
617–524–1718

MICHIGAN

**W. J. Beal Botanical Garden
    and MSU Campus**
Michigan State University
East Lansing, MI 48823
517–355–0348

**Cranbrook House and
    Gardens**
380 Lone Pine Rd.
P.O. Box 801
Bloomfield Hills, MI 48013
313–645–3149

Dow Gardens
1018 W. Main St.
Midland, MI 48640
517–631–2677

Englerth Gardens
22 St.
Hopkins, MI 49010

Fernwood Botanic Gardens
1720 Range Line Rd.
Niles, MI 49120
616–695–6491

Matthaei Botanical Garden
University of Michigan
1800 North Dixboro Rd.
Ann Arbor, MI 48105
313–764–1168

MINNESOTA

Busse Gardens
Route 2, Box 238
Cokato, MN 55321
612–286–2654

**Minnesota Landscape
    Arboretum and
    Horticultural Research
    Center**
University of Minnesota
3675 Arboretum Dr.
P.O. Box 39

Chanhassen, MN 55317
612–443–2460

MISSISSIPPI

The Crosby Arboretum
3702 Hardy St.
Hattiesburg, MS 39401
601–264–5249

MISSOURI

Gilberg Perennial Farms
2906 Ossenfort Rd.
Glencoe, MO 63038

Missouri Botanical Garden
4344 Shaw Rd.
St. Louis, MO 63110
Mailing Address: P.O. Box
   299
St. Louis, MO 63166
314–577–5100

**Woodland and Floral
   Garden**
University of Missouri
Columbia, MO 62511

NEBRASKA

**Nebraska Statewide
   Arboretum**
111 Forestry Science
   Laboratory
University of Nebraska
Lincoln, NB 68508
402–472–2971

NEW HAMPSHIRE

Fuller Gardens
10 Willow St.
North Hampton, NH 03862
603–964–5414

NEW JERSEY

Leonard J. Buck Garden
Somerset County Park
   Commission
R.D. 2, Layton Rd.
Far Hills, NJ 07931
201–234–2677

**Rutgers University
   Research and Display
   Gardens**
P.O. Box 2312
Cook College
New Brunswick, NJ 08903
210–932–9325

Skylands
Ringwood State Park
P.O. Box 302
Ringwood, NJ 07456

NEW YORK

Bailey Arboretum
Bayville Rd.
Locust Valley, NY 11560
516–676–4497

Brooklyn Botanic Garden
1000 Washington Ave.
Brooklyn, NY 11225
718–622–4433

**Mary Flagler Cary
   Arboretum**
Institute of Ecosystem
   Studies
Box AB
Millbrook, NY 12545
914–677–5358

The Cloisters
The Metropolitan Museum
   of Art
Fort Tryon Park
New York, NY 10040
212–923–3700

The Conservatory Garden
Central Park
105th St. and Fifth Ave.
New York, NY 10003
212–360–8236

Cornell Plantations
1 Plantations Rd.
Ithaca, NY 14850
607–256–3020

Minn's Gardens
Dept. of Floriculture
   and Ornamental
   Horticulture
Cornell University
Ithaca, NY 14850

**The New York Botanical
   Garden**
Bronx, NY 10458
212–220–8700

Old Westbury Gardens
71 Old Westbury Rd.
Old Westbury, NY 11568
516–333–0048

**Pepsico World
   Headquarters**
Anderson Hill Rd.
Purchase, NY 10577

**Queens Botanical
   Garden**
43–50 Main St.
Flushing, NY 11355
718–886–3800

Sonnenberg Gardens
151 Charlotte Street
Canandaigua, NY 14424
716–394–4922

**SUNY Agricultural &
   Technical College**
Dept. of Ornamental
   Horticulture
Farmingdale, NY 11735

Wave Hill
675 W. 252nd St.
Bronx, NY 10471
212–549–2055

NORTH CAROLINA

**Biltmore House and
    Gardens**
Asheville, NC 28802
704–274–1776
Additional information:
    The Biltmore Co.
    Marketing Dept.
1 Biltmore Plaza
Asheville, NC 28802

**The North Carolina
    Botanical Garden and
    Coker Arboretum**
UNC-CH Totten Center
457-A Laurel Hill Rd.
Chapel Hill, NC 27514
919–967–2246

**North Carolina State
    University**
Raleigh, NC 27695

**University Botanic Gardens
    at Asheville, Inc.**
Univ. of North Carolina,
    Asheville
W. T. Weaver Rd.
Asheville, NC 28804
704–252–5190

OHIO

Cox Arboretum
6733 Springboro Pike
Dayton, OH 45449
513–434–9005

**Garden Center of Greater
    Cleveland**
11030 East Blvd.

Cleveland, OH 44106
216–721–1600

**Gardenview Horticultural
    Park**
16711 Pearl Rd.
Strongsville, OH 44136
216–238–6653

**Inniswood Botanical
    Garden and Nature
    Preserve**
940 Hempstead Rd.
Westerville, OH 43081
614–895–6216

Kingwood Center
900 Park Ave. West
Mansfield, OH 44906
419–522–0211

Mt. Airy Arboretum
5083 Colerain Ave.
Cincinnati, OH 45239
513–541–8176

**Stan Hywet Hall and
    Gardens**
714 North Portage Path
Akron, OH 44303
216–836–5533

**Sunnybrook Farms and
    Homestead Garden**
9448 Mayfield Rd.
Chesterland, OH 44026
216–729–7232

OKLAHOMA

Tulsa Garden Center, Inc.
2435 South Peoria St.
Tulsa, OK 74114
918–749–6401

**Will Rogers Horticultural
    Gardens**
3500 NW 36th St.

Oklahoma City, OK 73112
405–943–3977

OREGON

Berry Botanic Garden
11505 SW Summerville Ave.
Portland, OR 97219
503–636–4112

PENNSYLVANIA

**Ambler Campus of Temple
    University**
Dept. of Horticulture and
    Landscape Design
Temple University
Ambler, PA 19002
215–643–1200, ext. 365

**Arthur Hoyt Scott
    Horticulture Foundation**
Swarthmore College
Swarthmore, PA 19081
215–447–7025

**Bowman's Hill Wild
    Flower Preserve**
Washington Crossing
    Historic Park
Washington Crossing, PA
    18977
215–862–2924

Longwood Gardens
P.O. Box 501
Kennett Square, PA 19348
215–388–6741

RHODE ISLAND

Wilcox Park
17 ½ High Street
Westerly, RI 02891
401–348–8362

SOUTH CAROLINA

**Park Seed Company
Gardens**
Hwy. 254 North
Greenwood, SC 29647
803–374–3341

TENNESSEE

Memphis Botanic Garden
750 Cherry Rd.
Memphis, TN 38117
901–685–1566

**Tennessee Botanical
Gardens and Fine Arts
Center at Cheekwood**
Forrest Park Dr.
Nashville, TN 37205
615–352–5310

TEXAS

**Fort Worth Botanic
Garden**
3220 Botanic Garden Dr.
Fort Worth, TX 76107
817–870–7686

**San Antonio Botanical
Center**
555 Funston Pl.
San Antonio, TX 78209
512–821–5115

VIRGINIA

**American Horticultural
Society: River Farm**
7931 East Boulevard Dr.
Alexandria, VA 22308
Mailing address: P.O. Box
0105
Mount Vernon, VA 22121

**Andre Viette Farm and
Nursery**
Rte. 1, Box 16
(Route 608)
Fishersville, VA 22939
703–943–2315

**Lewis Ginter Botanical
Garden**
Richmond, VA 23220
804–262–9887

Monticello
P.O. Box 316

Charlottesville, VA 22902
804–295–8181/2657

Mount Vernon
Mount Vernon Ladies
Association
Mount Vernon, VA 22121
703–780–2000

Maymont
1700 Hampton St.
Richmond, VA 23220
804–358–7166

Norfolk Botanical Gardens
Norfolk, VA 23518
804–853–6972

**Virginia Polytechnic Inst.
and State University**
Dept. of Horticulture
Blacksburg, VA 24161

WISCONSIN

**Boerner Botanical Gardens
in Whitnall Park**
5879 South 92nd St.
Hales Corners, WI 53130
414–425–1130/529–1870

GLOSSARY

ALTERNATE: Arranged singly at intervals along the stem, not opposite or whorled. E.g., alternate leaves.

ANTHER: The pollen-bearing part of a stamen.

APETALOUS: Lacking petals.

APOMIXIS: Asexual reproduction by seed. The resulting plants are genetically identical to the parent plant.

ASCENDING: Growing obliquely upward. E.g., an ascending stem.

ASYMMETRICAL FLOWER: An irregular flower, bilaterally but not radially symmetrical.

AXIL: The angle between a petiole or peduncle and the stem that bears it. E.g., a leaf axil.

BACKCROSS: The crossing of a hybrid with one of its parents.

BANNER: The upper petal of a papilionaceous flower, as in the Leguminosae (Pea family). See STANDARD.

BASAL: Arising from the base or lower part of a plant. E.g., basal leaves.

BERRY: A fleshy, pulpy fruit containing seeds.

BI-: Twice. E.g., bipinnate, biternate.

BIFID: Cleft into two lobes, usually at the apex. E.g., a bifid leaf.

BLADE: The expanded part of a leaf or petal.

BLOOM: A pale, powdery, usually waxy, coating on leaves and other organs.

BRACT: A modified or reduced leaf, often associated with a flower or inflorescence.

BULBIL: A small bulblike structure found in the axil of a leaf or flower, as in *Yucca*.

CALYX (CALYCES): The outer series of a perianth, composed of free or united sepals.

CAMPANULATE: Bell shaped. E.g., a campanulate corolla.

CAPSULE: A dry, dehiscent fruit composed of two or more carpels.

CARPEL: One of the seed-bearing units of a pistil or ovary.

CILIATE: Fringed with marginal hairs.

CINCINNUS: A one-sided scorpioid cyme.

CLASPING: Partly or completely surrounding the stem. E.g., a clasping leaf.

CLAW: The narrowed, basal part of a petal.

CLEFT: Cut halfway or less into lobes. Terms such as "cleft," "dissected," "divided," and "lobed" all have precise meanings but are often used quite loosely.

CLONE: A vegetatively propagated plant genetically identical to its parent.

COLUMN: The fused staminal tube of the Malvaceae (Mallow family). Part of the corolla in *Asclepias* and *Tricyrtis*.

COMPOUND INFLORESCENCE: E.g., a compound umbel, composed of several secondary umbels.

COMPOUND LEAF: A leaf composed of two or more leaflets, pinnately compound when the leaflets are borne on both sides of the main axis, palmately compound when the leaflets arise from the end of a common petiole.

CONVOLUTE: Rolled up lengthwise, with one edge inside the other.

CORDATE: Heart shaped, as applied to leaf blades or bases.

CORM: A bulblike, compressed underground stem.

COROLLA: The inner series of a perianth, composed of petals, either separate or fused into a tube.

COROLLA TUBE: The tubular base of the corolla.

CORONA: A circular appendage or group of appendages between the corolla and the stamens, as in *Asclepias*.

CORYMB: A flat-topped or convex, indeterminate inflorescence.

CRENATE: Round toothed.

CRENULATE: With small, rounded teeth.

CRISPED: Irregularly ruffled along the margin.

CROWN: The persistent base of a perennial—where stems and roots meet.

CRUCIFORM: Cross shaped, as in the flowers of the Cruciferae (Mustard family).

CULTIVAR: See Introduction.

CUTTING: A vegetative part of a plant cut for purposes of propagation. E.g., a stem cutting, a root cutting.

CYATHIUM (CYATHIA): The unit of inflorescence in *Euphorbia,* which includes one female and several male flowers, and other structures, surrounded by small bracts.

CYME: A more or less flat-topped, determinate inflorescence.

DEADHEAD: See Appendix: Gardening with Perennials.

DECIDUOUS: Falling off at the end of a growth period or season. E.g., deciduous sepals, deciduous leaves.

DECUMBENT: Reclining on the ground, with the tip ascending or erect. E.g., a decumbent stem.

DECURRENT: Attached to the stem over a certain length. E.g., a decurrent leaf base or petiole.

DECUSSATE: Opposite leaves alternating at right angles with the pair above and below.

DEFLEXED: See REFLEXED.

DEHISCENT: Splitting open at maturity along definite lines. E.g., a dehiscent seedpod.

DENTATE: Toothed. Strictly, with sharp teeth at right angles to the margin.

DETERMINATE: Said of an inflorescence in which the oldest flower is borne at the end of the main axis or centrally and which will not continue to produce new flowers terminally. E.g., a cyme.

DIFFUSE: Loosely branching or spreading.

DISK: The central part of the flower head in the Compositae (Sunflower family).

DISK FLORET: One of the tubular flowers composing the disk in Compositae (Sunflower family).

DISKOID: Having only disk flowers.

DISSECTED: Deeply cut into narrow segments.

DIVIDED: Cut to the base, or nearly so, into lobes.

ELLIPTIC: Shaped like an ellipse, wider at the center and tapering to equal tips.

ENTIRE: Not toothed or lobed. E.g., an entire leaf.

EQUITANT: Said of leaves folded inward and in two ranks, as in *Iris.*

EVEN PINNATE: Pinnate, with no terminal leaflet.

ETIOLATED: With weak, spindly growth caused by inadequate light conditions.

EXSERTED: Projecting outward and beyond. E.g., exserted stamens.

FARINOSE: Covered with a granular or mealy coating, as in certain species of *Primula.*

FILAMENT: The structure supporting the anther in a stamen.

FILAMENTOUS: Threadlike or composed of threads.

FILIFORM: Threadlike, slender with a rounded cross section.

FLORET: A small flower, part of an inflorescence.

FOLLICLE: A dry, dehiscent fruit, with one carpel, opening along one side only.

FRUIT: A mature ovary and its related structures.

FUNNELFORM: Funnel shaped. E.g., a funnelform corolla.

GLABROUS: Smooth, hairless.

GLAND: A secreting organ.

GLANDULAR HAIR: A hair tipped with a gland or glands.

GLAUCOUS: Covered with a waxy bloom, whitish or bluish and usually easily rubbed off.

GLOBOSE: Roughly spherical.

HABIT: The overall appearance or shape of a plant. E.g., an erect habit.

HASTATE: Shaped like an arrowhead, with the basal lobes pointing outward.

HEAD: An individual inflorescence in the Compositae (Sunflower family). By extension, dense inflorescences, as in *Scabiosa*.

HELICOID CYME: A coiled, determinate inflorescence, with flowers borne only on one side.

HIRSUTE: With rough, stiff hairs.

HISPID: With stiff, bristly hairs.

HOOD: Part of the corona, in *Asclepias*.

HORT.: Of gardens. Appended to invalid scientific names or to Latin names traditionally but incorrectly applied.

INCISED: Deeply cut with sharp, irregular teeth.

INDETERMINATE: Said of an inflorescence in which the youngest flower is borne at the end of the main axis or centrally, and which may continue to produce new flowers terminally.

INFLORESCENCE: A grouping of flowers in a definite pattern. E.g., an umbel, a panicle.

INTERNODE: A section of stem between two nodes.

INVOLUCRE: One or more whorls of bracts usually beneath a flower or inflorescence.

INVOLUTE: With margins rolled inward and upward over the upper surface. E.g., an involute leaf.

IRREGULAR FLOWER: A flower which is bilaterally but not radially symmetrical.

KEEL: The lower, united petals in a papilionaceous flower. A projecting central rib on the underside of a leaf.

LANCEOLATE: Lance shaped, longer than broad and tapering to a point at the tip.

LEAFLET: One of the divisions of a compound leaf.

LIGULATE: Strap shaped.

LIMB: The expanded part of the corolla.

LINEAR: Narrow, with parallel or nearly parallel sides.

LIP: The upper or lower part of a two-lipped corolla or calyx.

LOBE: A division or segment of a leaf, sepal, petal, or other organ.

LOBED: Cut into lobes, usually less than halfway.

LYRATE: Pinnatifid, with an enlarged terminal lobe and smaller lateral lobes.

MIDRIB: The main central vein of a leaf.

MONOCARPIC: Blooming and fruiting only once and then dying.

NATURALIZE: To adapt to a nonnative environment. To become naturalized.

NECTARY: A nectar-secreting gland or other organ, usually inside the base of the corolla.

NODE: The area on a stem, sometimes swollen, where leaves are attached.

OBLANCEOLATE: Inversely lanceolate, broader at the tip, tapering to the base.

OBLONG: Much longer than wide, with nearly parallel sides.

OBOVATE: Inversely ovate, broader at the tip than at the base.

ODD PINNATE: Pinnate, with a single terminal leaflet.

OFFSET: A lateral branch or plantlet developing from the base of the parent plant.

OPPOSITE: Arranged in opposing pairs along the stem. E.g., opposite leaves.

ORBICULAR: Roughly circular in outline.

OVATE: Egg shaped in outline, broader at the base than at the tip.

OVOID: Egg shaped three dimensionally.

PALATE: A projection on the lower lip of a two-lipped corolla obstructing the throat, as in *Linaria* and *Mimulus*.

PALMATE: With segments, veins, or leaflets radiating from a common point.

PALMATELY: In a palmate manner.

PANICLE: A branching, indeterminate inflorescence, with more than one flower per branch.

PAPILIONACEOUS FLOWER: The butterflylike flower of certain members of the Leguminosae (Pea family). Consisting of five petals, the uppermost or banner, two laterals or wings, and two lower ones united into a keel.

PAPILLA (PAPILLAE): A small, nipple-shaped protuberance.

PARTED: Deeply cut, more than halfway, into lobes.

PEA STICK: See Appendix: Gardening with Perennials.

PEDICEL: The stalk of an individual flower in an inflorescence.

PEDUNCLE: The stalk of an inflorescence or of a solitary flower.

PELTATE: Said of a leaf attached more or less centrally to its stalk. The leaf is usually in the shape of a shield or umbrella.

PENTAMEROUS: With parts in fives or multiples of five.

PERFOLIATE: Said of a leaf the base of which completely surrounds the stem, or of opposite leaves joined at the base and surrounding the stem.

PERIANTH: The combined outer and inner series of a flower; the calyx and the corolla or the tepals.

PERSISTENT: Remaining attached.

PETAL: One of the parts of the corolla of a flower, usually colored and conspicuous.

PETALOID: Petal-like.

PETIOLE: The stalk of a leaf.

PINNATE: With segments, veins, or leaflets arranged on both sides of a main axis.

PINNATELY: In a pinnate manner.

PINNATIFID: Pinnately cleft or divided.

PINNATISECT: Pinnately cut all the way to the midrib.

PISTIL: The female reproductive organ in a flower, composed of a stigma, style, and ovary.

POD: A general term for a dry, dehiscent fruit, particularly a fruit of a member of the Leguminosae (Pea family).

PRICKLE: A small, pointed outgrowth from the epidermis.

PROPAGATION: The reproduction of a plant by seed or vegetative means.

PROSTRATE: Lying flat on the ground. E.g., a prostrate stem.

PUBESCENT: Hairy. Strictly, covered with short, soft hairs.

RACEME: An unbranched, indeterminate inflorescence, with one flower per pedicel.

RADIATE: Having only ray florets.

RANKED: In a vertical row. E.g., two-ranked leaves, as in *Iris*.

RAY OR RAY FLORET: A ligulate flower, one of the marginal florets in a flower head of the Compositae.

RECURVED: Curved downward or backward.

REFLEXED: Sharply curved downward or backward.

REGULAR: Radially symmetrical. E.g., a regular flower.

RENIFORM: Kidney shaped.

RESUPINATE: Upside down, as the flowers in *Alonsoa*.

REVOLUTE: With the margins rolled inward and downward over the lower surface.

RHIZOME: A horizontal stem running underground or on the surface.

RHOMBIC: Roughly diamond shaped.

ROSETTE: A crowded circle of basal leaves.

ROTATE: Wheel shaped. E.g., a rotate corolla.

RUNCINATE: With coarse, sharp teeth or lobes pointing backward toward the base of the leaf.

RUNNER: A slender, trailing stem, rooting at the nodes.

SAGITTATE: Shaped like an arrowhead, with the basal lobes pointing backward.

SALVERFORM: Said of a corolla with a slender tube expanding into a flat limb, as in *Phlox*.

SCAPE: A leafless flower stalk arising from ground level.

SCORPIOID CYME: A coiled, determinate inflorescence, with flowers or branches alternating on opposite sides of the axis.

SCREE: A sloping, free-draining bed of crushed rock, gravel, grit, and sand, with only a small proportion of soil, used for growing temperamental alpines.

SEGMENT: A part of a leaf, petal, or other organ. E.g., a lobe.

SEPAL: One of the parts of the calyx.

SERRATE: Sharp toothed. Strictly, with the teeth pointing forward toward the apex.

SERRULATE: With small, sharp teeth.

SESSILE: Without a stalk. E.g., a sessile leaf, a sessile flower.

SHEATHING: Said of a leaf base or petiole which surrounds and encloses the stem.

SILICLE: A dry, dehiscent, two-carpeled fruit, as in the Cruciferae (Mustard family).

SIMPLE: Not compound. E.g., a simple leaf.

SINUATE: With a very wavy margin.

SINUS: A recess between two lobes, as in a leaf or petal.

SOLITARY: Borne singly. E.g., a solitary flower.

SPADIX: A dense flower spike, surrounded by a spathe, as in the Araceae (Arum family).

SPATHE: A large, sheathing bract enclosing the spadix, as in the Araceae (Arum family). A sheathing floral bract, as in *Iris*.

SPATULATE: In the shape of a spatula or a spoon.

SPIKE: An indeterminate inflorescence, with sessile flowers.

SPIKELET: A small or secondary spike.

SPINE: A hard, sharp-pointed, deep-seated outgrowth from a stem or other organ.

SPUR: A tubular or saclike projection of a petal or sepal.

STAMEN: The male reproductive organ in a flower, composed of an anther borne on a filament.

STAMINODE: A sterile stamen, often enlarged and petaloid.

STANDARD: See BANNER. Also the upper petal in *Impatiens*. One of the three inner perianth segments in *Iris*.

STIGMA: The apical end of the pistil, which receives the pollen.

STIPULE: A small scalelike or leaflike structure sometimes found at the base of a leaf petiole.

STOLON: A slender, trailing stem, rooting at the nodes.

STRIATE: With longitudinal stripes, grooves, or ridges.

STRICT: Stiffly erect.

STYLE: The slender stalk of a pistil, connecting the stigma and ovary.

SUBSHRUB: See Introduction.

SUBTEND: To be placed below. E.g., a bract subtending a flower.

SUCKER: See Offset.

TAPROOT: The long, primary root of some plants, such as *Lupinus*.

TENDRIL: A twisting, modified leaf, used for attachment or support.

TEPAL: A perianth segment not clearly differentiated into a petal or sepal, as in many members of the Iridaceae (Iris family).

TERNATE: Divided into three segments or with three leaflets.

TERNATELY: In a ternate manner.

TETRAPLOID: Having twice the usual number of chromosomes.

THROAT: The expanded part of the corolla between the tube and the limb.

THYRSE: A dense, ovoid panicle.

TOMENTOSE: Densely woolly.

TRI-: Three times. E.g., tripinnate.

TRIFOLIATE: Having three leaves.

TUBER: A food-storing, thickened underground stem.

TUBERCLE: A small, rounded projection, as on a leaf.

UMBEL: A flat-topped or convex indeterminate inflorescence, with more or less equal pedicels arising from a single point.

UNDULATE: With wavy margins—less so than sinuate.

URCEOLATE: Urn shaped. E.g., an urceolate corolla.

VALVE: One of the parts into which a dehiscent fruit splits.

VARIEGATED: Said of leaves lacking chlorophyll in some part and thus patterned, commonly in white or yellow.

VEGETATIVE: Asexual. E.g., vegetative propagation. Pertaining to the nonreproductive parts of a plant.

VENTRICOSE: Enlarged or inflated on one side. E.g., a ventricose corolla.

VERTICILLASTER: A false whorl composed of a pair of opposite cymes, as in the Labiatae (Mint family).

WHORL: A circle of three or more leaves or flowers around a stem.

WHORLED: In a whorl.

WING: A lateral petal in a papilionaceous flower, also in *Impatiens.*

WINGED: With flat appendages extending outward. E.g., a winged stem, a winged seed.

WOODY: Containing lignified tissue.

XEROPHYTE: A plant adapted to an arid environment.

BIBLIOGRAPHY

Asterisks indicate recommended reading.

Aden, Paul. "The Cultivation of Hostas." *The Garden.* Journal of the Royal Horticultural Society. May 1986.

————. *The Hosta Book.* Portland, OR: Timber Press, 1988.

American Penstemon Society. *Manual for Beginners.* 3rd edition. 1981.

* Bailey, L. H. *Manual of Cultivated Plants.* New York: Macmillan Publishing Co., Inc., 1977.

Barker, David. "Epimedium." *Bull. of the Hardy Plant Society.* June 1985.

Barton, J. Barbara. *Gardening by Mail 2: A Source Book.* Sebastopol, CA: Tusker Press, 1987.

Beckett, Kenneth A. "Bergenias." *The Garden.* J. of the R.H.S. December 1983.

* ————. *Growing Hardy Perennials.* London: Croom Helm Ltd., 1981.

————. "Ligularia." *The Garden.* J. of the R.H.S. March 1981.

Benham, Steve. "*Diascia*—A Survey of the Species in Cultivation." *The Plantsman.* June 1987.

Black, Marvin. "Hardy Euphorbias for the Border." *Pacific Horticulture.* Spring 1984.

Bloom, Alan. "Achilleas." *The Garden.* J. of the R.H.S. June 1979.

————. "Aconitums." *The Garden.* J. of the R.H.S. July 1979.

————. "*Aster* Species." *The Garden.* J. of the R.H.S. February 1980.

————. "Herbaceous Potentillas." *The Garden.* J. of the R.H.S. January 1977.

————. *Perennials for Your Garden.* Chicago: Floraprint U.S.A., 1981.

————. "Polygonums." *The Garden.* J. of the R.H.S. September 1977.

Blunt, Wilfrid. "More Poppycock." *The Garden.* J. of the R.H.S. November 1975.

Bond, John. "Agapanthus Trial." *The Garden.* J. of the R.H.S. August 1978.

————. "Ranunculus." *The Garden.* J. of the R.H.S. November 1976.

Bowden, Wray. "Perennial Tetraploid Lobelia Hybrids." *The Garden.* J. of the R.H.S. February 1984.

Bramwell, David and Zoe. *Wild Flowers of the Canary Islands.* Cheltenham, Gloucestershire: Stanley Thornes Ltd., 1974.

Brearley, Christopher. "Crested Irises of North America." *The Plantsman.* September 1985.

Brickell, Christopher, and Fay Sharmon. *The Vanishing Garden.* London: John Murray, 1986.

Brooks, A. E. *Australian Native Plants for Home Gardens.* Melbourne: Lothian Publishing Co. Pty Ltd., 1979.

Brown, Robert C. "Two for the Space of One." *Bull. of the Hardy Plant Society.* June 1986.

* Bubel, Nancy. *The New Seed-Starters Handbook.* Emmaus, PA: Rodale Press, 1988.

Buckley, A. R. *Canadian Garden Perennials.* Saanichton, B.C.: Hancock House Publishers Ltd., 1977.

Cassidy, G. E. and S. Linnegar. *Growing Irises.* London: Croom Helm Ltd., 1982.

* Chatto, Beth. *The Damp Garden.* London: J. M. Dent & Sons, Ltd., 1982.

* ————. *The Dry Garden.* London: J. M. Dent & Sons, Ltd., 1978.

Cheek, Roy. "New Zealand Flax." *The Garden.* J. of the R.H.S. March 1979.

* Clapham, A. R., T. G. Tutin, and E. F. Warburg. *Flora of the British Isles.* Cambridge: Cambridge Univ. Press, 1987.

Clark, David. *Pelargoniums.* Kew Gardening Guides. Portland, OR: Timber Press, 1988.

Colley, J. Cobb and Baldassare Mineo. "Lewisias for the Garden." *Pacific Horticulture.* Summer 1985.

Cribb, Philip. "Orchids Hardy in the British Isles." *The Plantsman.* March 1987.

Crook, H. Clifford. *Campanulas.* Sakonnet, RI: Theophrastus, 1977.

Eddison, Sydney. "Nicotianas Worth Growing." *Horticulture.* May 1988.

———. "Primrose Primer." *Fine Gardening.* May/June 1988.

Edwards, Colin. *Delphiniums.* London: J. M. Dent & Sons Ltd., 1981.

* Eliovson, Sima. *Wild Flowers of Southern Africa.* 7th edition. Johannesburg: Macmillan South Africa, 1984.

Elliot, Jack. "Some Liliaceae." *Bull. of the Hardy Plant Society.* December 1984.

Elliot, Joe. "*Alstroemeria* Ligtu Hybrids." *The Garden.* J. of the R.H.S. July 1984.

* Elliot, W. Rodger and David L. Jones. *Encyclopaedia of Australian Plants Suitable for Cultivation.* Melbourne: Lothian Publishing Company Pty. Ltd., 1983–86.

Evans, Alfred. *The Peat Garden and its Plants.* London: J. M. Dent & Sons, Ltd., 1974.

———. "The Rock Gardener's Dilemma." *The Garden.* J. of the R.H.S. May 1987.

Evans, Ronald L. *Handbook of Cultivated Sedums.* Northwood, Middlesex: Science Reviews Limited, 1983.

* Everett, Thomas H. *The New York Botanical Garden Illustrated Encyclopedia of Horticulture.* New York: Garland Publishing, Inc., 1981.

Fish, Margery. *Cottage Garden Flowers.* London: Faber & Faber Limited, 1980.

Flintoff, Jerry. "A Gardener's Guide to Epimediums." *Pacific Horticulture.* Winter 1983.

Gentry, Howard Scott. *Agaves of Continental North America.* Tucson: University of Arizona Press, 1982.

Gould, Ralph. "Notes on Coleus at Wisley." *The Garden.* J. of the R.H.S. October 1987.

Grey-Wilson, C. "A Survey of *Impatiens* in Cultivation." *The Plantsman.* September 1983.

Gulmon, S. L. and H. A. Mooney. "Alstroemerias: Colorful Perennials for Summer-Dry Climates." *Pacific Horticulture.* Spring 1980.

Hainsworth, Peter. "Meconopsis." *Bull. of the Hardy Plant Society.* June 1986.

Harmon, Stanley M. "Liatris." *American Horticulturist.* June 1987.

* Harper, Pamela and Frederick McGourty. *Perennials: How to Select, Grow and Enjoy.* Tucson: HP Books, Inc., 1985.

* Hartmann, Hudson T. and Dale E. Kester. *Plant Propagation.* 3rd edition. Englewood Cliffs, NJ: Prentice Hall, Inc., 1975.

Haw, Stephen. "*Bletilla striata.*" *The Garden.* J. of the R.H.S. July 1985.

———. "The Origins of the Garden Chrysanthemum." *The Garden.* J. of the R.H.S. November 1986.

Hebb, Robert S. *Low Maintenance Perennials.* New York: Quadrangle/The New York Times Book Co., 1975.

Heywood, V. H. *Flowering Plants of the World.* New York: Mayflower Books Inc., 1978.

Higgins, Vera. *Crassulas in Cultivation.* London: Blandford Press, 1964.

Hillard, O. M. and B. L. Burtt. "A Revision of *Diascia* Section Racemosae." *Journal of South African Botany* 50 (1984).

Hiroe, Minosuke. *Umbelliferae of Asia.* Kyoto: Kyoto University, 1958.

* Hobhouse, Penelope. *Color in Your Garden.* London: Collins, 1985.

Horst, R. Kenneth. *Westcott's Plant Disease Handbook.* 4th edition. New York: Van Nostrand Reinhold Company, 1979.

* *Hortus Third.* New York: Macmillan Publishing Co., Inc., 1976.

Hudak, Joseph. *Gardening with Perennials.* Portland, OR: Timber Press, 1985.

Ingwersen, Will. "Some Origanums for the Garden." *The Plantsman*. December 1981.

* Innes, Clive. *The World of Iridaceae*. Ashington, Sussex: Holly Gate International Ltd., 1985.

International Code of Botanical Nomenclature. 14th International Botanical Congress. Konigstein, FRG: Koeltz Scientific Books, 1988.

International Code of Nomenclature for Cultivated Plants. International Commission for the Nomenclature of Cultivated Plants of the I.U.B.S. Utrecht, Netherlands: Int. Bureau for Plant Taxonomy & Nomenclature, 1980.

Jepson, Carl E. and Leland F. Allen *Wild Flowers of Zion and Bryce Canyon*. Salt Lake City, Utah: Zion-Bryce Natural History Association, 1958.

Kearney, Thomas H. and Robert H. Peebles *Arizona Flora*. Berkeley: University of California Press, 1960.

Kelaidis, Panayoti. "Fiery Phloxes of Chihuahua." *Pacific Horticulture*. Winter 1984.

Kelly, John. "*Diascia* 'Ruby Field.' " Letter to the Editor. *The Plantsman*. September 1987.

Kohlein, Fritz. *Iris*. Portland, OR: Timber Press, 1987.

———. *Saxifrages and Related Genera*. Portland, OR: Timber Press, 1985.

Lloyd, Christopher. *The Adventurous Gardener*. New York: Random House, 1983.

———. *The Well-Chosen Garden*. London: Mermaid Books, 1985.

Macoboy, Stirling. *Perennials for Bed and Border*. Sydney: Lansdowne Press, 1983.

Mathew, Brian. "Hellebores." *The Garden*. J. of the R.H.S. March 1988.

———. *The Iris*. London: B. T. Batsford Ltd., 1981.

———. "A Survey of Hellebores." *The Plantsman*. June 1981.

———. "Pulmonarias in Gardens." *The Plantsman*. September 1982.

* Mathias, Mildred E., editor. *Flowering Plants in the Landscape*. Berkeley: University of California Press, 1982.

McClintock, Elizabeth and Victor Reiter. "*Puya alpestris* and *Puya berteroniana.* " *Pacific Horticulture*. Summer 1982.

Morley, Brian. "*Helichrysum bracteatum* and Allies." *The Garden*. J. of the R.H.S. December 1978.

Munz, Philip A. *A California Flora and Supplement*. Berkeley: University of California Press, 1973.

Oliver-Smith, Paul. "Mertensia." *Bull. of the Hardy Plant Society*. December 1984.

Peterson, Roger Tory and Margaret McKenny. *A Field Guide to Wildflowers of Northeastern and Northcentral North America*. Boston: Houghton Mifflin Company, 1968.

* Pirone, Pascal P. *Diseases and Pests of Ornamental Plants*. 5th edition. New York: John Wiley & Sons, 1978.

Polunin, Oleg. *Flowers of Europe*. London: Oxford University Press, 1969.

Polunin, Oleg and Adam Stainton *Flowers of the Himalayas*. Oxford: Oxford University Press, 1984.

Rickett, Harold William. *Wild Flowers of the United States*. New York: The New York Botanical Garden/ McGraw-Hill Book Company, 1965–1973.

Rix, Martyn. "A *Nepeta* in Kashmir." *The Plantsman*. September 1986.

———. "The Genus Acanthus L." *The Plantsman*. December 1980.

Rountree, Lester. *Hardy Californians*. Salt Lake City: Peregrine Smith, Inc., 1980.

Schilling, Tony. "A Survey of Cultivated Himalayan and Sino-Himalayan *Hedychium* Species." *The Plantsman*. December 1982.

Schmidt, Marjorie G. *Growing California Native Plants*. Berkeley: University of California Press, 1980.

———. "The Vancouverias." *Pacific Horticulture*. Winter 1977.

Schulz, Peggy. *All About Geraniums*. Garden City, NY: Doubleday & Company, Inc., 1965.

Sinnes, A. Cort. *All About Perennials.* San Francisco: Ortho Books, 1981.

Smith, Iain. "The Virtue of Honesty." *The Hardy Plant.* June 1985.

Snyder, Leon C. *Flowers for Northern Gardens.* Minneapolis: University of Minnesota Press, 1983.

Stout, A. B. *Daylilies.* Millwood, NY: Sagapress, Inc., 1986.

Straley, Gerald B. "Meconopsis for the Garden." *Pacific Horticulture.* Spring 1987.

* Sunset *New Western Garden Book.* Menlo Park, CA: Lane Publishing Co., 1979.

Tait, William A. "Herbaceous Perennials for the Autumn Woodland." *The Garden.* J. of the R.H.S. October 1987.

———. "Honesty, Bittercress and Ladies' Smocks." *The Garden.* J. of the R.H.S. August 1986.

Taylor, George. *Meconopsis.* 2nd edition. London: Waterstone & Saga Press, 1985.

Taylor, Jane. "Kniphofia." *The Garden.* J. of the R.H.S. December 1986.

———. "Kniphofia—A Survey." *The Plantsman.* December 1985.

* *Taylor's Guide to Perennials.* New York: Chanticleer Press, 1986.

* *The Royal Horticultural Society Dictionary of Gardening.* Oxford: Clarendon Press, 1984.

Thomas, Graham S. "Bugbane by Any Other Name." *The Garden.* J. of the R.H.S. June 1975.

* ———. *Perennial Garden Plants.* 2nd edition. London: J. M. Dent & Sons Ltd., 1982.

Turner, Roger. "A Review of Spurges for the Garden." *The Plantsman.* December 1983.

Tutin, T. G., et al. *Flora Europea.* Cambridge: Cambridge University Press, 1864–1980.

Tyree, Art. "Superpoppy." *Pacific Horticulture.* Fall 1981.

Weaver, Richard E., Jr. "In Praise of Epimediums." *Arnoldia.* March/April 1979.

———. "The Hellebores." *Arnoldia.* January/February 1979.

Webb, William J. *The Pelargonium Family.* Dover, NH: Croom Helm, 1984.

White, Anne Blanco. "An Iris for All Seasons." *The Garden.* J. of the R.H.S. December 1985.

Willis, J. C. *A Dictionary of the Flowering Plants and Ferns.* 8th edition. Cambridge: Cambridge University Press, 1985.

Wright, Michael. *The Complete Handbook of Garden Plants.* New York: Facts on File Publications, 1984.

Wilson, Helen Van Pelt. *The Joy of Geraniums.* New York: M. Barrows & Company, Inc., 1965.

Wrigley, J. W. and M. Fagg. *Australian Native Plants.* 2nd edition. Sydney: Collins, 1983.

* Wyman, Donald. *Wyman's Gardening Encyclopedia.* New York: Macmillan Publishing Co., Inc., 1971.

INDEX OF SYNONYMS

Acanthus latifolius: A. mollis 'Latifolius'
Acanthus longifolius: A. balcanicus
Acanthus lusitanicus Hort.: *A. mollis* 'Latifolius'
Acanthus spinosus: A. spinosissimus
Achillea borealis: A. millefolium var. *californica*
Achillea eupatorium: A. filipendulina
Aconitum autumnale: A. henryi 'Spark's Variety'
Aconitum californicum: A. henryi 'Spark's Variety'
Aconitum cammarum: A. x *bicolor*
Aconitum carmichaelii var. *wilsonii: A. carmichaelii wilsonii*
Aconitum fischeri: A. carmichaelii
Aconitum lycoctonum: A. vulparia
Aconitum napellus 'Spark's Variety': *A. henryi* 'Spark's Variety'
Aconitum napellus bicolor: A. x *bicolor*
Aconitum stoerkianum: A. x *bicolor*
Actaea alba: A. pachypoda
Actaea spicata var. *rubra: A. rubra*
Adenophora communis: A. liliifolia
Adenophora farreri: A. confusa
Adenophora stylosa: A. liliifolia
Adonis dahurica: A. amurensis
Aeonium pseudotabuliforme Hort.: *Aeonium undulatum*
Aethionema jacunda: A. coridifolium
Aethionema pulchellum: A. grandiflorum
Aethionema warleyense: A. x *warleyense*
Aethionema 'Warley Rose': *A.* x *warleyense*
Agapanthus campanulatus: A. campanulatus campanulatus
Agapanthus orientalis: A. praecox orientalis
Agapanthus umbellatus: A. praecox
Agapanthus umbellatus globosus: A. campanulatus patens
Agapanthus umbellatus Hort.: *A. africanus*
Agapanthus umbellatus minimus: A. praecox minimus
Agathaea coelestis: Felicia amelloides

Agave americana var. *americana: A. americana*
Agave fernandi-regis: A. victoriae-reginae
Agave huachucencis: A. parryi var. *huachucencis*
Agrostemma coronaria: Lynchis coronaria
Ajuga alpina: A. genevensis
Ajuga repens: A. reptans
Ajuga rugosa: A. genevensis
Aloe hanburiana: A. striata
Aloe perfoliata var. *vera: A. barbadensis*
Aloe vera: A. barbadensis
Alonsoa grandiflora Hort.: *A. warscewiczii*
Alpinia nutans Hort.: *A. zerumbet*
Alpinia speciosa: A. zerumbet
Alstroemeria pulchella: A. psittacina
Althaea kragujevacensis: A. officinalis
Althaea narbonensis: A. cannabina
Althaea taurinensis: A. officinalis
Althaea rosea: Alcea rosea
Althaea zebrina: Malva sylvestris 'Zebrina'
Alyssum corymbosum: Aurinia corymbosa
Alyssum edentulum: Aurinia petraea
Alyssum pedemontanum: A. montanum
Alyssum saxatile: Aurinia saxatilis
Amaracus dictamnus: Origanum dictamnus
Ammocalis rosea: Catharanthus roseus
Amsonia salicifolia: A. tabernaemontana salicifolia
Anacyclus pyrethrum var. *depressum: A. depressus*
Anagallis grandiflora: A. monelli linifolia
Anagallis linifolia: A. monelli linifolia
Anaphalis cinnamomea: A. margaritacea yedoensis
Anaphalis yedoensis: A. margaritacea yedoensis
Anchusa italica: A. azurea
Anchusa myosotidiflora: Brunnera macrophylla
Anemone capensis: A. tenuifolia
Anemone elegans: A. x *hybrida*

Anemone japonica: A. hupehensis var.
  japonica
Anemone japonica Hort.: *A.* x *hybrida*
Anemone nipponica: A. hupehensis var.
  japonica
Anemone ranunculoides var. *pleniflora:*
  A. ranunculoides 'Flore-Pleno'
Anemone stellata: A. hortensis
Anemone vitifolia Hort.: *A. tomentosa*
Angelica officinalis: A. archangelica
Angelonia grandiflora Hort.: *A. salicariifolia*
Anigozanthos coccineus: A. flavidus
Anthemis biebersteiniana: A. marschalliana
Anthemis frutescens Hort.: *Chrysanthemum*
  frutescens
Anthemis rudolphiana: A. marschalliana
Anthericum algeriense: A. liliago major
Anthericum liliastrum: Paradisia liliastrum
Aquilegia akitensis: A. flabellata
Aquilegia atropurpurea: A. viridiflora
Aquilegia californica: A. formosa var.
  truncata
Aquilegia fauriei: A. flabellata
Aquilegia japonica: A. flabellata
Aquilegia lutea: A. viridiflora
Arabis albida: A. caucasica
Arabis alpina Hort.: *A. caucasica*
Arabis billardieri: A. caucasica
Arabis mollis Hort.: *A. procurrens*
Archangelica officinalis: Angelica
  archangelica
Arctotis calendulacea: Arctotheca calendula
Arctotis grandis: A. stoechadifolia var.
  grandis
Arctotis scapigera: A. acaulis
Arisaema atrorubens: A. triphyllum
Aristea major: A. thyrsiflora
Armeria caespitosa: A. juniperifolia
Armeria cephalotes: A. pseudoarmeria
Armeria formosa Hort.: *A. pseudoarmeria*
Armeria latifolia: A. pseudoarmeria
Armeria laucheana Hort.: *A. maritima*
  'Laucheana'
Armeria maritima forma *laucheana:*
  A. maritima 'Laucheana'
Armeria montana: A. plantaginea
Armeria rigida: A. plantaginea
Armeria stenophylla: A. plantaginea
Arnebia echioides: Echioides longiflorum

Artemisia albula: A. ludoviciana albula
Artemisia canescens, see *A. splendens* Hort.
Artemisia gnaphalodes: A. ludoviciana
Artemisia ludoviciana var. *gnaphalodes:*
  A. ludoviciana
Artemisia palmeri Hort.: *A. ludoviciana*
Artemisia purshiana: A. ludoviciana
Artemisia procera: A. abrotanum
Artemisia splendens, see *A. splendens* Hort.
Artemisia versicolor, see *A. splendens* Hort.
Arum italicum italicum: A. italicum
  'Pictum'
Arum pictum marmoratum Hort.:
  A. italicum 'Marmoratum'
Aruncus sylvester: A. dioicus
Asperula odorata: Galium odoratum
Asperula suberosa: A. gussonii
Asphodelus liburnicus: Asphodeline liburnica
Asphodelus luteus: Asphodeline lutea
X *Asterago lutea:* X *Solidaster luteus*
Aster corymbosus: A. divaricatus
Aster douglasii: A. subspicatus
Aster hybridus luteus: X *Solidaster luteus*
Aster luteus: X *Solidaster luteus*
Aster multiflorus: A. ericoides
Aster subcaeruleus: A. tongolensis
Astilbe chinensis taquetii 'Superba':
  A. taquetii 'Superba'
Astrantia helleborifolia: A. maxima
Astrantia major involucrata Hort.: *A. major*
  carinthiaca
Baptisia caerulea: B. australis
Baptisia exaltata: B. australis
Beleperone guttata: Justicia brandegeana
Bergenia beesiana: B. purpurascens
Bergenia bifolia: B. crassifolia
Bergenia delavayi: B. purpurascens
Bergenia ligulata: B. ciliata
Betonica grandiflora: Stachys grandiflora
Betonica macrantha: Stachys grandiflora
Betonica officinalis: Stachys officinalis
Bidens atrosanguinea: Cosmos atrosanguineus
Blandfordia flammea: B. grandiflora
Blandfordia marginata: B. punicea
Bletia hyacinthina: Bletilla striata
Bletia striata: Bletilla striata
Bletilla hyacinthina: B. striata
Bocconia cordata: Macleaya cordata
Bocconia japonica: Macleaya cordata

Bocconia microcarpa: *Macleaya microcarpa*
Boltonia glastifolia: *B. asteroides*
Boltonia latisquama: *B. asteroides* var. *latisquama*
Brauneria purpurea: *Echinacea purpurea*
Bryophyllum fedtschenkoi: *Kalanchoe fedtschenkoi*
Bulbine frutescens: *B. caulescens*
Bulbinella robusta: *B. floribunda*
Bulbinella robusta var. *latifolia*: *B. floribunda*
Bulbinella setosa: *B. floribunda*
Bulbinella caudata: *B. cauda-felis*
Buphthalmum salicifolium: *Inula* 'Golden Beauty'
Buphthalmum speciosum: *Telekia speciosa*
Calamintha nepetoides: *C. nepeta nepeta*
Caltha parnassifolia: *C. palustris*
Campanula bellardii: *C. cochleariifolia*
Campanula garganica: *C. elatines* var. *garganica*
Campanula grandis: *C. persicifolia*
Campanula latiloba: *C. persicifolia*
Campanula muralis: *C. portenschlagiana*
Campanula pusilla: *C. cochleariifolia*
Campanula turbinata: *C. carpatica* var. *turbinata*
Canna x *hortensis*: *C.* x *generalis*
Carlina acaulis 'Caulescens': *C. acaulis simplex*
Carlina acaulis caulescens Hort.: *C. acaulis simplex*
Cautleya lutea: *C. gracilis*
Cautleya robusta Hort.: *C. spicata*
Centaurea argentea: *C. gymnocarpa*
Centaurea candidissima: *C. cineraria*
Centaurea dealbata 'John Coutts': *C. hypoleuca* 'John Coutts'
Centaurea maritima: *Senecio cinerea*
Centaurea rutifolia: *C. cineraria*
Centaurea steenbergii Hort.: *C. dealbata steenbergii*
Cephalaria tatarica Hort.: *C. gigantea*
Cerastium columnae: *Cerastium tomentosum*
Chamaenerion angustifolium: *Epilobium angustifolium*
Chartolepis glastifolia: *Centaurea glastifolia*
Cheiranthus allionii: *Erysimum allionii* Hort.
Cheiranthus alpinus: *Erysimum alpinum*

Cheiranthus 'Bowles Purple': *Cheiranthus* 'Bowles Mauve'
Cheiranthus linifolius: *Erysimum linifolium*
Cheiranthus mutabilis: *C. semperflorens*
Cheiranthus senoneri: *C. cheiri*
Chelone barbata: *Penstemon barbatus*
Chrysanthemum densum amanum: *Tanacetum densum* 'Amanum'
Chrysanthemum erubescens Hort.: *C.* x *rubellum* Hort.
Chrysanthemum x *hortorum*: *C.* x *morifolium*
Chrysanthemum maximum Hort.: *C.* x *superbum*
Chrysanthemum serotinum: *C. uliginosum*
Chrysanthemum vulgare: *Tanacetum vulgare*
Chrysanthemum zawadskii latilobum: *C.* x *rubellum* Hort.
Chrysobactron hookeri: *Bulbinella hookeri*
Cicerbita: *Lactuca*
Cicerbita alpina: *Lactuca alpina*
Cimicifuga cordifolia: *C. racemosa cordifolia*
Cimicifuga foetida var. *intermedia*: *C. simplex*
Cimicifuga ramosa: *C. simplex ramosa*
Cineraria candidissima Hort.: *Senecio vira-vira*
Cineraria maritima var. *candidissima* Hort.: *Senecio vira-vira*
Cirsium acaule: *Carlina acaulis simplex*
Clematis davidiana: *C. heracleifolia davidiana*
Clematis douglasii scottii: *C. scottii*
Clematis mandshurica: *C. recta mandshurica*
Cnicus atropurpureus: *Cirsium rivulare atropurpureum*
Cnicus centauroides: *Centaurea cynaroides*
Coleus aromaticus: *C. amboinicus*
Coleus rehneltianus: *C. pumilus*
Conoclinium coelestinum: *Eupatorium coelestinum*
Cotyledon caespitosa: *Dudleya caespitosa*
Cotyledon californica: *Dudleya caespitosa*
Cotyledon viscida var. *insularis*: *Dudleya virens*
Craspedia uniflora: *C. glauca*
Crassula falcata: *C. perfoliata* var. *falcata*
Crassula quadrifolia: *C. multicava*
Crinitaria linosyris: *Aster linosyris*

Crucianella stylosa: Phuopsis stylosa
Cryptostemma calendulaceum: Arctotheca
    calendula
Cynoglossum longiflorum: Lindelofia
    longiflora
Cypripedium hirsutum: C. reginae
Cypripedium parviflorum: C. calceolus var.
    parviflorum
Cypripedium parviflorum var. *pubescens:*
    C. calceolus var. *pubescens*
Cypripedium pubescens: C. calceolus var.
    pubescens
Cypripedium spectabile: C. reginae
Delphinium chinense: D. grandiflorum
Delphinium sinense: D. grandiflorum
Delphinium sulphureum Hort.:
    D. semibarbatum
Delphinium zalil: D. semibarbatum
Dendranthema chanetti: Chrysanthemum
    chanetti
Dendranthema indicum: Chrysanthemum
    indicum
Dendranthema lavandulifolium:
    Chrysanthemum lavandulifolium
Diascia elegans Hort.: *D. vigilis*
Dietes catenulata: D. vegeta
Dietes iridoides: D. vegeta
Digitalis ambigua: D. grandiflora
Digitalis canariensis: Isoplexis canariensis
Dimorphotheca barbarae: Osteospermum
    barberae
Dimorphotheca ecklonis: Osteospermum
    ecklonis
Dimorphotheca fruticosa: Osteospermum
    fruticosum
Dracocephalum govianum: Nepeta
    governiana
Dracocephalum sibiricum: Nepeta sibirica
Drejeralla guttata: Justicia brandegeana
Dudleya grandis Hort.: *Dudleya brittonii*
Dudleya ingens Hort.: *Dudleya brittonii*
Echeveria albida: Dudleya virens
Echeveria cotyledon: Dudleya caespitosa
Echeveria laxa: Dudleya caespitosa
Echeveria pulverulenta: Dudleya pulverulenta
Echinops commutatus: Echinops exaltatus
Echinops ritro tenuifolius: E. ritro ruthenicus
Echinops ruthenicus: E. ritro ruthenicus
Echium bourgaeanum: E. wildpretii

Elvetria: Orthrosanthus
Epilobium rosmarinifolium: E. dodonaei
Epimedium alpinum 'Rubrum':
    E. x rubrum
Epimedium x coccineum: E. x rubrum
Epimedium grandiflorum var. *niveum:*
    E. x youngianum 'Niveum'
Epimedium hexandrum: Vancouveria
    hexandra
Epimedium lilacinum Hort.:
    E. x youngianum 'Roseum'
Epimedium macranthum: E. grandiflorum
Epimedium macranthum var. *niveum:*
    E. x youngianum 'Niveum'
Epimedium niveum: E. x youngianum
    'Niveum'
Epimedium pinnatum 'Sulphureum':
    E. x versicolor 'Sulphureum'
Epimedium sulphureum: E. x versicolor
    'Sulphureum'
Eremurus aurantiacus: E. stenophyllus
Eremurus bungei: E. stenophyllus
Eremurus x shelfordii Hort.: *E. x*
    isabellinus
Eremurus stenophyllus bungei:
    E. stenophyllus
Eremurus stenophyllus var. *bungei:*
    E. stenophyllus
Eremurus x warei Hort.: *E. x isabellinus*
Erigeron grandiflorus: E. speciosus
    macranthus
Erigeron hispidus: E. glaucus
Erigeron macranthus: E. speciosus
    macranthus
Erigeron mucronatus: E. karvinskianus
Eriogonum rubescens: E. grande var.
    rubescens
Eriophyllum caespitosum: E. lanatum
Epipactis latifolia: E. helleborine
Erodium olympicum: E. absinthoides
Ervum gracile: Vicia unijuga
Eryngium balsanae: E. eburneum
Eryngium paniculatum: E. eburneum
Eryngium pandanifolium: E. descaisneana
Eryngium tripartitum Hort.:
    E. x tripartitum
Erysimum asperum: E. allionii Hort.
Erysimum linifolium 'E. A. Bowles':
    Cheiranthus 'Bowles Mauve'

Erysimum perofskianum Hort.: *E. allionii* Hort.

Eupatorium ageratoides: E. rugosum

Eupatorium fraseri Hort.: *E. rugosum*

Eupatorium frasieri: E. rugosum

Eupatorium urticifolium: E. rugosum

Euphorbia biglandulosa: E. rigida

Euphorbia characias: E. characias characias

Euphorbia epithymoides: E. polychroma

Euphorbia robbiae: E. amygdaloides var. *robbiae*

Euphorbia veneta: E. characias wulfenii

Euphorbia wulfenii: E. characias wulfenii

Farfugium grande: Ligularia tussilaginea

Felicia capensis: F. amelloides

Filipendula hexapetala: F. vulgaris

Filipendula lobata: F. rubra

Fissipes acaulis: Cypripedium acaule

Francoa glabrata: F. ramosa

Francoa ramosa: F. appendiculata

Francoa sonchifolia: F. appendiculata

Funkia: Hosta

Funkia fortunei robusta: Hosta sieboldiana

Funkia glauca: Hosta sieboldiana

Funkia japonica: Hosta plantaginea

Funkia lanceolata: Hosta lancifolia

Funkia ovata albopicta: Hosta fortunei 'Albo-picta'

Funkia ovata aurea: Hosta fortunei 'Albo-picta'

Funkia sieboldiana condensata: Hosta tokudama

Funkia sieboldii: Hosta sieboldiana

Funkia subcordata: Hosta plantaginea

Funkia undulata: Hosta undulata

Galax aphylla: G. urceolata

Galeobdolon: Lamiastrum

Galeobdolon luteum: Lamiastrum galeobdolon

Galium triandrum: Asperula tinctoria

Gazania leucolaena: G. ringens var. *leucolaena*

Gazania longiscapa: G. linearis

Gazania pavonia: G. krebsiana

Gazania pinnata: G. pectinata

Gazania ringens var. *uniflora: G. ringens* var. *leucolaena*

Gazania splendens Hort.: *G. ringens*

Gazania uniflora: G. ringens var. *leucolaena*

Gentiana cordifolia: G. septemfida

Gentiana septemfida lagodechiana: G. lagodechiana

Geranium anemonifolium: Geranium palmatum

Geranium armenum: G. psilostemon

Geranium endressii 'A. T. Johnson': G. x *oxonianum* 'A. T. Johnson'

Geranium grandiflorum: G. himalayense

Geranium grandiflorum alpinum Hort.: G. *himalayense*

Geranium sanguineum lancastriense: G. *sanguineum* var. *striatum*

Geranium sanguineum var. *lancastriense:* G. *s.* var. *striatum*

Geranium sanguineum var. *prostratum: G. s.* var. *striatum*

Geum chilense: G. quellyon

Geum chiloense: G. quellyon

Geum coccineum Hort.: *G. quellyon*

Glandularia: Verbena

Glandularia canadensis: Verbena canadensis

Glaucium luteum: G. flavum

Gnaphalium lanatum: Helichrysum petiolare

Gnaphalium leontopodium: Leontopodium alpinum

Gunnera tinctoria: G. chilensis

Gypsophila dubia: G. repens

Hedychium acuminatum: H. spicatum var. *acuminatum*

Hedychium coronarium var. *flavescens:* H. *flavescens*

Hedychium gardnerianum: H. gardneranum

Hedychium maximum: H. coronarium var. *maximum*

Heeria: Heterocentron

Heeria elegans: Heterocentron elegans

Heeria rosea: Heterocentron macrostachyum

Helianthemum chamaecistus: H. *nummularium*

Helianthemum glaucum: H. croceum

Helianthemum grandiflorum: H. *nummularium grandiflorum*

Helianthemum poliifolium: H. apenninum

Helianthemum pulverulentum: H. *apenninum*

Helianthemum rhodanthum: H. apenninum var. *roseum*

Helianthemum variabile: H. nummularium

Helianthemum velutinum: H. apenninum
Helianthemum vulgare: H. nummularium
Helianthus orgyalis: Helianthus salicifolius
Helianthus scaberrimus: H. rigidus
Helichrysum petiolatum: H. petiolare
Heliopsis laevis: H. helianthoides
Heliopsis scabra: H. helianthoides scabra
Heliotropium corymbosum: H. arborescens
Heliotropium peruvianum: H. arborescens
Helleborus alnifolius: H. niger macranthus
Helleborus corsicus: H. argutifolius
Helleborus lividus corsicus: H. argutifolius
Helleborus niger alnifolius: H. niger
    macranthus
Hemerocallis aurantiaca littorea: H. littorea
Hemerocallis flava: H. lilioasphodelus
Hemerocallis graminea: H. dumortieri
Hemerocallis hybrida: H. x hybrida
Hemerocallis sieboldii: H. dumortieri
Heracleum lanatum: H. sphondylium
    montanum
Hesperaloe yuccifolia: H. parviflora
Hesperoyucca whipplei: Yucca whipplei
Heterocentron roseum: H. macrostachyum
Heterotheca mariana: Chrysopsis mariana
Heterotheca villosa: Chrysopsis villosa
Hexastylis arifolia: Asarum arifolium
Hexastylis shuttleworthii: Asarum
    shuttleworthii
Hexastylis virginica: Asarum virginicum
Hibiscus californicus: H. lasiocarpus
Hibiscus grandiflorus Hort.: *H. moscheutos*
    hybrids
Hibiscus incanus: H. lasiocarpus
Hibiscus lasiocarpus var. *californicus:*
    H. lasiocarpus
Hibiscus meehanii Hort.: *H. moscheutos*
    hybrids
Hibiscus speciosus: H. coccineus
Hieracium brunneocroceum: H. aurantiacum
Hieracium tomentosum: H. lanatum
Hieracium waldsteinii Hort.: *H. lanatum*
Hieracium welwitschii Hort.: *H. lanatum*
Hosta albomarginata: H. sieboldii
Hosta caerulea: H. ventricosa
Hosta erromena: H. undulata 'Erromena'
Hosta fortunei robusta: H. sieboldiana
Hosta fortunei viridis-marginata: H. fortunei
    'Albo-picta'

Hosta glauca: H. sieboldii, H. tokudama
Hosta 'Hyacinthina': *H. fortunei* var.
    hyacinthina
Hosta japonica: H. lancifolia, H. plantaginea
Hosta lancifolia marginata: H. sieboldii
Hosta lancifolia tardiflora: H. tardiflora
Hosta lancifolia var. *fortis: H. undulata*
    'Erromena'
Hosta lancifolia var. *undulata: H. undulata*
Hosta 'Makaimo Minor': *H. nakaiana*
Hosta media-picta: H. undulata
Hosta nigrescens elatior: H. 'Krossa Regal'
Hosta ovata: H. ventricosa
Hosta sieboldiana glauca: H. tokudama
Hosta spathulata: H. plantaginea
Hosta sparsa: H. tardiflora
Hosta subcordata: H. plantaginea
Hosta 'Thomas Hogg': *H. decorata*
Hosta variegata: H. undulata
Hylomecon vernalis: H. japonicum
Hymenocyclus croceus: Malephora crocea
Hymenocyclus luteus: Malephora lutea
Hymenocyclus purpureocroceus: Malephora
    crocea var. *purpureocrocea*
Hyssopus aristata: H. officinalis
Hyssopus vulgaris: H. officinalis
Iberis garrexiana: I. sempervirens
Iberis jacunda: Aethionema coridifolium
Imantophyllum miniatum: Clivia miniata
Impatiens herzogii: I. hawkeri
Impatiens holstii: I. wallerana
Impatiens mooreana: I. hawkeri
Impatiens schlechteri: I. hawkeri
Impatiens sultanii: I. wallerana
Inula afghanica Hort.: *I. magnifica*
Inula glandulosa: I. orientalis
Iris aequiloba: I. pumila
Iris bastardii: I. pseudacorus
Iris dichotoma: Pardanthopsis dichotomus,
    see *Belamcanda*
Iris douglasiana var. *watsoniana* Hort.:
    I. douglasiana
Iris florentina: I. 'Florentina'
Iris foliosa: I. brevicaulis, see Louisiana Iris
Iris fulva: I. cuprea, see Louisiana Iris
Iris x *germanica* var. *florentina: I.* 'Florentina'
Iris glauca: I. pallida
Iris lutea: I. pseudacorus
Iris kaemperi Hort.: *I. ensata*

Iris lamancei: I. brevicaulis
Iris odorissima: I. pallida
I. orientalis: I. sanguinea, see *I. sibirica*
Iris pallida 'Variegata': *I. pallida dalmatica*
    'Variegata'
Iris pallido-coerulea: I. pallida
Iris robinsoniana: Dietes robinsoniana
Iris sibirica var. *orientalis: I. sanguinea,* see
    I. sibirica
Iris stylosa: I. unguicularis
Iris taurica: I. pumila
Iris tuberosa: Hermodactylus tuberosus
Iris watsoniana: I. douglasiana
Isotoma petraea: Laurentia petraea
Jacobinia suberecta: Dicliptera suberecta
Jasione perennis: J. laevis
Jasione pyrenaica: J. laevis
Kalanchoe globulifera var. *coccinea:*
    K. blossfeldiana
Kentranthus: Centranthus
Kirengeshoma palmata erecta: K. p. koreana
Kleinia aizoides: Senecio aizoides, see
    S. mandraliscae
Kleinia mandraliscae: Senecio mandraliscae
Kniphofia alooides: K. uvaria
Kniphofia alooides 'Maxima': *K. praecox*
Kniphofia macowanii: K. triangularis
Kniphofia nelsonii: K. triangularis
Kniphofia uvaria 'Grandiflora': *K. praecox*
Kniphofia uvaria 'Nobilis': *K. praecox*
Lamiastrum luteum: L. galeobdolon
Lamium galeobdolon: Lamiastrum
    galeobdolon
Lathyrus gmelinii: L. luteus
Lathyrus maritimus: L. japonicus
Lathyrus maritimus japonicus: L. japonicus
Laurentia axillaris: Isotoma axillaris
Leontopodium sibiricum: Leontopodium
    leontopodioides
Lepachys: Ratibida, see *Rudbeckia*
Lepachys pinnata: Ratibida pinnata
Leptandra virginica: Veronicastrum
    virginicum
Leptosyne gigantea: Coreopsis gigantea
Leptosyne maritima: Coreopsis maritima
Leucanthemum vulgare: Chrysanthemum
    leucanthemum
Leuzea centauroides: Centaurea cynaroides
Lewisia finchae: L. cotyledon

Lewisia purdyii: L. cotyledon
Liatris callilepis Hort.: *L. spicata*
Liatris scariosa Hort.: *L. aspera*
Ligularia clivorum: L. dentata
Ligularia kaempferi: L. tussilaginea
Ligularia tangutica: Senecio tanguticus
Limonium dumosum Hort.: *Goniolimon*
    tataricum var. *angustifolium*
Limoniun tataricum: Goniolimon tataricum
Linaria dalmatica: Linaria genistifolia
    dalmatica
Lindelofia spectabilis: L. longiflora
Linosyris vulgaris: Aster linosyris
Linum alpinum: L. perenne alpinum
Linum julicum: L. perenne alpinum
Linum lewisii: L. perenne lewisii
Liriope graminifolia: L. spicata
Liriope graminifolia densiflora: Liriope
    muscari
Liriope majestica Hort.: *L. muscari*
    'Majestic'
Liriope muscari densiflora Hort.: *L. muscari*
Liriope muscari var. *munroei* Hort.:
    L. muscari 'Munroi's White'
Liriope platyphylla: L. muscari
Lithospermum angustifolium: L. incisum, see
    L. caroliniense
Lithospermum caroliniensis: L. caroliniense
Lithospermum croceum: L. caroliniense
Lithospermum doerfleri: Moltkia doerfleri
Lithospermum linearifolium: L. incisum, see
    L. caroliniense
Lithospermum mandanense: L. incisum, see
    L. caroliniense
Lithospermum petraeum: Moltkia petraea
Lobelia x *hybrida: L.* x *gerardii*
Lobelia fulgens: L. splendens
Lobelia x *milleri: L.* x *gerardii*
Lobelia x *vedrariensis: L.* x *gerardii*
Lochnera rosea: Catharanthus roseus
Lunaria biennis: L. annua, see *L. rediva*
Lychnis vulgaris Hort.: *L. viscaria*
Lysimachia verticillata: L. punctata
Malva mauritiana: M. sylvestris mauritiana
Malva zebrina: M. sylvestris 'Zebrina'
Marrubium candidissimum: Marrubium
    incanum
Matricaria capensis Hort.: *Chrysanthemum*
    parthenium

Matricaria eximia Hort.: *Chrysanthemum*
  parthenium
Matricaria parthenoides Hort.:
  Chrysanthemum parthenium
Meconopsis baileyi: M. betonicifolia
Megapterium missouriensis: Oenothera
  missouriensis
Megasea: Bergenia
Mentha gentilis: M. x *gentilis* 'Variegata'
Mentha rotundifolia 'Variegata':
  M. suaveolens 'Variegata'
Mesembryanthemum edule: Carpobrotus
  edulis
Mimulus bartonianus Hort.: *M. lewisii*
Mimulus grandiflorus: M. guttatus
Mimulus langsdorfii: M. guttatus
Mimulus luteus Hort.: *M. guttatus*
Mimulus tigrinus: M. x *hybridus*
Mondo jaburan: Ophiopogon jaburan
Mondo japonicum: Ophiopogon japonicus
Moraea bicolor: Dietes bicolor
Moraea catenulata: Dietes vegeta
Moraea chimboracensis: Orthrosanthus
  chimboracensis
Moraea iridoides: Dietes vegeta
Moraea robinsoniana: Dietes robinsoniana
Moraea vegeta: Dietes vegeta
Moschosma riparium: Iboza riparia
Mulgedium: Lactuca
Mulgedium alpinum: Lactuca alpina
Mulgedium bourgaei: Lactuca bourgaei
Nepeta gigantea Hort.: *N.* 'Six Hills
  Giant'
Nepeta govaniana: N. governiana
Nepeta macrantha: N. sibirica
Nepeta mussinii Hort.: *N.* x *faassenii*
Nicotiana affinis: N. alata
Nierembergia caerulea: N. hippomanica var.
  violacea
Nierembergia frutescens: N. scoparia
Nierembergia hippomanica Hort.: *N. h.* var.
  violacea
Nierembergia hippomanica var. *caerulea:*
  N. h. var. *violacea*
Nierembergia rivularis: N. repens
Nolana atriplicifolia: N. paradoxa
Nolana grandiflora: N. paradoxa
Nolana lanceolata: N. acuminata
Nolana prostrata: N. humifusa

Nordmannia cordifolia: Trachystemon
  orientalis
Oakesiella puberula: Uvularia caroliniana
Oakesiella sessilifolia: Uvularia sessilifolia
Oenothera cineus: O. tetragona fraseri
Oenothera fruticosa fraseri: O. tetragona
  fraseri
Oenothera fruticosa youngii: O. tetragona
Oenothera glauca: O. tetragona, O. tetragona
  fraseri
Oenothera macrocarpa: O. missouriensis
Oenothera speciosa childsii: O. berlandieri
Oenothera sulphurea Hort.: *O. odorata*
Oenothera youngii Hort.: *O. tetragona*
Ophiopogon arabicus Hort.: *O. planiscapus*
  'Arabicus'
Ophiopogon muscari: Liriope muscari
Ophiopogon planiscapus 'Nigrescens': *O. p.*
  'Arabicus'
Ophiopogon planiscapus 'Nigricans': *O. p.*
  'Arabicus'
Orobus aurantiacus: Lathyrus luteus aureus
Orobus lathyroides: Vicia unijuga
Orobus luteus: Lathyrus luteus
Orobus vernus: Lathyrus vernus
Oreocome candollei: Selinum candollei
Origanum vulgare 'Aureum': *Origanum*
  vulgare var. *aureum*
Paeonia albiflora: P. lactiflora
Paeonia anomala: P. x *smouthii*
Paeonia anomala smouthii: P. x *smouthii*
Paeonia chinensis Hort.: *P. lactiflora*
Paeonia edulis: P. lactiflora
Paeonia fragrans: P. lactiflora
Paeonia laciniata: P. x *smouthii*
Paeonia sinensis Hort.: *P. lactiflora*
Paeonia triternata: P. daurica
Papaver bracteatum: P. orientale
Papaver macounii: P. nudicaule
Papaver miyabeanum: P. nudicaule
Parahebe perfoliata: Veronica perfoliata
Pardanthus chinensis: Belamcanda chinensis
Parthenium matricaria: Chrysanthemum
  parthenium
Patersonia fragilis: P. glauca
Patrinia palmata: P. triloba
Pelargonium terebinthinaceum: P. graveolens
Penstemon 'Flathead Lake': *P.* x *johnsoniae*
Penstemon x *gloxinoides: P. gloxinoides* Hort.

Penstemon x *hybridus: P. gloxinoides* Hort.
Penstemon pubescens: P. hirsutus
Penstemon viscosa Hort.: *P. russeliana*
Pentas carnea: P. lanceolata
Petasites vulgaris: P. x *hybridus*
Phlomis laciniata: Eremostachys laciniata
Phlomis leonurus: Leonotis leonurus
Phlox amoena Hort.: *P.* x *procumbens,* see
    P. stolonifera
Phlox aristata: P. pilosa, see *P. divaricata*
Phlox canadensis: P. divaricata
Phlox decussata: P. paniculata
Phlox reptans: P. stolonifera
Phlox suffruticosa Hort.: *P. caroliniana*
Phormium cookianum: P. colensoi
Physalis franchetii: P. alkekengi
Physostegia virginiana 'Bouquet Rose': *P. v.*
    speciosa 'Rose Bouquet'
Physostegia virginiana 'Rose Bouquet': *P. v.*
    speciosa 'Rose Bouquet'
Phytolacca decandra: P. americana
Piquetia pillansii: Kensitia pillansii
Pimpinella magna 'Rosea': *P. major* 'Rubra'
Pimpinella magna 'Rubra': *P. major* 'Rubra'
Plumbago larpentae: Ceratostigma
    plumbaginoides
Podophyllum emodi: P. hexandrum
Polemonium amoenum: P. carneum
Polemonium caeruleum 'Album':
    P. caeruleum lacteum
Polemonium filicinum: P. foliosissimum
Polemonium haydenii: P. pulcherrimum
Polemonium lindleyii: P. pulcherrimum
Polygonatum canaliculatum: P. biflorum
Polygonatum falcatum 'Variegatum':
    P. odoratum thunbergii 'Variegatum'
Polygonatum giganteum Hort.:
    P. commutatum
Polygonatum japonicum: P. odoratum
    thunbergii
Polygonatum multiflorum Hort.:
    P. x *hybridum*
Polygonatum multiflorum striatum:
    P. x *hybridum* 'Variegatum'
Polygonatum officinale: P. odoratum
Polygonatum thunbergii: P. odoratum
    thunbergii
Polygonum compactum: P. cuspidatum
    'Compactum'

Polygonum filiforme: Tovara virginiana
    filiformis
Polygonum macrophyllum:
    P. sphaerostachyum, see *P. bistorta*
    'Superbum'
Polygonum oxyphyllum: P. amplexicaule,
    P. a. 'Album'
Polygonum reynoutria Hort.: *P. cuspidatum*
    'Compactum'
Polygonum sieboldii: P. cuspidatum
Polygonum virginianum: Tovara virginiana
Porteranthus trifoliatus: Gillenia trifoliata
Potentilla argyrophylla atrosanguinea:
    P. atrosanguinea
Potentilla coccinea: P. nepalensis
Potentilla formosa: P. nepalensis
Potentilla tonguei: P. x *tonguei*
Potentilla tormentilla-formosa: P. x *tonguei*
Potentilla warrenii Hort.: *P. recta* 'Warrenii'
Potentilla willmottiae: P. nepalensis 'Miss
    Willmott'
Potentilla verna: P. tabernaemontani
Poterium canadense: Sanguisorba canadensis
Poterium obtusum: Sanguisorba obtusa
Poterium tenuifolium: Sanguisorba tenuifolia
Primula acaulis: P. vulgaris
Primula alpina: P. auricula
Primula cachemiriana: P. denticulata
Primula hirta: P. rubra, see *P. auricula*
Primula hybrida: P. vulgaris
Primula littoniana: P. vialii
Primula lutea: P. auricula
Primula officinalis: P. veris
Primula x *variabilis: P.* x *tomasinii,* see
    P. veris
Prunella grandiflora hastifolia: P. g.
    pyrenaica, see *P. webbiana* Hort.
Prunella grandiflora webbiana: P. webbiana
    Hort.
Ptilotrichum spinosum: Alyssum spinosum
Pulmonaria azurea: P. angustifolia
Pulmonaria lutea Hort.: *Symphytum*
    grandiflorum
Pulmonaria maculata: P. officinalis
Pulmonaria maritima: Mertensia maritima
Pulmonaria montana: P. rubra
Pulsatilla amoena: Anemone pulsatilla
Pulsatilla nuttalliana: Anemone nuttalliana
Pulsatilla vulgaris: Anemone pulsatilla

Puya whytei: P. alpestris
Pyrethrum parthenium: Chrysanthemum
    parthenium
Pyrethrum roseum: Chrysanthemum
    coccineum
Ranunculus acris multiplex: R. acris
    'Flore-Pleno'
Ranunculus acris plenus: R. acris
    'Flore-Pleno'
Ranunculus bulbosus 'Speciosus Plenus':
    R. speciosus plenus Hort.
Ranunculus gouanii 'Plenus': R. speciosus
    plenus Hort.
Ratibida, see Rudbeckia
Rectanthera: Callisia
Reinwardtia tetragyna: R. indica
Reinwardtia trigyna: R. indica
Reynoutria japonica: Polygonum cuspidatum
Reynoutria sachalinensis: Polygonum
    sachalinense
Rhaponticum cynaroides: Centaurea
    cynaroides
Rhaponticum cynaroides scariosum:
    Centaurea rhaponticum
Rheum palmatum 'Atropurpureum':
    R. p. tanguticum
Rheum palmatum 'Rubrum':
    R. p. 'Atrosanguineum'
Rhodiola rosea: Sedum rosea
Richardia aethiopica Hort.: Zantedeschia
    aethiopica
Richardia africana: Zantedeschia aethiopica
Rochea falcata: Crassula perfoliata var.
    falcata
Roscoea superba: R. purpurea procera
Rudbeckia deamii: R. fulgida deamii
Rudbeckia newmanii: R. fulgida speciosa
Rudbeckia pinnata: Ratibida pinnata, see
    Rudbeckia
Rudbeckia purpurea: Echinacea purpurea
Rudbeckia speciosa Hort.: R. fulgida
    speciosa
Rudbeckia speciosa sullivantii: R. fulgida
    sullivantii
Ruellia amoena: R. graecizans
Ruellia longiflora: R. graecizans
Salvia ambigens: S. guaranitica
Salvia azurea pitcheri: S. azurea var.
    grandiflora

Salvia coerulea: S. guaranitica
Salvia forskaohlei: S. forskahlei
Salvia nemerosa Hort.: S. x superba
Salvia pitcheri: S. azurea var. grandiflora
Salvia rutilans: S. elegans
Salvia x sylvestris: see S. x superba
Salvia virgata Hort.: S. x superba
Salvia virgata nemerosa Hort.: S. x superba
Sanguinaria canadensis plena: S. c.
    'Multiplex'
Satureja grandiflora: Calamintha grandiflora
Saxifraga: See also Bergenia
Saxifraga fortunei: S. cortusifolia var.
    fortunei
Saxifraga peltata: Peltiphyllum peltatum
Saxifraga sarmentosa: Saxifraga stolonifera
Saxifraga umbrosa Hort.: S. x urbium
Scabiosa macedonica: Knautia macedonica
Scabiosa rumelica: Knautia macedonica
Schizocentron elegans: Heterocentron elegans
Schizocodon soldanelloides: Shortia
    soldanelloides
Schizocodon uniflorus: Shortia uniflora
Scrophularia aquatica 'Variegata':
    S. auriculata 'Variegata'
Scrophularia nodosa 'Variegata':
    S. auriculata 'Variegata'
Scutellaria canescens: S. incana
Sedum maximowiczii: Sedum aizoon
Sedum rhodiola: S. rosea
Sedum telephium maximum
    'Atropurpureum': S. maximum
    'Atropurpureum'
Sedum telephium purpureum: S. purpureum
Sedum woodwardii: Sedum aizoon
Selinum tenuifolium: S. candollei
Senecio artemisiifolius: S. adonidifolius
Senecio carpathicus: S. abrotanifolius
Senecio clivorum: Ligularia dentata
Senecio cruentus Hort.: S. x hybridus
Senecio kaempferi: Ligularia tussilaginea
Senecio ledebourii: Ligularia macrophylla
Senecio leucostachys: S. vira-vira
Senecio maritima: S. cinerea
Senecio pzrewalskii: Ligularia pzrewalskii
Senecio tiroliensis: S. abrotanifolius
Senecio veitchianus: Ligularia veitchiana
Setcreasea purpurea: S. pallida 'Purple
    Heart'

Setcreasea striata: Callisia elegans
Setcreasea tampicana: S. pallida 'Purple Heart'
Silene cucubalus: S. vulgaris
Silene glauca: S. vulgaris
Silene inflata: S. vulgaris
Silene latifolia: S. vulgaris
Silene maritima: S. vulgaris maritima
Silene wallichiana: S. vulgaris
Sisyrinchium angustifolium bellum: S. bellum
Sisyrinchium cyaneum: Orthrosanthus multiflorus
Sisyrinchium eastwoodiae: S. bellum
Sisyrinchium moritzianum: Orthrosanthus chimboracensis
Sisyrinchium polystachys: Orthrosanthus polystachys
X Solidaster hybridus: X Solidaster luteus
Sonchus jacquinii: S. congestus
Spiraea aruncus: Aruncus dioicus
Spiraea camtschatica: Filipendula camtschatica
Spiraea digitata: Filipendula palmata
Spiraea digitata nana Hort.: Filipendula palmata 'Nana'
Spiraea filipendula: Filipendula vulgaris
Spiraea gigantea Hort.: Filipendula camtschatica
Spiraea lobata: Filipendula rubra
Spiraea palmata: Filipendula palmata, F. purpurea, F. rubra
Spiraea palmata 'Elegans': Filipendula purpurea 'Elegans'
Spiraea ulmaria: Filipendula ulmaria
Spiraea venusta: Filipendula rubra
Spiraea venusta Hort.: Filipendula rubra 'Venusta'
Spironema: Callisia
Spironema fragrans: Callisia fragrans
Spironema melnickoffii: Callisia fragrans 'Melnickoff'
Stachys betonica: S. officinalis
Stachys hirsuta: S. densiflora
Stachys lanata: S. byzantina
Stachys macrantha: S. grandiflora
Stachys olympica: S. byzantina
Statice caespitosa: Armeria juniperifolia
Statice latifolia: Limonium latifolium

Statice perezii: Limonium perezii
Statice tatarica: Goniolimon tataricum
Steironema ciliatum: Lysimachia ciliata
Stokesia cyanea: S. laevis
Strelitzia parvifolia: S. reginae
Stylophyllum virens: Dudleya virens
Symphytum peregrinum: P. x uplandicum
Tanacetum serotinum: Chrysanthemum uliginosum
Tellima odorata: T. grandiflora
Thalictrum adiantifolium Hort.: T. minus
Thalictrum dipterocarpum Hort.: T. delavayi
Thalictrum flavum speciosum: T. flavum glaucum
Thalictrum glaucum: T. flavum glaucum
Thalictrum speciosissimum: T. flavum glaucum
Thermopsis caroliniana Hort.: T. villosa
Thermopsis lanceolata: T. lupinoides, see T. montana
Tiarella cordifolia var. collina: T. wherryi
Tradescantia dracaenoides: Callisia fragrans
Tradescantia laekenensis Hort.: T. albiflora 'Laekenensis'
Tradescantia reginae: Dichorisandra reginae
Tradescantia striata Hort.: T. albiflora 'Variegata'
Tradescantia tricolor Hort.: T. albiflora
Tradescantia virginiana Hort.: T. x andersoniana
Tradescantia viridis Hort.: T. albiflora
Trichinium exaltatum: Ptilotus exaltatus
Tricyrtis bakeri Hort.: T. latifolia
Trillium californicum: T. ovatum
Trillium flavum: T. erectum
Trillium luteum: T. viride var. luteum
Trillium sessile var. californicum: T. chloropetalum
Trillium sessile var. luteum: T. viride var. luteum
Tritoma: Kniphofia
Tritoma uvaria: Kniphofia uvaria
Trollius x hybridus: T. x cultorum
Tulbaghia cepacea: T. violacea
Tweedia caerulea: Oxypetalum caeruleum
Ulmaria lobata: Filipendula rubra
Uvularia puberula: U. caroliniana
Uvularia pudica: U. caroliniana

Vagnera racemosa: Smilacina racemosa
Valeriana coccinea: Centranthus ruber
Valeriana rosea Hort.: *Centranthus ruber*
   'Roseus'
Valeriana rubra: Centranthus ruber
Vancouveria parviflora: V. planipetala
Venidium calendulaceum: V. decurrens
Venidium fastuosum: Arctotis fastuosa
Verbascum 'Broussa': *V. bombyciferum*
Verbascum broussa Hort.: *V. bombyciferum*
Verbena aubletia: V. canadensis
Verbena x *hortensis: V.* x *hybrida*
Verbena patagonica: V. bonariensis
Verbena venosa: V. rigida
Veronica austriaca teucrium: V. latifolia
Veronica maritima: V. longifolia
Veronica rupestris: V. prostrata

Veronica teucrium: V. latifolia
Veronica virginica: Veronicastrum
   virginicum
Vesicaria utriculata: Alyssoides utriculata,
   see *Aurinia*
Vinca rosea: Catharanthus roseus
Viola rugulosa: V. canadensis rugulosa, see
   V. canadensis
Viola tricolor hortensis: V. x *wittrockiana*
Viscaria viscosa: Lychnis viscaria
Viscaria vulgaris: Lychnis viscaria
Viorna scottii: Clematis scottii
Yucca angustifolia: Y. glauca
Zantedeschia africana Hort.: *Z. aethiopica*
Zantedeschia melanoleuca: Z. albomaculata
Zauschneria californica var. *microphylla:*
   Z. cana

INDEX OF COMMON NAMES

Absinthe: *Artemisia absinthum*

Adam's-Needle: *Yucca filamentosa, Yucca smalliana*

African Daisy: *Arctotis, A. acaulis, Gerbera jamesonii*

African Iris: *Dietes vegeta*

Airplane Plant: *Crassula perfoliata* var. *falcata*

Algerian Marsh Orchid: *Dactylorhiza elata*

Alkali Grass: *Zigadenus elegans*

Allegheny Foamflower: *Tiarella cordifolia*

Allegheny Monkey Flower: *Mimulus ringens*

Allwood Pink: *Dianthus* x *allwoodii* Hort.

Alpine Poppy: *Papaver alpinum*

Alpine Wallflower: *Erysimum linifolium*

Alumroot: *Heuchera*

American Aloe: *Agave americana*

American Cow Parsley: *Heracleum sphondylium montanum*

American Germander: *Teucrium canadense*

American White Hellebore: *Veratrum viride*

Archangel: *Angelica archangelica, Lamium album*

Arctic Daisy: *Chrysanthemum arcticum*

Arctic Poppy: *Papaver nudicaule*

Artichoke: *Cynara scolymus*

Asiatic Poppy: *Meconopsis*

Asphodel: *Asphodelus*

August Lily: *Hosta plantaginea*

Autumn Monkshood: *Aconitum henryi* 'Spark's Variety'

Avens: *Geum*

Azure Monkshood: *Aconitum carmichaelii*

Baby Primrose: *Primula malacoides*

Baby's Breath: *Gypsophila, G. paniculata*

Bachelor's Buttons: *Bellis perennis*

Balloon Flower: *Platycodon grandiflorus*

Balmony: *Chelone glabra*

Balsamroot: *Balsamorhiza, B. hookeri*

Banana Yucca: *Yucca baccata*

Baneberry: *Actaea*

Barbados Aloe: *Aloe barbadensis*

Barbara's Buttons: *Marshallia grandiflora*

Barberton Daisy: *Gerbera jamesonii*

Barrenwort: *Epimedium*

Basket-of-Gold: *Aurinia saxatilis*

Beach Fleabane: *Erigeron glaucus*

Beach Pea: *Lathyrus japonicus*

Beach Wormwood: *Artemisia stellerana*

Beard-Tongue: *Penstemon*

Bear Grass: *Yucca smalliana, Xerophyllum asphodeloides*

Bear's-Breech: *Acanthus, A. mollis*

Beauty-of-the-Night: *Mirabilis jalapa*

Bedding Dahlia: *Dahlia merckii*

Bedding Geranium: *Pelargonium* x *hortorum*

Beebalm: *Monarda didyma*

Bee's Primrose: *Primula beesiana*

Beetleweed: *Galax urceolata*

Bell Agapanthus: *Agapanthus campanulatus*

Bellflower: *Campanula*

Bell Tree Dahlia: *Dahlia imperialis*

Bellwort: *Uvularia grandiflora*

Bethlehem Sage: *Pulmonaria saccharata*

Betony: *Stachys, S. officinalis*

Big Betony: *Stachys grandiflora*

Big Blue Lilyturf: *Liriope muscari*

Bigelow Sneezeweed: *Helenium bigelovii*

Bigflower Self-Heal: *Prunella grandiflora*

Bird-of-Paradise: *Strelitzia reginae*

Bishop's Hat: *Epimedium*

Bittercress: *Cardamine*

Bitterwort: *Gentiana lutea*

Bleeding-Heart: *Dicentra spectabilis*

Black Anther Flax Lily: *Dianella revoluta*

Blackberry Lily: *Belamcanda chinensis*

Black Cohosh: *Cimicifuga racemosa*

Black Cosmos: *Cosmos atrosanguineus*

Black-Eyed Susan: *Rudbeckia*

Black Knapweed: *Centaurea nigra*

Blackroot: *Veronicastrum virginicum*

Black Snakeroot: *Cimicifuga racemosa*

Black-Throated Calla: *Zantedeschia albomaculata*

Bladder Campion: *Silene vulgaris*

Blanket Flower: *Gaillardia*

Blazing Star: *Liatris*

Bleeding-Heart: *Dicentra*
Blister-Cress: *Erysimum*
Bloodflower: *Asclepias curassavica*
Bloodroot: *Sanguinaria canadensis*
Bloody-Butcher: *Trillium recurvatum*
Bloody Cranesbill: *Geranium sanguineum*
Blue African Lily: *Agapanthus, A. africanus,
    A. praecox*
Bluebell: *Campanula rotundifolia*
Bluebells: *Mertensia*
Bluebells-of-Scotland: *Campanula
    rotundifolia*
Blue-Daisy: *Felicia amelloides*
Blue-Eyed Arctotis: *Arctotis stoechadifolia*
Blue-Eyed Grass: *Sisyrinchium bellum*
Blue-Eyed Mary: *Omphalodes verna*
Blue False Indigo: *Baptisia australis*
Blue Flag: *Iris versicolor*
Blue Ginger: *Dichorisandra thyrsiflora*
Blue Lungwort: *Pulmonaria angustifolia*
Blue-Marguerite: *Felicia amelloides*
Blue Poppy: *Meconopsis*
Blue Sage: *Salvia azurea*
Blue Sow Thistle: *Lactuca alpina,
    L. bourgaei*
Blue Spiderwort: *Commelina coelestis*
Blue-Spiked Rampion: *Phyteuma
    betonicifolium*
Blue Star: *Amsonia tabernaemontana*
Blue Vervain: *Verbena hastata*
Blue Wild Indigo: *Baptisia australis*
Blue Yucca: *Yucca baccata*
Bog Rhubarb: *Petasites* x *hybridus*
Bonnet Bellflower: *Codonopsis*
Boneset: *Eupatorium*
Bonytip Fleabane: *Erigeron karvinskianus*
Border Carnation: *Dianthus* x *allwoodii*
    Hort.
Border Phlox: *Phlox paniculata*
Bottle Gentian: *Gentiana andrewsii*
Bouncing Bet: *Saponaria officinalis*
Bowman's Root: *Gillenia trifoliata,
    Veronicastrum virginicum*
Brass Buttons: *Cotula coronopifolia*
Bridal Wreath: *Francoa appendiculata*
Bristle Aster: *Aster liniarifolius*
British Columbia Wild Ginger: *Asarum
    caudatum*
Brown Beth: *Trillium erectum*

Bugbane: *Cimicifuga, C. racemosa*
Bugleweed: *Ajuga*
Burnet: *Sanguisorba*
Burning Bush: *Dictamnus albus*
Bush Violet: *Browallia speciosa*
Butter-and-Eggs: *Linaria vulgaris*
Butterbur: *Petasites, P.* x *hybridus*
Buttercup: *Ranunculus*
Butterfly Dock: *Petasites* x *hybridus*
Butterfly Lily: *Hedychium coronarium*
Butterfly Weed: *Asclepias tuberosa*
Button Snake-Root: *Eryngium yuccifolium*
Buzy Lizzy: *Impatiens wallerana*
Cactus Geranium: *Pelargonium echinatum*
Calamint: *Calamintha, C. grandiflora*
California Fuchsia: *Zauschneria,
    Z. californica*
California-Poppy: *Eschscholzia californica*
California Rockcress: *Arabis blepharophylla*
Calla Lily: *Zantedeschia, Z. aethiopica*
Campion: *Lychnis, Silene*
Canada Snakeroot: *Asarum canadense*
Canada Violet: *Viola canadensis*
Canada Wild Ginger: *Asarum canadense*
Canadian Burnet: *Sanguisorba canadensis*
Candelabra Tree: *Dahlia imperialis*
Candytuft: *Iberis*
Canterbury Bells: *Campanula medium*
Cape Anemone: *Anemone tenuifolia*
Cape Fuchsia: *Phygelius capensis*
Cape Weed: *Arctotheca calendula*
Cardinal Flower: *Lobelia cardinalis*
Cardoon: *Cynara cardunculus*
Carnation: *Dianthus*
Carolina Lupine: *Thermopsis villosa*
Carolina Phlox: *Phlox caroliniana*
Caroline Gromwell: *Lithospermum
    caroliniense*
Carpathian Bellflower: *Campanula carpatica*
Carpet Bugleweed: *Ajuga reptans*
Catmint: *Nepeta*
Catnip: *Nepeta cataria*
Cat's Valerian: *Valeriana officinalis*
Cattail Gayfeather: *Liatris pycnostachya*
Caucasian Inula: *Inula orientalis*
Caucasian Leopard's Bane: *Doronicum
    cordatum*
Caucasian Rockcress: *Arabis caucasica*
Century Plant: *Agave, A. americana*

Chalk Plant: *Gypsophila paniculata*
Chamomile: *Anthemis*
Chatterbox: *Epipactis gigantea*
Cheddar Pink: *Dianthus gratianopolitanus*
Cherry Pie: *Heliotropium arborescens*
Cheeses: *Malva sylvestris*
Chicory: *Cichorium intybus*
Chihuahuan Phlox: *Phlox mesoleuca*
Chiming Bells: *Mertensia ciliata*
Chimney Bellflower: *Campanula pyramidalis*
Chinese Ground Orchid: *Bletilla striata*
Chinese-Lantern Lily: *Sandersonia aurantiaca*
Chinese Lantern Plant: *Physalis alkekengi*
Chinese Peony: *Paeonia lactiflora*
Chinese Ragwort: *Senecio tanguticus*
Chocolate Root: *Geum rivale*
Christmas Bells: *Blandfordia, Sandersonia aurantiaca*
Christmas Rose: *Helleborus niger*
Cinquefoil: *Potentilla*
Circle Flower: *Lysimachia punctata*
Citron Daylily: *Hemerocallis citrina*
Closed Gentian: *Gentiana andrewsii*
Clove: *Dianthus*
Clustered Bellflower: *Campanula glomerata*
Coast Trillium: *Trillium ovatum*
Cobweb Houseleek: *Sempervivum arachnoideum*
Cohosh: *Actaea pachypoda*
Colewort: *Crambe cordifolia*
Columbine: *Aquilegia*
Comfrey: *Symphytum*
Common Agapanthus: *Agapanthus praecox*
Common Bugleweed: *Ajuga reptans*
Common Calla: *Zantedeschia aethiopica*
Common Coleus: *Coleus x hybridus*
Common Foxglove: *Digitalis purpurea*
Common Garden Peony: *Paeonia lactiflora*
Common Globeflower: *Trollius europeus*
Common Horehound: *Marrubium vulgare*
Common Houseleek: *Sempervivum tectorum*
Common Lungwort: *Pulmonaria officinalis*
Common Monkey Flower: *Mimulus guttatus*
Common Monkshood: *Aconitum napellus*
Common Peony: *Paeonia officinalis*
Common Primrose: *Primula vulgaris*
Common Rose Mallow: *Hibiscus moscheutos*
Common Shooting Star: *Dodecatheon meadia*

Common Sneezeweed: *Helenium autumnale*
Common Tansy: *Tanacetum vulgare*
Common Thyme: *Thymus vulgaris*
Common Torch Lily: *Kniphofia uvaria*
Common Valerian: *Valeriana officinalis*
Common Wormwood: *Artemisia absinthum*
Common Yarrow: *Achillea millefolium*
Compass Plant: *Silphium laciniatum*
Coneflower: *Rudbeckia*
Coral Aloe: *Aloe striata*
Coral Bells: *Heuchera sanguinea*
Corn Lily: *Veratrum californicum*
Corsican Hellebore: *Helleborus argutifolius*
Cottage Pink: *Dianthus x allwoodii* Hort., *Dianthus plumarius*
Cow Parsnip: *Heracleum*
Cowslip: *Caltha palustris, Primula veris, Pulmonaria*
Cowslip Lungwort: *Pulmonaria angustifolia*
Cranesbill: *Geranium*
Creeping Bellflower: *Campanula rapunculoides*
Creeping Gypsophila: *Gypsophila repens*
Creeping Lilyturf: *Liriope spicata*
Creeping Phlox: *Phlox stolonifera*
Creeping Polemonium: *Polemonium reptans*
Creeping Vervain: *Verbena canadensis*
Crested Gentian: *Gentiana septemfida*
Crested Iris: *Iris cristata*
Crimson Flag: *Schizostylis coccinea*
Crocodile-Jaws: *Aloe humilis*
Crosswort: *Phuopsis stylosa*
Crown Vetch: *Coronilla, C. varia*
Cuckoo Flower: *Cardamine pratensis*
Culver's Root: *Veronicastrum virginicum*
Cupflower: *Nierembergia, N. hippomanica* var. *violacea*
Cupid's Dart: *Catananche caerulea*
Cup Plant: *Silphium perfoliatum*
Curry Plant: *Helichrysum angustifolium*
Cushion Spurge: *Euphorbia polychroma*
Cutleaf Coneflower: *Rudbeckia laciniata*
Cyclamen-Leaved Ginger: *Asarum hartwegii*
Cypress Spurge: *Euphorbia cyparissias*
Damask Violet: *Hesperis matronalis*
Dame's Rocket: *Hesperis matronalis*
Dame's Violet: *Hesperis matronalis*
Danewort: *Sambucus ebulus*
Dark-Eye Sunflower: *Helianthus atrorubens*

Dark Mullein: *Verbascum nigrum*
Datil: *Yucca baccata*
Daylily: *Hemerocallis*
Deadnettle: *Lamium*
Deer Grass: *Rhexia virginica*
Dense Blazing Star: *Liatris spicata*
Desert Candle: *Eremurus*
Desert Hollyhock: *Sphaeralcea ambigua*
Desert Mallow: *Sphaeralcea ambigua*
Desert Marigold: *Baileya multiradiata*
Devil's Paintbrush: *Hieracium aurantiacum*
Dewflower: *Drosanthemum speciosum*
Digger's Speedwell: *Veronica perfoliata*
Dittany: *Dictamnus albus*
Dittany-of-Crete: *Origanum dictamnus*
Doll's Eyes: *Actaea pachypoda*
Double Orange Daisy: *Erigeron aurantiacus*
Dragon Arum: *Arisaema dracontium*
Dragon Plant: *Dracunculus vulgaris*
Dragonroot: *Arisaema dracontium*
Dropwort: *Filipendula vulgaris*
Dusty Miller: *Artemisia stellerana,
    Centaurea gymnocarpa, C. cineraria,
    C. ragusina.*
Dutchman's-Breeches: *Dicentra cucullaria*
Dwarf Agapanthus: *Agapanthus africanus*
Dwarf Coleus: *Coleus pumilus*
Dwarf Elder: *Sambucus ebulus*
Dwarf Lilyturf: *Ophiopogon japonicus*
Dyer's Woodruff: *Asperula tinctoria*
Early Daylily: *Hemerocallis dumortieri*
Edelweiss: *Leontopodium alpinum*
Edging Candytuft: *Iberis sempervirens*
Egyptian Star: *Pentas lanceolata*
Elecampane: *Inula helenium*
English Daisy: *Bellis perennis*
English Monkshood: *Aconitum napellus*
English Primrose: *Primula* x *polyantha,
    P. vulgaris*
English Wallflower: *Cheiranthus cheiri*
European Crowfoot: *Aquilegia vulgaris*
European Meadowsweet: *Filipendula
    ulmaria*
European Purple Loosestrife: *Lythrum
    salicaria*
European White Hellebore: *Veratrum album*
European Wild Ginger: *Asarum europeum*
European Wood Anemone: *Anemone
    nemerosa*

Evening Primrose: *Oenothera*
Fairy-Bells: *Disporum*
Fairy Crassula: *Crassula multicava*
Fairy Primrose: *Primula malacoides*
False Alum Root: *Tellima grandiflora*
False Anemone: *Anemonopsis macrophylla*
False Dragonhead: *Physostegia virginiana*
False Hellebore: *Veratrum*
False Indigo: *Baptisia*
False Lupine: *Thermopsis*
False Miterwort: *Tiarella*
False Rockcress: *Aubrieta deltoidea*
False Solomon's Seal: *Smilacina racemosa*
False Spikenard: *Smilacina racemosa*
False Sunflower: *Heliopsis*
Fat Solomon: *Smilacina racemosa* var.
    amplexicaulis
Feltbush: *Kalanchoe beharensis*
Felt Plant: *Kalanchoe beharensis*
Felwort: *Gentiana lutea*
Fennel: *Foeniculum vulgare*
Fernleaf Peony: *Paeonia tenuifolia*
Fern-Leaf Yarrow: *Achillea filipendulina*
Feverfew: *Chrysanthemum parthenium*
Field Daisy: *Chrysanthemum leucanthemum*
Finger Bowl Geranium: *Pelargonium
    crispum*
Fire-Pink: *Silene virginica*
Fireweed: *Epilobium, E. angustifolium*
Fish Geranium: *Pelargonium* x *hortorum*
Flag Iris: *Iris* x *germanica*
Flannelflower: *Actinotus helianthi*
Flat-Topped Aster: *Aster umbellatus*
Flax: *Linum*
Flax Lily: *Dianella, Phormium*
Fleabane: *Erigeron*
Florists' Chrysanthemum: *Chrysanthemum
    x morifolium*
Florists' Violet: *Viola odorata*
Flowering Bush Coleus: *Coleus thyrsoideus*
Flowering Spurge: *Euphorbia corollata*
Flowering Tobacco: *Nicotiana alata*
Foamflower: *Tiarella cordifolia*
Fortnight Lily: *Dietes vegeta*
Four-O'Clock: *Mirabilis jalapa*
Foxglove: *Digitalis*
Fox's-Brush: *Centranthus ruber*
Foxtail Agave: *Agave attenuata*
Foxtail Lily: *Eremurus*

Fragrant Plantain Lily: *Hosta plantaginea*
Fraxinella: *Dictamnus albus*
French Honeysuckle: *Hedysarum coronarium*
Fringe Cups: *Tellima grandiflora*
Fringed Bleeding-Heart: *Dicentra eximia*
Fringed Loosestrife: *Lysimachia ciliata*
Fringe Bell: *Shortia soldanelloides*
Fringe Galax: *Shortia soldanelloides*
Funkia: *Hosta*
Garden Chrysanthemum: *Chrysanthemum x morifolium*
Garden Columbine: *Aquilegia vulgaris*
Garden Heliotrope: *Valeriana officinalis*
Garden Phlox: *Phlox paniculata*
Garden Verbena: *Verbena x hybrida*
Garden Violet: *Viola odorata*
Garland Flower: *Hedychium coronarium*
Gas Plant: *Dictamnnus albus*
Gayfeather: *Liatris*
Geneva Bugleweed: *Ajuga genevensis*
Gentian: *Gentiana*
Gentian Sage: *Salvia patens*
Gentian Speedwell: *Veronica gentianoides*
Geranium: *Pelargonium*
German Catchfly: *Lychnis viscaria*
Germander: *Teucrium*
German Iris: *Iris x germanica*
German Primrose: *Primula obconica*
Giant Bellflower: *Ostrowskia magnifica*
Giant Butterbur: *Petasites japonicus giganteus*
Giant Desert Candle: *Eremurus robustus*
Giant Fennel: *Ferula communis*
Giant Helleborine: *Epipactis gigantea*
Giant Hogweed: *Heracleum mantegazzianum*
Giant Solomon's Seal: *Polygonatum commutatum*
Gibraltar Candytuft: *Iberis gibraltarica*
Ginger Lily: *Hedychium*
Gladdon Iris: *Iris foetidissima*
Gladwyn Iris: *Iris foetidissima*
Globeflower: *Trollius*
Globe Mallow: *Sphaeralcea*
Globe Thistle: *Echinops*
Goatsbeard: *Aruncus dioicus*
Goat's Rue: *Galega officinalis*

Goldbunch Leopard's Bane: *Doronicum pardalianches*
Gold Dust: *Aurinia saxatilis*
Golden Apple Mint: *Mentha x gentilis* 'Variegata'
Golden Aster: *Chrysopsis, C. villosa*
Golden Banner: *Thermopsis montana*
Golden Buttons: *Tanacetum vulgare*
Golden Calla: *Zantedeschia elliottiana*
Golden Columbine: *Aquilegia chrysantha*
Golden Drop: *Onosma echioides*
Golden Groundsel: *Ligularia dentata, Senecio aureus*
Golden Marguerite: *Anthemis tinctoria*
Golden Monkey Flower: *Mimulus luteus*
Goldenrod: *Solidago*
Goldenstar: *Chrysogonum virginianum*
Goldentuft: *Aurinia saxatilis*
Gooseneck Loosestrife: *Lysimachia clethroides*
Granny's Bonnet: *Aquilegia vulgaris*
Grass Pink: *Dianthus plumarius*
Gray-Headed Coneflower: *Ratibida pinnata*
Great Blue Lobelia: *Lobelia siphilitica*
Greater Spearwort: *Ranunculus lingua*
Great Leopard's Bane: *Doronicum pardalianches*
Great Scarlet Poppy: *Papaver bracteatum*
Great Solomon's Seal: *Polygonatum commutatum*
Great Yellow Gentian: *Gentiana lutea*
Great Willow Herb: *Epilobium angustifolium*
Grecian Foxglove: *Digitalis lanata*
Greek Valerian: *Polemonium reptans*
Greek Windflower: *Anemone blanda*
Green Dragon: *Arisaema dracontium*
Grim-the-Collier: *Hieracium aurantiacum*
Ground Clematis: *Clematis recta*
Ground Morning-Glory: *Convolvulus cneorum*
Groundsel: *Senecio*
Hairy Goldaster: *Chrysopsis villosa*
Hairy Toad-Lily: *Tricyrtis hirta*
Hairy Puccoon: *Lithospermum caroliniense*
Halberd-Leaved Rose Mallow: *Hibiscus militaris*
Hardhead: *Centaurea*
Hardy Ageratum: *Eupatorium coelestinum*

Hardy Gloxinia: *Incarvillea, I. delavayi*
Harebell: *Campanula rotundifolia*
Harebell Poppy: *Meconopsis quintuplinervia*
Hawk's Beard: *Crepis incana*
Hawkweed: *Hieracium*
Heart-Leaved Bergenia: *Bergenia cordifolia*
Heath Aster: *Aster ericoides*
Hedgehog: *Agave stricta, Aloe humilis*
Hedgehog Coneflower: *Echinacea purpurea*
Helen's Flower: *Helenium*
Heliotrope: *Heliotropium arborescens*
Hellebore: *Helleborus*
Helleborine: *Epipactis*
Helmet Flower: *Aconitum*
Hen-and-Chickens: *Echeveria, Sempervivum*
Herb-of-Grace: *Ruta graveolens*
Heronsbill: *Erodium*
High Daisy: *Chrysanthemum uliginosum*
High Mallow: *Malva sylvestris*
Himalayan Blue Poppy: *Meconopsis betonicifolia*
Himalayan Desert Candle: *Eremurus himalaicus*
Himalayan Elecampane: *Inula royleana*
Himalayan Fleece-Flower: *Polygonum affine*
Himalayan Primrose: *Primula denticulata*
Hoary Gromwell: *Lithospermum canescens*
Hollyhock: *Alcea, A. rosea*
Hollyhock Mallow: *Malva alcea*
Honeybush: *Melianthus major*
Hooker Inula: *Inula hookeri*
Horned Poppy: *Glaucium flavum*
Horned Rampion: *Phyteuma*
Horned Violet: *Viola cornuta*
Horsemint: *Monarda punctata*
Horseshoe Geranium: *Pelargonium x hortorum*
Hottentot Fig: *Carpobrotus edulis*
Hound's Tongue: *Cynoglossum nervosum*
Hungarian Clover: *Trifolium pannonicum*
Hungarian Daisy: *Chrysanthemum uliginosum*
Hungarian Speedwell: *Veronica latifolia*
Hybrid Daylily: *Hemerocallis x hybrida*
Hyssop: *Hyssopus officinalis*
Iceland Poppy: *Papaver nudicaule*
Ice Plant: *Carpobrotus, Drosanthemum, Lampranthus, Malephora, Oscularia*
Inch Plant: *Callisia*

Indian Paint: *Lithospermum canescens*
Indian Physic: *Gillenia trifoliata*
Indian Pink: *Spigelia marilandica*
Indian Poke: *Veratrum viride*
Indian Shot: *Canna indica*
Indian Squaw Grass: *Xerophyllum tenax*
Indian Turnip: *Arisaema triphyllum*
Inside-Out Flower: *Vancouveria planipetala*
Island Alumroot: *Heuchera maxima*
Italian Alkanet: *Anchusa azurea*
Italian Arum: *Arum italicum*
Italian Aster: *Aster amellus*
Italian Bugloss: *Anchusa azurea*
Ivy-Leaved Geranium: *Pelargonium peltatum*
Jack-in-the-Pulpit: *Arisaema triphyllum*
Jacob's Ladder: *Polemonium, P. caeruleum, P. reptans*
Jacob's Rod: *Asphodeline, A. lutea*
Japanese Anemone: *Anemone hupehensis, A. x hybrida*
Japanese Burnet: *Sanguisorba obtusa*
Japanese Butterbur: *Petasites japonicus*
Japanese Iris: *Iris ensata*
Japanese Meadowsweet: *Filipendula purpurea*
Japanese Pearly Everlasting: *Anaphalis margaritacea yedoensis*
Japanese Primrose: *Primula japonica*
Japanese Roof Iris: *Iris tectorum*
Japanese Star Primrose: *Primula sieboldii*
Japanese Water Iris: *Iris ensata*
Jasmine Tobacco: *Nicotiana alata*
Jerusalem Cowslip: *Pulmonaria officinalis*
Jerusalem Cross: *Lychnis chalcedonica*
Jerusalem Sage: *Phlomis fruticosa, Pulmonaria*
Joe-Pye Weed: *Eupatorium purpureum*
Joseph and Mary: *Pulmonaria longifolia*
Jupiter's-Beard: *Centranthus ruber*
Kaffir Lily: *Clivia, C. miniata, Schizostylis coccinea*
Kahili Ginger: *Hedychium gardneranum*
Kamchatka Bugbane: *Cimicifuga simplex*
Kangaroo Paw: *Anigozanthos*
Kansas Gayfeather: *Liatris pycnostachya*
Keys-of-Heaven: *Centranthus ruber*
Kingcup: *Caltha palustris*
King's Spear: *Asphodeline lutea, Eremurus*

Knapweed: *Centaurea*
Knotweed: *Polgonum*
Lace Aloe: *Aloe aristata*
Ladybells: *Adenophora*
Lady's-Mantle: *Alchemilla, A. mollis*
Lady's Slipper: *Cypripedium*
Lady's Smock: *Cardamine pratensis*
Lady Washington Geranium: *Pelargonium*
    x *domesticum*
Lamb's-Ears: *Stachys byzantina*
Languid Ladies: *Mertensia ciliata*
Larkspur: *Delphinium*
Leadwort: *Ceratostigma plumbaginoides*
Lebanon Stonecress: *Aethionema*
    coridifolium
Ledebour Globeflower: *Trollius ledebourii*
    Hort.
Lemon Daylily: *Hemerocallis lilioasphodelus*
Lemon Lily: *Hemerocallis lilioasphodelus*
Lemon-Scented Geranium: *Pelargonium*
    crispum
Lemon Thyme: *Thymus* x *citriodorus*
Lenten Rose: *Helleborus orientalis*
Leopard Flower: *Belamcanda chinensis*
Leopard's Bane: *Doronicum*
Licorice Plant: *Helichrysum petiolare*
Lilac Pink: *Dianthus superbus*
Lily of the Nile: *Agapanthus, A. africanus*
Lily-of-the-Valley: *Convallaria majalis*
Lilyturf: *Liriope*
Lion's-Ear: *Leonotis leonurus*
Little Brown Jugs: *Asarum arifolium*
London Pride: *Saxifraga* x *urbium*
Long Purple Flag: *Patersonia longiscapa*
Longspur Epimedium: *Epimedium*
    grandiflorum
Loosestrife: *Lysimachia, Lythrum*
Lord's-Candlestick: *Yucca gloriosa*
Lungwort: *Pulmonaria*
Lupine: *Lupinus*
Madagascar Periwinkle: *Catharanthus*
    roseus
Madeiran Marsh Orchid: *Dactylorhiza*
    foliosa
Madwort: *Alyssum*
Maguey: *Agave americana*
Maiden Pink: *Dianthus deltoides*
Maiden's Tears: *Silene vulgaris*
Mallow: *Malva, M. alcea*

Mallow Rose: *Hibiscus moscheutos*
Maltese Cross: *Lychnis chalcedonica*
Marguerite: *Chrysanthemum frutescens*
Marjoram: *Origanum*
Marsh Blue Violet: *Viola cucullata*
Marsh Mallow: *Hibiscus moscheutos*
    palustris, Althaea officinalis
Marsh Marigold: *Caltha, C. palustris*
Marsh Orchid: *Dactylorhiza*
Martha Washington Geranium: *Pelargonium*
    x *domesticum*
Marvel-of-Peru: *Mirabilis jalapa*
Maryland Aster: *Chrysopsis mariana*
Mask Flower: *Alonsoa warscewiczii*
Masterwort: *Astrantia, Heracleum*
    sphondylium montanum
Matilija-Poppy: *Romneya coulteri*
Mayapple: *Podophyllum peltatum*
Mayflower Daylily: *Hemerocallis multiflora*
Meadow Phlox: *Phlox maculata*
Meadow Rue: *Thalictrum*
Meadowsweet: *Filipendula*
Mealy-Cup Sage: *Salvia farinacea*
Medicinal Aloe: *Aloe barbadensis*
Merrybells: *Uvularia grandiflora*
Mexican Bush Sage: *Salvia leucantha*
Mexican Dayflower: *Commelina coelestis*
Mexican Tulip Poppy: *Hunnemannia*
    fumariifolia
Michaelmas Daisy: *Aster novae-angliae, Aster*
    novi-belgi
Milkweed: *Asclepias*
Miniature Hollyhock: *Sidalcea malviflora*
Mint: *Mentha*
Missouri Primrose: *Oenothera missouriensis*
Mist Flower: *Eupatorium coelestinum*
Misty Plume Bush: *Iboza riparia*
Miyabe: *Chrysanthemum weyrichii*
Moccasin Flower: *Cypripedium acaule*
Molly-the-Witch: *Paeonia mlokosewitschii*
Mondo Grass: *Ophiopogon japonicus*
Monkey Flower: *Mimulus*
Monkey Plant: *Ruellia makoyana*
Monkshood: *Aconitum*
Morning Flag: *Orthrosanthus*
Morning Star: *Orthrosanthus*
Mother-of-Thousands: *Saxifraga stolonifera*
Motherwort: *Leonurus cardiaca*
Mottled Wild Ginger: *Asarum shuttleworthii*

Mountain Asphodel: *Xerophyllum asphodeloides*
Mountain Bluebell: *Mertensia ciliata*
Mountain Bluets: *Centaurea montana*
Mountain Death Camas: *Zigadenus elegans*
Mountain Flax: *Phormium colensoi*
Mountain Fleece: *Polygonum amplexicaule*
Mountain Thermopsis: *Thermopsis montana*
Mountain Thistle: *Lactuca alpina*
Mourning Widow: *Geranium phaeum*
Mrs Robb's-Bonnet: *Euphorbia amygdaloides* var. *robbiae*
Mugwort: *Artemisia*
Mulla Mulla: *Ptilotus exaltatus*
Mullein: *Verbascum*
Mullein Pink: *Lychnis coronaria*
Musk Mallow: *Malva moschata*
Myrrh: *Myrrhis odorata*
Namaqualand Daisy: *Venidium*
Narrow-Leaved Plantain Lily: *Hosta lancifolia*
Narrow-Leaved Puccoon: *Lithospermum incisum*
Navelwort: *Omphalodes*
Nepal Cinquefoil: *Potentilla nepalensis*
New England Aster: *Aster novae-angliae*
New York Aster: *Aster novi-belgi*
New York Ironweed: *Vernonia noveboracensis*
New Zealand Flax: *Phormium tenax*
Nippon-Bells: *Shortia uniflora*
Nippon Daisy: *Chrysanthemum nipponicum*
Nippon Oxeye Daisy: *Chrysanthemum nipponicum*
Nodding Trillium: *Trillium cernuum*
Northern Shorewort: *Mertensia maritima*
Obedient Plant: *Physostegia virginiana*
Oconee-Bells: *Shortia galacifolia*
Octopus Agave: *Agave vilmoriniana*
Old Maid: *Catharanthus roseus*
Old-Man: *Artemisia abrotanum*
Old-Man-and-Woman: *Sempervivum tectorum*
Old-Woman: *Artemisia stellerana*
Orange Coneflower: *Rudbeckia fulgida*
Orange Daylily: *Hemerocallis aurantiaca, Hemerocallis fulva*
Orange Fleabane: *Erigeron aurantiacus*
Orange Sneezeweed: *Helenium hoopesii*

Oregon Fleabane: *Erigeron speciosus*
Oregon Sunflower: *Balsamorhiza sagittata*
Oriental Poppy: *Papaver orientale*
Orris: *Iris pallida*
Orris Root: *Iris* 'Florentina'
Oswego Tea: *Monarda didyma*
Our-Lord's-Candle: *Yucca whipplei*
Ox-eye Chamomile: *Anthemis tinctoria*
Oxeye Daisy: *Telekia speciosa, Chrysanthemum leucanthemum*
Oysterleaf: *Mertensia maritima*
Ozark Sundrop: *Oenothera missouriensis*
Painted Daisy: *Chrysanthemum coccineum*
Painted Trillium: *Trillium undulatum*
Palm Lily: *Yucca gloriosa*
Panda Plant: *Kalanchoe tomentosa*
Pansy: *Viola* x *wittrockiana*
Pansy-Flowered Geranium: *Pelargonium* x *domesticum*
Paris Daisy: *Chrysanthemum frutescens*
Paroo Lily: *Dianella caerulea*
Parrot Flower: *Alstroemeria psittacina*
Partridge-Breast: *Aloe variegata*
Pasque-Flower: *Anemone pulsatilla*
Peach-Leaved Bellflower: *Campanula persicifolia*
Peacock Anemone: *Anemone pavonina*
Peony: *Paeonia*
Pearly Everlasting: *Anaphalis*
Peppermint-Scented Geranium: *Pelargonium tomentosum*
Pepperroot: *Dentaria*
Perennial Candytuft: *Iberis sempervirens*
Perennial Cornflower: *Centaurea montana*
Perennial Honesty: *Lunaria rediviva*
Periwinkle Phlox: *Phlox adsurgens*
Persian Cornflower: *Centaurea dealbata*
Persian Epimedium: *Epimedium pinnatum*
Persian Insect Flower: *Chrysanthemum coccineum*
Persian Stonecress: *Aethionema grandiflorum*
Peruvian Lily: *Alstroemeria*
Pheasant's Eye: *Adonis, A. amurensis*
Pigsqueak: *Bergenia crassifolia*
Pincushion Flower: *Scabiosa caucasica*
Pineapple Mint: *Mentha suaveolens*
Pink: *Dianthus*
Pinkball Thrift: *Armeria pseudoarmeria*
Pink Calla: *Zantedeschia rehmannii*

Pink Lady's Slipper: *Cypripedium acaule*
Pinkroot: *Spigelia marilandica*
Pinwheel: *Aeonium haworthii*
Plantain: *Plantago, P. major*
Plantain Leopard's Bane: *Doronicum plantagineum*
Plantain Lily: *Hosta*
Plantain Thrift: *Armeria plantaginea*
Plumbago: *Ceratostigma plumbaginoides*
Plume Poppy: *Macleaya cordata*
Poison Flag: *Iris versicolor*
Poison Primrose: *Primula obconica*
Poke: *Phytolacca americana*
Pokeberry: *Phytolacca americana*
Poker Plant: *Kniphofia uvaria*
Pokeweed: *Phytolacca, P. americana*
Polyanthus Primrose: *Primula* x *polyantha*
Poppy: *Papaver*
Poppy Anemone: *Anemone coronaria*
Poppy-of-the-Dawn: *Eomecon chionantha*
Prairie Dock: *Silphium terebinthinaceum*
Prairie Mallow: *Sidalcea malviflora*
Pride of Madeira: *Echium fastuosum*
Primrose: *Primula*
Prince's Plume: *Stanleya pinnata*
Prophet Flower: *Echioides longiflorum*
Puccoon: *Lithospermum*
Purple Coneflower: *Echinacea purpurea*
Purple Heart: *Setcreasea purpurea* 'Purple Heart'
Purple Morning Flag: *Orthrosanthus multiflorus*
Purple Mullein: *Verbascum phoeniceum*
Purple Trillium: *Trillium erectum, Trillium recurvatum*
Purple Wake-Robin: *Trillium recurvatum*
Pussy-Ears: *Kalanchoe tomentosa*
Pussy-Tails: *Ptilotus exaltatus*
Pyrenees Chrysanthemum: *Chrysanthemum* x *superbum*
Pyrenees Monkshood: *Aconitum anthora*
Pyrethrum: *Chrysanthemum coccineum*
Queen-of-the-Meadow: *Filipendula ulmaria*
Queen-of-the-Prairie: *Filipendula rubra*
Queen's Spiderwort: *Dichorisandra reginae*
Queen's Gilliflower: *Hesperis matronalis*
Rockcress: *Arabis*
Rattlesnake-Master: *Eryngium yuccifolium*
Red Baneberry: *Actaea rubra*

Red Buckwheat: *Eriogonum grande* var. *rubescens*
Red Calla: *Zantedeschia rehmannii*
Red Flowering Tobacco: *Nicotiana* x *sanderae*
Red Ginger: *Alpinia purpurata*
Red Ginger Lily: *Hedychium coccineum*
Red Hot Poker: *Kniphofia uvaria*
Red Puccoon: *Sanguinaria canadensis*
Red Root: *Wachendorfia thyrsiflora*
Red Valerian: *Centranthus ruber*
Redwood Ivy: *Vancouveria planipetala*
Red Yucca: *Hesperaloe parviflora*
Regal Pelargonium: *Pelargonium* x *domesticum*
Renga Lily: *Arthropodium cirrhatum*
Rest Harrow: *Ononis rotundifolia*
Rhubarb: *Rheum*
Rockcress: *Arabis*
Rock Soapwort: *Saponaria ocymoides*
Rocky Mountain Columbine: *Aquilegia caerulea*
Rogue's Gilliflower: *Hesperis matronalis*
Roman Candle: *Yucca gloriosa*
Romero: *Trichostema lanatum*
Rose Campion: *Lychnis coronaria*
Rose Mallow: *Hibiscus*
Rose Periwinkle: *Catharanthus roseus*
Roseroot: *Sedum rosea*
Rose-Scented Geranium: *Pelargonium graveolens*
Rose-Scented Pelargonium: *Pelargonium capitatum*
Rose Verbena: *Verbena canadensis*
Rosinweed: *Silphium*
Rough Gentian: *Gentiana scabra*
Roundleaf Violet: *Viola rotundifolia*
Rover Bellflower: *Campanula rapunculoides*
Ruby Cinquefoil: *Potentilla atrosanguineum*
Russian Comfrey: *Symphytum* x *uplandicum*
Russian Sage: *Perovskia atriplicifolia*
Rusty Foxglove: *Digitalis ferruginea*
Saffron Buckwheat: *Eriogonum crocatum*
Sage: *Salvia*
Saucer Plant: *Aeonium undulatum*
Savoryleaf Aster: *Aster liniarifolius*
Saxifrage: *Saxifraga*
Scabious: *Scabiosa, S. caucasica*

Scarlet Lightning: *Lychnis chalcedonica*
Scarlet Monkey Flower: *Mimulus cardinalis*
Scarlet Paintbrush: *Crassula perfoliata* var.
   falcata
Scarlet-Seeded Iris: *Iris foetidissima*
Scoke: *Phytolacca americana*
Scotch Mint: *Mentha* x *gentilis* 'Variegata'
Scotch Pink: *Dianthus plumarius*
Sea Campion: *Silene vulgaris* subsp.
   maritima
Sea Dahlia: *Coreopsis maritima*
Sea Fig: *Carpobrotus chilensis*
Sea Holly: *Eryngium maritimum*
Sea Hollyhock: *Hibiscus moscheutos palustris*
Sea Kale: *Crambe maritima*
Sea Lavender: *Limonium, L. latifolium*
Sea Mertensia: *Mertensia maritima*
Sea Pea: *Lathyrus japonicus*
Sea Pink: *Armeria maritima*
Sea Poppy: *Glaucium flavum*
Sea Ragwort: *Senecio cinerea*
Seaside Daisy: *Erigeron glaucus*
Self-Heal: *Prunella*
Senna: *Cassia*
Setterwort: *Helleborus foetidus*
Shaggy Hawkweed: *Hieracium villosum*
Shasta Daisy: *Chrysanthemum* x *superbum*
Sheep's-Bit: *Jasione laevis*
Shellflower: *Alpinia zerumbet*
Shelford Foxtail: *Eremurus* x *isabellinus*
Shelford Hybrid: *Eremurus* x *isabellinus*
Shell Ginger: *Alpinia zerumbet*
Shepherd's Crook: *Lysimachia clethroides*
Shepherd's Scabious: *Jasione laevis*
Shooting Star: *Dodecatheon*
Short Purple Flag: *Patersonia glauca*
Show Pelargonium: *Pelargonium*
   x *domesticum*
Showy Groundsel: *Senecio pulcher*
Showy Lady's Slipper: *Cypripedium reginae*
Showy Leopard's Bane: *Doronicum*
   plantagineum
Showy Primrose: *Oenothera speciosa*
Showy Stonecrop: *Sedum spectabilis*
Shrimp Plant: *Justicia brandegeana*
Siberian Bugloss: *Brunnera macrophylla*
Siberian Iris: *Iris sibirica*
Siberian Meadowsweet: *Filipendula palmata*
Siberian Wallflower: *Erysimum allionii*

Sickle Plant: *Crassula perfoliata* var. *falcata*
Siebold Primrose: *Primula sieboldii*
Sierra Shooting Star: *Dodecatheon jeffreyi*
Silverbush: *Convolvulus cneorum*
Silver Dollar Plant: *Lunaria annua*
Silver Groundsel: *Senecio cinerea*
Simpler's Joy: *Verbena hastata*
Skullcap: *Scutellaria*
Skunk Cabbage: *Veratrum californicum*
Skunkleaf Polemonium: *Polemonium*
   pulcherrimum
Small Solomon's Seal: *Polygonatum biflorum*
Small Yellow Foxglove: *Digitalis lutea*
Snakeberry: *Actaea rubra*
Snakehead: *Chelone glabra*
Snake's Head Iris: *Hermodactylus tuberosus*
Sneezeweed: *Achillea ptarmica, Helenium*
Sneezewort: *Achillea ptarmica*
Snowdrop Anemone: *Anemone sylvestris*
Snowflake: *Lamium album*
Snow-in-Summer: *Cerastium tomentosum*
Snow Poppy: *Eomecon chionantha*
Snow Trillium: *Trillium grandiflorum*
Soapweed: *Yucca glauca*
Soapwell: *Yucca glauca*
Soapwort: *Saponaria*
Society Garlic: *Tulbaghia violacea*
Soldier Rose Mallow: *Hibiscus militaris*
Solomon's Seal: *Polygonatum*
Southern Star: *Oxypetalum caeruleum*
Southernwood: *Artemisia abrotanum*
Spanish-Bayonet: *Yucca baccata*
Spanish-Dagger: *Yucca gloriosa*
Spanish Buttons: *Centaurea nigra*
Spanish Shawl: *Heterocentron elegans*
Speedwell: *Veronica*
Spider Aloe: *Aloe humilis*
Spider Plant: *Anthericum*
Spiderwort: *Tradescantia*
Spiked Rampion: *Phyteuma spicatum*
Spike Gayfeather: *Liatris spicata*
Spike Speedwell: *Veronica spicata*
Spotted Beebalm: *Monarda punctata*
Spotted Calla: *Zantedeschia albomaculata*
Spotted Dead Nettle: *Lamium maculatum*
Spotted Dog: *Pulmonaria longifolia*
Spring Adonis: *Adonis vernalis*
Spring Vetchling: *Lathyrus vernus*
Spurge: *Euphorbia*

Squawroot: *Trillium erectum*
St. Bernard's Lily: *Anthericum liliago*
St. Bruno's Lily: *Paradisea liliastrum*
St. John's Chamomile: *Anthemis sancti-johannis*
Staghorn Cinquefoil: *Potentilla* x *tonguei*
Star Cluster: *Pentas lanceolata*
Starflower: *Smilacina stellata*
Statice: *Limonium latifolium*
Stiff Aster: *Aster liniarifolius*
Stiff Sunflower: *Helianthus rigidus*
Stinking Benjamin: *Trillium erectum*
Stinking Hellebore: *Helleborus foetidus*
Stinking Iris: *Iris foetidissima*
Stokes' Aster: *Stokesia laevis*
Stonecress: *Aethionema*
Stonecrop: *Sedum*
Storksbill: *Pelargonium*
Strawberry Begonia: *Saxifraga stolonifera*
Strawberry Geranium: *Saxifraga stolonifera*
Stream Orchid: *Epipactis gigantea*
Striped Inch Plant: *Callisia elegans*
Sulfur Buckwheat: *Eriogonum umbellatum* var. *polyanthum*
Sulfur Cinquefoil: *Potentilla recta* 'Warrenii'
Summer-Blooming Phlox: *Phlox paniculata*
Suncup: *Oenothera*
Sundrops: *Oenothera tetragona*
Sunflower: *Helianthus*
Sun Rose: *Helianthemum*
Swamp Milkweed: *Asclepias incarnata*
Swamp Rose Mallow: *Hibiscus moscheutos*
Sweet Cicely: *Myrrhis odorata*
Sweet Coltsfoot: *Petasites fragrans*
Sweetheart Geranium: *Pelargonium echinatum*
Sweet Pea: *Lathyrus odoratus*
Sweet Rocket: *Hesperis matronalis*
Sweet-Scented Geranium: *Pelargonium graveolens*
Sweet Violet: *Viola odorata*
Sweet White Violet: *Viola blanda*
Sweet William: *Dianthus barbatus*
Sweet Woodruff: *Galium odoratum*
Swordleaf Inula: *Inula ensifolia*
Tall Cupflower: *Nierembergia scoparia*
Tansy: *Tanacetum*
Taurus Cerastium: *Cerastium biebersteinii*
Tawny Daylily: *Hemerocallis fulva*

Texas Sage: *Salvia coccinea*
Thick-Leaved Phlox: *Phlox caroliniana*
Thin-Leaf Sunflower: *Helianthus decapetalus*
Thistle: *Cirsium*
Thoroughwax: *Bupleurum*
Thread-Leaf Coreopsis: *Coreopsis verticillata*
Three-Birds-Flying: *Linaria triornithophora*
Thrift: *Armeria, A. maritima*
Throatwort: *Trachelium caeruleum*
Thyme: *Thymus*
Tibetan Primrose: *Primula florindae*
Tickseed: *Coreopsis*
Tiger Aloe: *Aloe variegata*
Toadflax: *Linaria*
Toad-Lily: *Tricyrtis*
Toothwort: *Dentaria*
Torch Lily: *Kniphofia*
Torch Plant: *Aloe aristata*
Touch-Me-Not: *Impatiens*
Tower of Jewels: *Echium wildpretii*
Transvaal Daisy: *Gerbera jamesonii*
Treacleberry: *Smilacina racemosa*
Treasure Flower: *Gazania ringens*
Tree Celandine: *Macleaya cordata*
Tree Dahlia: *Dahlia imperialis*
True Solomon's Seal: *Polygonatum commutatum*
Tufted Pansy: *Viola cornuta*
Tufted Violet: *Viola cornuta*
Turkeybeard: *Xerophyllum asphodeloides*
Turtlehead: *Chelone, C. glabra*
Tussock Bellflower: *Campanula carpatica*
Trailing Arctotis: *Arctotis stoechadifolia*
Trailing Geranium: *Pelargonium peltatum*
Twinspur: *Diascia*
Umbrella Dracaena: *Dianella ensifolia*
Umbrella Plant: *Peltiphyllum peltatum*
Valerian: *Valeriana*
Vancouver Fern: *Vancouveria hexandra*
Variegated Ginger Mint: *Mentha* x *gentilis* 'Variegata'
Variegated Horse-Radish: *Armoracia rusticana variegata*
Velvet Centaurea: *Centaurea gymnocarpa*
Velvet Elephant-Ear: *Kalanchoe beharensis*
Velvetleaf: *Kalanchoe beharensis*
Vervain: *Verbena, V. rigida*
Vetch: *Vicia*
Viola: *Viola* x *williamsii*

Violet: *Viola*
Virginia Bluebells: *Mertensia virginica*
Virginia Cowslip: *Mertensia virginica*
Virginia Lion's Heart: *Physostegia virginiana*
Virginia Meadow Beauty: *Rhexia virginica*
Virginia Wild Ginger: *Asarum virginicum*
Vittadinia: *Erigeron karvinskianus*
Wake-Robin: *Trillium*
Wallflower: *Cheiranthus*
Wall Rockcress: *Arabis caucasica*
Wandering Jew: *Tradescantia albiflora*
Wand-Flower: *Galax urceolata*
Wand Loosestrife: *Lythrum virgatum*
Water Avens: *Geum rivale*
Water Figwort: *Scrophularia auriculata* 'Variegata'
Water Flag: *Iris pseudacorus*
Wavy-Leaf Plantain Lily: *Hosta undulata*
Wedding Lily: *Dietes robinsoniana*
Welsh Poppy: *Meconopsis cambrica*
Western Bleeding-Heart: *Dicentra formosa*
White Baneberry: *Actaea pachypoda*
White Daisy: *Chrysanthemum leucanthemum*
White Dead Nettle: *Lamium album*
White Camas: *Zigadenus elegans*
White False Indigo: *Baptisia leucantha*
White Ginger Lily: *Hedychium coronarium*
White Lilyturf: *Ophiopogon jaburan*
White Mugwort: *Artemisia lactiflora*
White Snakeroot: *Eupatorium rugosum*
White Wake-Robin: *Trillium grandiflorum*
White Wood Aster: *Aster divaricatus*
Widow Iris: *Hermodactylus tuberosus*
Wild Bergamot: *Monarda*
Wild Bleeding-Heart: *Dicentra eximia*
Wild Blue Phlox: *Phlox divaricata*
Wild Buckwheat: *Eriogonum*
Wild Columbine: *Aquilegia canadensis*
Wild Ginger: *Asarum*
Wild Hollyhock: *Sphaeralcea*
Wild Iris: *Iris versicolor*
Wild Parsnip: *Angelica archangelica*

Wild Pink: *Silene caroliniana*
Wild Senna: *Cassia hebecarpa, C. marilandica*
Wild Sweet William: *Phlox divaricata, P. maculata*
Willow Bellflower: *Campanula persicifolia*
Willow Gentian: *Gentiana asclepiadea*
Windflower: *Anemone*
Winter Begonia: *Bergenia ciliata*
Winter-Blooming Bergenia: *Bergenia crassifolia*
Winter Heliotrope: *Petasites fragrans*
Winter Iris: *Iris unguicularis*
Winter Wallflower: *Cheiranthus* x *kewensis*
Whorlflower: *Morina longifolia*
Wolfsbane: *Aconitum*
Wood Germander: *Teucrium scorodonia*
Woodruff: *Asperula*
Wood Sage: *Teucrium canadense, T. scorodonia*
Wood Trillium: *Trillium viride*
Woolly-Bears: *Ptilotus exaltatus*
Woolly Blue-Curls: *Trichostema lanatum*
Woolly Speedwell: *Veronica incana*
Woolly Yarrow: *Achillea tomentosa*
Wormwood: *Artemisia*
Woundwort: *Stachys*
Yarrow: *Achillea*
Yellow Archangel: *Lamiastrum galeobdolon*
Yellow Asphodel: *Asphodeline lutea*
Yellow Calla: *Zantedeschia elliottiana*
Yellow Flag: *Iris pseudacorus*
Yellow Flax: *Reinwardtia indica*
Yellow Foxglove: *Digitalis grandiflora*
Yellow Hardhead: *Centaurea macrocephala*
Yellow Iris: *Iris pseudacorus*
Yellow Lady's Slipper: *Cypripedium calceolus*
Yellow Loosestrife: *Lysimachia punctata*
Yellow Puccoon: *Lithospermum canescens*
Yellow Toad-Lily: *Tricyrtis flava*
Zonal Pelargonium: *Pelargonium* x *hortorum*

ABOUT THE AUTHORS

RUTH ROGERS CLAUSEN was trained as a horticulturist in England and as a botanist in the United States. She has spent the last twenty-five years in horticulture, working for commercial firms and public institutions in this country. A well-known lecturer, she teaches at the New York Botanical Garden. She is also a garden designer and consultant.

NICOLAS H. EKSTROM is a director of the Horticultural Society of New York. As a landscape designer and consultant, he has worked for both private and public clients. He maintains an extensive library of horticultural and botanical photographs for his own lectures and research and for publication.